Contents

PART 2

Paper 2.4

Financial Management and Control

ACCA Textbook

Official Publisher

PUBLICATIONS

British Library Cataloguing-in-Publication Data

A catalogue record for this book is available from the British Library.

Published by Foulks Lynch Ltd
4, The Griffin Centre
Staines Road
Feltham
Middlesex
TW14 0HS

ISBN 0 7483 6264 9

© Foulks Lynch Ltd, 2003

Printed and bound in Great Britain.

Acknowledgements

We are grateful to the Association of Chartered Certified Accountants and the Chartered Institute of Management Accountants for permission to reproduce past examination questions. The answers have been prepared by Foulks Lynch Ltd.

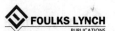
FOULKS LYNCH
PUBLICATIONS

Introduction

This Textbook is the ACCA's official text for Paper 2.4 *Financial Management and Control*, and is part of the ACCA's official series produced for students taking the ACCA examinations.

This new edition, updated for 2004 exams, has been produced with direct guidance from the examiner. It covers the syllabus and study guide in great detail, giving appropriate weighting to the various topics. Targeted very closely on the examination, this textbook is written in a way that will help you assimilate the information easily. Numerous practice questions and exam type questions at the end of each chapter reinforce your knowledge.

DEFINITION

- **Definitions.** The text defines key words and concepts, placing them in the margin, with a clear heading, as on the left. The purpose of including these definitions is to focus your attention on the point being covered.

KEY POINT

- **Key points**. In the margin you will see key points at regular intervals. The purpose of these is to summarise concisely the key material being covered.

ACTIVITY 1

- **Activities**. The text involves you in the learning process with a series of activities designed to catch your attention and make you concentrate and respond. The feedback to activities is at the end of each chapter.

SELF-TEST QUESTIONS

- **Self-test questions**. At the end of each chapter there is a series of self-test questions. The purpose of these is to help you revise some of the key elements of the chapter. All the answers to these questions can be found in the text.

EXAM-TYPE QUESTIONS

- **End of chapter questions**. At the end of each chapter we include examination-type questions. These will give you a very good idea of the sort of thing the examiner will ask and will test your understanding of what has been covered.

Syllabus and study guide

Objectives of the study guide

This study guide is designed to help you plan your studies and to provide a more detailed interpretation of the syllabus for Paper 2.4 *Financial Management and Control*. It contains both the syllabus and the study guide, which you can follow when preparing for the examination.

The syllabus outlines the content of the paper. The study guide takes the syllabus content and expands it into study sessions of similar length. These sessions indicate what the examiner expects of candidates for each part of the syllabus, and therefore gives you guidance in the skills you are expected to demonstrate in the examinations.

Syllabus content

1   FINANCIAL MANAGEMENT OBJECTIVES

Chapter 3

a   The nature, purpose and scope of financial management.

b   The relationship between financial management, management accounting and financial accounting.

c   The relationship of financial objectives and organisational strategy.

d   Problems of multiple stakeholders in financial management and the consequent multiple objectives.

e   Objectives (financial and otherwise) in not-for-profit organisations.

2   THE FINANCIAL MANAGEMENT ENVIRONMENT   Chapters 1, 2 & 4

a   Financial intermediation and credit creation.

b   Money and capital markets

   i   Domestic and international

   ii   Stock markets (both major markets and small firm markets).

c   The Efficient Markets Hypothesis.

d   Rates of interest and yield curves.

e   The impact of fiscal and monetary policy on business.

f   Regulation of business (for example, pricing restrictions, green policies and corporate governance).

3   MANAGEMENT OF WORKING CAPITAL

Chapters 5, 6 & 7

a   The nature and scope of working capital management.

b   Funding requirements for working capital.

c   Working capital needs of different types of business.

d   The relationship of working capital management to business solvency.

e   Management of stock, debtors, short term funds, cash, overdrafts and creditors.

f   Techniques of working capital management (including ratio analysis, EOQ, JIT, credit evaluation, terms of credit, cash discounts, factoring and invoice discounting, debtors cycles, efficient short term fund investing, cash forecasting and budgets, Miller-Orr models, basic foreign exchange methods, probabilities and risk assessment, terms of trade with creditors).

4   SOURCES OF FINANCE

Chapters 8, 9 & 10

a   Sources and relative costs (including issue costs) of various types of finance and their suitability to different circumstances and organisations (large and small, listed and unlisted) including:

   i   access to funds and the nature of business risk

   ii   the nature and importance of internally generated funds

   iii   capital markets (types of share capital, new issues, rights issues, loan capital, convertibles, warrants)

   iv   the effect of dividend policy on financing needs

   v   bank finance (short, medium and long term, including leasing)

   vi   trade credit

   vii   government sources: grants, regional and national aid schemes and tax incentives.

   viii   problems of small company financing (collateral, maturity funding gap, risk)

   ix   problems of companies with low initial earnings (R&D, Internet, and other high-technology businesses)

   x   venture capital and financial sources particularly suited to the small company

xi   international money and capital markets, including an introduction to international banking and the finance of foreign trade.

b   Requirements of finance (for what purpose, how much and for how long) in relation to business operational and strategic objectives.

c   The importance of the choice of capital structure: equity versus debt and basic analysis of the term profile of funds.

d   Financial gearing and other key financial ratios and analysis of their significance to the organisation.

e   Appropriate sources of finance, taking into account:

i   cost of finance

ii   timing of cash payments

iii   effect on gearing and other ratios

iv   effect on company's existing investors.

5   CAPITAL APPRAISAL INVESTMENT

Chapter 10, 11, 12 & 13

a   Discounted cash flow techniques

i   simple and compound interest

ii   net present value

iii   annuities and perpetuities

iv   internal rate of return

v   future value

vi   nominal interest

b   Appraisal of domestic capital investment opportunities for profit making and not-for-profit organisations through the use of appropriate methods and techniques

i   the risk/return relationship

ii   return on capital employed

iii   payback

iv   internal rate of return

v   net present value

vi   single and multi-period capital rationing

vii   lease or buy decisions

viii   asset replacement using equivalent annual cost.

Including (in categories (i)-(viii)) the effects of taxation, inflation, risk and uncertainty (probabilities, sensitivity analysis, simulation).

6   COSTING SYSTEMS AND TECHNIQUES

Chapters 15 & 25

a   The purpose of costing as an aid to planning, monitoring and control of business activity.

b   Different approaches to costing.

c   Costing information requirements and limitations in not-for-profit organisations.

d   Behavioural implications of different costing approaches including performance evaluation.

e   Implications of costing approaches for profit reporting, the pricing of products and internal activities/services.

7   STANDARD COSTING AND VARIANCE ANALYSIS

Chapters 15, 16, 17 & 18

a   Standard costing

i   determination of standards

ii   identification and calculation of sales variances (including quantity and mix), cost variances (including mix and yield); absorption and marginal approaches

iii   significance and relevance of variances

iv   operating statements

v   interpretation and relevance of variance calculations to business performance.

b   Planning and operational variances.

c   Behavioural implications of standard costing and variance reporting.

8   BUDGETING AND BUDGETARY CONTROL

Chapters 21, 22, 23 & 24

a   Objectives of budgetary planning and control systems including aspects of behavioural implications.

b   Evaluation of budgetary systems such as fixed and flexible, zero based and incremental, periodic, continuous and activity based.

c   Development, implementation and coordination of budgeting systems: functional, subsidiary and master/principal budgets (including cash budgeting); budget review.

d   Calculation and cause of variances as aids to controlling performance.

e   Quantitative aids to budgeting and the concepts of correlation, basic time series analysis (seasonality) and forecasting; use of computer based models.

f   Behavioural implications of budgeting and budgetary control.

9   PERFORMANCE MEASUREMENT

a   Measurement of productivity, activity, profitability and quality of service.

b   Relationship of measure to type of entity and range of measures, both monetary and non-monetary.

c   Indices to allow for price and performance changes through time.

d   Evaluating performance against objectives and plans, and identifying areas of concern from the information produced.

e   The impact of cost centres, revenue centres, profit centres and investment centres on management appraisal.

f   Difference between business performance and management performance.

g   Benchmarking.

Excluded topics

The following topics are specifically excluded from the syllabus:

*   Calculations involving the derivation of cost of capital in discounting problems. Candidates will always be supplied with an appropriate discount rate.

*   Calculations relating to Modigliani and Miller propositions.

Key areas of the syllabus

The core of the syllabus is aimed at developing the skills required in supporting managerial decision making. They reflect the core competencies needed for students to satisfy the aim of the paper identified above. The core areas are:

*   financial management objectives
*   management of working capital
*   sources of finance
*   capital investment appraisal
*   costing systems
*   standard costing and variance analysis
*   budgeting and budgetary control
*   performance management.

Additional information

Present value and annuity tables will be provided in the examination. The study guide provides more detailed guidance on the syllabus.

Study guide

1   THE ECONOMIC ENVIRONMENT I

Syllabus reference 2e   **Chapter 1**

Macroeconomic Objectives

*   identify and explain the main macro-economic policy targets
*   explain how government economic policy may affect planning and decision-making in business
*   define and explain the role of fiscal, monetary, interest rate and exchange rate policy

Fiscal Policy

*   identify the main tools of fiscal policy
*   explain how public expenditure is financed and the meaning of PSBR
*   explain how PSBR and taxation policy interact with other economic indicators
*   identify the implications of fiscal policy for business

2   THE ECONOMIC ENVIRONMENT II

Syllabus reference 2d, 2e, 2f   **Chapter 1, 2**

Monetary, inflation and exchange rate policy

*   identify the main tools of monetary policy
*   identify the factors which influence inflation and exchange rates, including the impact of interest rates
*   identify the implications of monetary, inflation and exchange rate policy for business

Aspects of government intervention and regulation

*   explain the requirement for and the role of competition policy
*   explain the requirement for and the role of official aid intervention
*   explain the requirement for and the role of Green policies
*   identify examples of government intervention and regulation

3   THE NATURE AND SCOPE OF FINANCIAL MANAGEMENT

Syllabus reference 1a, 1b, 1c, 1d, 1e   **Chapter 3**

*   broadly describe the relationship between financial management, management accounting and financial accounting
*   discuss the nature and scope of financial objectives for private sector companies in the context of organisational objectives
*   discuss the role of social and non-financial objectives in private sector companies and identify their financial implications
*   identify objectives (financial and otherwise) in not-for-profit organisations and identify the extent to which they differ from private sector companies
*   discuss the problems of multiple stakeholders in financial management and the consequent multiple objectives and scope for conflict

4   THE FINANCIAL MANAGEMENT FRAMEWORK

Syllabus reference 2a, 2b(i), (ii), 2c, 4a(xi), 5a(i)   **Chapter 4**

*   identify the general role of financial intermediaries
*   explain the role of commercial banks as providers of funds (including the creation of credit)
*   discuss the risk/return trade-off
*   identify the international money and capital markets and outline their operation
*   explain the functions of a stock market and corporate bond market
*   explain the key features of different types of security in terms of the risk/return trade-off

- outline the Efficient Markets Hypothesis and assess its broad implications for corporate policy and financial management
- explain the Separation Theorem
- explain the functions of and identify the links between the money and capital markets

5 MANAGEMENT OF WORKING CAPITAL I

Syllabus reference 3a, 3b, 3c, 3d, 3e, 3f   Chapter 5

General issues

- explain the nature and scope of working capital management
- distinguish between cash flow and profits
- explain the requirement for effective working capital management
- explain the relationship between working capital management and business solvency
- distinguish between the working capital needs of different types of business

Management of stock

- calculate and interpret stock ratios
- explain the role of stock in the working capital cycle
- apply the tools and techniques of stock management
- analyse and evaluate the results of stock management techniques

6 MANAGEMENT OF WORKING CAPITAL II

Syllabus reference 3e, 3f   Chapter 6

Management of creditors

- explain the role of creditors in the working capital cycle
- explain the availability of credit and the role of the guarantee
- identify the risks of taking increased credit and buying under extended credit terms
- explain how methods of paying suppliers may influence cash flows of both parties
- discuss the particular problems of managing overseas accounts payable
- calculate and interpret creditor ratios
- apply the tools and techniques of creditor management
- analyse and evaluate the results of creditor management techniques

Management of debtors

- explain the role of debtors in the working capital cycle
- explain how the credit-worthiness of customers may be assessed
- evaluate the balance of risks and costs of customer default against the profitability of marginal business

- explain the role of factoring and invoice discounting
- explain the role of early settlement discounts
- discuss the particular problems of managing overseas debtors
- calculate and interpret debtor ratios
- apply the tools and techniques of debtor management
- analyse and evaluate the results of debtor management techniques

7 MANAGEMENT OF WORKING CAPITAL III

Syllabus reference 3e, 3f   Chapter 7

Management of cash

- explain the role of cash in the working capital cycle
- calculate optimal cash balances
- describe the functions of, and evaluate the benefits from, centralised cash control and Treasury Management
- calculate and interpret cash ratios
- apply the tools and techniques of cash management
- analyse and evaluate the results of cash management techniques

8 SOURCES OF FINANCE I: SMALL AND MEDIUM SIZED ENTERPRISES (SMEs)

Syllabus reference 4a(i), (ii), (v), (vi), (vii) (viii), (ix), (x), 4b, 4c, 4d, 4e(i), (ii), (iii), (iv)   Chapter 8

- explain financing in terms of the risk/return trade-off
- describe the requirements for finance of SMEs (purpose, how much, how long)
- describe the nature of the financing problem for small businesses in terms of the funding gap, the maturity gap and inadequate security
- identify the role of risk and the lack of information on small companies to help explain the problems of SME financing
- explain the role of information provision provided by financial statements
- describe the particular financing problems of low-earning/high growth companies
- describe the response of government agencies and financial institutions to the SME financing problem
- explain what other measures may be taken to ease the financial problems of SMEs such as trade creditors, factoring, leasing, hire purchase, AIM listing, business angels and venture capital
- describe how capital structure decisions in SMEs may differ from larger organisations
- describe appropriate sources of finance for SMEs
- calculate and interpret appropriate ratios

9 SOURCES OF FINANCE II: EQUITY FINANCING

Syllabus reference 4a(iii), (iv), 4c, 4d, 4e(i), (ii), (iii), (iv)
Chapter 8

- describe ways in which a company may obtain a stock market listing
- describe how stock markets operate, including the AIM
- explain the requirements of stock market investors in terms of returns on investment
- calculate, analyse and evaluate appropriate financial ratios (e.g. EPS, PE ratio, dividend yield, etc.)
- outline and apply the dividend valuation model, including the growth adjustment
- explain the importance of internally generated funds
- describe the advantages and disadvantages of rights issues
- calculate the price of rights
- explain the purpose and impact of a bonus issue, scrip dividends and stock splits

10 SOURCES OF FINANCE III: DEBT AND NEAR-DEBT FINANCING

Syllabus reference 4a(i), (iii), (v), (vi), (xi), 4b, 4c, 4d, 4e(i), (ii), (iii), (iv)
Chapter 8, 9

- explain the features of different types of preference shares and the reasons for their issue
- explain the features of different types of long-term straight debt and the reasons for their issue
- explain the features of convertible debt and warrants and the reasons for their issue
- broadly describe the reasons for the choice of financing between preference shares, debt and near-debt instruments in terms of the risk/return trade-off
- assess the effect on EPS of conversion and option rights
- broadly describe international debt markets and the financing of foreign trade
- calculate and interpret appropriate ratios

11 SOURCES OF FINANCE IV: THE CAPITAL STRUCTURE DECISION

Syllabus reference 4c, 4d, 4e(i), (ii), (iii), (iv)
Chapter 10

- explain and calculate the level of financial gearing
- distinguish between operational and financial gearing
- outline the effects of gearing on the value of shares, company risk and required return
- explain how a company may determine its capital structure in terms of interest charges, dividends, risk and redemption requirements

- explain the role of short term financing in the capital structure decision
- explain the relationship between the management of working capital and the long term capital structure decision
- calculate and interpret appropriate ratios

12 INVESTMENT DECISIONS

Syllabus reference 5b(ii), (iii)
Chapter 11

- define and distinguish between capital and revenue expenditure
- compare and contrast fixed asset investment and working capital investment
- describe the impact of investment projects on financial statements
- calculate payback and assess its usefulness as a measure of investment worth
- calculate ROCE and assess its usefulness as a measure of investment worth

13 INTEREST AND DISCOUNTING

Syllabus reference 5a(i), (iii), (v), (vi)

- explain the difference between simple and compound interest
- explain the relationship between inflation and interest rates, distinguishing between nominal and real interest rates, and calculate nominal interest rates
- explain what is meant by future values and calculate future values, including application of the annuity formula
- explain what is meant by discounting and calculate present values, including the application of the annuity and perpetuity formula, and the use of present value and annuity tables
- explain the importance of the time value of money and the role of the cost of capital in appraising investments

14 INVESTMENT APPRAISAL USING DCF METHODS

Syllabus reference 5a(ii), (iv), 5b(ii), (iii), (iv), (v), (viii)
Chapter 11

- explain the importance of the time value of money and the role of the cost of capital in appraising investments
- identify and evaluate relevant cash flows of potential investments
- calculate present values to derive the NPV and IRR measures of investment worth
- explain the superiority of DCF methods over payback and ROCE
- assess the merits of IRR and NPV
- apply DCF methods to asset replacement decisions

15 PROJECT APPRAISAL ALLOWING FOR INFLATION AND TAXATION

Syllabus reference 5b   **Chapter 12**

Inflation

- distinguish general inflation from specific price increases and assess their impact on cash flows
- evaluate capital investment projects on a real terms basis
- evaluate capital investment projects on a nominal terms basis

Taxation

- calculate the effect of capital allowances and Corporation Tax on project cash flows
- evaluate the profitability of capital investment projects on a post-tax basis

16 PROJECT APPRAISAL ALLOWING FOR RISK   **Chapter 13**

Syllabus reference 5b

- distinguish between risk and uncertainty
- identify the sources of risk affecting project profitability
- evaluate the sensitivity of project NPV to changes in key variables
- apply the probability approach to calculating expected NPV of a project and the associated standard deviation
- explain the role of simulation in generating a probability distribution for the NPV of a project
- identify risk reduction strategies for projects
- evaluate the usefulness of risk assessment methods

17 CAPITAL RATIONING

Syllabus reference 5b(vi)   **Chapter 14**

- distinguish between hard and soft capital rationing
- apply profitability index techniques for single period divisible projects
- evaluate projects involving single and multi-period capital rationing

18 LEASING DECISIONS

Syllabus reference 5b(vii)   **Chapter 14**

- distinguish between operating and finance leases
- apply DCF methods to projects involving buy or lease problems
- assess the relative advantages and disadvantages of different types of lease
- describe the impact of leasing on company gearing

19 COSTING SYSTEMS AND TECHNIQUES

Syllabus reference 6a, 6b, 6c, 6d, 6e   Chapter 15

- outline and distinguish between the nature and scope of management accounting and the role of costing in meeting the needs of management
- describe the purpose of costing as an aid to planning, monitoring and controlling business activity
- different approaches to costing
  - marginal costing and absorption costing
  - service costing
  - theory of constraints and throughput accounting
  - activity based costing; use of cost drivers and activities
  - life cycle costing
  - target costing
- describe the costing information requirements and limitations in not-for-profit organisations
- broadly outline the behavioural implications of different costing approaches including performance evaluation
- explain the potential for different costing approaches to influence profit reporting and the pricing of products and internal services
- explain the role of costing systems in decision making

20 STANDARD COSTING I

Syllabus reference 7a(i), (ii), (iii), (v), 7c, 8d
                                        Chapter 19

- explain the uses of standard costs and the methods by which they are derived and subsequently reviewed
- calculate and evaluate capacity limitations when setting standards
- describe the types of standard (ideal, attainable, current and basic) and their behavioural implications
- calculate basic labour, material, overhead (variable and fixed) and sales variances, including problems of labour idle time
- explain the reasons for variances
- assess appropriate management action arising from the variances identified

21 STANDARD COSTING II

Syllabus reference 7a(ii), (iii), (iv), (v), 7b, 8d
                                        Chapter 19, 20

- prepare reconciliations using operating statements which
  - reconcile budgeted and actual profit figures, and/or
  - reconcile the actual sales less the standard cost of sales with the actual profit
- calculate and explain operational and planning variances

- demonstrate how absorption and marginal approaches can be used in standard costing
- calculate mix and yield variances for materials
- calculate mix and quantity variances for sales
- demonstrate an understanding of the inter-relationships between variances
- explain the reasons for variances
- assess appropriate management action arising from the variances identified

22 BUDGETARY PLANNING AND CONTROL I

Syllabus reference 8a, 8c, 8g   Chapter 21, 22

- identify the purposes of budgetary planning and control systems
- describe the planning and control cycle, and the control process
- explain the implications of controllability for responsibility reporting
- prepare, review and explain a budget preparation timetable
- prepare and evaluate functional, subsidiary and master budgets, including cash budgets
- explain the processes involved with the development and implementation of budgets
- explain the process of participation in budget setting and how this can address motivational problems

23 BUDGETARY PLANNING AND CONTROL II

Syllabus reference 8b, 8f, 8g   Chapter 22

- prepare and evaluate fixed and flexible budgets and evaluate the resulting variances
- prepare flexed budgets when standard fixed overhead absorption is employed
- assess the behavioural implications of budgetary control and performance evaluation, including participation in budget setting

24 BUDGETARY PLANNING AND CONTROL III

Syllabus reference 8b   Chapter 23

- describe and evaluate the main features of zero based budgeting systems
- describe the areas/organisations in which zero based budgeting may be applied
- describe and evaluate incremental budgeting and discuss the differences with zero based budgeting
- describe and evaluate periodic and continuous budgeting systems

25 QUANTITATIVE AIDS TO BUDGETING

Syllabus reference 8e   Chapter 24

- describe and apply the techniques of

  - high-low method
  - least squares regression
  - scatter diagrams and correlation
  - forecasting with least squares regression
  - time series to identify trends and seasonality
  - forecasting with time series
- evaluate the results of quantitative aids

26 INDICES

Syllabus reference 9c   Chapter 25

- explain the purpose of index numbers, and calculate and interpret simple index numbers for one or more variables
- deflate time-related data using an index
- construct a chained index series
- explain the term 'average index', distinguishing between simple and weighted averages
- calculate Laspeyres and Paasche price and quantity indices
- describe the relative merits of Laspeyres and Paasche indices

27 PERFORMANCE MEASUREMENT

Syllabus reference 9a, b, c, d, e, f, g   Chapter 26

- outline the essential features of responsibility accounting for various types of entity
- describe the range of management performance measures available for various types of entity
- calculate and explain the concepts of return on investment and residual income
- explain and give examples of appropriate non-monetary performance measures
- describe the various types of responsibility centre and the impact of these on management appraisal
- discuss the potential conflict in the use of a measure for both business and management performance
- analyse the application of financial performance measures including cost, profit, return on capital employed
- assess and illustrate the measurement of profitability, activity and productivity
- discuss the measurement of quality and service
- identify areas of concern from information supplied and performance measures calculated
- describe the features of benchmarking and its application to performance appraisal

The examination

Format of the examination

Paper-based examination

	Number of marks
Section A: One compulsory scenario based question	50
Section B: Choice of 2 from 4 questions (25 marks each)	50
	100
Total time allowed: 3 hours	

The overall balance in the examination will be approximately 60% computational and 40% non-computational.

Examination tips

- Spend the first few minutes of the examination **reading the paper**.

- Where you have a **choice of questions**, decide which ones you will do.

- **Divide the time** you spend on questions in proportion to the marks on offer. One suggestion is to allocate 1½ minutes to each mark available, so a 10 mark question should be completed in 15 minutes.

- Unless you know exactly how to answer the question, spend some time **planning** your answer. Stick to the question and **tailor your answer** to what you are asked.

- **Fully explain** all your points but be **concise**. Set out all workings **clearly and neatly**, and state briefly what you are doing. Don't write out the question.

- If you do not understand what a question is asking, **state your assumptions**. Even if you do not answer precisely in the way the examiner hoped, you should be given some credit, if your assumptions are reasonable.

- If you **get completely stuck** with a question, leave space in your answer book and **return to it later**.

- Towards the end of the examination spend the last **five minutes** reading through your answers and **making any additions or corrections**.

- Before you finish, you must fill in the required information on the front of your answer booklet.

Answering the questions

- **Multiple-choice questions**: Read the questions carefully and work through any calculations required. If you don't know the answer, eliminate those options you know are incorrect and see if the answer becomes more obvious. Remember that only one answer to a multiple choice question can be right!

- **Objective test questions** might ask for numerical answers, but could also involve paragraphs of text which require you to fill in a number of missing blanks, or for you to write a definition of a word or phrase, or to enter a formula. Others may give a definition followed by a list of possible key words relating to that description.

- **Essay questions**: Make a quick plan in your answer book and under each main point list all the relevant facts you can think of. Then write out your answer

developing each point fully. Your essay should have a clear structure; it should contain a brief introduction, a main section and a conclusion. Be concise. It is better to write a little about a lot of different points than a great deal about one or two points.

- **Case studies**: To write a good case study, first identify the area in which there is a problem, outline the main principles/theories you are going to use to answer the question, and then apply the principles/theories to the case. Include relevant points only and then reach a conclusion and, if asked for, recommendations. If you can, compare the facts to real-life examples – this may gain you additional marks in the exam.

- **Computations**: It is essential to include all your workings in your answers. Many computational questions require the use of a standard format: company profit and loss account, balance sheet and cash flow statement for example. Be sure you know these formats thoroughly before the examination and use the layouts that you see in the answers given in this book and in model answers. If you are asked to comment or make recommendations on a computation, you must do so. There are important marks to be gained here. Even if your computation contains mistakes, you may still gain marks if your reasoning is correct.

- **Reports, memos and other documents**: Some questions ask you to present your answer in the form of a report or a memo or other document. Use the correct format - there could be easy marks to gain here.

 FOULKS LYNCH
PUBLICATIONS

Study skills and revision guidance

This section aims to give guidance on how to study for your ACCA exams and to give ideas on how to improve your existing study techniques.

Preparing to study

Set your objectives

Before starting to study decide what you want to achieve – the type of pass you wish to obtain. This will decide the level of commitment and time you need to dedicate to your studies.

Devise a study plan

• Determine which times of the week you will study.

• Split these times into sessions of at least one hour for study of new material. Any shorter periods could be used for revision or practice.

• Put the times you plan to study onto a study plan for the weeks from now until the exam and set yourself targets for each period of study – in your sessions make sure you cover the course, course assignments and revision.

• If you are studying for more than one paper at a time, try to vary your subjects, this can help you to keep interested and see subjects as part of wider knowledge.

• When working through your course, compare your progress with your plan and, if necessary, re-plan your work (perhaps including extra sessions) or, if you are ahead, do some extra revision/practice questions.

Effective studying

Active reading

You are not expected to learn the text by rote, rather, you must understand what you are reading and be able to use it to pass the exam and develop good practice. A good technique to use is SQ3Rs – Survey, Question, Read, Recall, Review:

1 **Survey** the chapter – look at the headings and read the introduction, summary and objectives, so as to get an overview of what the chapter deals with.

2 **Question** – whilst undertaking the survey, ask yourself the questions that you hope the chapter will answer for you.

3 **Read** through the chapter thoroughly, answering the questions and making sure you can meet the objectives. Attempt the exercises and activities in the text, and work through all the examples.

4 **Recall** – at the end of each section and at the end of the chapter, try to recall the main ideas of the section/chapter without referring to the text. This is best done after a short break of a couple of minutes after the reading stage.

5 **Review** – check that your recall notes are correct.

You may also find it helpful to reread the chapter and try to see the topic(s) it deals with as a whole.

FOULKS LYNCH
PUBLICATIONS

Note-taking

Taking notes is a useful way of learning, but do not simply copy out the text. The notes must:

- be in your own words
- be concise
- cover the key points
- be well-organised
- be modified as you study further chapters in this text or in related ones.

Trying to summarise a chapter without referring to the text can be a useful way of determining which areas you know and which you don't.

Three ways of taking notes:

- **summarise the key points** of a chapter.

- **make linear notes** – a list of headings, divided up with subheadings listing the key points. If you use linear notes, you can use different colours to highlight key points and keep topic areas together. Use plenty of space to make your notes easy to use.

- **try a diagrammatic form** – the most common of which is a mind-map. To make a mind-map, put the main heading in the centre of the paper and put a circle around it. Then draw short lines radiating from this to the main sub-headings, which again have circles around them. Then continue the process from the sub-headings to sub-sub-headings, advantages, disadvantages, etc.

Highlighting and underlining

You may find it useful to underline or highlight key points in your study text – but do be selective. You may also wish to make notes in the margins.

Revision

The best approach to revision is to revise the course as you work through it. Also try to leave four to six weeks before the exam for final revision. Make sure you cover the whole syllabus and pay special attention to those areas where your knowledge is weak. Here are some recommendations:

- **Read through the text and your notes again** and condense your notes into key phrases. It may help to put key revision points onto index cards to look at when you have a few minutes to spare.

- **Review any assignments** you have completed and look at where you lost marks – put more work into those areas where you were weak.

- **Practise exam standard questions** under timed conditions. If you are short of time, list the points that you would cover in your answer and then read the model answer, but do try and complete at least a few questions under exam conditions.

- Also **practise producing answer plans** and comparing them to the model answer.

- If you are stuck on a topic find somebody (a tutor) to explain it to you.

- **Read good newspapers and professional journals**, especially ACCA's *Student Accountant* – this can give you an advantage in the exam.

- Ensure you **know the structure of the exam** – how many questions and of what type you will be expected to answer. During your revision attempt all the different styles of questions you may be asked.

Formulae and tables

Formulae

Regression analysis

$$a = \frac{\sum y}{n} - \frac{b\sum x}{n}$$

$$b = \frac{n\sum xy - \sum x \sum y}{n\sum x^2 - \left(\sum x\right)^2}$$

$$r = \frac{n\sum xy - \sum x \sum y}{\sqrt{\left(n\sum x^2 - \left(\sum x\right)^2\right)\left(n\sum y^2 - \left(\sum y\right)^2\right)}}$$

Economic order quantity $= \sqrt{\dfrac{2C_0 D}{C_h}}$

Economic batch quantity $= \sqrt{\dfrac{2C_0 D}{C_h\left(1 - \dfrac{D}{R}\right)}}$

Discount factor $= \dfrac{1}{(1+r)}$

Annuities

Future value $= A\left(\dfrac{(1+r)^n - 1}{r}\right)$

Present value $= \dfrac{A}{r}\left(1 - \dfrac{1}{(1+r)^n}\right)$

Indices

Laspeyre price index $= \dfrac{\sum(p_1 \times q_0)}{\sum(p_0 \times q_0)} \times 100$

Paasche price index $= \dfrac{\sum(p_1 \times q_1)}{\sum(p_0 \times q_1)} \times 100$

Laspeyre quantity index $= \dfrac{\sum(q_1 \times p_0)}{\sum(q_0 \times p_0)} \times 100$

Paasche quantity index $= \dfrac{\sum(q_1 \times p_1)}{\sum(q_0 \times p_1)} \times 100$

Present value table

Present value of 1 i.e. $(1+r)^{-n}$

where   r   = discount rate

       n   = number of periods until payment

Periods					Discount rate (r)						
(n)	1%	2%	3%	4%	5%	6%	7%	8%	9%	10%	
1	0.990	0.980	0.971	0.962	0.952	0.943	0.935	0.926	0.917	0.909	1
2	0.980	0.961	0.943	0.925	0.907	0.890	0.873	0.857	0.842	0.826	2
3	0.971	0.942	0.915	0.889	0.864	0.840	0.816	0.794	0.772	0.751	3
4	0.961	0.924	0.888	0.855	0.823	0.792	0.763	0.735	0.708	0.683	4
5	0.951	0.906	0.863	0.822	0.784	0.747	0.713	0.681	0.650	0.621	5
6	0.942	0.888	0.837	0.790	0.746	0.705	0.666	0.630	0.596	0.564	6
7	0.933	0.871	0.813	0.760	0.711	0.665	0.623	0.583	0.547	0.513	7
8	0.923	0.853	0.789	0.731	0.677	0.627	0.582	0.540	0.502	0.467	8
9	0.914	0.837	0.766	0.703	0.645	0.592	0.544	0.500	0.460	0.424	9
10	0.905	0.820	0.744	0.676	0.614	0.558	0.508	0.463	0.422	0.386	10
11	0.896	0.804	0.722	0.650	0.585	0.527	0.475	0.429	0.388	0.350	11
12	0.887	0.788	0.701	0.625	0.557	0.497	0.444	0.397	0.356	0.319	12
13	0.879	0.773	0.681	0.601	0.530	0.469	0.415	0.368	0.326	0.290	13
14	0.870	0.758	0.661	0.577	0.505	0.442	0.388	0.340	0.299	0.263	14
15	0.861	0.743	0.642	0.555	0.481	0.417	0.362	0.315	0.275	0.239	15
(n)	11%	12%	13%	14%	15%	16%	17%	18%	19%	20%	
1	0.901	0.893	0.885	0.877	0.870	0.862	0.855	0.847	0.840	0.833	1
2	0.812	0.797	0.783	0.769	0.756	0.743	0.731	0.718	0.706	0.694	2
3	0.731	0.712	0.693	0.675	0.658	0.641	0.624	0.609	0.593	0.579	3
4	0.659	0.636	0.613	0.592	0.572	0.552	0.534	0.516	0.499	0.482	4
5	0.593	0.567	0.543	0.519	0.497	0.476	0.456	0.437	0.419	0.402	5
6	0.535	0.507	0.480	0.456	0.432	0.410	0.390	0.370	0.352	0.335	6
7	0.482	0.452	0.425	0.400	0.376	0.354	0.333	0.314	0.296	0.279	7
8	0.434	0.404	0.376	0.351	0.327	0.305	0.285	0.266	0.249	0.233	8
9	0.391	0.361	0.333	0.308	0.284	0.263	0.243	0.225	0.209	0.194	9
10	0.352	0.322	0.295	0.270	0.247	0.227	0.208	0.191	0.176	0.162	10
11	0.317	0.287	0.261	0.237	0.215	0.195	0.178	0.162	0.148	0.135	11
12	0.286	0.257	0.231	0.208	0.187	0.168	0.152	0.137	0.124	0.112	12
13	0.258	0.229	0.204	0.182	0.163	0.145	0.130	0.116	0.104	0.093	13
14	0.232	0.205	0.181	0.160	0.141	0.125	0.111	0.099	0.088	0.078	14
15	0.209	0.183	0.160	0.140	0.123	0.108	0.095	0.084	0.074	0.065	15

FOULKS LYNCH
PUBLICATIONS

Annuity table

Present value of an annuity of 1 i.e. $\dfrac{1-(1+r)^{-n}}{r}$

where   r   = discount rate

       n   = number of periods

Periods (n)	Discount rate (r) 1%	2%	3%	4%	5%	6%	7%	8%	9%	10%	
1	0.990	0.980	0.971	0.962	0.952	0.943	0.935	0.926	0.917	0.909	1
2	1.970	1.942	1.913	1.886	1.859	1.833	1.808	1.783	1.759	1.736	2
3	2.941	2.884	20829	2.775	2.723	2.673	2.624	2.577	2.531	2.487	3
4	3.902	3.808	3.717	3.630	3.546	3.465	3.387	3.312	3.240	3.170	4
5	4.853	4.713	4.580	4.452	4.329	4.212	4.100	3.993	3.890	3.791	5
6	5.795	5.601	5.417	5.242	5.076	4.917	4.767	4.623	4.486	4.355	6
7	6.728	6.472	6.230	6.002	5.786	5.582	5.389	5.206	5.033	4.868	7
8	7.652	7.325	7.020	6.733	6.463	6.210	5.971	5.747	5.535	5.335	8
9	8.566	8.162	7.786	7.435	7.108	6.802	6.515	6.247	5.995	5.759	9
10	9.471	8.983	8.530	8.111	7.722	7.360	7.024	6.710	6.418	6.145	10
11	10.37	9.787	9.253	8.760	8.306	7.887	7.499	7.139	6.805	6.495	11
12	11.26	10.58	9.954	9.385	8.863	8.384	7.943	7.536	7.161	6.814	12
13	12.13	11.35	10.63	9.986	9.394	8.853	8.358	7.904	7.487	7.103	13
14	13.00	12.11	11.30	10.56	9.899	9.295	8.745	8.244	7.786	7.367	14
15	13.87	12.85	11.94	11.12	10.38	9.712	9.108	8.559	8.061	7.606	15

(n)	11%	12%	13%	14%	15%	16%	17%	18%	19%	20%	
1	0.901	0.893	0.885	0.877	0.870	0.862	0.855	0.847	0.840	0.833	1
2	1.713	1.690	1.668	1.647	1.626	1.605	1.585	1.566	1.547	1.528	2
3	2.444	2.402	2.361	2.322	2.283	2.246	2.210	2.174	2.140	2.106	3
4	3.102	3.037	2.974	2.914	2.855	2.798	2.743	2.690	2.639	2.589	4
5	3.696	3.605	3.517	3.433	3.352	3.274	3.199	3.127	3.058	2.991	5
6	4.231	4.111	3.998	3.889	3.784	3.685	3.589	3.498	3.410	3.326	6
7	4.712	4.564	4.423	4.288	4.160	4.039	3.922	3.812	3.706	3.605	7
8	5.146	4.968	4.799	4.639	4.487	4.344	4.207	4.078	3.954	3.837	8
9	5.537	5.328	5.132	4.946	4.772	4.607	4.451	4.303	4.163	4.031	9
10	5.889	5.650	5.426	5.216	5.019	4.833	4.659	4.494	4.339	4.192	10
11	6.207	5.938	5.687	5.453	5.234	5.029	4.836	4.656	4.486	4.327	11
12	6.492	6.194	5.918	5.660	5.421	5.197	4.988	4.793	4.611	4.439	12
13	6.750	6.424	6.122	5.842	5.583	5.342	5.118	4.910	4.715	4.533	13
14	6.982	6.628	6.302	6.002	5.724	5.468	5.229	5.008	4.802	4.611	14
15	7.191	6.811	6.462	6.142	5.847	5.575	5.324	5.092	4.876	4.675	15

Chapter 1
THE ECONOMIC ENVIRONMENT

The economic environment in which an organisation operates affects all financial management decision making. In this chapter we look at how a government's fiscal and monetary policies may impact on business.

Objectives

When you have studied this chapter you should be able to do the following:

- identify and explain the main macroeconomic policy targets

- explain how government economic policy may affect planning and decision-making in business

- define and explain the role of fiscal, monetary, interest rate and exchange rate policy

- identify the main tools of fiscal policy

- explain how public expenditure is financed and the meaning of PSBR

- explain how PSBR and taxation policy interact with other economic indicators

- identify the implications of fiscal policy for business

- identify the main tools of monetary policy

- identify the factors which influence inflation and exchange rates, including the impact of interest rates

- identify the implications of monetary, inflation and exchange rate policy for business.

1 Financial management and control

1.1 Introduction

Paper 2.4 comprises two main areas:

- financial management methods, used to analyse sources of finance and capital investment possibilities

- the use of management accounting techniques in business planning and control.

First, however, we shall look at the economic environment within which organisations operate.

2 Macroeconomic policy

2.1 The objectives of macroeconomic policy

Macroeconomic policy is the management of the economy by government in such a way as to influence the performance and behaviour of the economy as a whole.

The principal objectives of macroeconomic policy will be to achieve the following:

- full employment of resources, especially of the labour force

- price stability

- economic growth (This is measured by changes in national income from one year to the next)

- balance of payments equilibrium
- an appropriate distribution of income and wealth.

ACTIVITY 1

Before reading further consider how these objectives may conflict and compare your thoughts with the notes below.

There is no feedback to this activity.

2.2 Conflicts between objectives

Both economic theory and the experience of managing the economy suggest that the simultaneous achievement of all macroeconomic objectives may be extremely difficult. Two examples of possible conflict may be cited here.

There may be conflict between **full employment** and **price stability**. It is suggested that inflation and employment are inversely related. The achievement of full employment may therefore lead to excessive inflation through an excess level of aggregate demand in the economy.

Rapid **economic growth** may, in the short term at least, have damaging consequences for the **balance of payments** since rapidly rising incomes may lead to a rising level of imports.

Thus the conduct of macroeconomic policy involves trade-offs; governments may have to sacrifice the achievement of some objective in order to achieve another. The identification of targets for policy should reflect this. Government reputation and business confidence will both be damaged if the government is seen to be pursuing policy targets which are widely regarded as incompatible. Policy objectives may **conflict** and hence governments have to consider **trade-offs** between objectives.

KEY POINT

Policy objectives may **conflict** and hence governments have to consider **trade-offs** between objectives.

2.3 Impact of macroeconomic policies on the business sector

In order for macroeconomic policy to work, its instruments must have an impact on economic activity. This means that it must affect the business sector. It does so in two broad forms.

Macroeconomic policy may influence the level of aggregate demand and thus activity in the economy as a whole.

Aggregate demand is the total demand for goods and services in the economy.

Note: National income is aggregate demand that has been satisfied by the provision of goods and services etc.

The broad thrust of macroeconomic policy is to influence the level of aggregate demand (AD) in the economy. This is because the level of AD is central to the determination of the level of unemployment and the rate of inflation. If AD is too low, unemployment might result; if AD is too high, inflation induced by excess demand might result. Changes in AD will affect all businesses to varying degrees. Thus effective business planning requires that businesses can:

- predict the likely thrust of macroeconomic policy in the short to medium term
- predict the consequences for sales growth of the overall stance of macroeconomic policy and any likely changes in it.

The more stable government policy is, the easier it is for businesses to plan, especially in terms of investment, employment and future output capacity.

DEFINITION

Aggregate demand is the total demand for goods and services in the economy.

KEY POINT

Both **business costs** and **sales revenues** may be affected by macroeconomic policy.

Macroeconomic policy may influence the costs of the business sector.

Not only will the demand for goods and services be affected by macroeconomic policy: it also has important implications for the costs and revenues of businesses. Three important areas may be identified.

- **Macroeconomic policy** may involve changes in **exchange rates.** This will have the effect of raising the domestic price of imported goods. Most businesses use some imported goods in the production process; hence this leads to a rise in production costs.

- **Fiscal policy** involves the use of **taxation**: changes in tax rates or the structure of taxation will affect businesses. For example, a change in the employer's national insurance contribution will have a direct effect on labour costs for all businesses. Changes in indirect taxes (for example, a rise in VAT or excise duties) will either have to be absorbed or the business will have to attempt to pass on the tax to its customers.

- **Monetary policy** involves changes in **interest rates**; these changes will directly affect firms in two ways:

    - Costs of servicing debts will change especially for highly geared firms

    - The viability of investment will be affected since all models of investment appraisal include the rate of interest as one, if not the main, variable.

3   Monetary policy

It is clear that money is crucial to the way in which a modern economy functions. **Money** is any financial asset which has liquidity and fulfils the task of a medium of exchange. **Monetary policy** is concerned with influencing the overall monetary conditions in the economy. It is for this reason that governments may wish to concern themselves with monetary conditions in the economy. In particular, monetary policy may be concerned with:

(a) The **volume** of money in circulation. The stock of money in the economy (the 'money supply') is believed to have important effects on the volume of expenditure in the economy. This in turn may influence the level of output in the economy or the level of prices.

(b) The **price** of money. The price of money is the rate of interest. If governments wish to influence the amount of money held in the economy or the demand for credit, they may attempt to influence the level of interest rates.

The monetary authorities may be able to control either the supply of money in the economy or the level of interest rates but it cannot do both simultaneously. In practice, attempts by governments (such as the Thatcher government in the UK) to control the economy by controlling the money supply have failed and have been abandoned. However, growth in the money supply is monitored, because excessive growth could be destabilising.

3.1   The measurement of the money supply (stock)

Currently, in the UK, two measures of money supply are monitored.

(a) **M0**: a **narrow** money measure, incorporating:

    1   notes and coins in circulation with the public

    2   till money held by banks and building societies

    3   operational balances held by commercial banks at the Bank of England.

(b) **M4**: a **broad** money measure, incorporating:

1   notes and coins in circulation with the public

2   all sterling deposits held by the private sector at UK banks and building societies.

3.2 Problems with the operation of monetary policy

Two particular problems with the use of monetary policy are:

- the choice of targets
- the effects of interest rate changes.

The choice of targets

A fundamental problem of monetary policy concerns the choice of variable to operate on. The ultimate objective of monetary policy is to influence some important variable in the economy – the level of demand, the rate of inflation, the exchange rate for the currency, etc. However monetary policy has to do this by targeting some intermediate variable which, it is believed, influences, in some predictable way, the ultimate object of the policy.

The broad choice here is between targeting the **stock of money** or the **rate of interest**.

The effects of interest rates

The problem for the monetary authorities is that controlling the level of interest rates is rather easier than controlling the overall stock of money but the effects of doing so are less certain.

If governments choose to target interest rates as the principal means of conducting monetary policy this may have a series of undesirable effects. These principally relate to the indiscriminate nature of interest rate changes and to the external consequences of monetary policy.

When interest rates are changed it is expected that the general level of demand in the economy will be affected. Thus a rise in interest rates will discourage expenditure by raising the cost of credit. However, the effects will vary:

1   **Investment may be affected more than consumption**. The rate of interest is the main cost of investment whether it is financed by internal funds or by debt. However, most consumption is not financed by credit and hence is less affected by interest rate changes. Since the level of investment in the economy is an important determinant of economic growth and international competitiveness there may be serious long-term implications arising from high interest rates.

2   Even where consumption is affected by rising interest rates, the **effects are uneven**. The demand for consumer durable goods and houses is most affected since these are normally credit based purchases. Hence active interest policy may induce instability in some sectors of business.

The second problem arises from the openness of modern economies and their economic interdependence. There is now a very high degree of capital mobility between economies: large sums of short-term capital move from one financial centre to another in pursuit of higher interest rates. Changes in domestic interest rates relative to those in other financial centres will produce large inflows and outflows of short-term capital. Inflows of capital represent a demand for sterling and hence push up the exchange rate; outflows represent sales of sterling and hence depress the exchange rate. This may bring about unacceptable movements in the exchange rate.

3.3 Monetary policy in the UK

It is useful to look at the current monetary policy in the UK. Similar policies are pursued in the US and the eurozone countries.

In the UK, the central bank has been given responsibility by the government for controlling short-term interest rates. Short-term interest rates are controlled with a view to influencing the rate of inflation in the economy, over the long term. In broad terms, an increase in interest rates is likely to reduce demand in the economy and so lower inflationary pressures, whereas a reduction in interest rates should give a boost to spending in the economy, but could result in more inflation. The aim of economic policy is to find a suitable balance between economic growth and the risks from inflation.

Central governments can control short-term interest rates through their activities in the money markets. This is because the commercial banks need to borrow regularly from the central bank. The central bank lends to the commercial banks at a rate of its own choosing (a rate known in the UK as the repo rate). This borrowing rate for banks affects the interest rates that the banks set for their own customers. Action by a central bank to raise or lower interest rates normally results in an immediate increase or reduction in bank base rates.

KEY POINT

Changes in monetary policy will impact upon business activities by influencing the **availability** of finance, the **cost** of finance, the level of **consumer demand**, the level of **inflation** and the level of **exchange rates**.

3.4 Impact of changes in monetary policy on business decision making

Changes in monetary policy will influence the following factors.

*   **The availability of finance**. Credit restrictions achieved via the banking system or by direct legislation will reduce the availability of loans. This can make it difficult for small, medium-sized new businesses to raise finance. The threat of such restrictions in the future will influence financial decisions by companies, making them more likely to seek long-term finance for projects.

*   **The cost of finance**. Any restrictions on the stock of money, or restrictions on credit, will raise the cost of borrowing, making fewer investment projects worthwhile and discouraging expansion by companies. Also, any increase in the level of general interest rates will increase shareholders' required rate of return, so unless companies can increase their return share prices will fall as interest rates rise. Thus, in times of 'tight' money and high interest rates organisations are less likely to borrow money and will probably contract rather than expand operations.

*   **The level of consumer demand**. Periods of credit control and high interest rates reduce consumer demand. Individuals find it more difficult and more expensive to borrow to fund consumption, whilst saving becomes more attractive. This is another reason for organisations to have to contract operations.

*   **The level of inflation**. Monetary policy is often used to control inflation. Rising price levels and uncertainty as to future rates of inflation make financial decisions more difficult and more important. As prices of different commodities change at different rates the timing of purchase, sale, borrowing and repayment of debt become critical to the success of organisations and their projects. This is discussed further below.

*   **The level of exchange rates**. Monetary policy which increases the level of domestic interest rates is likely to raise exchange rates as capital is attracted into the country. Very many organisations now deal with both suppliers and customers abroad and thus cannot ignore the effect of future exchange rate movements. Financial managers must consider methods of hedging exchange rate risk and the effect of changes in exchange rates on their positions as importers and exporters.

FOULKS LYNCH
PUBLICATIONS

3.5   Impact of inflation on business cashflows and profits

The real effects on the level of profits and the cashflow position of a business of a sustained rate of inflation depends on the form that inflation is taking and the nature of the markets in which the company is operating. One way of analysing inflation is to distinguish between demand pull inflation and cost push inflation.

- **Demand pull inflation** might occur when excess aggregate monetary demand in the economy and hence demand for particular goods and services enables companies to raise prices and expand profit margins.

- **Cost push inflation** will occur when there are increases in production costs independent of the state of demand, e.g. rising raw material costs or rising labour costs. The initial effect is to reduce profit margins and the extent to which these can be restored depends on the ability of companies to pass on cost increases as price increases for customers.

One would expect that the effect of cost push inflation on company profits and cashflow would always be negative, but that with demand pull inflation profits and cashflow might be increased, at least in nominal terms and in the short run. In practice, however, even demand pull inflation may have negative effects on profits and cashflow.

Demand pull inflation may in any case work through cost. This is especially true if companies use pricing strategies in which prices are determined by cost plus some mark-up. In these circumstances demand pull inflation may work via costs.

- Excess demand for goods leads companies to expand output.

- This leads to excess demand for factors of production, especially labour, so costs (e.g. wages) rise.

- Companies pass on the increased cost as higher prices.

In most cases inflation will **reduce profits and cashflow,** especially in the long run.

4   Fiscal policy

Fiscal policy is the manipulation of the government budget in order to influence the level of activity in the economy. It can be described as the aspects of economic policy relating to government spending, taxation and government borrowing.

All governments engage in public expenditure, although levels vary somewhat from country to country. This expenditure must be financed either by taxation or by borrowing. Thus the existence of public expenditure itself raises issues of policy, notably how to tax and whom to tax. But, in addition, the process of expenditure and taxation permits the use of fiscal policy in a wider sense: the government budget can be manipulated to influence the level of aggregate demand in the economy and hence the level of economic activity.

The principal questions related to fiscal policy are as follows:

- How is government expenditure financed?

- What are the consequences of government borrowing?

- What are the limitations and problems of fiscal policy?

4.1   Taxation

The obvious means by which public expenditure can be financed is by taxation. The government receives some income from direct charges in the public sector (e.g. health prescription charges) and from trading profits of some public sector undertakings, but the bulk of its income comes from taxation.

Taxes are divided into broad groups.

- **Direct taxes** are taxes levied directly on income receivers whether they are individuals or organisations. These include income tax, national insurance contributions, corporation tax, inheritance tax.

- **Indirect taxes** are levied on one set of individuals or organisations but may be partly or wholly passed on to others and are largely related to consumption not income. These include VAT and excise duties. By their very nature, indirect taxes tend to be regressive which means they have a relatively greater impact on individuals with lower incomes.

Impacts of excessive taxation

Taxation can raise very large flows of income for the government. However excessive taxation may have undesirable economic consequences. Those most frequently cited are as follows.

- Personal disincentives to work and effort. This may be related mainly to the form of taxation, e.g. progressive income tax (earn more, pay more), rather than the overall level of taxation.

- Discouragement to business, especially the incentive to invest and engage in research and development, which results from high business taxation.

- Disincentive to foreign investment: multinational firms may be dissuaded from investing in economies with high tax regimes.

- A reduction in tax revenue may occur if taxpayers are dissuaded from undertaking extra income-generating work and are encouraged to seek tax-avoidance schemes.

If the tax rate exceeds a certain level, the total tax revenue falls. It should be noted that these disincentive effects, while apparently clear in principle, are difficult to identify in the real world and hence their impact is uncertain.

4.2   Government borrowing

The government budget (including central and local government) is a statement of public expenditure and income over a period of one year. Expenditure can be financed either by taxation or by borrowing. The relationship of expenditure to taxation indicates the state of the budget. Three budget positions can be identified.

- A **balanced budget:** total expenditure is matched by total taxation income.

- A **deficit budget:** total expenditure exceeds total taxation income and the deficit must be financed by borrowing.

- A **surplus budget:** total expenditure is less than total taxation income and the surplus can be used to pay back public debt incurred as a result of previous deficits.

Broadly the government can undertake two types of borrowing:

- It can borrow directly or indirectly **from the public** by issuing relatively illiquid debt. This includes National Savings certificates, premium bonds, long-term government stock. This is referred to as 'funding' the debt.

- It can borrow **from the banking system** by issuing relatively liquid debt such as Treasury bills. This is referred to as 'unfunded' debt.

Long-term government stock is issued for long-term financing requirements, whereas Treasury bills are issued to fund short-term cash flow requirements.

4.3   Problems of fiscal policy

Two difficulties associated with fiscal policy have dominated debates about macroeconomic management in recent years:

- the problem of 'crowding out'
- the incentive effects of taxation.

Both have had a major impact on the way in which fiscal policy has been conducted, especially in the UK and USA.

Crowding out

It is suggested that fiscal policy can lead to 'financial crowding out', whereby government borrowing leads to a fall in private investment since it would lead to higher interest rates. This argument has come in for some criticism.

KEY POINT

Doubts exist over the likely size of any crowding out effect of government borrowing on other borrowers but a very large PSBR may well lead to a **fall in private investment**.

However, when the economy is depressed, and there is not much new private sector investment, government spending programmes could help to give a boost to the economy.

Incentives

It is likely that all taxes have some effect. Indeed, the structure of taxes is designed to influence particular economic activities: in particular, taxes on spending are used to alter the pattern of consumption. Here are two examples.

- High excise duties on alcohol and tobacco products reflect social and health policy priorities.
- The recent decision in the UK to use excise duties to raise the real price of petrol over time is designed to discourage the use of private cars because of the environmental effects.

Thus taxes as instruments of fiscal policy can fulfil a variety of useful functions.

KEY POINT

High taxes can lead to personal and business **disincentives** to work and investment.

However, there has been a growing concern among some economists that taxes have undesirable side effects on the economy, notably on incentives. As we have seen, it is argued that high taxes, especially when they are steeply progressive, act as a disincentive to work and effort. Moreover some taxes have more specific effects. For example, employer national insurance payments raise the cost of labour and probably reduce employment.

Conclusion

This chapter has given a brief overview of the ways in which monetary and fiscal policies can impact on the financial management decisions of a business.

**SELF-TEST
QUESTIONS**

Macroeconomic policy

1   What are the principal objectives of macroeconomic policy? How may these conflict? (2.1, 2.2)
2   What implications does macroeconomic policy have for the costs of businesses? (2.3)

Monetary policy

3   Define monetary policy and explain its principal elements. (3)
4   Why can a central bank determine the price of money or the stock of money, but not both? (3)

Fiscal policy

5   Discuss the possible impacts of excessive taxation. (4.1)

6   What is meant by 'financial crowding out'? (4.3)

Chapter 2

GOVERNMENT INTERVENTION AND REGULATION

CHAPTER CONTENTS

In this chapter we shall continue our look at the economic environment in which an organisation operates by considering how governments can intervene in the management of business. We also consider other external regulations affecting the management of businesses.

Objectives

When you have studied this chapter you should be able to do the following:

- explain the requirement for and the role of competition policy
- explain the requirement for and the role of official aid intervention
- explain the requirement for and the role of green policies
- identify examples of government intervention and regulation.

1 Regulation of business

We saw in Chapter 1 how the government can have an impact in general terms on business operations through its macroeconomic policies, and we now turn to some of the more specific measures that may be taken to regulate business.

In particular, we shall consider pricing restrictions, green policies and corporate governance.

1.1 Pricing restrictions

It is not the government's place to set prices for goods and services provided by businesses in the private sector. In a competitive marketplace, prices will be set within the industry according to demand and supply. All producers have to accept the prevailing market price, unless they are able to add distinguishing features to their products (e.g. branding, superior technology) that enable them to charge higher prices.

However, some markets are characterised by various degrees of market power, in particular monopolies, whereby producers become price **makers** rather than price **takers**

The absence of competition results in disadvantages to the economy as a whole.

- **Economic inefficiency:** output is produced at a higher cost than necessary. For example, there may be no incentive to reduce costs by improving technology used.

- **Monopolies may be able to engage in price discrimination:** charging different prices to different customers for the same good or service, e.g. peak and off-peak pricing. This may act against the interests of customers.

- **Disincentive to innovate:** the absence of competition may reduce the incentive to develop new products or new production processes.

- **Pricing practices**: monopolies may adopt pricing practices to make it uneconomic for new firms to enter the industry thus reducing competition in the long run. These potential problems of companies with monopoly power must be considered in the light of some possible advantages that may be associated with such firms.

- **Large firms may secure economies of scale**: it is possible that there are significant economies of scale, reducing production costs, but that these require large firms and hence the number of firms in an industry is restricted. In this case the benefits of economies of scale may offset the inefficiencies involved.

- **The special case of natural monopolies**: this is the case where the economies of scale in the provision of some basic infrastructure are so great that only one producer is feasible. This may be the case of the public utilities in energy and water.

- **Research and development**: it may be that monopoly profits are both the reward for, and the source of finance for, technological and organisational innovation. Thus some static welfare losses have to be accepted in order to ensure a dynamic and innovative business sector.

Economic theory concludes that, all other things being equal, economic welfare is maximised when markets are competitive.

1.2 Fair competition: public provision and regulation

The response to the problems associated with monopoly power can take a variety of forms. The first of these is **public provision**. This is where an economic activity is nationalised. The advantages of this are as follows:

- unfair pricing practices and/or excessive prices can be eliminated

- cost advantages of economies of scale can be reaped.

Traditionally, public utilities have presented the most convincing case for nationalisation because they are natural monopolies. However, nationalised industries may have disadvantages, notably a greater potential for cost-inefficiency.

The alternative response to the dangers of monopoly is regulation.

Self regulation is common in many professions where the profession itself establishes codes of conduct and rules of behaviour (e.g. the Law Society, the British Medical Association).

The alternative is some form of **public or legal regulation**. An example in the UK is the establishment of regulatory bodies for the privatised utilities such as OFTEL and OFGAS. These were established in recognition of the monopoly power of the privatised utilities and have a degree of power over both prices and services in these industries.

Another UK regulatory body is the Financial Services Authority (FSA) which has responsibility for regulating the financial services, banking and insurance markets. The FSA does not have to control monopolies, but it is concerned with ensuring fair competition and protecting the public against unfair treatment by financial organisations.

1.3 Fair competition: the control of monopoly

Formal competition policy in the UK has centred upon two broad issues.

- monopolies and mergers

- restrictive practices.

The concern for monopolies is with firms which have a degree of monopoly power (defined as having more than 25% of the market for a good or service) or with mergers which may produce a new company with more than 25% of market share. The underlying presumption is that monopolies are likely to be inefficient and may act against the interest of customers.

The concern over restrictive practices is with trading practices of firms which may be deemed to be uncompetitive and act against the interests of consumers.

KEY POINT

A government can try to prohibit anti-competitive agreements and the abuse by companies of a dominant position in their markets.

In the UK, over the last fifty years, there have been various statutes passed to help control the impact of monopolies and restrictive practices. For example, the 1998 *Competition Act* prohibits:

(a)   anti-competitive agreements (such as price-fixing cartels); and

(b)   abuse of a dominant position in a market.

ACTIVITY 1

Taking as an example any commercial organisation with which you are familiar, what are the advantages and disadvantages of a high level of competition in its product markets and resource markets?

Feedback to this activity is at the end of the chapter.

2   Official aid intervention

The political and social objectives of a government, as well as its economic objectives, could be pursued through official aid intervention such as grants and subsidies.

DEFINITION

Externalities are costs (benefits) which are not paid (received) by the producers or consumers of the product but by other members of society.

3   Green policies

Externalities are costs (benefits) which are not paid (received) by the producers or consumers of the product but by other members of society.

The need for green policies arises from the existence of external environmental costs associated with some forms of production or consumption. An example of each is given below:

- **Production:** river pollution from various manufacturing processes

- **Consumption:** motor vehicle emissions causing air pollution and health hazards.

If external costs (and benefits) exist in the production or consumption process and if they are large in relation to private costs and benefits, the price system may be a poor mechanism for the allocation of resources. This is because private producers and consumers ignore (and indeed may be unaware of) the external effects of their activities.

KEY POINT

Externalities lead to a **misallocation of resources** and imply the need for policies to correct this. In particular, **green policies** are needed to tackle externalities that affect the **environment**.

Thus the price system, in which prices are determined by the interaction of supply and demand and which determines the allocation of resources, may lead to a misallocation of resources.

It is likely that policies to control damage to the environment will become more and more common as concern for the environment increases. The UK already has a differential tax on leaded and unleaded petrol and the government has taken the decision to use taxes to raise the real price of petrol each year. There is also a continuing debate in the EU over the possible introduction of a wider 'carbon tax'.

Externalities lead to a **misallocation of resources** and imply the need for policies to correct this. In particular, **green policies** are needed to tackle externalities that affect the **environment**.

4   Corporate governance

KEY POINT

Corporate governance is the system by which companies are directed and controlled.

A further constraint on a company's activities is the system of corporate governance regulation which has been introduced in the UK over the past ten years. In the late 1980s there was widespread belief that the traditional UK system enshrined in the *Companies Acts*, with the board of directors responsible for a company and the auditors appointed by the shareholders but remunerated by the directors, was insufficient to control modern companies.

 FOULKS LYNCH
PUBLICATIONS

4.1 A brief history of corporate governance in the UK

In the UK, the first initiatives for improving corporate governance were made by the Cadbury Committee. This was set up in 1991 by the Financial Reporting Council (FRC), the Stock Exchange and the accountancy profession to examine the reporting and control functions of boards of directors and the role of auditors and shareholders. Its full title was 'The Committee on the Financial Aspects of Corporate Governance', chaired by Sir Adrian Cadbury. In the wake of a number of large company disasters a better title might have been 'The Committee on How to Stop Fraud'.

The Cadbury Report entitled *The Financial Aspects of Corporate Governance* was issued in 1992. It contains a Code of Best Practice, which was supported by the London Stock Exchange and adopted as a voluntary code of best practice by UK listed companies.

Corporate governance issues have been continually reviewed, and the Cadbury Code was followed by the Greenbury Report and the Hampel Report. After the Hampel Committee reported, a Combined Code of Corporate Governance was drawn up. Like the original Cadbury Code, this is a voluntary code of practice for listed companies, but supported by the London Stock Exchange, and any deviations from recommended practice have to be reported and explained in the annual report and accounts.

The Combined Code has not provided an answer to the problems of corporate governance, and many problems remain.

- The Secretary of State for Trade and Industry commissioned the Higgs Report, into the role of non-executive directors. Higgs reported early in 2003, and most of the Higgs proposals were written into a new Combined Code, issued in July 2003.

- The Smith Report was commissioned into the responsibilities of audit committees and the need to ensure the independence of the external auditors. Smith reported early in 2003 to the Financial Reporting Council, and the report's proposals were written into the new Combined Code.

- The government introduced the Directors Remuneration Report Regulations in August 2002. These were issued as a statutory instrument, amending the Companies Act 1985. Quoted companies are now required by law to produce an annual report on directors' remuneration and on the company's policy on directors' remuneration. This report must be put to a shareholder vote for approval at the AGM.

4.2 Key issues in corporate governance

Broadly the Combined Code covers:

- Membership of the board to achieve a suitable balance of power. The chairman and chief executive officer should not be the same individual. There should be a sufficient number of non-executive directors on the board, and most of these should be independent.

- Non-executives on the board should prevent the board from being dominated by the executive directors. The role of the non-executives is seen as critical in preventing a listed company from being run for the personal benefit of its senior executive directors, and amendments to the Combined Code in 2003 included measures to increase the influence of the non-executives on the board.

- A remuneration committee to be established to decide on the remuneration of executive directors. Service contracts for directors should not normally exceed one year. Efforts to give shareholders greater influence over directors' remuneration have since resulted in the Directors' Remuneration Report Regulations.

- The role of the audit committee of the board.. This should consist of non-executive directors, and should work with the external auditors.

- The responsibility of the board of directors for monitoring all aspects of risk, not just the internal control system. When the Combined Code was first issued, the Turnbull Committee was set up by the ICAEW to report on the risk management element of corporate governance. The Turnbull report produced recommendations, and a risk report is now provided by listed companies in their annual report and accounts.

4.3   Audit committees

An **audit committee** is a committee of the board of directors, normally consisting of three to five directors with no operating responsibility in financial management, whose primary function is to assist the board to fulfil its stewardship responsibilities by reviewing the **systems of internal control**, the **audit process** and the **financial information** which is provided to shareholders.

Most UK listed companies now have an audit committee. An **audit committee** is a committee of the board of directors, normally consisting of three to five directors with no operating responsibility in financial management, whose primary function is to assist the board to fulfil its stewardship responsibilities by reviewing the **systems of internal control**, the **audit process** and the **financial information** which is provided to shareholders.

(a)   *Objectives and advantages*

Three main objectives are usually associated with audit committees:

(i)   Increasing public confidence in the credibility and objectivity of published financial information (including unaudited interim statements).

(ii)   Assisting directors (particularly non-executive directors) in meeting their responsibilities in respect of financial reporting.

(iii) Strengthening the independent position of a company's external auditor by providing an additional channel of communication.

In addition:

(iv)   They may improve the quality of management accounting; being better placed to criticise internal functions.

(v)   They should lead to better communication between the directors, external auditors and management.

(b)   *Disadvantages*

Audit committees may lead to:

(i)   fear that their purpose is to catch management out

(ii)   non-executive directors being over-burdened with detail

(iii) a 'two-tier' board of directors.

Finally, there is undoubtedly additional cost in terms of, at the least, time involved.

It seems likely that following the publication of the Smith report in 2003, the responsibilities of the audit committee will be enhanced.

4.4   Directors' remuneration

Following the success of the work of the Cadbury Committee, in 1995 the Confederation of British Industry (CBI) set up a committee under the chairmanship of Sir Richard Greenbury, the chairman of Marks and Spencer, to recommend best practice guidelines for UK company directors' pay. The CBI hoped that the

FOULKS LYNCH
PUBLICATIONS

Greenbury committee's work would prevent the government from legislating in what had become a controversial area.

The concern about directors' pay was that 'fat cat' directors were paying themselves excessive amounts, and the size of their rewards seemed to bear no relationship to the performance of the company. A view was expressed that a substantial proportion of executive directors' pay should be performance-related, so that the best interests of directors (higher rewards) would be compatible with the best interests of shareholders (higher profits, dividends and share price).

The Greenbury Report recommends that:

(a) The board of directors of listed companies should set up a remuneration committee of non-executive directors to determine specific remuneration packages for each executive director.

(b) The remuneration committee should report each year to the shareholders, in the company's annual report, giving the company's policy on executive directors' remuneration, and giving full details of each individual director's remuneration package. This recommendation is included in the UK Listing Rules and is a compulsory requirement for listed companies. The provisions in the UK Listing Rules have now been replaced by the even stricter legal requirements of the Directors' Remuneration Report Regulations 2002.

(c) Remuneration committees must provide the packages needed to attract, retain and motivate directors, but should take a robust line on payment of compensation where performance has been unsatisfactory.

Greenbury's recommendations were included in the Combined Code, first published in 1998. When the Code was updated in 2003, some new guidelines were introduced. For example, remuneration packages should not include excessive payoffs in the event of the directors' dismissal.

4.5   Future developments

Developments in corporate governance are likely to happen regularly. Not all developments have been mentioned here. One such development was the Public Interest Disclosure Act 1998, also known as the whistleblowers' charter. When an employee 'blows the whistle' on suspected malpractice within a company or other organisation, he or she is protected by law from victimisation (redundancy, demotion, being overlooked for promotion). Companies found guilty of victimisation will be liable to pay large sums in compensation to the individual. Already, large amount of money have been paid by UK companies to victimised whistleblowing employees.

ACTIVITY 2

Government intervention in the running of business is always a topical issue – try and collect newspaper/magazine articles looking at this area from different viewpoints. Some of the changes to corporate governance practice that are being recommended have met strong opposition from many senior business executives. Which side of the argument are you on?

There is no feedback to this activity.

Conclusion

This chapter has continued our look at government policy towards business by looking at more specific forms of business regulation through both government action and corporate governance.

SELF-TEST
QUESTIONS

Regulation of business

1   What are the principal ways in which the government can discourage the misuse of monopoly power? (1.2, 1.3)

2   What are the two main strands of UK competition policy? (1.3)

3   Sketch the institutional framework of regulation. (1.3)

Green policies

4   How might governments attempt to reduce the level of pollution caused by manufacturing firms? (3)

Corporate governance

5   What is meant by corporate governance? (4)

6   What are the key issues in corporate governance? (4.2)

FEEDBACK TO
ACTIVITY **1**

Advantages	*Disadvantages*
Greater production efficiency.	No monopoly profits
When labour is scarce, there is likely to be greater pressure for technological innovation and automation	Risk of price-cutting by competitors to levels that are not sustainable in the long term
Firms should be more customer-oriented	Higher resource costs
Competition in the product market could stimulate innocaiton and growth	Shortages in key resources

Chapter 3
FINANCIAL MANAGEMENT OBJECTIVES

This chapter introduces the role of the financial manager, who is concerned with the long-term achievement of corporate objectives by the efficient allocation of financial resources. The main area of concern here is the establishment of objectives, with consideration of the particular complexities of multiple stakeholders and not-for-profit organisations.

Much of the material is introductory, with more detailed discussion to follow in later chapters.

Objectives

When you have studied this chapter you should be able to do the following:

- broadly describe the relationship between financial management, management accounting and financial accounting

- discuss the nature and scope of financial objectives for private sector companies in the context of organisational objectives

- discuss the role of social and non-financial objectives in private sector companies and identify their financial implications

- identify objectives (financial and otherwise) in not-for-profit organisations and identify the extent to which they differ from private sector companies

- discuss the problems of multiple stakeholders in financial management and the consequent multiple objectives and scope for conflict.

1 The nature, purpose and scope of financial management

The role of the financial manager is separated into three main areas.

- the raising of finance

- the efficient allocation of financial resources

- maintaining control over the resources to ensure objectives are met.

A different way of describing corporate finance is that it determines which investments should the firm undertake; how, when, where and how much finance should be raised; and how the organisation's profits should be used or allocated.

1.1 Raising finance

The organisation must have the right amount of finance available at the right time to work towards its objectives. The financial manager must therefore be fully conversant with the short, medium and long-term funds required to invest in fixed assets and working capital.

Once the funding requirements have been identified, the financial manager will need to seek out the most appropriate sources of finance, taking account of cost, availability, term of finance and risk.

One of the most common sources of finance will be the internally generated surpluses from operations. When deciding as to the extent to which this is used, considerations will include dividend policy and the impact on capital structure.

External funds may be raised from a variety of financial institutions and individuals, in the form of both equity and debt finance, and the financial manager must try to match the characteristics of the chosen source(s) to the requirements of the firm.

1.2   Allocation of resources

The funds raised must be allocated in the most efficient and productive manner in meeting corporate objectives. Both past and forecast data must be analysed to identify the most appropriate areas to receive additional financial resource.

The financial manager must advise on the allocation of funds in terms of total investment, how this is split between fixed and current assets (working capital), and the levels of risk and return expected.

1.3   Control over resources

It is important that the use of allocated resources is continually monitored to ensure that the various activities undertaken by the organisation continue to make maximum contribution to the achievement of the organisational objectives. To this end, the efficiency of investments must be measured, in terms of a comparison between actual results and those forecast, or necessary, for the achievement of long-term objectives.

Each of these areas of financial management will be examined in greater detail as you work through the text.

1.4   Financial management, management accounting and financial accounting

Management accounting and financial management are both concerned with the use of resources to achieve a given target. Much of the information used and reported is common to both functions.

The main difference is in the time scales. Whilst financial management has targets, or objectives, that are generally long-term by nature, management accounting usually operates within a 12 month time horizon. The management accountant will be concerned with providing information for the more day-to-day functions of control and decision making. This will involve budgeting, cost accounting, variance analysis, and evaluation of alternative uses of short-term resources.

Financial accounting is not directly involved in the day to day planning, control and decision making of an organisation. Rather, it is concerned with providing information about the historical results of past plans and decisions. The purpose is to keep the owners (shareholders) and other interested parties informed as to the overall financial position of the business, and will not be concerned with the detailed information used internally by management accountants and financial managers.

2   Organisational strategy and financial objectives

2.1   The importance of financial strategy to the organisation

An organisation's **strategy** is a course of action, including the specification of resources required, to achieve a specific objective.

Financial strategy is that part of the overall organisational strategy that falls within the scope of the financial manager.

An organisation's financial managers must plan their courses of action to achieve the organisation's financial objectives. Financial managers concern themselves with questions such as the following:

- From which sources should funds be raised?

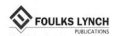

- Should proposed investments be undertaken?
- How large a dividend should be paid?
- How should working capital be controlled, e.g. should discounts be offered to debtors for prompt payment?
- Should hedging strategies be adopted to avoid currency risk or interest rate risk?

This text sets out to examine these questions and many more to enable financial managers to carry out their work. Without a financial strategy, the financial managers' work would be impossible.

2.2   Financial strategy and overall corporate strategy

Each level of a business can have its own strategy. Three levels are commonly identified.

Corporate strategy concerns the decisions to be made by senior management such as the particular business that the company is in, and whether new markets should be entered or current markets withdrawn from. Such decisions can often have important financial implications. If, for example, a decision is taken to enter a new market, should an existing company in that market be bought, or should a new company be started from scratch?

Business strategy concerns the decisions to be made by the separate strategic business units within the group. Each unit will try to maximise its competitive positions within its chosen market.

Operational strategy concerns how the different functional areas within a strategic business unit plan their operations to satisfy the corporate and business strategies being followed. We are of course most interested in the decisions facing the finance functions.

2.3   Financial objectives

The financial manager must try to ensure the achievement of the company's objectives. We will now look at the process whereby a firm will decide upon its objectives.

In order to apply analytical techniques to financial management, some more precise definitions of objectives are essential. These are considered by looking at:

- the concepts of maximising and satisficing
- the problem of multiple stakeholders.

3   Maximising and satisficing

Maximising involves seeking the best possible outcome.

Satisficing involves finding a merely adequate outcome.

Management could, on the one hand, constantly seek the maximum level of profitability, even though this might involve exposure to risk and much higher management work-loads. On the other hand, management might decide to hold profits at a satisfactory level, avoid risky ventures and reduce work-loads.

Within a company, management might seek to maximise the return to some groups (e.g. shareholders) and satisfy the requirements of other groups (e.g. employees). The discussion about objectives is really about which group's returns management is trying to maximise.

The issue is clouded by the fact that the management may itself be unclear about the difference between maximising and satisficing. Thus management may believe that it is, say, **maximising** shareholder returns, when in fact it has reduced effort and accepted a merely **satisfactory** level of shareholder return.

Nevertheless, the objectives, if not the applications, of maximising as compared to satisficing should be clear.

4   The problem of multiple stakeholders

It is generally accepted that the strategic objective of a profit-seeking organisation is the long-term goal of **maximising the wealth of the owners (usually shareholders)** of the organisation. However, a firm has many other stakeholders long and short-term, with many conflicting interests.

A stakeholder is someone with an interest in what the organisation does. The interests of some stakeholders are strong and can affect the objectives set for the organisation by its leaders.

ACTIVITY 1

Before reading further – list all those who you feel are stakeholders in a company.

Identify a key objective for each stakeholder you have listed.

Feedback to this activity is at the end of the chapter

In spite of the existence of other stakeholders, an assumption commonly applied in financial management is that the main objective of a company is to maximize the wealth of its ordinary shareholders (equity shareholders).

4.1   Non-financial objectives

The influence of the various parties with interests in the firm results in firms adopting many non-financial objectives, examples of which are:

- growth
- diversification
- survival
- maintaining a contented workforce
- becoming research and development leaders
- providing top quality service to customers
- maintaining respect for the environment.

Some of these objectives may be viewed as specific to individual parties. For example, engineering managers may stress research and development, whereas others may be seen as straight surrogates for profit, and thus for shareholder wealth (e.g. customer service). Finally, areas such as respect for the environment may be social constraints rather than objectives. In other words, managers may be limited by environmental considerations in the actions they take, while not regarding sound environmental policies as an objective in themselves.

List the non-financial objectives of a firm with which you are familiar – and look at how they conflict.

There is no feedback to this activity.

5   Shareholders as stakeholders

Within any economic system, the equity investors provide the risk finance.

Shareholders' wealth is affected by two main factors: the **rate of return** earned on the shares, and the **risk** attached to earning that return. For a quoted company, expectations about these two factors will play a major part in determining the market price of the shares.

The market value of shares will not necessarily be increased by increasing the expected rate of return, if this is achieved by increasing the risk of the company's operations. Indeed many risk-averse shareholders may sell out, causing a drop in market value. There is therefore a trade-off between risk and return.

The nature of risk is explained later. At this stage, you should understand the nature of return to shareholders and how it is usually measured.

5.1   Measuring return

Return can be measured by earnings or dividends, and capital appreciation.

Earnings per share (EPS)

The profit, or earnings, measure is familiar to accountants, and the earnings per share is often used as a measure of returns to equity.

$$\text{Earnings per share (EPS)} = \frac{\text{Attributable equity profit for the period}}{\text{Number of equity shares in issue}}$$

The disadvantage of EPS is that it does not represent the income of the shareholder. Rather, it represents the investor's share of profits generated by the company according to an accounting formula.

Whilst there is obviously a correlation between earnings applicable to individual shareholders, and their wealth, they are not equal.

Dividend yield

$$\text{Dividend yield} = \frac{\text{Actual dividend paid per share}}{\text{Market price per share}} \times 100\%$$

The dividend yield provides a direct measure of the wealth received by a shareholder. It is, however, incomplete in that it ignores the capital gain on the share which most investors would expect.

Dividend yield and capital growth

The addition of capital growth provides a more complete measure of return.

Example

One year ago the share price of C plc was 220p. A dividend of 40p has just been paid and the price is now 242p. What percentage return has been earned over the past year?

Solution

Step 1 Work out the current value of the share, including dividend.

	Pence
Current market price	242
Current dividend	40
Total value of holding now	282

Step 2 Calculate the increase in value over the year, as a percentage of the initial share price.

Value one year ago	220p

$$\text{Rate of return} = \frac{282 - 220}{220} = 0.28, \text{ or} \qquad 28\%$$

Alternative solution

	%
Dividend yield $\frac{40}{220} =$	18
Capital growth $\frac{242 - 220}{220} =$	10
Total rate of return	28%

The actual return received will depend on the shareholder's marginal rate of income tax and the capital gains tax suffered on any realised capital gain.

Whether shareholders prefer high dividend income or high capital gains will depend very much on their tax position. This problem is considered later in the context of dividend policy.

For the moment however, it is concluded that the best measure of returns to equity investors is dividend yield plus capital growth. Obviously, in making decisions about the future it is the **anticipated** dividend yield and capital growth that become important.

However, the concept of earnings per share will not be ignored in this text. Much financial evaluation is in terms of earnings, and they obviously have a major impact on both company decisions and share prices.

6   Managerial objectives

It is traditional to say that the principal objective of a company is maximisation of shareholder wealth. However, the actions taken by a company are decided upon by its managers (directors). We should not forget that the managers will have their own objectives which could conflict with those of the shareholders and other interested parties.

Managers could be interested in maximising the sales revenue of the firm or the number of employees so as to increase their own prestige and improve their career prospects. Alternatively they could be interested in maximising their personal short-term financial return by increasing salaries or managerial 'perks'. It is also important to note that different groups of managers may be following differing objectives. Marketing management may be interested in maximising sales revenue, whilst production managers may be more interested in developing the technological side of the firm as far as possible.

KEY POINT

The **total return** earned by an investor comprises two elements: **income** and **capital growth**.

KEY POINT

Managers may take decisions that will further their achievement of their own objectives which can conflict with those of other stakeholders.

Although the firm is owned by the shareholders the day-to-day control is in the hands of the managers (this situation being referred to as the divorce of ownership and control) and they are in an ideal position to follow their own objectives at the expense of other parties. Whilst, in theory, shareholders can replace the management of a company by voting out the directors at the AGM, in practice the fragmented nature of shareholdings makes this unlikely.

6.1   Conflicts of interest

Specific examples of the conflicts of interest that might occur between managers and shareholders include the following:

Takeovers

Managers in a target company often devote large amounts of time and money to 'defending' their companies against takeover. However, research has shown that shareholders in companies that are successfully taken over often earn large financial returns. On the other hand managers of companies that are taken over frequently lose their jobs. This is a common example of the conflict of interest between the two groups.

Time horizon

Managers know that their performance is usually judged on their short-term achievements. Shareholder wealth on the other hand is affected by the long-term performance of the firm. Managers can frequently be observed to be taking a short-term view of the firm which is in their own best interest but not in that of the shareholders.

Risk

Shareholders appraise risks by looking at the overall risk of their investments in a wide range of shares. They do not have 'all their eggs in one basket' and can afford a more aggressive attitude toward risk-taking than managers, whose career prospects and short-term financial remuneration depend on the success of their individual firm.

DEFINITION

Gearing is the ratio of a company's debt finance to its equity finance.

Gearing

The higher a company's gearing ratio, the higher the risk faced by the shareholders. This is covered in considerable detail later in the text.

As managers are likely to be more cautious over risk than shareholders they might wish to adopt lower levels of gearing than would be optimal for the shareholders.

Rewards

Senior managers might seek to ensure that they are highly rewarded, regardless of whether their company is doing well or badly. Shareholders are more likely to want directors to be paid well only if the company achieves a good performance.

KEY POINT

Managers' objectives will often be concerned with the short-term stability of the firm (and thus their jobs) which may conflict with the longer-term growth objectives of the shareholders.

6.2   The distinction between long-term and short-term objectives

Note the example above where managers' short-term objectives could be different from shareholders' long-term objectives. The assumed objective of financial managers is the maximisation of long-term shareholder value but it would be foolish to ignore short-term influences. The minimum short-term objective that managers seek would be stability: risks would be eliminated wherever possible and large movements in the share price would be avoided.

If a company encounters a recession it may find that it starts to make losses and could have to reassess its objectives; the long-term objective continues to be to report a steady growth in earnings per share but the short-term objective is simply to survive.

Managers' objectives will often be concerned with the short-term stability of the   firm (and thus their jobs) which may conflict with the longer-term growth objectives of the shareholders. The effect of **conflict of interest** between managers and shareholders can be minimised by the design of a **remuneration scheme** that encourages decisions that are in the interest of the shareholders.

6.3   Management remuneration packages

As discussed above, the objectives of shareholders and managers may not coincide and managers may engage in policies and practices which would not be consistent with those desired by shareholders.

A way of helping to avoid the problem of conflicting objectives is by the introduction of carefully designed remuneration packages for managers which would motivate them to take decisions which were consistent with the objectives of the shareholders.

Important factors to include in such schemes are as follows:

- The schemes should be easy to monitor, clearly defined and impossible to manipulate by managers.

- Management compensation should be linked to changes in shareholder wealth, if possible reflecting the managers' contribution to increased shareholder wealth.

- The time horizon of managers should match that of shareholders. For example, if shareholders require long-term share price maximisation managers should be encouraged to take decisions in line with this objective and not decisions that maximise short-term profits.

- Shareholders' and managers' attitudes to risk should be encouraged to be similar although this is extremely difficult since shareholders can spread their risk by investing in many different companies, but managers cannot easily do this.

Types of remuneration scheme include the following:

(a)   *A bonus based upon a minimum level of pre-tax profit*

This scheme would be easy to set up and monitor.

Disadvantages are that the scheme may lead to managers taking decisions that would result in profits being earned in the short term at the expense of long-term profitability. It could also lead to managers under-achieving, i.e. relaxing as soon as the minimum is achieved. The scheme might also tempt managers to use creative accounting to boost the profit figure.

(b)   *A share option scheme or the award of shares*

This scheme has the advantage that it will encourage managers to maximise the value of the shares of the company, i.e. the wealth of the shareholders. Such schemes are normally set up over a relatively long period, thereby encouraging managers to make decisions to invest in profitable projects which should result in an increase in the price of the company shares. However, efficient managers may be penalised at times when share prices in general are falling.

An alternative is therefore to reward managers by giving them fully-paid shares in the company as part of a bonus arrangement.

(c)   *A bonus based on turnover growth*

Turnover growth could be achieved at the expense of profitability, e.g. by reducing selling prices or by selecting high revenue product lines which may not necessarily be the most profitable. Maximising turnover is unlikely to maximise shareholder wealth.

(d) Profit related pay

The UK government used to encourage companies to establish profit related pay schemes by permitting employees to receive a limited amount of tax-free pay related to profit performance. However, this is no longer available.

(e) Avoiding rewards for failure

An executive's contract should perhaps restrict his entitlement to a 'pay off' if he is persuaded to resign for reasons of poor performance.

The effect of **conflict of interest** between managers and shareholders can be minimised by the design of a **remuneration scheme** that encourages decisions that are in the interest of the shareholders.

ACTIVITY 3

Do you know of any reward systems intended to foster goal congruence in companies with which you are familiar, e.g. bonus payments, share options, profit related pay? Try to decide whether you believe that such schemes are in fact an effective means of motivation.

There is no feedback to this activity.

6.4   Conclusions on corporate objectives

In the real world organisations undoubtedly follow objectives other than the maximisation of shareholder wealth. The return to equity holders will be an important consideration in financial decisions but it is unlikely to be the only one.

It is important, however, not to overplay the above conflicts. Most managers know that, if they let the shareholders down, share prices will fall and this could result in difficulty in raising further finance, unwanted takeover bids and the end of managerial careers. Also the increasing concentration of shares in the hands of institutional investors such as insurance companies and pension funds means that the divorce of ownership and control is far from complete.

KEY POINT

Institutional investors, because of their large shareholdings, are considered to hold great potential power over company management.

Actions of institutions, particularly in times of takeover bids, can determine the future of the firm and their objectives must be carefully considered by managers.

A compromise view of corporate objectives would be that, for a listed company, shareholder wealth will be the paramount objective but it will be tempered by the influences and objectives of other parties.

For the purpose of studying financial management you are recommended initially to accept the 'classical' objective of the maximisation of shareholder wealth for the purpose of theory building but when it comes to the evaluation and criticism of the theories then to be prepared to relax this objective.

7   Not-for-profit organisations

7.1   Objectives of 'not-for-profit' organisations

Organisations such as charities and trade unions are not run to make profits, but to benefit prescribed groups of people. Since the services provided are limited primarily by the funds available, the key objective is to raise the maximum possible sum each year (net of fund raising expenses) and to spend this sum as effectively as possible on the target group (with the minimum of administration costs).

Not-for-profit organisations will normally set targets for particular aspects of each accounting period's finances such as the following:

- total to be raised in grants and voluntary income
- maximum percentage that fund raising expenses represents of this total
- amounts to be spent on specified projects

• maximum permitted administration costs.

The actual figures achieved can then be compared with these targets and control action taken if necessary.

7.2   Financial objectives in public corporations

This category of organisation includes such bodies as nationalised industries and local government organisations. They represent a significant part of the UK economy and sound financial management is essential if their affairs are to be conducted efficiently. The major problem here lies in obtaining a measurable objective.

For a company listed on the stock market we can take the maximisation of shareholder wealth as a working objective and know that the achievement of this objective can be monitored with reference to share price and dividend payments. For a public corporation the situation is more complex. There are two questions to be answered:

• In whose interests are they run?

• What are the objectives of the interested parties?

Presumably such organisations are run in the interests of society as a whole and therefore we should seek to attain the position where the gap between the benefits they provide to society and the costs of their operation is the widest (in positive terms). The cost is relatively easily measured in accounting terms. However, many of the benefits are intangible. For example, the benefits of such bodies as the National Health Service or Local Education Authorities are almost impossible to quantify.

Because of the problem of quantifying the non-monetary objectives of such organisations most public bodies operate under objectives determined by the government (and hence ultimately by the electorate). Such objectives might include any or all of the following:

• obtaining a given accounting rate of return

• cash limits

• meeting budget

• breaking even in the long run.

ACTIVITY 4

Each time you read an article or hear a news item on an public sector organisation's policy or action consider which objective it is trying to achieve.

There is no feedback to this activity.

7.3   Value for money (VFM)

VFM aims to maximise the benefits available at the lowest cost to the taxpayer.

Value for money (VFM) is a notoriously elusive concept and yet it is assumed that everyone recognises it when they see it. The term is frequently bandied about but rarely defined. It is generally taken to mean the pursuit of economy, efficiency and effectiveness.

What do the words 'economy', 'effectiveness' and 'efficiency' mean?

A diagram helps to explain.

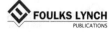

DEFINITIONS

Economy is the terms and conditions under which the authority acquires human and material resources. An economical operation acquires resources of the appropriate quality and provides a service to the appropriate standard at the lowest cost.
Efficiency is the relationship between the goods or services produced and the resources used to produce them. An efficient operation produces the maximum output for any given set of resource inputs; or, it has minimum inputs for any given quantity and quality of services provided.
Effectiveness is the extent to which a programme achieves its established goals or other intended effects.

'**Economy**' is achieved by minimising the cost of inputs required to achieve a defined level of output. (Whether this level of output is sufficient to achieve the organisation's objectives is another matter.)

'**Efficiency**' can be seen as a ratio of outputs to inputs. If we achieve a high level of output in relation to the amount of resources we put in, we have been efficient. (Once again, there is no guarantee that the outputs achieved are sufficient to meet the organisation's objectives.).

'**Effectiveness**' is a measure of outputs. Effectiveness is achieved if the outputs produced match the predetermined objectives. (Whether this is done economically or efficiently is another matter.)

Somewhat more formal definitions of these terms are given in the margin.

The three 'E's' are the fundamental prerequisites of achieving VFM. Their importance cannot be over-emphasised, so much so that external auditors in some parts of the public sector, i.e. local government, are now charged with the responsibility of ensuring that bodies have made adequate arrangements for securing economy, efficiency and effectiveness in the use of public funds.

The problem of accurately measuring VFM cannot be fully resolved in the public sector. Unlike the private sector, there is generally no profit yardstick against which to measure success; and, in most areas of public service provision, no commercial pressure to respond to. Certain indicators have been developed, the following being a few typical examples.

(a)   Cost in providing a certain service per unit (per week/per '000 population/per mile, etc), e.g. cost of providing secondary education per '000 population.

(b)   Service provided per unit (per week/per '000 population etc), e.g. home help hours per '000 population.

(c)   Inputs compared to outputs, e.g. administrative costs per Revenue audit undertaken

(d)   Other, e.g. complaints received.

Care must be taken, however, not to derive false meanings from limited data.

Qualitative judgements about services provided must not be attempted from input information; other factors must also be considered. For example, a government department may have staff who are well-trained and educated, but who are poorly managed and thus a low standard of service results.

Performance indicators are useful, particularly when making comparisons between departments/regions/authorities. However, no two areas are identical and allowance must be made for this and the limitations outlined above.

Conclusion

This chapter has introduced the financial manager's role, and in particular the importance of setting clear objectives as targets to work towards. It has recognised the difficulties arising from multiple stakeholders and not-for profit organisations.

SELF-TEST
QUESTIONS

The nature, purpose and scope of financial management

1   What are the three main areas of concern for the financial manager? (1)

2   How does the work of the financial manager differ from that of the management and financial accountants? (1.4)

The problem of multiple stakeholders

3   Give at least five other interested parties (stakeholders) whose objectives may also need to be considered. (4)

Managerial objectives

4   How may the potential conflict between management and shareholder objectives be minimised? (6.3)

Not-for-profit organisations

5   What sort of targets might not-for-profit organisations set for themselves? (7.1)

6   Distinguish between the three E's. (7.3)

EXAM-TYPE
QUESTION

Private v public sector objectives

Assume that you are a financial manager in a state owned enterprise that is about to have its majority ownership transferred from the government to the private sector and to become a listed company on the Stock Exchange.

Discuss the differences in financial objectives that you are likely to face and the changes in emphasis that are likely to occur in your strategic and operational decisions as a finance manager.   **(25 marks)**

For the answer to this question, see the 'Answers' section at the end of the book

---

FEEDBACK TO
ACTIVITY **1**

Stakeholders

The community at large

The general public can be a stakeholder group, especially when their lives are affected by an organisation's decisions. For example, local residents will be affected by proposals to build a new motorway or add a new runway to an airport. The goals of the community will be broad but will include such aspects as legal and social responsibilities, pollution control and employee welfare.

Company employees

Company employees are a major stakeholder group, and might be represented by trade unions. Their interests are likely to include working conditions, pay and job security.

Company managers/directors

Senior managers are in an ideal position to follow their own aims at the expense of other stakeholders. Their goals will be both long-term (defending against takeovers, sales maximisation) and short-term (profit margins leading to increased bonuses). The power of directors as a stakeholder group is recognised by codes of corporate governance.

Customers

Satisfaction of customer needs will be achieved through the provision of value for money products and services.

Suppliers

Suppliers to the organisation will have short-term goals such as prompt payment terms alongside long-term requirements including contracts and regular business. The importance of the needs of suppliers will depend upon both their relative size and the number of suppliers.

Finance providers

Providers of finance (banks, loan creditors) will primarily be interested in the ability of the firm to repay the finance including interest. As a result it will be the firm's ability to generate cash both in the long term and in the short term that will be the basis of the goals of these providers.

The government

The government has an interest in what companies do. Company activities are central to the success of the economy. Companies provide jobs and pay taxes. Actions by companies could breach the law or damage the environment and governments therefore need to control what they do.

As the objectives of other stakeholders are likely to conflict with those of the shareholders it will be impossible to maximise shareholder wealth and satisfy the objectives of other parties at the same time. In this situation the firm will face multiple, conflicting objectives, and satisficing of interested parties' objectives becomes the only practical approach for management. If this strategy is adopted then the firm will seek to earn a satisfactory return for its shareholders while at the same time (for example) paying reasonable wages and being a 'good citizen' of the community in which it operates.

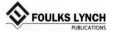

Chapter 4
THE FINANCIAL MANAGEMENT ENVIRONMENT

In the previous chapter we identified one of the main areas of concern to the financial manager as being the raising of finance. In this chapter we look at the institutions and markets that can help in this respect.

Objectives

When you have studied this chapter you should be able to do the following:

- identify the general role of financial intermediaries

- explain the role of commercial banks as providers of funds (including the creation of credit)

- discuss the risk/return trade-off

- identify the international money and capital markets and outline their operation

- explain the functions of a stock market and corporate bond market

- explain the key features of different types of security in terms of the risk/return trade-off

- outline the Efficient Markets Hypothesis (EMH) and assess its broad implications for corporate policy and financial management

- explain the Separation Theorem

- explain the functions of, and identify the links between, the money and capital markets.

1   Financial intermediation

DEFINITION

Intermediation refers to the process whereby potential borrowers are brought together with potential lenders by a third party, the intermediary.

Intermediation refers to the process whereby potential borrowers are brought together with potential lenders by a third party, the intermediary. There are many types of institutions and other organisations that act as intermediaries in matching firms and individuals who need finance with those who wish to invest.

1.1   Clearing banks

The familiar high street banks provide a payment and cheque clearing mechanism. They offer various accounts to investors and provide large amounts of short to medium-term loans to the business sector and the personal sector. They also offer a wide range of financial services to their customers. These are discussed further in a later section.

KEY POINT

- Clearing banks
- Investment banks
- Savings banks
- Building societies
- Finance companies
- Pension funds
- Insurance companies
- Investment/unit trusts

1.2   Investment banks

Investment banks, sometimes called merchant banks, concentrate on the following.

(a)   Financial advice to business firms

Few manufacturing or commercial companies of any size can now afford to be without the advice of a merchant bank. Such advice is necessary in order to obtain investment capital, to invest surplus funds, to guard against takeover, or to take over others. Increasingly, the merchant banks have themselves become actively involved in the financial management of their business clients and have had an influence over the direction these affairs have taken.

(b) Providing finance to business

Merchant banks also compete in the services of leasing, factoring, hire-purchase and general lending. They are also the gateway to the capital market for long-term funds because they are likely to have specialised departments handling capital issues as 'issuing houses'.

(c) Foreign trade

A number of merchant banks are active in the promotion of foreign trade by providing marine insurance, credits, and assistance in appointing foreign agents and in arranging foreign payments.

Not all merchant banks are large and not all offer a wide range of services: the term is now rather misused. However, it is expected that a merchant bank will operate without the large branch network necessary for a clearing bank, it will work closely with its business clients, and will be more ready to take business risks and promote business enterprise than a clearing bank. It is probably fair to say that a merchant bank is essentially in the general business of creating wealth and of helping those who show that they are capable of successful business enterprise.

1.3 Savings banks

Public sector savings banks (e.g. the National Savings Bank in the UK) are used to collect funds from the small personal saver, which are mainly invested in government securities.

1.4 Building societies

These take deposits from the household sector and lend to individuals buying their own homes. They have recently grown rapidly in the UK and now provide many of the services offered by the clearing banks. They are not involved, however, in providing funds for the business sector. Over recent years many have converted to banks.

1.5 Finance companies

These come in three main varieties:

(a) **Finance houses**, providing medium-term instalment credit to the business and personal sector. These are usually owned by business sector firms or by other financial intermediaries. The trend is toward them offering services similar to the clearing banks.

(b) **Leasing companies**, leasing capital equipment to the business sector. They are usually subsidiaries of other financial institutions.

(c) **Factoring companies**, providing loans to companies secured on trade debtors, are usually bank subsidiaries. Other debt collection and credit control services are usually on offer.

1.6 Pension funds

These collect funds from employers and employees to provide pensions on retirement or death. As their outgoings are relatively predictable they can afford to invest funds for long periods of time.

1.7 Insurance companies

These use premium income from policyholders to invest mainly in long-term assets such as bonds, equities and property. Their outgoings from their long-term business (life assurance and pensions) and their short-term activities (fire, accident, motor insurance, etc) are once again relatively predictable and therefore they can afford to tie up a large proportion of their funds for a long period of time.

1.8   Investment trusts and unit trusts

Investment trusts are limited liability companies collecting funds by selling shares and bonds and investing the proceeds, mainly in the ordinary shares of other companies. Funds at their disposal are limited to the amount of securities in issue plus retained profits, and hence they are often referred to as 'closed end funds'. Unit trusts on the other hand, although investing in a similar way, find that their funds vary according to whether investors are buying new units or cashing in old ones. Both offer substantial diversification opportunities to the personal investor.

2   The banking system

2.1   The clearing banks

The clearing banks participate in systems which simplify daily payments so that all the thousands of individual customer payments are reduced to a few transfers of credit between the banks.

The work of these institutions can best be understood through a consideration of the main items in their balance sheets.

2.2   Clearing bank liabilities

The money for which the banks are responsible comes chiefly from their customers' sight and time deposits – mostly current and deposit accounts with which most people are familiar. An important additional item relates to Certificates of Deposit. These are issued generally for a minimum amount of £50,000 and a maximum of £500,000 with an initial term to maturity of from three months to five years.

2.3   Clearing bank assets

Customers' money, as already explained, is re-lent in a variety of ways. The main aim of the banks is to have a range of lending instruments of varying terms so that money can be recovered quickly and yet, at the same time, earn the maximum return. Some funds, however, have to be kept in balances at the central bank (e.g. the Bank of England) for use in settling inter-bank debts through the Clearing House.

Banks have a far wider function than simply handling cheques and individuals' accounts and other deposits. The money they receive is lent out in a variety of ways, in order to achieve maximum return but with sufficient liquidity to repay customers as required.

The banks' lending takes the following main forms:

1   Inter-bank lending

Short-term lendings between banks are referred to as 'inter-bank' loans. The inter-bank markets in sterling and eurocurrencies are the largest of the short-term lending markets (money markets).

2   Buying Treasury bills

The clearing banks and discount houses also hold the government's own short-term securities (Treasury bills), which operate in much the same way as commercial bills.

3   Buying commercial or trade bills

These constitute a definite agreement to pay a certain sum of money at an agreed place and time. A bill is really a sophisticated IOU which is of very great value in foreign trade because it allows exporters to give credit to foreign buyers and yet obtain payments from banks as soon as goods are shipped. The necessary arrangements are nearly always handled by merchant banks. A commercial bill can be held until payment is due (unusual), or discounted with a bank or discount house (normal), or used to pay another debt (not common in modern practice).

4 Loans to customers

The clearing banks lend widely to individuals, private business customers, companies and organisations in the public sector. They do so by overdraft term facilities and loans repayable in instalments during an agreed period. In the UK, until fairly recently, they were reluctant to lend directly for more than short periods, but increasingly they have become involved in longer-term finance (up to about eight years) for business firms and even, under American influence, in the long-term mortgage market.

5 Trade investments

There are many specialist financial and lending activities that the banks are reluctant to handle through their general branches. They prefer to finance these indirectly through the ownership and overall control of specialist subsidiaries. Such activities include the following:

- **Hire purchase**, much of it for the purchase of motor vehicles.

- **Leasing**, i.e. hiring vehicles or equipment as opposed to purchase or hire-purchase, a practice encouraged by the peculiarities of the British taxation system.

- **Factoring and invoice discounting**, i.e. lending to business firms on the security of approved trade debts or taking over responsibility for the collection of trade debts. This is a method that allows a firm to give credit in competitive markets and still be paid for goods in order to keep necessary cash flowing through the firm.

2.4 Credit creation

This section considers the process for creating credit (in effect, creating money) under a modern banking system where banks keep only part of their assets in the form of cash to repay investors. The rest of the assets are in the form of investments which cannot easily be converted into cash.

Bank Z – Balance sheet at day 1

	£		£
Share capital	100	Fixed assets	100
Customer deposits	1,000	Cash	1,000
	1,100		1,100

In this simple example, share capital finances fixed assets, and so can be ignored. The customer deposits represent current accounts of customers. The bank therefore has a liability to repay all of these on demand.

However, since not all customers want their cash out at once, the bank only has to hold say 1/10 (£100) in the form of 'cash' (in practice, mainly deposits at the central bank). The rest can be loaned to other customers. If the bank loans £900 to customers, the balance sheet will look as follows.

Bank Z – Balance sheet at day 2

	£		£
Share capital	100	Fixed assets	100
Customer deposits	1,000	Loans	900
		Cash	100
	1,100		1,100

Note that there is now only £100 cash in the bank. The remaining £900 is in circulation and will eventually be spent and deposited back with the bank. The balance sheet will now look as follows.

Bank Z – Balance sheet at day 3

	£		£
Share capital	100	Fixed assets	100
Customer deposits		Loans	900
(1,000 + 900)	1,900	Cash (100 + 900)	1,000
	———		———
	2,000		2,000
	———		———

2.5   How much money is there in the above system?

The vital point to grasp is that the economy in the above example started with £1,000 cash (ignoring the cash used to subscribe for the share capital and buy the fixed assets). This cash was held outside the banking system and could be spent. There was therefore £1,000 of money in the economy in the form of cash.

Day 1

When that cash is deposited in the bank on Day 1, the **money** in the economy becomes the £1,000 of **deposits**. Remember that money is what can be spent – it is the means of exchange. Thus when the cash is in the bank it is not the **cash** that will be spent but the **customer deposits**. People will write out cheques and spend their bank balance – their deposits.

Day 2

When the bank loans out £900 on Day 2, the amount of **money** in the economy is £1,900, i.e. the £1,000 of deposits as above plus the £900 cash that is now back in circulation and can be spent.

Day 3

When this £900 is deposited back at the bank the money in the economy is still £1,900 – the amount of customer deposits at the bank.

Day 4 to, say, day 20

We can now extend the example because the bank only needs to keep 10% of its deposits in the form of cash. The bank can continue to lend money, have it re-deposited and then lend it again until customer deposits reach £10,000. The balance sheet will now be as follows.

Bank Z – Balance sheet at day 20

	£		£
Share capital	100	Fixed assets	100
Customer deposits	10,000	Loans	9,000
		Cash	1,000
	———		———
	10,100		10,100
	———		———

The money in the economy is now £10,000 – the customer deposits.

3   Money and capital markets

3.1   Financial markets

The financial markets, both capital and money markets, are places where those requiring finance (deficit units) can meet with those able to supply it (surplus units). They offer both primary and secondary markets.

DEFINITIONS

Primary markets deal in new issues of loanable funds. They raise new finance for the deficit units.

Secondary markets allow surplus units to sell their investments on to other investors.

KEY POINT

Secondary markets provide the investor with the means to achieve diversification, risk shifting, hedging and arbitrage.

DEFINITION

Hedging is the reduction or elimination of risk and uncertainty.

DEFINITION

Arbitrage is the process of buying a security at a low price in one market and simultaneously selling in another market at a higher price to make a profit.

KEY POINT

Capital markets deal in longer-term finance, mainly via a stock exchange.

3.2   The role of financial markets

Primary markets provide a focal point for borrowers and lenders to meet. The forces of supply and demand should ensure that funds find their way to their most productive usage.

Secondary markets allow holders of financial claims to realise their investment before the maturity date by selling them to other investors. They therefore increase the willingness of surplus units to invest their funds. A well-developed secondary market should also reduce the price volatility of securities, as regular trading in 'secondhand' securities should ensure smoother price changes. This should further encourage investors to supply funds.

Financial markets help investors achieve the following ends.

(a)   Diversification

By giving investors the opportunity to invest in a wide range of enterprises it allows them to spread their risk. This is the familiar 'Don't put all your eggs in one basket' strategy.

(b)   Risk shifting

Deficit units, particularly companies, issue various types of security on the financial markets to give investors a choice of the degree of risk they take. For example company loan stocks secured on the assets of the business offer low risk with relatively low returns, whereas equities carry much higher risk with correspondingly higher returns.

(c)   Hedging

Financial markets offer participants the opportunity to reduce risk through hedging which involves taking out counterbalancing contracts to offset existing risks. For example, if a UK exporter is awaiting payment in francs from a French customer he is subject to the risk that the French franc may decline in value over the credit period. To hedge this risk he could enter a counterbalancing contract and arrange to sell the French francs forward (agree to exchange them for pounds at a fixed future date at a fixed exchange rate). In this way he has used the foreign exchange market to insure his future sterling receipt. Similar hedging possibilities are available on interest rates and on equity prices.

(d)   Arbitrage

Although it is only the primary markets that raise new funds for deficit units, well-developed secondary markets are required to fulfil the above roles for lenders and borrowers. Without these opportunities more surplus units would be tempted to keep their funds 'under the bed' rather than putting them at the disposal of deficit units. However, the emergence of **disintermediation (reduction in the use of intermediaries) and securitisation (conversation into marketable securities),** where companies lend and borrow funds directly between themselves, has provided a further means of dealing with cash flow surpluses and deficits.

Secondary markets provide the investor with the means to achieve diversification, risk shifting, hedging and arbitrage.

3.3   The capital markets

Capital markets deal in longer-term finance, mainly via a stock exchange.

The major types of securities dealt on capital markets are as follows:

- public sector and foreign stocks
- company securities
- Eurobonds.

Eurobonds are bonds denominated in a currency other than that of the national currency of the issuing company (nothing to do with Europe!). They are also called international bonds.

As stock markets are of crucial importance in meeting the financial needs of business and government, their operation is dealt with in more detail later.

3.4   The money markets

Money markets deal in shorter-term funds, usually in the form of unsecured loans and other types of credit. No physical location exists, transactions being conducted by telephone or telex.

The money market is a market mainly for short-term and very short-term loans, in both sterling and foreign currencies, though some longer-term transactions are also undertaken. In fact, it is not one single market but a number of different markets which closely inter-connect with each other. The main participants in these markets are the central banks (e.g. Bank of England) and the commercial banks. Other participants include the finance houses, building societies, investment trusts and unit trusts, local authorities, large companies, and some private individuals.

3.5   Division of sources of finance

There are a number of possible classifications of funds, but for the purposes of this part of the text one distinction is of particular importance – namely the distinction between long-term and short-term funds.

The following classification is therefore applied.

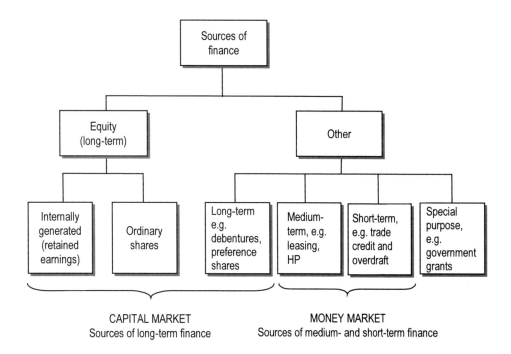

Each of these categories of finance will be considered in more detail in the chapters on sources of finance.

Definitions of long-term, medium-term and short-term finance are somewhat elastic but the following durations can be taken as a rough guide.

Short-term	Up to one year.
Medium-term	1 year to 7 years.
Long-term	7 years or more.

4   International capital markets

An international financial market exists where domestic funds are supplied to a foreign user or foreign funds are supplied to a domestic user. The currencies used need not be those of either the lender or the borrower.

The most important international markets are:

* the Euromarkets
* the foreign bond markets.

4.1   The Euromarkets

The term 'Euromarkets' is somewhat misleading, but the name has stuck. The markets originated in the 1950s, dealing in Eurodollars, but they have now grown to encompass other currencies including Euro-yen, Euro-sterling, Euro-Swiss and so on. Eurocurrency is money deposited with a bank outside its country of origin. For example, money in a US dollar account with a bank in London is eurodollars.

Note that these deposits need not be with European banks, although originally most of them were. Nowadays in fact active Euromarket centres are in London, New York, Tokyo, Singapore and Bahrain. Once in receipt of these Eurodeposits, banks then lend them to other customers and a Euromarket in the currency is created.

4.2   Types of Euromarket

The Eurocurrency market

This incorporates the short- to medium-term end of the Euromarket. It is a market for borrowing and lending eurocurrencies. Various types of deposits and loans are available.

Deposits vary from overnight to five years. Deposits can be in the form of straight-term deposits, with funds placed in a bank for a fixed maturity at a fixed interest rate. However, these carry the problem of interest rate penalties if early repayment is required.

Alternatively, deposits can be made in the form of negotiable **Certificates of Deposit** (CDs). There is an active secondary market in CDs and investors are therefore able to have access to their funds when required. Deposits can be made in individual currencies or in the form of 'currency cocktails' to allow depositors to take a diversified currency position. One common cocktail is the Special Drawing Right, consisting of US dollars, Deutschmarks, yen, French francs and sterling.

Euromarket **loans** may be in the form of straight bank loans, lines of credit (similar to overdraft facilities) and revolving commitments (a series of short-term loans over a given period with regular interest rate reviews). Small loans may be arranged with individual banks, but larger ones are usually arranged through syndicates of banks.

Much of the business on the Eurocurrency market is interbank, but there are also a large number of governments, local authorities and multinational companies involved. Firms wishing to use the market must have excellent credit standing and wish to borrow (or deposit) large sums of money.

The Eurobond market

A **Eurobond** is a bond issued in more than one country simultaneously, usually through a syndicate of international banks, denominated in a currency other than the national currency of the issuer.

This represents the long-term end of the Euromarket.

The bonds can be privately placed through the banks or quoted on stock exchanges. They may run for periods of between three and twenty years, and can be fixed or floating rate. Convertible Eurobonds (similar to domestic convertible loan stocks) and

Option Eurobonds (giving the holder the option to switch currencies for repayment and interest) are also used.

The major borrowers are large companies, international institutions like the World Bank, and the EC. The most common currencies are the US dollar, the euro, the Swiss franc, and to a smaller extent sterling.

5   Stock markets

The syllabus does not require you to have a detailed knowledge of any specific country's stock market or exchange. We may, however, make reference to the markets that operate in the UK for illustration purposes.

5.1   The role of a stock market

A country's stock market is the institution that embodies many of the processes of the capital market. Essentially it is the market for the issued securities of public companies, government bonds, loans issued by local authority and other publicly owned institutions, and some overseas stocks. Without the ability to sell long-term securities easily few people would be prepared to risk making their money available to business or public authorities.

A stock market assists the allocation of capital to industry; if the market thinks highly of a company, that company's shares will rise in value and it will be able to raise fresh capital through the new issue market at relatively low cost. On the other hand, less popular companies will have difficulty in raising new capital. Thus, successful firms are helped to grow and the unsuccessful to contract.

5.2   The role of speculation

Any consideration of a stock market has to face up to the problem of speculation, i.e. gambling. It is suggested that speculation can perform the following functions.

- It **smoothes price fluctuations.** Speculators, to be successful, have to be a little ahead of the rest of the market. The skilled speculator will be buying when others are still selling and selling when others are still buying. The speculator, therefore, removes the peaks and troughs of inevitable price fluctuations and so makes price changes less violent.

- Speculation ensures that **shares are readily marketable**. Almost all stock can be quickly bought and sold, at a price. Without the chance of profit there would be no professional operator willing to hold stock or agree to sell stock that is not immediately available. The fact that there are always buyers and sellers is of considerable importance to the ordinary individual investor who may have to sell unexpectedly at any time with little warning.

Stock markets help in the **determination of a fair price for assets,** and ensures assets are readily **marketable**.

5.3   Buying and selling shares

An investor will contact a **broker** in order to buy and sell shares. The broker may act as agent for the investor by contacting a **market-maker** (see below) or he may act as principal if he makes a market in those shares (i.e. buys and sells on his own behalf). In the latter case he is a **broker-dealer**.

Market-makers maintain stocks of securities in a number of quoted companies, appropriate to the level of trading in that security, and their income is generated by the profits they make by dealing in securities. A market maker undertakes to maintain an active market in shares that it trades, by continually quoting prices for buying and prices for selling the shares (bid and offer prices). If share prices didn't move, their profits would come from the difference (or 'spread') between the bid and offer prices. This profit is approximately represented by the difference between the 'bid' and 'offered'

price for a given security – the price at which a market-maker is prepared to buy the stock and the price at which he would be prepared to sell it.

For example, assume a quotation in respect of a fictitious company, Clynch plc.

The dealer might quote 145, 150.

This means he will buy the shares at £1.45 each and sell at £1.50 each.

KEY POINT

Share prices are dictated by the laws of supply and demand. If the future return/risk profile of the share is anticipated to improve, the demand for that share will be greater and the price higher.

Quotations are based on expectations of the general marketability of the shares and, as such, will probably vary constantly. For example, if an investor wants to buy 10,000 shares, the dealer might decide to raise his prices to encourage people to sell and thereby ensure that he will have sufficient shares to meet the order he has just received. Thus, his next quote might be 150, 155.

Conversely, if the investor wants to sell 10,000 shares, the dealer will be left with that number of additional shares, and he may wish to reduce his quotation to encourage people to buy; thus he may quote 140, 145.

If sufficient numbers of people wish to buy and sell the shares of Clynch plc, eventually a price will be found at which only marginal transactions are taking place.

If the general economic climate is reflected by each company's shares, it follows that there will be times when in general people wish to sell shares and hence prices drop, and other times when in general people are buying shares and prices rise.

Share prices are dictated by the laws of supply and demand. If the future return risk profile of the share is anticipated to improve, the demand for that share will be greater and the price higher.

Broker-dealers in the UK act as both brokers for clients and trade on their own account as dealers. In the UK, their activities in share dealing are restricted largely to listed companies whose shares are traded on SETS, the electronic 'trading book' of the London Stock Exchange.

5.4 Types of stock market

A country may have more than one securities market in operation. For illustration, the UK has the following:

(a) **The London Stock Exchange** – The main UK market for shares, on which the shares of large public companies are quoted and dealt. Costs of meeting entry requirements and reporting regulations are high.

(b) The **Alternative Investment Market (AIM)** – This is a separate market for the shares of smaller companies. Entry and reporting requirements are significantly less than those for the main market of the London Stock Exchange.

(c) An **'Ofex'** (off exchange) market in which shares in some public companies are traded, but through a specialist firm of brokers and not through a stock exchange.

6 The relationship between risk and return

Investment risk arises because returns are variable and uncertain. An increase in risk generally requires an increase in expected returns. For example, if we were comparing a Building Society investment with an investment in equities we would normally require a higher return from equities to compensate us for their extra risk. In a similar way if we were appraising equity investments in a food retailing company against a similar investment in a computer electronics firm we would usually demand higher returns from the electronics investment to reflect its higher risk.

6.1 The benefits of portfolio diversification

Investors generally hold a portfolio of investments, and for this reason this section will consider investment portfolios: however, the trade-off between risk and return also

applies to individual investments. A portfolio is simply a combination of investments. If an investor puts half of his funds into an engineering company and half into a retail shops firm then it is possible that any misfortunes in the engineering company (e.g. a strike) may be to some extent offset by the performance of the retail investment. It would be unlikely that both would suffer a strike in the same period.

6.2   Indifference curves

How do we determine which of a group of portfolios for which we know the risk and return is preferable? It all depends on the investor's attitude to risk against return, which may be depicted diagrammatically as 'indifference curves'. The following diagram shows three possible investments (R, S and T), their positions on the graph being determined by their return/risk combination. The investor who is trying to decide between them has indifference curves as shown.

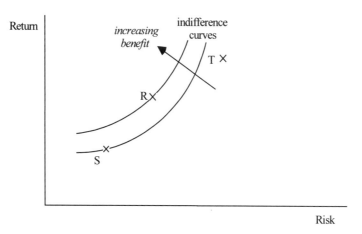

The indifference curves represent alternative combinations of risk and return between which the investor is indifferent. Obviously each investor will have different indifference curves, but they will tend to be of the slope indicated above. This is because most investors are averse to risk (risk averse), and will demand a higher return to compensate for higher risk.

Thus, the indifference curves represent the trade-off between risk and return for an individual investor.

In this example, the investor would prefer R to S as it is on a higher indifference curve – the lower level of risk for S does not adequately compensate for the lower level of return.

ACTIVITY 1

Would the investor prefer T to R on the above diagram?

Feedback to this activity is at the end of the chapter.

6.3   Portfolio selection with both risky and risk-free assets

A 'risk-free' security is one which shows no variability in its predicted returns. In other words its return is known with certainty. In practice it can be approximated by an investment in government stocks or bank deposit accounts at fixed interest (although varying rates of inflation would mean the real return on these investments becomes uncertain). A risk free security can be combined with risky assets to create a portfolio. The following diagram shows how portfolio risk and return varies when the portfolio is made up of varying proportions of risk-free securities (e.g. government stock) and a risky security (e.g. BP shares). For example, the point marked '0.8BP' represents a portfolio that comprises 80% BP shares and 20% government securities.

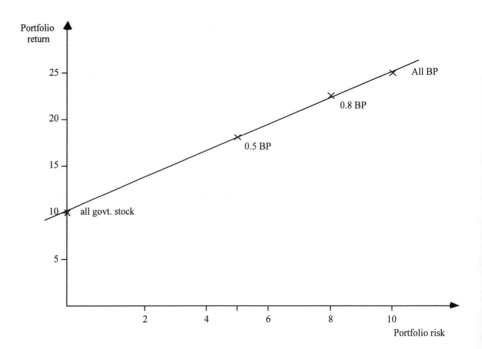

When combining a risk-free security with a risky security, there is a **straight line** trade-off between return and risk.

ACTIVITY 2

What sort of risk-free return is currently available at the time that you read this? You can obtain estimates from looking up the returns available from deposit accounts at banks and building societies, or from government stocks.

There is no feedback to this activity

6.4 Mixing many risky securities

(a) The expected return of a portfolio is equal to the weighted average of the returns of the individual securities in the portfolio.

(b) The risk of the portfolio depends on:

- the risk of each security in isolation

- the proportions in which the securities are mixed

- the correlations between every pair of securities in the portfolio i.e. the interrelationship between their riskiness.

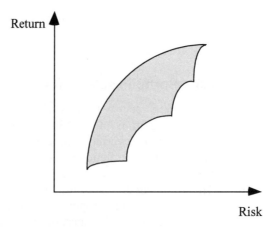

The shaded area shows the return and risk of all the possible portfolios constructed from the securities by mixing them in all possible proportions.

It is possible to identify which of these portfolios are really worth holding.

6.5   The efficient frontier

A rational risk-averse investor would define an **efficient portfolio** as one that has:

- a higher return than any other portfolio with the same risk

- a lower risk than any other with the same return.

So, out of all the possible portfolios which an investor could make out of his chosen securities, which would be chosen?

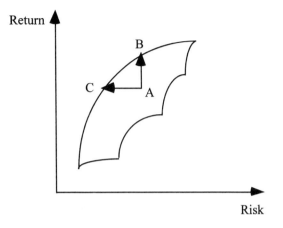

If we started with any portfolio A, in the middle of the opportunity set, then a better portfolio could be identified by moving upwards towards B (higher return, same risk) or to the left towards C (lower risk, same return).

Thinking in this way leads us to the conclusion that the efficient portfolios must lie along the top left hand edge of the opportunity set. This is called the **efficient frontier**.

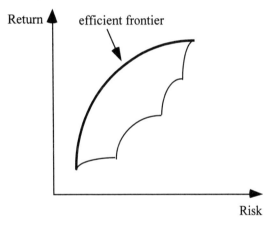

All other portfolios can now be ignored. Only the efficient ones need be considered. Logical investors would eliminate all others.

Notice the shape of this efficient frontier. As we attempt to increase return, risk begins to grow at an increasing rate.

An optimal portfolio could be identified for any investor by superimposing indifference curves on the efficient frontier.

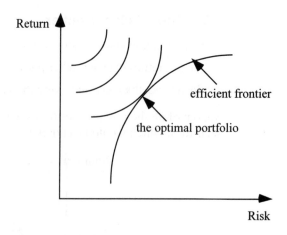

The optimal investment portfolio for an investor is one that optimises the mix of risk and return, given the investor's preferences and attitudes.

6.6   The capital market line

However, this so-called optimal portfolio has ignored the existence of fixed interest risk-free securities.

If this is included, the best portfolio is M in the following diagram, where a line drawn from R_F just touches the efficient frontier at a tangent:

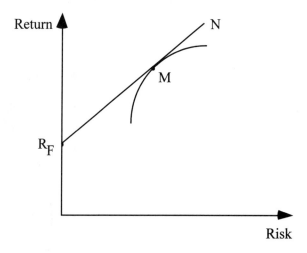

The surprising conclusion is that:

Out of all the possible portfolios that could be constructed from all risky investments, only one portfolio is worth considering – portfolio M.

A combination of R_F and M produces portfolios which are better than any others in terms of the return which is offered for any given level of risk.

However, given the existence of risk-free investment, investors would choose from those on the revised efficient frontier represented by line R_F M.

Portfolios on the line R_F M are achieved by mixing portfolio M with risk-free investments. Portfolios on the line M N are achieved by borrowing at the risk-free rate (remember we have assumed that the risk-free rate applies to borrowing as well as lending) and investing our own funds plus borrowed funds in portfolio M.

Portfolio M includes every risky security which is quoted on the market.

Portfolio M is in fact simply a slice of the whole stock market. The proportions of shares held in it are the same as the total market capitalisations of the shares on the stock market:

Portfolio M is called the market portfolio.

All rational risk-averse investors will hold the market portfolio, according to the model we have just constructed.

Note: It is not necessary for every investor to hold every share on the stock market. Close replicas of portfolio M may be generated by holding as few as fifteen shares. Investment in unit trusts will also achieve the same result.

However, all investors do not have the same attitude to risk. By using the market portfolio, and by either lending or borrowing suitably at the risk-free rate, the investor can choose any level of risk he likes and can predict the return which the market will give him. This return will be the best that he could possibly get for the risk taken.

By adding the investor indifference curves, we have:

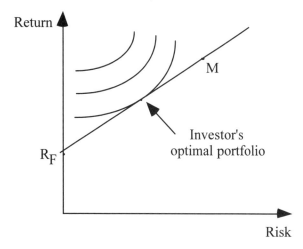

The trade-off between return and risk which is offered by this sensible use of the capital market is called the **capital market line**. This is effectively, as previously mentioned, our new efficient frontier.

6.7　Separation theorem

This ability to identify the portfolio of risky securities that an (risk averse) investor would wish to hold without needing to know his indifference curves is known as the **Separation Theorem** – the choice of optimal portfolio M is separated from the risk/return choice.

Separation theorem can be summarised as follows.

- We can separate the issue of what constitutes an optimal portfolio of risky assets (the market portfolio) from needing to know about the attitudes of individual investors to risk and return.

- This is because we can assume that an investor is able to adjust his own portfolio to suit his risk and return preferences by investing in a combination of the market portfolio and risk-free investments.

7　The efficient markets hypothesis (EMH)

7.1　Financial market efficiency

The efficiency of a financial market may be measured in various ways, the most relevant here being in terms of information processing. **Information processing efficiency** reflects the extent to which information regarding the future prospects of a security is reflected in its current price.

If all known information is reflected in a security's price then investment becomes a 'fair game'. All investors have the same chance, even if some of them have access to

more information, because under this concept of efficiency all information that can be known is already reflected in the share price.

Consider for example a pension fund manager who discovers that a particular company has made a scientific breakthrough that will lead to its expected profit doubling in the next few years.

- If the market were **not efficient** the manager could buy shares in the company at a cheap price from small investors who had not yet discovered the firm's new circumstances. In this situation the informed investor is gaining at the expense of the uninformed investor.

- In an **efficient** market, however, the share price of the company would reflect all information that could be known on the company and hence the informed investor would have to pay a 'fair' price for the shares.

Market efficiency is of great importance to financial management as it means that the results of management decisions will be quickly and accurately reflected in share prices. For example, if a firm undertakes an investment project which will generate a large surplus then in an efficient market it should see the value of its equity rise. Accordingly there have been many tests of the so-called efficient markets hypothesis (EMH) for the USA and the UK stock markets.

For the purposes of testing, the EMH is usually broken down into three categories, as follows:

- the weak form of the hypothesis

- the semi-strong form

- the strong form.

These are examined in the following sections. Each concerns the **type** of information which is reflected in share prices.

The efficient markets hypothesis argues that stock markets are efficient, in that information is reflected in share prices **accurately** and **rapidly**.

Weak form hypothesis

The **weak form of the hypothesis** states that share prices fully reflect information included in historical share price movements and patterns.

If this hypothesis is correct, then it should be impossible to predict future share price movements from historical patterns. For example, if a company's share price had increased steadily over the last few months to a current price of £2.50, this price will already fully reflect the information about growth. The next change in share price could be either upwards or downwards, with equal probability.

Because of this randomness in share price movements, this is frequently referred to as the **random walk hypothesis**. This means that the movements of share prices over time approximate to a random walk.

There is strong evidence to support the weak form of the efficient markets hypothesis, i.e. the hypothesis that share prices embody information included in historical share price movements and patterns.

Semi-strong form hypothesis

The **semi-strong form of the hypothesis** states that current share prices reflect not only historical share price information but also current information about the company to the extent that such information is publicly available.

This hypothesis can be tested by examining the way in which the market reacts to new information about a company, e.g. share splits, interim results, and so on.

Empirical evidence also tends to confirm the semi-strong form of the hypothesis.

Strong form hypothesis

The **strong form of the hypothesis** states that current share prices reflect not only historical share price patterns and current public knowledge, but also **all possible** information about the company, (including inside information).

This hypothesis can be tested by analysing market response to the release of previously confidential information about the company. If the hypothesis is correct then the mere publication of the information should have no impact on the share price. Consequently it should not be possible to make profits by dealing in response to 'inside' information.

The evidence is that the market does react when information is published. Profits could therefore be made by insider dealing (though this would be illegal in both the UK and the USA). Thus it appears that the strong form of the efficient markets hypothesis is not correct.

7.2   Implications of the EMH for financial managers

The above tests demonstrate that although the stock market is not completely efficient it is largely so. This has significant implications for financial management.

Timing of financial policy

Some financial managers argue that there is a right and a wrong time to issue new securities. New share issues should only be made when the market is at a high rather than a low. However, if the market is efficient how are financial managers to know if tomorrow's prices are going to be higher or lower than today's? Today's 'low' could turn out to be the highest the market will stand for the next five years. All current information is already reflected in share prices and unless the financial manager knows something the rest of the market does not then it is impossible to say in which direction the market will turn.

Project evaluation

When evaluating new projects financial managers usually use required rates of return drawn from securities traded on the capital market. For example, the rate of return required on a particular project may be determined by observing the rate of return required by shareholders of firms investing in projects of similar risks. This assumes that securities are fairly priced for the risk they carry – in other words that the stock market is efficient. If this is not the case then financial managers could be appraising projects on the wrong basis and therefore making bad investment decisions.

Creative accounting

In an efficient stock market share prices are based upon the expected future cash flows offered by securities and their level of risk. In turn these expectations reflect all current information. There is little point in firms attempting to distort current information to their advantage as investors will quickly see through any such attempts.

One American test of the semi-strong form of the hypothesis by Kaplan and Roll examined the impact on share prices of companies moving from accelerated to straight-line depreciation. This change only increased reported accounting earnings: actual cash flows remained unaltered as tax allowable depreciation remained unchanged. Initially share prices rose, possibly because the investors were not immediately informed of the changes, but within three months share prices fell as investors concluded that the cosmetic alterations to earnings were a sign of weakness rather than strength.

Other studies support this conclusion and it seems unlikely that investors can be 'fooled' by the manipulation of accounting profit figures or changes in capital structure resulting from capitalisation issues. Eventually (and usually sooner rather than later) investors will realise the cash flow consequences and alter share prices appropriately.

 FOULKS LYNCH
PUBLICATIONS

Mergers and takeovers

If shares are correctly priced this means that the rationale behind many mergers and takeovers may be questioned. If companies are acquired at their current equity valuation then the purchasers are effectively breaking even. If they are to make a significant gain on the acquisition then they must rely upon operating economies or rationalisation to provide the savings. If the acquirer pays current equity value plus a premium of, say, 25% (which is not uncommon) these savings would have to be considerable to make the takeover attractive.

You might be required to comment on the degree of efficiency in a particular securities market. The guidelines are as follows:

Degree of efficiency	*Characteristic*
Weak form	The share price does not respond to new information about the company, other than historical financial data (e.g. published financial statements)
Semi-strong form	The share price responds to new information about the company when it becomes publicly available.
Strong form	Share prices respond to developments even before they are known to the public.

Suppose for example that Dog plc is in secret takeover discussions with Cat plc, and agreement is now likely to be reached.

- If the market demonstrates only semi-strong form efficiency, there will be no significant change in the share price of either company before the proposed takeover agreement is announced.

- If the market demonstrates strong form efficiency, significant changes in the share prices of either or both companies would occur before the takeover agreement is announced.

8   Rates of interest and yield curves

8.1   Interest rates

Having looked at the factors affecting the value of, and thus returns on, equity shares, we now turn our attention to factors affecting the pattern of interest rates on different types of debt finance.

The main factors affecting the rate appropriate to a particular type of financial asset are as follows.

Duration of the loan

This is referred to as the **term structure** and is examined in more detail a little later.

Though they usually move up and down together, short-term interest rates (i.e. those for loans up to three months) are normally lower than longer-term rates of interest. The simple reason for this is that the longer the period of a loan the more the risk for the lender. Uncertainty is greater and the possibility of default increases, hence he will want a higher rate of return to compensate him for this enhanced degree of risk on a longer-term loan.

However, it is possible for short-term interest rates to be temporarily higher than longer-term rates, e.g. as the result of a foreign exchange crisis.

KEY POINT

The interest rate on a particular financial asset will be mainly influenced by its **term, risk, profitability,** and **size.**

FOULKS LYNCH
PUBLICATIONS

Risk

There is a trade-off between risk and return. Higher-risk borrowers will have to pay higher yields on their borrowing, to compensate lenders for the greater risk involved.

For this reason, a bank will charge a higher rate of interest on loans to borrowers from a high-risk category than to a low-risk category borrower. Banks will assess the creditworthiness of the borrower, and set a rate of interest on its loan at a certain mark-up above its base rate or LIBOR. In general, larger companies are charged at a lower rate of interest than smaller companies.

The need to make a profit on re-lending

Financial intermediaries make their profits from re-lending at a higher rate of interest than the cost of their borrowing. Intermediaries must pay various costs out of the differences, including bad debts and administration charges. What is left will be profit.

Size of the loan or deposit

The yield on assets might vary with the size of the loan or deposit.

- Time deposits above a certain amount will probably attract higher rates of interest than smaller-sized time deposits. The intermediary might be prepared to pay extra for the benefit of holding the liability as a single deposit (greater convenience of administration).

- The administrative convenience of handling wholesale loans rather than a large number of small retail loans partially explains the lower rates of interest charged by banks on larger loans. (The greater security in lending to a low-risk borrower could also be a factor.)

International factors

International interest rates will differ from country to country because of the different risks involved. The main risk is that the exchange rate may move against the investor reducing the capital value of the investment.

The interest rate on a particular financial asset will be mainly influenced by its **term, risk, profitability,** and **size.**

ACTIVITY 3

Get hold of a copy of a business section of a newspaper such as the Financial Times and find the money market interest rates for a variety of countries over various terms. Comment upon the patterns you can observe.

There is no feedback to this activity.

8.2   Yield curves

A yield curve is a diagrammatic representation of the **term structure** of interest rates. The **term structure of interest rates** refers to the way in which the yield of a security varies according to the term of the security, i.e. to the length of time before the borrowing will be repaid.

DEFINITION

The **term structure of interest rates** refers to the way in which the yield of a security varies according to the term of the security, i.e. to the length of time before the borrowing will be repaid.

Analysis of term structure is normally carried out by examining risk-free securities such as UK government stocks, also called gilts. Newspapers such as the *Financial Times* show the gross redemption yield and time to maturity of each gilt on a daily basis.

For example, the yields on three gilts may be shown as follows:

Name of gilt		*Gross redemption yield (%)*
Treasury 12%	20X0 (maturing shortly)	5.28
Treasury 13%	20X4	7.75
Treasury 8%	20X9	7.81

FOULKS LYNCH
PUBLICATIONS

These three exhibit the typical situation, with yields rising as the term to maturity increases. A graph can be drawn of the yield for each gilt against the number of years to maturity; the best curve through this set of points is called the yield curve.

The following is a typical yield curve:

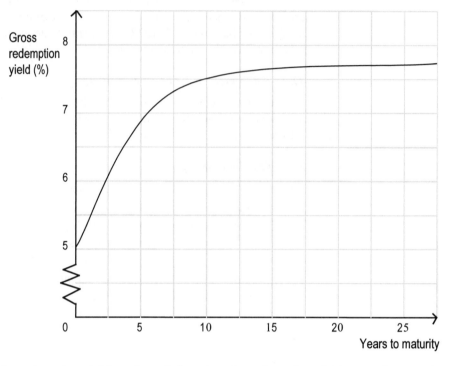

The redemption yield on shorts is less than the redemption yield on mediums and longs.

8.3 Why might the yield curve be this shape?

In general, redemption yields will rise as term to maturity increases as depicted by a typical yield curve.

A rising yield curve is called a 'normal' yield curve, provided the increase in interest rates is not steep.

A yield curve is said to be inverse when short-term rates are higher than longer-term rates.

8.4 Significance of yield curves to financial managers

Financial managers should inspect the current shape of the yield curve when deciding on the term of borrowings or deposits, since the curve encapsulates the market's expectations of future movements in interest rates.

For example, a yield curve sloping steeply upwards suggests that interest rates will rise in the future. The manager may therefore wish to avoid borrowing long-term on variable rates, since the interest charge may increase considerably over the term of the loan. Short-term variable rate borrowing or long-term fixed rate borrowing may instead be more appropriate.

Conclusion

This chapter has studied the functions of the various participants in the money and capital markets. It has considered the factors that influence the value of shares, including market efficiency, and those that determine the pattern of interest rates.

Financial intermediation

1   Describe the functions of a merchant bank. (1.2)

2   Give three other examples of intermediary institutions. (1)

The banking system

3   How do banks create money (credit)? (2.4)

Money and capital markets

4   Distinguish between money and capital markets (3.4, 3.5)

International capital markets

5   What is a Eurodollar (4.1)

The relationship between risk and return

6   What is the efficient frontier? (6.5)

The efficient markets hypothesis (EMH)

7   Describe what is meant by market efficiency. (7.1)

8   Define the three different forms of the EMH. Which form(s) is/are generally confirmed by empirical evidence? (7.1)

9   What are the implications of the EMH for financial management? (7.2)

Rates of interest and yield curves

10   What is an inverse yield curve? (8.3)

EXAM-TYPE
QUESTION

Stock markets

Explain briefly how stock markets work and assess their usefulness to business as a source of long-term capital.   **(25 marks)**

For the answer to this question, see the 'Answers' section at the end of the book.

FEEDBACK TO
ACTIVITY 1

No – R is on a higher indifference curve than T.

FOULKS LYNCH
PUBLICATIONS

Chapter 5

WORKING CAPITAL MANAGEMENT: INTRODUCTION

Working capital is the capital available for conducting the day to day operations of an organisation, represented by its net current assets. The managers have the responsibility to manage the levels of working capital in the best interests of the stakeholders.

This chapter starts with an examination of the general issues of working capital management, including ratio analysis. We then move on to look at the specific issues and techniques relating to the control of stock.

Objectives

By the time you have finished this chapter you should be able to do the following:

- explain the nature and scope of working capital management

- distinguish between cash flow and profits

- explain the requirement for effective working capital management

- explain the relationship between working capital management and business solvency

- distinguish between the working capital needs of different types of business

- calculate and interpret stock ratios

- explain the role of stock in the working capital cycle

- apply the tools and techniques of stock management

- analyse and evaluate the results of stock management techniques.

DEFINITIONS

Working capital normally refers to short-term net assets – stock, debtors and cash, less short-term creditors.

1 The nature and scope of working capital management

Working capital normally refers to short-term net assets – stock, debtors and cash, less short-term creditors. Working capital management is the management of all aspects of both current assets and current liabilities, to minimise the risk of insolvency while maximising the return on assets.

Working capital is an investment which affects cash flows.

- When stocks are purchased, cash is paid to acquire it.

- Debtors represent the cost of selling goods or services to customers, including the costs of the materials and the labour incurred.

The cash tied up in working capital is reduced to the extent that stocks are financed by trade creditors. If suppliers give a firm time to pay, the firm's cash flows are improved and working capital is reduced.

Investing in working capital has a cost, which can be expressed either as:

- the cost of funding it, or

- the lost investment opportunities because cash is tied up and unavailable for other uses.

1.1 Working capital management

Typically, current assets represent more than half the assets of companies and they tend to be of particular importance to small firms. Small businesses often fail as a result of failing to control working capital investment and business liquidity, and there is a direct link between sales growth and working capital management. Financial managers therefore spend a considerable amount of their time on working capital management.

The two fundamental questions to be answered in the area of working capital management are the following:

- How much should the firm invest in working capital?

- How should the investment in working capital be financed?

How to manage working capital investment can be considered in either of two ways:

- at the individual current asset or liability level, or

- in terms of total working capital requirement.

1.2 Total investment in working capital

For now, the total investment in working capital will be considered. Management of individual current asset and liability elements (i.e. stocks, debtors, cash and creditors) will be considered later.

Overall investment in working capital largely concerns trade-off. Here, the firm must consider the costs of investing in working capital (largely the financing cost) against the benefits it brings. With no investment in working capital there would be no stocks and no debtors, which would probably result in few sales and, therefore, little profit.

The decision regarding the level of overall investment in working capital is a cost/benefit trade-off – **liquidity v profitability**, or **cash flow v profits**.

Liquidity in the context of working capital management means having enough cash or ready access to cash to meet all payment obligations when these fall due. The main sources of liquidity are usually:

- cash in the bank

- short-term investments that can be cashed in easily and quickly

- cash inflows from normal trading operations (cash sales and payments by debtors for credit sales)

- an overdraft facility or other ready source of extra borrowing.

1.3 Cash flow v profits

Cash flow is the lifeblood of the thriving business. Effective and efficient management of the working capital investment is essential to maintaining control of business cash flow. Management must have full awareness of the profitability versus liquidity trade-off.

For example, healthy trading growth typically produces:
- increased profitability; and
- the need to increase investment in
  - fixed assets, and
  - working capital.

Here there is a trade-off under which trading growth and increased profitability squeezes cash. Ultimately, if not properly managed, increased trading can carry with it the spectre of overtrading and inability to pay the business creditors.

It is worthwhile stressing the difference between cash flow and profits. Companies fail, not because they are reporting insufficient profits, but because they have run out of cash to pay their liabilities (wages, amounts due to suppliers, overdraft interest, etc).

Some examples of transactions that have this 'trade-off' effect on cash flows and on profits are as follows.

(a) **Purchase of fixed assets for cash**. The cash will be paid in full to the supplier when the fixed asset is delivered. However profits will be charged gradually over the life of the asset in the form of depreciation.

(b) **Sale of goods on credit**. Profits will be credited in full once the sale has been confirmed; however the cash may not be received for some considerable period afterwards.

(c) **Some payments such as tax and dividend payments have no effect on profits** but do constitute a cash outflow.

Clearly, cash balances and cash flows need to be monitored just as closely as trading profits. The need for adequate cash flow information is vital to enable management to fulfil this responsibility.

2   Financing and working capital

Current assets have to be financed, with either short-term or long-term sources of finance. (By definition, working capital, which is current assets minus current liabilities, is the amount of current assets financed by long-term capital.) A firm's investment in working capital can be reduced by taking more short-term credit.

For example, suppose that a company has £200,000 of stocks and debtors. It can finance these assets in any of the following ways:

- With long-term funding of £200,000. The cost of doing this could be calculated by applying the firm's cost of capital to the £200,000 investment. However, this form of funding should help to ensure adequate liquidity.

- With short-term credit of £200,000. If the credit is provided by trade creditors, there is no cost. If it is provided by a bank overdraft, there is an interest cost on the overdraft balance. Excessive short-term funding creates a risk to cash flows and liquidity, because the stocks and debtors must continue to generate enough cash to meet the payment obligations to the short-term creditors.

- With a combination of long-term and short-term finance. This is what normally happens in practice, although the proportions of long-term and short-term funding can obviously vary.

A risk for rapidly-growing companies, particularly when profit margins are low, is that as they grow, they need larger investments in current assets (and fixed assets). If the increase in assets is financed largely by short-term credit, the risks of liquidity shortages will grow. Financing asset growth with short-term credit is called **overtrading**. Overtrading is explained in more detail later.

3   Working capital ratios

The adequacy of working capital management policies in maintaining liquidity can only be determined by a detailed analysis of current resources and requirements including regular cash flow forecasts. However, a broad indication of liquidity may be obtained by calculating various liquidity ratios.

These will be illustrated by reference to the following set of accounts.

Summarised balance sheets at 30 June

	20X7		20X6	
	£'000	£'000	£'000	£'000
Fixed assets (net book value)		130		139
Current assets:				
Stock	42		37	
Debtors	29		23	
Bank	3		5	
	74		65	
Creditors: amounts falling due within one year:				
Trade creditors	36		55	
Taxation	10		10	
	46		65	
Net current assets		28		–
Total assets less current liabilities		158		139
Creditors: amounts falling due beyond one year:				
5% secured loan stock		40		40
		118		99
Ordinary share capital (50p shares)		35		35
8% Preference shares (£1 shares)		25		25
Share premium account		17		17
Revaluation reserve		10		-
Profit and loss account		31		22
		118		99

Summarised profit and loss account for the year ended 30 June

	20X7		20X6	
	£'000	£'000	£'000	£'000
Sales		209		196
Opening stock	37		29	
Purchases	162		159	
	199		188	
Closing stock	42		37	
		157		151
Gross profit		52		45
Interest	2		2	
Depreciation	9		9	
Sundry expenses	14		11	
		25		22
Net profit		27		23
Taxation		10		10
Net profit after taxation		17		13
Dividends:				
Ordinary shares	6		5	
Preference shares	2		2	
		8		7
Retained profit		9		6

As with all ratio analysis, we need to compare the current year's ratios with target ratios, industry average ratios, or, as in this case, with last year's ratios.

3.1 Current and quick ratios

<table>
<tr><td>

DEFINITION

Current ratio =

$$\frac{\text{current assets}}{\text{current liabilities}}$$

Quick ratio =

$$\frac{\text{current assets less stock}}{\text{current liabilities}}$$

</td></tr>
</table>

$$\text{Current ratio} = \frac{\text{current assets}}{\text{current liabilities}}$$

$$\text{Quick ratio} = \frac{\text{current assets less stock}}{\text{current liabilities}}$$

The quick ratio excludes stock on the basis that the time scale over which this can be realised as cash may be considerably longer than the period within which trade creditors and other short-term creditors will require payment.

A higher ratio indicates better liquidity. However, a very high liquidity ratio could indicate excessive liquidity.

The current ratio

	20X7	*20X6*
	$\frac{74}{46} = 1.61$	$\frac{65}{65} = 1.0$

The quick (or acid test) ratio

	20X7	*20X6*
	$\frac{32}{46} = 0.7$	$\frac{28}{65} = 0.43$

KEY POINT

The **current** and **quick** ratios are measures of short-term liquidity which indicate the extent to which current assets cover current liabilities.

Both of these ratios show an improvement. The extent of the change between the two years seems surprising and would require further investigation. It would also be useful to know how these ratios compare with those of a similar business, since typical liquidity ratios for supermarkets, say, are quite different from those for heavy engineering firms.

In 20X7 current liabilities were well covered by current assets. Liabilities payable in the near future (trade creditors), however, are only half covered by cash and debtors (a liquid asset, close to cash).

In general, high current and quick ratios are considered 'good' in that they mean that an organisation has the resources to meet its commitments as they fall due. However, it may indicate that working capital is not being used efficiently, for example that there is too much idle cash that should be invested to earn a return.

Conventional wisdom has it that an ideal current ratio is 2 and an ideal quick ratio is 1. It is very tempting to draw definite conclusions from limited information or to say that the current ratio **should** be 2, or that the quick ratio **should** be 1. However, this is not very meaningful without taking into account the type of ratio expected in a similar business.

Any assessment of working capital ratios must take into account the **nature of the business** involved.

3.2 Cash operating cycle

DEFINITION

The **cash operating cycle** is the length of time which elapses between a business paying for its raw materials and the business's customers paying for the goods made from the raw materials.

The investment made in working capital is largely a function of sales and, therefore, it is useful to consider the problem in terms of a firm's working capital cycle, or cash operating cycle.

The **cash operating cycle** is the length of time which elapses between a business paying for its raw materials and the business's customers paying for the goods made from the raw materials.

The cash operating cycle

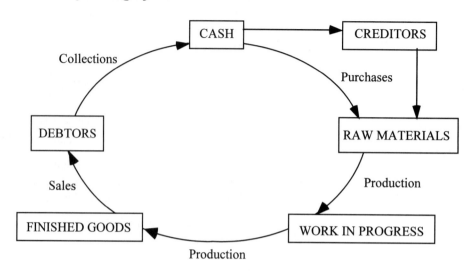

The cycle reflects a firm's investment in working capital as it moves through the production process towards sales. The investment in working capital gradually increases, firstly being only in raw materials, but then in labour and overheads as production progresses. This investment must be maintained throughout the production process, the holding period for finished goods and up to the final collection of cash from trade debtors. (*Note:* The net investment can be reduced by taking trade credit from suppliers.)

The faster a firm can 'push' items around the cycle the lower its investment in working capital will be.

3.3 Calculating the cash operating cycle

With some fairly basic financial information it is possible to measure the length of the cash operating cycle for a given firm.

For a **manufacturing business**, such as that illustrated in the diagram above, the cash operating cycle will be measured by:

Cash operating cycle = raw materials holding period + WIP holding period + finished goods holding period + debtors' collection period – creditors' payment period.

For a **wholesale** or **retail** business, there will be no raw materials or WIP holding periods, and the cycle simplifies to:

Cash operating cycle = stock holding period + debtors' collection period – creditors' payment period.

Summary

The cash operating cycle is measurable in days as:

> Stock turnover period
>
> plus Debtor days
>
> minus Creditor days

A longer stock turnover period, or allowing debtors longer to pay lengthens the operating cycle. It also increases the investment in stocks or debtors, tying up more cash in working capital.

A task for the financial manager is to maintain the length of the operating cycle at a level where the investment in working capital is not excessive, but at the same time liquidity is sufficient.

ACTIVITY 1

A company generally pays its suppliers six weeks after receiving an invoice, while its debtors usually pay within four weeks of invoicing. Raw materials stocks are held for a week before processing, which takes three weeks, begins. Finished goods stay in stock for an average of two weeks.

How long is the company's operating cycle?

Feedback to this activity is at the end of the chapter.

The periods relating to the individual current assets and liabilities are also useful ratios in their own right; we shall first consider them individually for our illustrative accounts (assuming its stock comprises only finished goods), and then combine them into the cash operating cycle.

DEFINITIONS

Stock holding period =

$\dfrac{\text{average stock held}}{\text{cost of sales}} \times 365 \text{ days}$

Stock turnover =

$\dfrac{\text{cost of sales}}{\text{average stock held}}$

KEY POINT

Companies have to strike a balance between being able to satisfy customers' requirements out of stock and the cost of having too much capital tied up in stock.

3.4   Stock holding period (stock turnover period)

$$\textbf{Stock holding period} = \frac{\text{average stock held}}{\text{cost of sales}} \times 365 \text{ days}$$

$$\textbf{Stock turnover} = \frac{\text{cost of sales}}{\text{average stock held}} \text{ times}$$

For our example, the stock holding periods are as follows.

20X7	*20X6*
$\dfrac{\frac{1}{2}(37+42)}{157} \times 365 \text{ days} = 92 \text{ days}$	$\dfrac{\frac{1}{2}(29+37)}{151} \times 365 \text{ days} = 80 \text{ days}$

The **stock holding period** has lengthened. In general, the shorter the stock holding period the better. It is very expensive to hold stock and thus minimum stock holding usually points to good management. However, not all industries can operate a just-in-time stock policy and unless the nature of the business is known, it is not possible to say whether either 92 days or 30 days is satisfactory or unsatisfactory. A jeweller will have a high stock holding period, but a fishmonger selling fresh fish has a very low stock holding period.

The **stock turnover ratio** is simply the inverse of the stock holding fraction.

20X7	*20X6*
$\dfrac{157}{\frac{1}{2}(37+42)} = 4.0 \text{ times each year}$	$\dfrac{151}{\frac{1}{2}(29+37)} = 4.6 \text{ times each year}$

These show that stock turnover has fallen. In 20X6 average stock was sold 4.6 times per year. In 20X7 it was sold 4.0 times per year.

3.5   Debtors' collection period (debtor days)

$$\text{Debtors' collection period} = \frac{\text{closing trade debtors}}{\text{average daily sales}}$$

DEFINITION

Debtors' collection period =

closing trade debtors
―――――――――
average daily sales

Businesses which sell goods on credit terms specify a credit period. Failure to send out invoices on time or to follow up late payers will have an adverse effect on the cash flow of the business. The debtors' collection period measures the average period of credit allowed to customers.

	20X7	*20X6*
Average daily sales	$\dfrac{£209,000}{365} = £573$	$\dfrac{£196,000}{365} = £537$
Closing trade debtors	£29,000	£23,000
Debtor days	$\dfrac{£29,000}{£573} = 50.6 \text{ days}$	$\dfrac{£23,000}{£537} = 42.8 \text{ days}$

Compared with 20X6 the debtors' collection period has worsened in 20X7. If the average credit allowed to customers was, say, thirty days, then something is clearly wrong. Further investigation might reveal delays in sending out invoices or failure to 'screen' new customers.

In general, the shorter the debtors' collection period the better because debtors are effectively 'borrowing' from the company. Remember, however, that the level of debtors reflects not only the ability of the credit controllers but also the sales and marketing strategy adopted, and the nature of the business. Any change in the level of debtors must therefore be assessed in the light of the level of sales.

DEFINITION

Debtors' collection period
formula =
Closing trade debtors
――――――――― × 365
Credit sales for year

Note: The quickest way to compute the debtor days is to use the following formula (we are assuming that all sales are on credit):

$$\frac{\text{Closing trade debtors}}{\text{Credit sales for year}} \times 365$$

20X7	*20X6*
$\dfrac{29,000}{209,000} \times 365 = 50.6 \text{ days}$	$\dfrac{23,000}{196,000} \times 365 = 42.8 \text{ days}$

Note: Instead of using the current value of trade debtors to calculate debtor days, the average value of debtors could also be used.

3.6   Creditors' payment period (creditor days)

DEFINITION

Creditors' payment period =

closing trade creditors
―――――――――
average daily purchases

OR

Closing trade creditors
――――――――― × 365
Credit purchases for year

$$\text{Creditors' payment period} = \frac{\text{Closing trade creditors}}{\text{Average daily purchases}}$$

This measures the average period of credit allowed by suppliers.

	20X7	*20X6*
Average daily purchases	$\dfrac{£162,000}{365} = £444$	$\dfrac{£159,000}{365} = £436$
Closing trade creditors	£36,000	£55,000
Creditors' payment period	81.1 days	126.2 days

The creditors' payment period has reduced substantially from last year. It is, however, in absolute terms still a high figure. Often, suppliers request payment within thirty days. The company is taking nearly three months. Trade creditors are thus financing

much of the working capital requirements of the business, which is beneficial to the company.

An increase in creditor days may be good in that it means that all available credit is being taken, but there are three potential disadvantages of taking extended credit

- Future supplies may be endangered.

- Availability of cash discounts is lost.

- Suppliers may quote a higher price for the goods knowing the company takes extended credit.

The quick calculation of creditors' payment period (creditor days) is:

$$\frac{\text{Closing trade creditors}}{\text{Credit purchases for year}} \times 365$$

<table>
<tr><td align="center">20X7</td><td align="center">20X6</td></tr>
<tr><td align="center">$\frac{36,000}{162,000} \times 365 = 81.1 \text{ days}$</td><td align="center">$\frac{55,000}{159,000} \times 365 = 126.3 \text{ days}$</td></tr>
</table>

Note: instead of using the current value of trade creditors to calculate creditor days, the average value of trade creditors could also be used.

3.7 The length of the cash operating cycle

We are now in a position to compute the length of the cash operating cycle for our example.

	20X7 days	20X6 days
Stock holding period	92	80
+		
Debtors' collection period	50.6	42.8
−		
Creditors' payment period	(81.1)	(126.2)
=		
Cash operating cycle	61.5 days	(3.4 days)

Our example shows that, in 20X7, there is approximately a 62 day gap between paying cash to suppliers for goods, and receiving the cash back from customers. However, in 20X6, there was the somewhat unusual situation where cash was received from the customers, on average, nearly 4 days before the payment to suppliers was needed.

The length of the cycle depends on the efficiency of management and the nature of the industry. The optimum level is the amount that results in no idle cash or unused stock, but that does not put a strain on liquid resources. Trying to shorten the cash cycle may have detrimental effects elsewhere, with the organisation lacking the cash to meet its commitments and losing sales since customers will generally prefer to buy from suppliers who are prepared to extend trade credit, and who have items held in stock when required.

KEY POINT

Any assessment of working capital ratios must take into account the **nature of the business** involved.

Again, any assessment of the acceptability or otherwise of the length of the cycle must take into account the nature of the business involved

A supermarket chain will tend to have a very low or negative cycle – they have very few, if any, credit customers, they have a high stock turnover and they can negotiate quite long credit periods with their suppliers.

A construction company will have a long cycle – their projects tend to be long-term, often extending over more than a year, and whilst progress payments may be made by the customer (if there is one), the bulk of the cash will be received towards the end of the project.

FOULKS LYNCH
PUBLICATIONS

It would be useful to have industry average figures with which to compare our results.

A general point to stress here again is that any assessment of the acceptability or otherwise of working capital ratios must take into account the nature of the business involved, types of goods sold, cash cycle experienced, the company's access to alternative finance sources and how predictable its cash flows are.

ACTIVITY 2

Try to find examples of differing working capital requirements for different organisations – why are their requirements different? (e.g. access to finance.)

There is no feedback to this activity.

ACTIVITY 3

Extracts from the profit and loss account for the year and the balance sheet as at the end of the year for a company show the following.

	£
Sales	250,000
Cost of goods sold	210,000
Purchases	140,000
Debtors	31,250
Creditors	21,000
Stock	92,500

Note: Assume all sales and purchases are on credit terms.

Calculate the length of the cash operating cycle.

Feedback to this activity is at the end of the chapter.

ACTIVITY 4

A company's annual sales are £8 million with a mark-up on cost of 60%. It normally pays creditors two months after purchases are made, holding one month's worth of demand in stock. It allows debtors $1\frac{1}{2}$ months' credit and its cash balance currently stands at £1,250,000. What are its current and quick ratios?

Feedback to this activity is at the end of the chapter.

4 The relationship of working capital management to business solvency

A firm needs a flow of cash to carry out the day-to-day transactions which form its business activity. Some cash payments (e.g. to small creditors) can be delayed without endangering the company's prospects but others must be paid on time.

- If debenture interest is not paid, the trust deed may allow the debenture holders to appoint a receiver to sell sufficient assets for the debenture to be repaid.

- Employees must be paid their wages and salaries on time, otherwise they will leave and the business will cease to function.

Cash must be in place to meet obligations as they fall due. If insufficient cash is available, the company will suffer from illiquidity. At the extreme, the company may fail due to illiquidity. A lot of academic research work has been carried out in recent years to try and develop warning indicators that a company might be going to fail through illiquidity, particularly by Professor Altman in developing Z-scores.

Profit earned will, to a certain extent, alleviate the effect of illiquidity, but the strain on operating cash flow will be accentuated by the need to provide for investment in fixed assets for the firm's future, dividends and interest for the providers of long-term capital, and taxation.

Management of cash flows therefore involves the interrelationship of the following items:

- profits
- working capital levels
- capital expenditure
- dividend policy
- taxation.

The emphasis in this section of the text is on the control of levels of working capital.

4.1   Short-term cash control

Control of cash over short periods is best achieved by preparing short-term cash forecasts for comparison with actual results. If the cash forecast shows an unacceptable cash balance or a cash deficit, then it will be necessary to review a number of items as follows:

- Profit levels, including changes in selling price or improvements in operating efficiency.
- Working capital requirements, i.e. stock holdings, credit periods given and taken, invoice processing procedures, etc.
- Fixed asset requirements, having regard to the timing and amounts of capital projects.
- Dividend policy.

4.2   Overcapitalisation

A firm is **overcapitalised** if its working capital is excessive for its needs.

Excessive stocks, debtors and cash will lead to a low return on investment, with long-term funds tied up in non-earning short-term assets.

Overcapitalisation can normally be identified by poor accounting ratios (such as liquidity ratios being too high or stock turnover periods being too long).

4.3   Overtrading

A firm is **overtrading** if it is trying to carry on too large a volume of activities with its current levels of working capital.

Often a company may try to grow too fast, reporting increasing profits while its overdraft soars. Remember that more companies fail when the economy is recovering from a recession than when the economy is entering a recession.

Overtrading is a serious problem that small but rapidly-expanding businesses can easily fall into. Signs of overtrading are:

- a rapid increase in stock levels, matched by a large increase in trade creditors or bank overdraft
- a deteriorating current ratio (ratio of current assets to current liabilities) and quick ratio (ratio of current assets excluding stocks) to current liabilities
- a significant slow-down in the average time for paying trade creditors
- sometimes, a large increase in debtors, with debtors also taking longer to pay. (Rapidly-growing businesses might sell on easy credit terms to win new customers.)

4.4 Control of orders received

Overtrading can cause grave financial problems, so it may be vital to limit the amount of business that is accepted. In a manufacturing firm, for instance, each order must be analysed to discover the following:

- its effect on factory capacity
- the amount of working capital tied up in the order
- the length of time for which the company must provide finance
- the estimated profit or contribution of the order.

Management will wish to select the most profitable orders and could perhaps formulate a selection factor relating the contribution to the total order value and the total financing period, e.g.:

$$\text{Selection factor} = \frac{\text{Contribution}}{\text{Order value} \times \text{Financing period}}$$

It might also be possible to limit the orders taken by a salesperson to a certain order value, with an overall ceiling any month. Beyond this, the salesperson must obtain approval from the sales manager. In that way, a profitable mix of orders could be selected which can be handled comfortably by the firm. Another aspect of orders is the relationship between quotations sent and orders received: if, say, 90% of quotations are accepted and firm orders received, the company may be under-pricing its products.

4.5 Control of purchase commitments

A firm's creditors can put the firm into liquidation if their demands for settlement are not satisfied. It is clearly important therefore to apply controls to the routines which create the liabilities, i.e. purchasing of material and plant, etc. The purchasing manager should verify that materials to be purchased will be resold or used in production within a reasonable time – say two months. In many cases this factor should carry greater weight than the savings that can be made by bulk-buying. The purchasing manager should, however, seek to negotiate with suppliers in an attempt to obtain bulk discounts by placing larger orders, but taking delivery over a long period – thereby reducing the total initial liability.

5 Management of stock

The **objective of stock management** is to ensure sufficient levels of stock to maintain an acceptable level of availability on demand whilst minimising the associated holding, administrative and stockout costs.

5.1 Costs of holding stock

Holding stock is an expensive business – it has been estimated that the cost of holding stock each year is one-third of its production or purchase cost.

Holding costs include:

- interest on capital
- storage space and equipment
- administration and staff costs
- leases.

On the other hand, running out of stock (known as a **stockout**) incurs a cost. If, for example, a shop is persistently out of stock on some lines, customers will start going elsewhere. **Stockout costs** are difficult to estimate, but they are an essential factor to consider in stock control.

Finally, **order set-up costs** are incurred each time a batch of stock is ordered. Administrative costs and, where production is internal, costs of setting up machinery will be affected in total by the frequency of orders.

The two major quantitative problems of determining re-order levels and order quantities are essentially problems of striking the optimum balance between holding costs, stockout costs and order set-up costs.

Before looking at theoretical approaches to determining optimum reorder quantities and levels – in particular, the Economic Order Quantity (EOQ) model - we shall briefly consider the practical systems and issues involves in the control of stock levels.

5.2 Stock management systems

Two bin system

This system utilises two bins, e.g. A and B. Stock is taken from A until A is empty. An order for a fixed quantity is placed and, in the meantime, stock is used from B. The standard stock for B is the expected demand in the lead-time (the time between the order being placed and the stock arriving), plus some 'buffer' stock.

When the new order arrives, B is filled up to its standard stock and the rest is placed in A. Stock is then drawn as required from A, and the process is repeated.

Single bin system

The same sort of approach is adopted by some firms for a single bin with a red line within the bin indicating the reorder level.

Control levels

In bin systems, where order quantities are constant, it is important to identify alterations to the estimates on which that quantity was based. The stock controller should be notified when the stock level exceeds a maximum or falls below a minimum.

- **Maximum** stock level would represent the normal peak holding i.e. buffer stocks plus the re-order quantity. If the maximum is exceeded, a review of estimated demand in the lead-time is needed.

- **Minimum** stock level usually corresponds with buffer stock. If stock falls below that level, emergency action to replenish may be required.

The levels would also be modified according to the relative importance/cost of a particular stock item.

The costs of a continual review of bin levels, as implied by the two-bin or one-bin system, may be excessive, and it may be more economic to operate a periodic review system.

Periodic review system (or constant order cycle system)

Stock levels are reviewed at **fixed intervals** eg, every four weeks. The stock in hand is then made up to a predetermined level, which takes account of likely demand before the next review and during the lead-time.

Thus a four-weekly review in a system where the lead-time was two weeks would demand that stock be made up to the likely maximum demand for the next six weeks.

Bin systems versus periodic review

Advantage of bin systems	Advantage of periodic review system
Stock can be kept at a lower level because of the ability to order whenever stocks fall to a low level, rather than having to wait for the next re-order date.	Order office load is more evenly spread and easier to plan. For this reason the system is popular with suppliers.

5.3   Slow-moving stocks

Certain items may have a high individual value, but be subject to infrequent demand. Slow-moving items may be ordered only when required, unless a minimum order quantity is imposed by the supplier.

A regular report of slow-moving items is useful in that management is made aware of changes in demand and of possible obsolescence. Arrangements may then be made to reduce or eliminate stock levels or, on confirmation of obsolescence, for disposal.

5.4   Just in time (JIT) systems

JIT is a series of manufacturing and supply chain techniques that aim to minimise stock levels and improve customer service by manufacturing not only at the exact time customers require, but also in the exact quantities they need and at competitive prices.

JIT extends much further than a concentration on stock levels. It centres around the elimination of waste. Waste is defined as any activity performed within a manufacturing company which does not add value to the product. Examples of waste are:

- raw material stock
- work-in-progress stock
- finished goods stock
- materials handling
- quality problems (rejects and reworks etc)
- queues and delays on the shop-floor
- long raw material lead-times
- long customer lead-times
- unnecessary clerical and accounting procedures.

JIT attempts to eliminate waste at every stage of the manufacturing process, notably by the elimination of:

- WIP, by reducing batch sizes (often to one)
- raw materials stock, by the suppliers delivering direct to the shop-floor just in time for use
- scrap and rework, by an emphasis on total quality control of design, of the process, and of the materials
- finished goods stock, by reducing lead-times so that all products are made to order
- material handling costs, by re-design of the shop-floor so that goods move directly between adjacent work centers.

The combination of these concepts in JIT results in:

- a smooth flow of work through the manufacturing plant
- a flexible production process which is responsive to the customer's requirements
- reduction in capital tied up in stocks.

5.5   The impact of JIT

A JIT manufacturer looks for a single supplier which can provide **high quality, frequent** and **reliable** deliveries, rather than the lowest price. In return, the supplier can expect more business under **long-term purchase orders**, thus providing **greater certainty** in forecasting activity levels.

Long-term contracts and single sourcing strengthen buyer-supplier relationships and tend to result in a higher quality product. Inventory problems are shifted back onto suppliers, with deliveries being made as required.

 FOULKS LYNCH
PUBLICATIONS

The spread of JIT in the production process inevitably affects those in delivery and transportation. Smaller, more frequent loads are required at shorter notice. The haulier is regarded as almost a partner to the manufacturer, but tighter schedules are required of hauliers, with penalties for non-delivery.

Reduction in stock levels reduces the time taken to count stock and the clerical cost.

For businesses that do not use JIT, there is an optimum order quantity for stock items, known as the economic order quantity or EOQ.

Buying stock items in this quantity minimises the combined costs of holding stock and ordering new stocks. With JIT, stockholding costs are close to zero, but stock ordering costs are high.

5.6   Economic order quantity (EOQ) model

We now turn to the theoretical side of stock control. Essentially, two stock problems need to be answered under either of two assumptions:

- when to re-order

- how much to re-order

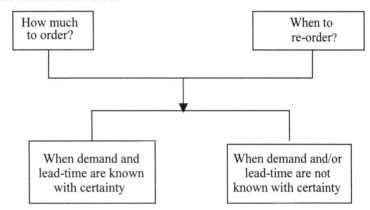

Pattern of stock levels

When new batches of an item in stock are purchased or made at periodic intervals the stock levels are assumed to exhibit the following pattern over time.

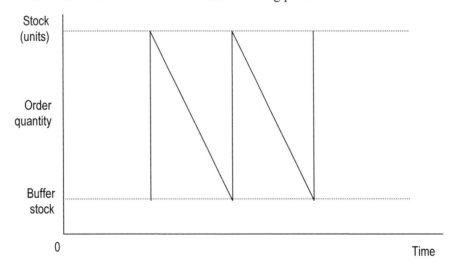

DEFINITION

Lead-time is the time between placing an order and delivery of the goods.

When should stock be re-ordered?

A gap (the lead-time) inevitably occurs between placing an order and its delivery. Where both that gap and the rate of demand are known with certainty, an exact decision on when to re-order can be made.

DEFINITION

Buffer stock is a basic level of
stock held for emergencies.

DEFINITION

Economic order quantity (EOQ)
is the quantity of stock ordered
each time which minimises annual
costs (order setup + holding
costs).

In the real world both will fluctuate randomly and so the order must be placed so as to leave some buffer stock if demand and lead-time follow the average pattern. The problem is again the balancing of **increased holding costs** if the buffer stock is **high**, against **increased stockout costs** if the buffer stock is **low**.

How much stock should be re-ordered?

Large order quantities cut order set-up and stockout costs each year. On the other hand, stock volumes will on average be higher and so holding costs increase. The problem is balancing one against the other.

Economic order quantity (EOQ) is the quantity of stock ordered each time which minimises annual costs (order setup + holding costs). Note that the EOQ is not affected by uncertainty of demand and lead-times, as long as demand is independent of stock levels.

Example

Watallington Ltd is a retailer of barrels. The company has an annual demand of 30,000 barrels. The barrels are purchased for stock in lots of 5,000 and cost £12 each. Fresh supplies can be obtained immediately, ordering and transport costs amounting to £200 per order. The annual cost of holding one barrel in stock is estimated to be £1.20.

The stock level situation could be represented graphically as follows:

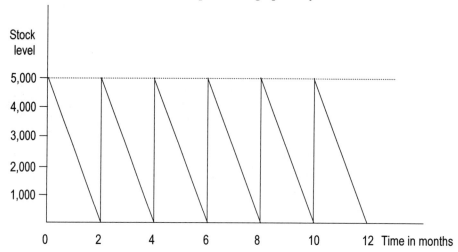

Thus Watallington Ltd orders 5,000 barrels at a time and these are used from stock at a uniform rate.

Every two months stock is zero and a new order is made. The average stock level is $\frac{5,000}{2}$ barrels, i.e. half the replenishment level.

Watallington's total annual stock costs are made up as follows.

		£
Ordering costs	$\frac{30,000}{5,000} \times £200$	1,200
Cost of holding stock	$\frac{5,000}{2} \times £1.20$	3,000
Total stock costs		4,200

5.7 How much stock to be re-ordered: the EOQ formula

You should remember from your previous studies that such situations offer minimum total stock costs when the order quantity is set at the economic order quantity or EOQ.

$$x = \sqrt{\frac{2CD}{H}}$$

where   C = fixed costs (order set-up costs) per order

D = expected annual sales volume

H = holding cost per stock unit per annum

For Watallington, EOQ $= \sqrt{\dfrac{2 \times 200 \times 30,000}{1.20}}$

= 3,162 barrels

Total annual costs for the company will comprise holding costs plus reordering costs.

= (Average stock × H) + (Number of reorders pa × C)

$= \left(\dfrac{3,162}{2} \times £1.20\right) + \left(\dfrac{30,000}{3,162} \times £200\right)$

= £1,897.20 + £1,897.53

= £3,794.73

ACTIVITY 5

Demand for a company's product is about 600,000 per annum. It costs £3 to keep one unit in stock for one year. Each time an order is placed, administrative costs of £40 are incurred.

How many units should the company order at a time?

Feedback to this activity is at the end of the chapter.

5.8 The effect of large order discounts on EOQ

Discounts may be offered for ordering in large quantities. If the order quantity to obtain the discount is above what would otherwise be the EOQ, is the discount still worth taking?

This problem may be solved by the following procedure.

Step 1   Calculate EOQ, ignoring discounts.

Step 2   If this is below the level for discounts, calculate total annual stock costs.

Step 3   Recalculate total annual stock costs using the order size required to just obtain the discount.

Step 4   Compare the cost of steps 2 and 3 with the saving from the discount, and select the minimum cost alternative.

Step 5   Repeat for all discount levels.

Example

In the Watallington illustration, suppose that a 2% discount is available on orders of at least 5,000 barrels and that a 2.5% discount is available if the order quantity is 7,500 barrels or above. With this information, would the economic order quantity still be 3,162?

Solution

	£
Steps 1 and 2 have already been carried out, and it is known that total annual cost at 3,162 barrels/batch =	3,795

Step 3   At order quantity 5,000, total costs are as follows.

$$\frac{5{,}000 \times £1.20}{2} + \frac{30{,}000 \times £200}{5{,}000}$$ 4,200

Extra costs of ordering in batches of 5,000	(405)
Less: Saving on discount 2% × £12 × 30,000	7,200

Step 4   Net cost saving   6,795

Hence batches of 5,000 are worthwhile.

Step 3   At order quantity 7,500, total costs are as follows.

$$\frac{7{,}500 \times £1.20}{2} + \frac{30{,}000 \times £200}{7{,}500}$$ 5,300

Costs at 5,000 batch size   4,200

Extra costs of ordering in batches of 7,500	(1,100)
Less: Saving on extra discount (2.5 – 2)% × £12 × 30,000	1,800

Step 4   Net cost saving   700

So a further saving can be made by ordering in batches of 7,500.

Tutorial note: often the 'holding cost' will reduce where quantity discounts are taken - because this cost often relates to the original cost of buying an item.

5.9   When to re-order stock

Having decided how much stock to re-order, the next problem is *when* to re-order. The firm needs to identify a level of stock which can be reached before an order needs to be placed. The **re-order level (ROL)** is the quantity of stock on hand when an order is placed. When demand and lead-time are known with certainty the re-order level may be calculated exactly.

ACTIVITY 6

Return to the original Watallington example. Assume that the company adopts the EDQ as its order quantity and that it now takes two weeks for an order be delivered. How frequently will the company place an order? How much stock will it have on hand when the order is placed?

Feedback to this activity is at the end of the chapter.

5.10   Re-order level with variable demand or variable lead-time

When **lead time and demand** are known with **certainty**, ROL = demand during lead-time. Where there is **uncertainty**, an optimum level of **buffer stock** must be found.

If there were certainty then the last unit of stock would be sold as the next delivery is made. In the real world, this ideal cannot be achieved. Demand will vary from period to period, and re-order levels must allow some buffer (or safety) stock, the size of which is a function of three factors.

FOULKS LYNCH
PUBLICATIONS

- variability of demand
- cost of holding stocks
- cost of stockouts.

The problem may be solved by calculating costs at various decision levels, using the following procedure.

Step 1   Estimate cost of holding one extra unit of stock for one year.

Step 2   Estimate cost of each stockout.

Step 3   Calculate expected number of stockouts per order associated with each level of stock.

Step 4   Calculate EOQ, and hence number of orders per annum.

Step 5   Calculate the total costs (stockout plus holding costs) per annum associated with each level of buffer stock, and select minimum cost options.

Example

Autobits Ltd is one of the few suppliers of an electronic ignition system for cars, and it sells 100 units each year. Each unit costs £40 to buy in from the manufacturer, and it is estimated that each order costs £10 to handle and that the cost of holding one unit in stock for one year is 25% of the cost price. The lead-time is always exactly one week. The weekly demand for units follows a probability distribution with a mean of 2, as follows:

Demand	Probability of demand
0	0.14
1	0.27
2	0.27
3	0.18
4	0.09
5	0.04
6	0.01

Autobits estimates that the stockout cost is £20 per unit.

Autobits must estimate when orders should be placed.

Solution

Step 1   Cost of holding one unit: £10 (£40 × 25%)

Step 2   Cost of stockout: £20

Step 3   Expected number of stockouts per order

The normal level of demand in the lead-time is 2 (average, or mean, demand). Define buffer stock as re-order level minus 2. For example, if buffer stock were zero, reordering would take place when stock fell to 2.

Buffer stock of 4 (6 − 2) would mean that, on the basis of the observations, a stockout would never occur. Thus, the range of buffer stock options is between 0 and 4 units i.e. re-order levels between 2 and 6.

The pay-off table between buffer stock and actual demand in terms of stockouts is as follows:

Pay-off table in terms of stockouts

Re-order level	2	3	4	5	6
Actual demand during lead-time					
2 or less	0	0	0	0	0
3	1	0	0	0	0
4	2	1	0	0	0
5	3	2	1	0	0
6	4	3	2	1	0

Multiplying, then, by the probability of that level of demand occurring, the expected number of stockouts is as follows:

Expected number of stockouts

Re-order level		2	3	4	5	6
Demand	Probability					
2 or less	0.68 *	0	0	0	0	0
3	0.18	0.18	0	0	0	0
4	0.09	0.18	0.09	0	0	0
5	0.04	0.12	0.08	0.04	0	0
6	0.01	0.04	0.03	0.02	0.01	0
Total = Expected stockouts per order		0.52	0.20	0.06	0.01	Nil

* calculated as 0.14 + 0.27 + 0.27 = 0.68

Step 4

$$EOQ = \sqrt{\frac{2CD}{H}}$$

$$= \sqrt{\frac{2 \times 10 \times 100}{10}}$$

$$= 14.142, \text{ or } 14$$

$$\text{Orders per annum} = \frac{100}{14}$$

$$= 7.142$$

Step 5

(i)	Re order level	2	3	4	5	6
(ii)	Buffer stocks ((i) –2)	0	1	2	3	4
(iii)	Annual cost of holding buffer stock ((ii) × £10)	0	£10.00	£20.00	£30.00	£40.00
(iv)	Stockouts per order (per step 3)	0.52	0.20	0.06	0.01	Nil
(v)	Annual cost of stockouts ((iv) × 7.142 × £20)	£74.28	£28.57	£8.57	£1.43	Nil
(vi)	Total buffer stock cost ((iii) + (v))	£74.28	£38.57	£28.57	£31.43	£40.00

Therefore the minimum cost solution is to hold a buffer stock of 2 i.e. re-order when stocks fall to 4.

From the above analysis, it is apparent that increasing buffer stock is worthwhile if the following conditions apply.

• Reduction in annual stockout costs > Unit holding cost

   or

• Stockout cost × Orders per annum × Decrease in expected number of stockouts per order > Unit holding cost.

Conclusion

This chapter has discussed the basic principles involved in working capital management, including financing issues and ratio analysis. The importance of liquidity to business survival and growth was emphasised. We also discussed stock management.

The nature and scope of working capital management

1   Working capital management is a trade-off between _____
    and _____. (1.2)

The relationship of working capital management to business solvency

2   Distinguish between over capitalisation and overtrading. (4.2, 4.3))

Management of stock

3   Briefly explain the basic principles of a JIT stock purchasing system. (5.4)
4   Which types of cost is the EOQ model trying to balance? (5.6)

Ewden plc

Ewden plc is a medium-sized company producing a range of engineering products which it sells to wholesale distributors. Recently, its sales have begun to rise rapidly following a general recovery in the economy as a whole. However, it is concerned about its liquidity position and is contemplating ways of improving its cash flow. Ewden's accounts for the past two years are summarised below.

Profit and loss account for the year ended 31 December

	20X2 £'000	20X3 £'000
Sales	12,000	16,000
Cost of sales	7,000	9,150
Operating profit	5,000	6,850
Interest	200	250
Profit before tax	4,800	6,600
Taxation*	1,000	1,600
Profit after tax	3,800	5,000
Dividends	1,500	2,000
Retained profit	2,300	3,000

*After capital allowances

Balance sheet as at 31 December

	20X2 £'000	20X2 £'000	20X3 £'000	20X3 £'000
Fixed assets (net)		9,000		12,000
Current assets				
Stock	1,400		2,200	
Debtors	1,600		2,600	
Cash	1,500		100	
		4,500		4,900
Current liabilities				
Overdraft	–		200	
Trade creditors	1,500		2,000	
Other creditors	500		200	
		(2,000)		(2,400)
10% Loan stock		(2,000)		(2,000)

Net assets	9,500	12,500
Ordinary shares (50p)	3,000	3,000
Profit and loss account	6,500	9,500
Shareholders' funds	9,500	12,500

In order to speed up collection from debtors, Ewden is considering two alternative policies. One option is to offer a 2% discount to customers who settle within 10 days of despatch of invoices rather than the normal 30 days offered. It is estimated that 50% of customers would take advantage of this offer. Alternatively, Ewden can utilise the services of a factor. The factor will operate on a service-only basis, administering and collecting payment from Ewden's customers. This is expected to generate administrative savings of £100,000 pa and, it is hoped, will also shorten the debtor days to an average of 45. The factor will make a service charge of 1.5% of Ewden's turnover. Ewden can borrow from its bankers at an interest rate of 18% pa.

Required:

(a)   Identify the reasons for the sharp decline in Ewden's liquidity and assess the extent to which the company can be said to be exhibiting the problem of 'overtrading'.

Illustrate your answer by reference to key performance and liquidity ratios computed from Ewden's accounts.   **(13 marks)**

(*Note:* it is not necessary to compile a FRS 1 statement.)

(b)   Determine the relative costs and benefits of the two methods of reducing debtors, and recommend an appropriate policy.   **(7 marks)**

(Total: 20 marks)

For the answer to this question, see the 'Answers' section at the end of the book.

FEEDBACK TO
ACTIVITY 1

Cash operating cycle = 4 + 1 + 3 + 2 – 6 weeks

= 4 weeks.

FEEDBACK TO
ACTIVITY 3

1   Creditors:

Average payment collection period

$$= \left(365 \times \frac{Creditors}{Purchases}\right) \qquad 365 \times \frac{21}{140} = \qquad (55 \text{ days})$$

2   Debtors:

Average collection period

$$= \left(365 \times \frac{Debtors}{Sales}\right) \qquad 365 \times \frac{31.25}{250} = \qquad 46 \text{ days}$$

3   Stock turnover:

$$= 365 \times \frac{Stock}{Cost \ of \ goods \ sold} \qquad 365 \times \frac{92.5}{210} = \qquad 161 \text{ days}$$

Length of cash operating cycle   152 days

FEEDBACK TO ACTIVITY 4

Step 1 Calculate annual cost of sales, using the cost structure.

	%	£m
Sales	160	8
Cost of sales	100	5
Gross profit	60	3

Step 2 Calculate creditors, debtors and stock.

$$\text{Creditors} = \frac{2}{12} \times \text{annual COS} = \frac{2}{12} \times £5m = £0.833m$$

$$\text{Debtors} = \frac{1.5}{12} \times \text{annual sales} = \frac{1.5}{12} \times £8m = £1m$$

$$\text{Stock} = \frac{1}{12} \times \text{annual COS} = \frac{1}{12} \times £5m = £0.417m$$

Step 3 Calculate the ratios.

$$\text{Current ratio} = \frac{\text{Stock + debtors + cash}}{\text{Creditors}} = \frac{0.417 + 1 + 1.25}{0.833} = 3.2$$

$$\text{Quick ratio} = \frac{\text{Debtors + cash}}{\text{Creditors}} = \frac{1 + 1.25}{0.833} = 2.7$$

FEEDBACK TO ACTIVITY 5

Use the formula $EOQ = \sqrt{\dfrac{2CD}{H}}$

Here $C = £40$

     $D = 600,000$

     $H = £3$

So EOQ $= \sqrt{\dfrac{2 \times 40 \times 600,000}{3}}$

     $= 4,000$ units

FEEDBACK TO ACTIVITY 6

(a) Annual demand is 30,000. The original EOQ is 3,162. The company will therefore place an order once every $\dfrac{3,162}{30,000} \times 365$ days ≈ 38 days.

(b) The company must be sure that there is sufficient stock on hand when it places an order to last the two weeks' lead-time. It must therefore place an order when there is two weeks' worth of demand in stock:

i.e. $\dfrac{2}{52} \times 30,000 \approx 1,154$ units.

FOULKS LYNCH
PUBLICATIONS

Chapter 6

WORKING CAPITAL MANAGEMENT: DEBTORS AND CREDITORS

Continuing the theme of the last chapter, we now look in more detail at the management of the two remaining components of working capital – debtors and creditors – both theoretically and practically.

Objectives

By the time you have finished this chapter you should be able to do the following-

- explain the role of creditors in the working capital cycle
- explain the availability of credit and the role of the guarantee
- identify the risks of taking increased credit and buying under extended credit terms
- explain how methods of paying suppliers may influence cash flows of both parties
- discuss the particular problems of managing overseas accounts payable
- calculate and interpret creditor ratios
- apply the tools and techniques of creditor management
- analyse and evaluate the results of creditor management techniques
- explain the role of debtors in the working capital cycle
- explain how the credit-worthiness of customers may be assessed
- evaluate the balance of risks and costs of customer default against the profitability of marginal business
- explain the role of factoring and invoice discounting
- explain the role of settlement discounts
- discuss the particular problems of managing overseas accounts receivable
- calculate and interpret debtor ratios
- apply the tools and techniques of debtor management
- analyse and evaluate the results of debtor management techniques.

1   Management of debtors

1.1   Extending trade credit

A firm must establish a policy for credit terms given to its customers. Ideally the firm would want to obtain cash with each order delivered, but that is impossible unless substantial settlement (or cash) discounts are offered as an inducement. It must be recognised that credit terms are part of the firm's marketing policy. If the trade or industry has adopted a common practice, then it is probably wise to keep in step with it.

A lenient credit policy may well attract additional custom, but at a disproportionate increase in cost. The optimum level of trade credit extended represents a balance between two factors:

- profit improvement from sales obtained by allowing credit
- the cost of credit allowed.

FOULKS LYNCH
PUBLICATIONS

KEY POINT

Management of debtors requires a credit policy to be **established**, properly **implemented** and continually **monitored**.

Management will be anxious to do the following:

- establish a credit policy in relation to normal periods of credit and individual credit limits
- develop a system which will control the implementation of credit policy
- prescribe reporting procedures which will monitor the efficiency of the system.

Management of debtors requires a credit policy to be established, properly implemented and continually monitored.

1.2 Establishing credit policy

The period of credit extended will be set by reference to:

- elasticity of demand for the company's products
- credit terms offered by competitors
- risk of bad debts resulting from extended credit periods
- financing costs and availability of finance
- costs of administering the credit system.

DEFINITION

Credit Assessment involves analysis of the prospective customer's current business situation and credit history, derived from information obtained from any available sources.

Individual credit limits depend on assessing the creditworthiness of a particular customer: in the first instance, whether the customer would be allowed credit at all; and secondly, the maximum amount that should be allowed. **Assessment** involves analysis of the prospective customer's current business situation and credit history, derived from information obtained from any available sources.

Credit policy must be reasonably flexible to reflect changes in economic conditions, actions by competitors and marketing strategy (e.g. the desire to 'kill off' a new competitor in the market).

ACTIVITY 1

A study of the debtors of XYZ Co Ltd has shown that it is possible to classify all debtors into certain classes with the following characteristics:

Category	Average collection period (days)	Bad debts (%)
A	15	0.5
B	20	2.5
C	30	5.0
D	40	9.5

The average standard profit/cost schedule for the company's range of products is as follows:

	£	£
Selling price		2.50
Less: Materials	1.00	
Wages	0.95	
Variable costs	0.30	
Fixed costs	0.05	
	___	2.30
Profit		0.20

The company has the opportunity of extending its sales by £1,000,000 per annum, split between categories C and D in the proportions 40:60. The company's short-term borrowing rate is 11½% per annum on a simple interest basis.

Evaluate the effect of the proposed increase in sales by carrying out the steps below.

Step 1   Calculate the **additional contribution** from the extra sales, split between the different categories of debtor. Assume that the contribution per £ of sales will be as shown on the standard cost card.

Step 2   For each category of debtor, work out the **bad debts** arising from the sales, using the given percentages. **Deduct** the bad debts from the additional contribution worked out in Step 1.

Step 3   For each category of debtor work out the (absolute) interest cost of allowing credit over the relevant period.

The cost equals: Annual interest rate × Additional debtors, where

Additional debtors =

$$\text{Additional annual sales} \times \frac{\text{Average collection period (days)}}{365}$$

Deduct this cost from the net additional contribution derived in Step 2.

The final result is the net profit or loss from expanding sales.

Feedback to this activity is at the end of the chapter.

Settlement discounts

A company may offer settlement discounts to its customers, by allowing debtors to pay less than their full debt if they pay sooner than the end of their credit period. The company must ensure that offering the discount is financially sensible, with the benefit of receiving the cash early exceeding the cost of the discount.

The mathematics of offering settlement discounts are very similar to the decision as to whether discounts should be taken from suppliers; this decision is examined later in this chapter.

1.3   Implementing credit policy

Implementation of a credit policy involves assessing **creditworthiness**, controlling **credit limits**, **invoicing** promptly and establishing procedures for **collection of overdue debts**

Assessing creditworthiness

A new customer's creditworthiness should be carefully assessed before extended credit terms are offered. Sources of information are:

- **Trade references.** The potential customer is asked to give names of two existing suppliers who will testify to the firm's credit standing. Note that there is a danger that firms will nominate only suppliers that are paid on time.

- **Bank references.** Permission is sought to approach the customer's bank to discuss his creditworthiness. Note that banks are often reluctant to give their customers bad references.

- **Credit agencies and credit associations.** These bodies will provide independent assessments of creditworthiness for a fee. Short reports may be obtained from regularly updated registers or special, more detailed, reports may be commissioned. Dun and Bradstreet is possibly the most well-known credit agency in this area, but there are others.

- **Reports from salesmen.** Salesmen are often the only representatives of the supplying firm who actually meet the potential customer's staff and see the

premises. They are therefore in a unique position to provide information on customer creditworthiness.

- **Information from competitors.** In 'close-knit' industries competing suppliers often exchange credit information on potential customers.

- **Financial statement analysis.** Recent accounts may be analysed to determine the customer's ability to pay.

- **Credit scoring**. This can be applied in all circumstances where credit is under consideration, but is more applicable where sales are direct to the public, and the use of the above evaluations are either not possible or are too expensive.

Example

A sample of a firm's past customers identifies the factors associated with bad debts. Age, sex, marital status, family size, occupation etc, may be significant factors. The firm allocates a points score to potential customers as follows:

Factor	Points score
Aged over 40	15
Married with fewer than three children	20
Home owner	20
At same address for over three years	15
At existing job for over two years	20
Car owner	10
Total	100

Past records show that there have been no records of payment difficulties with customers with a score of 80 or over, bad debts of 10% for scores between 35 and 80, and bad debts of 25% where customers had a score of less than 35. A 'cut-off' point of 35 would probably be established, and credit refused to any potential customer with a score of less than 35.

The factors which are considered most likely to influence creditworthiness are, of course, a matter of judgement, as are the respective weights which should be attached to each factor.

Preventing credit limits from being exceeded

Control of credit limits should occur at the order processing stage, i.e. the customer's ledger account will be adapted to reflect orders in the pipeline as well as invoiced sales.

Invoicing promptly

The customer's period of credit will relate to receipt of invoice, so it is essential to minimise the time-lag between despatch and invoicing, e.g. by streamlining authorisation and administrative procedures.

Collecting overdue debts

The longer a debt is allowed to run, the higher the probability of eventual default. A system of follow-up procedures is required, bearing in mind the risk of offending a valued customer to such an extent that their business is lost.

Techniques for 'chasing' overdue debts include the following:

- **Reminder letters.** These are often regarded as being a relatively poor way of obtaining payment, as many customers simply ignore them. Sending reminders by fax or email is usually more productive than using the post.

- **Telephone calls.** These are more expensive than reminder letters but where large sums are involved they can be an efficient way of speeding payment.

- **Withholding supplies.** Putting customers on the 'stop list' for further orders or spare parts can encourage rapid settlement of debts.

- **Debt collection agencies and trade associations.** These offer debt collection services on a fixed fee basis or on 'no collection no charge' terms. The quality of service provided varies considerably and care should be taken in selecting an agent.

- **Legal action.** This is often seen as a last resort. A solicitor's letter often prompts payment and many cases do not go to court. Court action is usually not cost effective but it can discourage other customers from delaying payment.

1.4   Monitoring the credit system

Management will require regular information to take corrective action and to measure the impact of giving credit on working capital investments. Typical management reports on the credit system will include the following points.

- **Age analysis** of outstanding debts.

- **Ratios,** compared with the previous period or target, to indicate trends in credit levels and the incidence of overdue and bad debts.

- **Statistical data** to identify causes of default and the incidence of bad debts among different classes of customer and types of trade.

1.5   Financing from debtors

Most businesses will have to extend credit to their customers to keep in line with industry practice and thus maintain sales. They must then wait until the customer pays to realise the cash. However, there are ways that the business may raise finance on the strength of its outstanding sales invoices, principally through the practices of:

- factoring

- invoice discounting.

2   Factoring debts

2.1   Factoring

DEFINITION

Factoring involves turning over responsibility for collecting the company's debts to a specialist institution (the factor).

DEFINITION

A factor is a financial institution that accelerates the cash conversion cycle for client companies, allowing them to gain access to debtors more quickly than if they waited for the normal trade credit period to elapse.

Many businesses use their own staff to collect debts. However, other arrangements can be made and other debt collection methods used. These include using the services of a factor.

A factor is a financial institution that accelerates the cash conversion cycle for client companies, allowing them to gain access to debtors more quickly than if they waited for the normal trade credit period to elapse.

There are three elements to a factor's services.

- **Providing finance**. A factor provides short-term finance to a business, based on the value of its unpaid invoices. A factor will pay an agreed proportion of the value of new invoices as soon as they are sent out to customers. It is repaid when the debt is eventually collected.

- **Administration of the sales ledger**. A factor also takes over the responsibility for administering the client's sales ledger and debt collection procedures.

- **Credit protection**. A factor might also agree to insure the debts of a client against bad debt risk. If a customer becomes a bad debt, the factor takes the loss.

Some companies realise that, although it is necessary to extend trade credit to customers for competitive reasons, they need payment earlier than agreed in order to assist their own cash flow. Factors exist to help such companies.

Factoring is most suitable for:

- small and medium-sized firms which often cannot afford sophisticated credit and sales accounting systems, and

- firms that are expanding rapidly. These often have a substantial and growing investment in stocks and debtors, which can be turned into cash by factoring the debts. Factoring debts can be a n more flexible source of financing working capital than an overdraft or bank loan.

Factoring is primarily designed to allow companies to accelerate cash flow, providing finance against outstanding trade debtors. This improves cash flow and liquidity

Factoring can be arranged on either a 'without recourse' basis or a 'with recourse' basis.

- When factoring is without recourse or 'non-recourse', the factor provides protection for the client against bad debts. The factor has no 'come-back' or recourse to the client if a customer defaults. When a customer of the client fails to pay a debt, the factor bears the loss and the client receives the money from the debt.

- When the service is with recourse ('recourse factoring'), the client must bear the loss from any bad debt, and so has to reimburse the factor for any money it has already received for the debt.

Credit protection is provided only when the service is non-recourse.

2.2   Sales ledger administration

A factor assumes the various functions of sales ledger administration, including:

- recording sales details in the sales ledger (i.e. in the accounts of the individual debtors)

- sending out statements

- sending out reminders, and

- collecting payment.

The factor might refer to this service as credit management and administration'. In some cases, the factor also sends out the invoices. However, it is more usual for the business (the factor's client) to send out the invoices, and to send a copy to the factor. The factor then enters the details in the sales ledger. Invoices must specify clearly that payments must be made to the factor.

The benefits for the client are the cost savings from reducing in-house administration and access to a more efficient, specialist credit management team. This is particularly valuable to a young fast-growing company, which may outgrow its administration system and otherwise be exposed to the liquidity risks of over-trading.

The fee for such an administration service would lie in the range of 0.75% to 2.5% of the value of sales turnover handled.

2.3   Credit protection from a factor

The factor can also provide a credit protection and evaluation service for clients, analysing customer characteristics before deciding on their credit-worthiness.

When factoring is without recourse, the factor is providing credit protection. Under this arrangement, the factor requires total control of credit approval and decides the credit limits for each customer of the client.

Example

Edden is a medium-sized company producing a range of engineering products which it sells to wholesale distributors. Recently, its sales have begun to rise rapidly due to

economic recovery. However, it is concerned about its liquidity position and is looking ways of improving cash flow.

Its sales are £16 million p.a., and average debtors are £3.3 million (representing about 75 days of sales).

One way of speeding up collection from debtors is to use a factor. The factor will operate on a service-only basis, administering and collecting payment from Edden's customers. This is expected to generate administrative savings of £100,000 each year. The factor has undertaken to pay outstanding debts after 45 days, regardless of whether the customers have actually paid or not. The factor will make a service charge of 1.75% of Edden's turnover. Edden can borrow at an interest rate of 8% pa.

Task

Determine the relative costs and benefits of using the factor.

Solution

Reduction in debtor days $= (75 - 45) = 30$ days

Reduction in debtors $= \frac{30}{365} \times £16m = $ **£1,315,068**

Interest saving $= (8\% \times £1,315,068) = £105,205$, say £105,000.

Administrative savings $= £100,000$

Service charge $= (1.75\% \times £16m) = £280,000$

Summary

	£
Service charge	(280,000)
Interest saved by reducing debtors	105,000
Administration costs saved	100,000
Net annual cost of the service	(75,000)

Edden will have to balance this cost against the security offered by improved cash flows and greater liquidity.

2.4   Provision of finance – finance factoring

Finance factoring is where the factor makes a cash advance to the client, as well as conducting sales ledger administration and debt collection services.

A factor will advance money to a client, based on a proportion (usually 80% to 85%) of approved invoices. Approved invoices are invoices to customers within credit limits. For example, a company with sales on 30-day credit terms from reliable customers of £500,000 per month might receive an advance of £400,000 (80%) £400,000 each month. Interest is charged on the money advanced. If the factor is a subsidiary of a bank, the interest rate is typically 1.5% to 3% above the bank's base rate, and charged on a daily basis.

When the customer eventually pays the debt to the factor, the client receives the balance of the payment less interest and other charges from the factor.

The following diagram show how this operates.

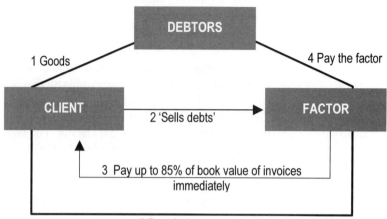

2.5 Non-recourse factoring: how the full service works

It might help now to go through the stages in a non-recourse factoring service, to see how all three services of the factor can link together.

- Most factoring agreements cover all sales by the client's business. The factor decides the credit limits for each customer of the client.

- The client business makes a sale and produces the invoice. (In some cases, the factor might produce the invoice itself from data supplied by the client.) The invoice must make it clear that payment must be made to the factor.

- The invoice goes to the customer and a copy goes to the factor.

- The factor is responsible for sales ledger administration, and recording the sale and debt in the customer's account in the sales ledger.

- The factor pays the client an agreed percentage amount of the invoice, typically 80% to 85% of the invoice value. (*Note*: Typically, the client will produce a number of invoices at the same time, so the factor provides finance for a number of invoices.) Payment of this advance is usually made within 24 hours.

- The factor issues statements to customers and collects payments. The debt collection service includes contacting late payers and chasing payment of overdue debts. (This happens with recourse factoring as well as non-recourse factoring.)

- When the factor receives payment, the factor pays the client the balance of the invoice amount, less charges.

- The factor provides regular reports on the status of the client's sales ledger, and the client can usually access customer account information on-line.

2.6 Advantages of factoring and problems with factoring

Advantages of factoring

The benefits of factoring are as follows.

- A business improves its cash flow, because the factor provides finance for up to 80% or more of debts within 24 hours of the invoices being issued. A bank providing an overdraft facility secured against a company's unpaid invoices will normally lend up to 50% only of the invoice value. (Factors will provide 80% or so because they set credit limits and are responsible for collecting the debts.)

- A factor saves the administration costs of keeping the sales ledger up-to-date and the costs of debt collection.

- A business can use the factor's credit control system to assess the creditworthiness of both new and existing customers.

- Non-recourse factoring is a convenient way of obtaining insurance against bad debts.

Problems with factoring

Although factors provide valuable services, companies are sometimes wary about using them. A possible problem with factoring is that the intervention of the factor between the factor's client and the debtor company could endanger trading relationships and damage goodwill. Customers might prefer to deal with the business, not a factor.

When a non-recourse factoring service is used, the client loses control over decisions about granting credit to its customers.

For this reason, some clients prefer to retain the risk of bad debts, and opt for a 'with recourse' factoring service. With this type of service, the client and not the factor decides whether extreme action (legal action) should be taken against a non-payer.

On top of this, when suppliers and customers of the client find out that the client is using a factor to collect debts, it may arouse fears that the company is beset by cash flow problems, raising fears about its viability. If so, its suppliers may impose more stringent payment terms, thus negating the benefits provided by the factor.

Using a factor can create problems with customers who may resent being chased for payment by a third party, and may question the supplier's financial stability.

ACTIVITY 2

A company has monthly credit sales of £200,000, and it gives customers 60 days credit. All customers take the full credit allowed. It has bad debts each year amounting to about 2.5% of sales turnover. It operates with a bank overdraft and pays interest at 8% on its overdraft balance.

The company s management is considering whether to use a factor to collect is debts, under a non-recourse factoring arrangement. A factor has indicated that it will take over the administration of the sales ledger and debt collection for a fee of 2% of annual credit sales turnover. This would save the company internal operating costs of £30,000 each year.

The factor would also charge 1.5% of turnover for credit insurance.

The factor will advance 80% of the value of invoices as soon as they are sent out, and charge interest at 7.75%.

If the services of the factor are used, it is anticipated that there will be no change in annual sales turnover and no change in the collection period of 60 days.

Required:

Assess the financial consequences of using the factor for non-recourse factoring and factor finance.

Feedback to this activity is at the end of the chapter.

3   Invoice discounting

Invoice discounting is a method of raising finance against the security of debtors without using the sales ledger administration services of a factor.

Firms of factors will also provide invoice discounting to clients.

With invoice discounting, the business retains control over its sales ledger, and confidentiality in its dealings with customers.

- The business sends out invoices, statements and reminders in the normal way, and collects the debts. With 'confidential invoice discounting', its customers are unaware that the business is using invoice discounting.

- The invoice discounter provides cash to the business for a proportion of the value of the invoice, as soon as it receives a copy of the invoice and agrees to discount it. The discounter will advance cash up to 80% of face value.

- When the business eventually collects the payment from its customer, the money must be paid into a bank account controlled by the invoice discounter. The invoice discounter then pays the business the remainder of the invoice, less interest and administration charges.

Invoice discounting can help a business that is trying to improve its cash flows, but does not want a factor to administer its sales ledger and collect its debts. It is therefore equivalent to the financing service provided by a factor.

Administration charges for this service are around 0.5–1% of a client's turnover. It is more risky than factoring since the client retains control over its credit policy. Consequently, such facilities are usually confined to established companies with an annual sales turnover above £500,000, and the business must be profitable. Interest costs are usually in the range 3–4% above base rate, although larger companies and those which arrange credit insurance may receive better terms.

The invoice discounter will check the sales ledger of the client regularly, perhaps every three months, to check that its debt collection procedures are adequate.

3.1   How invoice discounting works – example

At the beginning of August, Basildon plc sells goods for a total value of £300,000 to regular customers but decides that it requires payment earlier than the agreed 30-day credit period for these invoices. A discounter agrees to finance 80% of their face value, i.e. £240,000. Interest is 9% p.a. The invoices were due for payment in early September, but were subsequently settled in mid-September, exactly 45 days after the initial transactions. The invoice discounter's service charge is 1%. A special account is set up with a bank, into which all payments are made. The sequence of cash flows is:

August   Basildon receives cash advance of £240,000

Mid-September   Customers pay £300,000

Invoice discounter receives the full £300,000, paid into the special bank account Basildon receives the balance payable receivable less charges, i.e.

Service fee = 1% × £300,000 =	£3,000
Interest = 9% × £240,000 × 45/365 =	£2,664
Total charges	£5,663

Basildon receives:

Balance of payment from customer	£60,000
Less charges	£5,663
	£54,337

Summary

Total receipts by Basildon: £240,000 + £54,337	£294,337
Invoice discounter's fee and interest charges	£5,633

4 Management of trade creditors

4.1 Trade credit

Under **trade credit** a firm is able to obtain goods (or services) from a supplier without immediate payment, the supplier accepting that the firm will pay at a later date.

4.2 Trade credit periods

Trade credit periods vary from industry to industry and each industry will have what is a generally accepted norm which would be from seven days upwards. The usual terms of credit range from four weeks to the period between the date of purchase and the end of the month following the month of purchase. However, considerable scope for flexibility exists and longer credit periods are sometimes offered, particularly where the type of business activity requires a long period to convert materials into saleable products, e.g. farming.

4.3 Managing trade creditors

A proportion of the firm's suppliers will normally offer **settlement discounts** which should be taken up where possible by ensuring that special clearing treatment is given where settlement discount is allowed. However, if the firm is short of funds, it might wish to make maximum use of the credit period allowed by suppliers regardless of the settlement discounts offered.

It is a mistake to reduce working capital by holding on to creditors' money for a longer period than is allowed as, in the long term, this will affect the supplier's willingness to supply goods and raw materials, and cause further embarrassment to the firm.

Favourable credit terms are one of several factors which influence the choice of a supplier. Furthermore, the act of accepting settlement discounts has an opportunity cost, i.e. the cost of finance obtained from another source to replace that not obtained from creditors.

Whilst trade credit may be seen as a source of **free credit,** there will be **costs** associated with extending credit taken beyond the norm - lost discounts, loss of supplier goodwill, more stringent terms for future sales.

4.4 Costs of trade credit

In order to compare the cost of different sources of finance, all costs are usually converted to a **rate per annum** basis. The cost of extended trade credit is usually measured by **loss of discount**, but the calculation of its cost is complicated by such variables as the number of alternative sources of supply, and the general economic conditions.

Certain assumptions have to be made concerning (a) the maximum delay in payment which can be achieved before the supply of goods is withdrawn by the supplier, and (b) the availability of alternative sources of supply.

Example

A business is buying £1,000 worth of goods per month and can take 2.5% discount if it settles accounts within one month. It will lose that source of supply if it delays payment for more than three months. An alternative supply of goods will be difficult to obtain in the event of the business getting a bad name.

To work out the cost to the business of taking the extra two months' credit and losing the discount, carry out the following steps:

Step 1

Work out the discount available and the amount due if the discount were taken.

Discount available = 2.5% × £1,000 = £25

Amount due after discount = £1,000 − £25 = £975

Step 2

The effective interest cost of not taking the discount is:

$$\frac{\text{Discount available}}{\text{Discounted amount due}}$$

This applies to the maximum credit period available after losing the discount (i.e. three months less one month).

Interest cost of taking two months' credit $= \dfrac{£25}{£975} \approx 0.0256$ for a two month period.

The idea here is that the business is effectively borrowing £975 from the supplier for two months, and paying £1,000 back at the end, an interest charge of £25 on the 'loan'.

Step 3

Calculate the equivalent annual rate. For **simple interest**, this will be:

Interest cost for period × number of periods in a year × 100%.

For **compound interest**, the rate will be:

$(1 + \text{interest cost for period})^n - 1$, where 'n' is the number of periods in a year. As there are approximately six, sixty day periods in a year the simple annual cost would be: $0.0256 \times 6 \times 100\% \approx 15.4\%$. The compound annual cost is:

$$\left(1 + \frac{25}{975}\right)^6 - 1 = 0.164 \text{ or } 16.4\%$$

Note that this calculation contains only the explicit costs of trade credit. The implicit costs of delaying payment to the three month point should also be considered. For example, although suppliers may not cut off future supplies they may put a low priority on the quality of service given to late paying customers.

ACTIVITY 3

Work out the equivalent simple and compound annual costs of the following credit terms: 1.75% discount for payment within three weeks; alternatively, full payment must be made within eight weeks of the invoice date. Assume there are 50 weeks in a year.

Hint: Consider a £100 invoice.

Feedback to this activity is at the end of the chapter.

5 Foreign trade risk management

Whilst all of the basic management principles and techniques discussed so far apply equally to overseas debtors and creditors, there are additional risks that will need to be managed, including:

- export credit risk
- foreign exchange transaction exposure.

5.1 Export credit risk

Export credit risk is the risk of failure or delay in collecting payments due from foreign customers.

Possible causes of loss from such risk, which apply to all export trade of whatever size, include the following.

- **Illiquidity or insolvency** of the customer. This also of course occurs in domestic trading. But when an export customer cannot pay, suppliers have extra problems in protecting their positions in a foreign legal and banking system.
- Bankruptcy or **failure of a bank** in the remittance chain.
- A poorly specified **remittance channel**.
- **Inconvertibility** of the customer's currency, and lack of access to the currency in which payment is due. This can be caused by deliberate exchange controls or by an unplanned lack of foreign exchange in the customer's central bank.
- **Political risks**. Their causes can be internal (change of regime, civil war) or external (war, blockade) to the country concerned.

Exporters can protect themselves against these risks by the following means.

- Use **banks** in both countries to act as the collecting channel for the remittance and to control the shipping documents so that they are only released against payment or acceptance of negotiable instruments (bills of exchange or promissory notes).
- Commit the customer's bank through an **irrevocable letter of credit** (ILC).
- Require the ILC to be confirmed (effectively guaranteed) by a first class bank in the exporter's country. This makes the ILC a confirmed ILC (CILC)/
- Obtain support from **third parties**, for example:
  - get a guarantee of payment from a local bank
  - get a letter from the local finance ministry or central bank confirming availability of foreign currency.
- Take out export credit cover.
- Use an intermediary like a confirming, export finance, factoring or forfaiting house to handle the problems on their behalf; or possibly by giving no credit or selling only through agents who accept the credit risk (*del credere* agents) and are themselves financially strong.

None of these devices will enable the exporter to escape from certain hard facts of life:

- **The need to avoid giving credit to uncreditworthy customers.** Weak customers cannot obtain an ILC from their own bank, nor would they be cleared for credit by a credit insurer or intermediary.
- **The need to negotiate secure payment terms, procedures and mechanisms which customers do not find congenial.** An ILC and especially a CILC are costly to customers, and restrict their flexibility: if they are a bit short of cash at the end of the month, they must still pay out if their bank is committed.
- **Exporters can only collect under a letter of credit if they present exactly the required documents.** They will not be able to do this if they have sent the goods by air and the credit requires shipping documents; nor if they need to produce the

customer's inspection certificates and the customer's engineer is mysteriously unavailable to inspect or sign.

- **The need to insist that payment is in a convertible currency** and in a form which the customer's authorities will permit to become effective as a remittance to where the exporters need to have the funds, usually in their own country. Often this means making the sale subject to clearance under exchange controls or import licensing regulations.

5.2 Introductory points about foreign exchange

Many companies trade in foreign currencies, either buying from abroad in a foreign currency or denominating sales to export customers in a foreign currency. If so:

- they might need to buy foreign currency to pay a supplier, or
- they might need to convert foreign currency receipts into domestic currency.

Like domestic trade, foreign trade is arranged on credit terms. Companies usually know in advance what foreign currency they will need to pay out and what currencies they will be receiving. **Foreign exchange** risk arises in these situations:

- If a company has to obtain foreign currency at a future date to make a payment there is a risk that the cost of buying the currency will rise (from what it would cost now) if the exchange rate moves and the currency strengthens in value.

- If a company will want to convert currency earnings into a domestic currency at a future date, there is a risk that the value of the currency will fall (from its current value) if the exchange rate moves and the current falls in value.

Exposures to these risks of adverse changes in an exchange rate are known as (foreign exchange transaction exposures'.

These exposures can be 'hedged' (reduced or offset), using methods described below.

5.3 Foreign exchange transaction exposure

Transaction exposure leads to uncertainty as to future domestic currency cash flows arising from sales, purchases etc already made. The impact of this uncertainty can be minimised by the following means:

(a) Hedging
- currency forward or futures contracts
- money market hedge.

(b) Internal risk management methods
- leading and lagging
- settlement in domestic currency
- matching.

Example

Forex plc is expanding its operations into Switzerland and has ordered the construction of a factory near Nice. Final payment on the factory of 5,000,000 Swiss francs is due in three months' time. Foreign exchange and money market rates are given below:

	SFR/£
Spot	11.121 – 11.150
Three months forward	10.948 – 10.976

Note 1: The spot rate is the rate for buying or selling 'now' (or more exactly for settlement in two days' time). A forward rate is a rate agreed now for buying and selling, but for settlement at a future date.

Note 2: The customer can **buy** Swiss francs (SFR) at the **lower** rate and **sell** them at the **higher** rate.

	Borrowing	*Lending*
Euro-Swiss franc	11%	9%
Euro-sterling	15.5%	12%

Forex may adopt the following strategies to protect itself.

1   Hedge in the forward foreign exchange market

A forward contract is a contract between an individual or organisation and a banker whereby the two parties agree to exchange currencies on a **fixed future date** at an **exchange rate agreed now** (the **forward rate).**

Buy SFR 5,000,000 forward to guarantee their cost. To obtain the required amount this will cost:

$$\frac{5,000,000}{\text{SFR } 10.948/£} = £456,704 \text{ in three months' time}$$

2   Cover on the money markets

A money market hedge uses spot (current) exchange rates and fixed money market rates to achieve a fixed forward rate indirectly.

If the money market and foreign exchange markets are in equilibrium (interest rate parity) a money market hedge should give the same result as using the forward market.

To achieve this hedge, forex will need to borrow funds in the UK, convert them to Swiss francs (SFR) and invest them in Switzerland until they are required.

- Borrow £439,706 now @15.5% pa for three months.
- Convert the £s to SFR at spot rate to yield:

  £439,706 × SFR 11.121/£ = SFR 4,889,970.
- Invest the SFR for three months @ 9% pa to mature at:

$$\text{SFR } 4,889,970 \times (1 + \frac{0.09 \times 3 \text{ months}}{12 \text{ months}}) \approx \text{SFR } 5,000,000 \text{ in three months' time, which}$$

can be used to pay the Swiss supplier.

- Finally repay the £ loan which will mature at:

$$£439,706 \times (1 + \frac{0.155 \times 3 \text{ months}}{12 \text{ months}}) = £456,745 \text{ in three months' time.}$$

Note: Forex has invested in the strong currency (SFR) which has increased in value by approximately 1.5% over the period. The cost of this is that UK borrowing rates over a three-month period are roughly 1.6% higher than Swiss deposit rates. The net result is very close to the foreign exchange market cover and shows the markets are approximately in equilibrium; Forex has to effectively pay £456,745 compared to £456,704 under the forward hedge.

The initial £439,706 is obtained by working backwards, and amounts are rounded where appropriate.

3   Lead and lag

Leading is where a payment is made **in advance** of the required settlement date; **lagging** is when payment is **delayed.**

As the SFR is **strengthening** (the forward rate being lower than the spot rate) it could be advisable for Forex to pay early, e.g. buy SFR 5,000,000 spot and pay the bill now. This would cost:

$$\frac{\text{SFR } 5,000,000}{\text{SFR } 11.121/£} = £449,599 \text{ now}$$

To convert this to an effective cost in three months' time (i.e. to allow for the time value of money) we must assume the firm would have to borrow the funds for three months. This would then cost:

$$£449,599 \times (1 + \frac{0.155 \times 3 \text{ months}}{12 \text{ months}}) = £467,020 \text{ in three months' time.}$$

This appears a costly way of covering the exposure, but any discounts for early payment would also have to be taken into account. Note if the SFR had been weakening Forex would have attempted to pay late (a **lag payment**).

4   Pay in domestic currency

Forex could arrange with the supplier to pay in £. This would free Forex from foreign exchange transaction exposure but would load it onto the Swiss supplier. Marketing considerations would need to be taken into account.

5   Match

If a business has payments and receipts in the same currency, it may open up a bank account in that currency into which receipts are paid, and from which payments are made. This virtually eliminates transaction costs, and transaction exposure is confined to the net balance only - which may be realised when the rates are favourable.

Tutorial note: Bankers and corporate treasurers quote exchange rates by stating the 'fixed' currency first and the 'variable' currency second. So if we say that the US dollar is worth £1.50, we should refer to the sterling / dollar rate. Popular terminology, normally used by academics (including examiners!) is to put it the other way round, and to refer to the dollar / sterling rate. You need to be wary of how rates might be quoted in the exam.

ACTIVITY 4

A UK firm needs to pay a Singaporean supplier in three months' time. The current exchange rate is £1 = SGD 2.67. It is expected that the exchange rate will be £1 = SGD 2.65 in three months' time. The current sterling deposit interest rate is 10% pa. The company can either invest sufficient sterling now to pay the supplier SGD 20,000 at the forecast future exchange rate: or convert sterling into Singaporean dollars today, investing sufficient dollars to pay the bill in three months' time.

What must the Singaporean interest rate be for the firm to be indifferent between these two actions?

Feedback to this activity is at the end of the chapter.

Conclusion

This chapter has continued the topic of working capital management by looking at the particular issues arising in the management of debtors and creditors, including consideration of overseas aspects.

SELF-TEST QUESTIONS

Management of debtors

1   Give four factors that may influence the choice of credit period for a customer. (1.3)

2   Explain the term 'credit scoring'. (1.3)

Factoring debts

3   Describe the main features of debt factoring. (2.5)

Foreign trade risk management

4   How can export credit risk be protected against? (5.1)

Comfylot

Comfylot plc produces garden seats which are sold on both domestic and export markets. Sales during the next year are forecast to be £16 million, 70% to the UK domestic market and 30% to the export market, and are expected to occur steadily throughout the year. 80% of UK sales are on credit terms, with payment due in 30 days. On average UK domestic customers take 57 days to make payment. An initial deposit of 15% of the sales price is paid by all export customers.

All export sales are on 60 days credit with an average collection period for credit sales of 75 days. Bad debts are currently 0.75% of UK credit sales, and 1.25% of export sales (net of the deposit).

Comfylot wishes to investigate the effects of each of three possible operational changes:

(i)   Domestic credit management could be undertaken by a non-recourse factoring company. The factor would charge a service fee of 1.5% and would provide finance on 80% of the debts factored at a cost of base rate +2.5%. The finance element must be taken as part of the agreement with the factor. Using a factor would save an initial £85,000 per year in administration costs, but would lead to immediate redundancy payments of £15,000.

(ii)   As an alternative to using the factor a cash discount of 1.5% for payment in seven days could be offered on UK domestic sales. It is expected that 40% of domestic credit customers would use the cash discount. The discount would cost an additional £25,000 per year to administer, and would reduce bad debts to 0.50% of UK credit sales.

(iii)   Extra advertising could be undertaken to stimulate export sales. Comfylot has been approached by a European satellite TV company which believes that £300,000 of advertising could increase export sales in the coming year by up to 30%. There is a 0.2 chance of a 20% increase in export sales, a 0.5 chance of a 25% increase and a 0.3 chance of a 30% increase. Direct costs of production are 65% of the sales price. Administration costs would increase by £30,000, £40,000 and £50,000 for the 20%, 25% and 30% increases in export sales respectively. Increased export sales are likely to result in the average collection period of the credit element of all exports lengthening by five days, and bad debts will increase to 1.5% of all export credit sales.

Bank base rate is currently 13% per year, and Comfylot can borrow overdraft finance at 15% per year. These rates are not expected to change in the near future.

Taxation may be ignored.

Required:

Discuss whether any of the three suggested changes should be adopted by Comfylot plc. All relevant calculations must be shown.   **(20 marks)**

FEEDBACK TO ACTIVITY 1

	Ref to Steps	Category C £	Category C £	Category D £	Category D £
Additional contribution	(1)		40,000		60,000
Less: Additional costs:					
Bad debts	(2)	20,000		57,000	
Funding debtors	(3)	3,781		7,561	
			23,781		64,561
Additional profit and loss			16,219		(4,561)

Therefore, total additional profit = £16,219 – £4,561 = £11,658.

Note: It has been assumed that fixed costs will not increase as a result of the sales expansion.

Step 1   **Additional contribution**

(average per unit   =   £2.50 – (1.00 + 0.95 + 0.30) =   £0.25)

	Category C £	Category D £
Additional sales	40% × 1,000,000 = 400,000	60% × 1,000,000 = 600,000
Additional contribution	$\frac{0.25}{2.50}$ × 400,000 =40,000	$\frac{0.25}{2.50}$ × 600,000 =60,000

Step 2   **Bad debts**

Category C   5% × £400,000   =   £20,000

Category D   9.5% × £600,000   =   £57,000

Step 3   **Funding debtors**

Additional debtors	$\dfrac{30}{365}$ × 400,000 = 32,876	$\dfrac{40}{365}$ × 600,000 = 65,753

Cost of funding debtors

$11\frac{1}{2}$% × Additional debtors   = 3,781   = 7,561

It can be seen that additional profit is halved as a result of the additional financing required. In fact, the financing cost represents 1.26% of the additional sales value of Category D, while the bad debts represent 9.5%, a total of 10.76%.

FEEDBACK TO ACTIVITY 2

		Costs of factoring £	Savings £
Sales ledger administration	2% × £200,000 × 12	48,000	
Administration cost savings			30,000
Credit protection insurance	1.5% × £200,000 × 12	36,000	
Reduction in bad debt losses	2.5% × £200,000 × 12		60,000
Cost of factor finance	7.75% × 80% × £200,000 × 2 months	24,800	
Overdraft interest saved	8% × 80% × £200,000 × 2 months		25,600
Total		108,000	115,600
Net benefit from factoring	(115,600 – 108,800)		6,800

FOULKS LYNCH
PUBLICATIONS

FEEDBACK TO
ACTIVITY 3

Step 1

Work out the discount available and the amount due if the discount were taken.

Discount available on a £100 invoice = 1.75% × £100 = £1.75

Amount due after discount = £100 − £1.75 = £98.25

Step 2

The effective interest cost of not taking the discount is $\dfrac{£1.75}{£98.25} \approx 0.018$

for a (8 − 3) five-week period.

Step 3

Calculate the equivalent annual rate. There are ten five-week periods in a year.

The simple interest annual rate is therefore 0.018 × 10 × 100% = 18%.

The compound interest annual rate is $(1 + 0.018)^{10} − 1 \approx 0.195$ or 19.5%.

FEEDBACK TO
ACTIVITY 4

To be indifferent, the current sterling cost of each method must be the same. In each case, the company will invest slightly less than the final required amount, as the principal will accumulate interest over the deposit period.

Investing sterling

The final sum required will be $\dfrac{20,000}{2.65} \approx £7,547.17$, if the predicted exchange rate is correct.

The deposit will earn $\dfrac{10\%}{4}$ = 2.5% interest over the period.

Therefore the amount which must be invested is $\dfrac{£7,547.17}{1.025}$ = £7,363.09.

Investing Singaporean dollars

Let the Singaporean dollars interest rate be x% pa. The SGD deposit will earn $\dfrac{x\%}{4} = 0.25x\%$ interest over the period. Therefore the SGD amount which must be invested is SGD $\dfrac{20,000}{1+0.0025x}$.

The current sterling cost of this is $\dfrac{1}{2.67} \times \dfrac{20,000}{1+0.0025x}$.

For indifference, this must equal £7,363.09.

$$\dfrac{20,000}{1+0.0025x} = £7,363.09 \times 2.67 \,(= 19,659.45)$$

$$1 + 0.0025x = \dfrac{20,000}{19,659.45} = 1.017$$

$$x = \dfrac{1.017-1}{0.0025} = 6.8\% \text{ pa.}$$

Chapter 7
WORKING CAPITAL MANAGEMENT: CASH

We shall conclude our discussion of working capital management by considering cash management.

Objectives

By the time you have finished this chapter you should be able to do the following:

- explain the role of cash in the working capital cycle
- calculate optimal cash balances
- describe the functions of and evaluate the benefits from centralised cash control and treasury management
- calculate and interpret cash ratios
- apply the tools and techniques of cash management
- analyse and evaluate the results of cash management techniques.

1   Management of cash

Cash and bank balances should be kept to a minimum, as they (usually) earn nothing for the firm, but care must be taken to ensure that activities are not restricted through a shortage of ready cash to pay employees and creditors. Finance must obviously be set aside to meet taxation liabilities, pay dividends and invest in capital expenditure. However, until such payments become due, the cash may be profitably invested in short-term investments.

Managing cash usually involves the following issues:

- the preparation and use of cash budgets
- the management of short-term cash investments
- the management of overdrafts and bank loans
- the use of cash management models
- evaluating whether to use a centralised treasury department.

1.1   Cash budgets

The objectives of cash budgets are as follows.

- To integrate and appraise the effect of operating budgets on the firm's cash resources.
- To anticipate cash shortages and surpluses, and to allow time to plan how to deal with them.
- To provide a basis for comparison with actual, to identify unplanned occurrences.

A cash budget is essential for **control of day to day cash balances** and to allow efficient forward planning of the options for dealing with **short-term deficits and surpluses**.

Relationship of cash forecasts with cash budgets

The cash budget reflects the impact on cash resources of budgeted sales, costs and changes in asset structure, and is also confirmation that plans are financially viable.

It is important to distinguish between a budget and a forecast.

- A **cash forecast** is an estimate of cash receipts and payments for a future period under existing conditions before taking account of possible actions to modify cash flows, raise new capital, or invest surplus funds.

- A **cash budget** is a commitment to a plan for cash receipts and payments for a future period after taking any action necessary to bring the preliminary cash forecast into conformity with the overall plan of the business. Cash forecasts and cash budgets can both be prepared in any of the ways described.

Scope of cash budgets

The period covered by the budget and the frequency with which it is revised will depend on the purpose for which it is made.

A cash budget may be **long-term** or **short-term**, or it may be made in connection with a particular contract or **project**.

- A long-term cash budget will be made in connection with the long-term corporate plan, typically covering a period of three to five years. In some companies, however, the time horizon of budgeting may be less than a year, while in others (particularly those concerned with the exploitation of natural resources) budget periods in excess of five years may be necessary.

- A short-term cash budget relates to current operations. In a business which by choice or necessity gives very detailed attention to cash management, the shortest-term budget may be prepared daily or weekly and may cover perhaps one week or one month or more ahead.

- A project cash budget may be prepared in connection with a project or contract which is part of the business operations, but which needs to be assessed separately from the point of view of the cash resources it requires and its ability to pay for the use of those resources. Particular examples of this requirement are capital expenditure projects, research and development programmes and special marketing campaigns.

Preparation of cash budgets

An example showing the preparation of a cash receipts and payments budget will be fully explained in a later Chapter of this text.

1.2 Short-term cash investments

Short-term investment opportunities present themselves when cash surpluses arise. Companies may hold cash not only for transaction motives, but also for precautionary and speculative motives. **Transactions motive**: the need to hold cash to meet day-to-day operational requirements. **Precautionary motive**: the holding of buffer stocks of cash to cover unexpected business requirements. **Speculative motive**: cash may be held to exploit unanticipated business or investment opportunities. The company's attitude to risk and working capital management will determine the planned cash holdings.

- Firms with an aggressive working capital policy will plan to minimise funds held, and borrow whenever cash is needed.

- Firms with a defensive policy will set aside cash in an investment portfolio, which can be drawn upon when the need arises.

This section deals with the practical aspects of the management of a portfolio of short-term investments.

KEY POINT

Surplus cash comprises liquid balances held by a business which are neither needed to finance current business operations nor held permanently for short-term investment.

The availability of surplus cash is temporary, awaiting employment either in existing operations or in new investment opportunities (whether already identified or not).

The 'temporary' period can be of any duration from one day to the indefinite future date at which the new investment opportunity may be identified and seized.

The significance of this concept of balances held temporarily for conversion to other, more important, business uses is the absolute priority which must be given to the avoidance of risk over maximising returns. The usual principle of finding the optimal mix between risk and return does not apply here because the investment is secondary and incidental to the ultimate business use of the asset, not an end in itself.

Objectives in the investment of surplus cash

The objectives can be categorised as follows:

KEY POINT

When investing surplus cash the objectives of **liquidity** and **safety** take precedence over that of **profitability**.

- **Liquidity**: the cash must be available for use when needed.
- **Safety**: no risk of loss must be taken.
- **Profitability**: subject to the above, the aim is to earn the highest possible after tax returns.

Each of these objectives raises problems which will be explored now.

The liquidity problem

This problem is at first sight simple enough. If a company knows that it will need the funds in three days (or weeks or months), it simply invests them for just that period at the best rate available with safety. The solution is to match the maturity of the investment with the period for which the funds are surplus.

- The exact duration of the surplus period is not always known. It will be known if the cash is needed to meet a loan instalment, a large tax payment or a dividend. But it will not be known if the need is unidentified, or depends on the build-up of stock, the progress of construction work, or the hammering out of an acquisition deal.

- Expected future trends in interest rates (see below) affect the maturity of investments.

- Bridging finance may be available to bridge the gap between the time when the cash is needed and the subsequent date on which the investment matures.

- An investment may not need to be held to maturity if either an earlier withdrawal is permitted by the terms of the instrument without excessive penalty, or there is a secondary market and its disposal in that market causes no excessive loss. A good example of such an investment is a certificate of deposit (CD), where the investor 'lends' the bank a stated amount for a stated period, usually between one and six months. As evidence of the debt and its promise to pay interest the bank gives the investor a CD. There is an active market for CDs issued by the commercial banks and turning a CD into cash is easy and cheap.

The safety problem

Safety means there is no risk of loss. Superficially this again looks simple. The concept certainly includes the absence of credit risk. For example, the firm should not deposit with a bank which might conceivably fail within the maturity period and thus fail to repay the amount deposited.

However, safety is not necessarily to be defined as certainty of getting the original investment repaid at 100% of its original *sterling* money value. If the purpose for which the surplus cash is held is not itself fixed in sterling, then other criteria of safety may apply.

Examples

If the cash is being held to meet a future commitment, the ultimate amount of the commitment may be subject to inflationary rises (e.g. payment to building contractors for a new factory). In this case a safer investment instrument may be an index-linked gilt-edged bond with a maturity date about the expected date of the payment.

If the cash is being held to meet a future payment in a foreign currency, the only riskless investment would be one denominated in that currency.

The safety objective looks deceptively simple at first: go for the highest rate of return subject to the overriding criteria of safety and liquidity. However, here there are even more complications.

Factor being considered	Rule of thumb course of action
Fixed or variable rates	**Invest long** (fixed interest investments with late maturity dates – subject to the liquidity rule) if there are good reasons to expect interest rates to fall.
Term to maturity	**Invest short** (fixed interest investments with early maturity dates) or at variable rates if there are good grounds for expecting rates to go up.
Tax effects	Aim to optimise net cash flows *after tax*. Tax payments are a cash outflow. There are many tax-efficient investments for surplus cash, e.g. use of tax havens, or government securities which may be exempt from capital gains tax.
Use other currencies	Investing in currencies other than the company's operating currency in which it has the bulk of its assets and in which it reports to its owners, is clearly incompatible with the overriding requirement of safety, except in two possible sets of circumstances: • The investment is earmarked for a payment due in another currency (as seen earlier); or • Both principal and interest are sold forward or otherwise hedged against the operating currency (hedging is covered in greater detail later).
Difficulty in forecasting available funds	Segregate receipts and payments into the following categories: • The steadier and more forecastable flows, like cash takings in retail trades. There may be predictable peaks, say at the end of the week and in the pre-Christmas period. • The less predictable but not individually large items. • Controllable items like payments to normal suppliers. • Items like collections from major customers which are individually so large that it pays to spend some management time on them. • This segregation can even be taken to the point where separate bank accounts are used for the different categories.

Difficulty in finding the most favourable rates

Know the available instruments and their current relative benefits.

Shop around for the 'best buy' among investees who offer the most appropriate instrument.

1.3   Borrowing from the bank

Interest rates on bank loans and overdrafts are normally variable i.e. they alter in line with base rates. Fixed rate loans are available, but are less popular with firms (and providers of finance).

Bank overdrafts

A common source of short-term financing for many businesses is a bank overdraft. These are mainly provided by the clearing banks and represent permission by the bank to write cheques even though the firm has insufficient funds deposited in the account to meet the cheques.

An overdraft limit will be placed on this facility, but provided the limit is not exceeded, the firm is free to make as much or as little use of the overdraft as it desires.

The bank charges interest on amounts outstanding at any one time, and the bank may also require repayment of an overdraft at any time.

The **advantages of overdrafts** are the following:

• Flexibility – they can be used as required.

• Cheapness – interest is usually 2-5% above base rate (and all loan interest is a tax deductible expense).

The **disadvantages of overdrafts** are as follows:

• Overdrafts are legally repayable on demand. Normally, however, the bank will give customers assurances that they can rely on the facility for a certain time period, say six months.

• Security is usually required by way of fixed or floating charges on assets or sometimes, in private companies and partnerships, by personal guarantees from owners.

• Interest costs vary with bank base rates.

Overall, bank overdrafts are one of the most important sources of short-term finance for industry.

Bank loans

A bank loan represents a formal agreement between the bank and the borrower, that the bank will lend a specific sum for a specific period (one to seven years being the most common). Interest must be paid on the whole of this sum for the duration of the loan.

The source is, therefore, liable to be more expensive than the overdraft and is less flexible but, on the other hand, there is no danger that the source will be withdrawn before the expiry of the loan period. Interest rates and requirements for security will be similar to overdraft lending.

Comparison of bank loans and overdrafts

The difference can be shown as follows:

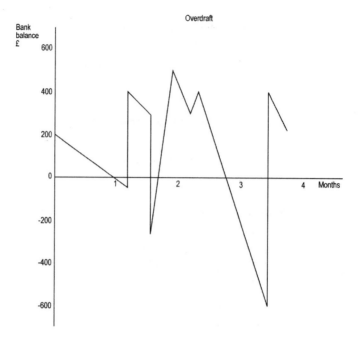

Bank loan

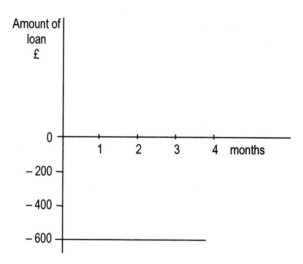

The company requires a maximum of £600 over the next four months. However, it is only halfway through month four that it actually requires the full amount. For the remainder of the period it will pay interest on an overdraft of substantially less than that, or it will pay no interest at all as it has a positive bank balance. If it borrows £600 by way of a bank loan at the beginning of the four months, it must pay interest for four months on the amount borrowed despite the fact that it rarely requires the full sum.

1.4 Cash management models

A number of different models have been developed for managing cash balances, in particular those developed by Baumol and by Miller-Orr.

All models assume that a business will have a certain amount of ready cash available, in a bank current account, for day to day transactions. In addition, an amount of buffer funds will be invested in deposit accounts, marketable securities etc that can be used to top up the current account, or absorb short-term surpluses from it, as appropriate.

The points addressed by the models are as follows:

- At what point should cash move between the current account and the buffer funds?

- How much cash should be moved?

- There are conflicting costs.

- Each time cash is moved in or out of the buffer funds, transaction costs will be incurred, which are often fixed.

- Any cash held within the current account has an opportunity cost associated with it, represented by the difference between the interest earned in the current account (if any) and that earned in the buffer funds.

Cash management models attempt to **minimise the total costs** associated with cash movements between a current account and short-term investments – the "opportunity" cost of lost interest plus transaction costs – by determining when, and how much, cash should be transferred each time.

Example

If the balances held in the current account are kept as low as possible, by frequent movements of cash in and out, in order to minimise the holding costs, this may lead to excessive transaction costs.

The models attempt to find an optimum cash management strategy that will minimise the total of these costs.

Baumol cash management model

The mechanics of this model are very similar to those of the EOQ model, which is covered in the stock control section of chapter 5.

If a company's cash resources are steadily used up by a constant daily demand for cash, Baumol suggested that the EOQ stock model could be applied to the situation so that the optimum regular cash injection, x, into the current account can be calculated.

$$x = \sqrt{\frac{2 \times \text{annual cash disbursements} \times \text{cost per sale of securities}}{\text{interest rate}}}$$

Where x = the optimum regular cash injection into the current account.

Example

A company faces a constant demand for cash totalling £200,000 pa. It replenishes its current account (which pays no interest) by selling constant amounts of gilts which are held as an investment earning 6% pa. The cost per sale of gilts is a fixed £15 per sale.

The optimum amount of gilts sold, x, for each cash injection into the current account will be:

$$x = \sqrt{\frac{2 \times 200,000 \times 15}{0.06}}$$

$$= \pounds10,000$$

Baumol's model suggests that when interest rates are high, the cash balance held without earning interest should be low, which seems sensible.

The problem with the model of course is its unrealistic assumption that firms face a constant demand for cash. In practice cash will be a net receipt one week and a net payment another week.

The Miller-Orr cash management model

A calculation question on this model is unlikely but a knowledge of its workings could be required.

The model takes into account uncertainty in both receipts and payments of cash. It is best explained with reference to the following diagram.

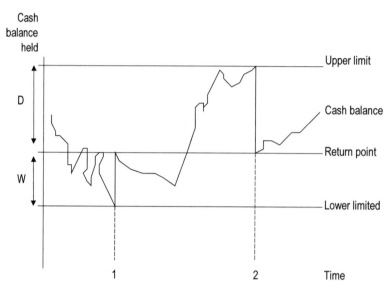

All cash receipts and payments are met from the cash balance and, as can be seen from the diagram, the cash balance of the firm is allowed to vary freely between two limits.

The **lower limit** has to be specified by the firm and the **upper limit** is calculated by the model. If the cash balance on any day goes outside these limits action must be taken.

1. **At point 1** the cash balance reaches the lower limit and must be replenished in some way, e.g. by the sale of marketable securities or withdrawal from a deposit account. The size of this withdrawal is indicated on the diagram (W), and it is the distance between the return point (usually set in Miller-Orr as the lower limit plus one third of the distance up to the upper limit) and the lower limit.

2. **At point 2** the cash balance reaches the upper limit and an amount (D) must be invested in marketable securities or placed in a deposit account. Again, this is calculated by the model as the distance between the upper limit and the return point.

The minimum cost upper limit is calculated by reference to **brokerage costs, holding costs** and the **variance of cash flows.** The model has some fairly restrictive assumptions, e.g. normally distributed cash flows but, in tests, Miller and Orr found it to be fairly robust and claim significant potential cost savings for companies.

Example

The usual Miller-Orr model sets the spread between the upper and lower cash balance limits as given left.

$$3 \left(\frac{\frac{3}{4} \times \text{transaction cost} \times \text{variance of cash flows}}{\text{interest rate}} \right)^{\frac{1}{3}}$$

So if a company sets its minimum cash balance at £5,000 and estimates the following:

- transaction cost = £15 per sale or purchase of gilts
- standard deviation of cash flows = £1,200 per day (so variance = £1.44m per day)
- interest rate = 7.3% pa = 0.02% per day.

Then the spread is calculated as: $3 \left(\dfrac{\frac{3}{4} \times 15 \times 1.44\,\mathrm{m}}{0.0002} \right)^{\frac{1}{3}}$

$= 3 \times £4,327$

$= £12,981$

Therefore:

lower limit (set by the company) = £5,000

upper limit = 5,000 + 12,981 = £17,981

return point = 5,000 + ($\frac{1}{3} \times$ 12,981) = £9,327

2   Treasury management

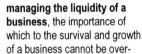
The term 'treasurer', and therefore 'treasury department', is an old one that has been resurrected in a modern context. It essentially covers the following activities:

- banking and exchange
- cash and currency management
- investment in short-term assets
- risk and insurance
- raising finance.

All these activities are concerned with **managing the liquidity of a business**, the importance of which to the survival and growth of a business cannot be over-emphasised.

2.1   Why have a treasury department?

The functions carried out by the treasurer have always existed, but have been absorbed historically within other finance functions. A number of reasons may be identified for the modern development of **separate treasury departments**:

- **size and internationalisation of companies**. These factors add to both the scale and the complexity of the treasury functions.
- **size and internationalisation of currency, debt and security markets**. These make the operations of raising finance, handling transactions in multiple currencies and investing much more complex. They also present opportunities for greater gains.
- **sophistication of business practice**. This process has been aided by modern communications, and as a result the treasurer is expected to take advantage of opportunities for making profits or minimising costs which did not exist a few years ago.

For these reasons, most large international corporations have moved towards setting up a separate treasury department.

KEY POINT

Treasury departments tend to rely heavily on **new technology** for information.

2.2   Treasury responsibilities

- The treasurer will generally report to the finance director (financial manager), with a specific emphasis on **borrowing** and **cash** and **currency management.**

- The treasurer will have a direct input into the finance director's management of debt capacity, debt and equity structure, resource allocation, equity strategy and currency strategy.

- The treasurer will be involved in investment appraisal, and the finance director will often consult the treasurer in matters relating to the review of **acquisitions and divestments, dividend policy and defence from takeover.**

Treasury departments are not large, since they are not involved in the detailed recording of transactions.

2.3   Centralisation of treasury activities

Should treasury activities in a large international group be centralised or decentralised?

- If they are **centralised**, each operating company holds only the minimum cash balance required for day to day operations, remitting the surplus to the centre for overall management.

- If they are **decentralised**, each operating company must appoint an officer responsible for that company's own treasury operations.

- Advantages of centralisation are as follows:

- **No need for treasury skills to be duplicated throughout the organisation.** One highly trained central department can assemble a highly skilled team, offering skills that could not be available if every company had their own treasury.

- **Necessary borrowings can be arranged in bulk,** at keener interest rates than for smaller amounts. Similarly bulk deposits of surplus funds will attract higher rates of interest than smaller amounts.

- The group's **foreign currency risk can be managed much more effectively** from a centralised treasury since only the treasury department can appreciate the total exposure situation. A total hedging policy is more efficiently carried out by head office rather than each company doing its own hedging.

- **Bank charges should be lower** since the carrying of both balances and overdrafts in the same currency should be eliminated.

KEY POINT

Centralised treasury management often results in a highly skilled team, cheaper borrowing, lower bank charges and more effective hedging of currency risk, but some motivational and local knowledge benefits may be lost.

Advantages of decentralisation are as follows:

- Greater autonomy leads to greater motivation. Individual companies will manage their cash balances more attentively if they are responsible for them rather than simply remitting them up to head office.

- Local operating units should have a better feel for local conditions than head office and can respond more quickly to local developments.

Centralised treasury management often results in a highly skilled team, cheaper borrowing, lower bank charges and more effective hedging of currency risk, but some motivational and local knowledge benefits may be lost.

Conclusion

This chapter has discussed the importance of cash management, discussing issues such as the investment of short-term cash surpluses, use of overdrafts, cash budgeting, cash management models and the importance of the treasury department.

Management of cash

1   Give at least two objectives of a cash budget. (1.1)

2   What are the three motives for holding cash? (1.2)

3   What are the objectives in the investment of surplus cash and how should they be prioritised? (1.2)

4   What are the costs that are taken into account in the Baumol and Miller-Orr models? (1.4)

Treasury management

5   Give three advantages of centralisation of treasury activities. (2.3)

Cash management

(a) 'Cash is no different from any other asset – if it is not being utilised properly it is going to result in lower profits.'

Discuss this statement, in particular referring to the motives for holding cash.
(8 marks)

(b) The AB Credit Collection Company Ltd employs agents who collect hire purchase instalments and other outstanding accounts on a door to door basis from Monday to Friday. The agents bank the cash collected to be remitted to head office once per week at the end of the week. The budget for next year shows that the total collections will be £5,200,000 and that the estimated bank overdraft rate is 9%. The collection manager has suggested that a daily remitting system should be introduced for collectors.

Comment on the significance of this system, stating clearly any assumptions you are required to make.
(12 marks)

(Total: 20 marks)

For the answer to this question, see the 'Answers' section at the end of the book.

Chapter 8
SOURCES OF FINANCE: EQUITY

In Chapter 3 we identified that one of the key areas of the financial manager's role is to raise appropriate finance to meet the organisation's funding requirements. Factors such as cost, availability, term of finance etc will need to be taken into account.

In this chapter we concentrate on the various methods of raising equity finance; the next chapter considers debt sources. In addition, the balance of long-term finance between equity and debt (the gearing level) is a very important consideration, and this will be examined in Chapter 10.

Objectives

By the time you have finished this chapter you should be able to do the following:

- explain financing in terms of the risk/return trade-off

- describe the financing problems of SMEs

- describe ways in which a company may obtain a stock market listing

- describe how stock markets operate

- explain the requirements of stock market investors in terms of returns on investment

- calculate, analyse and evaluate appropriate investment ratios

- outline and apply the dividend valuation model, including the growth adjustment

- describe the advantages and disadvantages of rights issues

- calculate the price of rights

- explain the purpose and impact of a bonus issue, scrip dividends and stock splits

- explain the features of different types of preference shares and the reasons for their issue.

1   Sources of finance

1.1   The need for finance for business

Companies need funds to bridge the gap between paying for production of finished goods and receiving money from their customers (**working capital**). They also need them for buying the fixed assets with which they operate such as machinery, land and buildings (**fixed capital**).

The major source of finance for companies is **retained earnings**, which can be used both for working capital and fixed assets, as they are funds which permanently belong to the business. However, these are insufficient for financing a business, particularly a new one, which has not yet had the opportunity to build up reserves of retained profits.

Short or medium-term finance is obtained from the money markets as explained below. The way in which a company can obtain long-term finance is by using the capital markets and issuing shares or debentures.

1.2 Criteria for choosing between sources of finance

A vast range of funding alternatives is open to companies and new developments occur every day. Before examining the various sources of finance available it is useful to consider some of the criteria which may be used to choose between them.

Cost

The higher the cost of funding, the lower the firm's profit. Debt finance tends to be **cheaper** than equity. This is because providers of debt take **less risks** than providers of equity and therefore earn less return. Interest on debt finance is also normally **corporation tax deductible**, while returns on equity are not.

Duration

Finance can be arranged for various time periods. Normally, but not invariably, long-term finance is **more expensive** than short-term finance. This is because lenders normally perceive the risks as being higher on long-term advances. Long-term finance does, however, carry the advantage of **security**, whereas sources of short-term finance can often be withdrawn at short notice. You should remember the 'rule of thumb' that says:

'Long-term assets should be financed by long-term funds and short-term assets (to some extent) by short-term funds.'

We would generally expect to see working capital financed partly by short-term facilities such as overdraft whilst fixed assets should be funded by long-term funds. This rule is commonly broken to gain access to cheap short-term funds but the risks involved should be appreciated.

Term structure of interest rates

The term **structure of interest rates** describes the relationship between interest rates charged for loans of differing maturities.

While short-term funds are usually cheaper than long-term funds, this situation is sometimes reversed and interest rates should be carefully checked.

Imagine the situation where the money markets expected interest rates to fall in the long term but remain high in the short term. In this situation borrowing short-term could prove quite expensive.

Gearing

Gearing is the ratio of debt to equity finance. Gearing will be investigated in depth later, but for now we should appreciate that although high gearing involves the use of cheap debt finance it does bring with it the risk of having to meet regular repayments of interest and principal on the loans. If these are not met the company could end up in liquidation.

On the other hand too little debt could result in earnings dilution. For example the issue of a large amount of equity to fund a new project could result in a decrease in earnings per share, despite an increase in total earnings.

Accessibility

Not all companies have access to all sources of finance. Small companies traditionally have problems in raising equity and long-term debt finance. These problems are investigated later but remember that many firms do not have an unlimited choice of funding arrangements.

A quoted company is one whose shares are dealt in on a recognised stock market, so shares in such a company represent a highly liquid asset. This, in turn, makes it much easier to attract new investors to buy new shares issued by the company because these investors know that they can always sell their shares if they wish to realise their investment.

Investment in shares of unquoted companies represents the acquisition of a highly illiquid investment. For this reason it is much more difficult for such a company to raise finance by new share issues.

The sections which follow relate to both quoted and unquoted companies. However, their different positions always need to be borne in mind.

2   Types of share capital

The term **equity** relates to **ordinary shares** only. There are other types of share capital relating to various types of **preference share**. These are not considered part of equity, as their characteristics bear more resemblance to debt finance. The main types of share capital are summarised below:

Type of share capital	Security or voting rights	Income	Amount of capital
Ordinary shares	Have voting rights in general meetings of the company. Rank after all creditors and preference shares in rights to assets on liquidation.	Dividends payable at the discretion of the directors (subject to sanction by shareholders) out of undistributed profits remaining after senior claims have been met. Amounts available for dividends but not paid out are retained in the company on behalf of the ordinary shareholders.	The right to all surplus funds after prior claims have been met.
Cumulative preference shares	Right to vote at a general meeting only when dividend is in arrears or when it is proposed to change the legal rights of the shares. Rank after all creditors but usually before ordinary shareholders in liquidation.	A fixed amount per year at the discretion of the directors, subject to sanction by shareholders and in accordance with rules regarding dividend payments. Arrears accumulate and must be paid before a dividend on ordinary shares may be paid. Note that unlike other forms of debt, the dividend paid on preference shares is not corporation tax deductible.	A fixed amount per share.
Non-cumulative preference shares	Likely to have some voting rights at all times rather than in specified circumstances as in the case of cumulative. Rank as cumulative in liquidation.	A fixed amount per year, as above. Arrears do not accumulate.	A fixed amount per share.

3   Raising equity finance

There are three main sources of equity finance:

- internally generated funds – retained earnings
- new external share issues – placings, offers for sale etc
- rights issues.

ACTIVITY 1

What would be the difference in terms of impact on shareholder base between raising equity finance through retained earnings and rights issues and raising equity finance via a new issue?

Feedback to this activity is at the end of the chapter.

3.1   Internally generated funds

DEFINITION

Internally generated funds comprise retained earnings (i.e. undistributed profits attributable to ordinary shareholders) plus non-cash charges against profits (e.g. depreciation).

KEY POINT

Internally generated funds are a cheap and immediate source of finance. However, the company's dividend policy must be taken into account when determining the level of usage

---

Internally generated funds comprise retained earnings (i.e. undistributed profits attributable to ordinary shareholders) plus non-cash charges against profits (e.g. depreciation). For an established company, internally generated funds can represent the single most important source of finance, for both short and long-term purposes.

Such finance is **cheap** and **quick** to raise, requiring no transaction costs, professional assistance or time delay. However, it is essential that the company's **dividend policy** is taken into account when determining how much of each year's earnings to retain.

Retained earnings are also a **continual source** of new funds, provided that the company is profitable and profits are not all paid out as dividends.

We shall explore this topic in more detail later. In general, however, shareholders of listed companies tend to prefer a stable growth dividend policy. Any unexpected cut in dividend, however potentially profitable, may lead to an adverse reaction in terms of a fall in share price.

Of course, for major investment projects, a greater amount of equity finance may be required than that available from internal sources. In this case some form of share issue will have to be made.

Internally generated funds are a cheap and immediate source of finance. However, the company's dividend policy must be taken into account when determining the level of usage.

3.2   New external share issues

KEY POINT

New shares can be issued by private negotiation, placing, or offer for sale, or by a rights issue.

There are several methods of issuing new shares according to the circumstances of the company.

New shares can be issued by **private negotiation**, **placing**, or **offer for sale**, or by a **rights issue.**

Type of Company	Company requirement	Method of issue	Type of investor
Unquoted	Finance without an immediate stock market quotation.	Private negotiation or placing. Enterprise Investment Scheme (EIS).	Individuals, merchant banks, finance corporations.
Unquoted or quoted	Finance with an immediate quotation. Finance with a new issue.	Stock Exchange or small firm market placing. Offer for sale. Offer for sale by tender. Intermediaries offer.	The investing public, pension funds, insurance companies and other institutions.
Quoted or unquoted	Limited finance without offering shares to non-shareholders.	Rights issue.	Holders of existing shares.

New issues for unquoted companies

Traditionally, unquoted companies obtained their funds from owner proprietors or rich patrons who were prepared to take a risk in order to show an above average return.

However, in the modern business environment, it can be difficult for small unquoted companies to raise equity finance from outside shareholders. A country's tax system may channel individual investors' money into institutions, and institutions are generally unenthusiastic about investing in unquoted companies for a number of reasons.

- The shares are not easily realisable.

- Costs can be kept down by investing in large parcels of shares rather than spreading investment over many small companies.

- Small firms are regarded as more risky (for example, they may lack proper financial control systems).

However, it is possible to arrange a **placing** of shares with an institution. Generally this is when there is at least a prospect of eventually obtaining a quotation on the Stock Exchange.

The small firm equity finance problem is dealt with in detail later in this chapter.

Becoming quoted (listed)

A company will wish to become listed on the stock exchange to increase its pool of potential investors. Only by being listed can a company offer its shares to the public.

The natural progression in recent years has been to seek a quotation on a small firm stock market, such as the UK's Alternative Investment Market (AIM), followed by a full listing on the major stock exchange.

The possible methods of obtaining a stock exchange listing in the UK are an offer for sale by prospectus, an offer for sale by tender, a placing or an introduction.

Offer for sale

Shares are offered at a fixed price to the general public (including institutions). Details of the offer document are published in a prospectus for the issue. The prospectus contains information about the company's past performance and future prospects, as specified by the rules for stock exchange companies. The rule book for UK companies

---

KEY POINT

A stock exchange listing in the UK can be obtained by: an offer for sale by prospectus; an offer for sale by tender; a placing; an intermediaries offer or an introduction.

DEFINITION

An **offer for sale** is an invitation to apply for shares in a company based upon information contained in a prospectus, either at a fixed price or by tender.

KEY POINT

The 'striking price' at which the shares are sold is determined by the demand for shares.

whose shares are listed on the main London Stock Exchange are the UK Listing Rules. These are issued by the UK Listing Authority, a department of the Financial Services Authority (FSA).

Offer for sale by tender

Shares are offered to the general public (including institutions) but no fixed price is specified. Potential investors bid for shares at a price of their choosing. The 'striking price' at which the shares are sold is determined by the demand for shares.

Placing

A placing may be used for smaller issues of shares (up to £15m in value). The bank advising the company selects institutional investors to whom the shares are 'placed' or sold. If the general public wish to acquire shares, they must buy them from the institutions.

Intermediaries offer

This is similar to a placing. An intermediaries offer is an offer of shares to intermediaries (e.g. brokers) for them to allocate to their own clients. The intermediaries will re-sell the shares to clients and will not retain any themselves. In contrast, with a placing, financial institutions buying the shares (e.g. pension funds) sill often buy them as investments.

Introduction

An introduction is used where there is no new issue of shares and the public already holds at least 25% of the shares in the company (the minimum requirement for a stock exchange listing). The shares become listed and members of the public can buy shares from the existing shareholders.

Institutional advisers on new share issues

As well as requiring the assistance of accountants in preparing the prospectus, new share issues may require the services of an **issuing house.** An issuing house is an investment bank specialising in new issue of shares.

(a)   **Issuing houses.** A company wishing to raise capital by offer for sale would first get in touch with one of the issuing houses which specialise in this kind of business.

In some cases, the issuing house earns a fee by organising public issues. In others, it purchases outright a block of shares from a company and then makes them an 'offer for sale' to the public on terms designed to bring in a profit to the issuing house.

There are between 50 and 60 members of the Issuing House Association, including all the important merchant banks. The fact that an issue is launched by one of these banks or other houses of high reputation is, in itself, a factor contributing to the chance of success of such a venture.

(b)   **Investment banks.** Investment banks also perform the functions of underwriting, marketing and pricing new issues.

- **Underwriting** – Large share issues are usually underwritten. An underwriter is someone (usually an investment institution) who is prepared to purchase shares in a share issue that other investors do not buy. For example, suppose that XYZ plc is issuing 50 million new shares at £2.50 each. If the issue is underwritten, the investment bank assisting the company with the issue will find one or more institutions who are prepared to buy up to a given quantity of the shares, if no one else wants them. In return for underwriting a portion of the new issue, an underwriter is paid a commission. If there are just one or two underwriters for an issue, the underwriters might off-load some of their risk by getting other institutions to *sub-underwrite* the issue. Sub-underwriters are also paid a commission.

DEFINITION

An **issuing house** is a commercial concern specialising in the issue in the capital market of shares of companies.

The effect of underwriting is to ensure that all the shares in a new issue will find a buyer. However, if a large quantity of the shares are left in the hands of the underwriters after the issue, the share price is likely to remain depressed until the underwriters have been able to sell off the shares they do not want in the secondary market.

- **Marketing** – the marketing and selling of a new issue is a business activity in its own right. The investment bank provides the expertise.

- **Pricing** – one of the most difficult decisions in making a new issue is that it should be priced correctly. If the price is too low, the issue will be over-subscribed, and existing shareholders will have had their holdings diluted more than is necessary. If the price is too high and the issue fails, the underwriters are left to subscribe to the shares. This will adversely affect the reputation of the issuing house and the company. Correct pricing is important, and the investment bank will be able to offer advice based on experience and expertise. One way round the issue price problem is an issue by tender.

3.3   Rights issues

A **rights issue** is an offer to the existing shareholders to subscribe for more shares, in proportion to their existing holding, usually at a relatively cheap price.

A rights issue can be made by a quoted or an unquoted company seeking limited finance without offering shares to non-shareholders.

In the UK company legislation requires an offer to be made to existing shareholders before it can be made to the public.

Any new shares issued by a UK public company to raise cash must therefore be offered to the existing shareholders in a rights issue, unless the existing shareholders have given their consent to new shares being issued by any method other than a rights issue.

In general, shareholders are usually prepared to allow their company to issue some new shares for cash without a rights issue, although shareholder consent is usually renewed each year at the annual general meeting.

Theoretical ex-rights price and the value of rights

When a rights issue is announced, the existing shareholders are given rights. A right is the right to buy a given number of new shares in the issue, at the issue price. For example, if a company announces a 1 for 4 rights issue at £3.25 per share, an ordinary shareholder with 50,000 shares will receive the right to buy 12,500 new shares at £3.25.

The price of the new shares should be below the current market price. For example, if a company announces a 1 for 4 rights issue at £3.25, the current share price will be higher than £3.25. Since the price of the new shares is lower than the current market price, it follows that the rights should have some value.

Example

ABC plc announces a 2 for 5 rights issue at £2 per share. There are currently 10 million shares in issue, and the current market price of the shares is £2.70.

ABC plc has a current market capitalisation of £27 million (10 million shares x £2.70). It plans to issue 4 million new shares at £2 each to raise £8 million. It therefore follows that in theory, after the rights issue, there will be 14 million shares in issue worth a total of £35 million (£27 million + £8 million). Since every share has the same market value, the theoretical market price per share after the issue will be £2.50 (£35 million/14 million shares). This is called the **theoretical ex-rights price** of the shares.

A method of calculating the theoretical ex-right price is as follows, using the figures in the example:

The rights issue is a 2 for 5 issue.

	£
5 existing shares have a current value of (5 × £2.70)	13.50
2 new shares will be issued for (× £2)	4.00
7 shares in total have a theoretical value of	17.50
Theoretical ex-rights price (£17.50/7)	£2.50

A formula for calculating the theoretical ex-rights price is:

$$\frac{\text{(Market value of shares already in issue)} + \text{(Proceeds from new share issue)}}{\text{Number of shares in issue after the rights issue ('ex rights')}}$$

The theoretical **value of rights** is the difference between the theoretical ex-rights price and the offer price of the new shares in the rights issue. In the example above, shareholders are being offered new shares for £2 when their theoretical value is £2.50, so in theory the value of the rights is £0.50 for each right to a new share.

Since rights have a value, they can be sold in the period between:

- the rights issue being announced and the rights to existing shareholders are issued, and

- the new issue actually taking place.

During this time, shareholders can sell their rights on the stock market, should they wish to do so.

The shareholders' options

The shareholders' options with a rights issue are to do one of the following.

1. **Take up their rights** by buying the specified proportion at the price offered. Purchasing further shares at a reduced price compensates shareholders for the drop in the ex-rights price of their existing shares.

2. **Renounce their rights and sell them in the market**. The sale of the shareholders' rights compensates them for the drop in the ex-rights price of their existing shares, e.g. the right to participate in Alpha's rights issue is worth (80p – 40p) = 40p, i.e. the difference between the rights price and the market value ex-rights.

3. **Renounce part of their rights and take up the remainder**. This results in a combination of (1) and (2) above.

4. **Do nothing**. They will be left with their original holding, which now has a reduced market value.

5. Shareholders **must take some action** on a rights issue if they are not to lose out as a result.

Example

Alpha plc has issued share capital of 100,000,000 shares with a current market value of £1 each. It announces a 1 for 2 rights issue at a price of 40p per share. It therefore plans to raise £20 million in new funds by issuing 50,000,000 new shares.

The theoretical ex-rights price is £0.80, calculated as follows.

	£
2 existing shares have a current value of (2 × £1)	2.00
1 new share will be issued for (× £0.40)	0.40

3 shares in total have a theoretical value of	2.40
	———
Theoretical ex-rights price (£2.40/3)	£0.80

The value of each right is £0.40, because new shares are being issued at £0.40 each when their theoretical market value is £0.80.

Let's assume that the rights can be sold in the stock market for £0.40 each. Suppose that investor B holds 1,000 shares in Alpha plc. His choices are as follows.

1 Take up his rights

Buy the new shares to which he is entitled. He can buy 500 new shares at £0.40, which will mean investing an additional £200 in the company.

	£
Current value of his 1,000 shares	1,000
Additional investment to buy 500 new shares	200
	———
Total theoretical value of investment	1,200
	———

Investor B will now have an investment of 1,500 shares that in theory will be worth £1,200 (£0.80 per share). The value of the total investment has gone up by £200, but this is the amount of the additional investment he has made to acquire the new shares.

2 Sell his rights

	£
Current value of his 1,000 shares	1,000
Theoretical value of his shares after the rights issue (× £0.80)	800
	———
Theoretical loss in investment value	200
Sale value of rights (500 rights × £0.40)	200
	———
Net gain/loss	0
	———

By selling his rights, investor B receives £200, but the value of his investment is likely to fall by £200, leaving him no better and no worse off overall.

3 Take up some rights and sell some rights

For example, suppose that investor B decides to buy 200 new shares in the issue for £80, and sell his rights to 300 shares for £120.

	£
Current value of his 1,000 shares	1,000
Purchase price of 200 new shares (× £0.40)	80
	———
	1,080
Theoretical value of 1,200 shares after the rights issue (× £0.80)	960
Loss in investment value	120
Sale value of rights (300 rights × £0.40)	120
	———
Net gain/loss	0
	———

The total value of his investment in theory will go up by £80, from £1,000 to £1,080, which is the amount of the additional investment he makes in new shares.

4 Take no action

If investor B takes no action, the value of his shares is likely to fall from £1,000 before the rights issue to £800 after the rights issue. Taking no action is therefore an

inadvisable option, because it results in a fall in investment value without any offsetting benefit from the sale of rights. However, for those shareholders who do nothing, the company will try to sell the shares to which they are entitled, and if the shares can be sold for more than their rights issue price, the surplus will be paid to the 'do nothing' shareholders.

3.4   Bonus issues, scrip dividends and share splits

Bonus issues

A bonus issue is a method of altering the share capital without raising cash. It is done by changing the company's reserves into share capital.

The rate of a bonus issue is normally expressed in terms of the number of new shares issued for each existing share held, e.g. one for two (one new share for each two shares currently held).

In the USA, capitalisation issues are usually expressed in terms of the number of shares held following the issue compared with the number previously held. Thus, a one for two scrip issue will be termed a **three for two split**. You need to be familiar with both UK and US terminology, as the majority of studies on this subject are to be found in American textbooks.

Example

UK terminology	Before	New	After	US terminology
1 for 2 scrip	2	1	3	3 for 2 split
2 for 5 scrip	5	2	7	7 for 5 split
3 for 10 scrip	10	3	13	13 for 10 split

A capitalisation issue does not change the shareholders' **proportionate** ownership of the company.

ACTIVITY 2

J Bloggs holds 1,000 shares in Deucalion plc which has a total issued capital of 4,000,000 shares. The directors decide to capitalise some of the revenue reserves by making a 1 for 4 scrip issue. Calculate J Bloggs' percentage share in the company before and after the scrip issue.

Feedback to this activity is at the end of the chapter

Scrip dividends

A **scrip dividend** is where a company allows its shareholders to take their dividends in the form of new shares rather than cash.

Do not confuse a scrip issue (which is a bonus issue) with a scrip dividend.

The advantage to the **shareholder** of a scrip dividend is that he can painlessly increase his shareholding in the company without having to pay broker's commissions or stamp duty on a share purchase.

The advantage to the **company** is that it does not have to find the cash to pay a dividend and in certain circumstances it can save tax.

Bonus issues, the balance sheet and investors' returns

The effect of a bonus issue on a company's balance sheet and on investors' returns is shown in the following example.

Example

Pyrrha plc has issued share capital of one million shares of 10p each. It generally pays a total dividend of £12,000. The company decides to issue bonus shares in the ratio of one for every two held. Note that the market value of the company will not change.

	Before bonus issue	*After 1 for 2 bonus issue*
Number of shares	1,000,000	1,500,000
Nominal value	10p	10p
Issued capital	100,000	150,000
Reserves (change into share capital after bonus issue)	100,000	50,000
Net assets	200,000	200,000
Net assets per share	20p	13.3p
Market capitalisation	£150,000	£150,000
Market price (market capitalisation/ number of shares)	15p	10p
Dividend per share	1.2p	0.8p
Dividend yield	8.0%	8.0%

The purposes of bonus issues are as follows:

- To increase marketability of the shares, since it will increase the number of shares in issue and hence reduce the market value of each share (in our example, from 15p to 10p each). This is the most common reason, and is peculiar to the UK. In the USA and Germany, for example, it is not uncommon to have single shares which are quoted at a price of the equivalent of several hundred pounds.

- To increase the amount of permanent capital of the business in line with growth in its assets. There is some merit in this argument, although it could also be argued that most shareholders would never expect the entire figure for 'retained earnings' in a balance sheet to be paid out by way of dividend.

Share splits

DEFINITION

A **share split** involves the division of existing shares into smaller denominations.

Like a bonus issue, a share split (also called a stock split) does not raise extra cash.

It simply makes the share capital more marketable, e.g. a company whose shares have a nominal value of £1 each but a markct value of £10 each may decide to split each £1 share into 10 shares of 10p each. The market value of each share then becomes £1.

The reverse procedure might be appropriate where the market value of a company's share is very low. This procedure is known as a **consolidation** of shares.

4   Choosing between sources of equity finance

Equity finance is not a single source of finance, but a group of alternative ways of raising risk-bearing funds. These may be summarised as follows:

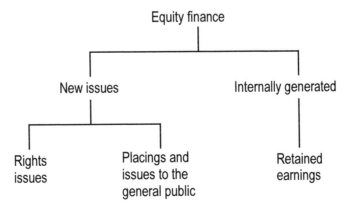

When choosing between sources of equity finance, account must be taken of factors such as the **accessibility** of the finance, the **amount** of finance, **costs** of the issue procedure, **pricing** of the issue, **control**, **taxation** and **dividend policy**.

4.1 Ability of company to raise finance by the means indicated

The ability of a company to raise equity finance is restricted by its access to the general market for funds. Thus, whilst **quoted** companies are able to use any of the sources, an **unquoted** company is restricted to rights issues and private placings. We shall examine the problem of equity finance for smaller companies later in this chapter.

Furthermore, there are statutory restrictions, for example those in the UK imposed by the Companies Act 1985. Only public limited companies may offer shares to the general public.

Obviously, the need to raise finance could be combined with a **flotation** (i.e. a private company going public and having its shares quoted on a recognised stock exchange). However, flotations will incur significant costs.

4.2 Amount of finance required

The amount of finance that can be raised by a **rights issue** from an **unquoted** company is limited by the number and resources of the existing shareholders. It is not possible to provide general estimates of the amounts that may be raised as the circumstances vary. For quoted companies, where rights may be sold, this is less problematic.

Larger sums can be raised by **placings**, but ultimately it is the offer of shares to the general public that opens up the full financial resources of the market.

4.3 Costs and complexity of issue procedures

Use of internally generated funds is easily the cheapest and simplest method. We have seen that, for new issues, placings are the most attractive on cost grounds, followed by rights issues, with public offers being by far the most expensive.

However, the costs go beyond those incorporated in the above computation. All new share issues will take management and administrative time within the company. This will be much greater for an offer for sale than for the other two alternatives.

4.4 Pricing

One of the most difficult problems in making a **new issue to the public** is setting the price correctly. If it is too high, the issue will not be fully taken up and will be left with the underwriters, and if it is underpriced some of the benefits of the project for which the finance is being raised will accrue to the new shareholders and not to the old.

The same pricing problem exists with a **placing** as with a new issue. There will be no danger of under-subscription, of course, because the placing is agreed before the issue is made. However, the price will have been negotiated so as to be attractive to the subscribing institutions. Almost inevitably, it will be below the issue price that it would obtain in the market, because of the attractions of lower issue costs.

A **rights issue**, on the other hand, completely by-passes the price problem. Since the shares are offered to existing shareholders, it does not matter if the price is well below the traded price. Indeed, it would be normal for this to be so. Any gain on the new shares would, by the nature of a rights issue, go to the existing shareholders.

The pricing of new issues is even more complex when the company is **unquoted**. A company coming to the market for the first time would have no existing market price to refer to and would have to value the shares from scratch.

KEY POINT

When choosing between sources of equity finance, account must be taken of factors such as the **accessibility** of the finance, the **amount** of finance, **costs** of the issue procedure, **pricing** of the issue, **control**, **taxation** and **dividend policy**.

4.5   Control of the company

There is no change in the shareholders with internally generated funds and rights issues, insofar as they are taken up by existing shareholders. On the other hand, **placings** and **sales** to the general public introduce new shareholders.

Which is preferable depends on the objectives of the fund-raising exercise. If the desire is to retain control for the existing shareholders, then the rights issue is preferable. If diversification of control is desired, then an issue to the public will be preferred.

4.6   Taxation

In general, there are no tax implications of raising equity finance.

4.7   Dividend policy

The use of internally generated funds may lead to a change in dividend policy which can, in practice, have a detrimental effect on share price. However, there is a theoretical argument that this should not be so. We shall examine this area more fully later in this chapter.

There can be no rigid rules concerning the choice of finance. Use of internally generated funds is the best choice, subject to sufficient availability and dividend policy considerations. Of the new issue options, the order of preference will generally be rights issue, placing and offer for sale to the general public. As funds available are consumed, so the next source is utilised.

5   Share valuations and investor ratios

A share price represents the amount that investors are currently prepared to pay to acquire a share in the company. Investors buy shares to obtain a return on investment. Clearly, there is a direct connection between a share's price and the value that investors put on the returns they expect to receive. We can even state that a share price equals the value of shareholders' expected future returns from the share.

Investor ratios can be used to measure the relationship of returns to share value. These ratios are based on historical returns, rather than expected future returns, but they are useful for monitoring and comparing different the shares of different companies.

The main investment ratios relating to ordinary shares are:

- **Earnings per share (EPS).** This is simply the total annual earnings of the company divided by the number of shares in issue. Although the detailed rules for calculating EPS are fairly complex, it is usually sufficient to assume that EPS is the total annual profit after interest, taxation and preference dividends, divided by the number of ordinary shares currently in issue. EPS is simply a measurement of the profit earned by the company for each share in issue.

- **P/E ratio**. The price/earnings ratio is the ratio of the current share price to annual earnings per share. For example, if the EPS is £0.60 and the share price is £6, the P/E ratio is 10. Share valuations are sometimes expressed in terms of P/E; for example, we might say that a company 's shares are valued on a P/E multiple of 12 when the average for companies in the industry is, say, 14.

- **Dividend yield**. This is the dividend in pence expressed as a proportion of the current share price. For example, if the annual dividend per share is 15p and the share price is £4, the dividend yield is (15/400) x 100% = 3.75%.

$$\text{Dividend yield} \quad = \quad \frac{\text{Annual dividend in pence}}{\text{Share price}} \times 100\%$$

The dividend yield shows the annual cash return on a company's shares for an investor buying the shares at today's price.

6   Dividend valuation model

In deciding whether to use retained profits as a source of new funds, the financial
manager needs to have an understanding of the effect of higher or lower dividends on
the share price. For example, a company might have made earnings of £300,000 in
total or £10 pence per share for its 3 million shares. Its directors could choose to retain
all the earnings as retained profits, and pay no dividend. Alternatively, it could pay a
dividend of 10 pence per share and have no retained earnings. More probably, it will
pay out some earnings as dividends and retain some for re-investment. So how would
any of the different dividend policies affect the share price?

In deciding whether to use retained profits as a source of new funds, the financial
manager needs to have an understanding of the effect of higher or lower dividends on
the share price. For example, a company might have made earnings of £300,000 in
total or £10 pence per share for its 3 million shares. Its directors could choose to retain
all the earnings as retained profits, and pay no dividend. Alternatively, it could pay a
dividend of 10 pence per share and have no retained earnings. More probably, it will
pay out some earnings as dividends and retain some for re-investment. So how would
any of the different dividend policies affect the share price?

To answer this question, we need to look into the dividend model of the valuation of
shares. The dividend model is based on the assumption that the current market value of
a share equals the value placed by investors on future expected cash returns on the
share. In other words, the share price equals the present value of all expected future
dividends.

Present value is calculated by discounting all expected future dividends into the
foreseeable future ('in perpetuity'). Discounting and discounting arithmetic are
explained in a later chapter. For the purpose of learning the dividend valuation model,
you just need to know the formulae.

6.1   The basic dividend valuation model: constant annual dividend

If we can assume that dividends are expected to remain the same every year and are
paid annually, and that the next dividend is payable in one year's time, the current
share price 'ex dividend' is:

$$\text{Share price} \quad = \quad \frac{\text{Annual dividend in pence}}{\text{Cost of equity}}$$

The cost of equity in this case is the dividend yield.

Example

A company is expected to pay an annual dividend of 18 pence per share into the
foreseeable future and the cost of equity is 9%. The next dividend is payable in one
year's time.

The expected share price will be: 18 pence/0.09 = 200 pence.

If the company is expected to pay a constant annual dividend and the next annual
dividend is payable very soon, the expected share price 'cum dividend' is:

$$\text{Share price cum div} \quad = \quad \frac{\text{Annual dividend in pence}}{\text{Cost of equity}} \quad + \quad \text{Current dividend}$$

6.2   The dividend growth model

When a company is expected to increase its annual dividend into the foreseeable future,
the current share price will reflect shareholders' expectations of the future increases in
annual returns. Growth in dividends can be expected when a company reinvests some
of its profits. In other words, dividend growth can come from paying less than 100% of
earnings in dividends. For example, if a company retains 60% of its earnings and pays
just 40% of its annual earnings in dividends, the retained profits are reinvested in the
business. If returns on the reinvested profits are, say, 10%, we can therefore expect
annual dividends to increase by 10% of 60%, or 6%.

The formula for calculating the present value of a company's shares, assuming:

- an annual cash dividend

- the next payment receivable in one year's time

- a constant expected percentage growth in the annual dividend into the foreseeable future

is:

$$P = \frac{d(1+g)}{(r-g)}$$

Where:

P   is the current share price (i.e. the price 'ex div', when there is no dividend currently payable on the share)

d   is the annual dividend that has just been paid

g   is the expected annual growth rate in dividends, expressed as a proportion (e.g. 4% = 0.04, 2.5% = 0.025 and so on)

so d (1 + g)   is next year's expected annual dividend

r   is the anticipated return on investment of the equity shareholders (the 'cost of equity'). This is expressed as a proportion.

This dividend valuation model for shares is sometimes called the Gordon growth model.

Example

A company has just paid an annual dividend of 24 pence. Shareholders expect annual dividends to grow by 1.5% into the foreseeable future. The return required by equity shareholders is 7.5%. What is the expected value of the company's shares?

Solution

$$P = \frac{24(1.015)}{(0.075 - 0.015)}$$

$$= 406 \text{ pence, or } £4.06.$$

6.3   Estimating the future annual growth rate in dividends

If you need to estimate an expected future rate of growth in annual dividends, you can use the formula:

$g = rB$

where g is the future rate of dividend growth

r is the return on new investments and

B is the proportion of earnings kept in the business as retained profits.

For example, if a company retains 45% of its profits and earns a return of 8% on its investments, the expected future annual growth rate in earnings and dividends should be .08 × 0.45 = 0.036 or 3.6%.

7   Dividend policy

Earlier, we recognised the link between the use of internally generated funds and a company's dividend policy. We now examine this link more closely.

If a company chooses to fund a new investment by a cut in dividend rather than by raising new equity finance, how will this affect the wealth of the existing shareholders?

- The **dividend irrelevancy theory** argues that existing shareholders will be **indifferent** between the two finance methods.

- Practical influences, including market imperfections, mean that changes in dividend policy, particularly reductions in dividends paid, **can have an adverse effect** on shareholder wealth.

7.1 Dividend irrelevancy theory

To illustrate the basic point we shall use an example of a company paying constant dividends, and make use of the DVM developed in the previous section.

The premise is this: if both new equity and retained earnings have the same cost then it should be irrelevant, in terms of shareholder wealth, where equity funds come from.

Example

Zeus plc has in issue 5,000,000 shares of £1 nominal value. These are currently quoted at £5 each ex-div. The dividend proposed for the current year is 50p per share. No increase in this dividend is anticipated unless new projects are accepted. There is no long-term debt.

The company can invest cash surpluses at 10% pa at the same level of risk as current operations.

Compute the effect on shareholders' wealth (cash and capital) of the following options being considered by the company:

(a) continuing with the current dividend and investment policy

(b) retaining an extra (i)£1m or (ii) £2.5m, in both cases investing it at 10% and paying out the returns as additional dividends

(c) paying out the normal dividend, and raising an additional £1m for investment at 10% by a rights issue.

Ignore taxation and issue costs.

Solution

Shareholder wealth is measured by cash in hand **plus** capital value. We need to assess the impact of each option on the shareholders' cash position and market value of their shares. The cash position will be affected by the level of current dividends received and cash contributions made. The capital position will be affected by the level of future dividends expected, and their required return.

As any new investment is not expected to change the level of risk, then it should have the same required return as prevails at the moment.

$$r = \frac{D}{P_0} = \frac{£0.50}{£5} = 10\%$$

		Market value £'000	*Cash* £'000	*Total wealth* £'000
(a)	*Continuing current policies*			
	MV = 5m × £5	25,000		
	Dividend = 5m × £0.50		2,500	27,500

(b) (i) *Retaining £1m and investing at 10%*

New future dividend = current dividend + investment returns
= 2,500 + 10% (1,000)
= 2,600 (new D)

FOULKS LYNCH
PUBLICATIONS

$$\text{New market value} \quad = \quad \frac{\text{new D}}{r}$$

$$= \quad \frac{2,600}{0.1} \qquad\qquad 26,000$$

Current dividend = normal dividend – retention   1,500   27,500

(ii) *Retaining £2.5m and investing at 10%*

New future dividend = current dividend + investment returns

$$= \quad 2,500 + 10\% \,(2,500)$$

$$= \quad 2,750 \text{ (new D)}$$

$$\text{New market value} \quad = \quad \frac{\text{new D}}{r}$$

$$= \quad \frac{2,750}{0.1} \qquad\qquad 27,500$$

Current dividend = normal dividend – retention   –   27,500

(c)   New future dividend = as (b) (i)   26,000
       Dividend – as (a)   2,500
       Subscribed for shares   (1,000)   27,500

The shareholders' wealth is the same in each case, illustrating the following two points:

- provided any cash retained is invested at the shareholders' required return, a cut in dividend of any size should not adversely affect the investor – **the cash lost now is exactly compensated by an increase in the value of their shares.** If the funds were actually invested at higher than the expected return for the level of risk, this would in fact increase shareholders' wealth.

- it theoretically makes no difference whether the new investment is funded by retention of dividend or new equity raised.

7.2   Arguments for the relevance of dividend policy

In theory the level of dividend is irrelevant and in a perfect capital market it is difficult to challenge the dividend irrelevancy position. However, once these assumptions are relaxed, certain practical influences emerge and the arguments need further review.

Dividend signalling

In reality, investors do not have perfect information concerning the future prospects of the company. Many authorities claim, therefore, that the pattern of dividend payments is a key consideration on the part of investors when estimating future performance.

For example, an increase in dividends would signal greater confidence in the future by managers and would lead investors to increase their estimate of future earnings and cause a rise in the share price. A sudden dividend cut on the other hand could have a serious impact upon equity value.

This argument implies that dividend policy is relevant. Firms should attempt to adopt a stable (and rising) dividend payout to maintain investors' confidence.

Preference for current income

Many investors require cash dividends to finance current consumption. This does not only apply to individual investors needing cash to live on but also to institutional investors, such as pension funds and insurance companies, who require regular cash inflows to meet day to day outgoings such as pension payments and insurance claims. This implies that many shareholders will prefer companies who pay regular cash dividends and will therefore value the shares of such a company more highly.

The proponents of the dividend irrelevancy argument challenge this argument and claim that investors requiring cash can generate 'home made dividends' by selling

shares. This argument has some attractions but it does ignore transaction costs. The sale of shares involves brokerage costs and can therefore be unattractive to many investors.

Taxation

In many situations income in the form of dividends is taxed in a different way from income in the form of capital gains. This distortion in the personal tax system can have an impact on investors' preferences.

From the corporate point of view this further complicates the dividend decision as different groups of shareholders are likely to prefer different payout patterns.

One suggestion is that companies are likely to attract a clientele of investors who favour their dividend policy (for tax and other reasons). In this case companies should be very cautious in making significant changes to dividend policy as it could upset their investors. Research in the USA tends to confirm this 'clientele effect' with high dividend payout firms attracting low income tax bracket investors and low dividend payout firms attracting high income tax bracket investors.

Conclusions on dividend irrelevancy arguments

Once market imperfections are introduced dividend policy does appear to have an impact upon shareholder wealth. If the clientele theory is taken into account three major points should be noted:

(a) Reductions in dividend can convey 'bad news' to shareholders (dividend signalling). Serious consideration should be given to other forms of finance before cutting dividends.

(b) Changes in dividend policy, particularly reductions, may conflict with investor liquidity requirements.

(c) Changes in dividend policy may upset investor tax planning.

KEY POINT

A change in dividend policy can affect shareholders perceptions and financial positions by:

- dividend signalling
- income preference
- taxation.

ACTIVITY 3

Read the Companies and Markets section of the Financial Times regularly, with particular regard to reported reactions of the markets to dividend announcements. Make a note of evidence of the dividend signalling hypothesis (e.g., when a cut in dividends results in a fall in share price).

There is no feedback to this activity

8   Financing problems of small businesses

8.1   Equity finance

Equity finance provided by wealthy individuals once formed an important source of expansion funds for the small business. More recently, however, small and medium sized enterprises (SMEs) have found themselves cut off from this source of capital for two main reasons:

- the increasing expense and difficulty of obtaining a quotation on a stock market. The attractiveness of a speculative equity investment in a company is much increased if there is a reasonable chance of a quotation, which gives the opportunity of selling the shares.

KEY POINT

SMEs have found it hard to raise equity finance due to **risk**, **marketability** and **tax** issues.

- in the UK the tax system has encouraged individuals to save with large institutions. These institutions prefer to invest in the shares of large companies rather than small ones or in non-corporate entities because of issues with marketability, risk and administrative costs.

Thus, wealthy individuals, who once provided a major source of venture capital (see below) for SMEs, have been persuaded by the tax system to channel their funds indirectly into large companies.

In the UK, the Wilson Committee on the provision of funds to industry and trade summarised the position in 1979, as follows:

'Compared to large firms, small firms are at a considerable disadvantage in financial markets . . . External equity is more difficult to find and may only be available on relatively unfavourable terms. Venture capital is particularly hard to obtain . . . Proprietors of small firms do not always have the same financial expertise as their larger competitors and information and advice about finance may not be easily accessible.'

8.2   Attempted solutions

Governments have tackled the increasing difficulties of financing small businesses by direct attacks on the two main problems as follows:

Making the shares marketable

Investment in small company shares has been encouraged by the development of **small firm markets** and various **tax incentives.**

The most important developments have been the creation of small firm markets, such as the Alternative Investment Market (AIM) in the UK.

In addition, in the UK, the Companies Act 1985 allows companies to purchase their own shares. This makes shares of small private companies more easily realisable and hence more attractive to the small investor. The position where a minority shareholder becomes trapped in such a company can be avoided.

Tax incentives

The Enterprise Investment Scheme (EIS)

The Wilson Committee's recommendations led to the development of the current Enterprise Investment Scheme which offers tax relief on investments in ordinary shares in qualifying unlisted trading companies, including those traded on the AIM. Individuals may invest up to £150,000 each tax year and qualify for 20% tax relief. Any gain on disposing of EIS shares after 5 years is exempt from capital gains tax. Income or capital gains tax relief is available on losses.

The scheme applies to any company trading in the UK and enables companies to raise up to £1m a year. Participating investors can become paid directors of the company and still qualify for the relief.

Venture Capital Trusts (VCTs)

VCTs are quoted companies similar to investment trusts. At least 70% of the underlying investments must be held in a spread of small unquoted trading companies within three years of the date of launch. Income tax relief is available at 20% on new subscriptions by individuals for ordinary shares in VCTs, to a maximum of £100,000 per annum.

Share incentive schemes

In the UK, there are schemes designed to encourage employees to hold shares in companies by which they are employed. All such schemes require Inland Revenue approval.

Other tax incentives for small businesses

These include the following:

- reduced rates of corporation tax for small companies
- increasing the VAT registration threshold.

8.3   Venture capital funds

The combination of increasing the prospective marketability of SME shares and tax relief schemes has led to the proliferation of venture capital funds, which provide equity capital for small and growing businesses.

One of the original, and still one of the best known, venture capital institutions in the UK is that forming part of the 3i Group. It takes a continuing interest in its client enterprises and does not require to withdraw the capital after, say, a five year period.

However, in recent years, most major sources of business finance have in some way become involved in the provision of venture capital, usually by setting up or participating in specialist 'venture capital funds'. The main spur to their growth has come from the incentives described above.

The result is that there is now no real shortage of venture capital for viable projects. The range of possible funds include those run by merchant and other banks, pension funds, individuals and local authorities.

8.4 Evaluation of a new project by a venture capital fund

The information required by a venture capital fund when assessing the viability of a new project can be classified as follows:

(1) **Financial aspects**

- project viability – cash flow/profit projections, NPV calculations
- financing requirements – in total, leaving the fund to decide the best package
- accounting system – to provide regular management accounting information
- availability of other sources of finance, including loans and grants from government bodies
- future policy as regards dividends and retention of profits – with high growth being preferred
- the intention of eventually obtaining a quotation – usually within 7-10 years
- the percentage stake which is offered in the firm – indicating the degree of control and risk.

(2) **Additional information affecting the proposal**

For most venture funds, evaluating financial information comes second to evaluating the **credibility of the firm's management**. A view must be formed as to whether the existing team has sufficient expertise to manage a growing firm, or whether specialist talent needs to be added.

The investor would then wish to see evidence that thorough **studies of the firm's markets** had been made, so that projected sales budgets were realistic. The single most common cause of failure in this sort of situation is over-optimism in sales projections. Relevant information includes market research, orders in hand, letters from potential customers and general projections of the market's prospects.

Information on **technical aspects** of the firm's products would then be useful, especially new designs which have not yet been tested.

The investor would also be interested in knowing **how much influence** it is envisaged it will have on the management decision-making in the firm. Nearly all venture funds will want a seat on the board.

8.5 Business angels

Although venture capital companies are the main providers of equity finance to small businesses, they are highly selective and normally do not invest in amounts under £100,000. An alternative source of smaller amounts of equity capital are private individuals, sometimes known as *business angels,* who normally have a business background.

Business angels are willing to make investments in small businesses in return for an equity stake. They can also offer the businesses the benefits of their own management

expertise. A number of *business angel networks* operate in the UK to match businesses seeking equity finance with potential investors.

8.6 Debt finance for small businesses

Traditionally, small businesses have borrowed by means of loans and overdrafts from clearing banks. The main problems have always been the **security** required by the bank for granting the loan, and the **risk averse attitude of banks** when faced with a decision relating to a new and untested project. In the UK, the requirement for a personal guarantee from the proprietor to cover the loan or overdraft advance has inhibited the expansion of many small businesses and contributed towards the problem of British ideas being developed abroad.

Whilst the UK government has attempted to make debt investment in small businesses more attractive by the introduction of its Loan Guarantee Scheme, this has not proved very successful due to its relatively high interest rate.

We will look further at the types of government financial assistance available to small businesses in the next chapter.

Conclusion

This chapter has started our look at the sources of finance – concentrating on equity finance.

Sources of finance

1 Give four criteria that may be used to choose between the various sources of debt and equity finance. (1.3)

Types of share capital

2 What is a "theoretical ex-rights price"? (3.3)

3 What is meant by the value of rights? (3.3)

4 What is the main purpose of a bonus issue? (3.4)

Raising equity finance

5 Write the formula for the dividend valuation model assuming constant annual dividends. (6.1)

6 Write the formula for the dividend growth model for the valuation of a share. (6.2)

Dividend valuation model

7 What initiatives have been taken to alleviate the problems of small companies seeking finance?(8.2)

G plc

G plc has a paid-up share capital of £1.2 million ordinary shares of £1 each, the current market price being £1.80 per share. It has no loan capital. Maintainable earnings before tax are £240,000. The company's effective tax rate of Corporation Tax is 50%. The company requires to raise a further £768,000 in order to achieve additional earnings of £112,000 per annum and proposes doing this by means of a rights issue. Suggested alternative prices per share for the rights issue are £1.60 and £1.28.

You are required:

(a)   to calculate for each alternative the theoretical market price per share of the enlarged capital after the issue (the 'ex-rights' price) and also the theoretical market value of a right
(9 marks)

(b)   to suggest what issue price is most likely to be adopted   **(5 marks)**

(c)   to state which factors might, in practice, invalidate the calculations you have made.   **(6 marks)**

(Total: 20 marks)

FEEDBACK TO
ACTIVITY **1**

Equity finance raised through retained earnings and rights issues will principally be provided by **existing** shareholders; new issues will result in a **wider shareholder base.**

FEEDBACK TO
ACTIVITY **2**

	Before	After
J Blogg's shareholding	1,000 shares	1,250 shares
Total issued capital	4,000,000 shares	5,000,000 shares
J Bloggs' percentage holding	0.025%	0.025%

Chapter 9
SOURCES OF FINANCE: DEBT

In this chapter we turn to non-equity sources of finance, mainly debt. Some sources are in fact 'hybrids', with some equity and some debt elements. Other forms of finance considered include grants and trade credit.

Objectives

By the time you have finished this chapter you should be able to do the following:

* describe the response of government agencies and financial institutions to the SME financing problem

* explain what other measures may be taken to ease the financial problems of SMEs such as trade creditors, factoring, leasing, hire purchase, AIM listing, business angels and venture capital

* explain the features of different types of long-term straight debt and the reasons for their issue

* explain the features of convertible debt and warrants and the reasons for their issue

* broadly describe the reasons for the choice of financing between preference shares, debt and near-debt instruments in terms of the risk/return trade-off

* assess the effect on EPS of conversion and option rights

* broadly describe international debt markets and the financing of foreign trade

* calculate and interpret appropriate ratios.

1   Forms of non-equity finance

The types of finance to be considered in this chapter can be summarised as follows.

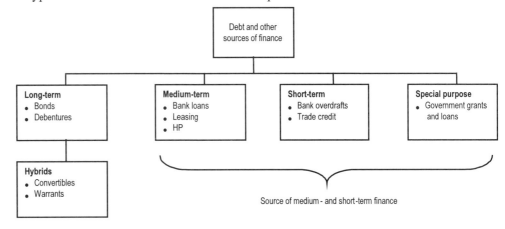

DEFINITION

A **debenture** is a written acknowledgement of a debt by a company, normally containing provisions as to payment of interest and the terms or repayment of principal. It may also be referred to as a **corporate bond** or **loan stock**.

2   Corporate bonds and debentures

Long-term debt (loan stock), usually in the form of debentures or bonds, is frequently used as a source of long-term finance as an alternative to equity.

A **debenture** is a written acknowledgement of a debt by a company, normally containing provisions as to payment of interest and the terms or repayment of principal. It may also be referred to as a **corporate bond** or **loan stock**.

Debentures are **traded** on stock markets in much the same way as shares, and may be **secured** or **unsecured**, and **redeemable** or **irredeemable**.

The term 'bonds' is now used generally to mean any kind of long-term marketable debt securities.

2.1   Secured debt

Secured debt will carry a charge over:

- one or more specific assets, usually lands and buildings, which are mortgaged in a **fixed charge**
- all assets – a **floating charge.**

On default, the debenture holders can appoint a receiver to administer the assets until the interest is paid. Alternatively the assets may be sold to repay the principal.

<aside>
KEY POINT

Debentures are **traded** on stock markets in much the same way as shares, and may be **secured** or **unsecured**, and **redeemable** or **irredeemable**.
</aside>

2.2   Irredeemable and redeemable debt

Irredeemable debt is not repayable at any specified time in the future. Instead, interest is payable ad infinitum. As well as some debentures, preference shares are often irredeemable.

If the debt is **redeemable** the principal will be repayable at a future date.

For example, if a company has "5% 2015 Debentures redeemable at par, quoted at £95 ex-int", this description refers to debentures that:

- pay interest at 5% on nominal value, i.e. £5 per £100 (this is known as the **coupon rate**)
- are redeemable in the year 2015
- will be repaid at par value, i.e. each £100 nominal value will be repaid at £100
- currently have a market value of £95 per £100, without rights to the current year's interest payment.

2.3   Characteristics of debentures and other long-term debt

Debentures from the viewpoint of the investor

(a) Debt is viewed as low risk because:

- it has a definite maturity and the holder has priority in interest payments and on liquidation
- income is fixed, so the holder receives the same interest whatever the earnings of the company.

(b) Debt holders do not usually have voting rights. Only if interest is not paid will holders take control of the company.

Debentures from the viewpoint of the company

(a) Advantages of debt:

- Debt is cheap. Because it is less risky than equity for an investor, debenture holders will accept a lower rate of return than shareholders. Also, **debt interest is an allowable expense for tax**. So if the cost of borrowing for a company is 6%, say, and the rate of corporation tax is 30%, the company can set the cost of the interest against tax, and the effective 'after tax' cost of the debt would be just 4.2% (6% × 70%).
- Cost is limited to the stipulated interest payment.
- There is no dilution of control when debt is issued.

(b) Disadvantages of debt:

- Interest must be paid whatever the earnings of the company, unlike dividends which can be paid in good years and not in bad. If interest is not paid, the trustees for the debenture holders can call in the receiver.

- Shareholders may be concerned that a geared company cannot pay all its interest and still pay a dividend and will raise the rate of return that they require from the company to compensate for this increase in risk. This may effectively put a limit on the amount of debt that can be raised.

- With fixed maturity dates, provision must be made for the repayment of debt.

- Long-term debt, with its commitment to fixed interest payments, may prove a burden especially if the general level of interest rates falls.

Deep discounted bonds and zero coupon bonds

Deep discounted bonds are those where the coupon rate being offered is below the market rate at the time of issue. If there is no annual interest payment, they are referred to as **zero coupon bonds**.

The return to the investor of these bonds is mainly in the form of a high redemption value. The attractions of these bonds to the company are as follows:

- the initial financing cash outlays are small

- the discount element of the bond is amortised and allowed annually against corporation tax.

From the investors' viewpoint, there are two other advantages:

- there is little chance of the bond being called early, as this would prove very expensive to the firm

- although the tax authorities amortise the discount element for tax purposes, the tax on this element of return to the investor is not normally payable until redemption.

3   Hybrids of debt and equity

Convertible loan stock is a loan which gives the holder the right to convert to other securities, normally ordinary shares, at a pre-determined price/rate and time.

Convertible debentures and **loan stock with warrants** represent forms of finance that are hybrids of debt and equity – they have elements of both.

3.1   Conversion rights and conversion premium

The **conversion rights** are either stated in terms of a **conversion ratio** (i.e. the number of ordinary shares into which £100 stock may be converted) or in terms of a **conversion price** (i.e. the right to convert into ordinary shares at a price of Xp) e.g.

- '£100 of stock may be converted into 25 ordinary shares' is a conversion ratio

- 'stock may be converted into shares at a value of 400p per share' is the equivalent conversion price.

Sometimes, the conversion price increases during the convertibility – this is done to stimulate early conversion. Another variation is to issue partly convertible stocks whereby only a portion of the stock – usually 50% – may be converted. Conversion rights usually cater for an adjustment in the event of capitalisation, rights issues, etc. Convertible preference shares are also possible.

A **conversion premium** exists when the market value of convertible stock exceeds the current market price of the shares into which they are or will become convertible. For example, suppose that £100 (nominal) of convertible stock is convertible into 10 shares of ABC plc. The stock has a market value of £102 and shares are currently priced at £9 each. The conversion premium for £100 of stock is therefore £12 (£102 – £90).

FOULKS LYNCH
PUBLICATIONS

3.2 Loan stock with warrants

A warrant gives the holder the right to subscribe at fixed future dates for a certain number of ordinary shares at a predetermined price.

The difference between a loan stock with warrants and a convertible debenture is that with a warrant the loan stock **itself** is not converted into equity, but bond holders make a **cash payment** to acquire the shares and **retain** their loan stock. This means that the loan stock will continue in existence until it is redeemed.

Warrants have value when the market price of shares rises above the price specified in the warrant. They are commonly used as a 'sweetener' for debt issues, allowing the firm to place a low interest rate on the loan. The cost to the firm is the right given to holders to buy equity at a (possibly) reduced price at the conversion date.

3.3 Attractions of convertibles and warrants as a source of finance

A **warrant** is merely an option, not linked to an underlying security, whilst a **convertible debenture** combines an option with a debenture.

Advantage	Comment
• Immediate finance at low cost	• Because of the conversion option, the loans can be raised at below normal interest rates
• Attractive, if share prices are depressed	• Where companies wish to raise equity finance, but share prices are currently depressed, convertibles offer a 'back-door' share issue method
• Self-liquidating	• Where loans are converted into shares, the problem of repayment disappears
• Exercise of warrants related to need for finance.	• Options would normally only be exercised where the share price has increased. If the options involve the payment of extra cash to the company, this creates extra funds when they are needed for expansion.

Example

(1) Raybeck plc issues 8% unsecured loan stock 20X1/X5 as part of the consideration for the acquisition of companies. With the loan stock are subscription rights (warrants) on the basis that holders of £100 loan stock could subscribe for up to 30 ordinary shares in Raybeck at a price of £8.75 per share. The option could be exercised any time between 20X2 and 20X5.

(2) Associated Engineering plc issues 7% convertible loan stock 20X8/X9. The conversion option is 80 ordinary shares for each £100 loan stock, and is exercisable between 20X1 and 20X5. If the option is not exercised, the debentures are redeemable at par between 20X8 and 20X9.

Describe the nature of these securities and comment on the exercise decisions that must be made by the investor.

Solution

Note the difference between these two issues. In the Raybeck case, the option is separate from the loan stock, which continues to exist whether or not the option is exercised. Also, the exercise of the option costs money. On the other hand, conversion of Associated Engineering loan stock is an actual replacement of the loan stock by shares, with no cash effect.

There are a number of variations on the theme of conversion rights including, for example, convertible preference shares. There is no need for you to memorise all the possibilities.

The warrants issued by Raybeck plc are worth exercising if the share price of Raybeck is above £8.75. For example if the share price rose to £10 then the value of the warrant would be:

Current market price – Exercise price = £10 – £8.75 = £1.25.

If share prices fell below £8.75 the warrant would be worthless. The above calculation is referred to as the **formula value of the warrant** or the **intrinsic value of the warrant**.

The conversion option on Associated Engineering's convertible is worth exercising if the share price rises above:

$$\frac{\text{Value of £100 loan stock}}{80 \text{ shares}}$$

Above this price, shareholders would receive equity of greater value than the £100 loan stock. Unlike a warrant, however, below this share price the value of the convertible does not fall to zero, but would settle at the market value of the security as a straight debenture.

The **formula value of a convertible** is the higher of its value as debt and its converted value.

3.4 The effect on EPS of conversions and option rights

Earnings per share (EPS) is a widely used measure of a company's performance, particularly over a number of years, and is a component of the very important Stock Exchange yardstick – the price earnings (PE) ratio. A key objective in the financial management of a quoted company is to record an increase in EPS over successive accounting periods.

$$\textbf{Earnings per share (in pence)} = \frac{\text{Net profit for the year after tax, minority interests, extraordinary items and preference dividends}}{\text{Weighted average number of equity shares in issue}}$$

The importance of EPS is reinforced by the issue of accounting standard FRS 14. The objective of FRS 14 is to ensure that a figure for earnings per share is prominently disclosed in the published accounts, and that the basis on which it is computed is comparable, within one company over a period of time, and between companies. This includes the disclosure of a 'diluted' EPS taking account of all conversion and option rights in existence.

Basic EPS

Example

M plc has the following summarised profit and loss account for 20X2:

	£'000
Profits before tax	6,000
Less: Tax	(1,300)
Profits after tax	4,700
Less: Minority interests	(700)
Profit for the financial year	4,000
Less: Dividends	(270)
Retained profit	3,730

An extract from the balance sheet as at 31 December 20X2 showed that issued share capital had been constant throughout the year as follows:

	£'000
£1 7% preference shares, fully paid	1,000
£1 ordinary shares, 75p paid	9,000
	10,000

Calculate the earnings per share for the year.

Solution

Earnings = Profit after tax, minority interests and preference dividends

= 4,000 − (7% −1,000)

= £3,930,000.

Number of issued equity shares = $\dfrac{£9\,\text{million}}{75p}$ = 12 million.

Therefore basic EPS = $\dfrac{£3.93m}{12m\ \text{shares}}$

= 32.75p per share

Diluted EPS

FRS 14 also requires disclosure of diluted EPS in addition to basic EPS. The principles of convertible loan stock and convertible preference shares are similar and will be dealt with together for the purposes of calculating diluted EPS.

Example

On 1 April 20X0, a company issued £1,250,000 8% convertible unsecured loan stock for cash at par. Each £100 nominal of the stock will be convertible in 20X3/X6 into the number of ordinary shares set out below.

On 31 December 20X3	124 shares
On 31 December 20X4	120 shares
On 31 December 20X5	115 shares
On 31 December 20X6	110 shares

Issued share capital: £500,000 in 10% cumulative preference shares of £1 and £1,000,000 in ordinary shares of 25p = 4,000,000 shares.

Corporation tax is 45%.

Trading results were as follows for the years ended 31 December:

	20X1 £	*20X0* £
Profit before interest and tax	1,100,000	991,818
Interest on 8% convertible unsecured loan stock	100,000	75,000
Profit before tax	1,000,000	916,818
Corporation tax	450,000	412,568
Profit after tax	550,000	504,250

Calculate (1) basic earnings per share and (2) diluted earnings per share.

Solution

		20X1 £	*20X0* £
(1)	Basic earnings per share		
	Profit after tax	550,000	504,250
	Less: Preference dividend	50,000	50,000
	Earnings	500,000	454,250
	Earnings per share based on 4,000,000 shares	12.5p	11.4p

(2)   Diluted earnings per share

	20X1		*20X0*	
	£	£	£	£
Earnings as above		500,000		454,250
Add: Interest on the convertible unsecured loan stock	100,000		75,000	
Less: Corporation tax	45,000		33,750	
		55,000		41,250
Adjusted earnings		555,000		495,500
Earnings per share based on 5,550,000 shares (20X0 – 5,162,500)		10p		9.6p

Notes:

(A) Up to 20X2 the **maximum** number of shares issuable after the end of the financial year will be at the rate of 124 shares per £100, viz: 1,550,000 shares, making a total of 5,550,000.

(B) The weighted average number of shares issued and issuable for 20X0 would have been one-quarter of 4,000,000 plus three-quarters of 5,550,000 i.e. 5,162,500.

3.5   Options and warrants to subscribe

The total number of shares issued on the exercise of the option or warrant is split into two as follows:

- the number of shares that would have been issued if the cash received had been used to buy shares at fair value (using the average price of the shares during the period)

- the remainder, which are treated like a bonus issue (i.e. as having been issued for no consideration).

The number of shares issued for no consideration is added to the number of shares when calculating fully diluted earnings per share.

Example

On 1 January 20X2 a company issues 1,000,000 shares under option. The net profit for the year is £500,000 and the company already has 4,000,000 ordinary shares in issue at that date.

During the year to 31 December 20X2 the average fair value of one ordinary share was £3 and the exercise price for shares under option was £2.

Calculate the earnings per share for the year ending 31 December 20X2.

Solution

Basic earnings per share: $\dfrac{500{,}000}{4{,}000{,}000} = 12.5\text{p}$

Diluted earnings per share:

	£
Number of ordinary shares in issue	4,000,000
Number of shares under option	1,000,000
Number of shares that would have been issued at fair value: $(1{,}000{,}000 \times 2/3)$	(666,667)
	4,333,333

Earnings per share: $\dfrac{500{,}000}{4{,}333{,}333} = 11.5\text{p}$

3.6   The order in which to include dilutive securities in the EPS calculation

Only potential ordinary shares that would dilute basic earnings per share should be taken into account when computing the diluted figure.

Where there is more than one issue of dilutive share the calculation is in two stages:

Step 1   For each issue, calculate earnings per incremental share.

Step 2   Adjust basic earnings per share for each issue from the most dilutive to the least dilutive.

When reading company accounts search for these hybrids and attempt the above calculations – you may need to guess some of the figures required for the calculations if the disclosure is poor.

There is no feedback to this activity.

4   Sources of short- and medium-term finance

With medium and short-term finance, the implication is that finance raised is to meet a specific current requirement which is not expected to continue indefinitely.

4.1   Identifying financing requirements

Unless the business is in continuing difficulties, the finance for a deficiency gap between cash inflows and outflows at a particular time should be required for a limited period only. For example, an **expansion in sales** may require an injection of funds to finance increased working capital, until the required level of cash is itself generated by the expansion. Similarly, a **seasonal period of low activity** may entail a need for short-term borrowing to cover inescapable fixed costs.

In considering the available sources of short and medium-term funds, two questions are asked:

• For what purpose are the funds required? and

• How long will the requirement last?

The most commonly used sources of medium and short-term finance are:

• leasing

• bank finance – loans and overdrafts

• trade credit

• debtor finance – factoring and invoice discounting.

Bank finance was discussed in Chapter 7, as part of cash management. The use of trade credit, debt factoring and invoice discounting as sources of finance was covered in Chapter 6. We shall now consider leasing.

5   Leasing

The popularity of leasing has grown over recent years to be a particularly important source of finance. Leasing is now common for vehicles, office and production equipment etc.

There are many different types of lease arrangement. In particular, lease-purchases are the modern equivalent of hire purchase (HP).

5.1   Characteristics of leasing

Leasing is a means of financing the use of capital equipment, the underlying principle being that use is more important that ownership. It is a medium-term financial arrangement, usually from one to ten years.

Leasing should be distinguished from short-term hire, contract hire and rental, which are all means of filling a temporary need. In the case of leasing, the firm intending to use the equipment selects its own supplier and then approaches the finance house which purchases the equipment and leases it to the user.

5.2   Operating leases and finance leases

There are fundamentally two types of lease agreement, as follows:

- operating leases
- capital or finance leases.

This section is concerned primarily with capital or finance leases.

The following criteria distinguish finance leases from operating leases.

Finance lease	*Operating lease*
One lease exists for the whole useful life of the asset.	The lease period is less than the useful life of the asset. The lessor relies on subsequent leasing or eventual sale of the asset to cover his capital outlay and show a profit.
The lessor does not usually deal directly in this type of asset.	The lessor may very well carry on a trade in this type of asset.
The lessor does not retain the risks or rewards of ownership.	The lessor is normally responsible for repairs and maintenance.
The lease agreement cannot be cancelled. The lessee has a liability for all payments.	The lease can sometimes be cancelled at short notice.
The substance of the transaction is the purchase of the asset by the lessee financed by a loan from the lessor, i.e. it is effectively a source of medium to long-term debt finance	The substance of the transaction is the short-term rental of an asset.

5.3   The finance lease agreement

A finance lease agreement is usually divided into two periods – primary and secondary.

(a)   The **primary** period is usually between 1 and 7 years (although 10 year primary periods, or even longer, may be possible) and it is in this period that the lessor would expect to recover the value of the equipment. The lessee is bound to pay the rental throughout the primary period.

(b)   During the **secondary** period, which will also usually be between 1 and 7 years, rentals are nominal only and the agreement can be terminated at any time without further payment. When the agreement is terminated, the lessee may ask the leasing company to sell the equipment to a third party. The agreement will usually allow the lessee to receive most of the proceeds of sale (75% to 95%).

The lessee in a finance lease is responsible for maintenance, insurance and operating costs in both periods and will normally take over the benefits of any guarantee or warranties.

6   Government assistance to small businesses

The UK government currently offers help to small firms in various business activities, including the raising of finance, innovation, information technology, exporting and training. Government financial assistance takes the form of **loan guarantees, grants and loans.**

6.1   Business links

The provision of business support services in England is coordinated through Business Links, which are local partnerships bringing together the services of the DTI, Training and Enterprise Councils, Chambers of Commerce, Enterprise Agencies, Local Authorities and other local bodies. There are currently 80 such partnerships. Similar support centres exist in the rest of the UK.

6.2   Financial assistance

Here we shall concentrate on the financial aspects of government assistance. Whilst you are not expected to have a detailed knowledge of particular government schemes, you should have a general awareness of the type of assistance offered.

Regional Selective Assistance (RSA)

This is a discretionary scheme available in those parts of the UK designated as Assisted Areas. It takes the form of grants to encourage firms to locate or expand in these areas. Projects must either create new employment or safeguard existing jobs.

In England, for example, RSA is available for projects involving capital expenditure of at least £500,000.

Enterprise grants

This is a selective scheme for firms employing less than 250 people. It is available for high quality projects in designated areas. Businesses may only receive one such grant.

Regional innovation grants

This is available in certain areas of the UK to encourage the development of new products and processes. It is available to individuals or businesses employing no more than 50 people. The scheme provides a fixed grant of up to 50% of eligible costs up to a maximum of £25,000.

Small firms training loans

These are available through the Department for Education and Employment and eight major banks in the UK. The scheme helps businesses with up to 50 employees pay for vocational education or training, by offering loans on deferred repayment terms:

- firms can borrow between £500 and £125,000 for between 1 and 7 years to cover education and training costs and, with restrictions, costs of consultancy advice on training matters

- the interest on the loan can be fixed or variable, and is paid by the Department for the first 6 to 12 months

- any education or training is eligible provided the firm can show that it will help them achieve their business objectives.

European Investment Bank (EIB) and European Investment Fund (EIF) schemes

The EIB provides loans to banks and leasing companies to help provide finance to small and medium-sized companies. The operators of EIB supported schemes include finance organisations such as Barclays Mercantile, Lombard Business Finance and Forward Trust.

The EIF provides loan guarantees in conjunction with some finance organisations' own environmental loan facilities. These facilities are designed to assist business to finance investments that produce a quantifiable environmental benefit (energy usage, raw material usage etc).

7   International finance

The primary function of banks is to act as financial intermediaries, that is to provide a link between net savers and net borrowers. In international banking the same function is fulfilled but across national boundaries. In addition international banks provide a range of banking services for their customers engaged in international business activity. These include:

- financing foreign trade

- financing capital investment

- providing local banking services in a range of countries

- trading in foreign exchange markets

- providing advice and information.

For their customers, the crucial services are those related to the international money and capital markets.

- **International money markets** are markets for short and medium-term funds. Business organisations with surplus funds can deposit these for periods ranging from overnight to five years. These funds are lent on to borrowers in these markets. The most important of the international money markets is the Eurocurrency market (see Chapter 4).

- **International capital markets** are markets for long-term funds. The instruments involved take a variety of forms including international bonds and Euro-equities.

The development of both international money markets and international capital markets have been closely linked to the development of the Euromarkets.

8   Comparing debt and equity finance

8.1   The advantages of debt over equity

Debt has three advantages over equity as a source of finance for the business: cheapness, flexibility and retention of control.

- In most situations debt is **cheaper** than equity on an after-tax basis. One reason for this is that it is generally less risky, so debt holders expect a lower return. Another reason is that **interest charges are tax deductible**.

    In other words the after-tax cost of debt is invariably cheaper for a company than the cost of equity capital (and preference share capital).

- Debt is also **more flexible** because it can in general terms be borrowed, repaid and re-borrowed in variable amounts at any time. Most debt contracts provide for borrowing, within limits, much at the borrower's option, and for repayment, although sometimes with a 'repayment penalty', at any time up to its contractual maturity.

- Debt is normally evidenced by a straightforward contract between borrower and lender, creating rights and obligations on both sides. Share capital (and particularly ordinary shares), however, carries with it the additional benefits of ownership of the business, including specifically the right to elect directors and appoint auditors.

8.2 The risks of debt

Repayment risk

Borrowing contains, by definition, an obligation to repay, whereas equity is usually irredeemable, with no obligation to pay. If a business cannot repay its debt when it falls due, it is insolvent.

Debt carries with it the risk that it cannot be repaid, and this risk increases with the amount of debt assumed. When the risk becomes unacceptable, either to the business itself or to its potential lenders, the business can be said to be at its maximum debt capacity.

Interest risk

Debt requires that in addition to principal (when due), interest is paid regularly throughout its life. Such interest can consume a significant portion of a business's trading profits, and can completely erode those trading profits so that it causes the business to suffer losses.

If too much debt is kept in shorter-term instruments, where the rate of interest can fluctuate with market rates, there is the added risk of having to pay at higher rates than that previously estimated.

Cost effect of interest risk

The 'cost effect' is created by some lending financial institutions who are prepared to accept a higher lending risk than, say, a normal commercial banking risk, but will charge more for it. Such a risk will usually be evidenced by an excessive level of debt in the borrowing business. Nonetheless, there is a financial point beyond which no lender will be prepared to lend. This is in the practical sense the limit of the business's debt capacity, as calculated externally. It may well, however, be rather higher than a business might see its own debt capacity.

Interest gearing effect of interest risk

$$\text{Interest gearing} = \frac{\text{Annual interest payments}}{\text{Annual pre - interest profit}}$$

The 'interest gearing effect' is based on the effect of changes in interest rates and pre-interest profits on the interest gearing ratio. In this case 'interest' is in effect net interest, calculated by deducting from interest payable on all debt the gross interest receivable on all interest-bearing investments.

The importance of interest gearing is twofold:

- Some, at least, of a firm's interest charge will be floating rather than fixed rate, in which case the actual amount of interest charges will, in a sense, be outside the borrower's control. The higher the absolute quantities of interest charges the more the risk of a general increase in rates wiping out the firm's profits.

- Since interest is relatively inelastic to changes in trading fortunes (ie, related mainly to the level of capital employed and not to changes in net profit), it creates greater variability in after-interest profits the higher its level.

Example

Two companies each made £100 pre-interest trading profits in year 1, but pay interest of £10 and £40 respectively (i.e. have interest gearing of 10% and 40% respectively):

Year 1	*Company A*	*Company B*
Pre-interest trading profits	100	100
Interest	10	40
Pre-tax trading profits	90	60

In year 2, however, interest charges remain the same in each case, but pre-interest trading profits halve to £50:

Year 2	*Company A*	*Company B*
Pre-interest trading profits	50	50
Interest	10	40
Pre-tax trading profits	40	10

The interest gearing risk is clear: a 50% fall in profits in Company A, with the lower interest gearing (10%), leads only to a 56% decline in pre-tax trading profits. In Company B, with a much higher interest gearing (40%) the decline in pre-tax profits is 83%.

The same effect would, of course, apply if interest charges were to increase as a result of a rise in interest rates generally, as opposed to a major change in trading profit, as in the example.

Higher interest gearing leads to greater volatility (i.e. risk) of post-interest profits. Higher interest gearing may then lead to lower shareholder satisfaction (and a lower share price, as a possible consequence), and greater risk in the business. This in itself does not mean there is a limit on debt capacity, but the level of interest gearing arising from a high level of debt may create an environment within which management may wish to reduce or limit further borrowing.

8.3   The choice of optimum gearing level

So whilst debt has some very obvious cost and flexibility advantages, it also introduces extra risks that will, initially at least, be borne by the shareholders. This extra risk is likely to result in additional required return for the shareholders, which will reduce, if not reverse, the effects of the cheaper cost of debt.

We return to the choice of capital structure in the next chapter.

Conclusion

In this chapter we have considered the various sources of debt and other non-equity forms of finance available to businesses, including government assistance. We have also introduced the idea of choosing an optimum balance of equity and debt finance, a topic which will be taken up in the next chapter.

Forms of non-equity finance

1   Give an example of a source of short-term, medium-term and long-term debt finance. (1)

Hybrids of debt and equity

2   What is the difference between convertible loan stock and loan stock with warrants? (3.2)

Leasing

3   Describe the primary and secondary periods of leasing agreements. (5.3)

Government assistance to small businesses

4   Describe the features of the small firms' Loan Guarantee Scheme in the UK. (6.2)

5   Describe the role of the European Investment Bank in the provision of finance for small businesses. (6.2)

Comparing debt and equity finance

6   What is meant by the interest gearing effect? (8.2)

EXAM-TYPE
QUESTION

Nolipival plc

(a)   Summarise the advantages to a company of issuing convertible loan stock rather than ordinary shares or debenture stock.   **(10 marks)**

(b)   State the circumstances under which there could be advantages to lenders and to borrowers respectively from issues of:

  (i)   debentures with a floating rate of interest;

  (ii)   zero-coupon bonds.   **(15 marks)**

Ignore taxation.   **(Total: 25 marks)**

For the answer to this question, see the 'Answers' section at the end of the book.

Chapter 10

CAPITAL STRUCTURE AND FINANCIAL RATIOS

At the end of the last chapter we introduced the question of the choice of an optimum capital structure, i.e. gearing level or ratio of debt to equity. Here we examine this further.

We start by looking at the various types of gearing measures and ratios. We shall then consider the impact of different levels of gearing on company risk and required return, and how a company may determine its capital structure. Finally we shall consider some other key financial ratios.

Objectives

By the time you have finished this chapter you should be able to do the following:

- explain and calculate the level of financial gearing

- distinguish between operational and financial gearing

- outline the effects of gearing on the value of shares, company risk and required return

- explain how a company may determine its capital structure in terms of interest charges, dividends, risk and redemption requirements

- explain the role of short-term financing in the capital structure decision

- explain the relationship between the management of working capital and the long-term capital structure decision

- calculate and interpret appropriate ratios.

1 Financial gearing

Financial gearing is one of the most widely used terms in accounting, and is concerned with the relationship between a company's borrowings and its shareholders' funds.

It can be used to measure the financial risk in a company's long-term capital structure.

Gearing calculations can be made in a number of ways, and may be based upon capital values or earnings/interest relationships. The main financial gearing ratios we shall refer to here are as follows:

- capital gearing – equity gearing and total gearing

- income (or interest) gearing.

All gearing ratios measure the same thing, but for comparison purposes it is essential that ratios are used consistently.

Note: To prevent confusion in an exam question, the examiner might specify the definition of gearing that candidates should use.

1.1 Capital gearing

Capital gearing is calculated from a company's financing structure as shown in its balance sheet.

Gearing is relevant to the long-term financial stability of a business. Two possible definitions of capital gearing will be considered, both of which consider the relationship between:

FOULKS LYNCH
PUBLICATIONS

(1) ordinary shareholders' funds (or equity interest); and

(2) fixed return capital – comprising long-term debt (bank loans, bonds) and preference share capital.

Long-term debt is usually taken as the value of loans and bonds that would appear as long-term creditors in the balance sheet. However, total long-term debt may also include long-term debt with less than 12 months now remaining to maturity and redemption.

Before looking at the two definitions of gearing we need to consider the basis for valuation of (1) and (2).

1.2 Book or market values?

Arguments for using market values

- When measuring rates of return on debt and equity it is generally accepted that market value is of far greater relevance than historic book values in measuring the value of the shareholders' or debt holders' investment.

- The market value represents the 'opportunity cost' of the investment made – it represents the proceeds foregone by the investor by choosing not to sell his shares/debentures now. It also represents the amount the company would have to pay if it wanted to redeem the capital now.

- If the investors in the company value the debt and equity in this way, it would be consistent also to measure gearing in terms of market values.

Arguments for using book values

- There are many instances where limits on gearing levels will be imposed on companies through their Memorandum or Articles, debenture trust deeds etc, and these will invariably be expressed in terms of book values.

- If market values were used, a sudden change in the market conditions that caused equity values to fall and debt to become more attractive could lead to the company suddenly finding itself in breach of its contractual obligations without having actually raised any more debt!

- Market values are not always available for all sources of finance – if the shares are unquoted, or with bank loans etc – whereas book values are always known.

Gearing ratios are very often computed on the basis of **book values**; you may be required to use market values as well/instead.

Accounts for illustration

Summarised balance sheet at 30 June

	20X1 £'000	20X1 £'000	20X0 £'000	20X0 £'000
Fixed assets (net book value)		130		13
Current assets:				
Stock	42		37	
Debtors	29		23	
Bank	3		5	
	74		65	

Creditors: amounts falling due within one year:		
Trade creditors	36	55
Taxation	10	10
	——	——
	46	65
	——	——
Net current assets	28	–
	——	——
Total assets less current liabilities	158	139
Creditors: amounts falling due beyond one year:		
5% secured loan stock	40	40
	——	——
	118	99
	——	——

	20X1	*20X0*
	£'000	*£'000*
Ordinary share capital (50p shares)	35	35
8% Preference shares (£1 shares)	25	25
Share premium account	17	17
Revaluation reserve	10	-
Profit and loss account	31	22
	——	——
	118	99
	——	——

Summarised profit and loss account for the year ended 30 June

	20X1		*20X0*	
	£'000	*£'000*	*£'000*	*£'000*
Sales		209		196
Opening stock	37		29	
Purchases	162		159	
	——		——	
	199		188	
Closing stock	42		37	
	——		——	
		157		151
		——		——
Gross profit		52		45
Interest	2		2	
Depreciation	9		9	
Sundry expenses	14		11	
	——		——	
		25		22
		——		——
Net profit		27		23
Taxation		10		10
		——		——
Net profit after taxation		17		13

Dividends:

	20X1	20X0
Ordinary shares	6	5
Preference shares	2	2
	8	7
Retained profit	9	6

The market values are/were as follows:

	20X1	20X0
ordinary shares (per share)	204p	195p
preference shares (per share)	80p	102p
5% loan stock (per £100 nominal value)	£108	£116

1.3 Equity gearing

DEFINITION

Equity gearing =

Preference share capital plus loans

Ordinary share capital and reserves

This is calculated as: $\dfrac{\text{Preference share capital plus long-term debt}}{\text{Ordinary share capital and reserves}}$

$$20X1 \qquad\qquad 20X0$$

Book values $\quad \dfrac{25+40}{118-25} \times 100 = 69.9\% \qquad \dfrac{25+40}{99-25} \times 100 = 87.8\%$

Market values $\dfrac{(0.8\times25)+(1.08\times40)}{2.04\times70} \times 100 = 44.3\% \dfrac{(1.02\times25)+(1.16\times40)}{1.95\times70} \times 100 = 52.7\%$

Note: If preference shares are treated as debt, equity gearing could also be described as the **debt/equity ratio**.

1.4 Total gearing (also referred to as capital gearing)

DEFINITION

Total gearing =

Preference share capital plus loans

Total long term capital

This is calculated as: $\dfrac{\text{Preference share capital plus long-term debt}}{\text{Total long term capital}}$

$$20X1 \qquad\qquad 20X0$$

Book values $\quad \dfrac{65}{158} \times 100 = 41.1\% \qquad \dfrac{65}{139} \times 100 = 46.8\%$

Market values $\quad \dfrac{63.2}{142.8+63.2} \times 100 = 30.7\% \quad \dfrac{71.9}{136.5+71.9} \times 100 = 34.5\%$

There is no real difference between the two calculations of gearing as the components of the numerator remain the same. Some prefer to use the equity gearing as it shows a more pronounced change if either fixed return capital or equity capital changes. Most use the second calculation as it is perhaps clearer to note the relationship of fixed interest finance to total finance.

However, you can see that there are significant differences between the actual figures derived, both between the two types (equity/total) and between the two bases (book/market value). This illustrates how important it is to ensure that like is being compared with like, whichever type and basis is used.

DEFINITION

Income (interest) gearing =

Debt interest
―――――――――――
Operating profits before
debt interest and tax

1.5   Income (or interest) gearing

This measure of gearing was introduced in the last chapter,

$$\frac{\text{Debt interest}}{\text{Operating profits before debt interest and tax}}$$

Note that just as preference shares are treated as debt in capital gearing ratios, their dividend is treated as debt interest.

For our example, the income gearing levels would be as follows:

20X1	20X0
$\frac{2+2}{27+2} \times 100 = 13.8\%$	$\frac{2+2}{23+2} \times 100 = 16.0\%$

Note: Interest gearing is the inverse of the **interest cover ratio**. (Interest cover = profits before interest and tax divided by interest charges).

1.6   Impact of financial gearing on returns to shareholders

We now return to a point made in the last chapter which is fundamental to the capital structure decision – that he presence of gearing has a direct effect on the variability (or risk) of returns to shareholders.

Example

Suppose there are two companies, A Ltd and B Ltd, with the same profit record but with different capital structures:

	A Ltd £	B Ltd £
Capital structure:		
10% Loan stock	20,000	-
Ordinary share capital and reserves	10,000	30,000
	30,000	30,000

	A Ltd Highly geared £	B Ltd No gearing £
Year 1 – Profits £4,000 before interest		
∴ Returns:		
10% Interest	2,000	-
Ordinary shares – balance	2,000	4,000
	4,000	4,000
Year 2 – Profits double to £8,000 before interest		
∴ Returns:		
10% Interest	2,000	-
Return to shareholders – balance	6,000	8,000
	8,000	8,000
Therefore, increase in return to ordinary shareholders	3 times	2 times

 FOULKS LYNCH PUBLICATIONS

Thus, the doubling of the profits in year 2 has the effect of tripling the return to the equity shareholders in the highly-geared company. The effect would be even more dramatic if the profits fell below £2,000 because then there would be no return at all to the ordinary shareholders in A Ltd. An investment in ordinary shares in a highly-geared company is a far more speculative investment than a purchase of ordinary shares in a low-geared company.

DEFINITION

Operating gearing is the relationship between **fixed and variable costs**.

2   Operating gearing

Before formalising the types of risk faced by shareholders we need to examine another type of gearing which will influence the level of variability of earnings before interest (and tax) – operating gearing.

Firms with high financial gearing are risky as fixed interest payments must be made irrespective of the level of earnings.

KEY POINT

Firms with high levels of fixed costs are usually described as having **high operating gearing**.

Operating gearing (also called operational gearing) measures the cost structure (fixed and variable) of the firm. Firms with high levels of fixed costs are usually described as having high operating gearing.

Operating gearing can be measured as the percentage change in earnings before interest and tax (EBIT) for a percentage change in sales, or as the ratio of fixed to variable costs.

Example

	Firm A £m	Firm B £m
Sales	5	5
Variable costs	3	1
Fixed costs	1	3
EBIT (Earnings before interest and tax)	1	1

What would be the impact of a 10% increase in sales volume on the EBIT of each firm?

Solution

Firm A New EBIT = ((5m − 3m) × 1.1) − 1m = £1.2m i.e. a 20% increase.

Firm B New EBIT = ((5m − 1m) × 1.1) − 3m = £1.4m i.e. a 40% increase.

Operating gearing would be as follows:

	Firm A	Firm B
$\dfrac{\% \text{ change in EBIT}}{\% \text{ change in sales}}$	$\dfrac{20\%}{10\%} = 2$	$\dfrac{40\%}{10\%} = 4$

Alternatively operating gearing could be calculated as follows:

	Firm A	Firm B
$\dfrac{\text{Fixed costs}}{\text{Variable costs}}$	$\dfrac{1}{3} = 0.33$	$\dfrac{3}{1} = 3$

Firm B carries a higher operating gearing because it has higher fixed costs. Its operating earnings are more volume-sensitive.

2.1 The relationship between financial and operating gearing

The above example illustrates that a company with higher operating gearing will have greater variability in EBIT relative to a given level of variability in sales.

The previous example illustrates that a company with higher financial gearing will have greater variability in returns to shareholders relative to a given level of variability in EBIT.

Thus if the sales of a company vary, the ultimate variability of returns to shareholders will be determined by the level of operating gearing – which determines the EBIT variability – as 'amplified' by the level of financial gearing.

So there is a trade off between operating and financial gearing. If a firm has a high degree of operating gearing, then unless sales were very stable, it would prefer to avoid financial gearing, and vice versa.

ACTIVITY 1

Plato plc has the following profit and loss account.

	£'000
Sales	10,000
Costs:	
Fixed	(2,000)
Variable=	(4,000)
EBIT	4,000

Suppose that £9m of 10% debentures are issued at par. Corporation tax is payable at 40%.
Assuming a 10% increase in sales, calculate the following ratios.

(a) The effect of operating gearing, as measured by: $\dfrac{\% \text{ change in EBIT}}{\% \text{ change in sales}}$

(b) The effect of financial gearing, as measured by:
$$\dfrac{\% \text{ change in earnings available to equity}}{\% \text{ change in EBIT}}$$

(c) The combined effect of both types of gearing, as measured by:
$$\dfrac{\% \text{ change in earnings available to equity}}{\% \text{ change in sales}}$$

(d) Comment on your results.

Feedback to this activity is at the end of the chapter.

3 Impact of capital structure on risk and required returns

3.1 The concept of a weighted average cost of capital

In our studies of sources of finance so far, each source of finance has been examined in isolation. However, the practical business situation is that there is a continuous raising of funds from various sources. These funds are used, partly in existing operations and partly to finance new projects. There is not normally any clear separation between funds from different sources and their application to specific projects.

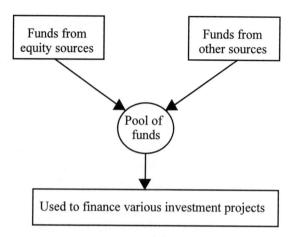

In order to provide a measure for evaluating these projects, the cost of the pool of funds is required. This is variously referred to as the combined or weighted average cost of capital (WACC).

The general approach is as follows:

Step 1   Calculate the cost of each source of finance.

Step 2   Weight these according to their importance in the financing mix, by reference to market values, for reasons discussed earlier.

The detailed calculation of individual costs of equity and debt finance is outside the scope of this syllabus, however, for the purposes of discussions regarding the effect of gearing on a company's cost of capital, a brief illustration of the computation of the WACC will be useful.

Example

Bacchante plc has a capital structure as follows:

	Cost of capital %	Market value £m
Bank loans	9	5
Debenture loans	12	6
Ordinary shares	15	39

The weighted average cost of capital will be calculated as follows:

Source	Market value £m	Proportions	Cost of capital %	Weighted cost %
Bank loans	5	0.10	× 9	0.90
Debentures	6	0.12	× 12	1.44
Ordinary shares	39	0.78	× 15	11.70
	50	1.00		14.04

3.2   The relative costs of debt and equity

In the above example, the costs of the debt finance (bank loans and debentures) were lower than that of the equity finance. This will be generally be so, for two main reasons:

- debt interest is tax-deductible

- the required return by debt holders is lower.

We have seen that an investment in debt is generally accepted as being of lower risk than one in equity. Interest is often fixed, its payment takes priority over dividend payments, and the loan itself may be secured on the company's assets.

It would therefore appear obvious that, in order to minimise its overall cost of capital, a company should include as much debt in its finance as possible, aiming for very high gearing levels (debt : equity ratio).

There is, however, a big flaw in this basic argument – it totally ignores the potential impact of increased gearing levels on the levels of risk perceived by both ordinary shareholders and, to a lesser extent, existing debt holders.

3.3   The risks faced by equity investors

Two types of risk are faced by the ordinary shareholder:

- business (or operating) risk
- financial (or gearing) risk.

The risk faced by the ordinary shareholders is the measure of the potential variation in their returns – i.e. future dividends (and therefore the future capital value of the shares as well). In the previous section we looked at this variability in terms of the levels of operating and financial gearing levels. This is now formalised in the definitions of the two types of risk faced by the ordinary shareholder as follows:

Business (or operating) risk

The basic earnings (before interest) of the company can fluctuate, caused by factors such as changes in market demand, actions of competitors, size of the company, quality of management decisions, the state of the economy etc.

For example, an oil prospecting venture will carry more business or operating risk than a property company.

As well as the factors affecting the basic sales income and costs, we have also seen that the level of operating gearing (fixed cost ratio) will impact here.

Financial (or gearing) risk

If a company has financial gearing, (debt in its capital structure), then a fixed interest charge must be deducted from the fluctuating earnings before the payment of dividends.

As we have seen, this has the effect of 'amplifying' fluctuations in the company's earnings, so that dividends face an additional risk, known as the finance or gearing risk.

Before reading further try and think what impact an increased level of gearing would have on a company's cost of capital.

There is no feedback to this activity.

3.4   The effect of gearing levels on a company's cost of capital (WACC)

An increase in gearing therefore leads to:

- additional risk for shareholders, and may well lead to an increase in their required return and thus the cost of equity but also
- a larger element of cheaper finance, debt.

How will these two opposing effects impact on the overall cost of capital, the WACC?

Whilst there have been many theories developed on this question, they are postulated under very restrictive (i.e. unrealistic) market and investor assumptions, and it is often felt that a 'trial and error' approach is more realistic.

Example

Grundig Plc is currently financed as follows:

	Cost %	Book value (£m)	Market value (£m)
Ordinary share capital	12.5	100	250
Debentures	6	60	50
		160	300

Grundig wishes to expand its business, for which a further £100m of finance is required. The following options are being considered:

Option (A) take on £50m debt plus £50m equity; or

Option (B) take on £80m debt plus £20m equity.

It is expected that the cost of the new debt will match that of the existing debt. However, due to the increased financial risk, it is estimated that the cost of equity will rise by 0.5% for option (A) and 2% for option (B).

Compute the effect on the WACC after the finance is raised under each of the options.

Solution

The existing WACC is $(250/300 \times 12.5\%) + (50/300 \times 6\%) = 11.42\%$

	Cost %	Option A (£m)	Option B (£m)
Ordinary share capital	12.5	300	270
Debentures	6	100	130
		400	400

New WACC under (A): $(300/400 \times 13\%) + (100/400 \times 6\%) = 11.25\%$

New WACC under (B): $(270/400 \times 14.5\%) + (130/400 \times 6\%) = 11.74\%$

Under Option A, which results in a moderate increase in gearing ratio, the WACC decreases – whilst the cost of equity did rise by a small amount, the effect of the increased tranche of cheap debt outweighed this.

Option B results in a much more significant rise in gearing – nearly doubling the percentage of debt – and is therefore accompanied by a far greater rise in the cost of equity. This now dominates, and the WACC rises.

3.5   Effects of gearing on the required return by debt holders

Whilst in the above example the cost of debt was assumed to remain at the current level throughout, it is quite possible that high levels of gearing would lead to an increase in this as well. As the element of fixed commitments to be paid out of variable earnings increases, there will be fears of liquidity problems and even insolvency, affecting the safety of the interest payments and possibly the loan capital itself.

This would tend to accelerate any increase in the WACC at high levels of gearing.

It is also possible that the cost of debt itself may rise with significantly increased gearing levels, as debt holders start to get worried about the firm's ability to meet the annual interest payments and/or repay the principal.

Changes in gearing levels affect the cost of equity due to the **change in gearing risk** and the **changes in proportions of funds.** Increased amounts of cheaper debt do not necessarily lead to a fall in the WACC.

4   Other factors influencing the capital structure decision

4.1   Growth and stability of sales

Where growth rates are high, equity is likely to be relatively cheap because of the attractiveness of the company. In addition, the cost of debt finance can easily be sustained, and the gearing effect will maximise the gain for equity.

If growth is stable, the ability to sustain high gearing levels increases.

4.2   Competitive structure of the industry

Sales are only one factor in determining profits. Another is the degree of competition and the profit margins in the industry.

4.3   Asset structure

Where the firm's asset structure largely consists of fixed assets, there will be a tendency to use long-term finance. If there is an emphasis on short-term assets, e.g. retailing, then short-term finance will be used.

4.4   Management attitudes towards control and risk

For quoted companies, issue of shares is attractive, with access to capital markets, less risk, and control being irrelevant.

For unquoted smaller companies, the issue of shares is often avoided in order to preserve control, and avoid dilution of equity.

4.5   Lender attitudes

The attitudes of lenders to the company and its financial structure dictate how much, and at what cost, the company can borrow.

4.6   Tax position

If a company is unlikely to be paying tax in the future it will not obtain the major benefit of debt finance (the corporation tax shield) but it may suffer agency and insolvency costs. In this situation debt financing would not be attractive.

4.7   Asset quality

Costs associated with financial distress/insolvency are likely to be higher for companies with a high proportion of intangible assets. Creditors know that it is easier to get their money back on land and buildings than it is on trademarks. In practice companies with large investments in property tend to be more highly geared than, for example, service companies.

4.8   Other reasons for borrowing

In the real world borrowing carries advantages that often outweigh the potential costs.

● arrangement costs on bank loans (the current source of much corporate debt) are significantly lower than flotation costs on new equity

● many small firms are unable to raise equity finance and borrowing becomes the only alternative if they wish to see their business grow

● other firms may wish to engage in borrowing overseas to hedge off foreign exchange exposure or to protect against political risk.

These considerations can often be as important as the theoretical arguments put forward above.

5 Other financial ratios

We have seen that debt and equity investors, both existing and future, will be interested in the gearing levels of a company. They need to determine the risk attached to their capital investment.

Other financial ratios that will be of interest to them will relate to the level and safety of their income from the investment, and we shall now look at the following ratios:

- Of particular interest to debt holders:Interest cover and interest yield
- Of particular interest to shareholders:Dividend and earnings-related ratios.

To illustrate these we shall use the accounts that were used earlier in this chapter to illustrate gearing ratios.

5.1 Debt holder ratios

Interest cover

Interest on loan stock (debenture stock) must be paid whether or not the company makes a profit. The ratio emphasises the cover (or security) for the interest by relating profit before interest and tax to interest paid.

20X1

$$\frac{52-9-14}{2} = \frac{29}{2} \text{ i.e. 14.5 times}$$

20X0

$$\frac{45-9-11}{2} = \frac{25}{2} \text{ i.e. 12.5 times}$$

The company is in a strong position as regards the payment of interest. Profit would have to drop considerably before any problem of paying interest arose.

In general, a high level of interest cover is 'good', with debt holders confident that profit is sufficient to pay interest and shareholders confident of their dividend. But a high interest cover ratio may also be interpreted as a company failing to exploit gearing opportunities to fund projects at a lower cost than from equity finance.

Interest yield

The interest yield is the interest or coupon rate expressed as a percentage of the market price.

On the 5% loan stock:

20X1

$$\frac{5}{108} \times 100 = 4.6\%$$

20X0

$$\frac{5}{116} \times 100 = 4.3\%$$

Note this measure totally ignores whether the debt is redeemable and how close redemption might be. It looks from the return as if the loan stock was bought at current market price and held for one year.

5.2 Shareholder ratios

An investor is interested in the income earned by the company for him and the return on his investment (the income earned related to the market price of the investment).

An investor in ordinary shares can look either at the company's earnings available to pay the ordinary dividend or at the actual ordinary dividend paid as measures of the income earned by the company for him. The ratios he would compute in each case would be as follows:

Dividends	*Earnings*
Dividend per share	Return on equity
Dividend cover	Earnings per share
Dividend yield	Price earnings ratio

In general, the higher each of these ratios is, the more attractive the shares will be to potential investors, who will be increasingly confident about the return the shares will give.

Some of these ratios were introduced in an earlier chapter.

Dividend per share

This relates to ordinary shares and is calculated as follows:

20X1

$$\frac{£6,000}{70,000} = 8.6 \text{ pence per share}$$

20X0

$$\frac{£5,000}{70,000} = 7.1 \text{ pence per share}$$

DEFINITION

Dividend cover =

$$\frac{\text{Profit available for ordinary shareholders}}{\text{dividend for the year (interim plus final)}}$$

Dividend cover

This is calculated by dividing profit available for ordinary shareholders by the dividend for the year (i.e. interim plus final). It is a measure of how many times the company's earnings could pay the dividend.

[20X1]

$$\frac{£17,000 - £2,000}{£6,000} = 2.5 \text{ times}$$

[20X0]

$$\frac{£13,000 - £2,000}{£5,000} = 2.2 \text{ times}$$

The profits available for ordinary shareholders are taken after deduction of the preference dividend. The cover represents the 'security' for the ordinary dividend – in this company the cover is reasonable.

KEY POINT

Dividend yield =

$$\frac{\text{dividend per share}}{\text{current share price}} \times 100\%$$

Dividend yield

This expresses dividend per share as a percentage of the current share price. The yield at today's date is:

[20X1]

$$\frac{8.6p}{204p} \times 100 = 4.2\%$$

[20X0]

$$\frac{7.1p}{195p} \times 100 = 3.6\%$$

DEFINITION

Return on equity =

$$\frac{\text{Profit after tax and preference dividends}}{\text{Ordinary shareholders' funds}} \times 100\%$$

Return on equity

This is a profitability ratio of particular relevance to the ordinary shareholders of a company. It is defined as:

$$\text{Return on equity} = \frac{\text{Profit after tax and preference dividends}}{\text{Ordinary shareholders' funds}} \times 100\%$$

[20X1]

$$\frac{£17,000 - £2,000}{£118,000 - £25,000} \times 100 = 16.1\%$$

[20X0]

$$\frac{£13,000 - £2,000}{£99,000 - £25,000} \times 100 = 14.9\%$$

Earnings per share (EPS)

We looked at EPS in an earlier chapter. For this company the calculation is as follows:

[20X1]

$$\frac{£17,000 - £2,000}{70,000} = 21.4\text{p per share}$$

[20X0]

$$\frac{£13,000 - £2,000}{70,000} = 15.7\text{p per share}$$

Price earnings ratio (PE ratio)

This is regarded as the most important investment ratio. It expresses the current share price (market value) as a multiple of the earnings per share.

20X1

$$\frac{204\text{p}}{21.4\text{p}} = 9.5 \text{ times}$$

20X0

$$\frac{195\text{p}}{15.7\text{p}} = 12.4 \text{ times}$$

The ratio of 9.5 times in 20X1 implies that if the current rate of EPS is maintained it will take nine and a half years to repay the cost of investing. The higher the PE ratio the longer the payback period. Thus we could conclude that the lower the PE ratio, the better the investment. However, this is not generally the case. High PE ratios are generally viewed as better than low ones.

The apparent paradox is resolved if the forward looking nature of stock exchange investments is considered. The PE ratio is based on current EPS but the stock market is pricing the share on expectations of future EPS. If the market considers that a company has significant growth prospects, the market price of the share will rise.

Conclusion

In this chapter we have considered the capital structure decision. We first looked at the various gearing ratios, capital/income and financial/operating. We examined the impact of gearing on risk, particularly those affecting the shareholder, namely business and finance risk. This led on to discussion of the choice of an optimum capital structure.

Finally we looked at some other financial ratios of interest to providers of finance.

SELF-TEST
QUESTIONS

Financial gearing

1 Distinguish between income and capital gearing. (1.1, 1.5)

Operating gearing

2 Give two ways in which operating gearing can be computed. (2)

Impact of capital structure on risk and required returns

3 What are the two main impacts on a company's cost of capital of an increase on gearing? (3.4)

Other factors influencing the capital structure decision

4 Outline four factors other than gearing risk that will be taken into account when deciding on financial structures. (4)

Other financial ratios

5 Why are high PE ratios generally regarded as better than low ones? (5.2)

EXAM-TYPE
QUESTION

Ratios – B Ltd

Below are the summarised accounts for B Ltd, a company with an accounting year ending on 30 September:

Summarised balance sheets

	20X1		20X2	
	£'000	£'000	£'000	£'000
Tangible fixed assets – at cost less depreciation		4,995		12,700
Current assets:				
Stocks	40,145		50,455	
Debtors	40,210		43,370	
Cash at bank	12,092		5,790	
	92,447		99,615	
Creditors – Amounts falling due within one year:				
Trade creditors	32,604		37,230	
Taxation	2,473		3,260	
Proposed dividend	1,785		1,985	
	36,862		42,475	
Net current assets		55,585		57,140
Total assets less current liabilities		60,580		69,840
Creditors – Amounts falling due after more than one year:				
10% debentures 20Y2/20Y5		19,840		19,840
		40,740		50,000
Capital and reserves:				
Called up share capital of 25p per share		9,920		9,920
Profit and loss account		30,820		40,080
Shareholders' funds		40,740		50,000

Summarised profit and loss accounts

	20X1	20X2
	£'000	£'000
Turnover	486,300	583,900
Operating profit	17,238	20,670
Interest payable	1,984	1,984
Profit on ordinary activities before taxation	15,254	18,686
Tax on profit on ordinary activities	5,734	7,026
Profit for the financial year	9,520	11,660
Dividends	2,240	2,400
	7,280	9,260
Retained profit brought forward	23,540	30,820
Retained profit carried forward	30,820	40,080

You are required:

(a) to calculate, for each year, two ratios for each of the following user groups, which are of particular significance to them:

(i)   shareholders

(ii) trade creditors.   **(8 marks)**

(b) to make brief comments upon the changes, between the two years, in the ratios calculated in (a) above.   **(8 marks)**

(Total: 16 marks)

For the answer to this question, see the 'Answers' section at the end of the book.

FEEDBACK TO
ACTIVITY **1**

	Original £'000	Inc 10% £'000	Difference £'000
Sales	10,000	11,000	1,000
Costs:			
Fixed	(2,000)	(2,000)	-
Variable	(4,000)	(4,400)	(400)
EBIT	4,000	4,600	600
Interest	(900)	(900)	-
Profit before tax	3,100	3,700	600
Corporation tax @ 40%	(1,240)	(1,480)	(240)
Earnings available to equity	1,860	2,220	360

Calculation of ratios

(a) Operating gearing $= \dfrac{600 \div 4,000}{1,000 \div 10,000} = \dfrac{0.15}{0.10} = 1.5 \text{ or } 150\%$

(b) Financial gearing $= \dfrac{360 \div 1,860}{600 \div 4,000} \approx \dfrac{0.19}{0.15} = 1.27 \text{ or } 127\%$

(c) Combined gearing $= \dfrac{360 \div 1,860}{1,000 \div 10,000} \approx \dfrac{0.19}{0.10} = 1.9 \text{ or } 190\%$

(d) Note that the combined gearing = Operating gearing $\times$ financial gearing
                                                            = 1.5 $\times$ 1.27 = 1.9 or 190%

Chapter 11
INTEREST AND DISCOUNTING

In this chapter we begin to examine a key area of finance: the appraisal of capital investments. We place ourselves in the position of managers faced with an investment opportunity, such as the launch of a new product, the construction of a new manufacturing facility etc. In most cases of this sort, a significant investment of capital is needed right away, whereas the projected revenues (or cost savings) will only arise later. How can managers assess whether the initial investment is justified?

In this chapter we shall look at the basic elements of financial arithmetic and interest calculations.

Objectives

By the time you have finished this chapter you should be able to:

- explain the difference between simple and compound interest
- explain the difference between nominal and effective interest rates and calculate effective interest rates
- explain what is meant by future values
- calculate future values including the application of the annuity formula
- explain what is meant by discounting
- calculate present values including the application of annuity and perpetuity formulae
- apply discounting principles to calculate the net present value of an investment project and interpret the results.

Note: to do calculations for compounding and future values, you need a calculator that has the functions to do this.

1   Introduction to simple and compound interest

Interest is earned on money invested. anyone investing money expects to earn a return on their investment, and this is usually measured as a percentage rate of return per annum.

A sum of money invested or borrowed is known as the **principal**.

When money is invested it earns interest. Similarly when money is borrowed, interest is payable.

Interest on an investment can be calculated as either simple interest or compound interest. simple interested is explained here, as well as compound interest, but it is much more important to be familiar with compound interest.

1.1   Simple interest

With **simple interest**, the interest is payable or recoverable each year but it is not added to the principal. For example, the interest payable (or receivable) on £100 at 15% pa for 1, 2 and 3 years will be £15, £30 and £45 respectively.

The usual notation is:

$$I = \frac{PRT}{100} \text{ or } P = \frac{100I}{RT} \text{ or } T = \frac{100I}{PR}, \text{ where:}$$

P = Principal

R = Interest rate % pa

T = Time in years

I = Interest in £

Example

A man invests £160 on 1 January each year. On 31 December simple interest is credited at 12% but this interest is put in a separate account and does not itself earn any interest. Find the total amount standing to his credit on 31 December following his fifth payment of £160.

Year (1 Jan)	Investment (£)		Interest (31 December)	
1		160	$\dfrac{12}{100} \times 160 =$	£19.20
2	160 + 160 =	320	$\dfrac{12}{100} \times 320 =$	£38.40
3	160 + 320 =	480	$\dfrac{12}{100} \times 480 =$	£57.60
4	160 + 480 =	640	$\dfrac{12}{100} \times 640 =$	£76.80
5	160 + 640 =	800	$\dfrac{12}{100} \times 800 =$	£96.00
Total				£288.00

Total amount at 31 December, Year 5 =

£(800 + 288) (Principal and simple interest)

= £1,088.

1.2   Compound interest

With **compound interest**, the interest is added each year to the principal and for the following year the interest is calculated on their sum. In other words, the interest on an investment rolls up, and interest is earned on the accumulated interest, as well as on the original principal amount.

For example, the compound interest on £1,000 at 10% pa for four years is calculated as follows.

Year	Principal (£)	Interest (£)		Total amount (£)	
1	1,000	$\dfrac{10}{100} \times 1,000 =$	100	1,000 + 100 =	1,100
2	1,100	$\dfrac{10}{100} \times 1,100 =$	110	1,100 + 110 =	1,210
3	1,210	$\dfrac{10}{100} \times 1,210 =$	121	1,210 + 121 =	1,331
4	1,331	$\dfrac{10}{100} \times 1,331 =$	133.1	1,331 + 133.1 =	1,464.1

An alternative way of writing this is now shown.

Year	Principal (£)		Total amount (£)
1	1,000	$1,000(1 + 0.1) =$	1,100
2	$1,000(1 + 0.1)$	$1,000(1 + 0.1)(1 + 0.1) = 1,000(1 + 0.1)^2 =$	1,210
3	$1,000(1 + 0.1)^2$	$1,000(1 + 0.1)^2(1 + 0.1) = 1,000(1 + 0.1)^3 =$	1,331
4	$1,000(1 + 0.1)^3$	$1,000(1 + 0.1)^3(1 + 0.1) = 1,000(1 + 0.1)^4 =$	1,464.1

So the amount (F) at the end of the *n*th year is given by.

$F = P(1+r)^n$

where 100r = rate % pa (in other words, when using this formula we express the interest rate as a decimal, such that 12%, for example, is expressed as 0.12 and 4.5% is written as 0.045).

Compound interest is generally given on all savings accounts.

1.3   Different types of investment problem

You might come across investment problems in any of the following forms.

- If you invest £X now for n time periods at an interest rate of r per time period, how much will your investment be worth at the end of time period r? For example, if you invest £1,000 now for 7 years at 3% per annum interest, what will your investment be worth at the end of year 7?

- If you want to have a fixed sum of money £X at the end of n time periods, how much would you need to invest now at an interest rate of r per time period in order to have £X at the end of that time? For example, if you want to have £10,000 in 5 years' time, what lump sum investment would you have to make now, earning 7.5% interest per annum, to have £10,000 at the end of 5 years?

- If you invest £A each time period for n time periods, earning interest at r per time period, what will the value of your investment be at the end of that time? For example, if you invest £40 a month in a savings account that pays interest at 0.25% (0.0025) per month, what will your investment be worth at the end of 5 years (= 60 time periods)?

- A fourth type of problem relates to the present value of annuities, and this is explained later.

1.4   Future values

A **future value** is the amount of money a sum invested now would be worth at a future date. In other words, if you invest a present lump sum now for n time periods at a rate of interest of r per time period, the future value is what your investment will be worth at the end of that time.

The formula for calculating a future value F has already been given.

Example

Calculate the compound interest on £624 at 4% pa for 10 years.

Solution

$F = P(1 + r)^n$

where P = £624, r = 0.04 and n = 10

$F = £624 (1 + 0.04)^{10}$

$= £624 (1.04)^{10}$

$= £923.67$

So the total interest earned in the period = £(923.67 − 624)

$= £299.67$

1.5 Present values

A present value of an investment can be described as the amount of money (a lump sum) that you would have to invest now for n time periods, earning interest at r per time period, to build up the value of your investment to £F at the end of that time.

So the amount (P) to be invested 'now' to earn F at the end of the *n*th year is given by.

$$P = F \times \frac{1}{(1+r)^n}$$

Example

Find the sum of money which, if invested now at 5% per annum interest (compound), will be worth £10,000 in 10 years' time.

Solution

$$P = F \times \frac{1}{(1+r)^n}$$

Where F = 10,000, r = 0.05 and n = 10

$$P = \frac{£10,000}{(1.05)^{10}}$$

$$P = £6,139.13$$

So £6,139.13 is the sum of money to be invested now. Put another way, £6,139.13 is the 'present value' equivalent of £10,000 in 10 years' time.

ACTIVITY 1

(a) You have £5,000 to invest now for 6 years at an interest rate of 5% per annum. What will be the value of the investment after 6 years?

(b) You want to put some money into a savings account now in order to have £7,500 after five years. You can earn interest at 4.5% per annum on your investment. What lump sum investment would you need to make?

Feedback to this activity is at the end of the chapter.

1.6 Future values and annuities

An **annuity** is a regular payment of the same amount each year. For example, you might invest £200 each year in a savings account for 10 years. The term 'annuity' is also used more generally to mean a constant amount invested every time period, not necessarily every year. so you might invest £25 each month in a savings account for three years, in which case you are investing an 'annuity' of £25 each month for 36 months.

When you invest an annuity at a given rate of interest r for n time periods, we can calculate what the total investment will be worth at the end of that time.

The future value of an annuity A can be calculated using the following formula:

Future value at end of year *n* =

$$A\left(\frac{(1+r)^n - 1}{r}\right)$$

where

A is the amount of the annuity (regular payment each time period)

r is the rate of interest

n is the number of years (or time periods)

This formula is given to you in the examination. So you don't need to remember it. However, you do need to be able to use it and apply it.

It is essential to note that this formula for the future value of an annuity is calculated on the assumption that the first annuity is invested at the end of the first time period, and the last annuity is invested at the very end of the final time period.

Example

An annuity will pay £100 for five years. What is its future value if the annual rate of interest is 10%?

The future value of the annuity is then calculated as follows:

$$£100 \times \frac{(1.10)^5 - 1}{0.10}$$

$$= £100 \times (1.61051 - 1)/0.10$$

$$= £100 \times (0.61051/0.10)$$

$$= £100 \times 6.1051$$

$$= £610.51$$

This assumes that the first £100 is invested at the end of the first year, and the fifth and final annual investment is made at the very end of the period, a the end of year 5, even though it does not have any time to earn any interest.

ACTIVITY 2

You plan to invest £50 each month for two years, starting at the end of this month. If you make 24 monthly investments at the end of each month, what will your total investment be worth at the end of two years? The rate of interest on your savings will be 0.25% per month. (0.25% = 0.0025).

Feedback to this activity is at the end of the chapter.

1.7   Annual percentage rate (APR)

It is common practice in the investment 'industry' to quote interest rates as an annual percentage. For example, a bank might offer interest of 8% per annum on a savings scheme, with interest payable every six months. What this means is that the bank will pay 4% interest every six months. This isn't an interest rate of 8% per annum. The annual interest rate is actually:

$(1.04)^2 - 1 = 0.0816$ or 8.16%.

Similarly, if a bank pays interest of 6% per annum, with interest payable every three months, this really means that the bank will pay interest of (6/4) 1.5% each quarter. So the real rate of interest is:

$(1.015)^4 - 1 = 0.06136 = 6.136\%$ per annum.

The 'real' rate of interest is referred to as the annual or annualised percentage rate or APR.

There are usually two rates quoted by financial institutions. The first is the **nominal rate**, and the other, the rate actually earned, is known as the annual percentage rate (APR) or the effective rate.

Example

An individual saves £40 each month with a building society, earning interest at 5% per annum, with interest paid every quarter. What will the investment be worth in total at the end of three years, and after 12 monthly investments – starting at the end of the first month?

Solution

The interest rate per quarter is 1.25%.

The future value of the annuity is:

$$£40 \times \frac{(1.0125)^{12} - 1}{0.0125}$$

$$= £40 \times (1.160755 - 1)/0.0125$$

$$= £40 \times (0.160755/0.0125)$$

$$= £40 \times 12.8604$$

$$= £514.42$$

1.8 Calculating a required annuity to achieve a future investment sum

The formula that is used to calculate the future value of an annuity can also be used to work out what annuity is required to build up an investment of £X at the end of a given time period.

Example

An individual wants to save a regular sum of money every six months for five years, so as to have a sum of £10,000 at the end of that time. There will be 10 equal amounts saved. The interest rate will be 6% per annum.

What amount must be saved every six months if the first amount is put into the savings account after six months?

Solution

(The interest rate every six months is 3% or 0.03.

$$£10,000 = £A \times \frac{(1.03)^{10} - 1}{0.03}$$

$$£10,000 = £A \times (1.343916 - 1)/0.03$$

$$£10,000 = £A \times (0.343916/0.03)$$

$$£10,000 = 11.4639A$$

$$A = £10,000/11.4639 = £872.30.$$

1.9   Calculating an annuity required to pay off a current loan

Another type of annuity calculation is to work out what the regular payments should be on a loan, to pay off the loan by the end of a given period of time. Typically, if you take out a bank loan at a fixed rate of interest, and make repayments of the loan every month, what would the size of the monthly repayments be?

Here the problem is not to work out what a stream of regular savings will be worth at the end of an investment period, but what stream of regular repayments will be needed to pay off a loan.

A formula for working this out is given in a formula sheet in the examination. It is a formula for the present value of an annuity:

$$\frac{A}{r}\left(1 - \frac{1}{(1+r)^n}\right)$$

Example

Paul has just borrowed £5,000 and he wants to pay the loan off in 12 monthly repayments. The interest rate on the loan is an APR of 6.168%. What should the monthly repayments be?

Solution

The APR is 6.168% and we need to convert this into a monthly interest rate. If you have a calculator that can do the calculation, you need the twelfth root of 1.06168, minus 1.

If you do not have a calculator that can do twelfth roots, you can divide the APR by 12. This gives 6.168%/12 = 0.514%. The monthly interest rate will be less than this, and probably a round number. A likely interest rate is 0.5%. you can check whether this is correct by working out:

$(1.005)^{12}-1$

This is $1.06168 - 1 = 0.06168$ or 6.168%.

The monthly interest rate is therefore 0.5% or 0.005.

Next we need to apply the formula. The present value of the monthly loan repayments is £5,000, the amount of the loan. The formula gives us:

$$£5,000 = A/0.005 \times \left[1 - \left(\frac{1}{1.005}\right)^{12}\right]$$

$£5,000 = A/0.005 \times [1 - (1/1.06168)]$

$£5,000 = A/0.005 \times [1 - 0.9419]$

$0.005\ (£5,000) = 0.0581A$

$£25 = 0.0581\ A$

$A = £430.29$

The same result could have been found more quickly using discount tables. Discounting and the use of discount tables are explained next.

2   Discounting techniques

2.1   Discounted cash flow

Discounting a cash flow takes account of the time value of money by bringing future cash flows back to what they are worth now (their present value).

A simple method of comparing two investment projects would be to compare the amount of cash generated from each – presumably, the project which generates the greater net cash inflow (taking into account all revenues and expenses) is to be preferred. However, such a simple method would fail to take into account the time value of money, the effect of which may be stated as the general rule below.

'There is a time preference for receiving the same sum of money sooner rather than later. Conversely, there is a time preference for paying the same sum of money later rather than sooner.' This is referred to as the time value of money

In simple terms, we would rather receive a sum of £100 now than in one year's time. There may be several reasons for this:

- Deferring the money is a risk. What if the funds are not available to pay us in one year's time?

- By receiving the money now we gain the chance to earn interest on it. For example, by placing it safely in a bank deposit account we might find that interest of £10 accumulates over the one-year period. If we wait for a year before receiving the £100 we lose the chance of earning this interest.

- Inflation may erode the value of the £100. In other words, with £100 now we can probably buy more than we could if we receive the same amount a year from now.

Different individuals and different businesses place different time values on money. For example, an individual with a very strong time value of money might refuse to defer his £100 unless he could exchange it for a much larger sum, say £150, in a year's time. Another individual might be prepared to accept a year's delay in return for just an extra £1; such an individual would have a low time value of money. For the first individual we conclude that £100 today is about equal in value to £150 in a year's time; for the second individual we conclude that £100 today is about equal in value to £101 in a year's time.

Another way of expressing the same thing is to say that for the first individual the present value of £150, receivable in one year's time, is £100; for the second individual the present value of £101, receivable in one year's time, is also £100.

We recognise the time value of money by discounting cash flows. There are two discounted cash flow (DCF) techniques:

- net present value (NPV)

- internal rate of return (IRR).

IRR will be considered in the next chapter.

2.2   Compound interest and discounting

The discounting process that is fundamental to DCF calculations is analogous to compound interest in reverse. A short compound interest calculation is included here as revision.

DEFINITION

Discounting a cash flow takes account of the time value of money by bringing future cash flows back to what they are worth now (their present value).

DEFINITION

The time value of money: the preference for receiving the same sum of money sooner rather than later or paying the same sum of money later rather than sooner.

KEY POINT

Discounted cash flow (DCF) techniques:
- net present value (NPV)
- internal rate of return (IRR).

KEY POINT

DCF calculations are analogous to compound interest in reverse.

Example

Barlow places £2,000 on deposit in a bank earning 5% compound interest per annum. You are required to find:

(a)   the amount that would have accumulated:

- after one year
- after two years
- after three years.

(b)   the amount that would have to be deposited if an amount of £2,500 has to be accumulated:

- after one year
- after two years
- after three years.

Solution

(a)   **Terminal values**

Although compound interest calculations can be produced using common sense, some may prefer to use a formula, as follows:

Final amount accumulated (terminal value), $S = P(1 + r)^n$

where

   P = Principal (initial amount deposited)

   r = interest rate per annum (as a decimal)

   n = number of years principal is left on deposit.

After 1 year, $S = £2,000 \times (1.05) = £2,100$

After 2 years, $S = £2,000 \times 1.05 \times 1.05 = £2,000 \times 1.05^2 = £2,205$

After 3 years, $S = £2,000 \times 1.05^3 = £2,315.25$

(b)   **Present values**

In this case the final amount, S, is known and the principal, P, is to be found. Again the formula could be used, rearranging it to become.

$$\text{Principal, } P = \frac{S}{(1+r)^n}$$

After 1 year

If £2,500 is required in 1 year's time, a principal, P, has to be invested such that:

   $P \times 1.05 = £2,500$

$$P = £2,500 \times \frac{1}{1.05} = £2,380.95$$

(If £2,381 is invested for a year at 5% interest, 5% of £2,380.95 or £119.05 is earned making the total amount £2,500 as required.)

FOULKS LYNCH
PUBLICATIONS

After 2 years

If £2,500 is required in 2 years' time.

$$P \times 1.05^2 = £2,500$$

$$P = £2,500 \times \frac{1}{1.05^2} = £2,267.57$$

(It can be checked that £2,267.57 will accumulate to £2,500 after 2 years.)

After 3 years

If £2,500 is required in 3 years' time.

$$P = £2,500 \times \frac{1}{1.05^3} = £2,159.59$$

This second group of calculations is the mechanics behind discounted cash flow calculations, the calculation of a present value. For example in (b) after 1 year one would be equally happy with receiving £2,500 in one year's time or £2,380.95 now. Although the immediate receipt is less than £2,500, if invested for a year at 5% it would amount to £2,500; hence the indifference between the two sums. £2,380.95 is called the **present value** (at 5%) of a sum of £2,500 payable or receivable in one year's time.

3 Net present value

To appraise a project which involves cash flows now and in the future we need to recognise the time value of money by discounting flows in the future back to their present value.

The discounting analysis we have looked at above is based on the investment preference, i.e. the ability to invest or borrow and receive or pay interest. The reason for this approach is that even where funds are not actually used and borrowed in this way, interest rates do provide a good measure of time preference.

If we treat outflows of cash as negative and inflows as positive the **net present value** (NPV) of a project is the sum of the present values of all flows which arise as a result of doing a project.

3.1 Formula

The present value (PV) of a single sum, S receivable in *n* years' time, given an interest rate (a discount rate) *r* is given by:

$$PV = S \times \frac{1}{(1+r)^n}$$

3.2 Illustrations

Find the present values of the following sums of money:

(a)   £1,000 receivable in 1 year's time given a discount rate of 10%.

(b)   £4,000 receivable in 2 years time given a discount rate of 5%.

(c)   £10,000 receivable in 5 years time given a discount rate of 8%.

In each case the process of reducing the cash flows to find that sum with which one would be equally happy now follows a procedure similar to compound interest backwards.

(a) $PV = £1,000 \times \dfrac{1}{1.10} = £909.09$

(One would be as happy with £909.09 now as with £1,000 in one year's time. With £909.09 available now to invest for one year at 10%, £90.91 interest is earned and the whole sum accumulates to £1,000 in one year's time.)

(b) $PV = £4,000 \times \dfrac{1}{(1.05)^2} = £3,628.12$

(Check for yourself that £3,628.12 will accumulate to £4,000 in two years if interest is earned at 5% pa.)

(c) $PV = £10,000 \times \dfrac{1}{(1.08)^5} = £6,806$

3.3   Present value factor tables

To make investment appraisal calculations simpler, tables are produced of present value factors (discount factors). These are similar to the tables of annuity factors mentioned earlier; again, they reflect both the interest rate and the time period concerned. For example, the factor corresponding to a sum of money payable in two years' time, with an interest rate of 10% per annum, is 0.826. This means that the present value of £1 receivable or payable in two years' time is £0.826, or 82.6p.

Example

A machine is being considered for purchase. It would cost £1.5m to buy, payable now, and would generate income of £0.9m in one year, £0.6m in two years and £0.5m in three years. Use the present value tables (mathematical tables) to estimate the net present value of this proposal.

Solution

$NPV (£000) = -1,500 + [900 \times 0.909] + [600 \times 0.826] + [500 \times 0.751] = 189$

3.4   Annuities

You have seen that an annuity means a regular payment of the same amount each year.

Illustration

Given a discount rate of 10%, find the present value of an annuity of £500 payable after one year, two years and three years.

The PV can be found from three separate calculations of the present value of a single sum:

$$PV = PV = \left[£500 \times \dfrac{1}{(1.10)}\right] + \left[£500 \times \dfrac{1}{(1.10)^2}\right] + \left[£500 \times \dfrac{1}{(1.10)^3}\right]$$

$$= £455 + £413 + £376 = £1,244$$

Note that in discounting calculations the convention is to take 'today' as being Time 0. Time 1 then refers to the end of Year 1 (or Month 1 if we are working in months). Similarly Time 2 refers to cash received or paid two years from 'today'.

ACTIVITY 3

Lindsay Ltd is unsure whether to invest in a new machine, with a cost of £1.5m. The net cash inflows from the machine are.

Time	1	2	3
Inflow (£000)	700	700	700

You are required to find the present value of the cash flow at the company's required rate of return of 10% and thus decide if the machine should be acquired. (Assume all cash flows occur annually in arrears on the anniversary of the initial investment.)

Feedback to this activity is at the end of the chapter.

3.5 What net present value means

Suppose, in an investment problem, we calculate the net present value of certain cash flows at 12% to be – £97, whereas at 8% the net present value of the same cash flows is + £108. Another way of expressing this is as follows:

If the funds were borrowed at 12% the investor would be £97 out of pocket.

If funds were borrowed at 8% the investor would be £108 in pocket.

In other words, a positive net present value is an indication of the surplus funds available to the investor now as a result of accepting the project.

3.6 Perpetuities

Sometimes it is necessary to calculate the present values of annuities which are expected to continue for an indefinitely long period of time, 'perpetuities'.
The cumulative present value factor tables only go up to 15 years and so a formula is required. The present value of £A receivable for n years given a discount rate r is:

$$\text{Present value} = A \times \frac{1}{r}\left(1 - \frac{1}{(1+r)^n}\right)$$

What happens to this formula as n becomes large? As n tends to infinity, $(1 + r)^n$ also tends to infinity and $\dfrac{1}{(1+r)^n}$ tends to zero. The cumulative discount factor tends to

$\dfrac{1}{r}(1-0)$ or $\dfrac{1}{r}$.

KEY POINT

To appraise a project which involves cash flows now and in the future we need to recognise the time value of money.

The present value of an annuity A receivable in arrears in perpetuity given a discount rate r is given by the following formula:

$$\text{PV of perpetuity} = \frac{A}{r} \left(= \frac{\text{Annual cash flow}}{\text{discount rate (as a decimal)}} \right)$$

Example

The present value of £5,000 receivable annually in arrears at a discount rate of 8% is:

$$\frac{£5,000}{0.08} = £62,500$$

4 Real rates, nominal rates and inflation

Compounding and discounting are normally at nominal rates of interest. These are interest rates reflecting market yields. A real rate of interest is the yield after allowing for inflation. For example, if the nominal or market yield on an investment is 8% and

the rate of inflation is 3% the real return is only about 5%. The exact relationship between nominal yield (money yield), the real yield and the annual rate of inflation is:

$(1 + N) = (1 + R)(1 + I)$

Where   N is the nominal rate of interest

            R is the real rate of interest and

            I is the annual rate of inflation.

Example

A bank pays 5% on a deposit account. Annual inflation is 3.6%.

(1.05) = $(1 + R)(1.036)$

$1 + R$ = $1.05/1.036$

          = 1.0135

The real rate on the deposit account is therefore 0.0135 or 1.35%.

Conclusion

In this chapter we have looked at interest calculations and have started to look at the key area of investment appraisal, which we will continue, in the next chapter.

SELF-TEST
QUESTIONS

Simple and compound interest

1   What is meant by simple interest? (1.1)

2   What is compound interest? (1.2)

3   What is an annuity? (1.6)

Discounting techniques

4   What is meant by discounting? (2.1)

Net present value

5   What is meant by net present value? (3.5)

EXAM-TYPE
QUESTION 1

Oracle plc

Oracle plc invests in a new machine at the beginning of Year 1 which costs £15,000. It is hoped that the net cash flows over the next five years will correspond to those given in the table below.

Year	1	2	3	4	5
Net cash flow	£1,500	£2,750	£4,000	£5,700	£7,500

You are required to calculate:

(i)   the net present value assuming a 15% cost of capital

(ii) the net present value assuming a 10% cost of capital.

(10 marks)

The extract below from present value tables is for your use.

Year	Discount factor		
	10%	15%	20%
1	0.909	0.870	0.833
2	0.826	0.756	0.694
3	0.751	0.658	0.579
4	0.683	0.572	0.482
5	0.621	0.497	0.402

FOULKS LYNCH
PUBLICATIONS

EXAM-TYPE
QUESTION **2**

Tom

(a) Tom is considering paying £80 into a fund on a monthly basis for 2 years
     starting in one year's time. The interest earned will be 0.5% per month. Once
     all these payments have been made, the investment will be transferred
     immediately to an account that will earn interest at 8% per annum until
     maturity. The fund matures five years after the last payment is made into it.

     Required:

     Calculate the terminal value of the fund in 7 years' time to the nearest £.

                                                                    (5 marks)

(b) Sally wishes to take out a loan for £4,000. She would have to make 24
     monthly payments and the APR would be 9.38%.

     Required:
     Calculate the monthly repayments for the loan.   **(5 marks)**
                                                            (Total: 10 marks)

For the answers to these questions, see the 'Answers' section at the end of the book.

FEEDBACK TO
ACTIVITY **1**

(a) $F = £5,000 (1 + 0.05)^6$

     $= £5,000 \times 1.3401$

     $= £6,700$

(b) Where F = 7,500, r = 0.045 and n = 5

     $P = \dfrac{£7,500}{(1.045)^5}$

     $P = £7,500/1.24618$

     $= £6,018$

FEEDBACK TO
ACTIVITY **2**

The future value of the annuity is

$£50 \times \dfrac{(1.0025)^{24} - 1}{0.0025}$

$= £50 \times (1.061757 - 1)/0.0025$

$= £50 \times (0.061757/0.0025)$

$= £100 \times 24.7028$

$= £247.03$

FEEDBACK TO
ACTIVITY **3**

Cash inflows from new machine.

$PV = \dfrac{£700,00}{1.10} + \dfrac{£700,00}{1.10^2} + \dfrac{£700,000}{1.10^3}$

$= £700,000 \times \left(\dfrac{1}{1.1} + \dfrac{1}{1.1^2} + \dfrac{1}{1.1^3} \right)$

$= £700,000 \times 2.48685 = £1,740,796$

Since the present value of the inflows exceeds the (present value of) the initial cost, the new machine project is worthwhile. (It has a net present value of £1,740,796 – £1,500,000 = £240,796.) Note that we do not have to discount the value of the initial investment, because it takes place 'today', i.e. Time 0. The discount factor relating to Time 0 is always 1, no matter what discount rate is being used, because payments 'today' are already expressed in present value terms.

Chapter 12
CAPITAL INVESTMENT APPRAISAL

This chapter is the first of four that look at the topic of capital expenditure and investment. The basics of one of the most important methods – discounted cash flow (DCF) – should be familiar to you from earlier studies. This chapter includes a revision of the basic principles and techniques of DCF. In the following chapters we shall be developing this in its application to specific investment decisions.

First, however, we need to look at other methods of investment appraisal which, whilst not being as theoretically sound as DCF, are often seen as of more practical use and are commonly used by organisations.

Objectives

By the time you have finished this chapter you should be able to do the following:

- define and distinguish between capital and revenue expenditure

- compare and contrast fixed asset investment and working capital investment

- describe the impact of investment projects on financial statements

- calculate payback and assess its usefulness as a measure of investment worth

- calculate ROCE and assess its usefulness as a measure of investment worth

- explain the importance of the time value of money and the role of the cost of capital in appraising investments

- identify and evaluate relevant cash flows of potential investments

- calculate present values to derive the NPV and IRR measures of investment worth

- explain the superiority of DCF methods over payback and ROCE

- assess the merits of IRR and NPV

- apply DCF methods to asset replacement decisions.

1   Investment appraisal: Introduction

1.1   Capital investment

Most businesses have to spend money from time to time on new fixed assets. Spending on fixed assets is capital expenditure. There are various reasons why capital expenditure might be either necessary or desirable, and these can be categorised into the following types.

(a)   **Maintenance** – This is spending on new fixed assets to replace worn-out assets or obsolete assets, or spending on existing fixed assets to improve safety and security features.

(b)   **Profitability** – This is spending on fixed assets to improve the profitability of the existing business, to achieve cost savings, quality improvement, improved productivity, and so on.

(c)   **Expansion** – This is spending to expand the business, to make new products, open new outlets, invest in research and development, etc.

(d)   **Indirect** – This is spending on fixed assets that will not have a direct impact on the business operations or its profits. It includes spending on office buildings, or

welfare facilities, etc. Capital spending of this nature is necessary, but a businesses should try to make sure that it gets good value for money from its spending.

In contrast to revenue expenditure, which is normally continual spending but in fairly small amounts, capital expenditure is irregular and often involves large amounts of spending. Because of the large amounts of money involved, it is usual for decisions about capital expenditure to be taken at a senior level within an organisation.

1.2   Capital budget

Large organisations will spend much more money on capital expenditure items, and much more regularly, than smaller organisations. Some organisations might have a long-term programme of capital spending that is reviewed and updated every year.

A capital budget is a programme of capital expenditure for the next few years, updated every year that sets out details of:

- Capital investment projects that have been authorised but not yet undertaken.

- Projects that likely to occur in the next few years, but that have not yet been authorised.

Before any individual investment project goes ahead, it should be authorised by an appropriate manager or committee within the organisation (or perhaps by the board of directors).

Basic stages in the capital budgeting cycle for a large organisation might be as follows:

Step 1   The requirements for capital expenditure in the business are forecast.

Step 2   Projects that might meet those requirements are identified.

Step 3   Alternative projects for meeting the requirements are appraised.

Step 4   The best alternatives are selected and approved.

Step 5   When a project has been approved, the capital expenditure is made.

Step 6   Actual spending is compared with planned spending, and the actual benefits obtained are monitored over time against the expected benefits. Deviations from estimates are examined.

1.3   The features of capital expenditure appraisal

Before any capital expenditure is authorised, the proposed spending (or 'capital project') should be evaluated. Management should be satisfied that the spending will be beneficial.

- If the purpose of a capital project is to improve profits, we need to be convinced that the expected profits are big enough to justify the spending. Will the investment provide a reasonable return?

- If the capital expenditure is for an essential purpose, such as to replace a worn-out machine or the acquire a new office building, we need to be convinced that the spending decision is the best option available, and that there are no cheaper or more effective spending options.

When a proposed capital projects evaluated, the costs and benefits of the project should be evaluated over its foreseeable life. This is usually the expected useful life of the fixed asset to be purchased, which will be several years. This means that estimates of future costs and benefits call for long-term forecasting.

A 'typical' capital project involves an immediate purchase of a fixed asset. The asset is then used for a number of years, during which it is used to increase sales revenue or to achieve savings in operating costs. There will also be running costs for the asset. At the

end of the asset's commercially useful life, it might have a 'residual value'. For example, it might be sold for scrap or in a second-hand market. (Items such as motor vehicles and printing machines often have a significant residual value.)

A problem with long-term forecasting of revenues, savings and costs is that forecasts can be inaccurate. However, although it is extremely difficult to produce reliable forecasts, every effort should be made to make them as reliable as possible.

- A business should try to avoid spending money on fixed assets on the basis of wildly optimistic and unrealistic forecasts.

- The assumptions on which the forecasts are based should be stated clearly. If the assumptions are clear, the forecasts can be assessed for reasonableness by the individuals who are asked to authorise the spending.

1.4   Methods of capital expenditure appraisal

When forecasts of costs and benefits have been made for a capital project, the estimates must be analysed to establish whether the project should go ahead. Should the business spend money now in order to earn returns over a number of years into the future?

Capital investment appraisal is an analysis of the expected financial returns from a capital project over its expected life.

There are several methods of carrying out a capital expenditure appraisal. The methods that will be described in this chapter are:

- Return on capital employed (ROCE)

- Payback

- The net present value method of discounted cash flow

- The internal rate of return method of discounted cash flow.

A common feature of all three methods is that they analyse the expected *cash flows* from the capital project, not the effects of the project on reported accounting profits.

Before describing the three techniques in detail, it will be helpful to look at the 'cash flow' nature of capital investment appraisal.

2   Return on capital employed (ROCE)

The return on capital employed (ROCE) – which may also be called the accounting rate of return (ARR) – expresses the profits from a project as a percentage of capital cost. However, what profits and what figure for capital cost are used may vary. The most common approach produces the definition given.

$$\text{ROCE} = \frac{\text{average annual (post depreciation) profits before interest and tax}}{\text{initial capital costs}} \times 100$$

In the absence of any instructions to the contrary, this is the method that you should use. Other methods discovered by a recent survey were:

- using average book value of the assets over their life

- using first year's profits

- using total profits over the whole of the project's life.

Example

A project involves the immediate purchase of an item of plant costing £110,000. It would generate annual cash flows of £24,400 for five years, starting in year 1. The

plant purchased would have a scrap value of £10,000 in five years, when the project terminates. Depreciation is on a straight line basis.

Calculate the ROCE.

Solution

Annual cash flows are taken to be profit before depreciation.

$$\text{Average annual depreciation} = (£110{,}000 - £10{,}000) \div 5$$

$$= £20{,}000$$

$$\text{Average annual profit} = £24{,}400 - £20{,}000$$

$$= £4{,}400$$

$$\text{ROCE} = \frac{\text{Average annual profit}}{\text{Initial capital cost}} \times 100$$

$$= \frac{£4{,}400}{£110{,}000} \times 100$$

$$= 4\%$$

2.1 Using average book values of investments

This variation on the calculation of an ROCE produces a figure which is, under certain circumstances, closer to the conventional financial accounting view of return on capital employed. But be careful when calculating a simple average in these circumstances! Note in the example below that the scrap value **increases** the average book value.

Example

Using the figures in the previous example, produce revised calculations based on the average book value of the investment.

Solution

$$\text{Average annual profits (as before)} = £4{,}400$$

$$\text{Average book value of assets} = \frac{\text{Initial capital cost} + \text{Final scrap value}}{2}$$

$$= \frac{£110{,}000 + £10{,}000}{2} = £60{,}000$$

$$\text{ROCE} = \frac{£4{,}400}{£60{,}000} \times 100 = 7.33\%$$

ACTIVITY 1

A project requires an initial investment of £800,000 and then earns net cash inflows as follows:

Year	1	2	3	4	5	6	7
Cash inflows (£'000)	100	200	400	400	300	200	150

In addition, at the end of the seven-year project the assets initially purchased will be sold for £100,000.

You are required to determine the project's return on capital employed using:

(a) initial capital invested

(b) average capital invested.

Feedback to this activity is at the end of the chapter.

2.2   Advantages of ROCE as an investment appraisal technique

ROCE as a method of investment appraisal has the following advantages:

- **Simplicity.** Being based on widely reported measures of return (profits) and asset (balance sheet values), it is easily understood and easily calculated.

- **Link with other accounting measures.** Annual ROCE, calculated to assess a business or sector of a business (and therefore the investment decisions made by that business), is a widely used measure. It is expressed in percentage terms with which managers and accountants are familiar.

2.3   Disadvantages of ROCE as an investment appraisal technique

There are a number of specific disadvantages of the ROCE as follows:

- It fails to take account of either the **project life** or the **timing of cash flows** (and time value of money) within that life.

- It will **vary with specific accounting policies**, and the extent to which project costs are capitalised. Profit measurement is thus 'subjective', and ROCE figures for identical projects would vary from business to business.

- It might ignore **working capital** requirements.

- Like all rate of return measures, it is not a measurement of **absolute gain** in wealth for the business owners.

- There is no definite **investment signal**. The decision to invest or not remains subjective in view of the lack of an objectively set target ROCE.

2.4   Accounting profits and cash flows

An investment involves the outlay of money 'now' in the expectation of getting more money back in the future. In capital investment appraisal, it is more appropriate to evaluate future cash flows – the money actually spent, saved and received - rather than accounting profits. Accounting profits do not properly reflect investment returns.

Suppose for example that a business is considering whether to buy a new fixed asset for £80,000 that is expected to increase profits before depreciation each year by £30,000 for four years. At the end of year 4, the asset will be worthless.

The business should assess whether the expected financial return from the asset is sufficiently high to justify buying it.

(a)   If we looked at the accounting returns from this investment, we might decide that annual depreciation should be £20,000 each year (£80,000/4 years). Annual profits would then be £10,000. We could then assess the project on the basis that it will add £10,000 each year to profit for the next four years. (We could estimate an expected average return on capital employed, or 'accounting rate of return'. Since the average balance sheet value of the asset over its useful life will be £40,000 after depreciation, we could say that the project will provide an average return on capital employed, in accounting terms, of 25% (£10,000/£40,000).

(b)   If we looked at the investment cash flows, the analysis is different. Here we would say that to invest in the project, the business would spend £80,000 now and would expect a cash return of £30,000 each year for the next four years.

Capital investment appraisal should be based on cash flows, because it is realistic to do so. Capital spending involves spending cash and getting cash back in return, over time.

2.5　Cash flows and relevant costs

The only cash flows that should be taken into consideration in capital investment appraisal are:

- cash flows that will happen in the future, and

- cash flows that will arise only if the capital project goes ahead.

These cash flows are direct revenues from the project and relevant costs. Relevant costs are future costs that will be incurred or saved as a direct consequence of undertaking the investment.

- Costs that have already been incurred are not relevant to a current decision. For example, suppose a company makes a non-returnable deposit as a down-payment for an item of equipment, and then re-considers whether it wants the equipment after all. The money that has already been spent and cannot be recovered and so is not relevant to the current decision about obtaining the equipment.

- Costs that will be incurred anyway, whether or not a capital project goes ahead, cannot be relevant to a decision about investing in the project. Fixed cost expenditures are an example of 'committed costs'. For the purpose of investment appraisal, a project should not be charged with an amount for a share of fixed costs that will be incurred anyway.

- Non-cash items of cost can never be relevant to investment appraisal. In particular, the depreciation charges on a fixed asset are not relevant costs for analysis because depreciation is not a cash expenditure.

Relevant costs in DCF analysis will be explained in more detail in the next chapter.

ACTIVITY 2

A company is evaluating a proposed expenditure on an item of equipment that would cost £160,000. A technical feasibility study has been carried out by consultants, at a cost of £15,000, into benefits from investing in the equipment. It has been estimated that the equipment would have a life of four years, and annual profits would be £8,000. Profits are after deducting annual depreciation of £40,000 and an annual charge of £25,000 for a share of fixed costs that will be incurred anyway.

Required:

What are the cash flows for this project that should be evaluated?

Feedback to this activity is at the end of the chapter.

3　Payback method of appraisal

3.1　Introduction

DEFINITION

Payback is the amount of time it is expected to take for the cash inflows from a capital investment project to equal the cash outflows.

It is the time that a project will take to pay back the money spent on it. It is based on expected cash flows form the project, not accounting profits.

The payback method of appraisal is used in one of two ways.

- A business might establish a rule for capital spending that no project should be undertaken unless it is expected to pay back within a given length of time. For example, a rule might be established that capital expenditure should not be undertaken unless payback is expected within, say, five years.

- When two alternative capital projects are being compared, and the decision is to undertake one or the other but not both, preference might be given to the project that is expected to pay back sooner.

Payback is commonly used as an initial screening method, and projects that meet the payback requirement are then evaluated using another investment appraisal method.

3.2 Calculating payback: constant annual cash flows

If the expected cash inflows from a project are an equal annual amount, the payback period is calculated simply as:

$$\text{Payback period} = \frac{\text{Initial payment}}{\text{Annual Cash Inflow}}$$

It is normally assumed that cash flows each year occur at an even rate throughout the year.

Example

An expenditure of £2 million is expected to generate cash inflows of £500,000 each year for the next seven years.

What is the payback period for the project?

Solution

$$\text{Payback} = \frac{£2,000,000}{£500,000} = \textbf{4 years}$$

The payback method provides a rough measure of the liquidity of a project, in other words how much annual cash flow it earns. It is not a measure of the profitability of a project over its life. In the example above, the fact that the project pays back within four years ignores the total amount of cash flows it will provide over seven years. A project costing £2 million and earning cash flows of £500,000 for just five years would have exactly the same payback period, even though it would not be as profitable.

A pay back period might not be an exact number of years.

Example

A project will involve spending £1.8 million now. Annual cash flows from the project would be £350,000.

What is the expected payback period?

Solution

$$\text{Payback} = \frac{£1,800,000}{£350,000} = \textbf{5.1429 years}$$

This can be stated in any of the following ways.

* Payback will be in 5.1 years.

* Payback will be in just over 5 years (or between 5 and 6 years).

* Payback will be in 5 years 2 months.

Payback in years and months is calculated by multiplying the decimal fraction of a year by 12 months. In this example, 0.1429 years = 1.7 months (0.1429 x 12 months), which is rounded to 2 months.

3.3 Calculating payback: uneven annual cash flows

Annual cash flows from a project are unlikely to be a constant annual amount, but are likely to vary from year to year.

Payback is calculated by finding out when the cumulative cash inflows from the project will pay back the money spent. Cumulative cash flows should be worked out by adding each year's cash flows, on a cumulative basis, to net cash flow to date for the project.

The simplest way of calculating payback is probably to set out the figures in a table.

An example will be used to illustrate how the table should be constructed.

Example

A project is expected to have the following cash flows.

Year	Cash flow
	£000
0	(2,000)
1	500
2	500
3	400
4	600
5	300
6	200

What is the expected payback period?

Solution

Figures in brackets are negative cash flows. In the table below a column is added for cumulative cash flows for the project to date. Figures in brackets are negative cash flows.

Each year's cumulative figure is simply the cumulative figure at the start of the year plus the figure for the current year. The cumulative figure each year is therefore the expected position as at the end of that year.

Year	Cash flow	Cumulative cash flow
	£000	£000
0	(2,000)	(2,000)
1	500	(1,500)
2	500	(1,000)
3	400	(600)
4	600	0
5	300	300
6	200	500

The payback period is exactly 4 years.

Payback is not always an exact number of years.

Example

A project would have the following cash flows.

Year	Cash flow
	£000
0	(1,900)
1	300
2	500
3	600
4	800
5	500

The payback period would be calculated as follows.

Year	Cash flow	Cumulative cash flow
	£000	£000
0	(1,900)	(1,900)
1	300	(1,600)
2	500	(1,100)
3	600	(500)
4	800	300
5	500	800

Payback is between the end of year 3 and the end of year 4 – in other words during year 4.

If we assume a constant rate of cash flow through the year, we could estimate that payback will be three years, plus (500/800) of year 4. This is because the cumulative cash flow is minus 500 at the star of the year and the year 4 cash flow would be 800.

We could therefore estimate that payback would be after 3.626 years or 3 years 8 months.

ACTIVITY 3

Calculate the payback period in years and months for the following project.

Year	Cash flow
	£000
0	(3,100)
1	1,000
2	900
3	800
4	500
5	500

How many units should the company order at a time so as to minimise the costs of stock ordering plus stock holding?

Feedback to this activity is at the end of the chapter.

3.4 Merits of payback method as an investment appraisal technique

KEY POINT

If cash inflows are uneven the payback has to be calculated by working out the cumulative cash flow over the life of a project.

The payback method of investment appraisal has some advantages.

(a) **Simplicity**

As a concept, it is easily understood and is easily calculated.

(b) **Rapidly-changing technology**

If new plant is likely to be scrapped in a short period because of obsolescence, a quick payback is essential.

(c) **Improving investment conditions**

When investment conditions are expected to improve in the near future, attention is directed to those projects which will release funds soonest, to take advantage of the improving climate.

(d) **Payback favours projects with a quick return**

It is often argued that these are to be preferred for three reasons:

(i)   Rapid project payback leads to rapid company growth – but in fact such a policy will lead to many profitable investment opportunities being

FOULKS LYNCH
PUBLICATIONS

overlooked because their payback period does not happen to be particularly swift.

(ii)   Rapid payback minimises risk (the logic being that the shorter the payback period, the less there is that can go wrong). Not all risks are related to time, but payback is able to provide a useful means of assessing time risks (and only time risk). It is likely that earlier cash flows can be estimated with greater certainty.

(iii)   Rapid payback maximises liquidity – but liquidity problems are best dealt with separately, through cash forecasting.

(e)   **Cash flows**

Unlike the other traditional methods it uses cash flows, rather than profits, and so is less likely to produce an unduly optimistic figure distorted by assorted accounting conventions which might permit certain costs to be carried forward and not affect profit initially.

3.5   Weaknesses of payback method

(a)   **Project returns may be ignored**

Cash flows arising after the payback period are totally ignored. Payback ignores profitability and concentrates on cash flows and liquidity.

(b)   **Timing ignored**

Cash flows are effectively categorised as pre-payback or post-payback – but no more accurate measure is made. In particular, the time value of money is ignored.

(c)   **Lack of objectivity**

There is no objective measure as to what length of time should be set as the minimum payback period. Investment decisions are therefore subjective.

(d)   **Project profitability is ignored**

Payback takes no account of the effects on business profits and periodic performance of the project, as evidenced in the financial statements. This is critical if the business is to be reasonably viewed by users of the accounts.

CONCLUSION

Payback is best seen as an initial screening tool – for example a business might set a rule that no project with a payback of more than five years is to be considered.

It is an appropriate measure for relatively straightforward projects e.g. those which involve an initial outlay followed by constant long-term receipts.

However in spite of its weaknesses and limitations the payback period is a useful most initial screening method of investment appraisal. It is normally used in conjunction with another method of capital investment appraisal, such as the NPV or IRR methods of discounted cash flow analysis.

4   Time value of money and DCF

Money is invested to earn a profit. For example, if an item of equipment costs £80,000 and would earn cash profits (profits ignoring depreciation) of £20,000 each year for four years, it would not be worth buying. This is because the total profit over four years (£80,000) would only just cover its cost.

Capital investments must make enough profits to justify their costs. In addition, the size of the profits or return must be large enough to make the investment worthwhile. In the example above, if the equipment costing £80,000 made total returns of £82,000 over four years, the total return on the investment would be £2,000, or an average of £500 per year. This would be a very low return on an investment of £80,000. More money could be earned putting the £80,000 on deposit with a bank to earn interest.

If a capital investment is to be justified, it needs to earn at least a minimum amount of profit, so that the return compensates the investor for both the amount invested and also for the *length* of time before the profits are made. For example, if a company could invest £80,000 now to earn revenue of £82,000 in one week's time, a profit of £2,000 in seven days would be a very good return. However, if it takes four years to earn the money, the return would be very low.

Money has a time value. By this we mean that it can be invested to earn interest or profits, so it is better to have £1 now than in one year's time. This is because £1 now can be invested for the next year to earn a return, whereas £1 in one year's time cannot. Another way of looking at the time value of money is to say that £1 in six years' time is worth less than £1 now. Similarly, £1 in five years' time is worth less than £1 now, but is worth more than £1 after six years.

DCF is an capital expenditure appraisal technique that takes into account the time value of money.

4.1   Discounted cash flow (DCF)

Discounted cash flow, or DCF, is an investment appraisal technique that takes into account both the timing of cash flows and also the total cash flows over a project's life.

- As with the payback method, DCF analysis is based on future cash flows, not accounting profits or losses.

- The timing of cash flows is taken into account by discounting them to a 'present value'. The effect of discounting is to give a higher value to each £1 of cash flows that occur earlier and a lower value to each £1 of cash flows occurring later in the project's life. £1 earned after one year will be worth more than £1 earned after two years, which in turn will be worth more than £1 earned after five years, and so on. Cash flows that occur in different years are re-stated on a common basis, at their present value.

Discounting was introduced in the previous chapter.

4.2   Discount factors and discount tables

A present value for a future cash flow is calculated by multiplying the future cash flow by a factor:

$$\frac{1}{1+r^{n}}$$

Check that you know how to do this on your calculator.

For example:

$$\frac{1}{1.10} = 0.909$$

$$\frac{1}{1.10^{2}} = 0.826$$

$$\frac{1}{1.10^{3}} = 0.751$$

However, there are tables that give you a list of these 'discount factors' without you having to do the calculation yourself.

To calculate a present value for a future cash flow, you simply multiply the future cash flow by the appropriate discount factor.

Any cash flows that take place 'now' (at the start of the project) take place in Year 0. The discount factor for Year 0 is 1.0, regardless of what the cost of capital is. Cash

flows 'now' therefore do not need to be discounted to a present value equivalent, because they are already at present value.

The cash flows for a project have been estimated as follows:

Year	£
0	(25,000)
1	6,000
2	10,000
3	8,000
4	7,000

The cost of capital is 6%. Discount factors at a cost of capital of 6% are:

Year	Discount factor at 6%
1	0.943
2	0.890
3	0.840
4	0.792

Required:

Convert these cash flows to a present value.

Add up the total of the present values for each of the years.

Feedback to this activity is at the end of the chapter.

4.3   The cost of capital

The cost of capital used by a business in DCF analysis is the cost of funds for the business. It is therefore the minimum return that the business should make from its own investments, to earn the cash flows out of which it can pay interest pr profits to its own providers of funds.

For the purpose of this text, the cost of capital is assumed to be a known figure.

5   Net present value method (NPV)

The **net present value** or **NPV** method of DCF analysis is to calculate a net present value for a proposed investment project. The NPV is the value obtained by discounting all the cash outflows and inflows for the project capital at the cost of capital, and adding them up. Cash outflows are negative and inflows are positive values. The sum of the present value of all the cash flows from the project is the 'net' present value amount.

The NPV is the sum of the present value (PV) of all the cash inflows from a project minus the PV of all the cash outflows.

- **If the NPV is positive**, it means that the cash inflows from a capital investment will yield a return in excess of the cost of capital. The project therefore seems financially attractive.

- **If the NPV is negative**, it means that the cash inflows from a capital investment will yield a return below the cost of capital. From a financial perspective, the project is therefore unattractive.

- **If the NPV is exactly zero**, the cash inflows from a capital investment will yield a return exactly equal to the cost of capital. The project is therefore just about financially attractive.

Example

Rug Limited is considering a capital investment in new equipment. The estimated cash flows are as follows.

Year	Cash flow
	£
0	(240,000)
1	80,000
2	120,000
3	70,000
4	40,000
5	20,000

The company's cost of capital is 9%.

Task

Calculate the NPV of the project to assess whether it should be undertaken.

The following are discount factors for a 9% cost of capital.

Year	Discount factor at 9%
1	0.917
2	0.842
3	0.772
4	0.708
5	0.650

Solution

Year	Cash flow	Discount factor at 9%	Present value
	£		£
0	(240,000)	1.000	(240,000)
1	80,000	0.917	73,360
2	120,000	0.842	101,040
3	70,000	0.772	54,040
4	40,000	0.708	28,320
5	20,000	0.650	13,000
Net present value			+ 29,760

The PV of cash inflows exceeds the PV of cash outflows by £29,760, which means that the project will earn a DCF return in excess of 9%. It should therefore be undertaken.

ACTIVITY 5

Fylingdales Fabrication is considering investing in a new delivery vehicle which will make savings over the current out-sourced service.

The cost of the vehicle is £35,000 and it will have a five-year life.

The savings it will make over the period are:

Cash flow:

	£
Yr 1	8,000
2	9,000
3	12,000
4	9,500
5	9,000

The firm currently has a return of 12% and this is considered to be its cost of capital.

Discount factors at 12%.

Yr 1	0.893
2	0.797
3	0.721
4	0.636
5	0.458

Required:

Calculate the NPV of the investment.

On the basis of the NPV you have calculated, recommend whether or not the investment should go ahead.

Feedback to this activity is at the end of the chapter.

5.1 Assumptions in DCF about the timing of cash flows

In DCF, certain assumptions are made about the timing of cash flows in each year of a project.

- A cash outlay at the beginning of an investment project ('now') occurs in year 0.

- A cash flows that occurs **during the course of a year** is assumed to occur all at once at the end of the year. For example, profits of £30,000 in Year 3 would be assumed to occur at the end of Year 3.

- If a cash flow occurs **at the beginning of a year**, it is assumed that the cash flow happens at the end of the previous year. For example, a cash outlay of £10,000 at the beginning of Year 2 would be treated as a cash flow in Year 1, occurring at the end of Year 1.

5.2 Investment in working capital

Some capital projects involve an investment in working capital as well as fixed assets. Working capital should be considered to consist of investments in stocks and debtors, minus trade creditors.

An investment in working capital slows up the receipt of cash. For example, suppose that a business buys an item for £10 for cash and resells it for £16. It has made a cash profit of £6 on the deal. However, if the item is sold for £16 on credit, the cash flow is different. Although the profit is £6, the business is actually £10 worse off for cash. This is because it has invested £16 in debtors (working capital).

An increase in working capital reduces cash flows and a reduction in working capital improves the cash flow in the year that it happens.

By convention, in DCF analysis, if a project will require an investment in working capital, the investment is treated as a cash outflow at the beginning of the year in which it occurs. The working capital is eventually released at the end of the project, when it becomes a cash inflow. (It is treated as a cash inflow because actual cash flows will exceed cash profits in the year by the amount of the reduction in working capital.)

Example

A company is considering whether to invest in a project to buy an item of equipment for £40,000. The project would require an investment of £8,000 in working capital. The cash profits from the project would be:

Year	Cash profit
	£
1	15,000
2	20,000
3	12,000
4	7,000

The equipment would have a resale value of £5,000 at the end of Year 4.

The cost of capital is 10%. Discount factors at 10% are:

Year	
1	0.909
2	0.826
3	0.751
4	0.683

Task

Calculate the NPV of the project and recommend whether or not, on financial grounds, you would recommend that the project should be undertaken.

Solution

Year	Equipt	Working capital	Cash profit	Total cash flow	Discount factor at 10%	Present value
	£	£	£	£		£
0	(40,000)	(8,000)		(48,000)	1.000	(48,000)
1			15,000	15,000	0.909	13,635
2			20,000	20,000	0.826	16,520
3			12,000	12,000	0.751	9,012
4	5,000	8,000	7,000	20,000	0.683	13,660
						+ 4,827

The NPV is positive, and from a financial perspective should therefore be undertaken.

6   Internal rate of return method (IRR)

Using the NPV method of discounted cash flow, present values are calculated by discounting cash flows at a given cost of capital, and the difference between the PV of costs and the PV of benefits is the NPV. In contrast, the **internal rate of return (IRR)** method of DCF analysis is to calculate the exact DCF rate of return that the project is expected to achieve. This is the cost of capital at which the NPV is zero.

If the expected rate of return (known as the internal rate of return or IRR, and also as the DCF yield) is higher than a target rate of return, the project is financially worth undertaking.

Calculating the IRR of a project can be done with a programmed calculator. Otherwise, it has to be estimated using a rather laborious technique called the interpolation method. The interpolation method produces an estimate of the IRR, although it is not arithmetically exact.

For a project with uneven cash flows, the IRR may be **approximated** by a formula which assumes a **linear relationship** between NPV and discount rate.

Graph of NPV v discount rate (showing non-linearity)

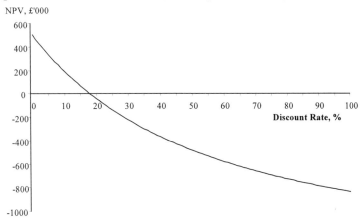

The steps in this method are as follows.

Step 1   Calculate two net present values for the project at two different costs of capital. You should decide which costs of capital to use. However, you want to find two costs of capital for which the NPV is close to 0, because the IRR will be a value close to them. Ideally, you should use one cost of capital where the NPV is positive and the other cost of capital where the NPV is negative, although this is not essential.

Step 2   Having found two costs of capital where the NPV is close to 0, we can then estimate the cost of capital at which the NPV is 0. In other words, we can estimate the IRR. This estimating technique is illustrated in the example below.

Example

A company is trying to decide whether to buy a machine for £13,500. The machine will create annual cash savings as follows.

Year	£
1	5,000
2	8,000
3	3,000

Task

Calculate the project's IRR.

Solution

Step 1   The first step is to calculate the NPV of the project at two different costs of capital. Ideally the NPV should be positive at one cost of capital and negative at the other.

So what costs of capital should we try?

One way of making a guess is to look at the profits from the project over its life. These are £16,000 over the three years. After deducting the capital expenditure of £13,500, this gives us a net return of £2,500, or an average of £833 each year of the project. £833 is about 6% of the capital outlay. The IRR is actually likely to be a bit higher than this, so we could start by trying 7%, 8% or 9%.

Here, 8% is used.

Year	Cash flow	Discount factor at 8%	PV
	£		£
0	(13,500)	1.000	(13,500)
1	5,000	0.926	4,630
2	8,000	0.857	6,856
3	3,000	0.794	2,382
			+ 368

The NPV is positive at 8%, so the IRR is higher than this. We need to find the NPV at a higher cost of capital. Let's try 11%.

Year	Cash flow	Discount factor at 11%	PV
	£		£
0	(13,500)	1.000	(13,500)
1	5,000	0.901	4,505
2	8,000	0.812	6,496
3	3,000	0.731	2,193
			(306)

The NPV is negative at 11%, so the IRR lies somewhere between 8% and 11%.

Step 2   The next step is to use the two NPV figures we have calculated to estimate the IRR.

We know that the NPV is + 368 at 8% and that it is - 306 at 11%.

Between 8% and 11%, the NPV therefore falls by 674 (368 + 306).

If we assume that the decline in NPV occurs in a straight line, we can estimate that the IRR must be:

$$8\% = \left[\frac{368}{674} \times (11-8)\% \right]$$

$$= 8\% + 1.6\% = 9.6\%.$$

An estimated IRR is therefore 9.6%.

6.1   Formula for calculating IRR

You might find the following formula for calculating the IRR useful.

If the NPV at A% is positive, + £P

and if the NPV at B% is negative, - £N

then

$$IRR = A\% \left[\frac{P}{(P+N)} \times (B+A)\% \right]$$

Ignore the minus sign for the negative NPV. For example, if P = + 60 and N = - 50, then P + N = 110.

Another example

A business undertakes high-risk investments and requires a minimum expected rate of return of 17% on its investments. A proposed capital investment has the following expected cash flows.

Year	£
0	(50,000)
1	18,000
2	25,000
3	20,000
4	10,000

Tasks

1   Calculate the NPV of the project if the cost of capital is 15%.

2   Calculate the NPV of the project if the cost of capital is 20%.

3   Use the NPVs you have calculated to estimate the IRR of the project.

4   Recommend, on financial grounds alone, whether this project should go ahead.

Discount factors:

Year	Discount factor at	
	15%	20%
1	0.870	0.833
2	0.756	0.694
3	0.658	0.579
4	0.572	0.482

Solution

Year	Cash flow	Discount factor at 15%	Present value at 15%	Discount factor at 20%	Present value at 20%
	£		£		£
0	(50,000)	1.000	(50,000)	1.000	(50,000)
1	18,000	0.870	15,660	0.833	14,994
2	25,000	0.756	18,900	0.694	17,350
3	20,000	0.658	13,160	0.579	11,580
4	10,000	0.572	5,720	0.482	4,820
NPV			+ 3,440		(1,256)

The IRR is above 15% but below 20%.

Using the interpolation method:

The NPV is + 3,440 at 15%.

The NPV is – 1,256 at 20%.

The NPV falls by 4,696 between 15% and 20%.

The estimated IRR is therefore:

$$IRR = 15\% + \left[\frac{3,440}{4,696} \times (20-15)\% \right]$$

$$= 15\% + 3.7\%$$

$$= 18.7\%$$

Recommendation

The project is expected to earn a DCF return in excess of the target rate of 17%, so (ignoring risk) on financial grounds it is a worthwhile investment.

6.2 IRR of even annual cash flows

A simpler approach can be used to find the IRR of simple projects in which the annual cash inflows are equal (as with the previous example). The IRR can be found via a cumulative discount factor, as the following exercise with the Thomson machine project shows.

NPV calculation

Time		Cash flow £'000	Discount Factor (c) %	Present Value £'000
0	Investment	(1,500)	1	(1,500)
1 – 3	Inflow	700	(b)	(a)
Net present value (£'000)				NIL

The aim is to find the discount rate (c) that produces an NPV of nil; therefore the PV of inflows (a) must equal the PV of outflows, £1,500,000. If the PV of inflows (a) is to be £1,500,000 and the size of each inflow is £700,000, the discount factor required must be 1,500,000 ÷ 700,000 = 2.143. The discount rate (c) for which this is the 3 year factor can be found by looking along the 3 year row of the cumulative discount factors shown **in the annuity table**. The figure of 2.140 appears under the 19% column suggesting an IRR of 19% is the closest.

The necessary procedure for exam purposes can be summarised as follows:

Step 1 – Find the cumulative discount factor, $\dfrac{\text{Initial investment}}{\text{Annual inflow}}$.

 FOULKS LYNCH PUBLICATIONS

Step 2 – Find the life of the project, n.

Step 3 – Look along the n year row of the cumulative discount factors till the closest value is found.

Step 4 – The column in which this figure appears is the IRR.

6.3   IRR of perpetuities

Just as it is possible to calculate the PV of a perpetuity so it is a simple matter to find the IRR of a project with equal annual inflows that are expected to be received for an indefinitely long period.

The IRR of a perpetuity $= \dfrac{\text{Annual inflow}}{\text{Initial investment}} \times 100$

This can be seen by looking at the formula for the PV of a perpetuity and considering the definition of internal rate of return.

Example

Find the IRR of an investment that costs £20,000 and generates £1,600 for an indefinitely long period.

$$\text{IRR} = \frac{\text{Annual inflow}}{\text{Initial investment}} \times 100 = \frac{£1,600}{£20,000} \times 100 = 8\%$$

Conclusion

This chapter lays the foundations for your studies of capital expenditure and investment. Whilst much of it may appear familiar, do make sure you are completely happy with these basics before moving on. In particular, be prepared to discuss the role that non-DCF techniques play, despite their theoretical drawbacks.

Return on capital employed (ROCE)

1   Define the accounting rate of return for a capital project (2)

2   What are relevant costs? (2.5)

Payback method of appraisal

3   What is the payback period for a project? (3.1)

4   What are the merits and disadvantages of using the payback method? (3.4, 3.5)

Time value of money and DCF

5   What is the time value of money? (4)

6   What is the formula for calculating the discount factor for year n when the cost of capital (expressed as a proportion) is r? (4.2)

Net present value method (NPV)

7   What is meant by the NPV of a capital project? (5)

8   What assumptions are used in DCF about the timing of cash flows? (5.1)

Internal rate of return method (IRR)

9   What is the IRR of an investment project? (6)

10   What formula should be used to estimate an IRR using the interpolation method? (6.1)

EXAM-TYPE
QUESTION

Basics

Basics Limited is considering whether to invest £90,000 in the purchase of a new item of equipment. The equipment would be paid for with a down-payment of £60,000 and the payment of the remaining £30,000 six weeks later. The company has already spent £8,000 on design and feasibility work, and the operational management team are keen to purchase the equipment quickly.

The equipment is expected to have a life of three years, after which time it should have a resale value of £5,000. The equipment will be depreciated by the straight-line method over three years. It has been estimated that an investment of £20,000 in working capital will be needed.

As a result of acquiring the equipment, it is expected that there will be an increase in annual cash profits, as follows:

Year	£
1	£37,000
2	£48,000
3	£26,000

Required:

(a)   Calculate the expected NPV of the investment, if the cost of capital is 8%.

(b)   Calculate the expected IRR of the investment, using the interpolation method and taking 12% as the cost of capital for calculating another NPV.

(7 marks)

(**Note**: The requirements of this question do not make up a full 25-mark question, but it is essential that you should be able to do these calculations confidently and correctly.)

For the answer to this question, see the 'Answers' section at the end of the book.

FEEDBACK TO
ACTIVITY 1

This uses **profits** rather than cash flows.

Average annual inflows = £1,750,000 ÷ 7 = £250,000

Average annual depreciation = (£800,000 – £100,000) ÷ 7 = £100,000

(A net £700,000 is being written off as depreciation over 7 years.)

Average annual profit = £250,000 – £100,000 = £150,000

The average capital invested is (800,000 + 100,000)/2 = £450,000

(a)   ROCE = $\dfrac{\text{Average annual profit}}{\text{Initial investment}} \times 100 = \dfrac{£150,000}{£800,000} \times 100 = 18.75\%$

(b)   ROCE = $\dfrac{\text{Average annual profit}}{\text{Average investment}} \times 100 = \dfrac{£150,000}{£450,000} \times 100 = 33.33\%$

FOULKS LYNCH
PUBLICATIONS

FEEDBACK TO ACTIVITY 2	The £15,000 already spent on the feasibility study is not relevant, because it has already been spent. (It is a 'sunk cost'.) Depreciation and apportioned fixed overheads are not relevant. Depreciation is not a cash flow and apportioned fixed overheads represent costs that will be incurred anyway.

	£
Estimated profit	8,000
Add back depreciation	40,000
Add back apportioned fixed costs	25,000
	———
Annual cash flows	73,000
	———

The project's cash flows to be evaluated are

Year		£
Now (Year 0)	Purchase equipment	(160,000)
1 - 4	Cash flow from profits	73,000 each year

FEEDBACK TO ACTIVITY 3

The payback period would be calculated as follows.

Year	Cash flow	Cumulative cash flow
	£000	£000
0	(3,100)	(3,100)
1	1,000	(2,100)
2	900	(1,200)
3	800	(400)
4	500	100
5	500	600

Payback is between the end of year 3 and the end of year 4 – in other words during year 4.

If we assume a constant rate of cash flow through the year, we could estimate that payback will be three years, plus (400/500) of year 4, which is 3.8 years.

0.8 years = 10 months (0.8 × 12)

We could therefore estimate that payback would be after 3 years 10 months.

FEEDBACK TO ACTIVITY 4

Year	Cash flow	Discount factor at 6%	Present value
	£		£
0	(25,000)	1.000	(25,000)
1	6,000	0.943	5,658
2	10,000	0.890	8,900
3	8,000	0.840	6,720
4	7,000	0.792	5,544
			———
			+ 1,822
			———

+ £1,822 is in fact the net present value of the project.

DCF Schedule (NPV method)

Discount rate 12%

Year	Outflow	Inflow	Discount factor at 12%	NPV
	£	£		£
0	(30,000)		1.000	(35,000)
1		8,000	0.893	7,144
2		9,000	0.797	7,173
3		12,000	0.712	8,544
4		9,500	0.636	6,042
5		9,000	0.568	5,112
			NPV	(985)

Recommendation

At the cost of capital of 12%, the NPV is negative, showing that the investment would earn a return below 12% per annum. On financial considerations, the recommendation is that the project should not be undertaken.

Chapter 13
FURTHER ASPECTS OF DCF

Having looked at the basics of discounted cash flow techniques, we now go on to look at cash flows in more detail, incorporating relevant cost principles, and the effects of taxation and inflation. We shall also discuss the potential conflict between NPV and IRR as criteria for investment decisions, and how public enterprises and other non-profit making organisations may approach their investment appraisal.

Objectives

By the time you have finished this chapter you should be able to do the following:

- explain the relationship between inflation and interest rates, distinguishing between real and nominal rates

- distinguish general inflation from specific price increases and assess their impact on cash flows

- evaluate capital investment projects on a real terms basis

- evaluate capital investment projects on a nominal terms basis

- calculate the effect of capital allowances and Corporation Tax on project cash flows

- evaluate the profitability of capital investment projects on a post-tax basis.

1   Relevant cash flows

1.1   Why evaluate cash flows rather than profits?

- Cash is what ultimately counts – profits are only a guide to cash availability: they cannot actually be spent.

- Profit measurement is subjective – the time period in which income and expenses are recorded, and so on, are a matter of judgement.

- Cash is used to pay dividends – dividends are the ultimate method of transferring wealth to equity shareholders.

In practice, the cash flow effects of a project are likely to be similar to the project's effects on profits. Major differences in cash and profit flows will be linked to the following

- changes in working capital

- asset purchase and depreciation

- deferred taxation

- capitalisation of research and development expenditure.

1.2   Determining relevant cash flows

The **relevant cash flows** are the **future incremental cash flows** of the organisation as a whole which arise as a result of the project's acceptance.

When deciding the amounts to be included in a DCF computation, it sometimes helps to tabulate the following for each cost/revenue element.

Cash flow if project accepted – Cash flow if project rejected = Relevant cash flow

In particular the following points should be noted.

- **Consider all alternatives** – questions will often ask for either project A or project B to be accepted. In these cases one or the other will generally be preferred. However, there are often other, still better, options available – sometimes simply doing nothing. These options should also be considered.

- **Identify 'sunk costs'** – money already spent or committed is irrelevant to the decision. We are concerned only with future cash flows.

- **Identify opportunity costs** – existing resources used should be included at their economic or opportunity cost, which is the cost incurred as a result of diverting the resource from its next best available use to the project under review. For example, if a project occupies premises which could otherwise be let at £1,000 pa, then that £1,000 could be regarded as a comparative cash outflow (in fact it is a cash inflow forgone).

- **Interest payments** – since the analysis is based on discounting, it would be double counting to include the interest payments on the finance used to fund the project in the cash flows. Interest payments arise because money has a time value and it is precisely this time value which discounting and compounding is designed to account for. The only exception is when appraising leasing or hire-purchase agreements. Tax relief on interest payments should also be ignored.

- **Dividend payments** – represent appropriation of the benefits of project acceptance rather than a relevant element in its appraisal. Incremental dividend cash flows should thus be ignored.

- **Taxation payments** – these are a cash outflow when they are paid. Capital allowances or tax losses may be treated as cash receipts at the point in time when they reduce a tax payment. This will be covered in more depth later in this chapter.

- **Scrap or terminal proceeds** – where any equipment used in a project is scrapped, the proceeds are a cash inflow.

- **Accounting treatment of costs** is often irrelevant (e.g. depreciation, stock valuation, methods of allocating overheads) because it has no bearing on cash flows, except to the extent that it may affect taxation payable. Overheads attributed to projects should, in the examination, be taken as absorbed figures unless specified otherwise. It should be assumed there is no change to actual overhead paid, and thus no relevant cash flow.

1.3 Comparing projects – differential cash flows

When deciding between two projects, only one of which can be accepted (i.e. mutually exclusive projects), two approaches are possible:

- discount the cash flows of each project **separately** and compare NPVs
- find the **differential** (or **incremental**) cash flow year by year, i.e. the **difference** between the cash flows of the two projects. Then use the discounted value of those differential cash flows to establish a preference.

Either approach will lead to the same conclusion.

Example

Two projects, A and B, are under consideration. Either A or B, but not both, may be accepted. The relevant discount rate is 10%.

You are required to recommend A or B by:

(a) discounting each cash flow separately; and

(b) discounting relative (incremental or differential) cash flows.

KEY POINT

Resources used should be included at their **economic or opportunity cost**, the benefit foregone from their next best use.

KEY POINT

Examples of costs that are **irrelevant** to DCF appraisals are depreciation, apportioned overheads, book values of assets, sunk costs, interest and dividends.

 FOULKS LYNCH PUBLICATIONS

The cash flows are as follows:

Time £	Project A £	Project B £
0	(1,500)	(2,500)
1	500	500
2	600	800
3	700	1,100
4	500	1,000
5	Nil	500

Solution

(a) *Discounting each cash flow separately*

Time	PV factor at 10%	[Project A] Cash flow £	PV £	[Project B] Cash flow £	PV £
0	1.000	(1,500)	(1,500)	(2,500)	(2,500)
1	0.909	500	455	500	455
2	0.826	600	496	800	661
3	0.751	700	526	1,100	826
4	0.683	500	341	1,000	683
5	0.621	Nil	Nil	500	310
NPV			318		435

Project B is preferred because its NPV exceeds that of A by £(435 – 318) = £117.

(b) *Discounting relative cash flows*

Time	Project A	Project B	Incremental cash flow B – A	PV factor at 10%	PV of incremental cash flow
0	(1,500)	(2,500)	(1,000)	1.000	(1,000)
1	500	500	Nil	0.909	Nil
2	600	800	200	0.826	165
3	700	1,100	400	0.751	300
4	500	1,000	500	0.683	341
5	Nil	500	500	0.621	311
NPV of incremental cash flow					117

In other words, the present value of the cash flows of project B are £117 greater than those of project A. B is preferred. Note the result is exactly the same in (a) and (b). This gives a useful short cut to computation when comparing two projects **as long as it is known in advance that one of the projects must be undertaken**. However, where this is not the case, care should be taken with the 'differential' approach or the technique may result in acceptance of a project with a negative NPV (the other project having a larger negative NPV).

ACTIVITY **1**

Smith Ltd has decided to increase its productive capacity to meet an anticipated increase in demand for its products. The extent of this increase in capacity has still to be determined, and a management meeting has been called to decide which of the following two mutually exclusive proposals – A and B – should be undertaken.

The following information is available.

	Proposal A £	Proposal B £
Capital expenditure:		
Buildings	50,000	100,000
Plant	200,000	300,000
Installation	10,000	15,000
Net income:		
Annual pre-depreciation profits (note (i))	70,000	95,000
Other relevant income/expenditure:		
Sales promotion (note (ii))	-	15,000
Plant scrap value	10,000	15,000
Buildings disposable value (note (iii))	30,000	60,000
Working capital required over the project life	50,000	65,000

Notes:

(i)   The investment life is ten years.

(ii)   An exceptional amount of expenditure on sales promotion of £15,000 will have to be spent in year two of proposal B. This has not been taken into account in calculating pre-depreciation profits.

(iii) It is the intention to dispose of the buildings in ten years' time.

Using an 8% discount rate, you are required to evaluate the two alternatives. State any assumptions you have made.

Feedback to this activity is at the end of the chapter.

ACTIVITY **2**

An investment in an item of equipment would cost £75,000. It is estimated that sales in the first year would be £60,000, rising by 5% a year for the next four years. Variable costs would be 50% of sales, annual fixed costs would be £20,000 in the first three years, rising to £30,000 in years 4 and 5. Of these fixed costs 40% would be avoidable if the project did not go ahead. The scrap value of the equipment at the end of year 5 would be £5,000. The project would also require an investment in working capital of £15,000 at the start of year 1 rising to £20,000 at the start of year 2 and to £25,000 at the start if year 4.

The company's cost of capital is 9%.

Required:

Calculate the NPV of the project and suggest whether it should be undertaken.

Assume that tax on profits is payable in the year that the profits arise.

Feedback to this activity is at the end of the chapter.

DEFINITION

Inflation may be defined as a general **increase in prices**, leading to a general **decline in the real value of money**.

2   DCF and inflation

Since capital investments provide a return over a period of several years, it might be important to consider the likely effect of inflation in costs and prices on the financial viability of an investment.

Inflation may be defined as a general **increase in prices**, leading to a general **decline in the real value of money**.

There will be two impacts of inflation on DCF project appraisal as follows:

- the **discount rate** given may include an allowance for a general rate of inflation
- the **cash flows** may be subject to inflation, possibly at different rates for different flows.

2.1 Effect of inflation on the discount rate

The discount rate used in investment appraisal reflects the finance providers' required rate of return (e.g. the rate of interest on a loan raised, or shareholders' required return if financed by equity).

In times of inflation, the fund providers will require a return made up of two elements.

- A return to compensate for **inflation** (to maintain purchasing power)
- A **real return** on top of this for the use of their funds.

The required return that incorporates both of these elements is known as a **money return**.

Example

An investor is prepared to invest £100 for one year. He requires a real return of 10%, in addition to an allowance for inflation, currently running at 5%.

Just to compensate for inflation, his money needs to increase by 5%, to £100 × 1.05 = £105.

To give a real return on top of this, it must further increase by 10%, to £105 × 1.1 = £115.5.

Thus his money must increase overall by 1.05 × 1.1 = 1.155 i.e. by **15.5%, the money rate of return.**

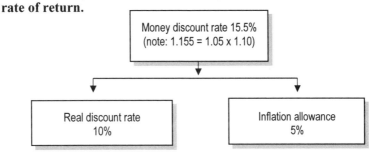

KEY POINT

The required return that incorporates both of these elements is known as a **money return**.

KEY POINT

Money discount rates (m) and cash flows **include the effect of inflation** (i).

Real discount rates (r) and cash flows **exclude the effect of inflation.**

ACTIVITY 3

Consider the level of interest rates current at the time that you are reading this. How much of the money interest rate is the real interest rate and how much the effects of inflation?

Feedback to this activity is at the end of the chapter.

2.2 Including inflation in DCF appraisals

DCF analysis can take place in either money or real terms, as long as the two are not muddled.

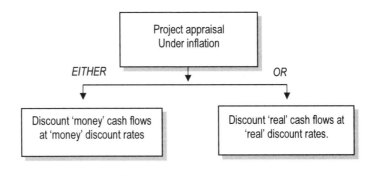

KEY POINT

DCF analysis can take place in either money or real terms, as long as the two are not muddled.

You may obtain 'real' rates of return using the following equation:

$$(1 + r) = \frac{(1 + m)}{(1 + i)}$$

where r is the real discount rate

m is the money discount rate

i is the inflation rate

Discounting real cash flows at a 'real' discount rate will only work if the same rate of inflation affects all cash flows and is equal to the rate incorporated into the money required return.

You may obtain real rates of return using the following equation:

$$(1+r) = \frac{(1+m)}{(1+i)}$$

where r is the real discount rate

m is the money discount rate

i is the inflation rate

In the last example:

$$(1+r) = \frac{(1+0.155)}{(1+0.05)} = 1.1,\text{ giving the real rate of return as 10\%.}$$

Example

A project has the following cash flows before allowing for inflation.

Year	Cash flow £
0	(750)
1	330
2	242
3	532

These are not, therefore, the flows expected if all figures grow in line with general inflation rates.

The money discount rate is 15.5%. The general rate of inflation is expected to remain constant at 5%.

You are required to evaluate the project in terms of:

(a) real cash flows and discount rates
(b) money cash flows and discount rates.

Solution

(a) *Real cash flows and discount rates*

Discount rate as per the question of 15.5% includes investor's/lender's inflation expectation of 5%. Hence 'real' discount rate, r, is given by:

$$1+r = \frac{1+m}{1+i}$$

$$1+r = \frac{1+0.155}{1+0.05} = 1.10$$

∴ r is 0.10 or 10%

Year	Cash flow £	PV factor @ 10%	Present value £
0	(750)	1.000	(750)
1	330	0.909	300
2	242	0.826	200
3	532	0.751	400
Net present value			150

(b)   *Money cash flows and discount rates*

The discount rate as per the question of 15.5% is the money discount rate. Cash flows, however, need to be increased by 5% compound each year from year 0, to allow for inflation.

Year	Real cash flow	Inflation factor	Money cash flow	Discount factor @ 15.5%	Present value
(i)	*(ii)*	*(iii)*	*(iv)* = *(ii)* × *(iii)*		
	£		£		
0	(750)	1	(750)	1.000	(750)
1	330	$1 + 0.05$	346	0.866	300
2	242	$(1 + 0.05)^2$	267	0.750	200
3	532	$(1 + 0.05)^3$	616	0.649	400
Net present value					150

Provided a constant rate of inflation applies to all factors, **either approach** yields identical conclusions (allowing for rounding).

2.3   Different rates of inflation for costs and revenues

In practice, inflation does not affect all costs to the same extent. Some may increase at above and some below the 'average' rate of inflation. Clearly, in relation to a given project, such variations are important and must be taken into account. This is much more easily dealt with by using money cash flows and discount rates.

Example

A company is considering a cost-saving project. This involves purchasing a machine costing £7,000, which will result in annual savings on wage costs of £1,000 and on material costs of £400.

The following forecasts are made of the rates of inflation each year for the next five years:

Wage costs	10%
Material costs	5%
General prices	6%

The cost of capital of the company, in money terms, is 15%.

Evaluate the project, assuming that the machine has a life of five years and no scrap value.

Solution

The first stage is to calculate money cash savings each year.

Year	Labour cash savings		Material cash savings		Total savings
	£	£	£	£	£
1	$1,000 \times 1.1$	1,100	400×1.05	420	1,520
2	$1,000 \times (1.1)^2$	1,210	$400 \times (1.05)^2$	441	1,651
3	$1,000 \times (1.1)^3$	1,331	$400 \times (1.05)^3$	463	1,794
4	$1,000 \times (1.1)^4$	1,464	$400 \times (1.05)^4$	486	1,950
5	$1,000 \times (1.1)^5$	1,610	$400 \times (1.05)^5$	510	2,120

Next evaluate the net present value.

Year	Cash flow £	PV factor @ 15%	PV of cash flow £
0	(7,000)	1.000	(7,000)
1	1,520	0.870	1,322
2	1,651	0.756	1,248
3	1,794	0.658	1,180
4	1,950	0.572	1,115
5	2,120	0.497	1,054
Net present value			(1,081)

Therefore the project is not worthwhile.

Note: the general rate of inflation has not been used in, and is irrelevant to, this calculation.

3   DCF and taxation

Taxation also has two major effects on DCF project appraisal.

- **Project cash flows will give rise to taxation** which itself has an impact on project appraisal. There will be differences between the cash flows earned and the level of profits on which the payment of taxation is based, particularly as regards capital expenditure, but in general cash receipts/payments will give rise to tax payable/relief.

- **Tax relief on interest payments** will reduce the effective rate of interest which a firm pays on its borrowings, and hence the opportunity cost of capital.

3.1   Incorporating taxation into DCF appraisals

The effects of taxation are complex, and are influenced by a number of factors including the following.

- the taxable profits and tax rate
- the company's accounting period and tax payment dates
- capital allowances
- losses available for set-off.

Whenever tax is relevant to an appraisal, **careful reading** of the question re tax rates, timings and capital allowances is essential. You must also state any assumptions.

Unless information is given to the contrary, the following assumptions should be adopted in the examination.

- taxable profits are the net project cash flows
- the current tax rate applies
- where a tax loss arises from the project, there are sufficient taxable profits elsewhere in the organisation to allow the loss to reduce any relevant (subsequent) tax payment (and thus may be treated as a cash inflow)
- the first capital allowance claim is immediate, with the first benefit one year later
- the company has sufficient taxable profits to obtain full benefit from capital allowances, and there are balancing adjustments on the disposal of all assets.

The timing of taxation cash flows

There are two possible assumptions about the timing of extra tax payments (due to higher profits or savings) or lower tax payments (due to losses or capital allowances).

- It could be assumed that the taxation cash flow occurs in the same year as the profit, loss or capital allowance giving rise to the higher or lower tax payment.

- Alternatively, it could be assumed that the taxation cash flow occurs one year after the profit, loss or capital allowance giving rise to the higher or lower tax payment.

There is no firm rule about which assumption should be used. If the tax cash flow occurs just a few months after the profit or loss, it could be assumed that they occur in the same year. If the tax cash flow occurs later, it is more appropriate to assume that it occurs one year in arrears. An examination question ought to state the assumption you should use, but if it doesn't state clearly the assumption you have chosen for your answer.

3.2   Capital allowances and tax cash flows

It is easy to get confused about the effect of capital allowances on taxation cash flows. The basic rules are as follows.

- If a business buys a capital asset in one year and sells it several years later, the total tax relief it will receive is the tax on the cost of the asset less its eventual disposal value. For example, if a business buys equipment for £100,000 in Year 0 and disposes of it in Year 5 for £20,000, it will receive tax relief on the net cost of £80,000. If the rate of corporation tax is 30%, the reduction in tax payments over the five years would be 30% x £80,000 = £24,000.

- Capital allowances are used to work out when the tax relief can be claimed. In other words, how will the reductions in tax payments be spread over the life of the asset?

- Capital allowances are usually calculated on a reducing balance basis each year. There is a capital allowance to claim each year, and the reduction in taxation is the capital allowance multiplied by the tax rate.

- When the asset is eventually disposed of, there is a balancing allowance or a balancing charge:

	£
Original cost of asset	X
Cumulative capital allowances claimed	(X)
Written down value of the asset	X
Disposal value of the asset	(X)
Balancing allowance or charge	X

If the written down value of the asset is more than its actual disposal value, there is a balancing allowance. Tax relief can be claimed on this. For example, suppose that an asset purchased for £100,000 is disposed of, and at the time of its disposal, cumulative capital allowances claimed on the asset over its life have been £68,000. The corporation tax rate is 30%.

- If the asset is disposed of for £20,000, there is a balancing allowance on disposal. The written down value of the asset (for capital allowance purposes) is £32,000, so there is a balancing allowance of £12,000. Since the tax rate is 30%, this will result in a tax saving of £3,600. Another way of looking at this is to say that the net cost of the asset is its original cost less its disposal value of £20,000. The net cost is £80,000, but capital allowances have been just £68,000. A further £12,000 should therefore be allowable.

- If the asset is disposed of for £40,000, there is a balancing charge on disposal. The written down value of the asset is lower than the actual disposal value by £8,000. The balancing charge will result in an additional tax payment of £2,400.

208 FINANCIAL MANAGEMENT AND CONTROL

If you have to work out capital allowances and their effects on tax payments, it helps to create a table of workings, as illustrated in the following example.

Example

A company buys an item of equipment for £160,000 on which capital allowances can be claimed at a reducing balance of 25% each year. The asset is eventually disposed of after five years for £. The rate of corporation tax is 30%.

The capital allowances and tax savings/payments are as follows.

Year	Written down value £	Capital allowance £	Tax saved/ (extra tax paid) at 30% £
0	160,000		
1	40,000	40,000	12,000
	120,000		
2	30,000	30,000	9,000
	90,000		
3	22,500	22,500	6,750
	67,500		
4	16,875	16,875	5,063
	50,625		
5	58,000		
	7,375		(2,213)
			30,600

Over the life of the asset, the net cost of the asset has been £160,000 less the disposal value of £58,000, i.e. £102,000. The total tax saved is 30% of £102,000 = £30,600, spread over the years as shown in the table.

Here, the assumption is that the first tax effect occurs in year 1.

Example

KL Ltd is considering manufacturing a new product. This requires machinery costing £20,000, with a life of four years and a terminal value of £5,000. Profits before depreciation from the project will be £8,000 pa. However, there will be cash flows which will differ from profits by the build-up of working capital during the first year of operations and its run-down during the fourth year, amounting to £2,000.

Tax allowances on the machine are 25% pa reducing balance. At the end of the project's life a balancing charge or allowance will arise equal to the difference between the scrap proceeds and the tax written down value.

Tax is payable one year after the end of the accounting year on which it is based, at a rate of 30%. The start of the project is also the start of the accounting year.

The cost of capital is 15%.

Should the project be accepted?

Solution

It is assumed that the tax on profits is payable one year after the year in which the profits occur. The timing of the tax effects of capital allowances are as shown in the table of workings below.

 FOULKS LYNCH
PUBLICATIONS

Given the wording of the question, it is assumed that the build up of working capital is a Year 1 cash flow, rather than a Year 0 cash flow.

Year	Profit	Working capital	Machine	Tax on profit	Tax saved from cap. allowances	Net cash flow
	£	£	£	£	£	£
0			(20,000)			(20,000)
1	8,000	(2,000)			1,500	7,500
2	8,000			(2,400)	1,125	6,725
3	8,000			(2,400)	844	6,444
4	8,000	2,000	5,000	(2,400)	633	13,233
5				(2,400)	398	(2,002)

Year	Net cash flow	Discount factor at 15%	Present value
	£		£
0	(20,000)	1.000	(20,000)
1	7,500	0.870	6,525
2	6,725	0.756	5,084
3	6,444	0.658	4,240
4	13,233	0.572	7,569
5	(2,002)	0.497	(995)
NPV			+ 2,423

The project is worthwhile.

Workings

Tax effect of capital allowances

Year		Written down value	Capital allowance	Tax saved/ (extra tax paid) at 30%
		£	£	£
0		20,000		
1		5,000	5,000	1,500
		15,000		
2		3,750	3,750	1,125
		11,250		
3		2,813	2,813	844
		8,437		
4		2,109	2,109	633
		6,328		
5	Disposal value	5,000		
	Balancing allowance	1,328		398
	Total tax reduction			4,500

It is assumed that the tax cash flows occur in the years shown in the table.

Note: It is important to remember that **capital allowances** themselves **are not cash flows** and so should not be included in the DCF analysis. The relevance of capital

allowances is in the amount by which **tax payments are reduced** as a result of the allowances.

Here is an example with a balancing charge at the end of the project.

A company is considering an investment in an item of equipment costing £80,000. The equipment would attract a 25% annual writing down allowance. The operating cash flows are forecast as:

		£
Year	1	30,000
	2	40,000
	3	20,000

These estimates do not allow for an investment of £25,000 in working capital that would be required. The project is expected to have a three-year life, at the end of which the equipment would have a sell-off value of £50,000 at the end of year 3. The rate of tax on profits is 30%. The company's cost of capital is 8%.

Required:

Calculate the NPV of the project and suggest whether it should be undertaken.

Feedback to this activity is at the end of this chapter.

4 NPV versus IRR

There are two methods of DCF analysis, the NPV and IRR methods. Which is better to use?

For deciding whether a project should be undertaken or not, both methods usually give the same decision, to invest or not to invest. However, they can give conflicting guidance when a choice has to be made between mutually exclusive projects. In such cases, the NPV method should be used.

4.1 Mutually exclusive investments

Organisations may often face decisions in which only one of two or more investments can be undertaken; these are called mutually exclusive investment decisions.

Example

Barlow Ltd is considering two short-term investment opportunities which they have called project A and project B, and which have the following cash flows:

Time		0	1
Project A (£'000)		(200)	240
Project B (£'000)		(100)	125

Barlow has a cost of capital of 10%. Find the NPVs and IRRs of the two projects.

Solution

		NPV £'000	*IRR* %
Project A:	$(240 \div 1.10) - 200$	18.18	20
Project B:	$(125 \div 1.10) - 100$	13.64	25

The IRRs could be found either by trial and error or by using the formula. It would be easier to notice that project A, over 1 year, earns £40,000 on an investment of £200,000 (a 20% return) whilst project B earns £25,000 on £100,000 (25%).

It can be seen that A has the higher NPV whilst B has the higher IRR – a conflict. How can we explain this?

Which should be used to decide?

The golden rule for deciding between mutually exclusive projects is to **accept the project with the higher NPV:**

- To **maximise shareholder wealth**, i.e. the market value of their shares, we wish to maximise **absolute** return, i.e. NPV. Whilst project B shows a higher **relative** return, it is on a smaller investment, yielding a lower absolute benefit. (It is assumed that you cannot do B twice – for example, A and B may be two different uses of an existing building).

- Project B will give a higher NPV for all discount rates **above 15%** – but this is **irrelevant** to an investor with a 10% discount rate.

- The higher IRR of project B indicates that project B will yield a positive NPV over a **wider range** of discount rates (0-25%) than A (0-20%) and this is therefore useful for **sensitivity analysis** where the discount rate is uncertain.

5 Capital expenditure decisions in non-profit seeking organisations

5.1 Capital budgeting in the public sector

Capital budgeting in the public sector is subject to different and/or additional criteria to those applied in purely commercial operations. The national budget – having been agreed, discussed and voted upon – will determine maximum resources to be allocated in the relevant period to services such as defence, education, health and social security. Sub-divisions of the services may have had to 'bid' for new projects during this process.

It is more likely that the methods described so far in this text will be utilised in choosing between investments at the lower level of decision-making rather than at the higher level. If, say, within a hospital service a choice has to be made between alternative forms of X-ray equipment then this can be done by equating future costs with capital cost to determine the best buy on purely financial criteria.

The bigger decision is likely to be: 'shall we build a new hospital and if so where and to serve what area?'

5.2 The use of cost benefit analysis (CBA)

Public sector investment requires substantial inputs computed in monetary costs but the return from the investment is frequently not directly assessable in monetary terms. These are social costs and benefits and some element of value judgement must be imposed upon them when deciding which project is to have use of the restricted resources available. Cost benefit analysis is a means of assessing the relative desirability of projects when the effects of all factors of time and cost are evaluated, including monetary and non-monetary values.

The political factor

A project may be desired by one political party but not by another. Hence, the degree of support may vary with a change of government.

Any public sector investment decision is subject to political and social factors which make the decision more difficult and uncertain in outcome than decisions in the private sector.

A project (say, a new airport) may be desirable for all political groups, in which case one element of the budgeting problem is removed. The decision then becomes a question of where and how soon.

5.3   The social net present value

Attempts have been made to subject the decision to quantitative analysis. One such method is to compute the social net present value (SNPV).

In principle this follows the computation of NPV in monetary terms (benefits – costs) used previously. The result here however hinges on weighting factors applied to the costs and benefits which are value judgements more open to opinion.

- How large a safety factor is to be built into a bridge construction to have an acceptable risk of collapse – indeed is there an **acceptable** risk of collapse?

- What quality of engineering is to be built into the bridge to avoid subsequent repair and maintenance?

- What is the value per minute saved by a commuter as a result of the new road bridge?

Example

Another London airport is to be built. Certain costs associated with four alternative sites can be determined with reasonable precision. These include the following:

- airport construction costs

- services

- road and rail extensions

- loss of agricultural land.

More subjective amounts might be allocated in respect of impact on residential conditions and schools and any gain or loss accruing to the location concerned as a result of the new traffic flow.

Conclusion

This chapter has looked at particular aspects of the application of DCF techniques. The nature of the cash flows to be included was examined, in terms of relevance, taxation and inflation. The choice between the two methods – NPV and IRR – for investment decisions was discussed, as were the particular problems in investment appraisal facing not-for-profit organisations, including the public sector.

SELF-TEST QUESTIONS	

Relevant cash flows

1   Why do we evaluate capital projects on the basis of forecast cash flows rather than profits? (1.1)

2   In what circumstances might using a differential approach to decide between two projects be misleading? (1.3)

DCF and inflation

3   How is it best to deal with varying inflation rates? (2.3)

DCF and taxation

4   What is the usual assumption about the timing of tax cash flows? (3.1)

Capital expenditure decisions in non-profit seeking organisations

5   What is meant by a social NPV? (5.3)

Breckall plc

You have been appointed finance director of Breckall plc. The company is considering investing in the production of an electronic security device, with an expected market life of five years.

The previous finance director has undertaken an analysis of the proposed project; the main features of her analysis are shown below.

She has recommended that the project should not be undertaken because the estimated annual accounting rate of return is only 12.3%.

Proposed Electronic Security Device Project

	Year 0 £'000	Year 1 £'000	Year 2 £'000	Year 3 £'000	Year 4 £'000	Year 5 £'000
Investment in depreciable fixed assets	4,500					
Cumulative investment in working capital	300	400	500	600	700	700
Sales		3,500	4,900	5,320	5,740	5,320
Materials		535	750	900	1,050	900
Labour		1,070	1,500	1,800	2,100	1,800
Overhead		50	100	100	100	100
Interest		576	576	576	576	576
Depreciation		900	900	900	900	900
		3,131	3,826	4,276	4,726	4,276
Taxable profit		369	1,074	1,044	1,014	1,044
Taxation		129	376	365	355	365
Profit after tax		240	698	679	659	679

Total initial investment is £4,800,000. The average annual after tax profit is £591,000.

All of the above cash flow and profit estimates have been prepared in terms of present day costs and prices, as the previous finance director assumed that the sales price could be increased to compensate for any increase in costs.

You have available the following additional information.

(a)   Selling prices, working capital requirements and overhead expenses are expected to increase by 5% per year.

(b)   Material costs and labour costs are expected to increase by 10% per year.

(c)   Capital allowances are allowable for taxation purposes against profits at 25% per year on a reducing balance basis.

(d)   Taxation of profits is at a rate of 35% payable one year in arrears.

(e)   The fixed assets have no expected scrap value at the end of five years.

(f)   The company's real after-tax cost of capital is estimated to be 8% per year, and money after-tax cost of capital 15% per year.

Assume that all receipts and payments arise at the end of the year to which they relate except those in year 0, which occur immediately.

Required:

(a)   Estimate the NPV of the proposed project. State clearly any assumptions that you make.   **(12 marks)**

(b)   Calculate by how much the discount rate would have to change to result in a net present value of approximately zero.   **(8 marks)**

(Total: 20 marks)

For the answer to this question, see the 'Answers' section at the end of the book

FEEDBACK TO ACTIVITY 1

Since the decision has been made to increase capacity (i.e. 'to do nothing' is not an alternative), the easiest approach is to discount the incremental cash flows.

		A £'000	B £'000	B – A £'000	8% Factor	PV £'000
0	Capital expenditure	(260)	(415)	(155)	1	(155)
0	Working capital	(50)	(65)	(15)	1	(15)
2	Promotion	-	(15)	(15)	0.857	(13)
1 – 10	Net income	70	95	25	6.710	168
10	Scrap proceeds	40	75	35	0.463	16
10	Working capital	50	65	15	0.463	7
	Net present value (£'000)					8

The present value of proposal B exceeds that of proposal A by £8,000 at 8% and therefore proposal B is preferred.

umptions

(a) The disposal value of buildings is realistic and that all other figures have been realistically appraised.

(b) Expenditure on working capital is incurred at the beginning of the project life and recovered at the end.

(c) Adequate funds are available for either proposal.

(d) All cash flows occur annually in arrears on the anniversary of the initial investment.

FEEDBACK TO ACTIVITY 2

Workings

Year	Sales £	Variable costs £	Avoidable fixed costs £	Net operating cash flows £
1	60,000	30,000	8,000	22,000
2	63,000	31,500	8,000	23,500
3	66,150	33,075	8,000	25,075
4	69,458	34,729	12,000	22,729
5	72,930	36,465	12,000	24,465

Solution

Year	Equipt £	Working capital £	Operating cash flows £	Net cash flow £	Discount factor at 9%	Present value £
0	(75,000)	(15,000)			1.000	(90,000)
1		(5,000)	22,000	17,000	0.917	15,589
2			23,500	23,500	0.842	19,787
3		(5,000)	25,075	20,075	0.772	15,498
4			22,729	22,729	0.708	16,092
5	5,000	25,000	24,465	54,465	0.650	35,402
NPV						+ 12,368

The NPV is positive, and on the basis of these figures the project would appear to be financially worthwhile.

Note on working capital

An investment in working capital, in the context of a capital investment appraisal means an investment in stocks and debtors less trade creditors. As you should be aware from your knowledge of cash flow statements, operating cash flows are:

- less than operating profit when there is an increase in stocks plus debtors less creditors
- more than operating profit when there is a decrease in stocks plus debtors less creditors.

The working capital adjustment in the cash flow calculation is therefore an adjustment to get from operating profit to operational cash flow. Here, the cash flow adjustment is assumed to occur at the start of the year, and so is shown as a cash flow for the end of the previous year.

The non-discounted net cash flows for working capital over the life of the project should always be 0, because the working capital investment is reduced to 0 at the end of the projects life.

FEEDBACK TO ACTIVITY 3

For example, when this answer was written, the gross yield on long (10 year) gilts was 5.45% while inflation was 1.6% pa.

m = money rate of interest = 5.45%

i = inflation rate = 1.6%

$$\therefore \text{ real rate of interest, r, is given by } 1+r = \frac{1+m}{1+i} = \frac{1.0545}{1.0160} = 1.0379$$

The real rate of interest is 3.8% pa.

FEEDBACK TO ACTIVITY 4

Workings

End of year	Written down value	Capital allowance £	Written down value £	Tax saving at 30% £
0			80,000	
1	(25% of 80,000)	20,000	60,000	6,000
2	(25% of 60,000)	15,000	45,000	4,500
3	(25% of 45,000)	11,250	33,750	
3	Balancing charge (50,000 – 33,750)	16,250		
		(5,000)		(1,500)
				9,000

Year	Equipt	Working capital	Operating cash flow	Tax on operating cash flow	Tax saved – capital allowances	Net cash flow	Discount factor at 8%	Present value £
0	(80,000)	(25,000)				(105,000)	1.000	(105,000)
1			30,000	(9,000)	6,000	27,000	0.926	25,002
2			40,000	(12,000)	4,500	32,500	0.857	27,853
3	50,000	25,000	20,000	(6,000)	(1,500)	87,500	0.794	69,475
NPV								17,330

Chapter 14

INVESTMENT APPRAISAL UNDER UNCERTAINTY

In the appraisal methods covered so far, we have made decisions based upon future cash flows, discount rates etc, that will almost certainly have been estimated. In this chapter we look at the techniques that may be used alongside the appraisal (usually DCF) to assess the effects of variations in those estimates. The technique to be used depends upon whether the variability can be quantified (risk) or not (uncertainty).

Objectives

By the time you have finished this chapter you should be able to do the following:

- distinguish between risk and uncertainty
- identify the sources of risk affecting project profitability
- evaluate the sensitivity of project NPV to changes in key variables
- apply the probability approach to calculating expected NPV of a project and the associated standard deviation
- apply decision tree analysis in project appraisal situations
- explain the role of simulation in generating a probability distribution for the NPV of a project
- identify risk reduction strategies for projects
- evaluate the usefulness of risk assessment methods.

1   Risk and uncertainty

The problems with investment appraisal as we have looked at it so far are as follows:

- all decisions are based on forecasts
- all forecasts are subject to varying degrees of uncertainty
- how can uncertainty be reflected in a financial evaluation?

D E F I N I T I O N

Risk – probabilities are attached to possible outcomes, giving an expected outcome that can be calculated mathematically.
Uncertainty – the future outcome cannot be predicted mathematically from available data.

The distinction between risk and uncertainty is that risk is quantifiable, whilst uncertainty is not. **Risk** – probabilities are attached to possible outcomes, giving an expected outcome that can be calculated mathematically. **Uncertainty** – the future outcome cannot be predicted mathematically from available data.

Although there is a clear distinction between these two problems that you should be aware of, in practice the words risk and uncertainty are used interchangeably.

1.1   Reducing the potential effects of uncertainty in projects

Techniques for reducing the effects of uncertainty in projects include:

- setting a minimum payback period
- making prudent estimates of cash flows to assess the worst possible situation
- assessing both best and worst possible situations to obtain a range of NPVs
- using **sensitivity analysis** to measure the 'margin of safety' on input data.

 FOULKS LYNCH PUBLICATIONS

1.2   Taking account of risk

Where the uncertainty can be quantified in terms of probability distributions (and it therefore strictly becomes risk) we can use **expected values** to obtain "representative" figures to use in project appraisals. However, this will not in itself indicate the degree of risk involved – two different projects can have the same expected values but may have been computed from underlying values with very different degrees of dispersion.

Simulation allows both the expected value and the degree of dispersion to be taken into account in decision-making.

These techniques are within your syllabus, and are covered in this chapter. There is, however, one other approach of which you should be aware, although the details of its application are outside the syllabus – the use of a **risk adjusted discount rate.**

Risk adjusted discount rates

This approach is commonly taken by investors. If, say, we were comparing a building society investment with one in equities we would normally require a higher return from equities to compensate us for their extra risk. In a similar way, if we were appraising shares in a food retailer against shares in a biotechnology firm we would usually demand higher returns from the latter to reflect its higher risk.

A **risk adjusted discount rate** can be employed in almost any situation involving risk. The practical problem is how much return we should demand for a given level of risk. To solve this problem we can turn to the stock exchange – a place where risk and return combinations (securities) are bought and sold every day. If, for example, we can better the return earned by investors on the stock market by investing in a physical asset offering the same level of risk, we can increase investor wealth and the investment should be adopted.

This approach leads to the development of the Capital Asset Pricing Model (CAPM) which will be studied later, in Paper 3.7.

2   Sensitivity analysis

Sensitivity analysis is a modelling and risk assessment procedure in which changes are made to significant variables in order to determine the effect of these changes on the planned outcome.

The figure reached in any capital investment decision calculation (a positive or negative NPV) is only as reliable as the estimates used to produce that figure. One only has to look at the revisions made to estimates of large capital sums in a major investment programme such as the Channel Tunnel between Folkestone and Calais to see how unreliable some of these estimates can be. Estimating the long-term benefits presents even greater problems.

One way of providing useful supplementary information for an investment decision is to consider a **range of figures** for various estimates and establish whether these give positive or negative NPVs. With spreadsheets, this exercise is easy to perform, sometimes being referred to as posing **'What if?'** questions. However, it is still important to determine what variations in estimates are reasonable and what are unlikely. This analysis is usually applied to one estimate at a time although it can be applied to each estimate simultaneously.

2.1   Percentage changes required to change decision

A more concise form of analysis takes each estimate in turn and assesses **the percentage change required to change an investment decision**. It is customary to apply it to single estimates although, if any relationship between variables is known, it can be applied to groups of figures. This form of sensitivity analysis is considered here.

Example

Bacher Ltd is considering investing £500,000 in equipment to produce a new type of ball. Sales of the product are expected to continue for three years at the end of which the equipment will have a scrap value of £80,000. Sales revenue of £600,000 per annum will be generated at a variable cost of £350,000. Annual fixed costs will increase by £40,000.

You are required:

(a) to determine whether, on the basis of the estimates given, the project should be undertaken, assuming that all cash flows occur at annual intervals and that Bacher Ltd has a cost of capital of 15%

(b) to find the percentage changes required in the following estimates for the investment decision to change:

  (i)   initial investment

  (ii) scrap value

  (iii) selling price

  (iv) sales volume

  (v)   cost of capital.

Solution

Although part (a) could be completed most efficiently by finding net annual inflows (£600,000 – £350,000 – £40,000) of £210,000, part (b) would be most effectively negotiated if the separate present values were found.

(a) **NPV calculation**

Time	Cash flow	15% Discount factor		Present value
	£000			£000
0	Equipment	(500)	1	(500)
1 – 3	Revenue	600		1,370
1 – 3	Variable costs	(350)	2.283	(799)
1 – 3	Fixed costs	(40)		(91)
3	Scrap value	80	0.658	53
Net present value (£'000)				33

The project should, on the basis of these estimates, be accepted.

(b) **Sensitivity analysis**

  (i) *Initial investment*

    For the decision to change, the NPV must fall by £33,000. For this to occur the cost of the equipment must rise by £33,000. This is a rise of:

$$\frac{33}{500} \times 100 \quad = 6.6\%$$

  (ii) *Scrap value*

    If the NPV is to fall by £33,000, the present value of scrap proceeds must fall by £33,000. The PV of scrap proceeds is currently £53,000. It must fall by:

$$\frac{33}{53} \times 100 = 62.26\%, \text{ say } 62\%$$

FOULKS LYNCH
PUBLICATIONS

(This would bring the scrap proceeds down by 62.26% to £30,192. The PV of the scrap proceeds would be £19,866, i.e. just over £33,000 less than in (a). There are some slight differences from rounding due to the use of 3 decimal place discount factors.)

Therefore to find the percentage change required in an estimate to change an investment decision, find:

$$\frac{\text{NPV of project}}{\text{PV of those figures that vary with estimate concerned}}$$

KEY POINT

Sensitivity to an estimate =

$$\frac{\text{NPV of project}}{\text{PV of those figures that vary with estimate concerned}} \times 100$$

(iii) *Sales price*

If sales price varies, sales revenue will vary (assuming no effect on demand). If the NPV of the project is to fall by £33,000, the selling price must fall by:

$$\frac{33}{1,370} \times 100 = 2.4\%$$

(iv) *Sales volume*

If sales volume falls, revenue and variable costs fall (contribution falls). If the NPV is to fall by £33,000, volume must fall by:

$$\frac{33}{(1,370-799)} \times 100 = 5.8\%$$

(v) *Cost of capital*

If NPV is to fall, cost of capital must rise. The figure which the cost of capital must rise to, that gives an NPV of zero, is the project's IRR. To find the IRR, which is probably not much above 15%, the NPV at 17% can be found using the summarised cash flows.

NPV (£'000) = − 500 + [210 × 2.210] + [80 × 0.624] = 14

KEY POINT

Sensitivity to cost of capital can be determined by computing the IRR.

The IRR is a little more than 17%, possibly 18%, but the formula can be used.

$$\text{IRR} \approx 15 + \left(\frac{33}{33-14}\right) \times (17-15)$$

$$\approx 18.47\%, \text{ say } 18.50\%$$

The cost of capital would have to increase from 15% to 18½% before the investment decision changes.

ACTIVITY 1

Using the data in the previous example about Bacher's new equipment, estimate the percentage changes in (a) unit variable cost and (b) annual fixed cost needed to change the investment decision.

Feedback to this activity is at the end of the chapter.

2.2 Strengths of sensitivity analysis

- No complicated theory to understand.

- Information will be presented to management in a form which facilitates subjective judgement to decide the likelihood of the various possible outcomes considered.

- Identifies areas which are crucial to the success of the project. If it is chosen those areas can be carefully monitored.

- Indicates just how critical are some of the forecasts which are considered to be uncertain.

2.3 Weaknesses of sensitivity analysis

- It assumes that changes to variables can be made independently, e.g. material prices will change independently of other variables. This is unlikely. If material prices went up the firm would probably increase selling price at the same time and there would be little effect on NPV. A technique called simulation (see later) allows us to change more than one variable at a time.

- It only identifies how far a variable needs to change, it does not look at the probability of such a change. In the above analysis, sales volume appears to be the most crucial variable, but if the firm were facing volatile raw material markets a 65% change in raw material prices would be far more likely than a 29% change in sales volume.

- It is not an optimising technique. It provides information on the basis of which decisions can be made. It does not point to the correct decision directly.

DEFINITION

An **expected value** is computed by multiplying the value of each possible outcome by the probability of that outcome, and summing the results.

3 Expected values

When considering an investment decision it may be possible to make several predictions about alternative future outcomes and to assign probabilities to each outcome. An **expected value** is computed by multiplying the value of each possible outcome by the probability of that outcome, and summing the results.

An expected value can therefore be defined as a weighted average value, calculated from probability estimates.

Example

Cash flows from a new restaurant venture may depend on whether a competitor decides to open up the same area. We make the following estimates:

Competitor opens up	Probability	Project NPV £	EV
Yes	0.3	(10,000)	(3,000)
No	0.7	20,000	14,000
			11,000

The expected net present value of this venture is $(0.3 \times -10,000) + (0.7 \times 20,000) =$ £11,000.

The expected value is the weighted average of the outcomes, with the weightings based on the probability estimates. The EV does not necessarily represent what the outcome will be, nor does it represent the most likely result (that is £20,000). What it really represents is the average pay-off per occasion if the project were repeated many times (i.e. a 'long-run' average).

There are two main problems with using expected values to make decisions in this way:

- the project will only be carried out once. It could result in a sizeable loss and there may be no second chance to win our money back.

- the probabilities used are simply subjective estimates of our belief, on a scale from 0 to 1. There is probably little data on which to base these estimates.

The simple decision rule using expected values is **to accept projects with a positive
expected NPV**. When choosing between projects accept those projects with the highest
expected NPVs.

3.1   Calculating expected values

These problems must be faced, and are discussed in detail in the following sections.
However, it is first necessary to know how to calculate and use expected values.

Example

Hofgarten Newsagents stocks a weekly magazine which advertises local second-hand
goods. Marie, the owner, can buy the magazines for 15p each and sell them at the retail
price of 25p. At the end of each week unsold magazines are obsolete and have no
value.

Marie estimates a probability distribution for weekly demand which looks like this:

Weekly demand in units	Probability
10	0.20
15	0.55
20	0.25
	────
	1.00
	────

(a)   What is the expected value of demand?

(b)   If Marie is to order a fixed quantity of magazines per week how many
       should that be? Assume no seasonal variations in demand.

Solution

(a)   EV of demand = $(10 \times 0.20) + (15 \times 0.55) + (20 \times 0.25) = 15.25$ units per week.

(b)   The first step is to set up a **decision matrix** of possible strategies (numbers
      bought) and possible demand, as follows:

Outcome (number demanded)	Strategy (number bought)		
	10	15	20
10			
15			
20			

The 'payoff' from each combination of action and outcome is then computed:

No sale → loss of 15p per magazine.

Sale   → profit of 25p – 15p = 10p per magazine.

Payoffs are shown for each combination of strategy and outcome.

Workings

(i)   If 10 magazines are bought, then 10 are sold no matter how many are demanded
        and the payoff is always $10 \times 10p = 100p$.

(ii)   If 15 magazines are bought and 10 are demanded, then 10 are sold at a profit of $10
        \times 10p = 100p$, and 5 are scrapped at a loss of $5 \times 15p = 75p$, making a net profit of
        25p.

(iii)   The other contributions are similarly calculated.

Probabilities are then applied to compute the expected value resulting from each
possible course of action.

In the same matrix, probability × payoff can be inserted in each cell and totalled to give the expected payoff.

Probability	Outcome	Expected payoff (number bought)		
	(number demanded)	10	15	20
0.20	10	20p	5p	(10p)
0.55	15	55p	82p	41.25p
0.25	20	25p	37p	50p
1.00	EV	100p	125p	81.25p

The expected values of each strategy are listed on the bottom line, in pence. From this it can be seen that the strategy which gives the highest expected payoff is to stock 15 magazines each week.

What does this expected value mean? It means that if the strategy is followed for many weeks, then on average the profit will be 125p per week. What actually happens is that eight weeks out of ten the payoff is likely to be 150p and two weeks out of ten it drops to 25p. This strategy produces the highest long-run profit for the firm.

The expected value technique is ideally suited to the sort of problem which is repetitive and involves only small outlays of money.

ACTIVITY 2

A company is considering whether to invest in equipment for providing a new service to its clients. The equipment will cost £100,000 and will have a disposal value of £20,000 after four years. Estimates of sales and incremental fixed cost cash expenditures are as follows.

Annual sales	Probability	Extra annual fixed cost cash expenditure	Probability
£		£	
600,000	0.4	200,000	0.7
700,000	0.4	250,000	0.3
800,000	0.2		

The company expects to achieve a contribution/sales ratio of 40% on all the services it provides. The project would need additional working capital of £30,000 from the start of year 0. It would have a four-year life.

The company's cost of capital is 9%.

Required

Calculate the expected NPV.

Feedback to this activity is at the end of the chapter.

3.2   Advantages of expected values

- Recognises that there are several possible outcomes and is, therefore, **more sophisticated** than single value forecasts.
- Enables the **probability** of the different outcomes to be quantified.
- Leads directly to a simple optimising decision rule.
- Calculations are relatively **simple**.

3.3　Limitations of expected values

- By asking for a series of forecasts the whole **forecasting procedure is complicated**. Inaccurate forecasting is already a major weakness in project evaluation. The probabilities used are also usually very subjective.

- The expected value is merely a weighted average of the probability distribution, indicating the **average payoff** if the project is repeated many times.

- The expected value gives no indication of the **dispersion** of possible outcomes about the expected value. The more widely spread out the possible results are, the more risky the investment is usually seen to be. The expected value ignores this aspect of the probability distribution.

- In ignoring risk, the expected value technique also **ignores the investor's attitude to risk**. Some investors are more likely to take risks than others.

The expected value technique is best suited to a problem which is **repetitive** and involves **relatively small** investments

3.4　Conclusions on expected values

The simple expected value decision rule is appropriate if three conditions are met or nearly met:

- there is a reasonable basis for making the forecasts and estimating the probability of different outcomes

- the decision is relatively small in relation to the business. Risk is then small in magnitude

- the decision is for a category of decisions that are often made. A technique which maximises average payoff is then valid.

4　Simulation in investment appraisal

Simulation is a modelling technique that can incorporate many combinations of variables in producing a range of possible outcomes and their probability distribution.

Sensitivity analysis considered the effect of changing one variable at a time. **Monte Carlo simulation** allows us to consider the effect of all possible combinations of variables.

Simulation involves the construction of a **mathematical model** to recreate, for example, a potential investment project. The model can include all random events that might affect the success or failure of such a project, like a competitor appearing, changes in consumer taste, changes in inflation or exchange rates etc.

It is then possible to formulate a distribution of the **possible cash flows** from the project from which the **probability of different outcomes** can be calculated.

This should result in better decisions than those based on the calculation of a single net present value or internal rate of return figure, because there are bound to be factors affecting the outcome which are beyond the company's control and will affect the cash flows used in the calculation.

4.1　The simulation process

The approach breaks down into three stages, and is greatly helped by the use of a computer.

DEFINITION

Simulation is a modelling technique that can incorporate many combinations of variables in producing a range of possible outcomes and their probability distribution.

Stage 1 Specify major variables

Variables will differ between investment projects but typical examples are as follows:

(1) *Market details*

- market size
- selling price
- market growth rate
- market share.

(2) *Investment costs*

- investment required
- residual value of investment.

(3) *Operating costs*

- variable costs
- fixed costs
- taxation
- useful life of plant.

Stage 2 Specify the relationships between variables to calculate an NPV

Sales revenue = market size × market share × selling price.

Net cash flow = sales revenue − (variable costs + fixed costs + taxation) etc.

Stage 3 Simulate the environment

To conduct the simulation we need to attach a probability distribution to each variable. For example, we may have the following estimates of variable cost.

Variable cost per unit £	4.00	4.50	5.00
Probability	0.3	0.5	0.2

Random numbers are then assigned to represent the above probability distribution.

Variable cost per unit £	4.00	4.50	5.00
Probability	0.3	0.5	0.2
Random number range	00-29	30-79	80-99

If two digit random numbers are then generated, the probability of occurrence of each range will reflect the underlying probability distribution.

Probability distributions and random number ranges are assigned to each variable. Care must be taken at this stage to allow for dependence between variables. For example, selling price and market share could clearly be related and it could be necessary to specify a probability distribution of market shares for each selling price.

Finally to simulate the project we need to do the following:

- draw a random number for each variable (note that most computers can generate random numbers)
- select the value of each variable corresponding with the selected random number and compute an NPV
- repeat the process many times until we have a probability distribution of returns.

Results of simulation

The results of a simulation exercise will be a probability distribution of NPVs.

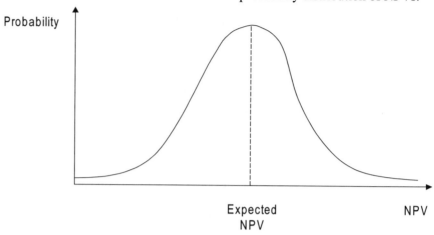

Instead of choosing between expected values, decision-makers can now take the dispersion of outcomes and the expected return into account.

4.2   Merits of simulation

The major advantages of simulation are as follows:

- It includes all possible outcomes in the decision making process
- It is a relatively easily understood technique
- It has a wide variety of applications (stock control, component replacement, corporate models etc.)

4.3   Drawbacks of simulations

However, it does have some significant drawbacks:

- models can become extremely complex, particularly where dependent probabilities are involved, and thus the time and costs involved in their construction can be more than is gained from the improved decisions.
- probability distributions may be difficult to formulate.

Conclusion

In this chapter we have looked at some of the techniques that may be employed within investment appraisal to recognise the effects of uncertainty and risk – sensitivity analysis (uncertainty), expected values and simulation (risk). As well as being able to apply these techniques in a given situation, you will be expected to appreciate the extent to which they are able to incorporate uncertainty into the decision-making process.

SELF-TEST
QUESTIONS

Risk and uncertainty

1   Give three examples of ways in which the effects of uncertainty can be reduced. (1.1)

Sensitivity analysis

2   Explain the basic purpose of sensitivity analysis. (2)

3   How do you calculate the sensitivity of a project to changes in sales volume? (2)

Expected values

4   Why is it said that expected values do not take account of risk? (3.4)

5   Under what circumstances is an expected value of greatest use in decision-making? (3.5)

Mentor Products plc

Mentor Products plc are considering the purchase of a new computer-controlled packing machine to replace the two machines which are currently used to pack products X. The new machine would result in reduced labour costs because of the more automated nature of the process and, in addition, would permit production levels to be increased by creating greater capacity at the packing stage. With an anticipated rise in the demand for product X, it has been estimated that the new machine will lead to increased profits in each of the next three years. Due to uncertainty in demand however, the annual cash flows (including savings) resulting from the purchase of the new machine cannot be fixed with certainty and have therefore been estimated probabilistically as follows:

Year 1 £'000	Prob.	Year 2 £'000	Prob.	Year 3 £'000	Prob.
10	0.3	10	0.1	10	0.3
15	0.4	20	0.2	20	0.5
20	0.3	40	0.3	30	0.2
		30	0.4		

Because of the overall uncertainty in the sales of product X, it has been decided that only three years' cash flows will be considered in deciding whether to purchase the new machine. After allowing for the scrap value of the existing machines, the net cost of the new machine will be £42,000.

The effects of taxation should be ignored.

You are required to do the following:

(a)   Ignoring the time value of money, identify which combinations of annual cash flows will lead to an overall negative net cash flow, and determine the total probability of this occurring.

(b)   On the basis of the average cash flow for each year, calculate the net present value of the new machine given that the company's cost of capital is 15%.

Relevant discount factors are as follows.

Year	Discount factor
1	0.870
2	0.756
3	0.658

(c)   Analyse the risk inherent in this situation by simulating the net present value calculation. You should use the random numbers given at the end of the question to simulate five sets of cash flows. On the basis of your simulation results, what is the expected net present value and what is the probability of the new machine yielding a negative net present value?

	Set 1	Set 2	Set 3	Set 4	Set 5	
Year 1	4	7	6	5	0	
Year 2	2	4	8	0	1	
Year 3	7	9	4	0	3	**(20 marks)**

For the answer to this question, see the 'Answers' section at the end of the book.

(a)   Change in unit variable cost

The project's NPV must fall by £33,000 therefore the PV of the variable costs must rise by £33,000. Since the PV of variable costs is £799,000, a rise of £33,000 is an increase of:

$$\frac{33}{799} \times 100 = 4.1\%$$

(b)   Change in annual fixed costs

Since the PV of fixed costs is £91,000, a rise of £33,000 is an increase of:

$$\frac{33}{91} \times 100 = 36\%$$

Annual sales £	Probability	EV £
600,000	0.4	240,000
700,000	0.4	280,000
800,000	0.2	160,000
EV of annual sales		680,000
C/S ratio		40%
EV of annual contribution		272,000

Extra annual fixed cost cash expenditure £	Probability	EV £
200,000	0.7	140,000
250,000	0.3	75,000
		215,000

The EV of annual cash profits is therefore £272,000 - £215,000 = £57,000.

Year	Equipment £	Working capital £	Profits £	Net cash flow £	Discount factor at 9%	Present value £
0	(100,000)	(30,000)		(130,000)	1.000	(130,000)
1 – 4			57,000	57,000	3.240	184,680
4	20,000	30,000		50,000	0.708	35,499
NPV						+ 90,080

The expected NPV is positive, and on the basis of expected values, the project should be undertaken.

Chapter 15

ASSET INVESTMENT DECISIONS AND CAPITAL RATIONING

This chapter starts with the application of discounted cash flow techniques to specific asset investment decisions – first, the financing choice between leasing and borrowing to buy, and second, the decision as to when to replace a particular asset. We then go on to look at the problem of allocation of capital between projects when it is in short supply, either in one period only or for more than one period.

Objectives

By the time you have finished this chapter you should be able to do the following:

- distinguish between hard and soft capital rationing
- apply profitability index techniques for single period divisible projects
- evaluate projects involving single and multi-period capital rationing
- distinguish between operating and finance leases
- apply DCF methods to projects involving buy or lease problems
- assess the relative advantages and disadvantages of different types of lease
- describe the impact of leasing on company gearing.

1 Lease or buy decisions

We saw earlier that leasing is a form of finance whereby an asset can be used within a business without it necessarily being bought outright. We are now looking at the problem of evaluating whether leasing is better than outright purchase with borrowed funds in a particular situation.

Thus, where the use of an asset is required for a new project, there are two decisions to be made:

- is the project itself worthwhile in the first place?
- if so, should the asset be leased or bought with a loan?

The analysis of these decisions has been a controversial area over the years, particularly as regards the discount rates to be used. The approach that follows is one of the most commonly used, and will certainly be acceptable in the examination. The following example will be used to illustrate the approach to a typical exam question.

In lease or buy questions you may have both an **investment** decision and a **finance** decision.

KEY POINT

In lease or buy questions you may have both an **investment** decision and a **finance** decision.

1.1 Example

A firm is considering acquiring a new machine to neutralise the toxic waste produced by its refining plant. The machine would cost £6.4 million and would have an economic life of five years. The machine will reduce operating costs of the firm by £2.4 million pa. Capital allowances of 25% pa on a declining balance basis are available for the investment. Taxation of 30% is payable on operating cash flows one year in arrears. It is considered that a discount rate of 20% would reflect the risk of the project's operating cash flows.

The firm intends to finance the new plant by means of a five-year fixed interest loan at 11.4% pa, principal repayable in five years' time. As an alternative a leasing company has proposed a finance lease over five years at £1.42 million per year payable in advance. Scrap value of the machine under each financing alternative will be zero.

You are required to advise the firm whether the project should be undertaken and, if so, which financing method to adopt.

1.2 Evaluating the investment decision

The project for which the asset is to be acquired should, initially at least, be evaluated independently of the method of finance.

(1)   It will have its own level of risk, for which an appropriate discount rate should be used. Unless told otherwise, this will often be approximated by the **company's existing cost of capital**, assuming its cash flows are of the same level of risk as those from existing operations.

(2)   The cash flows to which this discount rate should be applied will be the **project operating cash flows:**

- asset flows – initial cost and residual value
- working capital flows
- net cash operating inflows
- tax relief on capital allowances
- tax on operating inflows

The **investment decision** will be made by computing the NPV of the project's operating cash flows, ignoring all finance flows, at the company's cost of capital.

Note that this approach effectively assumes the purchase of the asset is funded from the existing pool of funds of the company, and will attract capital allowances. When appraising the method of finance, if these or any other aspects of the project flows are lost or altered, this will be included in the evaluation of its costs.

Applying these principles to the example, we are told that the project flows should be discounted at 20%. There are no working capital flows or residual value. Tax is at 30% with a one year time lag:

Time	0	1	2	3	4	5	6
	£m	£m	£m	£m	£m	£m	£m
Asset	(6.400)	0	0	0	0	0	0
Tax relief on CAs (W)		0.480	0.360	0.270	0.203	0.152	0.456
Operating cost savings		2.400	2.400	2.400	2.400	2.400	0
Tax on savings @ 30%			(0.720)	(0.720)	(0.720)	(0.720)	(0.720)
Net cash flow	(6.400)	2.880	2.040	1.9500	1.883	1.832	(0.264)
PV factor @ 20%	1	0.833	0.694	0.579	0.482	0.402	0.335
Present values	(6.400)	2.399	1.416	1.129	0.908	0.736	(0.088)

NPV of the project is therefore £100,000. Thus the project is worthwhile, although only marginally so.

Note that in some exam questions, this first step may already have been done, and you will simply be asked to make the finance decision.

Working

Time	Opening value £m	Allowance £m	Closing value £m	Tax saving (allowance × 0.30) £m
0	6.400	1.600	4.800	0.480
1	4.800	1.200	3.600	0.360
2	3.600	0.900	2.700	0.270
3	2.700	0.675	2.025	0.203
4	2.025	0.506	1.519	0.152
5	1.519	1.519 **	0	0.456

** balancing allowance

Note: all tax savings are lagged by one year. Timing of capital allowances can vary depending upon the date of purchase. This analysis assumes that Time 0 is at the beginning of the first year, and therefore the tax relief (on capital allowances and/or leasing payments) commences twelve months later (the typical assumption by examiners).

1.3   Evaluating the finance decision

The **finance decision** will be made by computing the NPV of the lease finance cash flows at the post-tax cost of borrowing and comparing it with the PV of the borrowing flows, which equate to the original cost of the asset.

One method of financing the asset is to borrow £6.4 million at a pre-tax interest rate of 11.4%. We need to compare the finance flows associated with this borrowing option with those arising from the leasing option to decide between them. Four questions arise.

How do we compare borrow and buy with leasing?

Using principles of maximisation of shareholder wealth discussed previously, we shall use an **NPV** approach.

What discount rate do we use?

If we assume that shareholders will view leasing and borrowing as being of similar risk (usually lower than that of the project itself), we will use the cost of borrowing as an appropriate rate. As the interest payments on the loan will attract tax relief, the appropriate rate to use is the **post-tax cost of borrowing.**

What are the finance flows?

The finance flows associated with the **borrow and buy** option comprise the interest payments, the principal repayment and the tax relief on the interest payments. However, from basic principles of discounting, if these are discounted at the post tax interest rate (cost of borrowing) they will come back to the original amount borrowed, i.e. £6.4m.

The finance flows associated with the **leasing** option will be:

- the lease payments

- the tax relief on the lease payments

- the lost tax relief on writing down allowances.

Note that since the capital allowances are included in the evaluation of the project, if a particular finance method eliminates these, the effect must be included as part of the cost of that method of finance.

So we need to discount the lease finance flows at the post tax cost of borrowing and compare the result with the original cost of the asset, £6.4m.

What is the post tax cost of borrowing?

The pre-tax cost of borrowing is 11.4%. The post-tax cost of borrowing can be approximated by multiplying this by (1 – tax rate) i.e. 11.4% × (1 – 0.3) = 7.98%, say 8% (strictly this ignores the impact of a one year time delay on tax relief but this is acceptable).

PV of lease flows

Time	0	1	2	3	4	5	6
	£m	£m	£m	£m	£m	£m	£m
Lease payments	(1.420)	(1.420)	(1.420)	(1.420)	(1.420)		
Tax relief on payments @ 30%		0.426	0.426	0.426	0.426	0.426	
Lost tax relief on CAs (W)		(0.480)	(0.360)	(0.270)	(0.203)	(0.152)	(0.456)
Net cash flow	(1.420)	(1.474)	(1.354)	(1.264)	(1.197)	0.274	(0.456)
PV factor @ 8%	1.000	0.926	0.857	0.794	0.735	0.681	0.630
Present values	(1.420)	(1.365)	(1.160)	(1.004)	(0.880	0.187	(0.287)

NPV of the lease flows is £(5.929m).

The lease costs have a negative PV of £5.929 million, implying that they are equivalent to taking out a loan of this amount now at a post-tax interest rate of 8%. This compares favourably with the borrowing and buying option, which has costs with a negative PV of £6.4m, i.e. the original loan required to buy the asset outright. Thus, leasing should be chosen.

1.4   Combining the investment and finance

Note that the profitability of the original investment will be improved if the leasing option is chosen, from an NPV of £100,000 (assuming finance costs with a PV of £6.4m) to:

$$£100,000 + £(6.4 - 5.929)m = £571,000$$

This makes it a less marginal decision.

Summary: lease or buy decisions

When faced with a decision about acquiring a new capital asset, and also a decision about whether to lease or buy the equipment, the steps should be as follows.

1   Start by ignoring the financing decision. Calculate whether the asset should be acquired, assuming that it is purchased. Discount the project cash flows at the company's after-tax cost of capital. The investment should normally only be considered if the NPV is positive.

2   Having calculated an NPV for the project cash flows, consider the financing alternatives.

3   The cash flows of cost of the option to purchase are the cost of the asset (Year 0) and its eventual disposal value, and the effect on tax payments of claiming capital allowances.

4   The cash flows of the option to lease are the annual lease payments, and the tax reductions from claiming these expenditures against tax.

5   Discount the two financing cash flows at the company's after-tax cost of borrowing. The preferred option is the option with the lower PV of cost.

2   Asset replacement decisions

Once the decision has been made to acquire an asset for a long-term project, it is quite likely that the asset will need to be replaced periodically throughout the life of the project. The decision we are concerned with here is – how often should the asset be replaced?

Within the UK, it is estimated that 50% to 60% of total investment incorporates replacement. Yet the evidence also suggests that replacement appraisal is somewhat haphazard. In particular:

*   there is a failure to take account of the time-scale problems

*   techniques such as payback and accounting rate of return are used, which are unsuitable for replacement decisions

*   taxation and investment incentives are ignored

*   inflation is ignored.

This section is concerned with developing a systematic approach to replacement analysis.

2.1   Factors in replacement decisions

The factors to be considered when making replacement decisions are as follows:

*   **Capital cost of new equipment** – the higher cost of equipment will have to be balanced against known or possible technical improvements.

*   **Operating costs** – operating costs will be expected to increase as the machinery deteriorates over time. This is referred to as **operating inferiority**, and is the result of:

    (1)   increased repair and maintenance costs

    (2)   loss of production due to 'down-time' resulting from increased repair and maintenance time

    (3)   lower quality and quantity of output.

        *   **Resale value** – the extent to which old equipment can be traded in for new.

        *   **Taxation and investment incentives**.

        *   **Inflation** – both the general price level change, and relative movements in the prices of input and outputs.

Determining the optimum replacement period (cycle) will largely be influenced by:

*   the capital cost/resale value of the asset – the longer the period, the less frequently these will occur

*   the annual operating costs of running the asset – the longer the period, the higher these will become.

2.2   The time-scale problems

A special feature of replacement problems is that it involves comparisons of alternatives with different time-scales. If the choice is between replacing an item of machinery every two years or every three years, it would be meaningless simply to compare the NPV of the two costs.

Cost over two years   PV = P

Cost over three years   PV = Q

Almost certainly P < Q. However, this does not take account of the cost of providing asset for the third year. One way of comparing asset replacement options is to conver the PV of cost over one replacement cycle to an equivalent annual PV of cost.

In other words, we compute the PV of costs over one cycle and then turn it into an equivalent annual cost using the annuity factor for the number of years in the replacement cycle. Thus, the costs associated with any particular cycle can be considered as equivalent to having to pay this EAC every year throughout the cycle ar throughout subsequent cycles.

The **equivalent annual cost** is the equal annual cash flow (annuity) to which a series of uneven cash flows is equivalent in PV terms.

DEFINITION

The **equivalent annual cost** is the equal annual cash flow (annuity) to which a series of uneven cash flows is equivalent in PV terms.

Example

A decision has to be made on replacement policy for vans. A van costs £12,000 and th following additional information applies:

Interval between replacement (years)	Trade in allowance £		Age at year end	Maintenance cost paid at year end £
1	9,000		Year of replacement	Nil
2	7,500		1	1,500
3	7,000		2	2,700

Calculate the optimal replacement policy at a cost of capital of 15%. There are no maintenance costs in the year of replacement. Ignore taxation and inflation.

Solution

It is assumed that a brand new van is owned at the beginning of the cycle, and therefo must be owned at the end of the cycle.

The costs incurred over a single cycle are computed and the EAC is found as follows.

(1) Replace every year

$$\text{NPV of a single cycle} = -£12,000 + \frac{£9,000}{1.15} = £(4,174)$$

1 year 'annuity' factor = 0.870

$$\text{Equivalent annual cost} = \frac{\text{NPV}}{\text{annuity factor}} = \frac{£(4,174)}{0.870} = £(4,798)$$

(2) Replace every two years

$$\text{NPV of a single cycle} = -£12,000 - \frac{£1,500}{1.15} + \frac{£7,500}{1.15^2} = £(7,633)$$

2 year 'annuity' factor = 1.626

$$\text{Equivalent annual cost} = \frac{£(7,633)}{1.626} = £(4,694)$$

(3) Replace every three years

$$\text{NPV of a single cycle} = -£12,000 - \frac{£1,500}{1.15} - \frac{£2,700}{1.15^2} + \frac{£7,000}{1.15^3} = £(10,743)$$

3 year 'annuity' factor = 2.283

$$\text{Equivalent annual cost} = \frac{£(10,743)}{2.283} = £(4,706)$$

Conclusion

The optimal replacement period is every two years.

Note that the equivalent annual cost is that sum that could be paid annually in arrears to finance the three replacement cycles. It is equivalent to the budget accounts that various public services encourage customers to open to spread the cost of those services more evenly. The present value of annual sums equal to the EAC's is the same as the PV of the various receipts and payments needed to buy and maintain a van.

The **optimum replacement period (cycle)** will be the period that has the lowest EAC.

A company with a cost of capital of 12% wishes to determine the optimum replacement policy for its computers. Each computer costs £5,000 and can either be traded in at the end of the first year for £3,000 (no maintenance cost paid) or traded in at the end of the second year for £1,500 (£800 maintenance paid after one year). Calculate the equivalent annual cost of each policy and recommend which should be implemented.

Feedback to this activity is at the end of the chapter.

3   Capital rationing

Capital rationing arises when an organisation is restricted in the amount of funds available to initiate all worthwhile projects (i.e. projects that have a positive net present value).

The fact that capital needs to be rationed is a situation that has to be appreciated when looking at capital budgeting.

There are two causes of capital rationing, as follows:

- **hard (external) capital rationing** – Although, theoretically, finance is always available at a price, in practice most lending institutions decide that there is a point beyond which they will not lend, at any price. This may provide an absolute limit to the funds available.

- **soft (internal) capital rationing** – Particularly following a period of economic depression, many firms may be more concerned with survival than growth. In order to minimise risk, they adopt conservative growth and financing policies. Also, they want to maintain stable dividends rather than use cash for expansion.

Whether the restriction is caused by internal or external causes does not affect the analysis.

Capital rationing might therefore exist for reasons other than inability to obtain additional capital.

- A company might be aware that when proposals are made for new capital investments, the managers who put forward the proposals are often over-optimistic in their expectations and with their forecasts. Imposing capital spending limits can be a way of weeding out weak or marginal projects, by making them compete for funds with stronger and more profitable projects. This can be a crude but effective way of reducing the risk of making poor investments.

- A company might be able to raise new finance externally, but decide on a strategy of organic growth. An advantage of organic growth is that the benefits of growth should all be enjoyed by the existing shareholders. However, a strategy of organic growth inevitably places restrictions on the amount of investment capital available.

- A company might be able to raise additional capital by borrowing externally. However, higher borrowing has implications for financial risk, through higher financial gearing. A company might therefore impose limits on its external borrowing by setting a limit to its gearing level.

3.1 Types of capital rationing

Two types of capital rationing may be distinguished:

- **Single period** – shortage of funds now, but funds are expected to be freely available in all later periods.
- **Multi-period** – where the period of funds shortage is expected to extend over a number of years, or even indefinitely.

3.2 Project divisibility

Projects may be divided into two categories.

- **Divisible projects** – either the whole project, or any fraction of the project, may be undertaken. If a fraction only is undertaken, then both initial investment and cash inflows are reduced **pro rata**. Quoted shares represent a divisible investment – varying numbers of shares may be purchased, with resultant prorating of investment returns.
- **Indivisible projects** – either the project must be undertaken in its entirety, or not at all. Decisions about introducing new product ranges are indivisible – either new products are introduced or they are not.

In reality, almost all projects are indivisible. However, the assumption of divisibility enables the easier use of mathematical tools. Its implications are reconsidered later.

The approaches to the combinations of rationing and project types that you will be expected to deal with are summarised as follows:

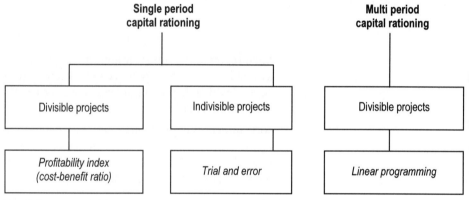

The **objective** of all capital rationing exercises is the maximisation of the total NPV of the chosen projects' cash flows at the cost of capital.

3.3 Single period capital rationing, divisible projects

Maximising NPV is achieved in these circumstances by ranking projects according to their **profitability index (cost-benefit ratio)**, then allocating funds accordingly until they are exhausted.

The **profitability index (PI)** of a project is the NPV per £ invested.

By comparing NPV with initial cash outflows, a measure of returns relative to size is obtained. This is comparable with the IRR approach. It suffers from the same criticisms as the latter in that it measures relative, not absolute, returns. In the capital rationing situation, however, this is what is required, since a selection of projects with the highest profitability indices will result in the maximum net present value for limited funds available.

Example

C Ltd, with a cost of capital of 10%, has £40,000 available for investment in Year 0. Four divisible projects are available.

Project	Outlay		Receipts (cash flows)		
	Year 0	Year 1	Year 2	Year 3	Year 4
	£	£	£	£	£
1	100,000	40,000	100,000	80,000	60,000
2	30,000	40,000	40,000	40,000	40,000
3	20,000	40,000	30,000	40,000	50,000
4	40,000	20,000	30,000	30,000	30,000

You are required to calculate the optimal investment policy.

KEY POINT

For a single period capital rationing between divisible projects, use the PI to rank projects.

Solution

Project	Net present value at 10%	Profitability indices – net present value per £1 of outlay at 10%	Ranking
	£	£	
1	120,255	1.203	III
2	96,894	3.230	II
3	105,479	5.274	I
4	46,079	1.152	IV

(Note: when reviewing your own workings to pre-worked NPV figures in this or any other text, allow for possible small differences due to rounding of present value factors.)

Summary of optimal plan for C Ltd:

Project	Fraction of project accepted	Outlay at time 0 £	Net present value £
3	1.00	20,000	105,479
2	2/3	20,000	64,596*
Capital used and available		40,000	
Net present value obtained			170,075

* Two-thirds of £96,894.

The opportunity cost of the capital rationing is £198,632 (368,707 – 170,075).

You might think that the IRR approach, as a measure of relative profitability, could be used to rank projects in a capital rationing situation. In fact this approach does not always give the correct ranking, but it may be used in the examination if profitability indices cannot be calculated from the information given.

3.4   Single period capital rationing, indivisible projects

In these circumstances, the objective can only be achieved by selecting from amongst the available projects on a trial and error basis. Because of the problem of indivisibility this may leave some funds unutilised.

Example

PQ Ltd has £50,000 available to invest. Its cost of capital is 10%. The following indivisible projects are available:

Project	Initial outlay £	Return pa to perpetuity £
1	20,000	1,500
2	10,000	1,500
3	15,000	3,000
4	30,000	5,400
5	25,000	4,800

Solution

The first stage is to calculate the NPV of the projects.

Project	Initial outlay £	PV of cash flows ** £	NPV £
1	20,000	15,000	(5,000)
2	10,000	15,000	5,000
3	15,000	30,000	15,000
4	30,000	54,000	24,000
5	25,000	48,000	23,000

$$** \text{ PV of perpetuity} = \frac{\text{Annual receipt}}{\text{Discount rate as a proportion}}$$

The approach is then one of considering all possible combinations of projects under the investment limit of £50,000.

The optimum selection of projects is as follows.

Projects	Initial outlay £	NPV £
2	10,000	5,000
3	15,000	15,000
5	25,000	23,000
	50,000	43,000

Unused funds	Nil
Funds available	50,000

This may be compared to the ranking, if these were divisible projects:

Project	Cost/benefit ratio			Ranking	Fraction of project accepted	NPV £
1	−5/20	=	−0.25	V	-	
2	5/10	=	0.50	IV	-	
3	15/15	=	1.00	I	1.00	15,000
4	24/30	=	0.80	III	1/3	8,000
5	23/25	=	0.92	II	1.00	23,000
						46,000

The projects selected do not coincide with this ranking because of the fact that they are not divisible. Given there is this constraint, and that for finance, no solution will give a higher NPV than £43,000.

3.5 Investment of surplus funds

In addition to specific investment opportunities, there may be a general opportunity to invest surplus funds on the market. Assuming equal risk levels, the rate of interest earned cannot, in the long run, be higher than the cost of the capital of the company, otherwise the cost of capital would be found to increase.

The rate of interest payable on surplus funds is therefore likely to be below the cost of capital. In a single period capital rationing situation, there is rarely any advantage in investing surplus funds at below the cost of capital (i.e. in projects with negative NPVs). However, if a project with a negative NPV has a cash inflow at year 0, rather than an outflow, investment could be worthwhile as it might free up funding for investment in other profitable projects which would otherwise be rejected under the capital rationing constraints.

As well as the specific investment opportunities available, consideration should also be given to **investing surplus funds** arising in one period, even at rates lower than the cost of capital, in order to increase funds available in later periods.

KEY POINT

For **multi-period** capital rationing, divisible projects, a **linear programming** approach may be suitable.

3.6 Multi-period capital rationing, divisible projects

This has already been defined as the situation where the cash shortage extends into a number of future periods. The problem is too complex to be suitable for a trial-and-error approach.

However, it may be defined so as to be suitable for a **linear programming** approach. For linear programming to be suitable, the following conditions must apply:

- The proportions undertaken of each of the projects available are the variables.

- Projects are assumed to be divisible.

- There are only two projects being considered (more than two projects requires the simplex technique which is not examinable in this paper).

- NPVs are linearly related to the proportion of each project accepted.

- Cash limits year by year form the constraints.

- The objective is to maximise the NPV of cash flows at the cost of capital.

You should also note that the linear programming problems examined assume that projects cannot be deferred, and have cash outflows extending over several periods. Multi-period rationing problems in the examination will generally be suitable for solution using linear programming.

To demonstrate the technique, an artificially simple example with only two projects will be examined.

Example

A company is proposing to invest in two projects. The projects are divisible, i.e. they can be accepted in whole or in part. If accepted in part, both cash outflows and subsequent cash receipts are reduced pro rata.

The two projects and associated cash flows are as follows:

Year	Project A Cash flow £	Project B Cash flow £
0	(10,000)	(20,000)
1	(20,000)	(10,000)
2	(30,000)	-
3	100,000	60,000

The company's cost of capital is 10%. All cash flows occur at exactly 12 month intervals, starting in year 0.

The funds available are restricted as follows:

Year 0	–	£20,000
Year 1	–	£25,000
Year 2	–	£20,000

Funds not utilised in one year will not be available in subsequent years. Projects cannot be deferred.

You are required to find the company's optimum investment policy.

Solution

It is first necessary to calculate the NPV of each project at 10%.

Year	10% discount factor	Project A Cash flow	Project A Present value	Project B Cash flow	Project B Present value
		£	£	£	£
0	1.000	(10,000)	(10,000)	(20,000)	(20,000)
1	0.909	(20,000)	(18,180)	(10,000)	(9,090)
2	0.826	(30,000)	(24,780)	-	-
3	0.751	100,000	75,100	60,000	45,060
NPV			22,140		15,970

Let a be the proportion of project A accepted.

Let b be the proportion of project B accepted.

The constraints are formulated as follows.

Year 0	10,000a	+	20,000b	≤	20,000	or	a	+	2b	≤	2
Year 1	20,000a	+	10,000b	≤	25,000	or	4a	+	2b	≤	5
Year 2	30,000a			≤	20,000	or	3a			≤	2

General non-negativity constraints: $0 \le a \le 1$
                                        $0 \le b \le 1$

The objective is to maximise NPVs from investment, i.e. $22,140a + 15,970b$

The problem may be viewed graphically:

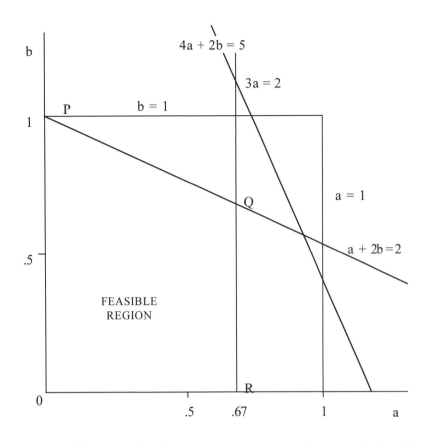

The feasible region (0PQR) has three corners as well as zero: P, Q and R. Proportions accepted, and resulting NPVs, are as follows:

Corner	Value of		Interpretation	NPV
	b	a		£
P	1	Nil	Accept B entirely and A not at all	15,970
Q	2/3	2/3	Accept 2/3 of each project	25,406
R	Nil	2/3	Accept 2/3 project A only	14,760

Clearly the optimum solution is to invest in 2/3 of each project – i.e. the solution suggested at point Q.

Workings

At Q two equations are satisfied.

$$a + 2b = 2 \text{-----------} (1)$$

$$3a = 2 \text{-----------} (2)$$

(2) becomes a   =   2/3

Substitute (2) in (1) 2b = 1 1/3------ (3)

b   =   2/3

Note that this solution leaves funds unused in year 1. This poses the question of whether it would be worthwhile to hold funds available from year 1 to year 2, even if they have to be invested below 10% – even say at Nil%.

ACTIVITY 2

Availability of investment opportunities below the cost of capital

In the above example, suppose £1,000 of the funds spare in year 1 can be held at a zero rate of interest until year 2.

Does this alter the optimal investment policy?

Feedback to this activity is at the end of the chapter.

3.7   More than two projects

The example above has enabled the problems to be handled computationally. Howeve
the technique is only relevant in reality where there are a number of projects, i.e. whei
there are more than two.

You are not likely to be asked to solve such problems numerically, but it will be helpf
if you can formulate the objective and constraint equations (i.e. the linear programmin
model).

Example

A company has four divisible projects available. The cash outlays and NPVs are as
follows:

Project	Outlay Year 0 £'000	Year 1 £'000	Net present value at 10% £'000
1	20	–	10
2	40	20	30
3	50	80	60
4	30	30	15

Capital rationing is expected to extend over the next two years, with £100,000 availabl
now and £80,000 next year before accepting any of the projects.

Solution

Let x_1 be the proportion of project (1) accepted

         x_2 be the proportion of project (2) accepted

         x_3 be the proportion of project (3) accepted

         x_4 be the proportion of project (4) accepted

Hence x_i can take any value between 0 and 1, i.e.

   $0 \geq x_i \geq 1$ where i = 1 – 4

Objective: to maximise net present value = $10x_1 + 30x_2 + 60x_3 + 15x_4$

Constraints:

Year	Funds available	Funds utilised
0	100 ≥	$20x_1 + 40x_2 + 50x_3 + 30x_4$
1	80 ≥	$20x_2 + 80x_3 + 30x_4$

Logic (non-negativity) constraints:

   $0 \geq x_1 \geq 1 \quad 0 \geq x_2 \geq 1$ etc.

The optimum solution can now be found by one of the standard techniques for
manipulating linear programming problems, e.g. the Simplex method.

Note: this method can also incorporate the investment of surplus funds as will be seen
in the Examination Type Questions at the end of the chapter.

Conclusion

This chapter has addressed three separate topics, linked by the use of DCF techniques.
Of the three, leasing is perhaps the most likely to be examined, although there is a
question on asset replacement in the Pilot Paper.

Lease or buy decisions

1   In a lease or buy problem, how is the investment decision made? (1.2)

2   In a lease or buy problem, how is the finance decision made? (1.3)

3   Why are the rates used in the two decisions likely to be different? (1.2, 1.3)

Asset replacement decisions

4   What is the objective in choosing an optimum replacement period? (2.1)

Capital rationing

5   How is the problem of single period rationing with indivisible projects tackled? (3.4)

6   Give at least four conditions for the linear programming technique to apply. (3.6)

Ceder Ltd

Ceder Ltd has details of two machines which could fulfil the company's future production plans. Only one of these machines will be purchased.

The 'standard' model costs £50,000, and the 'de-luxe' £88,000, payable immediately. Both machines would require the input of £10,000 working capital throughout their working lives, and both machines have no expected scrap value at the end of their expected working lives of four years for the standard machine and six years for the de-luxe machine.

The forecast pre-tax operating net cash flows associated with the two machines are:

	years hence					
	1	*2*	*3*	*4*	*5*	*6*
	£	£	£	£	£	£
Standard	20,500	22,860	24,210	23,410		
De-luxe	32,030	26,110	25,380	25,940	38,560	35,100

The de-luxe machine has only recently been introduced to the market and has not been fully tested in operating conditions. Because of the higher risk involved, the appropriate discount rate for the de-luxe machine is believed to be 14% per year, 2% higher than the discount rate for the standard machine.

The company is proposing to finance the purchase of either machine with a term loan at a fixed interest rate of 11% per year.

Taxation at 35% is payable on operating cash flows one year in arrears, and capital allowances are available at 25% per year on a reducing balance basis.

You are required:

(a)   to calculate for both the standard and the de-luxe machine:

(i) payback period

(ii) net present value.

Recommend, with reasons, which of the two machines Ceder Ltd should purchase.

(Relevant calculations must be shown.)

(b) If Ceder Ltd were offered the opportunity to lease the standard model machine over a four year period at a rental of £15,000 per year, not including maintenance costs, evaluate whether the company should lease or purchase the machine.   **(20 marks)**

Arctica

(a) For what *economic* reasons do central governments periodically impose limits on the capital expenditure of regional authorities?   **(6 marks)**

(b) How does the required return for public sector investment decisions differ from that in the private sector?   **(8 marks)**

(c) The regional authority of Arctica, the most northerly province of Northland (a member of the European Union which uses sterling as its currency) received many complaints from the general public during the past winter for its poor performance in clearing the local roads in snowy weather conditions. The roads department operates a fleet of five vehicles all beyond their optimum operating lifetimes and consequently having a high rate of breakdowns. Their second-hand value is estimated at £2,000 each. Modern replacements cost £50,000 each. After a life span of six years, it is expected that each vehicle could be resold for £5,000 after overhaul, or for £2,000 as scrap. The vehicles will require overhauls every two years costing £14,000 per vehicle.

A consultant, hired to assess the size of fleet required to provide an acceptable level of service to avoid future complaints, estimates that 10 vehicles would suffice in all but exceptional weather conditions. However, Arctica is concerned about the recent tightening by central government (on whom regional authorities rely for most of their capital funding), of controls over capital spending. The vehicles would only be needed for the six months from October to March, although they could be hired during the summer months for a maximum of five years to a nearby quarry for a fixed annual contract fee for all 10 vehicles of initially £200,000, but declining by £40,000 each year to reflect ageing of the fleet. However, Arctica is concerned that the quarry workings are approaching exhaustion and may be closed in the near future. Indeed, the quarry company will not sign a firm contract for a period exceeding two years out of a similar concern.

During the winter, the 10 vehicles would be kept on stand-by, to be driven, when needed, by refuse disposal truck drivers, assigned from normal duties and paid overtime wage rates if necessary. Incremental operating costs, including salt to treat the roads, will depend on winter weather conditions according to the following probability distribution:

Cost of drivers' wages, fuel, maintenance and salt

Winter weather	Probability	Annual cost (£m)
Severe	0.2	1.5
Average	0.5	0.8
Good	0.3	0.3

Instead of buying 10 vehicles, Arctica is considering contracting-out the whole operation. It has received an unofficial tender from a waste management company, Dumpex plc, which might be willing to perform the required services at an all-in fee of £1m pa, payable at the end of each year.

Central government guidelines require regional authorities to evaluate capital expenditures at a discount rate of 5% expressed in real terms. The real rate of return in the private sector for transport and related activities is currently 8% net of all taxes.

All estimates of costs and benefits have been made in constant price terms. As a public sector organisation, Arctica is not liable to pay taxes.

Required:

(i)   Is it financially more worthwhile for Arctica to purchase the new vehicles or to accept the tender from Dumpex?

   Explain your answer.   **(15 marks)**

(ii)   What is the maximum annual tender figure at which Arctica would contract out the operation?

   Explain your answer.   **(3 marks)**

(d)   Find the break-even value of the annual contract fee payable to Dumpex plc on the assumption that Arctica is unable to conclude any form of contract with the quarry company.

   Comment on your results.   **(9 marks)**

(e)   Discuss *three* alternative ways in which Arctica could finance this project.
                                                                        (9 marks)
                                                                    (Total: 50 marks)
                                                                    (ACCA June 95)

FEEDBACK TO ACTIVITY 1

(i)   Replace every year

$$\text{NPV of 1 cycle} = -£5,000 + \frac{£3,000}{1.12} = £(2,321)$$

$$\text{EAC} = \frac{£(2,321)}{0.893} = £(2,599)$$

(ii)   Replace every other year

$$\text{NPV of 1 cycle} = -£5,000 - \frac{£800}{1.12} + \frac{£1,500}{1.12^2} = £(4,518)$$

$$\text{EAC} = \frac{£(4,,518)}{1.690} = £(2,673)$$

Replacing every year is the cheaper option.

FEEDBACK TO ACTIVITY 2

The investment of £1,000 is itself a mini-project whose NPV is computed as follows:

Year	Cash flow £	Discount factor £
1	(1,000)	0.909
2	1,000	0.826
		(83)

As expected the NPV of this project is negative.

However the effect of undertaking this short-term investment is to tighten the cash constraint in year 1 (to £24,000) and relax it in year 2 (to £21,000).

Thus the problem becomes:

Constraints: Year 0 (unchanged) a + 2b ≤ 2
                      Year 1 20a + 10b ≤ 24
                      Year 2 30a ≤ 21
                      Non-negativity   0 ≤ a ≤ 1
                                            0 ≤ b ≤ 1

Objective:

To maximise $22,140a + 15,970b - 83$

Solving the equations at corner Q as before

$$a = 7/10$$

$$b = 13/20$$

Thus, the NPV $= (22{,}140 \times 7/10) + (15{,}970 \times 13/20) - 83$

$= \pounds25{,}795$

This represents a gain of £389 over the previous optimum solution, and hence it is worthwhile to accept the opportunity (provided possible) to retain the £1,000 despite having a rate of return (nil) below 10%.

Chapter 16
COSTING SYSTEMS AND TECHNIQUES – 1

This chapter marks the start of the management accounting part of the syllabus, and looks at the contribution of cost and management accounting to financial management and control.

Objectives

By the time you have finished this chapter you should be able to do the following:

*   outline and distinguish between the nature and scope of management accounting and the role of costing in meeting the needs of management

*   describe the purpose of costing as an aid to planning, monitoring and controlling business activity

*   describe different approaches to costing: absorption costing, marginal costing, activity-based costing and service costing

*   describe the costing information requirements and limitations in not-for-profit organisations

*   explain the potential for different costing approaches to influence profit reporting and the pricing of products and internal services

*   explain the role of costing systems in decision-making.

1   Management accounting

DEFINITION

Management accounting is the process of **identification, measurement, accumulation, analysis, preparation, interpretation** and **communication** of information used by management to **plan, evaluate** and **control** the activities of an organisation.

Management accounting is the process of **identification, measurement, accumulation, analysis, preparation, interpretation** and **communication** of information used by management to **plan, evaluate** and **control** the activities of an organisation. As the definition implies, the management accountant has a wide ranging area of responsibility involving professional knowledge and skill in the preparation and, in particular, the presentation of information to all levels of management in the organisation structure. This information will be used by management to assist in its activities of:

*   planning

*   decision-making

*   monitoring and control.

1.1   Planning

Information provided by the management accountant to assist in the planning process may relate to:

*   pricing

*   capital expenditure projects

*   product costs

*   markets and competition

*   past costs and revenues for budgeting purposes.

The management accountant will be heavily involved with the budgeting process itself, establishing procedures and timetables, and co-ordinating subsidiary budgets into an overall master budget.

 FOULKS LYNCH PUBLICATIONS

1.2 Decision-making

On a more day-to-day basis, the management accountant can assist in the decisions regarding production plans and other resource allocation problems by analysing cost information using techniques such as key factor analysis, opportunity costing, etc.

1.3 Monitoring and control

The production of performance reports will be the management accountant's responsibility, in which actual costs and revenues are compared with budgeted, with significant variances highlighted. Before presenting this to management, the management accountant will be expected to carry out investigations into the reasons for the variances and possible ways of rectifying adverse conditions.

In summary, the role of the management accountant can thus be described as one of a **gate-keeper** and an **information manager.**

1.4 The gate-keeper

The management accountant is often viewed as the keeper of the gate through which all transactions and information flow.

Management accountants have been trained to ensure that transactions must be properly authorised and payments not made until it is confirmed that the goods/services have been provided and that the price charged is that agreed. Consequently other managers may see the management accountant as the person who approves the transaction, though in non-financial decisions this is unlikely. The management accountant is merely responsible for ensuring that approval has been received.

The management accountant is likely, however, to control the flow of information within an organisation.

It is the management accountant who decides:

- which information concerning costs and revenues is collected
- the basis on which calculations and valuations are made
- how information is presented and with what frequency
- who receives the information.

1.5 The information manager

Accounting information is part of the overall information system of the organisation. Since management accounting uses numeric and other quantitative data in its reports and analysis, the management accountant is often seen as the focal point for such information.

Other managers will ask the management accountant to provide data in respect of certain decisions. These may be historical using data already available, or they may involve the prediction of future outcomes. In either case they make use of the quantitative data which is accessed via the management accounting system.

KEY POINT

In summary, the role of the management accountant can thus be described as one of a **gate-keeper** and an **information manager**.

2 Cost accounting

One of the major sources of data and information upon which the management accountant will draw is the costing records and accounts.

Cost accounting can therefore be seen as a subsidiary part of the wider area of management accounting. Cost accounting is the establishment of **budgets, standard costs** and **actual costs** of operations, processes, activities or products, and the analysis of **variances, profitability** or **social use** of funds. It involves the use of a comprehensive set of principles, methods and techniques in the determination and appropriate analysis of costs to meet the needs of, in particular, the management accountant.

DEFINITION

Cost accounting is the establishment of **budgets, standard costs** and **actual costs** of operations, processes, activities or products, and the analysis of **variances, profitability** or **social use** of funds.

FOULKS LYNCH
PUBLICATIONS

Consider the following simple trading and profit and loss account that may form part of the financial accounts.

XYZ Company
Trading and profit and loss account for the year ended . . .

		£	£
Sales			200,000
Cost of sales:	Materials consumed	80,000	
	Wages	40,000	
	Production expenses	15,000	
			135,000
Gross profit			65,000
Marketing expenses		15,000	
General administrative expenses		10,000	
Financing costs		4,000	
			29,000
Net profit before tax			36,000

The above statement may be adequate to provide outsiders with a superficial picture of the trading results of the business, but managers would need much more detail to answer questions such as these.

- What are our major products and which ones are most profitable?

- How much has our stock of raw materials increased?

- How does our labour cost per unit compare with last period?

- Are our personnel department expenses more than we expected?

The cost accountant will aim to maintain a system which will provide the answers to those (and many other) questions on a regular and **ad-hoc** basis. In addition, the cost accounts will contain detailed information concerning stocks of raw materials, work-in-progress and finished goods as a basis for the valuation necessary to prepare final accounts.

ACTIVITY 1

Before reading further list what you think the aims of costing might be and compare your answer with the section below.

Feedback to this activity is at the end of the chapter.

3   Costing issues

Note: If you are familiar with the basic techniques of cost accounting, you should be able to read through the first part of this chapter fairly quickly.

DEFINITION

A **cost unit** is a unit of product or service in relation to which costs are ascertained.

3.1   Cost units

One of the principal pieces of information provided by the costing system will be the cost of the products or other outputs of the business. A **cost unit** is a unit of product or service in relation to which costs are ascertained.

The ascertainment of the cost per cost unit is important in:

- pricing decisions

- assessing the viability of special orders

- measuring changes in costs and efficiency levels

- stock valuation
- budgeting.

Cost units may be identified for the control of both the productive and the support activities of a business. Some examples are given below.

Knowledge of the unit costs is essential in **pricing** and **product mix** decisions, **stock valuation** and for **budgeting** purposes.

Industry or activity	Cost unit
Manufacturing industries	
Brewers	Barrel/hectolitre
Brick-making	1,000 bricks
Coal mining	Ton/tonne
Paper	Ream
Sand and gravel	Cubic yard/metre
Service industries	
Hospitals	(a) Beds occupied
	(b) Out-patient
Professional service, e.g. accountants	Chargeable man-hour
Individual departments	
Personnel departments and welfare	Employee
Materials storage/handling	(a) Requisition units issued/received
	(b) Material movement values issued/received

ACTIVITY 2

What cost units are used in an organisation with which you are familiar?

There is no feedback to this activity.

3.2 Cost classification

Costs may be classified using a number of different criteria. Classification is the logical grouping of similar items and the purpose of classifying costs is so that meaningful cost accounting reports may be prepared based upon such costs.

The classification criterion chosen will depend on both the purpose of the classification and the type of organisation. Some classifications (e.g. by element) greatly assist the collection of costs. Different classifications are dealt with below.

Elements of cost

The initial classification of costs is according to the **elements** upon which expenditure is incurred:

- materials
- labour
- expenses.

Within the cost elements, costs can be further classified according to the **nature** of expenditure. This is the usual analysis in a financial accounting system, e.g. raw materials, consumable stores, wages, salaries, rent, rates, depreciation.

DEFINITION

Direct costs are costs which are incurred for, and can be conveniently identified with, a particular cost unit. The aggregate of direct materials, direct wages and direct expenses is known as **prime cost**.

Indirect costs are costs which cannot be associated with a particular unit of output. The total of indirect materials, indirect wages and indirect expenses represents **overheads**.

Direct and indirect costs

Direct costs are costs which are incurred for, and can be conveniently identified with, a particular cost unit. The aggregate of direct materials, direct wages and direct expenses is known as **prime cost**.

Indirect costs are costs which cannot be associated with a particular unit of output. The total of indirect materials, indirect wages and indirect expenses represents **overheads**.

To ascertain the total cost of a cost unit, indirect costs are allotted to cost centres and cost centre costs are shared over (absorbed by) cost units. The subject of allotment and absorption of overhead costs is revised later.

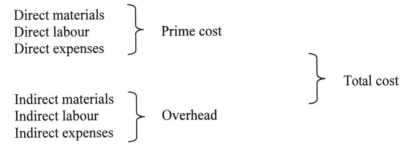

Functional analysis of cost

Overhead classification

Overheads are usually categorised into the principal activity groups:

- manufacturing
- administration
- selling
- distribution
- research.

Prime cost classification

Prime costs are usually regarded as being solely related to production, and so are not classified.

Normal and abnormal costs

An important feature of management reporting is that it should emphasise the areas of the business which require management attention and possible action.

Controllable and non-controllable costs

The need to emphasise abnormal costs to management has been explained above. The purpose of this is to encourage management action. The distinction between controllable and non-controllable costs is dependent on the person to whom any report is directed. The classification emphasises the costs which can be affected by the actions of a particular manager.

Relevant and irrelevant costs

In the context of decision-making management needs information to assist them in making the correct choice between alternatives. For these purposes and to ensure that valuable management time is not wasted only those costs affected by the management's decision are important. These are classified as relevant costs, and include opportunity costs.

To be relevant a cost must be future and incremental (i.e. changed by the decision) as discussed earlier in the context of investment appraisal.

Fixed and variable costs

The final classification, which is of great relevance in decision-making, is by behaviour. The analysis of costs between fixed, variable and semi-variable elements should be very familiar to you by now.

3.3   Impact of costing approaches on management information

As you work through the remainder of the text you should become aware of the ways in which the different costing approaches studied can impact on the various areas of management concern. Examples are given below:

(a)   **Cost accumulation and profit reporting**

Different costing methods produce different measurements of profit.

- The way in which costs are attributed to cost units – under marginal, absorption or ABC principles – can have significantly different effects on their valuation. This, in turn, will impact on reported profits.

- The absorption of fixed costs into cost units can lead to distortion of profits where stock levels are changing significantly.

- The use of activity based costing principles can lead to significantly different product costings from those obtained under traditional absorption costing.

(b)   **Decision-making**

- The use of an opportunity costing approach to evaluation of existing resources in a short-term opportunity will often lead to a much lower acceptable selling price than where traditional historical costing principles are applied.

- Product profit statements drawn up under different cost accumulation methods can give very different pictures of the relative profitability of potential products and therefore optimum production plans.

There is a danger that the information provided by costing systems can be misleading and prompt management into making inappropriate decisions. Decisions should be based on relevant costs only, and for capital investment decisions n the time value of money.

(c)   **Control and performance evaluation**

- The use of target costing and life cycle costing principles may focus attention on more relevant areas for cost control and reduction than traditional long-run variance analysis.

- The basis upon which standards are determined and the way in which budgets are managed will affect reported variances and can have significant behavioural effects on staff.

(d)   **Pricing**

Costing systems can influence pricing decisions. Where the aim of an organisation is to make a profit, it is reasonable to assume that products or services should be sold at a price in excess of their cost. Consequently, pricing decisions could be based on a cost-plus approach, by adding a profit mark-up to cost. However, pricing should be based on what the market will bear, and cost-plus pricing, for both selling externally and for internal transfers between profit centres of the business, has severe limitations and should be regarded as inferior in most circumstances to a market-based approach to pricing.

4   Absorption costing

Under the **absorption costing** method, in addition to direct costs, a share of indirect production costs (overheads) is attributed to cost units by means **of overhead absorption rates.**

Our first area of study concerns the traditional method of absorbing overheads into product costs, the detailed mechanics of which will be familiar to you from your earlier studies. Here we are more concerned with evaluation of this method against others, in particular marginal costing and activity based costing.

4.1   Overheads

In many businesses, particularly in the modern manufacturing environment, overheads represent a large element of cost, and can also present the largest accounting problem!

In this context, we are generally referring to production overheads. Marketing, general administration, R&D costs etc, that are not directly concerned with production, are not generally included in cost accumulation exercises, being treated as period costs.

Production overheads are the indirect materials, wages and expenses attributable to production and the service activities associated with production.

Indirect production costs are incurred in three main ways:

- **Production activities** – costs arising in production departments such as fuel, protective clothing, depreciation and supervision.
- **Service activities** – the cost of operating non-producing departments or sections within the factory, e.g. materials handling, production control, canteen.
- **Establishment costs** – general production overhead such as factory rent/rates, heating and lighting and production management salaries.

The **objectives** of accounting for overheads are as follows:

- To identify costs in relation to output products and services
- To identify costs in relation to activities and divisions of the organisation
- To control overhead costs.

The procedures described in the rest of this section are largely concerned with the first objective above. Their relationship to the other objectives is discussed subsequently. The steps involved are directed at establishing an **overhead absorption rate**. This rate is used to relate overheads to cost units.

Whilst such an overhead absorption rate may be a blanket rate for the whole enterprise, normally **departmental absorption rates** will be established for application to **cost units** passing through all the production cost centres.

4.2   Overhead absorption – revision example

The following example revises the basic processes of allocation, apportionment and absorption of overheads via cost centres, both production and service, studied in an earlier paper.

A **cost centre** is a production or service location, function, activity or item of equipment whose costs may be attributed to cost units.

The ABC Washing Machine Co produces a standard washing machine in three production departments (Machining, Assembling and Finishing) and two service departments (Materials handling and Production control).

Costs for last year, when 2,000 machines were produced, were as follows:

Materials

Machine shop	£240,000
Assembly	£160,000
Finishing	£40,000
Materials handling	£4,000

Wages

Machining	10,000 hours at £3.72
Assembly	5,000 hours at £2.88
Finishing	3,000 hours at £3.60
Materials handling	£8,000
Production control	£11,200

Other costs

Machine shop	£41,920
Assembly	£12,960
Finishing	£7,920
Materials handling	£8,000
Production control	£2,400

It is estimated that the benefit derived from the service departments is as follows:

Materials handling

Machine shop	60%
Assembly	30%
Finishing	10%

Production control

Machine shop	40%
Assembly	30%
Finishing	20%
Materials handling	10%

Required

(a) Prepare a statement showing the overhead allocated/apportioned to each of the production departments.

(b) Calculate the unit cost of a washing machine.

Solution

(a) *Overhead allocation and apportionment*

Materials and wages incurred by the production departments may be assumed to be direct costs and therefore excluded from the overhead distribution.

	Total	Machining	Assembly	Finishing	Production control	Materials handling
	£	£	£	£	£	£
Indirect materials	4,000	-	-	-	-	4,000
Indirect wages	19,200	-	-	-	11,200	8,000
Other	73,200	41,920	12,960	7,920	2,400	8,000
	96,400	41,920	12,960	7,920	13,600	20,000
Production control	-	5,440	4,080	2,720	(13,600)	1,360
Materials handling	-	12,816	6,408	2,136	-	(21,360)
	96,400	60,176	23,448	12,776	-	-

Overheads are **allocated/apportioned** to cost centres using any 'reasonable basis'. Costs accumulated in service cost centres are then **re-apportioned** to

production cost centres. The total costs in these are finally **absorbed** into cost units using an appropriate **absorption rate.**

Service department costs have been apportioned to production departments using the percentage benefit shown in the question.

(b)   Unit cost

	Machining £	Assembly £	Finishing £	Total £
Direct materials	240,000	160,000	40,000	440,000
Direct wages	37,200	14,400	10,800	62,400
Production overheads	60,176	23,448	12,776	96,400
	337,376	197,848	63,576	598,800
Units produced				2,000
Cost per unit				£299.40

5   Absorption rates

5.1   Single product absorption rate

The overhead absorption rate is the following fraction:

$$\frac{\text{Cost centre overhead in £}}{\text{Cost centre volume in units}}$$

In the ABC example the number of washing machines used was the measure of volume. This was acceptable because the question stated that a standard machine was produced. As all the machines were of the same type it is fair that each one should bear the same share of the costs of operating the departments which produced them.

5.2   More than one product

If, however, the ABC Washing Machine Co produced three types of machine (say regular, super and deluxe), then the amount of work (and therefore the cost) would be different for each type. The difference in direct cost can be measured; more or less materials would be requisitioned and more or less labour hours would be spent.

It would now be unreasonable to use units as the basis for absorbing overheads. It may take longer and more materials to produce a deluxe machine than a regular model and, therefore, the deluxe machine uses more of the production resources represented by overhead costs.

Thus, overhead may be absorbed in cost units by any of the following means:

- rate per unit
- percentage of prime cost (direct labour, direct material and direct expenses)
- percentage of direct wages
- direct labour hour rate
- machine hour rate.

Example

Facts are as in the ABC example. A separate absorption rate for each cost centre is to be calculated as follows.

- Machining: machine hour rate (each machine is manned by four operatives).
- Assembly: direct labour hour rate.
- Finishing: percentage of direct wages.

FOULKS LYNCH
PUBLICATIONS

Solution

Absorption rates

$$\text{Machining} = \frac{\text{Cost centre overhead}}{\text{Machine hours}} = \frac{£60,176}{10,000 \div 4} = £24.07 \text{ per machine hour}$$

$$\text{Assembly} = \frac{\text{Cost centre overhead}}{\text{Direct labour hours}} = \frac{£23,448}{5,000} = £4.69 \text{ per labour hour}$$

$$\text{Finishing} = \frac{\text{Cost centre overhead} \times 100}{\text{Direct wages}} = \frac{£12,776 \times 100}{£10,800} = 118.3\% \text{ of direct wages}$$

The overhead absorbed by a particular washing machine could then be accumulated.

Assume that a regular machine takes 1 hour machining, 2 hours assembly and 1 hour finishing.

Overhead absorbed

		£
Machining	1 hour × £24.07	24.07
Assembly	2 hours × £4.69	9.38
Finishing	118.3% of (1 × £3.60)	4.25
		37.70

5.3 Under/over-absorption of overheads

The washing machine illustration implies that absorption rates were calculated after the event, i.e. when overhead and volume for the period had been ascertained. This is not so. Unit costs are a continuous requirement for management information and will invariably reflect overhead absorption on a **predetermined basis**:

$$\text{Absorption rate} = \frac{\text{Budgeted overhead}}{\text{Budgeted volume}}$$

Generally, the rate is derived from the annual budget to avoid distortion caused by seasonal fluctuation and to provide a consistent basis for measuring variations.

Actual overhead and/or volume will rarely coincide exactly with budget and therefore a difference between overhead absorbed and overhead incurred will arise.

Example

In year 9 the budget for a machine shop shows:

    Overhead   £60,000

    Volume   12,000 machine hours

In January, year 9, the machine shop incurred £5,400 of overhead and 1,050 machine hours were worked.

Calculate the predetermined absorption rate and the overhead under- or over-absorbed in January.

$$\text{Absorption rate} = \frac{\text{Budgeted overhead}}{\text{Budgeted volume}} = \frac{£60,000}{12,000 \text{ machine hours}} = £5.00 \text{ per machine hour}$$

	£
Overhead incurred	5,400
Overhead absorbed (1,050 hours × £5.00)	5,250
Under-absorbed overhead	150

The under-absorption arises from a combination of two factors.

(1) Overhead costs were higher than budget ($\frac{£60,000}{12}$) for the month;

(2) Volume was greater than budget ($\frac{12,000 \text{ hours}}{12}$) for the month.

In practice a separate absorption rate may be calculated for fixed and variable overhead to enable the effect of cost and volume changes to be shown more clearly. Analysis of over/under-absorbed overhead is perhaps covered more appropriately under **standard costing**.

Note that overhead absorbed (sometimes called **recovered**) represents:

Actual production (machine hours in this instance)	×	Predetermined rate per unit (machine hours)

5.4   Appraisal of total absorption costing

Arguments for the use of absorption costing:

- It is necessary to include fixed overhead in stock values for financial statements. Routine cost accounting using absorption costing produces stock values which include a share of fixed overhead.

- For small jobbing business, overhead allotment is the only practicable way of obtaining job costs for estimating and profit analysis.

- Analysis of under/over-absorbed overhead is useful to identify inefficient utilisation of production resources.

Arguments against the use of absorption costing

- Allocation, apportionment and absorption methods are arbitrary. For example it is common to split heating costs on the basis of floor area – but clearly that is not the only acceptable method. Also, it may be difficult to justify absorption on labour hours rather than machine hours. This problem is increased when service departments exist and a basis of re-apportionment of their costs must be agreed on. Often the selection of the basis used for allocation, apportionment and absorption owes more to the debating skills of the various managers at costing meetings than to the underlying production and selling and distribution realities.

- It treats what are predominantly fixed costs as if they varied per unit. For example, rent or depreciation of the factory will be absorbed per labour hour, but, of course, it does not really change with the number of hours worked, or number of units of production produced.

- Under or over-absorption will almost certainly need adjusting for at the year end. Only if both expenditure and the activity level are exactly as budgeted will the 'correct' amount of overheads be absorbed into production. This is very unlikely.

Two alternative methods need to be considered that will go some way towards addressing these problems:

- marginal costing

- activity based costing.

6 Marginal costing

Marginal costing is the term applied when the routine cost accounting system incorporates the marginal principle. Under absorption costing the unit cost includes an absorbed amount calculated from total overheads, i.e. fixed plus variable. Under marginal costing only variable costs are charged to cost units. Fixed costs for a period are fully written off against contribution.

The fundamental difference between marginal and absorption costing is therefore one of timing. Under marginal costing fixed production overheads are charged **in the period incurred**. Under absorption costing fixed production overheads are absorbed into units made and charged **in the period of sale**.

6.1 Marginal and absorption costing profit statements compared

Example

Company A produces a single product with the following budget:

Selling price	£10
Direct materials	£3 per unit
Direct wages	£2 per unit
Variable overhead	£1 per unit
Fixed overhead	£10,000 per month.

The fixed overhead absorption rate is based on a volume of 5,000 units per month. Show the operating statement for the month, when 4,800 units were produced and sold under:

(a)   absorption costing;

(b)   marginal costing.

Assume that costs were as budget.

Solution

(a)   *Absorption costing*

	£
Sales (4,800 units)	48,000
Cost of sales (4,800 × £8) (W1)	38,400
	———
Operating margin	9,600
Under-absorbed overhead (W2)	(400)
	———
Operating profit	9,200
	———

Workings

(W1) Unit cost represents materials (£3) + wages (£2) + variable overhead (£1) + fixed overhead absorbed ($\frac{£10,000}{5,000}$) = £8 per unit.

The actual activity level is not the same as the budgeted level and thus the predetermined absorption rate of $\frac{£10,000}{5,000 \text{ units}}$, i.e. £2 per unit results in an under-absorption of fixed overheads which must be adjusted for in the operating statement.

(W2)
	£	
Fixed overhead incurred	10,000	
Fixed overhead absorbed	9,600	(4,800 × £2)
	———	
Under-absorption	400	
	———	

An adjustment for under or over-absorption of fixed overheads will be necessary if:

(i)   the actual activity level is different to that budgeted, or

(ii)   actual expenditure on fixed overheads is different to that budgeted.

(b)   *Marginal costing*

	£
Sales	48,000
Variable cost of sales (4,800 × £6)	28,800
Contribution	19,200
Fixed costs	10,000
Operating profit	9,200

6.2   Profit reconciliations: marginal and absorption costing

In the example above operating profit is the same under both methods. That will not be so, however, when production is more or less than sales, i.e. stocks of finished goods are maintained.

Under marginal costing stocks of work in progress and finished products will be valued at variable costs only. Where production and sales levels are not in sympathy and stock levels are fluctuating, the net profit will be different from that disclosed by an absorption method of costing which values stocks of work in progress and finished products to include an amount of absorbed fixed production overheads.

Example

Use the same price and cost information as in the above example but assume that production was 4,800 units and sales were 4,500 units. The company has no opening stocks. Show the operating statement for the month under:

(a)   absorption costing

(b)   marginal costing, and

(c)   reconcile the difference in reported profit.

Solution

(a)   *Absorption costing*

	£	£
Sales (4,500 × £10)		45,000
Cost of sales		
Opening stock	-	
Production cost (4,800 × £8)	38,400	
Closing stock (300 × £8)	(2,400)	
		(36,000)
Operating margin		9,000
Under-absorbed overhead		(400)
Operating profit		8,600

(b) *Marginal costing*

	£	£
Sales (4,500 × £10)		45,000
Cost of sales		
Opening stock	-	
Production cost (4,800 × £6)	28,800	
Closing stock (300 × £6)	(1,800)	
		(27,000)
Contribution		18,000
Fixed costs		10,000
Operating profit		8,000

(c) *Reconciliation of profit figures*

	£	£
Profit under marginal costing		8,000
Closing stock valuation under absorption costing (300 × £8)	2,400	
Closing stock valuation under marginal costing (300 × £6)	1,800	
Fixed costs absorbed into closing stock in absorption costing		600
Profit under absorption costing		8,600

6.3 Appraisal of marginal costing

Preparation of routine operating statements using marginal costing is considered more informative to management.

• **Contribution per unit** is a direct measure of how profit and volume relate. Profit per unit is a misleading figure: in the example the operating margin of £2 per unit arises because fixed overhead per unit is based on 5,000 units. If another basis were used, margin per unit would differ even though fixed overhead was the same amount in total.

• Build-up or run-down of stocks of finished goods will not distort comparison of period operating statements. Absorption costing statements may obscure the effect of increasing or decreasing sales. Note that in the first example if production had been 6,000 units, i.e. 4,800 sold plus 1,200 held in stock, the absorption costing statement would be as follows:

	£	£
Sales	48,000	
Cost of sales		
Production 6,000 × £8	48,000	
Closing stock 1,200 × £8	9,600	
		38,400
Operating margin		9,600
Over-absorbed fixed overhead (6,000 × £2) – £10,000		2,000
Operating profit		11,600

A marginal costing statement would, however, still show a profit of £9,200 because production and closing stocks are valued at the variable cost of £6 per unit.

- There is no arbitrary apportionment of fixed costs that may give misleading product cost comparisons.

7   Activity based costing

Whilst marginal costing gives useful information for decision-making, businesses will generally have to absorb both variable and fixed production overheads for external reporting (and possibly pricing) purposes.

However, it is generally accepted that in the modern manufacturing environment the traditional absorption methods, for example using direct labour or machine hours as a basis for absorption, can result in quite misleading product costs.

7.1   The traditional manufacturing environment

The traditional absorption costing method was considered adequate when manufacturing processes were continuous production lines being highly labour/machine intensive. A high proportion of total production costs were represented by direct costs. Indirect costs (factory supervision, machine running costs etc) were quite closely related to labour or machines; and even if overhead allocation was fairly arbitrary, it was an insignificant part of product cost and had little impact.

7.2   The modern manufacturing environment

With manufacturing processes being increasingly computerised, production moving away from continuous high volume runs to smaller customised batches and the resulting high proportion of indirect costs arising from production scheduling, quality control, marketing etc, the traditional method is no longer seen as giving acceptable results.

Activity based costing (ABC) is the process of cost attribution to cost units on the basis of benefit received from indirect activities, e.g. ordering, setting up, assuring quality.

The ABC system recognises that:

- activities consume resources and products consume activities

- direct labour and machine hours are not meaningful cost drivers for many overheads in modern manufacturing environments.

A **cost driver** is a factor that causes an activity to occur, and thus determines the size of the activity's costs.

An American university professor, Robert Kaplan of the Harvard Business School, was one of the original critics of the traditional method of absorbing indirect costs into product costs. Professor Kaplan has subsequently put forward an alternative approach to product costing. This alternative approach is based on linking overheads to the products which cause them and absorbing on the basis of the activities that 'drive' costs (the cost drivers). This approach is usually referred to as **activity based costing** (ABC).

ABC provides cost information which can be used in understanding what drives overhead costs for meaningful performance measurement, product costing and profitability analysis. The following diagram illustrates the ABC approach:

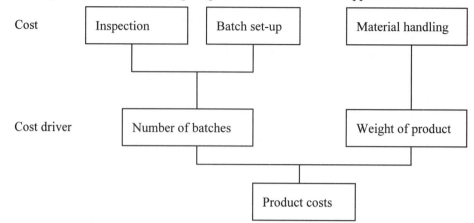

Therefore, the product that is produced in the smallest batches and has a relatively high weight, is deemed to be the most expensive. The number of batches and the weight of the product are the characteristics that drive costs, and are therefore used to absorb indirect costs into the cost of a product.

The use of an appropriate absorption base will not produce 'exact' measures of product cost but they will produce meaningful 'estimates'. With the evolution of manufacturing changing the structure of product cost from primarily variable to predominantly fixed costs and increasing the importance of overhead functions, the recognition of the shortfall of traditional costing is essential, and the use of a more meaningful system such as ABC should be promoted.

Typical overheads which are not driven by production volume are listed below:

- **Set-up costs** – driven by the number of manufacturing set-ups.

- **Order processing costs** – driven by the number of receiving orders raised.

- **Packing department costs** – driven by the number of packing orders.

- **Engineering department costs** – driven by the number of production orders.

7.3   The mechanics of ABC

Three stages can be identified:

Step 1   The **collection** of overhead costs in the same way as traditional overhead control accounts would operate.

Step 2   The **pooling** of costs based upon the activities which have consumed resources rather than on the basis of production departments or centres. The activities selected are based upon four classes of transaction:

- Logistical transactions – the moving and tracking of materials in and through the production process.

- Balancing transactions – matching resources with the demands of the production operation. This will include ensuring that resources are available when required.

- Quality transactions – ensuring output conforms with established specifications which will meet all market expectations.

- Change transactions – the need to respond to changes in customer demand, design changes, scheduling, supply and production methods.

Such transactions will frequently cross the traditional functional boundaries of an organisation.

Step 3   The various overhead transactions are then allocated to the products based upon a series of cost drivers which indicate how the product has made demands upon the various activities. The rates for charging out are based upon dividing the activity cost for a period by the cost driver volume. Thus the cost of the purchasing function will be divided by the number of purchase orders raised by each department.

Example

Oceanides has four departments who make use of the procurement function. The total cost of the function is £10,000,000 per annum. The four departments use the function in the following way.

Department	No of orders	Cost allocation £
A	200,000	6,666,667
B	50,000	1,666,667
C	40,000	1,333,333
D	10,000	333,333
	300,000	10,000,000

Simply dividing the total cost by the cost driver we get:

$$\frac{£10,000,000}{300,000} = £33.33 \text{ per order.}$$

ACTIVITY 3

Pelleas has the following indirect costs.	£	No. of cost drivers	
Quality control	90,000	450	inspections
Process set-up	135,000	450	set-ups
Purchasing	105,000	1,000	purchase orders
Customer order processing	120,000	2,000	customers
Occupancy costs	150,000	75,000	machine hours
	600,000		

Calculate the charge-out rates for each of the activities.

Feedback to this activity is at the end of the chapter.

7.4   Product costing with ABC

Having identified the overhead absorption rates based upon appropriate cost drivers, we are now in a position to attribute costs to products.

Example

Pelleas, (the company in the above activity), makes a standard product called the Melisande.

The cost details are as follows.

Unit material cost	£0.50
Unit labour cost	£0.40
Total production for the coming year	1,000,000 units
Number of production runs	50
No. of purchase orders required	50
Number of customer orders	10
Unit machine time	3 minutes

The product run is inspected once at the end of each production run.

Using the cost driver rates calculated in the activity, **you are required** to calculate the standard cost of a Melisande.

Solution

We need to draw up a grid for the overheads.

Function	Rate × Usage		£
Quality control	£200 × 50	=	10,000
Process set-up	£300 × 50	=	15,000
Purchasing	£105 × 50	=	5,250
Customer orders	£60 × 10	=	600
Occupancy	£2 × 50,000	=	100,000
			130,850

Dividing the total overhead cost by the number of units produced we get:

$$\frac{130,850}{1,000,000} = £0.13085 \text{ (say £0.13)}$$

Thus the standard unit cost for a Melisande is as follows.

	£
Material	0.50
Labour	0.40
Overhead	0.13
	1.03

7.5 Selecting the cost drivers

In the main, the cost driver will be measured in terms of volume of transactions. However, ABC also tries to identify costs that are not contributing to the value of the product/service so the following questions are relevant:

* What services does this activity provide?
* Who receives the services?
* Why do you require so many people?
* What might cause you to require more/less staff?
* Why does over/idle time exist?

Three types of cost driver have emerged:

* **Pure activity output volume** – where the basic transactions of the activity are identical in terms of their resource demands such as the purchasing of raw materials or a similar range of items.

* **Activity/output volume/complexity** – where the basic transactions differ in terms of their resource demands as when purchases are made from different overseas suppliers.

* **Situation** – where an underlying factor can be identified as driving the workload of an activity such as the number of suppliers when supplier vetting and liaison were vital components of the cost pool.

Examples of cost drivers

The following are examples of cost drivers in the **manufacturing sector**.

Activity	Cost driver
Material procurement	No. of purchase orders
Material handling	No. of movements
Quality control	No. of inspections
Engineering services	No. of change orders

Maintenance	No. of break-downs
Line set-up	No. of set-ups

For the **service sector** the following taken from the field of health care may serve as an example. The cost drivers form the basis of costs charged to patients.

Activity	*Cost driver*
Patient movement	No. of in-patients
Booking appointments	No. of patients
Patient reception	No. of patients
X-ray:	
equipment preparation	Time taken
patient preparation	Time taken
patient aftercare	Time taken
film processing	No. of images
Film reporting	No. of images

From Kirton "*ABC at Luton & Dunstable Hospital*"

7.6   The merits of ABC

- An improved, more accurate product cost may enable a company to concentrate on a more profitable mix of products or customers. ABC has been effectively used in identifying customers who are unprofitable to service.

  It is argued that traditional overhead apportionment leads to incorrect commitment of resources to products.

- ABC extends the variable cost rationale to both short and long-term costs by quantitatively addressing the cost behaviour patterns in terms of both short- run volume changes as well as long-term cost trends.

- It helps identify value added and non-value added costs so that the non-value added items can be appraised effectively with a view to elimination. As such it forces managers and supervisors to consider the drivers that effect costs and what these drivers contribute to the final product.

Thus the managers will have a better understanding of the economics of production and the economics of the activities performed by the company.

7.7   The weaknesses of ABC

Ahmed and Scapens *(Cost allocation: theory and practice 1991)* warned that ABC was unlikely to relate all overheads to specific activities. It also ignores the potential for conflict, especially where there is more than one potential cost driver.

More recently, the warning has been reiterated by emphasising that there is no such thing as a 100% accurate cost. At best, ABC will only improve the quality of cost information. The student should perhaps note Brimson's 1991 definition of product cost – 'a summation of the cost of all traceable activities to design, procure material, manufacture and distribute a product.'

Perhaps the key word in that definition is traceable, whether or not a cost can be traced objectively to the production/delivery of a good/service.

8 Service costing

So far we have considered the application of cost accumulation to production based businesses, which have a specific tangible product or cost unit against which to measure costs. Businesses or departments that provide a service do not tend to have such an easily identifiable cost unit, nor is it so easy to trace costs to specific output.

Examples of organisations where services are being **sold** include:

- the utilities – electricity, gas, water and telephone
- the professions – accountancy, architects etc
- passenger and freight transport
- broadcasting
- hospitals
- theatres
- education.

Examples of types of service **activities within businesses** (most of which will not earn any external revenue) include:

- canteens
- training departments
- maintenance departments
- power generating departments
- cleaning departments
- welfare departments
- stores.

8.1 Service costing units

Management needs to ascertain the cost of providing each unit of service for both decision-making and evaluation and control purposes.

- In **decision-making** the cost per unit is important for pricing decisions if the service is being sold, and for deciding if it is better to provide the service 'in-house' or buy it in if the service is part of a business.
- It is vital for **evaluation and cost control** purposes that management can compare (1) cost per unit in different locations or years, and (2) actual cost per unit with expected or budgeted cost per unit.

However the selection of cost unit is not always easy. Management must decide how to measure the service being provided and what measures of performance are most appropriate to the control of costs and how the costs can be collected.

ACTIVITY 4

List a number of service industries and service departments and determine their cost units.

There is no feedback to this activity.

8.2 Calculation of cost per unit of service

Direct and indirect costs must be identified or assigned to each service department and described under suitable headings. This will be achieved by coding suppliers invoices and by applying predetermined absorption rates. Management should also specify any additional information they require, e.g. splits into fixed and variable elements of cost.

9   Costing information in not-for-profit organisations

It is not always possible to state objectives in quantitative terms, or to measure the output of services, in not-for-profit organisations such as charities or public sector services.

Nevertheless, such organisations will incur costs, and many of the costing principles and techniques studied here will be of relevance. Particular areas of concern are discussed below.

9.1   Cost units

It is often more difficult to decide upon one principal measure of output in such organisations than in commercial concerns which sell specific products or services. Instead, a variety of cost units may be defined to measure the cost effectiveness of the various activities carried out by the organisations. For example, a college may use students, lecture-days and/or courses as cost units for cost control.

However, once such units have been defined, costs per unit can provide useful information for cost control. Comparisons with historical trends, or with similar cost data from similar activities in other organisations, may be made.

9.2   Performance measures

In a not-for-profit organisation, performance measures will need to measure both the quantity and the quality of outputs.

The former will often be easier than the latter. For example, in an outpatients' department of a hospital, it is relatively easy to measure the number of patients dealt with in a year; it is not so easy to measure the quality of care they received. This will require information that is outside the scope of the costing and other financial systems, such as patient surveys and recovery rates.

However, there are still many types of performance measure that can be used to evaluate performance. For example, in a college, the ratio of academic staff to students analysed by department, the cost per student and an analysis of student performance may provide useful indicators of operational performance.

Not-for-profit organisations' costing information requirements will be essentially similar to those of commercial concerns – detailed **analysis of costs** by department, activity, etc – although the definition of a **unique cost unit** to which these are attributed may be more difficult.

9.3   Planned versus actual results

Where an objective is stated in non-quantitative terms, the comparison between planned and actual level of achievement may need some degree of subjective judgement by a suitably qualified person or group of people. This is analogous to the judgement of creative competitions, such as gymnastics or piano playing.

Other procedures will be very similar to those used in commercial concerns. For example, school or hospital departments will generally have a budget to work towards, as dictated by funding available and prioritised needs of the various departments. Analysis of actual costs against these 'line' budgets can then be used to highlight areas of excessive expenditure.

10   Value analysis

Value analysis is a systematic interdisciplinary examination of factors affecting the cost of a product or service, in order to devise means of achieving the specified purpose **most economically** at the required standard of **quality** and **reliability**. It can be a particularly useful technique for controlling performance in not-for profit organisations, although it can be applied in a commercial environment too.

Value analysis is basically a form of cost reduction, i.e. a method of improving profitability by reducing costs without necessarily increasing prices; it is thus particularly useful to manufacturers or suppliers who are unable to fix their own price because of, for example, a competitive market.

However, the use of value analysis in all circumstances should be considered as it should be obvious that any failure to reduce costs will result in sub-optimisation of profitability.

Value analysis resulted from a realisation by manufacturers that they were incorporating features into their product which the user of the product did not require and was not prepared to pay for. For instance, few manufacturers of bath taps are prepared to produce taps in solid gold, as the demand for such expensive taps is very limited – most people are quite satisfied with brass.

In the same way, other not so obvious but equally *useless*, features can be incorporated into products.

Value analysis takes a critical look at each feature of a product, questioning its need and its use, and eliminating any unjustifiable features.

It is useful to distinguish two types of value – utility value and esteem value.

10.1 Utility value and esteem value

Utility value is the value an item has because of the uses to which it can be put. **Esteem value** is the value put on an item because of its beauty, craftsmanship etc.

Value analysis is basically concerned with those products which only have utility value and no esteem value.

The difference may be illustrated by reference to furniture. An individual who requires something to sit on may be satisfied with a crudely-made three-legged stool, or even a tree stump. He will be prepared to pay a very low sum of money for this. He may be prepared, however, to pay a great deal more money for a well-made fashionable reclining leather chair.

Both serve the same basic purposes – a seat – but while a tree stump only has utility value, the leather reclining chair has esteem value as well.

If a product has no esteem value, i.e. there is no need for aesthetic features, there is potential to reduce costs by excluding these.

10.2 The value analysis method

Value analysis is concerned with five basic areas:

Step 1   Establish the precise requirements of the customer. By a process of judicious enquiry it should be possible to discover precisely why customers want an item, whether the item has any esteem value, etc. Only in this way can the manufacturer be certain that each function incorporated into the product contributes some value to it.

Step 2   Establish and evaluate alternative ways of achieving the requirements of the customers. There may be methods of producing the item which have not

been considered, e.g. replacing metal panels with plastic. Each alternative method must be costed out in units of:

- **Materials** – amount required, acceptable level of wastage (can it be improved?), alternative, cheaper materials.

- **Labour** – can the cost be reduced by eliminating operations or changing production methods?

- **Other factors** – can new, cheaper processes be found? Would a cheaper finish be acceptable?

Step 3   Authorise any proposals put forward as a result of Step 2. The assessment in Step 2 may be carried out by middle management and, if so, it will require ratification by top management before implementation.

Step 4   Implementation of proposals.

Step 5   Evaluate feedback from new proposals to establish the benefits from the change.

Several benefits will result from value analysis:

- Many customers will be impressed by the interest shown in their requirements and this will lead to increased sales.

- A firm which adopts this approach is likely to attract better staff, due both to the prospects for an outlet for their ideas and the higher morale resulting from the team approach.

- There are economic and financial benefits arising from the elimination of unnecessary complexity and the better use of resources.

Example

ABC Ltd makes and sells two products, X and Y. Both products are manufactured through two consecutive processes – assembly and finishing. Raw material is input at the commencement of the assembly process. An activity based costing approach is used in the absorption of product specific conversion costs.

The following estimated information is available for the period ending 31 December 20X5.

	Product X	*Product Y*
Production/sales (units)	12,000	7,200
Selling price per unit	£75	£90
Direct material cost per unit	£20	£20
ABC variable conversion cost per unit		
- assembly	£20	£28
- finishing	£12	£24
Product specific fixed costs	£170,000	£90,000
Company fixed costs	£50,000	

ABC Ltd uses a minimum C/S ratio target of 25% when assessing the viability of a product. In addition, management wish to achieve an overall net profit margin of 12% on sales in this period in order to meet return on capital targets.

Explain how target costing may be used in achieving the required returns and suggest specific areas of investigation.

Solution

The information given will give the following estimated product and company results:

Per unit	Product X		Product Y		Company
	£	£	£	£	£
Selling price		75		90	
Less: variable costs					
materials	20		20		
conversion costs	32		52		

Per unit	Product X		Product Y		Company
	£	£	£	£	£
		(52)		(72)	
Contribution		23		18	
Contribution: sales ratio		30.7%		20%	

Total for period					
Sales		900,000		648,000	1,548,000
Contribution (sales × cont/unit)		276,000		129,600	
Product specific fixed costs		(170,000)		(90,000)	
Contribution		106,000		39,600	145,600
Company fixed costs					(50,000)
Net profit					95,600
Net profit margin on sales					6.2%

The company is falling considerably short of its 12% net profit margin target. If sales quantities and prices are to remain unchanged, costs must be reduced if the required return is to be reached.

KEY POINT

Value analysis takes a critical look at each feature of a product, questioning its need and its use, and eliminating any unjustifiable features.

Product Y is falling short of the C/S ratio target. Cost reduction exercises must be concentrated particularly on this product if its production is to continue to be seen to be worthwhile.

The design specification for each product and the production methods should be examined for potential areas of cost reduction that will not compromise the quality of the products.

- Can any materials be eliminated, e.g. cut down on packing materials?
- Can a cheaper material be substituted without affecting quality?
- Can part-assembled components be bought in to save on assembly time?
- Can the incidence of the cost drivers be reduced, in particular for product Y?
- Is there some degree of overlap between the product-related fixed costs that could be eliminated by combining service departments or resources?

Conclusion

This chapter has introduced the management accounting part of the syllabus by reviewing several costing systems and techniques, as an aid to planning, monitoring and control of business activity.

Both commercial and not-for-profit organisations' costing information needs have been considered, and the impact of the modern business environment on costing approaches has been discussed.

SELF-TEST
QUESTIONS

Management accounting/Cost accounting

1   Describe the relationship between management accounting and cost accounting. (1, 2)

Costing issues

2   Give examples of cost units for both a manufacturing and a service industry. (3.1)

Absorption rates

3   Why does over- or under-absorption of overhead occur in absorption costing? (5.3)

Marginal costing

4   Why do the reported profits differ between absorption and marginal costing? (6.1)

Activity based costing

5   What is activity-based costing? (7)

6   What is a cost driver? (7.2)

Costing information in not-for-profit organisations

7   Why might control be more difficult in not-for-profit organisations? (9)

Value analysis

8   What are the three main elements of value for money? (10)

EXAM-TYPE
QUESTION 1

RH Ltd

RH Ltd makes and sells one product, the standard production cost of which is as follows for one unit.

		£
Direct labour	3 hours at £6 per hour	18
Direct materials	4 kilograms at £7 per kg	28
Production overhead	Variable	3
Fixed		20
Standard production cost		69

Normal output is 16,000 units per annum and this figure is used for the fixed production overhead calculation.

Costs relating to selling, distribution and administration are as follows:

Variable	20 per cent of sales value
Fixed	£180,000 per annum

The only variance is a fixed production overhead volume variance. There are no units in finished goods stock at 1 October 20X2. The fixed overhead expenditure is spread evenly throughout the year. The selling price per unit is £140.

For the two six-monthly periods detailed below, the number of units to be produced and sold are budgeted as:

	Six months ending 31 March 20X3	Six months ending 30 September 20X3
Production	8,500	7,000
Sales	7,000	8,000

Required:

(a) Prepare statements for management showing sales, costs and profits for **each** of the six-monthly periods, using:

   (i) marginal costing,
   (ii) absorption costing.   **(15 marks)**

(b) Prepare an explanatory statement reconciling for **each** six-monthly period the profit using marginal costing with the profit using absorption costing. **(4 marks)**

(c) State and explain **three** business situations where the use of marginal costing may be beneficial to management in making a decision.   **(6 marks)**

(Total: 25 marks)

For the answer to this question, see the 'Answers' section at the end of the book.

EXAM-TYPE
QUESTION 2

ABC terms

(a) In the context of activity-based costing (ABC), it was stated in Management Accounting – Evolution not Revolution by Bromwich and Bhimani, that

   'Cost drivers attempt to link costs to the scope of output rather than the scale of output thereby generating less arbitrary product costs for decision-making.'

   Required:

   Explain the terms 'activity-based costing' and 'cost drivers'.   **(8 marks)**

(b) XYZ plc manufactures four products – namely A, B, C and D – using the same plant and processes.

   The following information relates to a production period:

Product	Volume	Material cost per unit	Direct labour per unit	Machine time per unit	Labour cost per unit
A	500	£5	½ hour	¼ hour	£3
B	5,000	£5	½ hour	¼ hour	£3
C	600	£16	2 hours	1 hour	£12
D	7,000	£17	1½ hours	1½ hours	£9

Total production overhead recorded by the cost accounting system is analysed under the following headings:

   Factory overhead applicable to machine-oriented activity is £37,424.

   Set-up costs are £4,355.

   The cost of ordering materials is £1,920.

   Handling materials is £7,580.

   Administration for spare parts is £8,600.

These overhead costs are absorbed by products on a machine hour rate of £4.80 per hour, giving an overhead cost per product of:

   A = £1.20 B = £1.20   C = £4.80   D = £7.20

However, investigation into the production overhead activities for the period reveals the following totals:

Product	Number of set-ups	Number of material orders	Number of times material was handled	Number of spare parts
A	1	1	2	2
B	6	4	10	5
C	2	1	3	1
D	8	4	12	4

Required:

(a) Compute an overhead cost per product using activity-based costing, tracing overheads to production units by means of cost drivers. **(6 marks)**

(b) Comment briefly on the differences disclosed between overheads traced by the present system and those traced by activity-based costing. **(3 marks)**

(Total: 17 marks)

For the answer to this question see the 'Answers' section at the end of the book.

FEEDBACK TO ACTIVITY 1

The aims of costing

The ultimate aim of the costing system, is to meet the needs of management in their key activities of planning, decision-making, monitoring and controlling activities.

Information will be provided by the costing system which can be used specifically to:

- disclose profitable and unprofitable activities
- identify waste and inefficiency
- analyse movements in profits
- estimate and fix selling prices
- value stocks
- develop budgets and standards
- evaluate the cost effects of policy decisions.

FEEDBACK TO ACTIVITY 2

Quality control	90,000	÷	450	= £200 per inspection
Process set-up	135,000	÷	450	= £300 per set-up
Purchasing	105,000	÷	1,000	= £105 per order
Customer order processing	120,000	÷	2,000	= £60 per customer
Occupancy costs	150,000	÷	75,000	= £2 per machine hour

Note that occupancy cost has been allocated on traditional machine hours. The cost driver there is time, and as such, a conventional ABC method is not applicable. The student should remember that ABC will never cater 100% for all overheads.

Chapter 17
COSTING SYSTEMS AND TECHNIQUES – 2

This chapter continues the description of costing systems and techniques, and explains throughput accounting, life cycle costing and target costing

Objectives

By the time you have finished this chapter you should be able to:

- explain the concept of throughput accounting

- explain the impact of life cycle costing on cost accumulation

- describe and apply target costing methods

- describe the interaction between life cycle and target costing.

1 The theory of constraints and bottlenecks in work flow

A bottlenck in a production system or work flow system is something that holds up the work flow and prevents output from being faster and higher. A bottleneck might be a machine whose capacity limits the throughput of the whole production process. It might be a key department with highly specialist skills that holds up the process.

To avoid large build-ups of inventory, the non-bottleneck areas should be balanced to produce what the bottleneck can absorb in the short term. Thus, if the bottleneck can only absorb 60% of the output of the non-bottleneck areas, then the output should be scaled down to that level, since any excess over that level is only going to increase the piles of work-in-progress inventory standing about. It has also been suggested that overhead should be absorbed on the basis of throughput based upon the duration of production from the initial input of raw materials and components to the delivery of the finished products. By adopting this approach, management can see how costs can be reduced by cutting the throughput time.

Eli Goldratt, famed for his book The Goal, coined the term 'theory of constraints' (TOC) to describe the process of identifying the constraints that restrict output and then taking steps to eliminate them.

The steps to follow in TOC are as follows.

Step 1

Identify the bottlenecks in the system. These are the constraints that restrict output from being increased.

Step 2

Concentrate on each bottleneck in turn to ensure that they are being fully and efficiently utilised.

Step 3

Scale down the throughput of non-bottleneck activities to match what can be dealt with by the bottlenecks.

Step 4

Remove bottlenecks if possible, e.g. by hiring in more skilled workers or buying a larger machine.

Step 5

Since TOC is a continuous improvement process, return to Step 1 and re-evaluate the system now that some bottlenecks have been removed.

Goldratt advises on the use of throughput accounting (TA) to apply TOC principles.

2   Throughput accounting

Throughput accounting is a method of accounting that focuses on throughput, and relates costs of production to throughput.

Throughput is 'the rate of production of a defined process over a stated period of time. Rates may be expressed in terms of units of products, batches produced, turnover, or other meaningful measurements.' (CIMA Official Terminology)

A basic concept in throughput accounting is that the production manager has a quantity of resources available, in the form of labour resources, capital equipment, buildings and so on. The cost of these resources is assumed to be time-related, and so fixed for a given period of time. Resources are used to create throughput. Direct materials are turned into finished items and sold, and the value of throughput can be measured as:

Sales revenue minus Direct materials costs

Notice in particular that throughput is only created when the finished output is sold. If items are produced and put into finished goods stock, no throughput is created. The aim is not production at any price. Throughput accounting focuses on the need to achieve sales with items produced, and stocks are only considered desirable to the extent that they can increase throughput. In this respect, the principles of throughput accounting are consistent with the principles of *just in time production (JIT)*.

2.1   Influences on throughput

Factors that affect the value of throughput in any period are:

- the selling price of items sold
- the purchase cost of direct materials
- efficiency in the usage of direct materials
- the volume of throughput.

Constraints on throughput could be:

- selling prices that are too high (thereby limiting sales demand) or too low (thereby restricting sales revenue)
- unreliable product quality (resulting in scrapped items or items returned by customers)
- unreliable supplies of key materials (so that production cannot be scheduled in an optimal way)
- a shortage of production resources (leading to bottlenecks).

Management should aim to maximise throughput with available resources. Some resources might be in short supply, and so act as a constraint on production. Shortages of resources are referred to as *bottlenecks*. A bottleneck is 'an activity within an organisation which has a lower capacity than preceding or subsequent activities, thereby limiting throughput.' (CIMA *Official Terminology*)

DEFINITION

Throughput is the rate of production of a defined process over a stated period of time. Rates may be expressed in terms of units of products, batches produced, turnover, or other meaningful measurements. *(CIMA Official Terminology)*

DEFINITION

A **bottleneck** is an activity within an organisation that has a lower capacity than preceding or subsequent activities, thereby limiting throughput. *(CIMA Official Terminology)*

FOULKS LYNCH
PUBLICATIONS

The task of management is to eliminate bottlenecks and other constraints. Removing a bottleneck in one part of the production process should result in higher throughput, although the bottleneck will often switch to another part of the production process. Management should then focus on eliminating the new bottleneck, in order to increase throughput still further.

2.2   Throughput accounting reports

Results in a given period can be reported to management in terms of throughput achieved, as follows.

Products	A	B	C	D	E	F
	£	£	£	£	£	£
Sales						
Direct materials						
Throughput						
Labour costs						
Other production overheads						
Administration costs						
Marketing costs						
Profit						

Any closing inventory is valued at direct materials cost only, and no direct labour or production overhead costs are added to stock values. You might see a similarity here between throughput accounting and marginal costing, but with only direct materials costs treated as a marginal cost item.

There is no profit, and so no value, in manufacturing for stock unless there is a clear link between producing for stock now in order to have the certainty of increasing future sales. This can happen, for example, when sales are seasonal. Stocks might be built up in advance of the high sales period, in order to meet sales demand when it eventually occurs. (If stocks are not built up in advance, the organisation will not have the resources to meet sales demand in the peak season.)

2.3   Throughput accounting performance measurements

In throughput accounting, only direct materials costs are regarded as variable costs. Direct labour costs and production overheads (conversion costs) are fixed costs, which may be grouped together and labelled as *'total factory costs'*.

Performance measures used in throughput accounting are:

- return per factory hour

- throughput accounting ratio

2.4   Return per factory hour

This is a measure of throughput per hour of the bottleneck resource, and is therefore:

$$\frac{\text{Sales minus direct materials cost}}{\text{Usage (in hours) of the bottleneck resource}}$$

This measurement of performance is similar in concept to the contribution per unit of scarce resource. This is a marginal costing concept, which is used for short-term decision making when a key resource is in scarce supply.

2.5   Throughput accounting ratio

The throughput accounting ratio is the ratio of the throughput earned and the cost per 'factory hour', where factory hour is measured as the usage in hours of the bottleneck resource. The ratio is therefore:

$$\frac{\text{Return per factory hour}}{\text{Total cost per factory hour}}$$

Management should try to achieve a high throughput ratio

Example

A company manufactures a single product which it sells for £10 per unit. The direct materials cost of the product is £3 per unit. Other factory costs total £50,000 each month. The bottleneck factor in production is the assembly of the unit, which is a labour-intensive process. There are 20,000 labour hours available in assembly each month, and each unit takes two hours to assemble.

Required. Calculate the budgeted rate per factory hour and the throughput ratio each month.

Solution

$$\text{Return per factory hour} = \frac{\text{Sales minus direct materials costs}}{\text{Usage of bottleneck resource}}$$

$$= \frac{£10 - £3}{2 \text{ hours}}$$

$$= £3.50$$

$$\text{Cost per factory hour} = \frac{\text{Total factory cost}}{\text{Bottleneck resource hours available}}$$

$$= \frac{£50,000}{20,000 \text{ hours}}$$

$$= £2.50$$

$$\text{Throughput accounting ratio} = \frac{\text{Return per factory hour}}{\text{Cost per factory hour}}$$

$$= \frac{£3.50}{£2.50}$$

$$= £1.40$$

X Limited manufactures a product that requires 1.5 hours of machining. Machine time is a bottleneck resource, due to the limited number of machines available. There are 10 machines available, and each machine can be used for up to 40 hours per week.

The product is sold for £85 per unit and the direct material cost per unit is £42.50. Total factory costs are £8,000 each week.

Required: Calculate:

(a)   the return per factory hour

(b)   the throughput accounting ratio

Feedback to this activity is at the end of the chapter.

2.6   Treatment of bottlenecks

Bottlenecks can be identified by profiling capacity usage through the system. Usually they will be areas of most heavy usage. Thus monitoring build-ups of inventory and traditional idle time and waiting time will indicate actual or impending bottlenecks.

Traditional efficiency measures will be important in managing bottlenecks. Changes in efficiency will indicate the presence of bottlenecks and the need for a response. This may take the form of creating short-term build-ups of stock to alleviate the problem. Another possible solution might be to prioritise the work at bottlenecks to ensure that throughput is achieved. Measures that highlight throughput per bottleneck capacity measures will need to be developed.

In view of the fact that the JIT philosophy sees all non-value adding activities as potential waste, TA looks for anything that will enhance saleable output. Thus, anything that will reduce costly lead times, set-up times and waiting times will enhance the throughput. Again, these need to be identified and reported on and monitored to see if they are being reduced.

2.7   Other factors

All constraints should be considered in the reporting process. If quality is a throughput constraint, then detailed quality cost reports on rework, scrap levels and returns need to be added to the performance measuring process. Equally, if delivery times are crucial, then failure to meet delivery times needs to be reported. The student should begin to see that the essence of throughput accounting is contingent on what is needed and the circumstances that prevail.

2.8   Assessment

TA will appear to the student to be going against the trend of emulating Japanese-style methods as described by H Thomas Johnson. It is a highly short-term perspective on costs, regarding only material as variable or directly activity-related. It neglects the costs of overhead and people. As a result, there will always be the risk of suboptimal profit performance. TA will really only work effectively where material remains a high proportion of the cost or selling price. Also, there must be a situation where demand is constant enough or high enough to always put pressure on output and production resources.

It is suggested that TA with its emphasis on direct material is an ideal complement to ABC which can draw attention to the overheads. In that way, a comprehensive cover of costs can be achieved.

It is suggested that TA with its emphasis on direct material is an ideal complement to ABC which can draw attention to the overheads. In that way, a comprehensive cover of costs can be achieved.

DEFINITION

Life cycle costing is the profiling of cost over a product's life, including the pre-production stage.

3 Life cycle costing

3.1 The product life cycle

Life cycle costing is the profiling of cost over a product's life, including the pre-production stage.

It is generally accepted that most products will have quite a distinct product life cycle, as illustrated below:

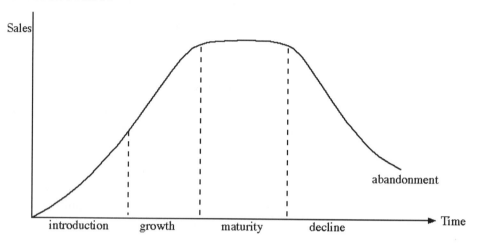

(1)   At the **introductory stage** the product is launched. Its success depends upon awareness and trial of the product by consumers. This stage is likely to be accompanied by extensive marketing and promotion. A high level of set-up costs will already have been incurred by this stage (**pre-production costs**), including research and development, product design and building of production facilities.

(2)   If the product is accepted, it will move into the **growth stage**, where sales volume increases dramatically, and unit costs fall as fixed costs are recovered over greater volumes. Marketing and promotion will continue through this stage.

(3)   As market saturation is approached, with sales growth slowing, the product is entering its **maturity stage.** Initially profits will continue to increase, as initial set-up and fixed costs are recovered and marketing and distribution economies achieved. However, price competition and product differentiation will start to erode profitability as firms compete for the limited new customers remaining.

(4)   Eventually, in the **decline stage**, the product will move towards obsolescence as it is replaced by new and better alternatives. The product will be **abandoned** when profits fall to an unacceptable level, or when further capital commitment is required. Meanwhile, a replacement product will need to have been developed, incurring new levels of R&D and other product set-up costs.

3.2 Relevance in today's manufacturing environment

- In an advanced manufacturing environment, where products have low labour content, and are designed to make use of standard components and minimise wastage, rectification and warranty costs, the **direct unit cost is relatively low.**

- A very high proportion of the total costs over the product's life cycle will be in the form of **initial development, design and production set-up costs,** and ongoing fixed costs that are committed to at this stage.

- In addition, in a globally competitive market, **product life cycles are decreasing**, making initial costs even more disproportionate in the early stages. The time scale between launch of one product and commencement of development of its successor can be very short, as can be seen in the modern car and computer industries.

The recognition of product life cycles, with corresponding strategic planning of new development, marketing and finance, is of great importance for modern businesses. A primary objective will be to match the high costs with revenues.

3.3   Life cycle costing

The commitment of a high proportion of a product's life cycle costs at the very early stages of the cycle has led to the need for accounting systems that compare the revenues from a product with *all* the costs incurred over the entire product life cycle.

Life cycle costing (LCC) is such a system. It **tracks and accumulates** the actual costs and revenues attributable to each product from inception to abandonment.

In this way:

- the final profitability of a given product is determined at the end of its life; whilst

- accumulated costs at any stage can be compared with life cycle budgeted costs, product by product, for the purposes of planning and control.

We can compare this approach with more traditional management accounting practices.

- Most accounting reporting systems are based upon periodic accounts, reporting product profitability in isolated calendar-based amounts, rather than focusing on the revenues and costs accumulated over the life cycle to date.

- Recognition of the commitment needed over the entire life cycle of a product will generally lead to more effective resource allocation than the traditional annual budgeting system.

- R&D, design, production set-up, marketing and customer service costs are traditionally reported on an aggregated basis for all products and recorded as a period expense. Life cycle costing traces these costs to individual products over their entire life cycles, to aid comparison with product revenues generated in later periods.

- Relationships between early decisions on product design and production methods and ultimate costs can therefore be identified and used for subsequent planning.

With **decreasing product lives**, it is important to recognise and monitor the relatively high pre-production and early stage costs product by product.

3.4   The use of cost tables in cost control

Cost tables are computerised cost relational databases that facilitate accurate estimates of costs of the many different combinations of component assemblies, manufacturing processes, etc, that may be considered during a product's design.

Cost tables are a valuable tool in improving control during the product life cycle. The 'Red Book' of costs used in the automobile industry in the west is a form of cost table.

Japanese firms use cost tables to both estimate the cost of new products, and control and reduce the costs of existing products. All component activities are included to enable decisions to be taken about alternative methods of manufacture especially where volumes and specifications may differ.

Cost tables can also be used for indirect activities as well as providing choices of design that require different mixes of direct and indirect costs.

Since it is estimated that between 50% and 80% of the total life cycle cost may be committed before production ever takes place, to have these accurate estimates of the cost at the outset is extremely valuable in a competitive market. Ways of reducing costs can be found and even as production progresses, further cost reduction can be encouraged.

4   Target costing

Target costing, as with several other effective new developments in management accounting, has come from Japan where manufacturers such as Sony and Toyota feel that it is responsible for improvements in their market share.

The **target cost** is a product cost estimate derived by subtracting a desired profit margin from a competitive market price. The target cost may be less than the planned initial product cost, but will be expected to be achieved by the time the product reaches the mature production stage.

The main theme behind target costing is not finding what a new product *does* cost but what it *should* cost.

- The starting point for target costing is an estimate of a selling price for a new product that will enable a firm to capture a required share of the market.

- The next step is to reduce this figure by the firm's required level of profit. This will take into account the return required on any new investment and on working capital requirements.

- This will produce a target cost figure for product designers to meet.

Conclusion

This chapter has explained three costing techniques that can have specific applications, in providing useful information to management for planning and control, performance measurement and decision-making purposes.

The theory of constraints and bottlenecks in work flow

1   What is the purpose of the theory of constraints? (1)

Throughput accounting

2   What is throughput? (2)

3   Define return per factory hour (2.4)

4   Define the throughput accounting ratio (2.5)

Life cycle costing

5   How does life cycle costing differ from the traditional costing approach? (3)

6   What are the four stages in a normal product life cycle? (3.1)

Target costing

7   What is target costing? (4)

Return per factory hour = (£85 - £42.50)/ 1.5 hours = £28.33

Cost per factory hour = £8,000/(10 x 40 hours) = £20

Throughput accounting ratio = £28.33/£20 = 1.4165

Chapter 18
STANDARD COSTING AND VARIANCE ANALYSIS

In this chapter we start the standard costing section of the syllabus. The early sections should be revision for you, but if you find that you are unsure on earlier work then you should revise that first and then return to this chapter.

After a quick revision of variances we are going to consider how they can be used in management control. We look at the main causes of variances, and in particular how the effects of inappropriate budgeting can be quantified in terms of planning variances. We also look at the main considerations that should be made in deciding whether to investigate the cause of a variance in the first place.

Objectives

By the time you have finished this chapter you should be able to do the following:

- explain the uses of standard costs and the methods by which they are derived and subsequently reviewed

- calculate and evaluate capacity limitations when setting standards

- describe the types of standard (ideal, attainable, current and basic) and their behavioural implications

- calculate basic labour, material, overhead (variable and fixed) and sales variances, including problems of labour idle time

- prepare reconciliations using operating statements which

  - reconcile budgeted and actual profit figures, and/or

  - reconcile the actual sales less the standard cost of sales with the actual profit

- demonstrate how absorption and marginal approaches can be used in standard costing

- explain the reasons for variances

- assess appropriate management action arising from the variances identified

- calculate and explain operational and planning variances

- demonstrate an understanding of the interrelationships between variances

- assess appropriate management action arising from the variances identified.

1   Standard costing

The definitions (given overleaf) highlight the principal purposes of running a standard costing system:

- to assist in **planning** and **budgeting** of a business's activities

- to assist in the **control** of the business activities

- to provide a basis for **performance measurement**

- to **motivate** management to work towards company objectives.

DEFINITION

Standard cost is a predetermined measurable quantity set in defined conditions and expressed in money. It is built up from an assessment of the value of each cost element. Its main uses are providing bases for **performance measurement**, **control** by exception reporting, valuing **stock** and establishing **selling prices**.

Standard costing is a method of cost accounting which incorporates standard costs and variances into the ledger accounts.

1.1 The operation of a standard costing system

The operation of a standard costing system requires:

- the accurate preparation of standard costs
- comparison of standard with actual costs
- the regular review of standards.

1.2 Preparing standard costs

Standard costs comprise two estimates which are multiplied to produce the standard cost of the output unit. These two estimates are:

- a physical measure of the resources required for each unit of output
- the price expected to be paid for each unit of the resource.

The first step is to identify the resources required for each output unit. This includes:

- each type of different raw material or component
- each grade and skill type of labour
- each type of machine.

For each of these an estimate must then be made of the quantity of materials, number of components, number of hours etc, required for each output unit (allowing for normal losses, wastage, inefficiency).

For each of these resources an estimate must be made of the expected cost per unit of the resource (i.e. per kg, per unit, per hour). When making these estimates regard must be given towards the likely level of inflation and price changes expected in the budget period.

These estimates are summarised on a standard cost card, which shows the standard cost for a single unit of a product.

1.3 Setting standard costs

There is a whole range of bases upon which standards may be set within a standard costing system. This choice will be affected by the use to which the standards will be put.

It is usual to identify four types of standard. The definitions are as follows:

KEY POINT

It is usual to identify four types of standard:
- Basic standard
- Ideal standard
- Attainable standard
- Current standard

- **Basic standard** – a standard established for use over a long period from which a current standard can be developed.
- **Ideal standard** – a standard which can be attained under the most favourable conditions, with no allowance for normal losses, waste and machine downtime.
- **Attainable standard** – a standard which can be attained if a standard unit of work is carried out efficiently, a machine properly operated or materials properly used. Allowances are made for normal losses, waste and machine downtime.
- **Current standard** – a standard established for use over a short period of time, related to current conditions.

Attainable standards are the most commonly used.

1.4 Comparing against actual performance

Standard costing is part of the cost control system.

There is one important feature of standard costing which must be remembered:

- standard costing carries out variance analysis using the normal, double entry ledger accounts.

This is done by recording in the ledgers:

- actual costs as inputs
- standard costs as outputs
- the difference as the variance.

Control is achieved by comparing actual performance with the standard that has been set, and explaining the cause of the difference.

The difference may be caused by a difference in the quantity of resources used, the cost per unit of the resource or a combination of both. These differences are known as variances.

1.5   Review of standard costs

The calculation of variances referred to above may identify that the standard is unachievable or that it is out of date. In such circumstances the standard is not providing a realistic target and it should be revised.

Similarly, changes in the method of operation will invalidate the standard previously set. It should be reviewed on a regular basis and where appropriate revised using the same principles as are used to set new standards.

2   Basic variance analysis

There are a few general points you should be reminded of before we start the revision of the individual variances.

- The purpose of calculating variances is to show the effect of the variances on **actual** profit compared to the **budget**. This overall effect is known as the **profit variance**.

- Variances which cause the actual profit to be *greater* than expected are known as **favourable** variances (denoted (F)) and those causing the actual profit to be **less** than expected are known as **adverse** (denoted (A)).

- The reconciliation between actual and budgeted profits using variances is presented as an **operating statement**. You should recall that profits can be measured on an **absorption** or **marginal** costing basis. The effect of this is that there are some differences in the calculation of variances relating to sales and fixed overheads and the way operating statements are presented.

- Variances are computed on the basis of a **flexed** budget. Thus total cost variances are computed as follows.

	£
Actual cost for actual production	x
Less standard cost **for actual production**	(x)
Cost variance	x

2.1   Basic variances – revision and definitions

The variances in the following example should all be familiar to you. If you feel confident on this topic, try the example yourself before looking at the answers below.

Example

Church Ltd manufactures a chemical additive called React. The following standard costs apply for the production for 100 cylinders:

		£
Materials	500kgs @ 80p per kg	400
Labour	20 hours @ £5.50 per hour	110
Variable overheads	20 hours @ £2.50 per hour	50
Fixed overheads	20 hours @ £5.00 per hour	100
		660

The monthly sales/production budget is 10,000 cylinders. Selling price = £9 per cylinder.

For the month of November the following data is available:

Produced/sold	10,600 cylinders
Sales value	£98,500
Material purchased and used (53,200kg)	£42,500
Labour worked and paid (2,040 hours)	£10,600
Variable overheads	£5,800
Fixed overheads	£11,000

You are required to compute the materials, labour, overhead and sales variances.

Direct material total cost variance

DEFINITION

Standard material cost of output produced - actual cost of material purchased.

A measurement of the difference between the standard material cost of the output produced and the actual material cost incurred.

$$\left(10,600 \times \frac{£400}{100}\right) - £42,500 = (£100) \text{ adverse}$$

Where the quantities of material purchased and used are different, the total variance should be calculated as the sum of the usage and price variances.

Direct material price variance

DEFINITION

Direct material price variance represents the difference between the actual price paid for purchased materials and their standard cost.

$$(53,200 \times £0.80) - £42,500 = £60 \text{ favourable}$$

The material price variance may also be calculated at the time of material withdrawal from stores. In this case, the stock accounts are maintained at actual cost, price variances being extracted at the time of material usage rather than of purchase:

(actual material used × standard cost) - actual cost of material used).

Direct material usage variance

Measures efficiency in the use of material, by comparing the standard cost of material used (£42,560) with the standard material cost of what has been produced (£42,400).

$$\left(10,600 \times \frac{£400}{100}\right) - (53,200 \times £0.80) = (£160) \text{ adverse}$$

or

Comparing the quality of material actually used with the quantity we would expect to use (standard), and multiplying this by the standard cost per kg (here 80p).

Direct labour total cost variance

Indicates the difference between the standard direct labour cost of the output which has been produced and the actual direct labour cost incurred.

$$\left(10,600 \times \frac{£110}{100}\right) - £10,600 = £1,060 \text{ favourable}$$

Direct labour rate variance

Indicates the actual cost of any change from the standard labour rate of remuneration.

$(2,040 \times £5.50) - £10,600 = £620$ favourable

Direct labour efficiency variance

Indicates the standard labour cost of any change from the standard level of labour efficiency.

((actual production in standard hours × standard direct labour hour rate per hour) - (actual direct labour hours worked × standard direct labour rate per hour)).

$(10,600 \times \dfrac{20}{100} \times £5.50) - (2040 \times £5.50) = £440$ favourable

Variable production overhead total cost variance

Represents the difference between the amount of variable production overhead which has been absorbed by output, and the actual cost.

$(10,600 \times {}^{50}\!/_{100}) - £5,800 = (£500)$ adverse

Variable production overhead expenditure variance

The difference between the actual variable production overhead costs and those in a budget flexed on labour hours.

(Actual cost incurred - (actual hours worked × standard variable production overhead absorption rate per hour)).

Start with hours worked	£
2,040 hours should cost (× 2.50)	5,100
did cost	5,800
Variable overhead expenditure variance	700 A

Variable production overhead efficiency variance

The difference between the variable overhead cost budget flexed on actual labour hours, and the variable overhead cost absorbed by output produced.

((Actual hours worked × standard variable production overhead absorption rate per hour) - (actual production in standard hours × variable absorption rate per hour)).

$(10,600 \times \dfrac{20}{100} \times £2.50) - (£2,040 \times £2.50) = £200$ favourable

Fixed production overhead total cost variance

The difference between the actual fixed production overhead incurred and the amount absorbed by output produced.

$(10,600 \times \dfrac{£100}{100}) - £11,000 = (£400)$ adverse

Fixed production overhead expenditure variance

The difference between the fixed production overhead costs in the period, and that which was incurred.

(budgeted fixed production overhead - actual fixed production overhead).

$10,000 - £11,000 = (£1,000)$ adverse

Fixed production overhead volume variance

The over or under-absorption of overhead cost caused by actual production volume differing from that budgeted.

$$(10,600 \times \frac{20}{100} \times £5) - £10,000 = £600 \text{ favourable}$$

Sales price variance

The change in revenue caused by the actual selling price differing from that budgeted.

$$98,500 - (10,600 \times £9) = £3,100 \text{ favourable}$$

Sales volume profit variance

The change in profit caused by sales volume differing from that budgeted.

$$[£10,600 \times £2.40] - \left[10,000 \times £(9 - \frac{660}{100})\right] = £1,440 \text{ favourable}$$

3   Additional revision points

3.1   Raw material stocks

Profit is often affected by the change in the level of stock and the extent to which this affects the calculation of direct materials variances depends on the methods chosen to value stock. Stocks may be valued using:

• the **standard** price for the material with the effect that **price variances** are calculated based on the **quantity purchased** rather than the quantity of materials **used**

• the **actual** price (as applies from using FIFO, LIFO, etc) with the effect that any price variance is recognised not at the time of purchase but at the time of **issue**.

3.2   Idle time

Basic variance analysis assumes that the number of labour hours **paid** equalled the number of hours **used** in production.

This may not be the case – even direct labour is often paid for non-productive hours, such as when waiting for machine set-up or repairs etc. This is known as **idle time**.

There will be three labour variances:

• rate variance (based on hours paid)

• idle time variance (idle time hours valued at standard rate)

• efficiency variance (based on hours worked).

ACTIVITY 1

Re-compute the labour variances for the earlier Church Ltd example if hours worked were 1,980 and hours paid were 2,040.

Feedback to this activity is at the end of the chapter.

3.3   When variable overhead cost varies with volume

If variable overhead cost changes not as a result of a change in direct labour hours, but as a result of a change in production volume it is not possible to calculate the sub-variances defined above.

Instead only the total variance can be calculated using the standard variable overhead cost per unit.

3.4   Fixed overhead capacity and efficiency variances

The fixed overhead volume variance can be analysed into a separate **capacity** variance and an **efficiency** variance.

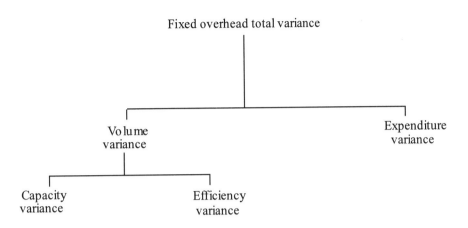

The capacity variance measures whether the workforce worked **more or less hours than budgeted for the period**.

Capacity variance = (Actual hours worked – Budgeted hours worked) × Absorption rate.

The **efficiency** variance measures whether the workforce **took more or less time than expected** in producing their output for the period.

Efficiency variance = (Standard hours worked for actual production – Actual hours worked) × Absorption rate.

Together, these two sub-variances explain why the level of activity was different from that budgeted, i.e. they combine to give the fixed overhead volume variance.

Compute the fixed overhead capacity and efficiency variances for the earlier Church Ltd example (keeping hours worked as 2,040).

Feedback to this activity is at the end of the chapter.

3.5   Fixed overhead variances and marginal costing

Under marginal costing the total fixed production overhead variance will always equal the fixed production overhead expenditure variance which is calculated in the same way as for absorption costing systems (above).

3.6   Sales margin volume variance

The use of absorption or marginal costing affects the calculation of the sales volume variance.

- Under absorption costing any difference in units is valued at the standard profit per unit.
- Under marginal costing such a difference in units is valued at the standard contribution per unit.

In neither case is the standard selling price used. This is because when volumes change so do production costs and the purpose of calculating the variance is to find the effect on **profit**.

3.7   The operating statement

The purpose of calculating variances is to identify the different effects of each item of cost/income on profit compared to the expected profit. These variances are summarised in a reconciliation statement, known as an operating statement.

In an absorption system:

- The statement commences with the **budgeted profit** which is based upon budgeted cost and activity levels.

- This is then adjusted by the **sales volume variance** to reflect any difference in actual and budgeted activity. The result, which is referred to as the 'Standard profit on actual sales' represents the profit which would be achieved if:

   (i)   the selling price was as budgeted

   (ii)   all variable costs were as per the standard unit cost

   (iii) all fixed costs were as budgeted.

- The **selling price** and **cost variances** are then included under the headings of adverse and favourable as appropriate. The total of these should reconcile the actual profit to the standard profit on actual sales.

A marginal costing operating statement evaluates:

- the volume variance using contribution per unit

- there is no fixed overhead volume variance.

ACTIVITY 3

Prepare the operating statement for Church Ltd on an absorption basis.

Feedback to this activity is at the end of the chapter.

4   Causes of variances

KEY POINT

There are generally four causes of variances:
- Bad budgeting
- Bad measurement or recording of actual results
- Random factors
- Operational factors

4.1   Bad budgeting

If insufficient time and resources are not applied when setting the standards and budgets they are likely to be inaccurate or inappropriate in relation to the prevailing circumstances.

In this case, it is important to extract the effects of bad budgeting before using variances as a means of judging the effectiveness of operations.

We will look at the way such an analysis may be carried out in terms of identifying planning and operational variances later in the chapter.

4.2   Bad measurement or recording of results

Any inaccuracies in measuring or recording actual results will have an obvious effect on the variances reported. Care must be taken when measuring:

- **activity achieved** – including adjustments for work in progress

- **resources used** – including adjustments for materials, etc held in production stores

- **costs of resources** – including adjustments for accruals and prepayments.

4.3   Random factors

A standard or budget is an average target for a period of time. It is therefore expected that actual results will fluctuate randomly about this target. Such fluctuations will be measured as variances, though they should not be of any significance.

Later in the chapter we shall consider how we can attempt to identify random variances and thus avoid the unnecessary time and costs involved with their investigation.

4.4   Operational factors

Assuming that the budget/standard is realistic, that the actual results recorded are accurate, and that the variance is not due to random factors, it will be due to the operations of a business not being performed as planned.

It will be in this area that the greatest degree of management control may be exercised, although a variance will not always be the result of a controllable cause (for example, when external prices have risen unexpectedly).

In many exam questions on this area the examiner, having asked you to compute some variances, then requires you to suggest possible reasons for them, usually operational reasons. The most important thing to do first is to look for clues in the information given to you as part of the question. When this source of ideas is exhausted, you must revert to your imagination.

4.5   Operational causes of variances

Materials price variance

This could be due to any of the following factors:

- different source of supply
- unexpected general price increase
- alteration in quantity discounts
- substitution of a different grade of material
- standard set at mid-year price so one would expect a favourable price variance in the early months and an adverse variance in the later months of the year.

Materials usage variance

This could be due to any of the following factors:

- higher/lower incidence of scrap
- alteration to product design
- substitution of a different grade of material.

Wages rate variance

This could be due to any of the following factors:

- unexpected national wage award
- overtime or bonus payments different from plan
- substitution of a different grade of labour.

Labour efficiency variance

This could be due to any of the following factors:

- improvement in methods of working conditions including better supervision
- consequences of the learning effect
- introduction of incentive scheme or staff training
- substitution of a different grade of labour.

Variable overhead variance

This could be due to any of the following factors:

- unexpected price changes for overhead items
- incorrect split between fixed and variable overheads.

Fixed overhead expenditure variance

This could be due to any of the following factors:

- changes in prices relating to fixed overhead items, e.g. rent increase

- seasonal effect, e.g. heat/light in winter. (This arises where the annual budget is divided into four equal quarters or thirteen equal four-weekly periods without allowances for seasonal factors. Over a whole year the seasonal effects would cancel out.)

Fixed overhead volume variance

This could be due to any of the following factors:

- change in production volume due to change in demand or alterations to stockholding policy

- changes in productivity of labour or machinery

- production lost through strikes, etc.

Operating profit variance due to selling prices

This could be due to any of the following factors:

- unplanned price increase

- unplanned price reduction, e.g. to try and attract additional business.

Operating profit variance due to sales volume

This is obviously caused by a change in sales volume, which in turn may be due to any of the following factors:

- unexpected fall in demand due to recession

- additional demand attracted by reduced prices

- failure to satisfy demand due to production difficulties.

4.6   Interdependence of variances

The cause of a particular variance may affect another variance in a corresponding or opposite way, for example cheaper material may lead to more being used.

5   Planning and operational variances

It was suggested above that a possible cause of variances is bad budgeting (an organisation is working to a reasonable level of efficiency but variances have been reported because its performance has been assessed by comparison with an unrealistic budget). More useful information can be obtained from variances if the original standards are examined at the end of an accounting period to determine whether or not they are realistic.

If it is found that the standards are unrealistic they can be revised, with hindsight, and performance compared with the revised standards.

Planning and operational variances represent a split of the original total cost variance which can then be subdivided into price and usage or rate and efficiency. Rather than use easily understood terms such as 'original budget' and 'revised budget' it is customary to resort to Latin and use the following terms:

Ex-ante budget   =   original budget

Ex-post budget   =   revised budget

The method of calculation is shown in the next few sections.

FOULKS LYNCH
PUBLICATIONS

Example

Rhodes Ltd manufactures Stops which it is estimated require 2 kg of material XYZ at £10/kg. In week 21 only 250 Stops were produced although budgeted production was 300. 450 kg were purchased and used in the week at a total cost of £5,100. Later it was found that the standard had failed to allow for a 10% price increase throughout the material supplier's industry. Rhodes Ltd carries no stocks.

(a)   Provide a traditional variance analysis.

(b)   Reanalyse the variances along planning and operational lines.

Solution

(a)   **Traditional analysis**

			£
Materials price:	$(450 \times £10) - £5,100$	=	600 (A)
Materials usage:	$((250 \times 2) - 450) \times £10$	=	500 (F)
Total variance:	$(250 \times 2 \times £10) - £5,100$	=	£100 (A)

(b)   **Planning and operational analysis**

Step 1

The essential working is to produce three lines:

1   Original flexed budget   (*ex-ante*).

2   Revised flexed budget   (*ex-post*).

3   Actual results.

Step 2

Split the previous total variance into planning and operational variances.

Total cost variance   =   (1) – (3)

Planning variance   =   (1) – (2)

Operational variance =   (2) – (3)

Step 3

Analyse the operational variance in an appropriate way, here into price and usage. You may be asked to split the planning variance also, although in this case there is little information content in the split.

Operational variances are analysed by using revised standards instead of the original standards.

If planning variances have to be analysed then the approach is to treat the revised standards as 'actual figures'.

Workings

(W1)   Original flexed budget (*ex-ante*)

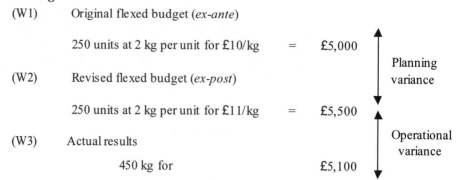

250 units at 2 kg per unit for £10/kg   =   £5,000

(W2)   Revised flexed budget (*ex-post*)

250 units at 2 kg per unit for £11/kg   =   £5,500

(W3)   Actual results

450 kg for   £5,100

Planning variance

Operational variance

Note: this is a similar approach to the 'line by line' method used to summarise traditional variances although in reverse order.

				£	
Planning variance	=	£5,000 – £5,500	=	500	(A)
Operational variance	=	£5,500 – £5,100	=	400	(F)
Total variance (as before)	=	£5,000 – £5,100	=	100	(A)

5.1   Further analysis of operational variances

KEY POINT

The operational variance can be split into **price** and **usage**.

KEY POINT

Operational price variance
=(Actual material used and bought x Revised standard price) – Actual cost of actual materials bought and used.

KEY POINT

Operational usage variance
=((Revised) standard materials used for actual production – Actual materials used) x Revised standard materials price.

The planning variance is purely attributable to the change in price and therefore cannot be analysed further. The operational variance can be split into **price** and **usage.** The price variance can be calculated by reference to the new, more realistic (ex-post) standard; the usage variance is recalculated in terms of the ex-post price standard.

- **Operational price variance**

    = (Actual material used and bought × Revised standard price) – Actual cost of actual materials bought and used.

    = (450 × £11) – £5,100   =   £150   (A)

- **Operational usage variance**

    = ((Revised) standard materials used for actual production – Actual materials used) × Revised standard materials price.

    = ((250 × 2) – 450) × £11   =   £550   (F)

    Note: The total operational variance of £400 favourable has been split into price and usage.

5.2   Points to note from example

(1)   Under the traditional analysis whoever was responsible for purchasing would have been held responsible for incurring the £600 unfavourable price variance. In fact, analysis (b) shows that £450 of this, effectively, was **uncontrollable**, due to an across-the-board increase. The variance arose mainly as a result of **poor forecasting.**

(2)   Usage variance is more favourable under (b) because of the effect of the additional value of the same saving in quantity.

(3)   The planning variance isolated under (b) is **uncontrollable** in terms of this report. No decision could have been made to avoid it. If, however, there existed a substitute for XYZ which under the *ex-ante* budget was more expensive, but turned out to be cheaper *ex-post*, the resulting variance would be controllable (see later).

FOULKS LYNCH
PUBLICATIONS

(4)   The calculations are such that **the two price variances will not add up to the previous traditional price variance.** This must be the case since the usage variance has changed.

5.3   Material price and usage planning variances

Example

The previous example could be developed further if it were found at the end of the week that the materials usage standard was inappropriate following a change in production methods that brought the standard usage down from 2 kg per unit to 1.9 kg per unit.

Produce planning and operational variances under these new circumstances.

Solution

Once again the three line working provides the key to the new split of the £100 adverse total materials cost variance.

Working

Original flexed budget (*ex-ante*)

250 units at 2 kg per unit for £10/kg   =   £5,000

Revised flexed budget (*ex-post*)

↑ Planning variance

250 units at 1.9 kg per unit for £11/kg   =   £5,225

Actual results

↕ Operational variance

450 kg for   £5,100

				£
Planning variance	=	£5,000 − £5,225	=	225 (A)
Operational variance	=	£5,225 − £5,100	=	125 (F)
Total variance (again)	=	£5,000 − £5,100	=	100 (A)

The analysis of the operational variance, £125 (F), is straightforward: actual costs are compared with the new standard of 1.9 kg at £11 per kg as follows:

Operational variances.

				£
Price	=	$(450 \times £11) − £5,100$	=	150 (A)
Usage	=	$((250 \times 1.9) − 450) \times £11$	=	275 (F)
Total operational variance				£125 (F)

Although little can be gained from splitting the planning variance in this instance, you may be asked to carry out the exercise. Price and usage variances are calculated as is conventional. The standards to use are the original standards. Treat the revised (*ex-post*) standards as if they were actual costs.

Planning variances

				£
Price	=	$((250 \times 1.9) \times £10) − £5,225$	=	475 (A)
Usage	=	$((250 \times 2) − (250 \times 1.9)) \times £10$	=	250 (F)
Total planning variance				225 (A)

FOULKS LYNCH
PUBLICATIONS

Operational variances are analysed by using **revised standards** instead of the original standards.

If planning variances have to be analysed then the approach is to treat the revised standards as 'actual figures'.

ACTIVITY 4	Hugh Ltd set a standard cost at £40 per unit. 10,000 units were produced with a total cost of £610,000. It is now felt that a more realistic standard cost would have been £68 per unit. Calculate the total, operational and planning variances.

Feedback to this activity is at the end of the chapter.

5.4   Planning and operational sales variances

Another example of a planning and operational variance calculation becoming renamed arises when the exercise is carried out in the context of a sales volume variance. In these circumstances the new names given to the planning and operational variances are as follows.

planning   ⇒   market volume variance

operational   ⇒   market share variance

The logic behind this is that the reason for the incorrect estimate of the budgeted sales was that the size of the total market (for all sellers) had been incorrectly estimated.

Example

Hudson Ltd has a sales budget of 400,000 units for the coming year based on 20% of the total market. On each unit, Hudson makes a profit of £3. Actual sales for the year were 450,000, but industry reports showed that the total market volume had been 2.2 million.

(a) Find the traditional sales (margin) volume variance.

(b) Split this into planning and operational variances (market volume and market share).

Solution

(a) Traditional sales volume variance

     = (Actual units sold − Budgeted sales) × Standard profit per unit

     = (450,000 − 400,000) × £3 = £150,000 (favourable).

(b) Planning and operational variances

     Once again a three line working helps. The revised (*ex-post*) budget would show that Hudson Ltd should expect to sell 20% of 2.2 million units = 440,000 units.

     Original budget (*ex-ante*)

     400,000 units @ £3 per unit = £1,200,000   Planning ('Market volume')

     Revised budget (*ex-post*)

     440,000 units @ £3 per unit = £1,320,000   Operational ('Market share')

     Actual results

     450,000 units @ £3 per unit = £1,350,000

£

Planning (or market volume) variance = £1,320,000 – £1,200,000   120,000 (F)

Operational (or market share) variance = £1,350,000 – £1,320,000   30,000 (F)

Total sales volume variance =   150,000

Most of the favourable sales volume variance can be attributed to the increase in the overall market volume, however, some can be put down to effort by the sales force which has increased its share of the market a little from 20% to $\left(\dfrac{450,000}{2,200,000} \right) = 20.5\%$.

5.5 Advantages and disadvantages of the analysis

The analysis of the traditional variances into planning and operational categories has distinct **advantages**:

- Variances are **more relevant**, especially in a turbulent environment.

- The operational variances give a **'fair' reflection** of the actual results achieved in the actual conditions that existed.

- Managers are, theoretically, **more likely to accept and be motivated** by the variances reported which provide a better measure of their performance.

- **It emphasises the importance of planning** and the relationship between planning and control and a better guide for cost control.

- The analysis helps in the **standard setting learning process**, which will hopefully result in more useful standards in the future.

The use of planning and operational variances is not widespread. Therefore, there may be perceived **disadvantages**:

- The establishment of *ex-post* budgets is **very difficult**. Managers whose performance is reported to be poor using such a budget are unlikely to accept them as performance measures because of the subjectivity in setting such budgets.

- There is a considerable amount of **administrative work** involved first to analyse the traditional variances and then to decide on which are controllable and which are uncontrollable.

- The analysis tends to **exaggerate the interrelationship of variances**, providing managers with a 'pre-packed' list of excuses for below standard performance. Poor performance is often excused as being the fault of a badly set budget.

6 Operating statements using planning and operational variances

You should remember that operating statements are used to reconcile budget profits and actual profits by detailing the variances for the period. By calculating planning and operating variances it is being recognised that part of the profit difference is due to budget errors, inappropriate standards, or non-controllable external factors. By identifying these as planning variances management's attention is focused on the controllable items.

The following example illustrates how the use of planning and operational variances improves the relevance to management of the operating statement.

Example

POV Ltd uses a standard costing system to control and report upon the production of its single product.

An abstract from the original standard cost card of the product is as follows:

	£	£
Selling price per unit	200	
Less: 4 kgs materials @ £20 per kg	80	
6 hours labour @ £7 per hour	42	
	—	122
Contribution per unit		78

For period 3, 2,500 units were budgeted to be produced and sold but the actual production and sales were 2,850 units.

The following information was also available:

(1) At the commencement of period 3 the normal material became unobtainable and it was necessary to use an alternative. Unfortunately, 0.5 kg per unit extra was required and it was thought that the material would be more difficult to work with. The price of the alternative was expected to be £16.50 per kg. In the event, actual usage was 12,450 kgs at £18 per kg.

(2) Weather conditions unexpectedly improved for the period with the result that a 50p per hour bad weather bonus, which had been allowed for in the original standard, did not have to be paid. Because of the difficulties expected with the alternative material, management agreed to pay the workers £8 per hour for period 3 only. During the period 18,800 hours were paid for.

After using conventional variances for some time, POV Ltd is contemplating extending its system to include planning and operational variances.

Required:

(a) Prepare a statement reconciling budgeted contribution for the period with actual contribution, using conventional material and labour variances.

(b) Prepare a similar reconciliation statement using planning and operational variances.

(c) Explain the meaning of the variances shown in statement (b).

Solution

(a) Reconciliation of budgeted and actual contribution using conventional variances

				£
Budgeted contribution:	2,500 × £78			195,000
Variances		*Favourable*	*Adverse*	
		£	£	
Sales volume		27,300		
Direct material	– Price	24,900		
	– Usage		21,000	
Direct labour	– Rate		18,800	
	– Efficiency		11,900	
		52,200	51,700	
				500
Actual contribution				195,500

Assumption: No sales price variance.

Workings

Conventional variances

(i) **Materials**

Price = (Actual material purchased × standard price) − (Actual cost of material purchased)

= (12,450 × £20) − (12,450 × £18)

= 249,000 − 224,100

= £24,900 (F)

Usage = (Standard quantity for actual production × standard price) − (Actual material used at standard price)

= (2,850 × 4 × £20) − (12,450 × £20)

= 228,000 − 249,000

= 21,000 (A)

(ii) **Labour**

Rate = (Actual hours worked × standard direct labour rate) − (Actual hours worked × actual hourly rate)

= (18,800 × 7) − (18,800 × 8)

= 131,600 − 150,400

= 18,800 (A)

Efficiency = (Standard hours of actual production × standard rate) − (Actual hours worked × standard rate)

= (2,850 × 6 × £7) − (18,800 × £7)

= 119,700 − 131,600

= 11,900 (A)

(iii) **Sales volume contribution**

= (Budgeted sales units × standard contribution per unit) − (Actual sales units × standard contribution per unit)

= (2,500 × £78) − (2,850 × £78)

= 195,000 − 222,300

= 27,300 (F)

Reconciliation statement using planning and operational variances

			£
Budgeted contribution for actual sales:	2,850 × £78		222,300.00

Planning variances	*Favourable* £	*Adverse* £	
Material – Price	44,887.5		
– Usage		28,500	
Labour – Rate: weather	8,550.00		
– Rate: material		25,650	
	53,437.50	54,150	
			(712.50)
Revised budgeted contribution (£77.75 × 2,850)			221,587.50

Operational variances		Favourable £	Adverse £
Material	– Price		18,675.00
	– Usage	6,187.50	
Labour	– Rate	0	
	– Efficiency		13,600.00
		6,187.50	32,275.00

26,087.50

Actual contribution   195,500.00

Workings

Planning variances

(i) **Material** = (Standard material cost) – (Revised standard material cost)

    Price = $(2,850 \times (4 + 0.5) \times £20) - (2,850 \times (4 + 0.5) \times £16.50)$

         = $256,500 - 211,612.50$

         = 44,887.50 (F)

    Usage = $(2,850 \times 4 \times £20) - (2,850 \times 4.5 \times £20)$

         = $228,000 - 256,500$

         = 28,500 (A)

(ii) **Labour rate**

    (1) Weather bonus

         = $(2,850 \times 6 \times £7) - (2,850 \times 6 \times £6.50)$

         = $119,700 - 111,150$

         = 8,550 (F)

    (2) **Alternative material difficulties**

         = $(2,850 \times 6 \times £6.50) - (2,850 \times 6 \times £8)$

         = $111,150 - 136,800$

         = 25,650 (A)

    ∴ Revised unit contribution is as follows.

	£	£
Selling price		200.00
Direct material: $4.5 \times £16.50$	74.25	
Direct labour: $6 \times £8$	48.00	
		(122.25)
Contribution		77.75

FOULKS LYNCH
PUBLICATIONS

Operational variances

(i) **Material**

Price $= (12{,}450 \times £16.50) - (12{,}450 \times £18)$

$= 205{,}425 - 224{,}100$

$= 18{,}675 \text{ (A)}$

Usage $= (2{,}850 \times 4.50 \times £16.50) - (12{,}450 \times £16.50)$

$= 211{,}612.5 - 205{,}425$

$= 6{,}187.5 \text{ (F)}$

(ii) **Labour**

Rate   0

Efficiency $= (2{,}850 \times 6 \times £8) - (18{,}800 \times £8)$

$= 136{,}800 - 150{,}400$

$= 13{,}600 \text{ (A)}$

(c) The analysis of variances in part (b) makes it possible to separate those variances which are non-controllable (the planning variances) from the variances which are controllable by the individual managers (the operational variances).

In this case the change in type of material used was unavoidable. Similarly, the change in weather conditions could not have been anticipated. The cost implications of these changes are reflected in the planning variances. Management's attention should be focused primarily on the operational variances.

In particular, why did the firm pay £18 per kg for material when this was expected to cost £16.50?

The operational material usage variance indicates that less material was used than expected – this could be due to the workers spending longer working with the material (as evidenced by the adverse efficiency variance).

7   Investigation of variances

We have identified four main causes of variances: bad budgeting, bad measurement/recording, random factors and operational causes. In order to get the greatest benefit from variance analysis, we need to determine which of these has contributed towards the variances isolated, by some form of investigation.

The **object** of the investigation is to provide more useful information for **performance assessment** and **cost control.**

- In the first case the investigation will ascertain whether or not the variance was the result of **bad budgeting** and its **controllability** in general.

- In the case of cost control the major aim is to establish the **specific cause** of the variance and particularly if it is merely the result of some **random variation** in costs. It is then hoped that some significant cost saving can be made.

KEY POINT

Whether a variance should be investigated depends upon its size

- Whether favourable/adverse
- Correction costs v benefits
- Ability to correct
- Past pattern
- Budget reliability
- Measurement/recording

7.1   When should a variance be investigated?

It is rarely practical, or even worthwhile, to investigate every variance produced in an analysis. The factors to consider when deciding whether or not to investigate a variance include the following:

(1) **Size of variance** – it might be assumed that greater cost savings will result from investigating larger variances which also have a major effect on a manager's performance report.

(2) **Favourable or adverse** – the general impression would be that only adverse variances should be investigated, although, by investigating favourable variances an organisation can:

- remove the effect of budget padding when assessing performance
- produce more realistic budgets in the future
- establish ways in which performance might be improved still further in the future.

(3) **Costs and benefits of correction** – if the likely cause of a variance is known but it is felt that it will cost too much to eliminate that cause, the variance may not be investigated. It may be that standards have to be revised.

(4) **Ability to correct a variance** – this is related to the previous factor, but now the point at issue is whether a cause of a variance will stay corrected once money has been spent to rectify that cause.

(5) **Past pattern of variances** – if a variance is merely the result of random variations in cost then no amount of remedial action will bring about a cost saving.

(6) **Reliability of budgets** – whilst establishing the extent to which a variance is due to bad budgeting will have all the benefits set out for planning and operational variances, if a variance is purely the result of a badly set budget there will be no major cost savings following the investigation.

(7) **Reliability of measurement and recording systems** – poor measurement and recording systems can give rise to a variance, for instance if closing stock is incorrectly recorded then an incorrect figure for materials usage is assumed and a variance might result. The benefits of investigation are similar to those of investigating the consequences of bad budgeting.

Several of these considerations give rise to criteria or techniques for variance investigation. Point (5) is taken into account by constructing **statistical control charts** whilst points (3) and (4) can be assessed using **decision trees.** The matter of mere size gives rise to a number of investigation criteria.

7.2   Size of variance

When an organisation has to decide whether or not a variance merits investigation one of several criteria can be adopted:

(1) **Fixed size of variance** – a firm might investigate any variance over £x,000. Whilst this is easy to administer it ignores the fact that a variance of £5,000 in a total cost of £20,000 is more likely to indicate a fault than a variance of £5,000 in a total cost of £200,000. Hence (2).

(2) **Fixed percentage rule** – a variance might be investigated if it is more than x% of the standard cost. Whilst this overcomes the weakness of method (1), it ignores the fact that some costs normally vary more than others. Hence (3).

(3) **Statistical decision rule** – now a variance is only investigated if a study of past patterns of variances suggests that a variance of this size only occurs x% of the time that a process is under control. If there is only, say, a 5% chance that a cost can differ from standard by as much as the size of a particular variance it is much

more likely that a problem has occurred that merits investigation. The problem comes with determining what the x% should be. The rule tends to be applied with ad hoc selections (5%, 1%, say) without taking into account the costs and benefits of correction or the ability to correct a variance.

A survey carried out in the USA reported that, of 100 large companies:

- 72% investigated variances based on managerial judgement
- 54% used a fixed absolute amount
- 43% used the fixed percentage rule
- 4% used statistical decision rules.

It would seem likely that the 4% excluded all those firms that used the decision rule, which is about to be illustrated, as part of the regular statistical quality control checks carried out by most manufacturing organisations or firms concerned with packaging material.

7.3   Pattern of variances – statistical control charts

Consider an operational process for which the mean time is 50 minutes with a standard deviation of 10 minutes. It is known from statistical theory that the pattern of actual times is likely to form a Normal distribution about the mean.

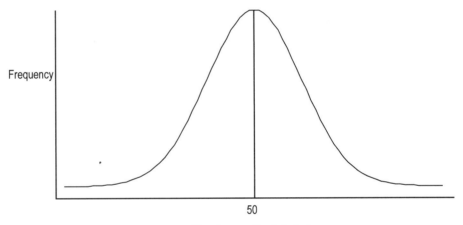

Furthermore, it is known that specific proportions of the times will be within specified standard deviations of the mean.

The values are approximately:

1 standard deviation	68%	(68.26%)
2 standard deviations	95%	(95.44%)
3 standard deviations	99.7%	(99.73%)

DEFINITION

Control limits are quantities/ values outside which managerial operation is triggered.

This information can be used to create a **statistical control chart.** The mean time forms the **standard**. The **control limits** are set a given number of standard deviations from the mean.

Consider, as an example, a process for which the standard time is 50 minutes. The control limits might be set at 30 and 70 minutes, and actual times recorded as follows:

Time to complete operation

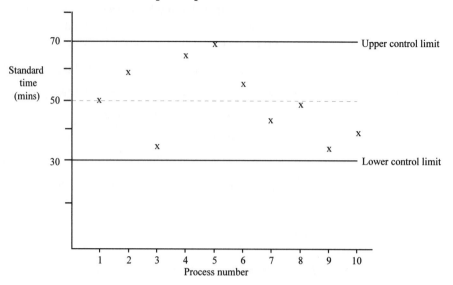

If the actual time taken falls within the bands the variance is not significant. For this reason the band limits are referred to as control limits. This poses two questions:

- How are control limits set?

- What action should be taken if results fall outside the control limits?

7.4 Setting control limits

Control limits should be set so that there is only a small chance of a random fluctuation falling outside them.

Distribution of time to complete

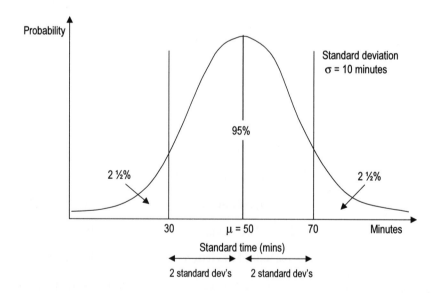

- In this example the control limits are set **two standard deviations from the mean.** Thus, 95% of the recorded process times should lie within the control limits.

- The actual time is recorded on the chart after the completion of each process. It will soon be apparent if the mean time is shifting from 50 minutes, as the recorded times move outside the control limits.

- If more than 5% of the observed results do lie outside the control limits, then the system may be referred to as being statistically out of control. At this stage management must decide what further action to take.

Merely determining initially whether variances represent random fluctuations or not does not tell us what to do about significant variances. The question is whether to investigate or not. In many cases the reason for a variance may be already known or easily ascertainable. In other cases, it must be a matter of weighing likely costs of investigation against likely benefits.

ACTIVITY 5

Donald Ltd has set the standard for a production process in such a way that small adverse variances would be expected to occur. Studies over several months have shown that, when no production difficulties arise, the average weekly variance is £150 adverse. They have also shown that the variances are normally distributed with a standard deviation of £100. Control limits are to be set such that the probability of a wasted investigation is 10% for adverse variances and 5% for favourable ones.

From normal distribution tables:

(1)   5% of probabilities occur more than 1.28 standard deviations above the mean.

(2)   10% of probabilities occur more than 1.645 standard deviations below the mean.

(a)   Suggest a reason why the standard has been set in this way.

(b)   Calculate the control limits.

Feedback to this activity is at the end of the chapter.

7.5   Costs, benefits and ability to correct variance

This approach to the investigation of a variance involves the application of decision theory. The investigation is done if its cost is less than the expected net benefits involved.

The cost-benefit analysis can be depicted by a decision tree as follows:

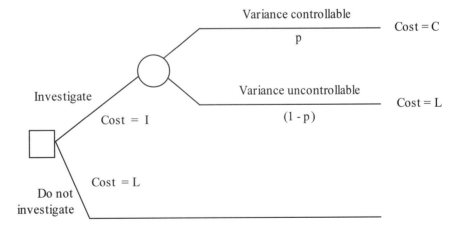

Key to symbols in decision tree

I   =   cost of investigating the variance

C   =   cost of correcting variance

L   =   cost incurred if variance not corrected

p   =   probability that the variance is controllable.

The variance will be investigated if:

> Cost of investigation + expected costs after investigation < cost if not investigated

> $I + Cp + L(1 - p) < L$.

KEY POINT

The cost-benefit decision-making rule is that the variance should be investigated if the **cost of doing so is less than the expected value** of the net benefit.

Example

Last month an adverse direct material usage variance of £1,000 arose.

On the basis of past experience, the cost of an investigation into the variance would be £400 and the cost of corrective action, if the situation is in fact controllable, is estimated to be £300. The net present value of the expected savings from taking the corrective action, assuming a controllable situation, is estimated to be £900. The probability that the variance is uncontrollable is estimated to be 0.3.

You are required to prepare a calculation to show whether the variance should be investigated.

Solution

Using the same tree and symbols as before:

I   =   £400

C   =   £300

L   =   £900

p   =   1 − 0.3

    =   0.7

Cost of investigating   =   £400 + (0.7 × £300) + (0.3 × £900) = £880

Cost of not investigating = £900

∴ It is just worth investigating.

7.6   Sensitivity

The illustration could be extended quite simply to determine the point of indifference between the 'investigate' or 'not to investigate' decision in terms of the value of:

- p, i.e. the probability of the variance being controllable
- the net present value of the expected savings (L).

The calculations, which equate expected values of investigating and not, are as follows:

Sensitivity to p

$$£400 + (p × £300) + ((1 − p) × £900) = £900$$

$$£400 + £300p + £900 − £900p$$

$$£1,300 − £600p = £900$$

$$p = \frac{400}{600} \text{ or } 0.67$$

Therefore, the estimate for the probability that the variance is uncontrollable could rise from 0.30 to 0.33 before the decision would change.

Sensitivity to L

$$400 + (300 \times 0.7) + (L \times 0.3) = L$$

$$400 + 210 + 0.3L = L$$

$$L = \frac{610}{0.7}$$

$$= 871.4$$

Therefore, with the probability estimate unchanged, the net present value of the expected savings could fall from £900 to about £871 before the decision would change.

7.7   Investigation of variances in practice

Part of the difficulty of applying, for example, the formal decision-making associated with costs versus benefits analysis is in determining the probabilities and net present values involved with a meaningful degree of **accuracy.**

In practice, only a limited number of organisations formally use the statistical or decision-making criteria outlined in the previous sections. Instead, reliance may be placed on **managerial judgement** or **simple percentage rules** (e.g. variances below x% are regarded as insignificant and not subjected to investigation). Whilst such approaches appear to be cruder, nevertheless they implicitly use the same concepts and may well in practice lead to similar decisions.

It would be wrong to assume that all variances reported to a manager come as a **surprise** to him or her. They represent the monetary evaluation of the effect on profit of differences between budget or standard and actual. Decisions will have been made by managers during the period and they will be fully aware of these. The variances, when they are reported, possibly quite a while after the events to which they relate, only **quantify in monetary values the effect of the decisions already made.** Any corrective action should have been taken as soon as possible after the event – the manager would not wait to see the size of the variance before taking action.

In such cases the investigation of perhaps a significant variance will be of little additional use in terms of information to the manager concerned.

Clearly any formalised rules about the investigation and significance of variances need to be **flexible** enough to cope with the specific circumstances that arise. The investigation of variances is the process of **increasing the information available to management** and this must always be a prime objective.

Conclusion

This chapter has provided a quick revision of standard costing and basic variances then looked at the relevance or otherwise of variances in providing management with useful information. Four basic causes of variances were identified and two of these were examined in greater detail: how the effects of **bad budgeting** can be isolated using **planning variances** and how the effects of **random factors** can be isolated using **statistical control charts**.

These techniques are part of the general topic of **variance investigation,** the overriding criterion of which is that variances should only be investigated if the **costs** of their investigation will be outweighed by the resulting **benefits** from their correction.

KEY POINT

Variances should only be investigated if the **costs** of their investigation will be outweighed by the resulting **benefits** from their correction.

Standard costing

1   Explain the operation of a standard costing system. (1)

2   How is a total cost computed? (1.2)

Additional revision points

3   If it is assumed that stocks of raw materials are held at standard cost, what implication does this have for the computation of the price and usage variances? (3.1)

4   Interpret what is meant by a favourable variable overhead efficiency variance. (3)

5   Explain the function of the sales margin volume variance. (3.6)

Causes of variances

6   Briefly describe the four main causes of variances. (4)

7   Give two illustrations of variance interdependencies. (4.6)

Planning and operational variances

8   What are market share and market volume variances? (5.4)

Investigation of variances

9   What factors contribute towards the variance investigation decision? Give at least five. (7.1)

10   Describe the use of statistical control charts in this context. (7.3)

Simplo Ltd

Simplo Ltd make and sell a single product. A standard marginal cost system is in operation. Feedback reporting takes planning and operational variances into consideration. It is implemented as follows:

(1)   Permanent non-controllable changes from the original standard are incorporated into a revised standard.

(2)   The budgeted effect of the standard revision is reported for each variance type.

(3)   The sales volume variance is valued at the revised standard contribution and is analysed to show the gain or loss in contribution arising from a range of contributory factors.

(4)   The remaining operational variances are then calculated.

Information relating to Period 6 is as follows:

(i)   A summary of the operating statement for Period 6 using the variance analysis approach detailed above is as follows:

	£	
Original budgeted contribution	51,200	
Budget revision variances (net)	13,120	(F)
Revised budgeted contribution	64,320	
Sales volume variance	16,080	(F)

FOULKS LYNCH
PUBLICATIONS

Revised standard contribution for sales achieved	80,400	
Other variances (net)	8,200	(A)
Actual contribution	72,200	

(F) = Favourable, (A) = Adverse.

(ii)   Original standard cost data per product unit.

	£	£
Selling price		100
Less: Direct material 5 kilos at £10	50	
Direct labour 3 hours at £6	18	
	—	68
Contribution		32

(iii)   The current market price is £110 per unit. Simplo Ltd sold at £106 per unit in an attempt to stimulate demand.

(iv)   Actual direct material used was 12,060 kilos at £10 per kilo. Any related variances are due to operational problems.

(v)   The original standard wage rate excluded an increase of £0.60 per hour subsequently agreed with the trade unions. Simplo Ltd made a short term operational decision to employ a slightly lower grade of labour, who were paid £6.20 per hour. The total hours paid were 7,600. These included 200 hours of idle time, of which 40% was due to a machine breakdown and the remainder to a power failure.

(vi) Budgeted production and sales quantity	1,600 units
Actual sales quantity	2,000 units
Actual production quantity	2,400 units.

Required:

(a)   Prepare a single operating statement for Period 6 which expands the summary statement shown in (i) above.

This single operating statement should clearly show:

(i)   the basis of calculation of the contribution figures for original budget, revised budget and revised standard for sales achieved;

(ii)   the analysis of the budget revision variance by variance type;

(iii)   the analysis of the sales volume variance showing the quantity and value of the gain or loss arising from each of the following factors:

- additional capacity available
- productivity reduction
- idle time
- stock increase not yet translated into sales.

(iv)   The analysis of the 'other variances' by variance type.

(b)   Prepare a brief report to the management of Simplo on the performance in Period 6 making full use of the information contained in the operating statement prepared in (a). Your report should indicate the relevance of the analysis utilised in the operating statement.   **(25 marks)**

For the answer to this question, see the 'Answers' section at the end of the book.

FEEDBACK TO ACTIVITY 1

	£	£
Actual hours paid at actual rate	10,600	
Rate variance		*620 fav*
Actual hours paid at standard rate (2,040 × £5.50)	11,220	
Idle time variance		*330 adv*
Actual hours worked at standard rate (1,980 × £5.50)	10,890	
Efficiency variance		*770 fav*
Standard hours worked at standard rate $(10,600 \times \frac{20}{100} \times £5.50)$	11,660	

FEEDBACK TO ACTIVITY 2

	£	£
Budgeted hours worked at standard rate	10,000	
Capacity variance		*200 fav*
Actual hours worked at standard rate (2,040 × £5.00)*Efficiency variance*	10,200	*400 fav*
Standard hours worked at standard rate $(10,600 \times \frac{20}{100} \times £5.00)$	10,600	

FEEDBACK TO ACTIVITY 3

				£
Budgeted profit	(10,000 @ £2.40)			24,000
Add: sales margin volume variance				1,440
Standard profit	(10,600 @ £2.40)			25,440

Less: other variances		Adv £	Fav £	
Sales price			3,100	
Materials	– price		60	
	– usage	160		
Labour	– rate		620	
	– efficiency		440	
Variable overheads	– expenditure	700		
	– efficiency		200	
Fixed overheads	– expenditure	1,000		
	– volume		600	
		1,860	5,020	3,160
Actual profit				28,600

Actual profit

	£	£	£
Sales value			98,500
Less			
Materials purchased and used		42,500	
Labour worked and paid		10,600	
Variable overheads		5,800	
Fixed overheads		11,000	
			(69,900)
			28,600

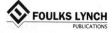

	£
Total variance	
Standard cost of 10,000 units at £40	400,000
Actual cost of 10,000 units	610,000
Total variance	210,000 A
Operational variance	
10,000 units at £68 (ex-post)	680,000
Actual cost	610,000
Operational variance	70,000 F
Planning variance	
Standard cost of 10,000 units at £40	400,000
10,000 units at £68 (ex-post)	680,000
Planning variance	280,000 A

Note

Total variance   =   Operational variance + Planning variance

£210,000 A   =   £70,000 F + £280,000 A

(a)   **Harshly set standards**

Whilst it is accepted that standards should not be set too toughly nor too loosely, it is thought that a standard slightly tougher than is actually expected to be achieved will motivate staff to work harder. This standard will have been set to get the best out of staff.

(b)   **Control limits**

When tackling questions to do with normal distributions it is useful to draw a diagram to represent the problem, as shown below.

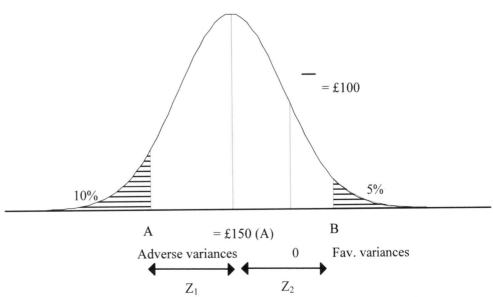

The tails of the distribution show the relevant 10% and 5% areas mentioned in the question. The values of Z_1 and Z_2 can be found from normal distribution tables.

Z_1 = 1.28 standard deviations

Z_2 = 1.645 standard deviations

Control limits.

A = £150 (Adverse) + (1.28 × £100) = £278 (Adverse)

B = £150 (Adverse) − (1.645 × £100) = £15 (Favourable)

Chapter 19
MIX VARIANCES

This chapter takes a closer look at materials variances where there is more than one type of material input and at sales variances where there is more than one product involved. This is a fairly short chapter to reflect the complexity of the material involved – but don't panic, work slowly through it and you should understand the main concepts fairly quickly.

It is important to note that the mix and yield/quantity analysis will only give meaningful results where there is some degree of interchangeability between the materials or products. You shouldn't automatically launch into the somewhat involved computations unless you are specifically told to do so or it is clearly relevant to the circumstances.

Objectives

By the time you have finished this chapter you should be able to do the following:

- calculate mix and yield variances for materials
- calculate mix and quantity variances for sales.

1   Materials mix and yield variances

KEY POINT

The calculation of a materials mix variance is only of relevance where materials can be interchanged to some extent.

1.1   Relationship to material price and usage variances

In many industrial situations, more than one material is used in the manufacturing cycle for a single product.

- If the various materials used cannot be substituted in any way for each other, the approach is to continue to look at each material quite separately.

- However, in many circumstances the materials used are to some extent **substitutes for each other**, i.e. the mix of materials used in the manufacturing can be altered without noticeably affecting the end product. It is in this situation that the calculation of a mix variance becomes appropriate.

In many circumstances the materials used are to some extent substitutes for each other. It is in this situation that the calculation of a mix variance becomes appropriate.

1.2   The basic principles

The following data will be used to illustrate the principles and computations involved.

Standard materials cost for 990 tonnes of production.

Material	Tonnes	Price per tonne £	£
A	550	6.00	3,300
B	330	5.00	1,650
C	220	4.50	990
	1,100		5,940
Less: Normal process loss (10%)	110		-
Standard cost for	990	=	5,940

This represents a standard material cost per tonne of £6.00.

Actual materials cost of 990 tonnes.

Material	Tonnes	Price per tonne £	£
A	444	7.50	3,330
B	446	6.00	2,676
C	240	4.50	1,080
	1,130		7,086
Less: Process loss	140		-
Actual cost for	990	=	7,086

1.3 The variances

Why has the production of 990 tonnes cost £7,086 in materials instead of £5,940? There are three reasons:

(1) The three materials have been bought at **different prices per tonne** than standard – the **price** variance.

(2) The three materials have been used in **different proportions** from standard – the **mix** variance.

(3) A **different total quantity** of materials from standard (for actual output) have been used – the **yield** variance.

The combination of (2) and (3) – mix and quantity – makes up the overall usage variance.

1.4 The computations

The analysis required can be summarised as follows:

(1)	(2)	(3)	(4)
Actual total quantity in actual proportions at actual prices	Actual total quantity in actual proportions at *standard* prices	Actual total quantity in *standard* proportions at standard prices	Standard total quantity in standard proportions at standard prices

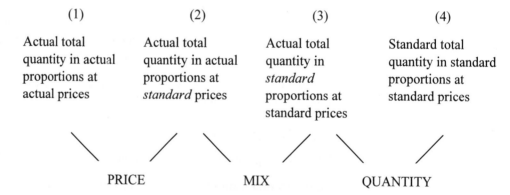

         PRICE   MIX   QUANTITY

The data for (1) and (4) are already given in our example – note that the standard data has already been flexed to the actual level of production. In other examples you may have to do this yourself.

We therefore need two additional tables, for (2) and (3).

Material	(2) Actual quantity used in actual proportions (mix) at standard prices			(3) Actual quantity used in standard proportions (mix) at standard prices		
	Tonnes	Standard price per tonne		Tonnes	Standard price per tonne	
		£	£		£	£
A	444	6.00	2,664	565	6.00	3,390
B	446	5.00	2,230	339	5.00	1,695
C	240	4.50	1,080	226	4.50	1,017
	1,130		5,974	1,130		6,102

The variance analysis is as follows:

Materials price variance

KEY POINT

Materials price variance
= (Actual material input x standard prices) – (Actual input x actual prices).

= (Actual material input × standard prices) – (Actual input × actual prices)

=   (2)   –   (1)

= £5,974 – £7,086

= £1,112(A)

Materials mix variance

KEY POINT

Materials mix variance
= (Total material input in standard mix x standard prices) – (Actual material input x standard prices).

= (Total material input in standard mix × standard prices) – (Actual material input × standard prices)

=   (3)   –   (2)

= £6,102 – £5,974

= £128 (F)

Materials yield variance

KEY POINT

Materials yield variance
= (Standard quantity of materials specified for actual production x standard prices) – (Actual total material input in standard proportions x standard prices).

= (Standard quantity of materials specified for actual production × standard prices) – (Actual total material input in standard proportions × standard prices)

= (4) – (3)

= £5,940 – £6,102

= £162 (A)

∴ **Usage variance**   =   £128 – £162   =   £34 (A)

1.5   Interpretation

The mix and yield variances can be interpreted as follows:

- The **mix variance** of £128F arises because, compared with the standard, less of the more expensive material (A) has been used and more of the cheaper materials (B and C).

- The **yield variance** of £162A represents the fact that 1,130 tonnes of material in total were input into the process and, with a normal loss of 10%, the expected yield of good production was 1,017 tonnes (0.9 × 1,130). However, good production only amounted to 990 tonnes. The yield was lower than expected by 27 tonnes which, evaluated at the standard product cost of £6 per tonne, gives a yield effect of £162A.

FOULKS LYNCH
PUBLICATIONS

These two variances are probably interrelated and should, therefore, be considered together. It is likely that the change to a cheaper mix of materials has resulted in the yield of good production being down compared with standard. The net effect of the two is an overall adverse usage variance for direct material of £34.

1.6 Splitting the materials mix variance

It is possible to show the build-up of material mix variance of £128F in total for materials A, B and C separately, by comparing the quantities in (2) and (3) line by line as follows:

Material	Actual quantity used tonnes	Actual quantity used in standard mix tonnes	Mix variance tonnes	Standard price per tonne £	Mix variance £
A	444	565	121 F	6.00	726 F
B	446	339	107 A	5.00	535 A
C	240	226	14 A	4.50	63 A
	1,130	1,130	Nil		128 F

The same total favourable mix variance (£128) is made up of favourable and adverse sub-variances. A reduction in the proportion of material A has given rise to a favourable variance and the increased usage of materials B and C has given rise to adverse variances.

The mechanics of the calculations are quite clear but how would a manager receiving such a breakdown of the total mix variance interpret the analysis? The manager might conclude that it was a good idea to reduce the proportion of A used as this produces a favourable variance, but a bad thing to increase the proportions of B and C with their resultant adverse effects.

Two points should be made here.

- As mentioned above, looking at mix variances in isolation from yield variances can be dangerous. If the manager tries to reduce the largest adverse variance, say, by using less of B, this may have adverse effects on the yield.

- Is using more of B and C necessarily a bad thing? They are **relatively cheaper** than A and therefore one might expect their increased relative use should give rise to a **favourable** variance.

The alternative analysis shown below reflects the second point.

1.7 Using average standard cost of input in mix valuations

Under this approach, each individual material mix element in tonnes is valued at the difference between:

- the individual standard prices of the materials, and
- the overall average standard cost of material input (in standard mix).

In the above example, the standard cost of material input is $\frac{£5,940}{1,100} = £5.40$ per tonne.

Now, if a material's own price is **higher** than this, it is a relatively **expensive** material, and thus **excess usage** over standard mix should give rise to an **adverse** variance.

This will be achieved by multiplying the **adverse** mix variance (in tonnes) by a **positive** difference between individual and average price resulting in an overall **adverse** cost variance.

The same logic is applied to ensure that under-usage of relatively cheap materials will give rise to an adverse variance, etc.

For our example, the computations would look like this:

Material	P_S Standard price per tonne £	P_A Average standard price per tonne £	$P_S - P_A$ Difference £	Q_S Actual quantity used in standard mix tonnes	Q_A Actual quantity used tonnes	$Q_S - Q_A$ Difference £	$(P_S - P_A)$ $(Q_S - Q_A)$ Mix variance £
A	6.00	5.40	0.60	565	444	121 F	72.60 F
B	5.00	5.40	(0.40)	339	446	107 A	42.80 F
C	4.50	5.40	(0.90)	226	240	14 A	12.60 F
				1,130	1,130	–	128.00 F

- Material A variance is favourable because less of an expensive material has been used.

- The increased usage of the relatively cheaper materials B and C would tend to reduce the overall cost of the mix and so produce the favourable variances.

- This approach is clear-cut. The effect of the change in the mix, compared with the standard, is favourable because it has reduced the overall average cost of the mix.

1.8   Breakdown of the yield variance

The total effect on the yield of good production is an interrelated consideration. Although it is possible to sub-analyse the yield variance, doing so is unlikely to produce any more meaningful information to management than the total yield variance on its own does. The yield variance is a measure of whether more or less good production has been achieved from the actual input, compared with the standard. Therefore, the yield is related more to output than to individual material inputs.

In summary, there is some doubt about the usefulness to management of any breakdown in the direct material mix or yield variances. If an analysis of the mix variances is undertaken, there are two methods of calculation. The approach using the comparison with the **average standard input price** seems to produce logical and unequivocal variances, but it should be noted that some authorities prefer the previous approach.

The Acton company produces a product by mixing three chemicals X, Y, Z in the proportions 4, 3, 3 respectively. Minor variations on these proportions are acceptable. The standard prices for the chemicals are as follows.

X	£3.20/litre
Y	£2.50/litre
Z	£3.60/litre

There is a 5% normal loss.

Last month's output was 210,000 litres.

The inputs were:

X	70,200 litres at £3.30
Y	69,800 litres at £2.45
Z	60,200 litres at £3.70

Calculate the material price, the material mix, the material yield and the material usage variances. Hence check the relationship between the mix, yield and usage variance.

Feedback to this activity is at the end of the chapter.

2   Sales mix and quantity variances

Where more than one product is sold, it is likely that each will have a different profit. If they are sold in a mix different from that budgeted, a sales mix profit variance will result. Even if the products are not possible substitutes, a change of sales mix may indicate a change in emphasis of selling effort by sales staff or marketing resources.

Example

Note: the profit figure used will be the standard profit (assuming an absorption costing system).

The Omega company sets the following sales budgets for three products:

			Budgeted profit £
A	400	units at a standard profit of £8	3,200
B	600	units at a standard profit of £6	3,600
C	1,000	units at a standard profit of £4	4,000
	2,000	units	£10,800

The company expects to sell A, B and C in the proportion of 4 : 6 : 10 respectively. Actual sales are achieved at the standard selling price, as follows:

			Actual profit £
A	300	units @ £8	2,400
B	700	units @ £6	4,200
C	1,200	units @ £4	4,800
	2,200	units	£11,400

In this example any differences in selling price have been ignored. If products are sold for anything other than their standard selling price this variance should be calculated **separately** first. Thereafter the calculation of the sales volume variance can be done at a standard margin (profit, as here, or contribution) per unit.

2.1   The variances

With the price variance being nil in this case, the question that remains to be answered is: Why have the sales for the period yielded £11,400 in standard profits instead of £5,940? There are two reasons:

(1) The three products have been sold in **different proportions** from standard – the **mix** variance.

(2) A **different total quantity** of sales from standard have been made – the **quantity** variance.

The combination of these makes up the overall **sales margin volume** variance.

2.2   The computations

A tabular approach, analogous to that used for materials, is strongly recommended, although other approaches will be shown. The column headings for the relevant tables are as follows:

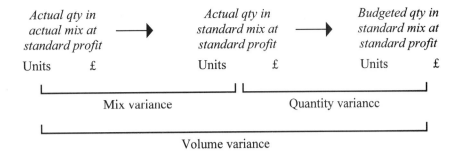

2.3   Solution

The previous figures show a favourable variance of £600 (£11,400 – £10,800) attributable to a change in sales volume which can be split into mix and quantity.

A useful working is the average standard profit per unit $= \dfrac{£10,800}{2,000} = £5.40.$

This can be used to evaluate the profits derived from any total sales quantity, provided the products are in standard mix and at standard profits per unit.

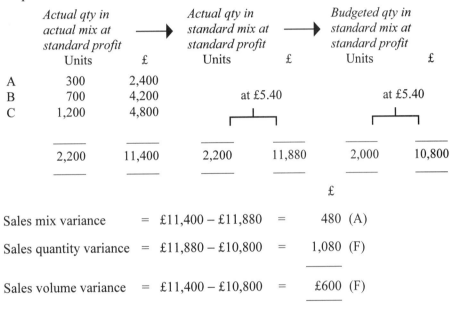

	Actual qty in actual mix at standard profit		Actual qty in standard mix at standard profit		Budgeted qty in standard mix at standard profit	
	Units	£	Units	£	Units	£
A	300	2,400				
B	700	4,200		at £5.40		at £5.40	
C	1,200	4,800				
	2,200	11,400	2,200	11,880	2,000	10,800

					£	
Sales mix variance	=	£11,400 – £11,880	=	480	(A)
Sales quantity variance	=	£11,880 – £10,800	=	1,080	(F)
Sales volume variance	=	£11,400 – £10,800	=	£600	(F)

2.4   Interpretation

Since the net effect of the quantity changes is always zero (i.e. we are considering the mix with the total sales of 2,200 units) the overall mix variance will be favourable if more products with a higher profit per unit are sold in place of products with a lower profit per unit, i.e. in this case the proportion of B and C, which have a lower profit per unit has been increased whereas A, which yields a higher profit per unit, has been reduced. Hence an overall adverse mix variance.

2.5   Splitting the sales mix variance

If any split of the mix variance is deemed necessary the following approach is suggested although the low additional information content of the split makes the exercise rather futile. The basic idea is to assess the effect of the change in proportion of each product by reference to the weighted average contribution earned if the standard mix is sold, i.e. as per budget (£5.40).

	Actual quantity in standard mix		Actual quantity in actual mix				£	
A	440		300	=	140 × £(8 − 5.40)	=	364	A
B	660		700	=	40 × £(6 − 5.40)	=	24	F
C	1,100		1,200	=	100 × £(4 − 5.40)	=	140	A
	2,200	⇐	2,200		Mix variance		480	A

This approach specifically demonstrates whether the change in proportion of each individual product increases or decreases the weighted average profit earned.

Hence in the case of A, as contribution is higher than the weighted average, the reduction in proportion of A will depress profits. With product C the profit per unit (£4) is below average. Hence an increase in proportion of C is *not* beneficial as it will reduce the weighted average contribution earned.

2.6   Usefulness of the sales mix variance

Variances are calculated for the purpose of control. Managers are provided with a variance analysis of their areas of responsibility so that they can improve their decisions. The sales margin mix variance must be judged by this objective.

Two situations are possible:

(1) The manager is responsible for two or more products which are to some extent substitutes for each other, e.g. ranges of cheap and expensive cosmetics. Since the mix variance represents shifts in demand between the product ranges, it has significance. As stated before, it is not relevant for non-substitutes.

(2) The manager is responsible for one line of products. Other managers are responsible for other totally different product lines. In this situation, to provide a product manager with a mix variance when he can control only one product is meaningless.

ACTIVITY 2

From the following information provide a comprehensive sales margin variance analysis.

	Product X	Product Y	Product Z
Budget			
Sales price	£20	£20	£10
Cost	£10	£15	£8
Units	100	700	200
Total profit	£1,000	£3,500	£400
Actual			
Sales price	£21	£24	£7
Units sold	200	700	100

Feedback to this activity is at the end of the chapter.

Conclusion

This chapter has explained how mix and yield (materials) or mix and quantity (sales) may be calculated and interpreted by management.

The whole topic of mix and yield/quantity variances can be confusing, with various tables of data and sub-analysis methods. It is easy to concentrate too much on the

mechanics and to overlook the fact that variance analysis is a way of presenting information to management so that individual managers can take decisions on the most appropriate courses of action. It is important that the manager receiving the variance report should understand the meaning of any mix and yield/quantity variances in it.

SELF-TEST
QUESTIONS

Materials mix and yield variances

1   In what circumstances is the mix/yield analysis of the materials usage variance most meaningful? (1.1)

2   Explain the meanings of the materials mix and yield variances. (1.3)

3   What is the purpose of sub-analysing the mix variance using an average price of input? (1.7)

Sales mix and quantity variances

4   What does the sales margin mix variance indicate? (2.1)

5   In what circumstances is the sales mix/quantity analysis variance most helpful to management? (2.6)

EXAM-TYPE
QUESTION

Chemical company

A chemical company has the following standards for producing 9 gallons of a machine lubricant.

5 gallons of material P @ £0.70 per gallon

5 gallons of material Q @ £0.92 per gallon.

No stocks of raw materials are kept. Purchases are made as needed so that all price variances relate to materials used. Actual results showed that 100,000 gallons of material were used during a particular period as follows.

45,000	gallons of material P at an actual cost per gallon used of £0.80	36,000
55,000	gallons of material Q at an actual cost per gallon used of £0.97	53,350
100,000		£89,350

During the period 92,070 gallons of the machine lubricant were produced.

Required:

(a) Calculate the total materials variance and analyse it into its price, yield and mix components.   **(10 marks)**

(b) Explain the circumstances under which a materials mix variance is relevant to managerial control.   **(10 marks)**
                                                              (Total: 20 marks)

For the answer to this question, see the 'Answers' section at the end of the book.

Materials price variance = (Actual price – standard price) × Actual quantity

		£
X (3.30 – 3.20) × 70,200	=	7,020 (A)
Y (2.45 – 2.50) × 69,800	=	3,490 (F)
Z (3.70 – 3.60) × 60,200	=	6,020 (A)
Price variance		9,550 (A)

Materials mix variance = (Actual mix – standard mix of actual) × Standard price

				£
0.4	X	(70,200 – 80,080) × 3.20	=	31,616 (F)
0.3	Y	(69,800 – 60,060) × 2.50	=	24,350 (A)
0.3	Z	(60,200 – 60,060) × 3.60	=	504 (A)
Mix variance		200,200 200,200		6,762 (F)

Materials yield variance = (Standard input for actual output – Actual mix in standard proportions) × Standard price

				£
0.4	X	(88,421 – 80,080) × 3.20	=	26,691 (F)
0.3	Y	(66,316 – 60,060) × 2.50	=	15,640 (F)
0.3	Z	(66,316 – 60,060) × 3.60	=	22,522 (F)
Yield variance		221,053 200,200		64,853 (F)

Standard input for actual output = $\dfrac{100}{95} \times 210,000 = 221,053$

Materials usage variance = (Standard input for actual output – Actual mix) × Standard price

		£
X (88,421 – 70,200) × 3.20 =		58,307 (F)
Y (66,316 – 69,800) × 2.50 =		8,710 (A)
Z (66,316 – 60,200) × 3.60 =		22,018 (F)
Usage variance		71,615 (F)

Check: mix variance + yield variance = usage variance

6,762 (F)   +   64,853 (F)   = 71,615 (F)

Sales price variance = (Actual price – Standard price) × Actual quantity sold

Product				£
X	(£21 – £20)	×200	=	200 (F)
Y	(£24 – £20)	×700	=	2,800 (F)
Z	(£7 – £10)	×100	=	300 (A)
				2,700 (F)

	Actual qty in actual mix at standard margin		Actual qty in standard mix at standard margin		Budgeted qty in standard mix at standard margin	
	Units	£	Units	£	Units	£
X	200	2,000				
Y	700	3,500	at £4.90		at £4.90	
Z	100	200				
	1,000	5,700	1,000	4,900	1,000	4,900

Budgeted profits	= £1,000 + £3,500 + £400 =	£4,900
Average profit/unit	= £4,900 ÷ 1,000 =	£4.90
		£
Sales mix variance	= £5,700 − £4,900 =	800 (F)
Sales quantity variance	= £4,900 − £4,900 =	-
Sales volume variance	= £5,700 − £4,900 =	800 (F)

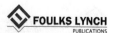

Chapter 20
BUDGETARY PLANNING AND CONTROL

In Chapter 3, we discussed the **objectives** a business may set for itself, both financial and non-financial. Once those objectives have been identified and prioritised, the **planning** process can begin.

These plans must then be communicated to those responsible for carrying them out, and an important part of the communication of short-term financial plans is the **annual budget**. It is also an essential tool in the **control** of business operations.

In this chapter we look at the planning and budget setting process, including the preparation of the various types of budget initially reviewing old material before moving onto new areas.

In the following chapters we look at the use of budgets as a means of control and motivation, alternative approaches to budget setting and the quantitative aids that may be used in the preparation of budgets.

Objectives

By the time you have finished this chapter you should be able to do the following:

- identify the purposes of budgetary planning and control systems
- describe the planning and control cycle, and the control process
- prepare, review and explain a budget preparation timetable
- prepare and evaluate functional, subsidiary and master budgets, including cash budgeting
- explain the processes involved with the development and implementation of budgets.

1   The planning process

1.1   Planning and objectives

You will recall from your earlier studies that firms need to plan to survive.

A frequently asked question in formulating the corporate plan is 'Where do we see ourselves in ten years time'? To answer this successfully the firm must consider:

- what it wants to achieve (its objectives)
- how it intends to get there (its strategy)
- what resources will be required (its operating plans)
- how well it is doing in comparison to the plan (control).

Corporate planning is a long-run activity which seeks to determine the direction in which the firm should be moving in the future. For corporate planning purposes it is essential that the objectives chosen are **quantified** and have a **timescale** attached to them. A statement such as 'maximise profits' or 'increase sales' would be of little use in corporate planning terms.

FOULKS LYNCH
PUBLICATIONS

The following would be far more helpful:

- achieve a growth in EPS of 5% per annum over the coming ten year period
- obtain a turnover of £x million within six years
- launch at least two new products per year, etc.

Some objectives may be difficult to quantify (e.g. contented workforce) but if no attempt is made there will be no yardstick against which to compare actual performance.

1.2 Importance of long-range planning for successful budgetary control

A budget is not (or should not be) the same as a forecast. A forecast is a statement of what is **expected** to happen; a budget is a statement of what it is reasonable to believe **can be made** to happen.

A system of budgetary control introduced in isolation without any form of corporate or long-range planning is unlikely to yield its full potential benefit.

For example, an organisation without a long-range plan may start with the sales forecast and try to improve the expected results slightly by increasing the advertising budget. This modified sales forecast then becomes the budget on which the other budgets are based.

This approach has several limitations, some of which are listed below.

(1) In the absence of specified long-term objectives, there are no criteria against which to evaluate possible courses of action. Managers do not know what they should be trying to achieve. Performance evaluation can only be on a superficial 'better/worse than last year' basis: no one has assessed the potential of the business.

(2) Many decisions, e.g. capital expenditure decisions or the decision to introduce a new product, can only be taken on a long-term basis. Long-term forecasts may be inaccurate, but they are better than no forecast at all. A company with no long-range forecasting would be in dire straits when, sooner or later, sales of its existing products decline.

(3) There is a limit to the influence a company can exert over events in the short term (e.g. by increased advertising). If it wishes to improve its position markedly, it must think long-term.

(4) Eventually some factor other than sales may become the limiting factor, e.g. shortage of materials or labour. If the company has not anticipated the situation, it may simply have to live with the problem. With adequate long-range planning it might be able to avoid or overcome it.

1.3 Overview of the planning process

The overall planning process is described in the following diagram with which you should already be familiar:

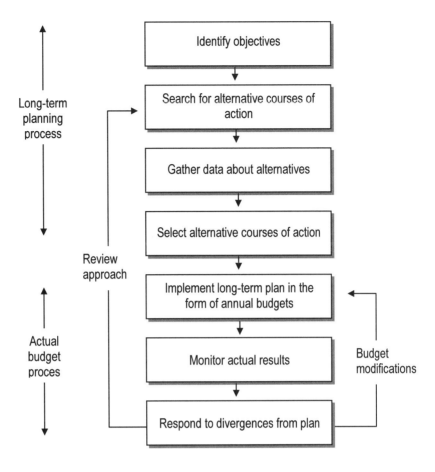

The seven stages are expanded below.

(1) Identify objectives

This first stage requires the company to specify objectives towards which it is working, as discussed earlier.

(2) Search for possible courses of action

A series of specific strategies should be developed dealing particularly with:

- developing new markets for existing products

- developing new products for existing markets

- developing new products for new markets.

(3) Gathering data about alternatives and measuring pay-offs

This is an information-gathering stage.

(4) Select course of action

Having made decisions, long-term plans based on those decisions are created.

(5) Implementation of long-term plans

This stage signals the move from long-term planning to annual budgeting. The budget provides the link between the strategic plans and their implementation in management decisions. The budget should be seen as an integral part of the long-term planning process.

(6) **Monitor actual outcomes**

This is the particular role of the cost accountant, keeping detailed financial and other records of actual performance compared with budget targets (variance accounting).

(7) **Respond to divergences from plan**

This is the control process in budgeting, responding to divergences from plan either through budget modifications or through identifying new courses of action.

2   Budgetary control process

The budgetary control process comprises two distinct elements:

(1) **Planning**

This involves the setting of the various budgets for the appropriate future period. Management at the various levels in an organisation should be involved in the budgetary planning stage for its own area of responsibility.

(2) **Control**

Control involves the comparison of the plan in the form of the budget with the actual results achieved for the appropriate period. Any significant divergences between the budgeted and the actual results should be reported to the appropriate management so that the necessary action can be taken.

ACTIVITY 1

Before continuing, see if you can remember what the functions of a budgetary control system are.

Feedback to this activity is at the end of the chapter.

2.1   Functions of a budgetary control system

Planning and co-ordination

Success in business is closely related to success in planning for the future. In this context the budget serves three functions:

- it provides a formal planning framework that ensures planning does take place

- it co-ordinates the various separate aspects of the business by providing a master plan (the **master budget**) for the business as a whole (this is particularly important in a large organisation engaged in making several different products, where otherwise it is too easy for individual managers to concentrate on their own aspects of the business)

- though not all decisions can be anticipated, the budget provides a framework of reference within which later operating decisions can be taken.

Authorising and delegating

Adoption of a budget by management explicitly authorises the decisions made within it. This serves two functions:

- the need continuously to ask for top management decisions is reduced;

- the responsibility for carrying out the decisions is delegated to individual managers.

Evaluating performance

One of the functions of accounting information is that it provides a basis for the measurement of managerial performance. By setting targets for each manager to achieve, the budget provides a bench-mark, against which his actual performance can be assessed objectively.

FOULKS LYNCH
PUBLICATIONS

Note, however, that before a budget can successfully be used for this purpose, it must be accepted as reasonable by the individual manager whose area of responsibility it covers and whose performance is to be evaluated.

Discerning trends

It is important that management should be made aware as soon as possible of any new trends, whether in relation to production or marketing. The budget, by providing specific expectations with which actual performance is continuously compared, supplies a mechanism for the early detection of any unexpected trend.

Communication and motivating

The application of budgeting within an organisation should lead to a good communications structure. Managers involved in the setting of budgets for their own responsibility need to have agreed strategies and policies communicated down to them. A good system of downwards communication should itself encourage good upwards and sideways communication in the organisation. Budgets that have been agreed by managers should provide some motivation towards their achievement.

Control

Once the budgets have been set and agreed for the future period under review, the formal control element of budgetary control is ready to start. This control involves the comparison of the plan in the form of the budget with the actual results achieved for the appropriate period. Any significant divergences between the budgeted and the actual results should be reported to the appropriate management so that the necessary action can be taken.

When the goals have been set for the organisation, the management uses the budgetary system to control the running of the business to evaluate the extent to which those goals are achieved. By a continuous comparison of actual performance with planned results, deviations or variances are quickly identified and appropriate action initiated. This is a fundamental aspect of the whole process: if targets were set but little or no attempt were made to measure the extent to which they were achieved, then the advantages of budgeting would be severely curtailed.

There is, however, a danger in adhering to the budget too inflexibly. Circumstances may change, and the budget should change accordingly or the control system should identify separately the variances arising due to the changed conditions. Organisations operate within a dynamic environment, and the control systems need to be appropriately flexible.

2.2 Setting up a budgetary control system

Before a budgetary control system can be introduced, it is essential that:

- Key **executives are committed** to the proposed system.
- The **long-term objectives** of the organisation have been defined (as previously discussed).
- There is an adequate **foundation of data** on which to base forecasts and costs.
- An **organisation chart** should be drawn up, clearly defining areas of authority and responsibility. The organisation can then be logically divided into *budget centres*, such that each manager has a budget for, and is given control information about, the area which he can control. This is the essence of **responsibility accounting.**
- A **budget committee** should be set up and a *budget manual* produced.
- The **budget period** should be set.

2.3   Budget centres

A **budget centre** is a clearly defined part of an organisation for the purposes of operating a budgetary control system. Each function within an organisation will be sub-divided into appropriate budget centres. In determining budget centres it is important to be able to define them in terms of management responsibility. The manager responsible for a budget centre (e.g. the machining department within the production function) will be involved in the planning stage of setting the budget for his area of responsibility and he will be the recipient of control information in due course.

2.4   Budget committee

A typical budget committee comprises the chief executive, the management accountant (acting as budget officer) and functional heads. The functions of the committee are to:

- agree policy with regard to budgets
- co-ordinate budgets
- suggest amendments to budgets (e.g. because there is inadequate profit)
- approve budgets after amendment, as necessary
- examine comparisons of budgeted and actual results and recommend corrective action if this has not already been taken.

The budget officer is secretary to the committee and is responsible for seeing that the timetables are adhered to and for providing the necessary specialist assistance to the functional managers in drawing up their budgets and analysing results.

2.5   Budget manual

A budget manual is a document that sets out instructions on the responsibilities and procedures of budget preparation.

2.6   Budget period

The **budget period** is the period of time for which a budget is prepared and over which the control aspect takes place. The length of such a period will depend on various factors.

- **The nature of the business** – in the ship-building or power supply industries budget periods of ten to twenty years may be appropriate.   Periods of less than one year may be appropriate for firms in the clothing and fashion industries.
- **The part of the business being budgeted** – capital expenditure will usually be budgeted for longer periods ahead than the production output.
- **The basis of control** – many businesses use a twelve month period as their basic budget period, but at the same time it is very common to find the annual budget broken down into quarterly or monthly sub-units. Such a breakdown is usually for control purposes because actual and budgeted results need to be monitored continuously. It is not practicable to wait until the end of a twelve month budget period before making control comparisons.

3   Structuring the budgets

The steps taken to structure the budgets are as follows:

(1) Prepare:

- sales forecast
- raw material availability forecast
- cash availability forecast, etc.

(2) Determine the principal budget factor.

(3) Decide whether the limitations can be removed, and at what cost, e.g. by additional advertising expenditure, by intensive recruitment and training, etc. This is a matter for the budget committee.

(4) Draw up budgets on the agreed basis.

3.1   The principal budget factor

The **principal budget factor** is a factor which will limit the activities of an undertaking and which is often the starting point in budget preparation. In most businesses, it is the **volume of the demand** for the product which limits the scale of operation. It is possible, however, for there to be some other limiting factor, e.g. labour, material, cash or machinery.

The limiting factor must be identified at the first stage of the budgeting process, since it will determine all the other budgets.

The determination and valuation of the principal budget factor is achieved using forecasting techniques. These are dealt with later in this text.

3.2   Drawing up the budget

Assuming that the level of demand is the principal budget factor, the various functional, departmental and master budgets will be drawn up in the following order.

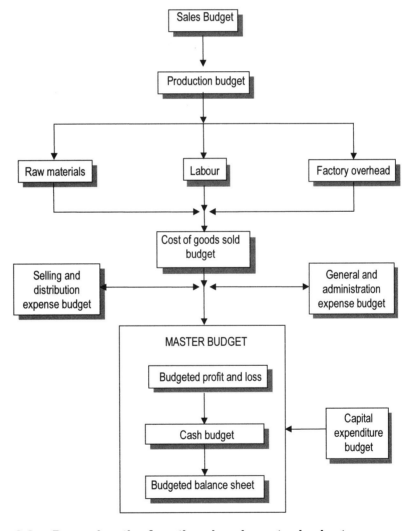

3.3   Preparing the functional and master budgets

We shall now revise the technique of budget preparation with a worked example.

Hash Ltd makes two products – PS and TG. Sales for next year are budgeted at 5,000 units of PS and 1,000 units of TG. Planned selling prices are £65 and £100 respectively.

332 FINANCIAL MANAGEMENT AND CONTROL

Hash Ltd has the following opening stock and required closing stock:

	PS units	TG units
Opening stock	100	50
Required closing stock	1,100	50

You are also given the following data about the materials required to produce PS and TG and the whittling and fettling processes involved in production:

	PS	TG
Finished products		
Kg of raw material X, per unit of finished product	12	12
Kg of raw material Y, per unit of finished product	6	8
Direct labour hours per unit of finished product	8	12

	Raw material X	Raw material Y
Direct materials		
Desired closing stock in kg	6,000	1,000
Opening stock in kg	5,000	5,000

Standard rates and prices

Direct labour	£2.20 per hour
Raw material X	£0.72 per kg
Raw material Y	£1.56 per kg
Production overheads	£
Variable	1.54 per labour hour
Fixed	0.54 per labour hour
	2.08 per labour hour

3.4 The sales budget

The sales budget represents the plan in terms of the quantity and value of sales, for sales management. In practice this is often the most difficult budget to calculate.

The sales budget for our example would be as follows.

	Total	PS	TG
Sales units	6,000	5,000	1,000
Sales value	£425,000	£325,000	£100,000

In practice a business would market many more than two products. Moreover, the sales budget would probably be supported by subsidiary budgets to show analysis according to, for example:

- responsibility, e.g. Northern area, Western area, etc
- type of customer, e.g. wholesale, retail, government, etc

3.5 The production budget

The production budget is usually expressed in quantity and represents the sales budget adjusted for opening/closing finished stocks and work in progress.

Production budget	PS units	TG units
Sales budget	5,000	1,000
Budgeted stock increase (1,100 – 100)/(50 – 50)	1,000	-
Production in units	6,000	1,000

3.6   Production costs budget

The production budget needs to be translated into *requirements* and *values* for:

- raw materials
- direct labour
- factory overheads.

3.7   The raw materials budget

(Remember that Hash Ltd is going to produce 6,000 units of PS and 1,000 units of TG.)

		X kg		Y kg
For production of PS	6,000 × 12 kg	72,000	6,000 × 6 kg	36,000
For production of TG	1,000 × 12 kg	12,000	1,000 × 8 kg	8,000
Raw materials used		84,000		44,000
Budgeted raw material stock increase/(decrease)	(6,000 – 5,000)	1,000	(1,000 – 5,000)	(4,000)
Raw materials purchased		85,000		40,000
		£		£
Budgeted value of purchases				
X £0.72 per kg × 85,000		61,200		
Y £1.56 per kg × 40,000				62,400

3.8   Labour budget

		Hours		£
For PS	6,000 × 8 hrs	48,000		
For TG	1,000 × 12 hrs	12,000		
		60,000	@ £2.20	132,000

3.9   Production overhead budget

		£
Variable costs	60,000 hours × £1.54	92,400
Fixed costs	60,000 hours × £0.54	32,400
		124,800

3.10   Cost of goods sold budget

Remember that we are calculating the cost of goods sold. So far we have calculated the amounts of material, labour and overheads used in **production**. To arrive at the figures for cost of goods sold you have to remember that production is used not just for sales but also to increase/decrease stock levels – hence the need to adjust for the **opening** and **closing** stock position of both **raw material** and **finished goods**.

Opening/closing stock of raw materials

	Closing			**Opening**	
	£	£			£
X	6,000 kg × £0.72	4,320		5,000 kg × £0.72	3,600
Y	1,000 kg × £1.56	1,560		5,000 kg × £1.56	7,800
		5,880			11,400

Opening/closing stock of finished goods

		PS £		TG £
Standard cost of finished goods. Materials.				
X	12 kg × £0.72	8.64	12 kg × £0.72	8.64
Y	6 kg × £1.56	9.36	8 kg × £1.56	12.48
		18.00		21.12
Wages	8 hours × £2.20	17.60	12 hours × £2.20	26.40
Overhead	8 hours × £2.08	16.64	12 hours × £2.08	24.96
		52.24		72.48
Closing stock in units		1,100		50
Stock value		£57,464		£3,624
Opening stock in units		100		50
Stock value		£5,224		£3,624

Cost of goods sold budget

We can now bring all the above elements together.

	£	£
Opening stocks		
Raw materials	11,400	
Finished goods (5,224 + 3,624)	8,848	
		20,248
Raw materials purchased (61,200 + 62,400)		123,600
Direct labour		132,000
Production overhead		124,800
		400,648
Less: Closing stocks		
Raw materials	5,880	
Finished goods (57,464 + 3,624)	61,088	
		66,968
		333,680

3.11 Non-production cost budgets

Marketing, administration and other non-production costs budgets will be a summary of the budget centres within those functions.

For the purposes of this example, the marketing/administration budget is assumed to be £45,000.

4   The master budget

The **master budget** is the budget into which all subsidiary budgets are consolidated. The master budget normally comprises:

- budgeted profit and loss account
- budgeted balance sheet
- budgeted cash flow statement (cash budget).

It is likely to be supported by a capital expenditure budget.

Cash budgets require detailed information about timings of cash flows, debtors and creditors, etc which we do not have for our current example. Their preparation will therefore be dealt with in a separate section.

4.1   Budgeted profit and loss account

The budgeted profit and loss account is prepared by summarising the operating budgets.

Master budget - profit and loss account

	£	£
Sales		425,000
Cost of sales		
Opening stocks	20,248	
Raw materials	123,600	
Direct labour	132,000	
Production overhead	124,800	
	400,648	
Closing stocks	66,968	
		333,680
Operating margin		91,320
Marketing/administration		45,000
Operating profit		46,320

Note: the above budgets are presented to highlight planned requirements rather than for costing purposes. Most businesses will obviously be more complex than that illustrated and supporting analyses would be prepared as required, e.g:

- production units by month or weeks

- raw materials by supplier

- direct labour by grade.

4.2   Budgeted balance sheet

The total company plan will include a statement to show the financial situation at the end of the budget period. Subsidiary budgets will be prepared to analyse movements in fixed and working capital during the budget period based on the operating budgets and reflecting financial policy formulated by the budget committee.

The activity that follows the cash budget example later in the text revises the types of computation required for the balance sheet.

4.3   Capital expenditure budget

The capital expenditure included in the master budget will essentially be an extract from the long-term capital budget.

- The **cash** required to finance the capital expenditure will be incorporated in the cash budget (as illustrated later).

- The **assets** relating to the capital expenditure will be incorporated in the budgeted balance sheet.

- The **depreciation** will be reflected in both the budgeted profit and loss account (annual charge) and the budgeted balance sheet (accumulated).

A capital expenditure budget is in many respects the most problematic budget to prepare in that the types of projects for which capital expenditure is to be incurred tend to have long time spans and uncertain outcomes.

5 Preparing the cash budget

DEFINITION

A **cash budget** is a detailed budget of estimated cash inflows and outflows incorporating both revenue and capital items.

A **cash budget** is a detailed budget of estimated cash inflows and outflows incorporating both revenue and capital items

The preparation of cash budgets or budgeted cash flow statements has two main objectives:

* to provide periodic budgeted cash balances for the budgeted balance sheet

* to anticipate cash shortages/surpluses and thus provide information to assist management in short and medium-term cash planning and longer-term financing for the organisation.

5.1 Method of preparation

* Forecast sales.

* Forecast time-lag on converting debtors to cash, and hence forecast cash receipts from credit sales.

* Determine stock levels, and hence purchase requirements.

* Forecast time-lag on paying suppliers, and thus cash payments for purchases.

* Incorporate other cash payments and receipts, including such items as capital expenditure and tax payments.

* Collate all this cash flow information, so as to determine the net cash flows.

5.2 Layout of the cash budget

A tabular layout should be used, with:

* **columns** for weeks, months or quarters (as appropriate)

* **rows** for cash inflows and outflows.

Example

A wholesale company ends its financial year on 30 June. You have been requested, in early July 20X5, to assist in the preparation of a cash forecast. The following information is available regarding the company's operations.

(a) Management believes that the 20X4/20X5 sales level and pattern are a reasonable estimate of 20X5/20X6 sales. Sales in 20X4/20X5 were as follows:

		£
20X4	July	360,000
	August	420,000
	September	600,000
	October	540,000
	November	480,000
	December	400,000
20X5	January	350,000
	February	550,000
	March	500,000
	April	400,000
	May	600,000
	June	800,000
	Total	6,000,000

(b) The accounts receivable at 30 June 20X5 total £380,000. Sales collections are generally made as follows:

During month of sale	60%
In first subsequent month	30%
In second subsequent month	9%
Uncollectable	1%

(c) The purchase cost of goods averages 60% of selling price. The cost of the stock on hand at 30 June 20X5 is £840,000, of which £30,000 is obsolete.

Arrangements have been made to sell the obsolete stock in July at half the normal selling price on a cash on delivery basis. The company wishes to maintain the stock, as of the first of each month, at a level of three months' sales as determined by the sales forecast for the next three months. All purchases are paid for on the tenth of the following month. Accounts payable for purchases at 30 June 20X5 total £370,000.

(d) Payments in respect of fixed and variable expenses are forecast for the first three months of 20X5/20X6 and are as follows.

	£
July	160,620
August	118,800
September	158,400

(e) It is anticipated that cash dividends of £40,000 will be paid each half-year, on the fifteenth day of September and March.

(f) During the year unusual advertising costs will be incurred that will require cash payments of £10,000 in August and £15,000 in September. The advertising costs are in addition to the expenses in item (d) above.

(g) Equipment replacements are made at a rate which requires a cash outlay of £3,000 per month. The equipment has an average estimated life of six years.

(h) A £60,000 payment for corporation tax is to be made on 15 September 20X5.

(i) At 30 June 20X5 the company had a bank loan with an unpaid balance of £280,000. The entire balance is due on 30 September 20X5, together with accumulated interest from 1 July 20X5 at the rate of 12% pa.

(j) The cash balance at 30 June 20X5 is £100,000.

You are required to prepare a cash forecast statement, by month, for the first three months of the 20X5/X6 financial year. The statement should show the amount of cash on hand (or deficiency of cash) at the end of each month. All computations and supporting schedules should be presented in clear and concise form.

Solution

Many of the costs can be entered straight on to the cash flow statement, e.g. expenses, dividends, capital expenditure etc.

FINANCIAL MANAGEMENT AND CONTROL

There are three supporting schedules needed.

(1) Cash received from sales

	Sales £	Cash received July £	August £	September £
May	600,000	54,000	-	-
June	800,000	240,000	72,000	-
July	360,000	216,000	108,000	32,400
August	420,000	-	252,000	126,000
September	600,000	-	-	360,000
		510,000	432,000	518,400

(2) Other receipts – Obsolete stock

Obsolete stock at cost $= $ £30,000

Normal sales price $= \dfrac{100}{60} \times$ £30,000 $=$ £50,000

Realised $\frac{1}{2} \times$ £50,000 $=$ £25,000

(3) Payments to trade creditors

		£	£	£
(i)	10 July – Balance b/d			370,000
(ii)	10 August – sales in July		360,000	
	Cost of goods sold (60%)		216,000	
	Less: Opening stock	(840,000)		
	Less: Obsolete stock	30,000		
		(810,000)		
	Add: Closing stock 60%			
	(420,000 + 600,000 + 540,000)	936,000		
			126,000	
				342,000
(iii)	10 September – sales in August		420,000	
	Cost of goods sold (60%)		252,000	
	Less: Opening stock	(936,000)		
	Add: Closing stock 60%			
	(600,000 + 540,000 + 480,000)	972,000		
			36,000	
				288,000

Cash budget

	July £	August £	September £
Receipts:			
Receipts from debtors	510,000	432,000	518,400
Obsolete stock	25,000	-	-
	535,000	432,000	518,400

	July £	August £	September £
Payments			
Payments to creditors	370,000	342,000	288,000
Expenses	160,620	118,800	158,400
Dividends	-	-	40,000
Advertising	-	10,000	15,000
Capital expenditure	3,000	3,000	3,000
Corporation tax	-	-	60,000
Bank loan	-	-	288,400
	533,620	473,800	852,800
Net cash inflow/(outflow)	1,380	(41,800)	(334,400)
Balance b/f	100,000	101,380	59,580
Balance/ (deficiency) at month end	101,380	59,580	(274,820)

ACTIVITY 2

Referring back to the cash budget example just completed, compute the following balances that would appear in the budgeted balance sheet as at 30 September 20X5.

(a)   Debtors

(b)   Trade creditors

(c)   Closing stock

Feedback to this activity is at the end of the chapter.

Conclusion

This chapter has considered the need for long-term planning and the conversion of these plans into short-term quantified statements, budgets.

The preparation of budgets can involve a lot of number crunching. The key to success in an examination question is clear workings, cross referenced to the main solution statement.

SELF-TEST
QUESTIONS

The planning process

1   Give at least four objectives, other than profit/shareholder wealth maximisation, that a business may pursue. (1.1)

2   What is the difference between a budget and a forecast? (1.2)

Budgetary control process

3   What are the functions of a budgetary control system? (2.1)

Structuring the budgets

4   What is the difference between a production costs budget and a cost of goods sold budget? (3.6. 3.10)

The master budget

5   How will the capital expenditure budget impact upon the three components of the master budget? (4.3)

FOULKS LYNCH
PUBLICATIONS

Cash budget

From the following statements, prepare a month-by-month cash budget for the six months to 31 December.   **(20 marks)**

(a) **Revenue budget (i.e. trading and profit and loss account)**

Six months to 31 December (all revenue/costs accrue evenly over the six months)

	£'000	£'000
Sales (cash received one month in arrears)		1,200
Cost of sales:		
Paid one month in arrears	900	
Paid in month of purchase	144	
Depreciation	72	
		1,116
Budgeted profit		84

(b) **Capital budget**

	£'000
Payments for new plant	
July	12
August	25
September	13
November	50
	100
Increase in stocks, payable August	20
	120

Receipts	
New issue of share capital (October)	30

(c) **Balance sheet**

	Actual 1 July £'000
Assets side	
Fixed assets	720
Stocks	100
Debtors	210
Cash	40
	1,070
Liabilities side	
Capital and reserves	856
Taxation (payable December)	30
Creditors – trade	160
Dividends (payable August)	24
	1,070

FEEDBACK TO ACTIVITY 1	The functions of a budgetary control system are:

- planning and co-ordination
- authorising and delegating
- evaluating performance
- discerning trends
- communicating and motivating
- control.

FEEDBACK TO ACTIVITY 2

(a) **Debtors**

Looking back at the working in (1) closing debtors will be made up as follows:

From August sales	10% x 420,000	42,000
From September sales	40% x 600,000	240,000
		282,000

This assumes the 1% uncollected amounts from previous months have been written off.

(b) **Trade creditors**

The goods purchased in September will be paid for in October, and will therefore represent our creditors. In September, we purchase goods for sale in December at a cost of 60% x £400,000 = £240,000.

(c) **Stock**

The closing stock at 30 September will represent October, November and December's sales, at cost.

60% (540,000 + 480,000 + 400,000) = £852,000.

Chapter 21
USING BUDGETS TO CONTROL AND MOTIVATE

KEY POINT

There are three basic behavioural aspects to consider in the budgeting process – participation in budget setting, budgets as targets, and using budgets in performance evaluation.

DEFINITION

A **fixed budget** is a budget which shows income/costs for a single level of activity (usually budgeted).

KEY POINT

A **flexible budget** is a budget which, by recognising different cost behaviour patterns, is designed to change as the volume of activity changes.

This chapter looks at how budgets are used.

First, as a means of **control**, by the extraction of variances derived from fixed, or more likely, flexed budgets.

Secondly, as a means of **motivation**. There are three basic behavioural aspects to consider in the budgeting process – participation in budget setting, budgets as targets, and using budgets in performance evaluation.

Objectives

By the time you have finished this chapter you should be able to do the following:

- explain the implications of controllability for responsibility reporting
- explain the process of participation in budget setting and how this can address motivational problems
- prepare and evaluate fixed and flexible budgets and evaluate the resulting variances
- prepare flexed budgets when standard fixed overhead absorption is employed
- assess the behavioural implications of budgetary control and performance evaluation, including participation in budget setting.

1 Fixed, flexible and flexed budgets

1.1 Fixed budgets

A **fixed budget** is a budget which shows income/costs for a single level of activity (usually budgeted). A fixed budget makes no attempt to separate costs into those which are fixed and those which are variable.

It is therefore unsuitable for use as a basis for comparison with actual costs where such costs are known to vary with activity and the level of activity differs from that budgeted.

Fixed budgets are mainly used:

- as an expression of a ceiling on indirect, discretionary expenditure
- for businesses in a service industry, where many costs are largely fixed over a budget period.

1.2 Flexible and flexed budgets

These terms are often used interchangeably.

Strictly a flexible budget is a set of fixed budgets for various levels of activity, or ranges of activity levels.

The activity levels for which separate budgets are prepared will be those at which some aspect of cost behaviour changes, for example:

- levels at which 'steps' in fixed costs change, e.g. where an extra supervisor or machine is needed
- levels at which variable costs per unit change, e.g. labour overtime, bulk discounts on materials, etc.

One of these fixed budgets will be used as the **original** budget, based upon the expected level of activity.

Once the actual level of activity is known, the appropriate part of the flexible budget (whether the original or not) can then be used as a basis for the preparation of a **flexed** budget for purposes of comparison and variance analysis.

However, for control and motivational purposes, the budget for activity-related items should generally be able to cope with variations in activity levels.

1.3 Performance reporting

The twin concepts of **responsibility accounting** and **management by exception** require reporting to managers when actual results for items under their control deviate from planned results. Under a system of **responsibility accounting** the organisation is divided into budget centres, each of which has a manager who is responsible for its performance. **Management by exception** is the practice of focusing on activities which require attention and ignoring those which appear to be conforming to expectations.

Many of the costs under a manager's control are variable and will therefore change if the level of activity is different from that in the budget. It would be unreasonable to criticise a manager for incurring higher costs if these were a result of a higher than planned volume of activity. Conversely, if the level of activity is low, costs can be expected to fall and the original budget must be amended to reflect this.

A budget performance report based on a flexed budget therefore compares actual costs with the costs budgeted for the level of activity actually achieved. It does not explain any change in budgeted volume, which should be reported on separately.

It should be noted, however, that flexible and flexed budgets recognise fixed and variable costs in relation to a single measure of activity. The reality is more complex.

* Costs may be affected by more than one such measure.

* Not all costs will be affected by the same activity measures.

Performance reports should also distinguish between **controllable fixed costs** and **uncontrollable fixed costs**.

Look at the example below, as a simplified performance report for an operating division.

	£'000
Sales	750
Variable costs	420
Contribution	330
Controllable fixed costs (or avoidable fixed costs)	110
	220
Uncontrollable fixed costs (share of general overhead)	150
Profit	70

In this example, the key **performance measure** for the division is neither the contribution margin nor the net profit. It is **contribution minus controllable fixed costs** or profit before deducting apportioned general overheads.

This basic approach might be required in your examination as a method of presenting a division's performance.

2   Performance reports using flexed budgets

You will recall from your earlier studies that a performance report for a particular product, department or function will be prepared as follows:

(1) A fixed budget is set at the beginning of the period, based on estimated production. This is the original budget.

(2) This is then **flexed** to correspond with the actual level of activity.

(3) The result is compared with actual costs, and differences (variances) are reported to the managers responsible.

2.1   Investigation of variances shown on the performance report

As discussed earlier, the variances shown on each manager's performance report will need to be reviewed:

- to determine whether they are significant relative to absolute/relative size, previous patterns of variances, etc and thus warrant investigation

- to determine the extent to which they may be attributed to bad planning or inaccurate measurement.

The variances may then be subject to further analysis, between:

- planning and operational variances

- price/rate/usage/efficiency (mainly operational variances)

as covered in the earlier standard costing chapters.

3   Behavioural aspects of budgeting

If budgetary control is to be successful, attention must be paid to behavioural aspects, i.e. the effect of the system on people in the organisation and *vice versa.* Poor performance and results are more often due to the method of implementation and subsequent operation of a system, with a failure to allow properly for the human side of the enterprise, than to the system itself. The management needs to be fully committed to the budgeting system, and through leadership and education lower levels of management in the organisation should be similarly committed and motivated.

Budgets are one important way of influencing the behaviour of managers within an organisation. There are very few, if any, decisions and actions that a manager in an organisation can take which do not have some financial effect and which will not subsequently be reflected in a comparison between budgeted and actual results. This all-embracing nature of budgets is probably the most important advantage that a budgetary system has over most other systems in a typical organisation.

3.1   Roles of budgets – from a behavioural aspect

As identified earlier, budgets can take on a number of different roles in any organisation and each has important behavioural implications. Each is now re-examined from a behavioural aspect.

(1) **Authorisation**

Once a budget has been agreed, it is not interpreted by many managers merely as an authorisation to 'spend up to the budget' but rather as an authorisation to 'spend the budget', otherwise there is a real fear that the following year's budget will be cut. Therefore, there is a tendency in an underspend situation, when approaching the end of the financial year, to spend money when it is not really necessary to do so ('use it or lose it').

(2) **Planning**

The budgeting system provides a formal, co-ordinated approach to short-term planning throughout the organisation. Each manager has a framework in which to

plan for his own area of responsibility. Without budgeting it is difficult to imagine an alternative system, affecting all parts of an organisation, in which such planning could take place.

(3) Forecasting

Short-term budgets covering the next one or two years may provide the basis for making forecasts beyond that period, e.g. in appraising a project with a five year life, data may be extracted from the budgets and used to make forecasts for another three years.

The danger with this approach is that, if the budgets are incorrect, the extrapolations beyond the budget period are also likely to be wrong and the financial analysis of the project may be unsound.

The budgets could be incorrect because 'slack' or 'bias' has been built into them, a topic to be discussed later.

(4) Communicating and co-ordinating

A budgeting system encourages good communications and co-ordination in an organisation. Information about objectives, strategies and policies has to be communicated down from top management and all the individual budgets in an organisation need to be co-ordinated in order to arrive at the master budget.

(5) Motivation

Agreed budgets should motivate individual managers towards their achievement, which in turn should assist the organisation in attaining its longer-term objectives. Motivational effects and the concept of budget difficulty are dealt with later.

(6) Evaluation of performance

A comparison between the predetermined budget and the actual results is the most common way in which an individual manager's performance is judged on a regular basis. The way this appraisal is made and how deviations are dealt with may influence how the individual manager behaves in the future. This role is also the subject of further discussion later.

3.2 Behavioural problems associated with implementing budgetary control

- There may be a general **fear and misunderstanding** about the purpose of budgetary control. It is often regarded as a penny-pinching exercise rather than recognised as a tool of management at all levels in an organisation structure.

    If this tends to be the attitude, a carefully planned campaign of education and understanding should be undertaken. Managers should be encouraged to discover what is in the budgetary control system for them.

- Employees may become **united against management** and devote their energies to finding excuses for not meeting targets.

    Targets that are realistic, and are seen by the employees as being realistic, are what is required. Good communications involving consultation and participation should help to minimise this problem.

- One of the key roles in any organisation is at the supervisor/foreman level where the continual interface between management and employees exists. The **leadership** and **motivational function** of a supervisor or foreman is very important if the work is to be done and targets are to be achieved.

- The breaking down of an organisation into many sub-areas of managerial responsibility can lead to **sub-optimisation problems** as far as the whole company is concerned, i.e. the optimisation of an individual manager's department or section at the expense of the organisation overall.

    Such dysfunctional behaviour should be minimised. It reflects a lack of goal congruence.

- If budgets are built up from the base of the organisation, with individual departmental budgets providing the input to the overall master budget, the **tendency to incorporate slack into budgets** needs to be carefully monitored.

- Some **desirable projects could be lost** because they were not foreseen and therefore not budgeted for. The system needs to be flexible enough to avoid this problem.

All of these problems really relate to criticisms of the manner in which budgetary control systems tend to be operated, rather than of budgetary control *per se.*

The three particular areas of behavioural aspects of budgeting need to be addressed.

- Budget setting   -   participation
- Budgets as targets   -   motivation
- Budgets as assessors   -   performance evaluation.

4   Participation in budget setting

4.1   Imposed budgets – Theory X

In some organisations budgets are set by higher levels of management and then communicated to the lower levels of management to whose areas of responsibility they relate.

Thus, such budgets are seen by those lower-level managers as being **imposed upon them** by their superiors in the organisational hierarchy without their being allowed to participate in the budget-setting process and therefore **without their being able directly to influence** the budget figures.

This approach to involvement in the budgetary system is consistent with Douglas McGregor's Theory X view of how people behave in organisations. The Theory X view is based on the assumptions that people in work environments are basically lazy and dislike work and any responsibility associated with it. They are motivated by money to meet their basic needs.

Therefore, the Theory X style of management is **authoritarian**, based on **direction and control** down through the organisation and typified by a host of rules and regulations.

4.2   Participative budgets – Theory Y

The other end of the spectrum is described by McGregor as **Theory Y**. This is a participative theory of management, assuming that people in a work environment do **seek more responsibility** and **do not have to be so tightly controlled**. Therefore, it is in organisations where a Theory Y style of management predominates that one is more likely to come across a fully participative approach to the setting of budgets.

The general argument is that the more individual managers are allowed to participate, i.e. to influence the budgets for which they are held responsible, the more likely it is that they will accept the targets in the budgets and strive actively towards the attainment of those targets.

Under the Theory Y, participative style of management, actual performances should be increased by the motivational impact of budgets. An important point to recognise is the difference between **actual** and **perceived** participation. It is the extent to which an individual manager **perceives** that he has influenced the budget that is crucial in that manager's acceptance of it.

4.3   Limitations to the participative theory

There are limitations on the extent of the effectiveness of participation in the budget-setting process.

(1) If budgets are used both in a motivational role and for the evaluation of managerial performance, then a serious conflict can arise. A manager, through participation, may be able to influence the very budget upon which he is subsequently evaluated.

By lowering the standard in the budget he has biased the budget and he may then appear to attain a better actual performance in any comparison with it. This is discussed further below.

(2) Some people in organisations, by the very nature of the make-up of their personality, do not wish to participate in the wider aspects of their jobs. They prefer an authoritarian style of leadership and do not strive for independence.

Participative approaches to budget-setting will be very limited in their effect in such circumstances.

(3) Participation will be less effective in organisational situations where a manager or employee feels that he has **little scope to influence** the actual results for the budgeted area of responsibility. The lower down in the organisation structure the budget holder is, the more constrained is he by factors imposed from above. For example, objectives, strategies and policies, as well as the sales forecast and budget, limit the extent that a subordinate manager in the production function has for real participation in the setting of the budget for his area of responsibility.

4.4 Budget bias

Budget bias, or budget 'slack', as it is sometimes referred to, is the common process of building room for manoeuvre when setting a budget by overstating the level of budgeted expenditure or by understating the level of budgeted sales.

The following are possible reasons for the creation of the bias in a budget, by the manager responsible for it:

- It should lead to the most favourable result when actual is compared with budget. Such a result should lead to the optimisation of personal gain for the individual manager.

- Where reward structures are based on comparisons of actual with budgeted results, bias can help to influence the outcome.

- In an uncertain business environment it is a way of relieving some of the pressures of a tight situation. The bias will allow some leeway if things do not go according to plan. An example at the factory floor level of this is where workers deliberately do not show how quickly a job can be completed when they are being closely studied by work study (time-and-motion) personnel. The standard time that results will leave the workers with room to manoeuvre in the case of non-standard or different work or where through more general dissatisfaction they do not want to work flat out.

- Some people may see the creation of bias in a budget as a way of 'legally' beating the system. Human behaviour generally in other fields tends to follow such an approach, e.g. the legal avoidance of tax is a way of getting round the (tax) system. Therefore, a manager may regard the creation of bias as a desirable personal objective and success in achieving it as motivational towards the best actual performance.

Budget bias can sometimes be in the opposite direction to that which has been described already. A manager in the marketing function may bias his budget in an optimistic way by overstating budgeted sales. This could be due to a desire to please senior management by showing an optimistic forecasted sales trend. Alternatively, a manager whose performance has been weak previously may wish to show a promising situation in order to gain approval by his superiors. The short-term approval will usually be at the risk of future disapproval if the optimistic result is not reflected in the actual results.

Finally there is the question 'Is budget bias or slack good or bad?' It depends how the budget is used.

- If the bias has the effect of motivating a manager to his best actual performance, there would appear to be a good reason for its existence.

- If budgets are used to make forecasts and consequent major decisions then, to the extent that the budgets are biased, there will be errors in the forecasts being made beyond the budget period. Erroneous decisions may then be made.

If budgets are to be made in this way the bias needs to be removed from any budgets before the forecasts are made. The effects of budget bias can be minimised by careful control, at the budget setting stage, over any changes in the budget from one year to the next which are not due to external factors.

5   Budgets as motivational targets

5.1   The right budget level

Budgets will invariably be seen as targets for managers to work towards. The question asked here is: 'at what level should budget target be set to gain optimum motivation and thus performance?'

- Empirical evidence suggests that if a budget is set such that it does not contain a suitable element of targetry (ie, difficulty), then actual performance should be a little better than the budget but it will not be optimised.

  In other words, managers do not usually work to their full potential if they know that a lower level of performance will still meet the budget (and they are evaluated on the basis of a favourable result compared with the budget).

- On the other hand, if the budget is too difficult, because it is based on idealistic levels of performance, managers become discouraged at what they regard as an unattainable standard. The effect of such demotivation is that actual performance falls short of what might reasonably have been expected.

The aim should be to agree a budget that falls between these two extremes and therefore incorporates just the right degree of difficulty which will lead to the optimal level of performance. At this level the budget should be challenging enough to motivate a manager to optimise on his performance without being too ambitious.

5.2   Expectations and aspirations budgets

The right level of difficulty is that element of targetry which is acceptable to that individual manager. This level of acceptability will differ from manager to manager, as each individual behaves and reacts in a different way in similar circumstances. This concept of budget difficulty can be demonstrated diagrammatically as follows.

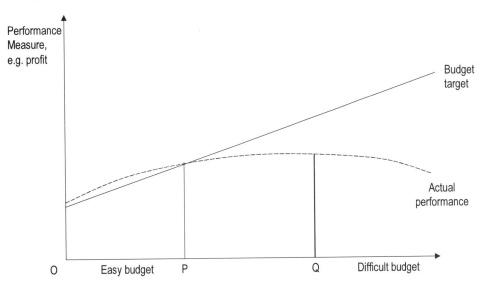

- A budget set at the point where OP represents the degree of difficulty or targetry in it is referred to as an **'expectations budget'** as budget and actual are likely to coincide. However, a relatively easy-to-achieve budget is likely to lead to a sub-optimal actual performance.

- In order to achieve a higher actual performance a more difficult budget needs to be set (an **'aspirations budget'**).

- A budget set at the point where OQ represents the degree of difficulty or targetry in it should lead to optimal performance (highest point on the 'actual' performance curve).

It should be noted that setting the budget at OQ would give rise to an adverse variance compared with budget. Senior management's interpretation of the reaction to such a variance needs to be carefully considered if the individual manager is not to react adversely in the future to not achieving the budgeted performance. It is in the overall company's best interest to optimise an individual manager's actual performance.

How the degree of difficulty, OQ, is determined is not at all easy in practice because it involves a knowledge of how each individual manager will react and behave. Attempts to quantify the degree of difficulty using work study assessments are a highly simplified approach to a very complex problem.

5.3   The need for two budgets

Attempts to use the budget as a motivating tool in the manner described may in fact lead to the need for two budgets.

(1) A summation of what all the individual managers have agreed to achieve (with the different degrees of budget difficulty incorporated into them).

(2) A budget which recognises that actual performance is likely to fall short of aspiration and is, therefore, a more realistic basis for planning purposes, e.g. placing capital expenditure contracts (budgets used for forecasting purposes).

Which of the above theories most reflects your experiences? Why? Ask other people for their views.

There is no feedback to this activity.

6   Budgets in managerial performance evaluation

In the previous section the motivating effect of budgets was considered, but it should be remembered that the budgets by themselves have a limited motivational effect. It is the reward structure that is linked to achieving the budget requirements, or lack of reward for non-achievement, which provides the real underlying motivational potential of budgets. The rewards need not be directly financial but could be in terms of future prospects of promotion.

A manager will need to regard the reward as being worthwhile if his behaviour is to be influenced so that he strives actively towards the achievement of the budget.

6.1   Budget performance reports

The choice of which particular performance measures to use is important to ensure that the individual manager sees the attainment of his targets as worthwhile for himself and at the same time in the best interests of the organisation as a whole. In practice, conflicts can and often do arise between individual managers' personal objectives and those of the organisation as a whole.

It has already been mentioned in an earlier section that it is a common practice to attempt to assess the performance of a manager by a comparison of budgeted and actual results for his area of responsibility in the organisation.

The way in which the information in budget reports is used in this way has to be considered. Different degrees of emphasis on the results of budget versus actual comparisons can lead to different attitudes and feelings among managers. There is a need to achieve the correct balance between:

- at the one extreme, an **over-emphasis** on results leading to pressure and feelings of injustice from the system

- at the other, **too little stress** on results leading to a budget irrelevancy attitude and low morale.

6.2   Hopwood's style of management evaluation

AG Hopwood reported in 1973 on his research in this area. He studied the manufacturing division of a US steelworks involving a sample of more then two hundred managers with cost centre responsibility. He identified the following three distinct styles of using budget/actual cost information in the evaluation of managerial performance:

(1) **Budget-constrained style**

   Here the primary emphasis is on the evaluation of a manager's performance in terms of meeting the budget in the short term.

(2) **Profit-conscious style**

   The performance of a manager is measured in terms of his ability to increase the overall effectiveness of his area of responsibility in the context of meeting the longer-term objectives of the organisation. At cost centre levels of responsibility the reduction of long-run average costs could be seen as achieving this. Short-term budgetary information needs to be used with care and in a flexible way to achieve this purpose.

(3) **Non-accounting style**

   A manager's evaluation is not based on budgetary information. Accounting information plays a relatively unimportant role in such a style. Other, non-accounting performance indicators are as important as the budget information.

A brief summary of the major effects that these three styles had on managers now follows.

- The budget-constrained style resulted in a great involvement in costs and cost information and a high degree of job-related pressure and tension. The latter often led to the manipulation of data for inclusion in accounting reports. Relations with both colleagues and the manager's superior were poor.

- The profit-conscious style showed good relations with colleagues and superiors. There was still a high involvement with costs but less job-related pressure. Consequently, the manipulation of accounting data was reduced.

- The non-accounting style showed very similar effects to the profit conscious style except for the much lower impact of costs and cost information on the manager. Hopwood found some evidence that better managerial performance was being achieved where a profit conscious or non-accounting style was in use. Poor performance was often associated with a budget constrained style.

6.3   Otley's research

Subsequent studies involving profit centre managers in the UK coal mining industry undertaken by DT Otley (published 1978) did not always mirror Hopwood's earlier results. One particular area of difference was that the UK study showed a closer link between the budget constrained style and good performance.

The manager evaluated on a rather tight budget constrained basis tended to meet the budget more closely than if it was evaluated in a less rigid way.

The results of these studies by Hopwood and Otley can be reconciled in terms that each took place in a different organisational environment. The US study involved highly interdependent cost centres in a highly integrated production function. The UK study involved largely independent profit centres. Any generalisations about evaluation styles must take into account the contingent variables associated with differing organisational structures.

Conclusion

This chapter has looked at the use of budgets as tools of control and motivation.

It is generally accepted that the use of **flexed** budgets in performance reports gives more meaningful results, although there are circumstances under which a **fixed** budget can be used successfully.

The potential effects of a budgetary control system on **management behaviour** must not be overlooked when planning its introduction and implementation.

The **participation** of lower management levels in the budget setting process can lead to greater commitment to meeting the targets set therein, although this may lead to **budget bias.**

The level at which the **budget targets** are set is a balance between setting it high enough to encourage better performance but not so high as to demotivate.

Finally, the use of budget information in **performance evaluation** must have regard to the reaction of management to the results.

SELF-TEST
QUESTIONS

Fixed, flexible and flexed budgets

1   Distinguish between fixed, flexible and flexed budgets. (1.1, 1.2)

2   Give three reasons why flexed budgets may be more useful than fixed budgets in performance reports. (1.3)

Behavioural aspects of budgeting

3   What are the potential behavioural problems associated with implementing budgetary control? (3.2)

Participation in budget setting

4   What is budget bias, and why might it arise? (4.4)

Budgets as motivational targets

5   Explain the meanings and uses of an expectations budget and an aspirations budget. (5.2)

Budgets in managerial performance evaluation

6   Complete the following table summarising Hopwood's findings on the effects of three different styles of management evaluation on management behaviour: (6.2)

Style	Effect on behaviour		
	Involvement in costs	Manipulation of data	Relations with colleagues
Budget constrained	*HIGH*		
Profit conscious			
Non-accounting			*GOOD*

Budget drawbacks

You are required to discuss separately each of the following statements.

(a)   Most budgeting systems are bureaucratic and reinforce organisational inertia
whereas what is required is continuous adaptation to deal with a volatile
environment.   **(7 marks)**

(b)   The typical flexible budget is virtually useless as a control device because for
convenience it is common practice for all the variable elements in the budget
to be flexed according to the same activity indicator whereas in reality the
elements vary according to different activity indicators.   **(6 marks)**

(c)   Participation by managers in setting budget levels is a laudable philosophy but
it is naive to think that participative approaches are always more effective than
authoritarian styles.   **(7 marks)**

(Total: 20 marks)

Chapter 22

ALTERNATIVE BUDGETARY SYSTEMS

So far, we have assumed a **periodic** approach to budgeting – a budget is set for a period, compared with actual results for the period, variances extracted and acted upon. Then a new budget is set for the next period, incorporating revised standards where necessary, and so on.

At the start of this chapter we challenge this approach by looking at the use of **continuous** or **rolling** budgets.

We then turn to the concepts behind setting the budget itself, and look at alternative approaches to the traditional approach of budgeting cost by function within cost centres, usually based upon the previous years' figures 'plus a bit'. **Zero based budgets, activity based budgets** and **planning, programming budgeting systems** all take a different slant on this process.

Objectives

By the time you have finished this chapter you should be able to do the following:

- describe and evaluate the main features of zero based budgeting systems
- describe the areas/organisations in which zero based budgeting may be applied
- describe and evaluate incremental budgeting and discuss the differences with zero based budgeting
- describe and evaluate periodic and continuous budgeting systems.

1　Continuous (rolling) budgets

Budgets are deemed by many organisations to be unchangeable and sacrosanct. The reasons are twofold.

(1) How **committed** would management be to the budget preparation process if they knew that senior management accepted that their budgets would need to be adjusted before the end of the budget term?

(2) The comparison of the **original** master budget with annual revenues and costs is a useful one – even if the organisation operated under very changed conditions from that originally planned. Also the use of **'revision (planning) variances'** can be used to bridge the gap and produce meaningful management performance reports.

However there are circumstances in which management may consider that the initial master budget is inadequate as a forecast of future outturn and/or as a control benchmark, and where alternative measures are required. For example, the environmental suppositions upon which strategic and budget planning are based may prove to be very unlike those conditions encountered during the budget term.

1.1　How should budgets be changed?

If change in the budget is required the options available to management are as follows.

- to **continue** with the original budget, making allowances as necessary
- to **adapt** the original budget to reflect the changed circumstances
- to adopt a **'rolling budget'** or forecast revision approach

- to **re-budget** from scratch.

The decision will depend partly upon the degree of error from the budgeted assumptions, and partly upon the ways management use the budget, e.g. as authority to spend, or as a limit on spending.

(1) If environmental states are not considerably different from those budgeted for, it may be pragmatic to retain the original budget and expect middle and junior managers to adapt to the changed situation within the structure of the original budget. This policy would maintain the integrity of the budgeting procedures and most likely be a practical and economic approach.

(2) If the different states evolved around only one or two assumptions (such as interest rates and a certain material input inflation), it might be wise and feasible to adapt the master budget to the new situation, particularly if the budgetary data are held in a sophisticated computer financial model. As the revised budget would be based on the original budget it is more likely to be accepted by managers who would appreciate the need to reflect new conditions.

(3) Rolling (continuous) budgets (and forecast revisions) are more likely to be practised as a matter of routine managerial philosophy, rather than as a response to a particular or unexpected situation.

(4) The bigger the divergence of actual conditions from those budgeted the more logical would be the decision to recognise the inadequacy of the original budget and the need to re-budget. Failure to do so might cause managers to waste limited resources or to use them inappropriately.

1.2 The effects of changing the budget

The many consequences of changing the annual budget can be reduced to a few major considerations:

- a weakening of the importance placed on the budget system

- increased time spent by managers on budget preparation

- the problem of gaining budget acceptance

- the lack of clear financial objectives

- the lack of meaningful management performance measures.

1.3 Rolling budgets

A **rolling budget** is 'a budget continuously updated by adding a further period, say a month or quarter and deducting the earliest period. Beneficial where future costs and/or activities cannot be forecast reliably'.

A typical rolling budget might be prepared as follows:

(1) A budget is prepared for the coming year (say January – December) broken down into suitable, say quarterly, control periods.

(2) At the end of the first control period (31 March) a comparison is made of that period's results against the budget. The conclusions drawn from this analysis are used to update the budgets for the remaining control periods and to add a budget for a further three months, so that the company once again has budgets available for the coming year (this time April – March).

(3) The planning process is repeated at the end of each three-month control period.

It is worth noting that the relatively recent development of sophisticated computer budgeting models has increased the use of rolling budgets and similar concepts in organisations. Often figures are now revised by computers with minimal intervention by managers.

1.4   Advantages of rolling budgets

- Budgets are more realistic and achievable since they are continuously revised to reflect changing circumstances.

- The annual disruption associated with the preparation of an annual budget is removed.

- The pressures (and stress) placed on managers to achieve unrealistic budget targets are eased.

- Variance feedback is more meaningful.

- It tends to reduce budgetary bias.

- It reduces the rigidity of the budget system and builds contingency and innovation into the preparation/feedback stages of the control system.

- The assessment of objectives and plans is continuous rather than being a one-off exercise.

- Without some form of budget revision, operational management may continue to invest and recruit, etc with the belief that management strategy holds firm.

- It might help to increase management commitment to the budget.

- The arbitrary and artificial distinction drawn between one financial year and the next is removed, since budgets always extend for a year ahead.

1.5   Disadvantages of rolling budgets

However the problems likely to be encountered with rolling budgets include the following.

- If it is difficult to plan ahead accurately (and it always is!) when once a year managers spend a lot of time and effort on the task, how likely is it that managers can do the same forecasts more accurately every month or quarter when they are involved in other responsibilities?

- There is a danger that the rolling budget will become the last budget 'plus or minus a bit' and will be representative of absolutely nothing in terms of corporate objectives and meaningless for performance control purposes.

- Managers will be faced with a greater work load and additional staff may be required.

- Managers may devote insufficient attention to preparing budgets which they know will shortly be revised.

- The organisation might be required to operate annual budgets (such as enterprises operating in the public sector).

2   Zero-based budgeting (ZBB)

2.1   Incremental budgeting

KEY POINT

Incremental budgeting can lead to perpetuation of past inefficiencies.

A common starting point for the preparation of the next annual budget is the current year's budget – incorporating current levels of operating activity and current budgeted allowances for current activities.

These are then adjusted for expected changes in the next year – incremental budgeting.

The main disadvantage of such an approach is that it implicitly assumes that all current activities are worth continuing, at the current levels. Past inefficiencies can thus be perpetuated.

DEFINITION

ZBB is a method of budgeting whereby all activities are re-evaluated each time a budget is prepared. Discrete levels of each activity are valued and a combination chosen to match funds available.

2.2 The principles of ZBB

ZBB is a method of budgeting whereby all activities are re-evaluated each time a budget is prepared. Discrete levels of each activity are valued and a combination chosen to match funds available.

ZBB makes no initial assumptions – each year's budgets are compiled by assessing each potential activity from scratch (zero base). The following types of questions are asked to evaluate, on a cost-benefit basis, each activity:

- Should the activity or function be performed at all?
- At what level should it be performed?
- Is it being performed in the optimum manner?
- How much will it cost?

KEY POINT

ZBB is most commonly applied to service activities and departments.

In this way, ZBB should identify any budgeting slack and eliminate it, in contrast to the incremental approach where it is likely to continue.

However, it is more costly to operate, and, if not used with care, can result in the cessation of activities that are beneficial in the long term.

It is most commonly applied to service activities and departments.

DEFINITION

A **decision package** is a document that identifies and describes a specific activity in such a manner that senior management can:

- evaluate it and rank it against other activities competing for limited resources
- decide whether to approve or disapprove it.

2.3 ZBB technique

(1) The first requirement in a ZBB process is the development of a **decision package**.

A **decision package** is a document that identifies and describes a specific activity in such a manner that senior management can:

- evaluate it and rank it against other activities competing for limited resources
- decide whether to approve or disapprove it.

Decision packages are developed by managers for their particular areas of responsibility and will contain information such as:

- the function of the department
- a performance measure for the department
- costs and benefits of operating a department at a range of different levels of funding
- consequences of not operating at those levels.

(2) The second requirement is the actual evaluation and ranking of the decision packages, using cost/benefit analysis.

(3) The result is a list of ranked projects or activities which senior management can use to evaluate needs and priorities in making budget approvals. The resources available to the organisation for the forthcoming budget period are thus allocated accordingly.

ACTIVITY 1

It is not easy to produce a decision package – try and prepare one for a function within your organisation.

There is no feedback to this activity

2.4 Review cycles

This in practice may be a formidable task, particularly with the interrelationships that exist within an organisation, and probably no organisation can afford to take the time to examine every activity in the necessary depth every year.

A review cycle covering each activity once every three or four years may be more practical.

2.5   Applications of ZBB

(1) ZBB is said to be particularly useful in local government. It may be easier to apply in that situation because it is possible to segregate and assess the benefits of each activity (e.g. refuse collection, schools, road maintenance) and the complicated links often found in industry are minimal.

(2) In the private sector its most productive use would seem to be in the area of non-manufacturing costs. In this area efficiency standards are difficult to develop and costs often tend to mushroom.

KEY POINT

Management need to be confident that the benefits to be derived from the adoption of a ZBB philosophy will outweigh the costs of its implementation.

2.6   Benefits of ZBB

Despite considerable practical problems associated with applying ZBB throughout the organisation, some important benefits are envisaged in its rationale:

- It helps to create an organisational environment where change is accepted.
- It helps management to focus on company objectives and goals.
- It concentrates the attention of management on the future rather than on the past.
- It helps to identify inefficient and obsolete operations within the organisation.
- It provides a framework to ensure the optimum utilisation of resources by establishing priorities in relation to operational activity.
- It can assist motivation of management at all levels.
- It provides a plan to follow when more financial resources become available.
- It establishes minimum requirements from departments.

It also has some disadvantages:

- It takes more management time than conventional systems, in part because managers need to learn what is required of them.
- There is a temptation to concentrate on short-term cost savings at the expense of longer-term benefits.
- It takes time to show the real benefits of implementing such a system.

2.7   Example

ZBB Ltd has two service departments – material handling and maintenance, which are in competition for budget funds which must not exceed £925,000 in the coming year. A zero base budgeting approach will be used whereby each department is to be treated as a decision package and will submit a number of levels of operation showing the minimum level at which its service could be offered and two additional levels which would improve the quality of the service from the minimum level.

The following data have been prepared for each department showing the three possible operating levels.

Materials handling department

Level 1. A squad of 30 labourers would work 40 hours per week for 48 weeks of the year. Each labourer would be paid a basic rate of £4 per hour for a 35 hour week. Overtime hours would attract a premium of 50% on the basic rate per hour. In addition, the company anticipates payments of 20% of gross wages in respect of employee benefits. Directly attributable variable overheads would be incurred at the rate of 12p per man hour. The squad would move 600,000 kilos per week to a warehouse at the end of the production process.

Level 2. In addition to the level 1 operation, the company would lease 10 fork lift trucks at a cost of £2,000 per truck per annum. This would provide a better service by

enabling the same volume of output as for level 1 to be moved to a customer collection point which would be 400 metres closer to the main factory gate. Each truck would be manned by a driver working a 48 week year. Each driver would receive a fixed weekly wage of £155.

Directly attributable overheads of £150 per truck per week would be incurred.

Level 3. A computer could be leased to plan the work of the squad of labourers in order to reduce their total work hours. The main benefit would be improvement in safety through reduction in the time that work-in-progress would lie unattended. The computer leasing costs would be £20,000 for the first quarter (3 months), reducing by 10% per quarter cumulatively thereafter.

The computer data would result in a 10% reduction in labourer hours, half of this reduction being a saving in overtime hours.

Maintenance department

Level 1. Two engineers would each be paid a salary of £18,000 per annum and would arrange for repairs to be carried out by outside contractors at an annual cost of £250,000.

Level 2. The company would employ a squad of 10 fitters who would carry out breakdown repairs and routine maintenance as required by the engineers. The fitters would each be paid a salary of £11,000 per annum.

Maintenance materials would cost £48,000 per annum and would be used at a constant rate throughout the year. The purchases could be made in batches of £4,000, £8,000, £12,000 or £16,000. Ordering costs would be £100 per order irrespective of order size and stock holding costs would be 15% per annum. The minimum cost order size would be implemented.

Overheads directly related to the maintenance operation would be a fixed amount of £50,000 per annum.

In addition to the maintenance squad it is estimated that £160,000 of outside contractor work would still have to be paid for.

Level 3. The company could increase its maintenance squad to 16 fitters which would enable the service to be extended to include a series of major overhauls of machinery. The additional fitters would be paid at the same salary as the existing squad members.

Maintenance materials would now cost £96,000 per annum and would be used at a constant rate throughout the year. Purchases could be made in batches of £8,000, £12,000 or £16,000. Ordering costs would be £100 per order (irrespective of order size) and stock holding costs would now be 13.33% per annum. In addition, suppliers would now offer discounts of 2% of purchase price for orders of £16,000. The minimum cost order size would be implemented.

Overheads directly related to the maintenance operation would increase by £20,000 from the level 2 figure.

It is estimated that £90,000 of outside contractor work would still have to be paid for.

Required:

(a) Determine the incremental cost for each of levels 1, 2 and 3 in each department.

(b) In order to choose which of the incremental levels of operation should be allocated the limited budgeted funds available, management have estimated a 'desirability factor' which should be applied to each increment. The ranking of the increments is then based on the 'incremental cost × desirability factor' score, whereby a high score is deemed more desirable than a low score. The desirability factors are estimated as follows.

	Material handling	*Maintenance*
Level 1	1.00	1.00
Level 2 (incremental)	0.60	0.80
Level 3 (incremental)	0.50	0.20

Use the above ranking process to calculate which of the levels of operation should be implemented in order that the budget of £925,000 is not exceeded.

Solution

(a) Materials handling department

Level 1

		£	£
Wages cost:	30 × 40 hours × 48 weeks × £4		230,400
	30 × 5 hours × 48 weeks × £2		14,400
			244,800
Employee benefits	20% × £244,800		48,960
Variable overhead	30 × 40 hours × 48 weeks × 12p		6,912
Incremental cost			300,672

Level 2

		£
Leasing:	10 trucks @ £2,000	20,000
Drivers' wages	10 drivers × 48 weeks × £155	74,400
Overhead	10 trucks × 48 weeks × £150	72,000
Incremental cost		166,400

Level 3

		£	£
Leasing:	(£20,000 + £18,000 + £16,200 + £14,580)		68,780
Savings.			
(30 men × 40 hours × 48 weeks × 10% = 5,760 hours)			
Wages cost:	5,760 hours × £4	23,040	
	2,880 hours × £2	5,760	
		28,800	
Employee benefits	20% × 28,800	5,760	
Variable overhead	5,760 hours × 12p	691	
			(35,251)
Incremental cost			33,529

Maintenance department

Level 1

		£
Engineers' salaries	2 × £18,000	36,000
Outside contractors		250,000
Incremental cost		286,000

Level 2

		£
Engineers' salaries	2 × £18,000	36,000
Fitters' salaries	10 × £11,000	110,000
Materials		48,000
Ordering costs (W1)		600
Stockholding costs (W1)		600

FOULKS LYNCH
PUBLICATIONS

Overheads	50,000
Outside contractors	160,000
	405,200
Less level one costs	(286,000)
Incremental cost	119,200

Level 3

		£
Engineers' salaries	2 × £18,000	36,000
Fitters' salaries	16 × £11,000	176,000
Materials		96,000
Ordering costs (W2)		600
Stockholding costs (W2)		1,045
Discount		(1,920)
Overheads		70,000
Outside contractors		90,000
		467,725
Less level two costs		(405,200)
Incremental cost		62,525

(b) Factor scores

		Material handling		Maintenance
Level 1:	(£300,672 × 1.00)	300,672	(£286,000 × 1.00)	286,000
Level 2:	(£166,400 × 0.60)	99,840	(£119,200 × 0.80)	95,360
Level 3:	(£33,529 × 0.50)	16,765	(£62,525 × 0.20)	12,505

The budget will be spent as follows.

		£
Material handling	Level 3	
	(£300,672 + £166,400 + £33,529)	500,601
Maintenance	Level 2	
	(£286,000 + £119,200)	405,200
		905,801

Workings

(W1)

Order size	No. of orders	Average stock	Ordering cost	Holding cost	Total cost
£4,000	12	£2,000	£1,200	£300	£1,500
£8,000	6	£4,000	£600	£600	£1,200
£12,000	4	£6,000	£400	£900	£1,300
£16,000	3	£8,000	£300	£1,200	£1,500

(W2)

Order size	No. of orders	Average stock	Ordering cost	Holding cost	Total cost
£8,000	12	£4,000	£1,200	£533.20	£1,733.20
£12,000	8	£6,000	£800	£799.80	£1,599.80
£16,000	6	£8,000	£600	£1,066.40	£1,666.40

The discount of 2% is worth (2% × £96,000) = £1,920 per annum. Therefore as net cost if orders are placed for £16,000 each time is negative, orders will be placed at this level.

As stock is thereby reduced by 2% the stock-holding cost is also reduced by 2% to £1,045.07.

2.8 Conclusions on ZBB

Costs v benefits

Theoretically ZBB is a very sound tool of management, and the likely success of such a system depends very largely on commitment to it in terms of management time and effort. This type of analytical approach to budgeting can be very costly in terms of time and money, and there should be some attempt to measure the benefits that could be obtained.

Budgeting cycle duration

Under a traditional approach to budgeting, which accepts current levels of expenditure, budgeting is very often a time-consuming activity. Some large organisations in the UK begin the budgetary planning stage for the next year very early in the current year – and that is with a traditional approach. The adoption of a system of ZBB would undoubtedly lengthen the cycle considerably.

A piecemeal approach

Few, if any, large organisations in this country have adopted ZBB for all their parts for every year, and it is doubtful whether this would ever be completely feasible. However, a selective approach as to which parts of the organisation are to be subjected to a ZBB procedure in any one year may be a practical compromise, even if by doing this some of the advantages may be clearly curtailed.

The following summary is taken from Horngren:

Some generalisations concerning ZBB experiences

While it is difficult to conclude on the appropriateness and effectiveness of this technique in different organisational settings, the following comparative outline represents an attempt to integrate some of these experiences.

	Private sector	*Public sector*
(1) Extent of use	The use of ZBB has spread rapidly in both sectors since the early 1970s. Furthermore, there is no indication that there is a levelling off of interest in ZBB or its use.	
(2) Where and how it is primarily being used.	As a management tool in planning for and controlling the staff and support functions. A ZBB review is normally conducted for a relatively small portion of a corporation's total budget.	As the main system of budget justification (and, in most cases, presentation) for all functions within an organisation.
(3) Perceived effectiveness of ZBB as a tool in reducing costs/ personnel and shifting resource allocations.	There have been some examples of cost/personnel savings and shifts in resource allocation resulting from the use of ZBB, but these have not been widespread.	To date there have been no substantive examples of savings or shifts in resource allocation which resulted from the use of ZBB.

FOULKS LYNCH
PUBLICATIONS

| (4) Most frequently mentioned benefit and problem associated with the use of ZBB | Benefit – Increased participation of managers in the budget preparation process.

Problem – Time and effort required to develop, implement and operate the system. |
| (5) Incidence of post audits of ZBB | Many user organisations in both sectors have conducted a review of the process at various stages in its implementation and use. However, these reviews tend to be informal, providing limited insight into the 'real' cost effectiveness of the process. |

The extent to which these observations are valid is still open to debate and the test of time. Owing to the 'newness' of the technique the above comments are based on the short-run experiences of users.'

3　Activity based budgeting (ABB)

DEFINITION

ABB is a method of budgeting based on an activity framework and utilising cost driver data in the budget-setting and variance feedback processes.

Activity based budgeting extends the use of activity-based costing (ABC) from individual product costing, for pricing and output decisions, to the overall planning and control system of the business.

The basic approach of ABB is as follows:

(1) The work of each department for which a budget is to be prepared is analysed by its major activities, for which cost drivers may be identified.

(2) The budgeted cost of resources used by each activity is determined (from recent historical data) and, where appropriate, cost per unit of activity is calculated.

(3) Future costs can then be budgeted by deciding on future activity levels and working back to the required resource input.

3.1　ABB activity matrix example

The following 'activity matrix' shows the resources used (rows) and major functions/activities (columns) of the stores department of a manufacturing business.

The total current annual costs of each resource consumed by the department are shown in the final column. They have then been spread back over the various activities to establish the cost pools. The allocation of resource costs between activities will, to some extent, be subjective.

• Each of the first four activities has an identifiable cost driver, and the total resource cost driver rates can be determined (cost per unit of activity).

• The last two activities that occur within the department are non-volume related, and are sometimes referred to as "sustaining costs". They are necessary functions and should not be ignored in the budgeting process. However, they should not be attributed to particular cost drivers, as this would not reflect their true cost behaviour and would result in inappropriate budgets being set.

Activity cost matrix for stores department

Activity:	Goods inwards	Goods out	Stock orders	Monthly stock counting	Records maintenance	Supervision	Total
Cost driver:	Deliveries	Stores requisitions	Orders	Counts	-	-	
Resource	£'000	£'000	£'000	£'000	£'000	£'000	£'000
Management salary	-	-	-	1.5	3.5	25	30
Storekeepers' wages	50	30	10	4	20	-	114
Overtime	15	-	-	5	5	-	25
Stationery, etc	1	2	2	1	3	-	9
Other	6	4	2	1	2	4	19
Total	72	36	14	12.5	33.5	29	197
Volume of activity	450	375	100	12	-	-	
Cost per activity unit	£160	£96	£140	£1,042	£33,500	£29,000	

The budget for the stores department for next year will be set by deciding upon the expected number of deliveries, stores requisitions, orders, etc and costing these up accordingly. Sustaining costs will effectively be treated as fixed costs.

3.2 Advantages of ABB

- The costs of activities are identified. Each delivery of goods costs £160 to process. This should be taken into account when determining optimum order sizes, etc. Is it necessary to have monthly stock counts at a cost of £1,042 each? To what extent can the stock records be relied upon if counts are reduced?

- It takes into account the impact of activity levels on resource costs, of assistance in cost reduction programmes and in setting realistic cost targets.

- Activity unit costs allow easier analysis of cost trends over time and intra-departmental comparisons.

- Resource allocation decisions are assisted by the activity related cost information arising from an ABB system.

- ABB links directly to a total quality management (TQM) programme by relating the cost of an activity to the level of service provided (e.g. stores requisitions processed) – do the user departments feel they are getting a cost-effective service?

4   Planning, programming budgeting systems (PPBS)

PPBS were developed specifically to serve the budgeting requirements of **non-profit making organisations,** such as government departments.

Traditionally, budgets for such organisations will be drawn up on a departmental basis – each departmental manager submitting their budget for staff, premises, establishment and other costs.

One of the main criticisms of such an approach in these types of organisation is their lack of information on the activities actually being performed by the departments – the costs are analysed by nature rather than purpose.

The objectives of these organisations will not be focused upon levels of output and profitability, but on the cost-effective performance of a given programme of activities. It is the aim of PPBS to ensure that the budgeting process is structured accordingly.

KEY POINT

Resource allocation decisions are assisted by the activity related cost information arising from an ABB system.

KEY POINT

Under PPBS budgets are structured according to a **programme of activities** rather than departmentally.

FOULKS LYNCH PUBLICATIONS

4.1　The technique of PPBS

(1) Under a PPBS budgets are constructed on the basis of **programmes** that are set in order to achieve the organisational objectives.

(2) Each programme is then evaluated to identify the most cost-effective means of carrying it out, and, by a cost-benefit approach, to determine its level of priority in the allocation of resources.

(3) Resources are thus allocated to programmes rather than to individual departments

Programmes will often involve several departments. Each department's 'budget' will therefore be made up of its share of the allocated resource for each programme in which it is involved. However, the structure of the budget will in fact be by programme, rather than department.

Thus programmes will cut across departmental barriers and once this philosophy has been accepted it will allow the scarce resources of an organisation, which may well be located in a single department, to be put to the best use. Identifying such scarce resources allows for the expansion of that critical department, possibly at the expense of departments now seen to be overstaffed. The approach also focuses people's minds on the long-term commitments of an organisation that those programmes represent.

Examples

Two organisations that have dabbled with PPBS are the American Forestry Service and the US Department of Defence.

A 'programme' that the former might wish to implement would be to increase access the Forestry Service property over a two year period. This would involve effort from:

- the publicity department to heighten awareness
- the Forestry Service's roads department to make areas more accessible
- maintenance departments to equip picnic areas
- building departments to provide kiosks or larger refreshment facilities.

The service would produce a budget for its 'Increased Access' programme which would include the costs incurred on the programme by all these departments. The person responsible for 'driving' that programme would compare actual costs with his budget in the conventional way – this would require a more detailed costing system than would formerly have been used.

4.2　Conclusions on PPBS

PPBS were first used in the USA in the 1960's and initially were seen to be effective. Their advantages were seen as:

- providing management information that related more directly to the work of an organisation
- allowing scarce resources to be identified, put to best use, and eliminated as a budgeting constraint
- allowing programmes to be assessed in terms of their efficiency and effectiveness
- highlighting long-term commitments of an organisation.

However after its initial apparent success it was felt that PPBS had contributed to the subsequent poor performance in the Department of Defence. The department, like the Forestry Service, modified the process adopting hybrid approaches to budgeting. Whether PPBS could be said to be entirely to blame is doubtful. Some of the cause of criticism in these government agencies must be attributed to the difficulties of reconciling the different priorities of different political parties and special interest groups.

Conclusion

This chapter has challenged some of the traditional aspects of budgeting.

You should recognise that many organisations use a combination of traditional and alternative approaches when setting their budgets.

SELF-TEST QUESTIONS

Continuous (rolling) budgets

1   How are rolling budgets prepared? (1.3)

2   Give three advantages and three disadvantages of a rolling budget approach. (1.4, 1.5)

Zero-based budgeting (ZBB)

3   What steps are taken in carrying out a ZBB exercise? (2.3)

Activity based budgeting (ABB)

4   Explain the principles of ABB. (3)

Planning, programming budgeting systems (PPBS)

5   What are the main benefits to be derived from a PPBS approach? (4.2)

EXAM-TYPE QUESTION

A manufacturing company

A manufacturing company intends to introduce zero base budgeting in respect of its service departments.

Required:

(a)   Explain how zero base budgeting differs from incremental budgeting and explain the role of committed, engineered and discretionary costs in the operation of zero based budgeting.   **(8 marks)**

(b)   Give specific examples of committed, engineered and discretionary costs for each of the following service departments:

(i)   Safety.

(ii)   Maintenance.

(iii)   Accounting.   **(9 marks)**

(c)   Prepare a brief summary which explains ways in which profitability may improve by increasing the proportion of funds allocated to each of the service departments named in (b) above.   **(8 marks)**

(Total: 25 marks)

For the answer to this question, see the 'Answers' section at the end of the book.

Chapter 23

QUANTITATIVE AIDS TO BUDGETING

Budgeting requires the prediction, or forecasting, of future revenues and costs. In this chapter we consider some of the techniques used in forecasting for budgeting purposes. The techniques discussed should be familiar to you but you need to consider their use in budget preparation.

The two main areas of consideration are the **prediction of costs**, mainly based upon the assumption of a linear relationship between costs and activity level, and **time series analysis**, most commonly used for forecasting sales.

Objectives

By the time you have finished this chapter you should be able to do the following:

- describe and apply the techniques of:

  - least squares regression

  - scatter diagrams and correlation

  - forecasting with least squares regression

  - time series to identify trends and seasonality

  - forecasting with time series.

- evaluate the results of quantitative aids.

1   Forecasting

Budgeting for future profit or cashflows requires us to forecast future costs and revenues, at varying levels of activity. How do we use past experience to make forecasts?

A system of forecasting must be designed, with the following components:

(1) **Data**. Any forecast will take into consideration results which have been obtained in the past. No situation is static and the most up-to-date results are the most relevant to the forecasting model.

(2) **Models**. The forecaster must try to make a model which will fit the situation under review. He will need to plot graphs of past results to look for patterns, trends, seasonal fluctuations and other cycles which might appear from past results, which must be reflected in the model.

(3) **Future conditions**. The projections of the model must then be evaluated in the light of any outside factors or changed conditions.

(4) **Errors**. Any forecast is, at best, a close approximation of an actual result, and the forecaster will want to make allowances for errors. Statistical theory can be applied to errors in forecasting by assuming that errors came from a normal distribution with a mean of zero. This enables the forecaster to calculate the tolerances on the forecast.

1.1   The uses of forecasts

- **Budgeting**

  Without being able to forecast revenues and costs, firms would be unable to implement any budgetary control system. All budgets are based on forecasted figures, even if these figures are based on intuition. Obviously, the more accurate the forecasts, the more accurate and useful will be the budgets and hence the control on costs.

- **Setting of standards**

  If an organisation uses standard costing as a control method, it needs to set the standards as accurately as possible taking into account the management philosophy of standard setting, i.e. low but obtainable, or high as an incentive. Such costs and selling prices included in the standard will all be forecast figures.

1.2   Decision-making

A common approach to decision-making is 'what if?' analysis. To evaluate the various future operating policies open to management, models will be used to predict the outcomes in terms of revenues, costs, cash flows and profits. Computers are likely to be used to assist in this exercise.

1.3   The techniques of forecasting

In this chapter we shall be looking at two main areas of forecasting:

Cost prediction

Using historical data on costs at various activity levels to arrive at a straight line relationship between them, which is then extrapolated to forecast costs for future activity levels.

Time series analysis

Again using historical data to predict future values, but with time (rather than activity level) being the underlying independent variable. The data will generally exhibit variations about a central trend, which may or may not be linear.

In the context of budgeting, time series analysis will be most commonly used for sales forecasting.

Again much of this material is developed from your earlier studies and so a brief resume of the main points is given here.

2   Cost prediction

There are five main methods that can be used to predict future figures from the analysis of past data:

- the engineering approach
- the account analysis approach
- scatter diagrams
- the high low method
- regression analysis.

2.1   The engineering approach

This approach is based on building up a complete specification of all inputs (e.g. materials, labour, overheads) required to produce given levels of output; these are then costed out at expected input prices. This approach is therefore based on the technical specification, which is then costed out using expected input prices.

This approach works reasonably well in a single product or start-up situation – indeed in the latter it may be the only feasible approach. However, it is difficult to apply in a multi-product situation, especially where there are joint costs, or the exact output mix is not known.

2.2   The account analysis approach

Rather than using the technical information, this approach uses the information contained in the ledger accounts. These are analysed and categorised as either fixed or variable (or semi-fixed or semi-variable). Thus, for example, materials purchase accounts would represent variable costs, office salaries a fixed cost. Since the ledger accounts are not designed for use in this way, some reorganisation and reclassification of accounts may be required.

You should note that this is the approach implicit in many examination questions.

The problems with this approach are several.

- Inspection does not always indicate the true nature of costs. For example, today factory wages would normally be a fixed cost, with only overtime and/or bonuses as the variable element.

- Accounts are by their nature summaries, and often contain transactions of different categories.

- It rests on historical information with the problems noted above.

3   Scatter diagrams

You should recall that information about two variables that are considered to be related in some way can be plotted on a scatter diagram.

3.1   Independent/dependent variables

The independent variable is marked along the horizontal (x) axis and the dependent variable along the vertical (y) axis.

You are advised to think in terms of the x-axis being the cause, and the y-axis the effect.

3.2   Correlation

One advantage of a scatter diagram is that it is possible to see quite easily if the points indicate that a relationship exists between the variables, i.e. to see if any **correlation** exists between them.

Scatter graphs of non-linear correlation can assume many different types of curve.

- If the points lie exactly on a straight line, then the correlation is said to be **perfect linear correlation**. In practice this rarely occurs and it is more usual for the points to be scattered in a band, the narrower the band the higher the degree of correlation.

- **Positive correlation** exists where the values of the variables increase together.

- **Negative correlation** exists where one variable increases as the other decreases in value.

KEY POINT

The engineering approach is based on the technical specification for the output which is then costed out using expected input prices.

KEY POINT

The account analysis approach uses analysed historical ledger accounts.
Information as a basis for predicting future costs.

KEY POINT

Information about two variables that are considered to be related in some way can be plotted on a **scatter diagram**.

KEY POINT

You are advised to think in terms of the **x-axis** being the **cause**, and the **y-axis** the **effect**.

FOULKS LYNCH
PUBLICATIONS

3.3   Line of best fit

To obtain a description of the relationship between two variables in the form of an equation in order to forecast values, it is necessary to fit a straight line through the points on the scatter diagram which best represents all of the plotted points.

The equation for any straight line is of the form:

$$y \quad = \quad a + bx$$

where x and y are the variables and a and b are constants for the particular line in question.

> a is called the **intercept** on the y-axis and measures the point at which the line will cut the y-axis.
>
> b is called the **gradient** of the line and measures its degree of slope.
>
> a and b can take any value, including zero, and may be positive or negative.

If we are trying to predict total cost from past data of costs and activity levels then in the general equation y = a + bx:

> y is total cost
>
> a is fixed costs
>
> b is variable cost per unit
>
> x is the activity level, i.e. quantity produced.

E.g. the line for total cost where fixed costs = £1,000 per month and variable costs = £20 per unit would thus be represented as:

> y = £1,000 + £20x

How do we predict the values of a and b that 'best fit' the historical data?

Methods include the following:

- **Fitting a line 'by eye'** which appears to suit all the points plotted. This method has the disadvantage that if there is a large amount of scatter no two people's lines will coincide and it is, therefore, only suitable where the amount of scatter is small, or where the degree of accuracy of the prediction is not critical.

- The **high low** approach (discussed below).

- **Least squares regression**, the most mathematically correct method (discussed later in this chapter).

4   High low (or range) method

This and the next method that follows are based on an analysis of historical information of costs at different activity levels. What we need to do is to separately identify the fixed and variable cost elements so that each can be predicted for anticipated future activity levels.

The variable cost is estimated by calculating the average unit cost between the highest and lowest volumes and the fixed and total cost function can then be derived.

For example, if the costs of producing the highest and lowest levels of production (10 units and 12 units) are £30 and £35 respectively then the variable costs per unit are £5/2 units or £2.50. The fixed costs are thus £5 and the total cost = £5 + £2.50x where x = production level.

4.1   Example

	Production (units)	Total cost (£)
High	120	3,500
Low	100	3,000
Change	20	500

$$\text{Variable cost} \quad = \quad \frac{£500}{20} = £25 \text{ per unit}$$

$$\text{Fixed cost} \quad = \quad £3,000 - 100 \times £25 = £500$$

$$\text{Total cost} \quad = \quad £500 + £25 \times \text{units}$$

4.2   Limitations

The limitations of the high low method are as follows:

- Its reliance on historical data, assuming that (i) activity is the only factor affecting costs and (ii) historical costs reliably predict future costs.

- The use of only two values, the highest and the lowest, means that the results may be distorted because of random variations in these values.

5   Regression analysis

You should be familiar with regression analysis from your earlier studies. However, it is an area which students find difficult and as such it is repeated here. Least squares regression, like the high low method, is used to predict a linear relationship between two variables. Unlike the high low method it uses all past data to calculate the line of best fit.

5.1   Why 'least squares'?

The criterion for determining 'best fit' is that of minimising the sum of the squared vertical distances from each point to the line. Squaring these deviations overcomes problems that might arise because some deviations would be positive and some negative, depending on whether the point was above or below the line. It is not necessary to go into the theory of this method any more deeply at this level. The following diagram illustrates the basic idea.

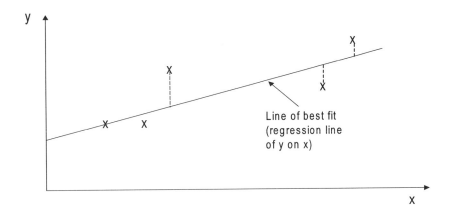

Line of best fit (regression line of y on x)

FINANCIAL MANAGEMENT AND CONTROL

5.2 Computing the regression line of y on x

Assuming that the equation of the regression line of y on x is:

$$y = a + bx,$$

as it will be if we are trying to predict cost (y) from activity level (x), it is necessary to calculate the values of a and b so that the equation can be completely determined.

The following formulae are used; a knowledge of their derivation is not necessary. They do not need to be memorised since they are supplied in the exams.

$$a = \bar{y} - b\bar{x} = \frac{\Sigma y}{n} - \frac{b\Sigma x}{n}$$

$$b = \frac{n\Sigma xy - \Sigma x \Sigma y}{n\Sigma x^2 - (\Sigma x)^2}$$

n is the number of pairs of x, y values, i.e. the number of points on the scatter graph.

The value of b must be calculated first as it is needed to calculate a.

Example

The following table shows the number of units of a good produced and the total costs incurred.

Units produced	Total costs
100	40,000
200	45,000
300	50,000
400	65,000
500	70,000
600	70,000
700	80,000

Calculate the regression line for y on x.

Solution

Notes on the calculation

- A scatter diagram is always a useful aid in answering questions on correlation and regression. Even if it is not specifically requested, a sketch diagram can be included as part of a solution.

- The calculation can be reduced to a series of steps.

Step 1 Tabulate the data and determine which is the dependent variable, y, and which the independent, x.

Step 2 Calculate Σx, Σy, Σx^2, Σxy (leave room for a column for Σy^2 which may well be needed subsequently).

Step 3 Substitute in the formulae in order to find b and a in that order.

Step 4 Substitute a and b in the regression equation.

The calculation is set out as follows, where x is the activity level in units of hundreds and y is the cost in units of £1,000.

x	y	xy	x^2
1	40	40	1
2	45	90	4
3	50	150	9
4	65	260	16
5	70	350	25

6	70	420	36
7	80	560	49
28	420	1,870	140	$n = 7$

$$b = \frac{n\Sigma xy - \Sigma x \Sigma y}{n\Sigma x^2 - (\Sigma x)^2}$$

(Try to avoid rounding at this stage since, although n Σxy and $\Sigma x \Sigma y$ are large, their difference is much smaller.)

$$= \frac{(7\times1,870)-(28\times420)}{(7\times140)-(28\times28)}$$

$$= \frac{13,090-11,760}{980-784}$$

$$= \frac{1,330}{196}$$

$$= 6.79$$

$$a = \frac{\Sigma y}{n} - \frac{b\Sigma x}{n}$$

$$= \frac{420}{7} - (6.79\times\frac{28}{7})$$

$$= 60 - 27.16$$

$$= 32.84$$

∴ the regression line for y on x is:

y =   32.84 + 6.79x   (x in hundreds of units produced, y in £1,000's).

(Always specify what x and y are very carefully.)

This line would be used to estimate the total costs for a given level of output. If, say, 250 units were made we can predict the expected yield by using the regression line where $x = 2.5$.

y =   32.84 + 6.79 × 2.5

=   32.84 + 16.975

=   49.815

i.e. we predict total costs of £49,815 for production of 250 units.

5.3   Using the regression line for forecasting

In the previous example, having found the equation of the line of best fit, we used this to forecast the total cost for a given level of activity.

The validity of such forecasts will be dependent upon two main factors.

- Whether there is sufficient **correlation** between the variables to support a linear relationship within the range of the data used.
- Whether the forecast represents an **interpolation** or an **extrapolation**.

5.4   Correlation

Through regression analysis it is possible to derive a linear relationship between two variables and hence estimate unknown values. However, this does not measure the degree of correlation between the variables, i.e. how strong the connection is between the two variables. It is possible to find a line of best fit through any assortment of data points. This doesn't mean that we are justified in using the equation of that line for prediction.

Thus the logical approach to take should be as follows:

Step 1

Is there a causal relationship between two variables? (Correlation)

If yes

Step 2

Deduce the coefficient 'a' and 'b' in order to establish a line of best fit in the form

   y = a + bx. (Regression)

↓

Step 3

Use the equation to forecast the value of an unknown variable given that the value of the other variable can be ascertained for the period for which the forecast is to be made.

Example

If there is a correlation between the demand for sun roofs in a given year and the sales of new cars in the previous year, then this year's car sales could be used to predict sun roof demand for next year.

5.5   Correlation coefficient

Earlier in the chapter we discussed correlation and how two variables can be plotted together on a scatter diagram and the correlation between the variables intuitively estimated by simply looking at the diagram. However, a more scientific measure of the strength of the correlation is available by calculating the correlation coefficient.

Pearson's correlation coefficient, also called the 'product moment correlation coefficient', r, is computed as:

$$ r = \frac{n\sum xy - \sum x \sum y}{\sqrt{(n\sum x^2 - (\sum x)^2)(n\sum y^2 - (\sum y)^2)}} $$

where x and y represent pairs of data for two variables x and y, and n is the number of pairs of data used in the analysis.

This formula does not have to be memorised, since it is also supplied in the exam, but practice is needed at applying it to data and interpreting the result.

Example

Units produced	Total costs
	£
100	40,000
200	45,000
300	50,000
400	65,000
500	70,000
600	70,000
700	80,000

The totals required are as follows:

$\sum x = 28$, $\sum y = 420$, $\sum xy = 1,870$, $\sum x^2 = 140$, $\sum y^2 = 26,550$, $n = 7$

$$\text{Thus}\quad r = \frac{(7 \times 1,870) - (28 \times 420)}{\sqrt{((7 \times 140) - (28 \times 28))((7 \times 26,550) - (420 \times 420))}}$$

$$= \frac{13,090 - 11,760}{\sqrt{(980 - 784)(185,850 - 176,400)}}$$

$$= \frac{1,330}{\sqrt{(196 \times 9,450)}} = 0.98$$

5.6   Interpretation of coefficient of correlation

Having calculated the value of r, it is necessary to interpret this result. Does $r = 0.98$ mean that there is high correlation, low correlation or no correlation? The following points should be noted:

(1) The value of r varies between +1 and −1 where.

  $r = +1$ means perfect positive linear correlation;

  $r = 0$ means no correlation

  $r = -1$ means perfect negative linear correlation.

  So in this case the value of 0.98 indicates a high degree of positive correlation between the variables.

KEY POINT

The closer that r is to +1 (or − 1) the higher the degree of positive (or negative) correlation.

(2) In general, the closer that r is to +1 (or − 1) the higher the degree of positive (or negative) correlation. This will be confirmed by the scatter diagram where the points will lie in a narrow band for such values.

(3) It must be realised that r only measures the amount of linear correlation, i.e. the tendency to a straight line relationship. It is quite possible to have strong non-linear correlation and yet have a value of r close to zero. This is one reason why it is important in practice to draw the scatter graph first.

(4) The more data points the further r may be from 1 and still indicate good correlation. If there are few data points, as here, we would wish to see r very close to 1 (clearly if there were only 2 points they will lie exactly on the line of best fit).

(5) Even if the correlation is deemed sufficiently high to justify a linear relationship within the range of the data used, this may not be continued outside the range, as will now be discussed.

5.7   Interpolation and extrapolation

As has been shown, regression lines can be used to calculate intermediate values of
variables, i.e. values within the known range. This is known as interpolation and it is
one of the main uses of regression lines.

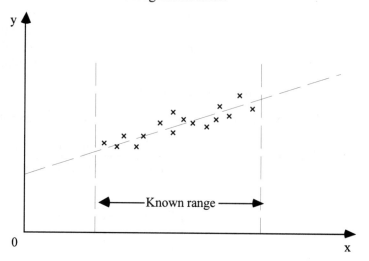

It is also possible to extend regression lines beyond the range of values used in their
calculation. It is then possible to calculate values of the variables that are outside the
limits of the original data. This is known as extrapolation.

The problem with extrapolation is that it assumes that the relationship already
calculated is still valid. This may or may not be so.

For example, if output was increased outside the given range there might come a point
where economies of scale reduce costs and total costs might actually fall.

The resultant diagram could be of this form.

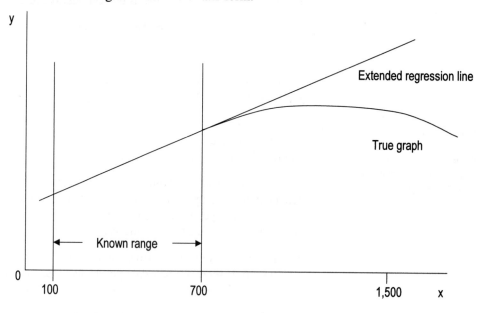

Therefore the cost of making 1,500 units as estimated from the regression line may be
very different from that actually achieved in practice.

Generally speaking, extrapolation must be treated with caution, since once outside the
range of known values other factors may influence the situation, and the relationship
which has been approximated as linear over a limited range may not be linear outside
that range. Nevertheless, extrapolation of a time series is a valuable and widely used
technique for forecasting.

5.8   Spurious correlation

You should be aware of the big danger involved in correlation analysis. Two variables, when compared, may show a high degree of correlation but they may still have no direct connection. Such correlation is termed spurious or nonsense correlation and unless two variables can reasonably be assumed to have some direct connection the correlation coefficient found will be meaningless, however high it may be.

The following are examples of variables between which there is high but spurious correlation:

(a) Salaries of school teachers and consumption of alcohol.

(b) Number of television licences and the number of admissions to mental hospitals.

Such examples clearly have no direct causal relationship. However, there may be some other variable which is a causal factor common to both of the original variables. For example, the general rise in living standards and real incomes is responsible both for the increase in teachers' salaries and for the increase in the consumption of alcohol.

6   Time series analysis

A **time series** is a set of observations taken at equal intervals of time (monthly, quarterly, annually etc).

Again time series analysis is covered in Paper 1.2 – but because students sometimes experience difficulty it is repeated here – even if you think you understand this technique do review this section to ensure that you do.

We have looked at the prediction of future costs from known levels of future activity, often production. However, the production levels may well be dictated by future sales demand, which will therefore need to be forecast first. This may be done by the means of time series analysis.

Unlike the general scatter diagrams considered above, the graph of a time series always has time as the independent variable, i.e. on the horizontal axis.

As well as periodic sales, examples of time series include monthly unemployment figures, daily average temperatures, annual populations, etc.

6.1   A time series graph

The following graph depicts the sales for Bloggs Brothers Engineering Ltd for the 14 years from 20X1 to 20Y4.

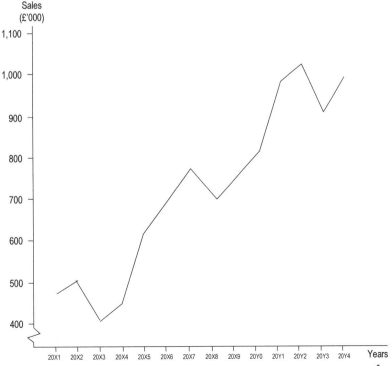

6.2   The components of a time series

A time series is influenced by a number of factors, the most important of which are described below.

(1) Long-term trends

This is the way in which the graph of a time series appears to be moving over a long interval of time when the short-term fluctuations have been smoothed out. The rise or fall is due to factors which change slowly, e.g:

- increase or decrease in population
- technological improvements
- competition from abroad.

(2) Cyclical variations

This is the wave-like appearance of a time series graph when taken over a number of years. Generally, it is due to the influence of booms and slumps in industry. The period in time from one peak to the next is often approximately 5 to 7 years.

(3) Seasonal variations

This is a regular rise and fall over specified intervals of time. The interval of time can be any length – hours, days, weeks etc, and the variations are of a periodic type with a fairly definite period, e.g:

- rises in the number of goods sold before Christmas and at sale times
- rises in the demand for gas and electricity at certain times during the day
- rises in the number of customers using a restaurant at lunch-time and dinner time.

These are referred to under the general heading of 'seasonal' variations as a common example is the steady rise and fall of, for example, sales over the four seasons of the year.

However, as can be seen from the examples, the term is also used to cover regular variations over other short periods of time.

They should not be confused with cyclical variations (2) which are long-term fluctuations with an interval between successive peaks greater than one year.

(4) Residual or random variations

This covers any other variation which cannot be ascribed to (1), (2) or (3) above. This is taken as happening entirely at random due to unpredictable causes, e.g:

- strikes
- fires
- sudden changes in taxes.

Random variations are, by definition, not possible to predict, i.e. build into a model. We can simply isolate the other three components and whatever is left will be the random variations.

Not all time series will contain all four elements. For example, not all sales figures show seasonal variations.

6.3   Separating the components

It is essential to be able to disentangle these various influences and measure each one separately. The main reasons for analysing a time series in this way are as follows:

- To be able to predict future values of the variable, i.e. to make forecasts.

- To attempt to control future events.

- To 'seasonally adjust' or 'de-seasonalise' a set of data, that is to remove the seasonal effect. For example, seasonally adjusted unemployment values are more useful than actual unemployment values in studying the effects of the national economy and Government policies on unemployment.

6.4   Additive and multiplicative models

To analyse a time series, it is necessary to make an assumption about how the four components described combine to give the total effect.

(1)   The simplest method is to assume that the components are added together, i.e. if:

A	=	Actual value for the period
T	=	Trend component
C	=	Cyclical component
S	=	Seasonal component
R	=	Residual component

then $A = T + C + S + R$. This is called an additive model.

(2)   Another method is to assume that the components are multiplied together, i.e:

$$A = T \times C \times S \times R$$

This is called a multiplicative model.

The additive model is the simplest, and is satisfactory when the fluctuations about the trend are within a constant band width. If, as is more usual, the fluctuations about the trend increase as the trend increases, the multiplicative model is more appropriate. Illustrated diagrammatically:

(1) y

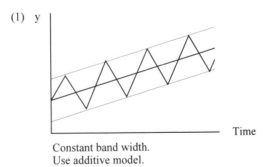

Constant band width.
Use additive model.

(2) y

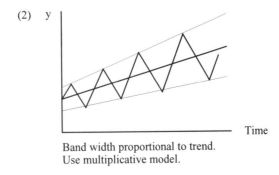

Band width proportional to trend.
Use multiplicative model.

6.5   Isolating the trend

(1) The trend can be obtained by using **regression analysis** to obtain the line of best fit through the points on the graph, taking x as the year numbers (1, 2, 3.... etc) and y as the vertical variable.

(2) It is not necessary for the trend to be a straight line, as **non-linear regression** can be used, but for this method it is necessary to assume an appropriate mathematical form for the trend, such as parabola, hyperbola, exponential, etc. If the trend does not conform to any of these, the method cannot be used.

(3) An alternative, which requires no assumption to be made about the nature of the curve, is to smooth out the fluctuations by **moving averages**.

The simplest way to explain the method is by means of an example.

6.6   Moving averages

Example

The following are the actual annual sales figures for the Bloggs Brothers Engineering Ltd graph shown earlier.

Year	Sales (£'000)
20X1	491
20X2	519
20X3	407
20X4	452
20X5	607
20X6	681
20X7	764
20X8	696
20X9	751
20Y0	802
20Y1	970
20Y2	1,026
20Y3	903
20Y4	998

Using the method of moving averages the general trend of sales will be established.

Solution

Step 1   First, it is advisable to look at the graph of the time series shown earlier and reproduced below, so that an overall picture can be gained and the cyclical movements seen.

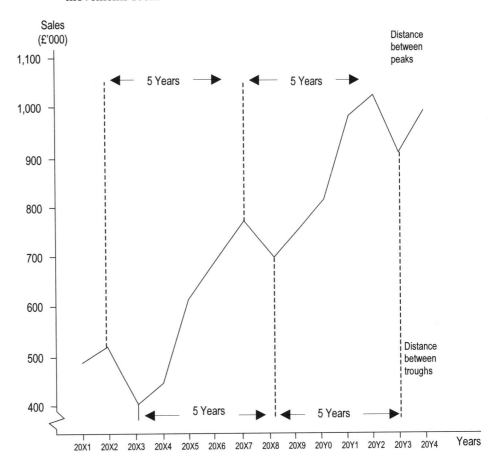

In order to calculate the trend figures it is necessary to establish the span of the cycle. From the graph it can easily be seen that the distance in time between successive peaks (and successive troughs) is 5 years. Therefore a 5 point moving average must be calculated.

Note: in an examination it will usually be obvious what length cycle to use and it will be unnecessary to draw the graph unless asked.

Step 2   A table of the following form is now drawn up:

Year	Sales (£'000)	5 yearly moving total	5 yearly moving average
20X1	491	-	-
20X2	519	-	-
20X3	407	2,476	495
20X4	452	2,666	533
20X5	607	2,911	582
20X6	681	3,200	640
20X7	764	3,499	700
20X8	696	3,694	739
20X9	751	3,983	797
20Y0	802	4,245	849
20Y1	970	4,452	890
20Y2	1,026	4,699	940
20Y3	903	-	-
20Y4	998	-	-

Notes on the calculation

As the name implies, the five yearly moving total is the sum of successive groups of 5 years' sales, i.e:

$$491 + 519 + 407 + 452 + 607 \quad = \quad 2{,}476$$

Then, advancing by one year.

$$519 + 407 + 452 + 607 + 681 \quad = \quad 2{,}666, \text{ etc.}$$

etc

$$802 + 970 + 1{,}026 + 903 + 998 \quad = \quad 4{,}699$$

These moving totals are divided by 5 to give the moving averages, i.e:

$$2{,}476 \div 5 \quad = \quad 495$$
$$2{,}666 \div 5 \quad = \quad 533$$

$$4{,}699 \div 5 \quad = \quad 940$$

Averages are always plotted in the middle of the time period, i.e. 495 is the average of the figures for 20X1, 20X2, 20X3, 20X4 and 20X5 and so it is plotted at the end of 20X3, this being the mid-point of the time interval from the end of 20X1 to the end of 20X5. Similarly, 533 is plotted at the end of 20X4, and 940 is plotted at the end of 20Y2.

Step 3   The trend figures, i.e. the five yearly moving averages, can now be drawn onto the original graph alongside the raw data.

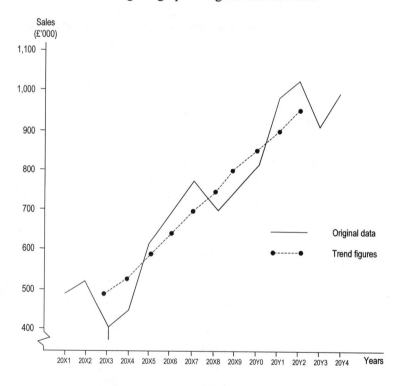

6.7   Seasonal variations

As we have seen, the other 'predictable' components of a time series, the cyclical and seasonal variations, could have very different cycle spans. Cyclical variations may only repeat themselves every 5 to 7 years, whereas seasonal variations could have a span of only a week.

Thus the data used to isolate both of these components for one series would need to be extensive – 15 years' worth of weekly sales, for example, would comprise 780 data values.

Whilst this is perfectly manageable with the help of a computer, it is highly unlikely that you would be able to tackle these within the time constraints of an exam!

It is thus more likely that either:

- data will be annual, and only cyclical variations will be isolated, i.e. assume the model

$$A = T + C + R \qquad \text{or} \qquad A = T \times C \times R$$

or

- data will be shorter term (daily, quarterly) and only seasonal variations will be isolated, i.e. assume the model

$$A = T + S + R \qquad \text{or} \qquad A = T \times S \times R$$

The method for isolating cyclical or seasonal variations is identical; here we shall look at an example that allows us to isolate seasonal variations, and also looks at the problem of centring the trend.

Example

The following table gives the takings (£000) of a shopkeeper in each quarter of 4 successive years.

Qtrs	1	2	3	4
20X1	13	22	58	23
20X2	16	28	61	25
20X3	17	29	61	26
20X4	18	30	65	29

Calculate the trend figures and quarterly variations, using moving averages and the additive model and draw a graph to show the overall trend and the original data.

Solution

As discussed above the model to be used with shorter term data is:

$$A \qquad = \qquad T + S + R$$

The approach taken is as follows.

(1) Isolate the trend (T), by moving averages.

(2) Subtract those figures from the actual data (A–T) leaving seasonal (S) + random (R) variations.

(3) These are then averaged to remove R, leaving S.

(4) Plot the graph of A and T.

1 Year & quarter	2 Takings (£'000) A	3 4 quarterly moving average	4 Centred value T	5 Quarterly + Residual variation (A–T) = S + R
1	13	-	-	-
2	22		-	-
20X1		29		
3	58		30	28
		30		
4	23		31	–8
		31		
1	16		32	–16
		32		
2	28		33	–5
20X2		33		
3	61		33	28
		33		
4	25		33	–8
		33		
1	17		33	–16
		33		
2	29		33	–4
20X3		33		
3	61		34	27
		34		
4	26		34	–8
		34		
1	18		35	–17
		35		
2	30		36	–6
20X4		36		
3	65		-	-
4	29	-	-	-

Notes on the calculations above
- **Column 3**

To smooth out quarterly fluctuations, calculate a 4-point moving average, since there are 4 quarters (or seasons) in a year.

i.e, $\dfrac{13 + 22 + 58 + 23}{4}$ = $\dfrac{116}{4}$ =   29

then, advancing by one quarter.

$\dfrac{22 + 58 + 23 + 16}{4}$ = $\dfrac{119}{4}$ = 30 (rounding to nearest whole number)

etc

$\dfrac{18 + 30 + 65 + 29}{4}$ = $\dfrac{142}{4}$ = 36 (rounding to nearest whole number).

KEY POINT

Where it is appropriate to use an even-numbered point moving average the data will need to be **centred**.

But there is a problem. 29 is the average of the figures for the four quarters of 20X1 and so if plotted, would be at the mid-point of the interval from the end of the first quarter to the end of the fourth quarter, i.e. half-way through the third quarter of 20X1. But, to find A – T, it is essential that A and T both relate to the same point in time. The four-quarterly moving averages do not correspond with any of the A values, the first coming between the second and third A values and so on down. To overcome this, the moving averages are 'centred', i.e. averaged in twos. The first centred moving average will then coincide with the third A value and so on.

FOULKS LYNCH
PUBLICATIONS

Note: that centring is necessary because the cycle has an even number of values (4) per cycle. Where there is an odd number of values per cycle, as in the previous example, the moving averages themselves correspond in time with A values, and centring should not be done.

- **Column 4**

The centring is as follows:

i.e. $\dfrac{29+30}{2}$ = 30 (rounding up)

$\dfrac{30+31}{2}$ = 31 (rounding up)

$\dfrac{35+36}{2}$ = 36 (rounding up).

The first average now corresponds in time with the original value for the 3rd quarter, and so on.

These are the trend values.

- **Column 5**

A – T = S + R, hence the figures for the quarterly + residual variations are the differences between the actual figures and the centred values.

i.e. 58 – 30 =   28

23 – 31 =   –8

30 – 36 =   –6

Isolating seasonal variations

In order to establish the seasonal variation, another table must be drawn up to remove the residual variation *R*. This collates the corresponding values of S + R for each season from different years, and averages them.

	Quarter 1	Quarter 2	Quarter 3	Quarter 4
20X1	–	–	28	–8
20X2	–16	–5	28	–8
20X3	–16	–4	27	–8
20X4	–17	–6	–	–
Totals	–49	–15	83	–24
Average seasonal variation	–16	–5	28	–8

The individual variations have been averaged out for each quarter of the cycle.

e.g. Quarter 1 $\dfrac{-16+(-16)+(-17)}{3}$ = $\dfrac{-49}{3}$ = –16

Quarter 2 $\dfrac{-5+(-4)+(-6)}{3}$ = $\dfrac{-15}{3}$ = –5

Strictly, the quarterly variations should total to zero, but –16 + (–5) + 28 + (–8) = –1. As a rule, the total excess (–1 here) should be split evenly between the seasonal variations. However, the adjustment would only be –1 ÷ 4, i.e. –0.25 which means using a spurious

accuracy of two decimal places. To avoid this one value only need be adjusted, choosing the greatest value as this will give the lowest relative adjustment error.

1st	Quarter	=		−16
2nd	Quarter	=		−5
3rd	Quarter	=	28 + 1 =	29
4th	Quarter	=		−8
				0

Draw the graph:

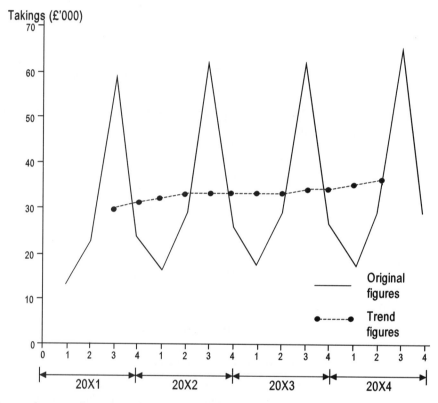

As can be seen from the calculations and the graph, the takings show a slight upward trend and the seasonal (quarterly) variations are considerable.

6.8   Seasonally adjusted figures

A popular way of presenting a time series is to give the seasonally adjusted or de-seasonalised figures.

This is a very simple process once the seasonal variations are known.

For the additive model:

Seasonally adjusted data = Original data − Seasonal variation = A − S.

For the multiplicative model:

Seasonally adjusted data = Original data ÷ Seasonal indices = A ÷ S.

The main purpose in calculating seasonally adjusted figures is to remove the seasonal influence from the original data so that non-seasonal influences can be seen more clearly.

Example: additive model

The same shopkeeper as in the last example found his takings for the four quarters of 20X5 were £19,000, £32,000, £65,000 and £30,000 respectively. Has the upward trend continued?

Solution

De-seasonalising the figures gives:

		Seasonally adjusted Figures (£'000)
Quarter 1	19 – (–16) =	35
Quarter 2	32 – (–5) =	37
Quarter 3	65 – 29 =	36
Quarter 4	30 – (–8) =	38

So, as can be seen from comparing the seasonally adjusted figures with the trend figures calculated earlier, the takings are indeed still increasing, i.e. there is an upward trend.

Example: multiplicative model

The following data will be seasonally adjusted using 'seasonal indices.'

	Quarter			
	1	*2*	*3*	*4*
Sales (£'000)	59	50	61	92
Seasonal variation	–2%	–21%	–9%	+30%

If $A = T \times S \times R$, the de-seasonalised data is A/S.

A decrease of – 2% means a factor of 0.98. Similarly, an increase of 30% means a factor of 1.3. Hence the seasonal factors are 0.98, 0.79, 0.91, 1.30 respectively. The actual data, A, must be divided by these values to remove the seasonal effect.

A	*Seasonal factor (S)*	*Seasonally adjusted figure (= A/S)*
59	0.98	60
50	0.79	63
61	0.91	67
92	1.30	71

While actual sales are lowest in summer and highest in winter, the seasonally adjusted values show a fairly steady increase throughout the year.

6.9   Forecasting with time series

It has been shown in the above sections how data can be de-seasonalised in order to identify the underlying trend. However, it is often the case that predictions are required to be made about the future, but taking into account seasonal factors.

First, the trend value(s) need to be forecast. This can be done in two ways.

- By fitting a line of best fit (straight or curved) by eye (preferably through the trend found by moving averages).

- By using linear regression. This was considered earlier in the chapter.

The line is then extended to the right (or future time values used in the regression line) in order to estimate future trend values.

Second, this 'trend' value is then adjusted in order to take account of the seasonal factors.

Hence, the forecast $= T_e + S$, where $T_e =$ extrapolated trend.

Residual variations are by nature random and therefore unforecastable.

Example

Using the data from the shopkeeper predict the takings of the shop for the first and second quarters of 20X5.

Solution

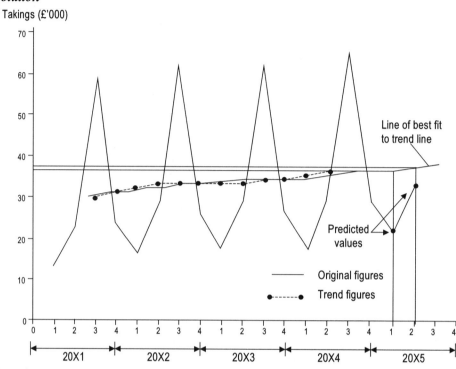

From the graph it can be seen that the trend line predicts values as follows:

Quarter in 20X5	(i) Trend value	(ii) Seasonal variation	(i) + (ii) Final prediction
1	37,000	−16,000	21,000
2	38,000	−5,000	33,000

The predicted values of £21,000 and £33,000 have been plotted on the graph.

For the multiplicative model, the extrapolated trend must be multiplied by the appropriate seasonal factor.

Thus in the multiplicative example above, if the predicted trend value for the first quarter of the following year was £65,000, the appropriate seasonal factor for this quarter being 0.98, the forecast of actual sales would be £65,000 × 0.98 = £64,000 (to the nearest £000).

6.10 Limitations of time series analysis

Time series analysis is based on the assumption that what has happened in the past can be used to predict what will happen in the future, and that identifiable trends in the past will continue into the future. These assumptions can be wrong.

- Significant changes might occur quite quickly, so that what happens in the future will be completely different from the past. For example, new technology could revolutionise practices and products within an industry. Equally, sudden changes

could occur in product markets or geographical markets, making the past a poor guide to the future. A company might change its mix of products or services, which could affect its future prospects.

- Financial figures collected over a long period of time for time series analysis will be affected by changing price levels. The level of costs and revenues several years ago are not properly comparable with current or future costs and prices, due to inflation. Historical costs need to be adjusted for time series analysis.

Indices and index numbers can be used to adjust historical figures to the same basis for comparison and forecasting purposes. The use of index numbers is explained in the next chapter.

Conclusion

This chapter has looked at the quantitative techniques that you may be required to employ in cost and revenue forecasting for budgeting purposes.

First, we considered the prediction of costs, mainly based upon the assumption of a linear relationship between costs and activity level. The techniques centre around the determination of a 'line of best fit', from judgmental means from a scatter diagram, through the 'high low' method using limited historical cost data, to linear regression (the mathematical approach that uses all available data).

Then we turned to time series analysis, which does not necessarily start from the premise of a linear relationship. The trend may be extracted by the method of moving averages (or regression if it is approximately linear). The cyclical or seasonal variations are then derived by averaging the deviations of the time series from the trend. Each of these elements is then forecast individually. The combined results give the overall predictions for future values of the time series.

SELF-TEST QUESTIONS

Scatter diagrams

1   In a scatter diagram, the .... variable is on the x-axis and the .... variable is on the y-axis. Fill in the gaps. (3.1)

2   If the equation y = a + bx is applied to total cost, what will a, b , x and y represent? (3.2)

Regression analysis

3   Before using a regression line for prediction purposes, what factors should be considered? (5.3)

4   Give an example of spurious correlation. (5.8)

Time series analysis

5   What does the method of moving averages try to achieve? (6.5)

6   How would the predicted trend value be adjusted for seasonal variations under (i) the additive model and (ii) the multiplicative model? (6.9)

EXAM-TYPE QUESTION

D & E Ltd

D & E Ltd produce brakes for the motor industry. Its management accountant is investigating the relationship between electricity costs and volume of production. The following data for the last ten quarters has been derived, the cost figures having been adjusted (i.e. deflated) to take into account price changes.

Quarter	1	2	3	4	5	6	7	8	9	10
Production X ('000 units)	30	20	10	60	40	25	13	50	44	28
Electricity costs Y (£'000)	10	11	6	18	13	10	10	20	17	15

(Source; Internal company records of D & E Ltd)

$\Sigma X^2 = 12,614$ $\Sigma Y^2 = 1,864$ $\Sigma XY = 4,728$

You are required:

(a) to draw a scatter diagram of the data on squared paper;   **(4 marks)**

(b) to find the least squares regression line for electricity costs on production and explain this result;   **(8 marks)**

(c) to predict the electricity costs of D & E Ltd for the next two quarters (time periods 11 and 12) in which production is planned to be 15,000 and 55,000 standard units respectively;   **(4 marks)**

(d) to assess the likely reliability of these forecasts;   **(4 marks)**

(e) explain briefly how time series analysis can assist the management accountant.

(Total: 20 marks)

For the answer to this question, see the 'Answers' section at the end of the book.

Chapter 24
INDEX NUMBERS

Indexing is a technique for comparing, over time, changes in some property of a group of items (price, quantity consumed, etc.) by expressing the property each year as a percentage of some earlier year, a base year.

Examples of index numbers are frequently seen in everyday life. The best-known is probably the retail price index (RPI), which measures changes in the prices of goods and services supplied to retail customers. This index is often thought of as a 'cost of living' index. Index numbers may also measure quantity changes (e.g. volumes of production or trade) or changes in values (e.g. retail sales, value of exports).

In this chapter you will learn about simple indices, weighted indices, chain base indices, Laspeyre indices and Paasche indices.

Objectives

By the time you have finished this chapter you should be able to:

- explain the purpose of index numbers, and calculate and interpret simple index numbers for one or more variable

- deflate time-related data using an index

- construct a chained index series

- explain the term 'average index', distinguishing between simple and weighted averages

- calculate Laspeyre and Paasche price and quantity indices

- discuss the relative merits of Laspeyre and Paasche indices.

1   The purpose of index numbers

1.1   Inflation

Inflation is the process whereby the price of commodities steadily rises over time.

DEFINITION

Inflation is the process whereby the price of commodities steadily rises over time.

Inflation often makes information difficult to interpret. If data simply shows, for example, the cost of raw materials used, it may be difficult to assess changes in quantities used when the prices of the raw materials are subject to inflation. If management wishes to interpret changes in quantities of materials used they must first adjust the expenditure figures for price changes.

1.2   Index numbers

An **index number** shows the rate of change of a variable from one specified time to another.

DEFINITION

An **index number** shows the rate of change of a variable from one specified time to another.

Most accountants acknowledge that the accounts of businesses are distorted when no allowance is made for the effects of inflation. The use of index numbers is often required for the preparation of inflation-adjusted accounts. This chapter considers the range of possible methods by which such index numbers might be calculated.

1.3   Types of index number

The following types of index number will be considered:

- simple indices

- weighted indices
- chain base indices
- Laspeyre indices
- Paasche indices.

2 Simple indices

2.1 Price and quantity percentage relatives

Price and quantity percentage relatives (also called percentage relatives) are based on a single item. There are two types: price relatives and quantity relatives.

A **price relative** shows changes in the price of an item over time.

A **quantity relative** shows changes in quantities over time.

The formulae for calculating these relatives are as follows:

$$\text{Simple price index} = \frac{p_1}{p_0} \times 100$$

$$\text{Simple quantity index} = \frac{q_1}{q_0} \times 100$$

Where:

p_0 is the price at time 0

p_1 is the price at time 1

q_0 is the quantity at time 0

q_1 is the quantity at time 1

The concept of time 0, time 1 and so on is simply a scale counting from any given point in time. Thus, for example, if the scale started on 1 January 20X0 it would be as follows:

The starting point is chosen to be most convenient for the problem under consideration.

Example

If a commodity costs £2.60 in 20X4 and £3.68 in 20X5, calculate the simple price index for 20X5, using 20X4 as base year (i.e. time 0).

Solution

$$\text{Simple price index} = \frac{p_1}{p_0} \times 100 = \frac{3.68}{2.60} \times 100 = 141.5$$

This means that the price has increased by 41.5% of its base year value, i.e. its 20X4 value.

Example

6,500 items were sold in 20X8 compared with 6,000 in 20X7. Calculate the simple quantity index for 20X8 using 20X7 as base year.

Solution

Simple quantity index = $\dfrac{q_1}{q_0} \times 100 = \dfrac{6,500}{6,000} \times 100 = 108.3$

This means that the quantity sold has increased by 8.3% of its 20X7 figure.

ACTIVITY 1

A product which cost £12.50 in 20X0, cost £13.65 in 20X1. Calculate the simple price index for 20X1 based on 20X0.

Feedback to this activity is at the end of the chapter.

2.2   Multi-item indices

KEY POINT

Usually, an index number is required to show the variation in a number of items at once.

By using appropriate weights, price relatives can be combined to give a multi-item price index.

Usually, an index number is required to show the variation in a number of items at once rather than just one as in the examples above. The RPI is such an index and consists of a list of items as diverse as the price of bread, the cost of watch repairs, car repairs and cinema tickets.

By using appropriate weights, price relatives can be combined to give a multi-item price index.

3   Weighted indices

3.1   Weighted average of price relatives

DEFINITION

An index number based on **price relatives** compares the price of each item in one year with the price of each item in the base year.

An index number based on **price relatives** compares the price of each item in one year with the price of each item in the base year, expressing each as a percentage relative, and then finds the weighted average of the percentage relatives.

Example

From the following information, construct an index of the weighted average of price relatives, with 20X5 as the base year.

	Price (pence)		
Item	*20X5*	*20X6*	*Weights*
A	10	20	100
B	25	26	182
C	35	33	132
D	12	13	13
			427

Solution

Index of the weighted average of price relatives

$$= \dfrac{\sum W\left(\dfrac{p_1}{p_0} \times 100\right)}{\sum W} = \dfrac{52,783.5}{427} = 123.6$$

Where W = weight, p_1 = prices in 20X6, p_0 = prices in 20X5.

FOULKS LYNCH
PUBLICATIONS

Workings

p_0	p_1	Price relative $\dfrac{p_1}{p_0} \times 100$	W	$W \times (\dfrac{p_1}{p_0} \times 100)$
10	20	200.0	100	20,000.0
25	26	104.0	182	18,928.0
35	33	94.3	132	12,447.6
12	13	108.3	13	1,407.9
			427	52,783.5
			ΣW	$\Sigma W \times \dfrac{p_1}{p_0} \times 100$

3.2 Selecting weights

The weights applied to price relatives should, in general, reflect the amount spent or total value of each item purchased, rather than simply the quantities purchased (however standardised). The reason is that this eliminates the effect of a relatively low-priced item having a very high price relative from only a small price rise.

Example

The price of peas and bread, and the amount consumed in both years, is as follows:

Item	20X5 price	20X6 price	Units consumed (both years)
Peas	2p	3p	2
Bread	15p	16p	5

You are required:

(a)   to construct a price-relative index using:

   (i)   quantity weights

   (ii)   value weights

(b)   to explain why the value weighted price relative is the more useful.

Solution

(a) (i) Using quantity weights

Item	20X5 p_0 pence	20X6 p_1 pence	q^*	Quantity weight only $W_A(= q)$	Value weight W_B $(= p_0 \times q)$
Peas	2	3	2	2	$2 \times 2 = 4$
Bread	15	16	5	5	$15 \times 5 = 75$
				7	79
				ΣW_A	ΣW_B

Same consumption pattern for both years

Item	$\dfrac{p_1}{p_0} \times 100$	$W_A \times \dfrac{p_1}{p_0} \times 100$	$W_B \times \dfrac{p_1}{p_0} \times 100$
Peas	150.0	300.0	600.0
Bread	106.7	533.5	8,002.5
		833.5	8,602.5
		$\Sigma W_A \times \dfrac{p_1}{p_0} \times 100$	$\Sigma W_B \times \dfrac{p_1}{p_0} \times 100$

Therefore, using quantity weights only, the index is as follows:

$$\frac{\sum W_A\left(\frac{p_1}{p_0}\times100\right)}{\sum W_A} = \frac{833.5}{7} = 119.1$$

(This would imply an average increase in prices of 19.1%.)

(a) (ii) **Using value weights, the index is:**

$$\frac{\sum W_B\left(\frac{p_1}{p_0}\times100\right)}{\sum W_B} = \frac{8,602.5}{79} = 108.9$$

(This implies an average increase of 8.9%.)

(b) The fact that the value weighted average of price relatives is the more realistic can be shown by considering total expenditure:

Item	Expenditure 20X5		Expenditure 20X6		% increase
Peas	2×2	4p	2×3	6p	50%
Bread	5×15	75p	5×16	80p	6.7%
Total Budget		79p		86p	8.86%

Thus, an equal *money* price rise for two items will cause a higher percentage price rise for the lower-priced item which is compensated for when the weights used are the value or expenditure on each item, since this reduces the importance of the lower priced item.

Algebraically, as $W = q \times p_0$ then the weighted average of price relatives, which is:

$$\frac{\sum W\left(\frac{p_1}{p_0}\times100\right)}{\sum W}, \text{ becomes } \frac{\sum qp_0 \times \frac{p_1}{p_0}}{\sum qp_0}\times100 = \frac{\sum qp_1}{\sum qp_0}\times100$$

ACTIVITY 2

A production process uses 10 sacks of product A and 30 of product B per year. The costs are as follows:

Item	20X1	20X2
Product A	£6.50	£6.90
Product B	£2.20	£2.50

Construct a price relative index using:

(a) quantity weights

(b) value weights.

Feedback to this activity is at the end of the chapter.

3.3 Simple average index

If there had been no weighting then a simple average index or an aggregate index would have been formed. This method simply adds all the prices together and takes no account of volumes sold.

3.4   The retail price index (RPI)

The UK **retail price index** measures the percentage changes month by month in the average level of prices of goods and services purchased by most households in the UK.

It is not, strictly speaking, a cost of living index, as it includes non-essential items such as leisure and entertainment and there are a number of payments not included, such as income tax, national insurance contributions, savings, charitable subscriptions, etc., but it is the best measure of the cost of living available.

For the prices, a representative list (basket) of items and services has been selected, and prices are collected (where appropriate) by a monthly sample survey among retail outlets in some 180 urban and rural centres. The prices noted are those actually charged, where these differ from published prices.

The index is calculated as a weighted average of price relatives, the weights being the proportional parts of each £1,000 spent by the average household on each item (i.e. value weights). These weights are updated annually and are obtained from the *Family Expenditure Survey* which is a continuous survey among an annual sample of about 7,000 householders, who are asked to keep a diary of all their expenditure for a period of two weeks. For the purpose of the RPI, very high and very low income families are excluded from the calculations.

The RPI is used for the following purposes:

- measurement of cost of living

- measurement of inflation, used for wage negotiations, etc.

- index-linked pensions, wages

- current cost accounting

- deflation of monetary series to obtain value in 'real terms', time series deflation.

3.5   The index of industrial production

The **index of industrial production** measures changes in the general level of output of UK industry as a whole, so it is used as an indicator of the country's overall industrial performance.

For the purposes of the index, UK industry is split into 880 categories, which are classified in 20 groups to comprise the whole of the manufacturing, mining, construction and energy sectors of the economy.

The index is a weighted average of quantity relatives. Each of the 20 groups is given a weight in proportion to the value of its net output, the sum of the weights of all 20 groups being 1,000. The quantities used are, as close as is possible, the actual output figures for each group.

The most common use of the index is to gauge the level of recession or economic growth occurring in the manufacturing sector of the UK.

3.6   Deflating a monetary series

Deflating a monetary series shows the 'real term' effect.

If wages, for example, increase at exactly the same rate as inflation, the earner's purchasing power is not changed. In real terms, the wage has remained constant. The following example illustrates the method, using the RPI as the measure of inflation to deflate a set of sales values.

Example

Year	Actual sales (£'000)	RPI	Deflated sales (£'000)
1	275	100	$\dfrac{275}{100} \times 100 = 275$
2	305	112	$\dfrac{305}{112} \times 100 = 272$
3	336	122	$\dfrac{336}{122} \times 100 = 275$
4	344	127	$\dfrac{344}{127} \times 100 = 271$
5	363	133	$\dfrac{363}{133} \times 100 = 273$

It will be seen that although actual sales have increased in value by a fairly large amount, in real terms there has been a slight decrease.

Note: Deflated sales $= \dfrac{\text{Actual sales}}{\text{RPI}} \times 100$

KEY POINT

Deflated sales =
$\dfrac{\text{Actual sales}}{\text{RPI}} \times 100$

4 Chain base index numbers

If a series of index numbers are required for different years, such that the rate of change of the variable from one year to the next can be studied, the chain base method is used. This means that each index number is calculated using the previous year as base. If the rate of change is *increasing* then the index numbers will be rising; if it is *constant*, the numbers will remain the same and if it is *decreasing* the numbers will be falling.

DEFINITION

Chain base index numbers are calculated using the previous year as base.

Example

A shopkeeper received the following amounts from the sale of radios:

20X1	£1,000
20X2	£1,100
20X3	£1,210
20X4	£1,331
20X5	£1,464

Is it correct to say that the annual rate of increase in revenue from sales of radios is getting larger?

Solution

Year	Sales	Chain base index
20X1	£1,000	
20X2	£1,100	$\dfrac{1,100}{1,000} \times 100 = 110$
20X3	£1,210	$\dfrac{1,210}{1,100} \times 100 = 110$
20X4	£1,331	$\dfrac{1,331}{1,210} \times 100 = 110$
20X5	£1,464	$\dfrac{1,464}{1,331} \times 100 = 110$

FOULKS LYNCH
PUBLICATIONS

Although the sales revenue from radios has increased each year, the chain base index numbers have remained static at 110. Therefore, the annual rate of increase of sales revenue from radios is remaining constant rather than increasing.

The chain base is also a suitable index to calculate when the weights ascribed to the various items in the index are changing rapidly. Over a period of years, this index would have modified itself to take account of these changes whereas in a fixed-base method after a number of years the whole index would have to be revised to allow for the changed weighting.

4.1 Revision of indices

It is normal to periodically revise the commodities and weights used as a basis for index calculation. In order to maintain comparability, the new index is linked to the old series so as to establish one single index series with periodic revision of the weights.

The weights used in the RPI are now revised annually. However, other indices, both in the UK and overseas, may not be subject to regular revision.

5 Laspeyre and Paasche indices

These are sometimes referred to as aggregative indices.

An aggregate price index compares the total expenditure in one year (i.e. at that year's prices) on a particular collection of goods with the total expenditure in the base year, at base year prices, on the same collection of goods.

By using the term total expenditure, this statement assumes that the weights used are the quantities purchased.

Given this assumption, a choice of weights arises between the quantity purchased in the **base year** and the quantity purchased in the **current year** for which the index is being prepared. Both choices are acceptable and both have their respective merits and demerits. The resultant indices are named after their 'inventors'.

The Laspeyre price index uses base year quantities, the Paasche uses current year quantities. The Paasche index, for instance, compares the cost of buying current year quantities at current year prices with buying them at base year prices.

5.1 Formulae

Laspeyre price index $= \dfrac{\Sigma(p_1 \times q_0)}{\Sigma(p_0 \times q_0)} \times 100$ (using base year quantities as weights).

Paasche price index $= \dfrac{\Sigma(p_1 \times q_1)}{\Sigma(p_0 \times q_1)} \times 100$ (using current year quantities as weights).

Example

The Laspeyre and Paasche price indices will be calculated for the following data, using 20X4 as base year:

	20X4		*20X5*	
Item	*Price (p_0)*	*Quantity (q_0)*	*Price (p_1)*	*Quantity (q_1)*
Milk	19p a pint	50,000 pints	26p a pint	70,000 pints
Bread	39p a loaf	30,000 loaves	40p a loaf	40,000 loaves
Soap	42p a pack	20,000 packs	64p a pack	25,000 packs
Sugar	60p a kilo	10,000 kilos	68p a kilo	8,000 kilos
Eggs	84p a box	3,000 boxes	72p a box	2,500 boxes

Solution

(a)   **Laspeyre index**

Item	Weight (q_0)	Price (p_0)	$p_0 \times q_0$ £	Price (p_1)	$p_1 \times q_0$ £
Milk	50,000	19p	9,500	26p	13,000
Bread	30,000	39p	11,700	40p	12,000
Soap	20,000	42p	8,400	64p	12,800
Sugar	10,000	60p	6,000	68p	6,800
Eggs	3,000	84p	2,520	72p	2,160
			38,120		46,760

$\Sigma p_1 q_0$ = 46,760 = last year's buying pattern at today's prices.

$\Sigma p_0 q_0$ = 38,120 = last year's buying pattern at last year's prices.

$\therefore$ Index $= \dfrac{\Sigma p_1 q_0}{\Sigma p_0 q_0} \times 100$

$= \dfrac{46,760}{38,120} \times 100$

$= 122.7$

The cost of buying 20X4 quantities at 20X5 prices shows an increase of 22.7% over 20X4 costs.

(b)   **Paasche index**

Item	Weight (q_1)	Price (p_0)	$p_0 \times q_1$ £	Price (p_1)	$p_1 \times q_1$ £
Milk	70,000	19p	13,300	26p	18,200
Bread	40,000	39p	15,600	40p	16,000
Soap	25,000	42p	10,500	64p	16,000
Sugar	8,000	60p	4,800	68p	5,440
Eggs	2,500	84p	2,100	72p	1,800
			46,300		57,440

$\Sigma p_0 q_1$ = 46,300 = today's buying pattern at last year's prices.

$\Sigma p_1 q_1$ = 57,440 = today's buying pattern at today's prices.

$\therefore$ Index $= \dfrac{57,440}{46,300} \times 100$

$= 124.1$

The 20X5 index shows an increase of 24.1% over 20X4 prices when buying 20X5 quantities.

Note: In calculating either type of index, a common mistake made by students is to add all the prices and all the quantities and multiply the two totals, i.e. $\Sigma p \times \Sigma q$ is calculated instead of $\Sigma(p \times q)$. To do so is quite wrong and will be penalised in the marking of the examination.

5.2   Comparison of Laspeyre and Paasche indices

In a period of inflation, there is a general increase in prices. In addition, there will be relative price changes. Thus, for example, in the 1980s petrol became relatively more expensive and electric goods became relatively cheaper.

The effect of these changes is a changing pattern of consumption, with consumers switching to relatively less expensive goods, e.g. from large cars to small cars, and buying more electric goods.

This switching minimises the effect of inflation on individual consumers. However, if a Laspeyre index is used it will fail to take account of the changing pattern of consumption. As a result, a Laspeyre index tends to overstate the real impact of inflation on individuals.

On the other hand, a Paasche index involves recalculating data for all preceding years each year. With a large number of indices to maintain, this is not practicable. Also, because a Paasche index is based on current consumption patterns it tends to understate the overall effect of inflation on consumers.

5.3　Relative merits of types of indices

The relative merits and demerits of the indices are summarised below.

Laspeyre index – Advantages

1　Cheaper, as the obtaining of new quantities each year may be costly.

2　Easier to calculate where a series of years are being compared, since the denominator remains the same for all years, e.g. 20X7 index would be calculated

$$\frac{\sum q_7 p_0}{\sum q_0 p_0} \times 100$$

where p_7 = prices in 20X7 and p_0 prices in 20X0.

3　Each year in a series of Laspeyre indices is directly comparable with all previous years.

Laspeyre index – Disadvantages

1　The major disadvantage of using Laspeyre indices is that an out-of-date consumption pattern may be used. In practice this is overcome by a periodic revision of the base year to keep it up-to-date, but this makes very long-term comparison almost impossible as the continuity of the series is destroyed.

2　As prices rise, quantities purchased tend to diminish if there are alternative goods available. This decrease is not reflected in the Laspeyre index which tends, therefore, to overestimate the effect of rising prices.

Paasche index– Advantages

1　Since current year weights are used, it results in an index being based on the current pattern of consumption so that a less frequent revision of base year is needed.

Paasche index– Disadvantages

1　Where a series of years is involved, the amount of calculation is greater as both numerator and denominator need calculating each year, e.g. 20X7 index would be calculated:

$$\frac{\sum q_7 p_7}{\sum q_0 p_7} \times 100$$

where:　p_7 = prices in 20X7,

　　　q_7 = quantities in 20X7 and

　　　p_0 = prices in 20X0

2   Each Paasche index in a series is only directly comparable with the base year (i.e. 20X7 does not bear comparison with 20X6; only with base year 20X0).

3   The Paasche index can only be constructed if up-to-date information is available. The RPI is a Paasche index but, although it is produced monthly, quantities are only updated annually.

4   Rising prices have the opposite effect on the weights and the Paasche index therefore tends to underestimate the effect of inflation.

5.4   Quantity index

A **quantity index** measures changes in the volume of goods produced or sold.

An example is the UK **Index of Industrial Production** explained earlier.

Just as a price index needs to be weighted with the quantities purchased, so a quantity index must be weighted with prices. A change in the volume of gold or other precious metal would have a greater effect on the economy that the same change in the volume of sand and gravel produced, because volume for volume it is much more valuable.

A quantity index is therefore calculated in the same way as a price index, with the role of price and quantity reversed.

$$\text{Laspeyre quantity index} = \frac{\Sigma q_n p_0}{\Sigma q_0 p_0} \times 100$$

$$\text{Paasche quantity index} = \frac{\Sigma q_n p_n}{\Sigma q_0 p_n} \times 100$$

Example

Laspeyre and Paasche quantity indices will be calculated for the data given earlier. From the previous example:

$\Sigma q_1 p_0 = \Sigma p_0 q_1 = 46{,}300$

$\Sigma q_0 p_0 = \Sigma p_0 q_0 = 38{,}120$

$\Sigma q_1 p_1 = \Sigma p_1 q_1 = 57{,}440$

$\Sigma q_0 p_1 = \Sigma p_1 q_0 = 46{,}760$

Solution

Hence the Laspeyre index for 20X5 with 20X4 as base is $\dfrac{46{,}300}{38{,}120} \times 100 = 121.5$

and the Paasche index for 20X5 with 20X4 as base is $\dfrac{57{,}440}{46{,}760} \times 100 = 122.8$

5.5   Value index

For a price index or a quantity index the weights are the same in both the numerator and the denominator of the formula. A value index uses current year weights for the numerator and base year weights for the denominator:

$$\text{Value index for year 1} = \frac{\Sigma p_1 q_1}{\Sigma p_0 q_0} \times 100$$

$\Sigma p_1 q_1$ = value of all goods in year 1

$\Sigma p_0 q_0$ = value of all goods in the base year

Using the data given earlier:

$$\text{Value index for 20X5 with 20X4 as base} = \frac{57{,}440}{38{,}120} \times 100 = 150.7$$

Hence the value of all goods purchased increased by 50.7% from 20X4 to 20X5.

ACTIVITY 3

Taking 20X0 as the base year, calculate base year and current year weighted index numbers for prices and quantities for year 20X1 for the following data.

	20X0		20X1	
Item	Price (£)	Quantity	Price (£)	Quantity
A	0.20	20	0.22	24
B	0.25	12	0.28	16
C	1.00	3	0.98	2

Feedback to this activity is at the end of the chapter.

Conclusion

This chapter has considered index numbers and looked at the calculation of several indices as well as considering their practical uses.

SELF-TEST QUESTIONS

The purpose of index numbers

1   What is the purpose of an index number? (1.2)

Simple indices

2   Distinguish between a price relative and a quantity relative.(2.1)

Multi-item indices

3   What is the Retail Prices Index (RPI)? (2.2)

4   What does the index of industrial production seek to measure? (3.5)

Laspeyre and Paasche indices

5   What is the formula for a Laspeyre price index? (5.1)

6   Distinguish between a Laspeyre and a Paasche index. (5.2)

7   Give one advantage of the Laspeyre index over the Paasche index (5.3).

Constructing an index number

(a) What are the main considerations to be borne in mind when constructing an index number?   **(4 marks)**

(b) The table below shows the total weekly expenditure on four commodities in June 20X1 and June 20X8, based on a representative sample of 1,000 households.

You are required to compute a Laspeyre index showing the extent of the rise in prices of all four commodities.   **(3 marks)**

(c) Explain briefly the major weakness of the Laspeyre index in this case, and suggest an alternative.   **(3 marks)**

(Total: 10 marks)

Commodities	Quantities purchased (lbs)	Total expenditure £
June 20X1		
Butter	3,500	280
Potatoes	8,500	85
Apples	2,000	100
Meat	6,000	1,200
	20,000	1,665
June 20X8		
Butter	3,500	700
Potatoes	7,000	700
Apples	2,500	250
Meat	6,500	3,250
	19,500	4,900

For the answer to this question, see the 'Answers' section at the end of the book.

Simple price index = $\frac{p_1}{p_0} \times 100$ where p_1 is the price in 20X1 and p_0 is the price in 20X0:

$$= \frac{13.65}{12.50} \times 100$$

$$= 1.092 \times 100$$

$$= 109.20$$

This means that the price has increased by 9.2% on its base year price of £12.50.

FOULKS LYNCH
PUBLICATIONS

Let's start by preparing a table of all the information required to answer the question:

Item	p_0 20X1	p_1 20X2	q	Quantity weight only $W_A (= q)$	Value weight $W_B (= p_0 \times q)$
Product A	6.5	6.9	10	10	65
Product B	2.2	2.5	30	30	66
Σ				40	131

Item	$\dfrac{p_1}{p_0} \times 100$	$W_A \dfrac{p_1}{p_0} \times 100$	$W_B \dfrac{p_1}{p_0} \times 100$
Product A	106.2	1,062	6,903.0
Product B	113.6	3,408	7,497.6
Σ		4,470	14,400.6

(a) To calculate the index using quantity weights, we need to insert the data into the formula:

$$\frac{\Sigma W_A \times \dfrac{p_1}{p_0} \times 100}{\Sigma W_A} = \frac{4,470}{40} = 111.75$$

(b) To calculate the index using value weights, we need to insert the data into the formula:

$$\frac{\Sigma W_B \times \dfrac{p_1}{p_0} \times 100}{\Sigma W_B} = \frac{14,400.6}{131} = 109.93$$

Item	p_0	q_0	p_1	q_1	$p_0 q_0$	$p_0 q_1$	$p_1 q_0$	$p_1 q_1$
A	0.20	20	0.22	24	4.0	4.8	4.40	5.28
B	0.25	12	0.28	16	3.0	4.0	3.36	4.48
C	1.00	3	0.98	2	3.0	2.0	2.94	1.96
					10.0	10.8	10.70	11.72

Laspeyre price index for 20X1 $= \dfrac{\Sigma p_1 q_0}{\Sigma p_0 q_0} \times 100 = \dfrac{10.7}{10.0} \times 100 = 107.0$

Paasche price index for 20X1 $= \dfrac{\Sigma p_1 q_1}{\Sigma p_0 q_1} \times 100 = \dfrac{11.72}{10.8} \times 100 = 108.5$

Laspeyre quantity index for 20X1 $= \dfrac{\Sigma q_1 p_0}{\Sigma q_0 p_0} \times 100 = \dfrac{10.8}{10.0} \times 100 = 108.0$

Paasche quantity index for 20X1 $= \dfrac{\Sigma q_1 p_1}{\Sigma q_0 p_1} \times 100 = \dfrac{11.72}{10.70} \times 100 = 109.5$

Thus prices increased by 7% or 8.5% and quantities by 8% or 9.5% depending on which method of weighting is used.

Chapter 25
PERFORMANCE MEASUREMENT

To control an organisation and ensure it attains its goals we must pose and answer the following questions:

- What do we intend to happen?
- What has happened?
- Who is responsible for what has happened?
- How does what has happened compare with what we intended?
- What action is necessary?

To answer these questions each organisation needs:

- a responsibility accounting system
- an internal control system
- a selection of performance measures.

This chapter deals with these and looks at performance measurement in a range of organisations.

Objectives

By the time you have finished this chapter you should be able to:

- outline the essential features of responsibility accounting for various types of entity
- describe the various types of responsibility centre and the impact of these on management appraisal
- describe the range of management performance measures available for various types of entity
- calculate and explain the concepts of return on investment and residual income
- explain and give examples of appropriate non-monetary performance measures
- discuss the potential conflicts in the use of a measure for both business and management performance
- analyse the application of financial performance measures including cost, profit, return on capital employed
- assess and illustrate the measurement of profitability, activity and productivity
- discuss the measurement of quality and service
- identify areas of concern from information supplied and performance measures calculated
- describe the features of benchmarking and its application to performance appraisal.

1   Responsibility accounting

1.1   In a typical organisation, lower levels of management report on an area of the business to more senior managers. Each manager is in charge of a 'responsibility centre'.

DEFINITIONS

Responsibility centre is a segment of an organisation whose manager is accountable for a specified set of activities.

Responsibility accounting is a system where the plans or budgets for each responsibility centre are compared with the actual level achieved, and explanations are sought for any discrepancies.

A **responsibility centre** is a segment of an organisation whose manager is accountable for a specified set of activities.

Responsibility accounting is a system where the plans or budgets for each responsibility centre are compared with the actual level achieved, and explanations are sought for any discrepancies.

Management will need information concerning:

- cost units
- cost centres
- profit centres
- investment centres.

1.2   Cost units

DEFINITION

A **cost unit** is a unit of product or service in relation to which costs are ascertained.

A **cost unit** is a unit of product or service in relation to which costs are ascertained.

The ascertainment of the cost per cost unit is important for a variety of reasons, such as:

- making decisions about pricing, acceptance of orders, and so on
- measuring changes in costs and relative levels of efficiency
- inventory valuation for financial reporting
- planning future costs (budgeting and standard costs).

1.3   Cost centres

DEFINITION

A **cost centre** is a production or service location, function, activity or item of equipment whose costs may be attributed to cost units.

A **cost centre** is a production or service location, function, activity or item of equipment whose costs may be attributed to cost units.

In other words, it is a part of a business for which costs can be identified and then allocated to cost units. It might be a whole department (e.g. packaging) or just a sub-division (e.g. a few machines).

1.4   Profit centre

DEFINITION

A **profit centre** is a production or service location, function, activity or item of equipment whose costs and revenues can be ascertained.

A **profit centre** is a production or service location, function, activity or item of equipment whose costs and revenues can be ascertained.

A profit centre is similar to a cost centre but it also earns revenue and thus profits which can be identified separately.

1.5   Investment centre

DEFINITION

An **investment centre** is a production or service location, function, activity or item of equipment for which costs, revenues and investment can be ascertained.

An **investment centre** is a production or service location, function, activity or item of equipment for which costs, revenues and investment can be ascertained.

An investment centre is similar to a profit centre but the investment can be identified separately as well as costs and revenues.

The type of responsibility centre a manager is in charge of will affect his/her appraisal. For example, a manager of a cost centre will only be appraised on costs, a manager of a profit centre will be assessed on costs and revenues, and a manager of an investment centre will also be assessed on investments undertaken.

ACTIVITY 1

Suggest suitable cost units, cost centres, profit centres and investment centres for the following industry sectors.

(a)   Hotel and catering

(b)   Professional services (accountants, architects)

(c)   Manufacturing.

Feedback to this activity is at the end of the chapter.

2   Designing a responsibility accounting system

2.1   Controllable and uncontrollable costs

Performance reports should concentrate only on **controllable costs**. Controllable costs are those costs controllable by a particular manager in a given time period. Over a long enough time-span all costs are controllable by someone in the organisation. For example, factory rental may be fixed for a number of years but there may eventually come an opportunity to move to other premises. Such a cost, therefore, is controllable in the long term by a manager fairly high in the organisation structure. However, in the short term it is uncontrollable even by senior managers, and certainly uncontrollable by managers lower down the organisational hierarchy.

There is no clear-cut distinction between controllable and non-controllable costs for a given manager, who may in any case be exercising control jointly with another manager. The aim under a responsibility accounting system will be to assign and report on the cost to the person having primary responsibility. The most effective control is thereby achieved, since immediate action can be taken.

Some authorities would favour the alternative idea that reports should include all costs caused by a department, whether controllable or uncontrollable by the departmental manager. The idea here is that, even if he has no direct control, he might influence the manager who does have control. There is the danger of providing the manager with too much information and confusing him but, on the other hand, the uncontrollable element could be regarded as 'for information only', and in this way the manager obtains a fuller picture.

Example

An illustration of the two different approaches is provided by raw materials. The production manager will have control over usage, but not over price, when buying is done by a separate department. For this reason the price and usage variances are separated and, under the first approach, the production manager would be told only about the usage variance, a separate report being made to the purchasing manager about the price variance. The alternative argument is that if the production manager is also told about the price variance, he may attempt to persuade the purchasing manager to try alternative sources of supply.

What are the potential dangers of including uncontrollable costs in a performance report?

Feedback to this activity is at the end of the chapter.

2.2   The problem of dual responsibility

A common problem is that the responsibility for a particular cost or item is shared between two (or more) managers. For example, the responsibility for payroll costs may be shared between the personnel and production departments; material costs between purchasing and production departments; and so on. The reporting system should be designed so that the responsibility for performance achievements (i.e. better or worse than budget) is identified as that of a single manager.

The following guidelines may be applied:

When manager controls	Make responsible for
Quantity and price	All expenditure variances
Quantity but not price	Variances due to usage
Price but not quantity	Variances due to input prices
Neither quantity nor price	Nothing: the variances are uncontrollable from the point of view of that manager

2.3   Guidelines for reporting

There are several specific problems in relation to reporting which must be identified and dealt with.

Levels of reporting

The problem is how far down the management structure should responsibility centres be identified for reporting purposes? On the one hand, lower reporting levels encourage delegation and identify responsibility closer to the production process. On the other hand, more responsibility centres increase the number of reports and hence the cost of their production. One solution may be to combine small responsibility centres into groups (e.g. departments) for reporting purposes.

Frequency of reports and information to be reported

The frequency of reports should be linked to the purposes for which they are required. This may well mean a variety of reports being produced to different time-scales for different purposes, e.g. some control information will be required weekly, or even daily. However, comprehensive budget reports are only likely to be required monthly.

The related problem is the content of such reports. It has been suggested that in computerised information systems the problem is often too much, rather than too little, information. Generally, as reporting proceeds up the management pyramid, the breadth of the report should increase, and the detail should decrease.

3   Performance criteria

3.1   Design of the system

The managers of every organisation will need to develop their own set of performance measures to help them gain and retain competitive advantage. The set of measures they adopt will be affected by the interaction of three contingent variables:

- the competitive environment they face
- their chosen strategy, e.g. cost leadership or product differentiation
- the type of business they are running.

The design of the system is linked to these variables. The three steps are as follows:

1   The first stage is to determine the competitive environment that the organisation faces. If it is relatively turbulent and competitive (dynamic) the managers will need to build an interactive information system (by exception), focusing on strategic threats and uncertainties. Regular dialogue between top management and operating staff will facilitate organisational learning. If the conditions are stable, management can rely on delegated control of day-to-day operations to ensure sustained competitive success.

2   What is measured depends on strategic intentions. Where an organisation decides to differentiate itself in the market on the basis of service quality, then it should design measures to monitor and control the quality of the service. If the strategy is based on technology and innovation, then it should be measuring its performance in these areas relative to its competitors.

3   The third stage is to decide what type of business you are dealing with. Some measures may be feasible in one sector of the business, but not in others. Even when the strategy and what should be measured are known, it may not be that easy to see how to measure it.

The performance dimensions that are used also fall into distinct categories. Financial performance and competitiveness are set to measure the results of the organisation's strategy. All companies will wish to measure the results of their strategy. Innovation, quality measurements, resource utilisation and flexibility are measures of factors which determine competitive success and will vary between companies.

| ACTIVITY 3 | If an organisation is following a cost leadership strategy, what will their performance measurement focus on? |

Feedback to this activity is at the end of the chapter.

3.2   Performance measures

There is a large number of performance measures which may be used. These may be classified into various groups.

Quantitative and qualitative measures

Quantitative measures are those which may be expressed in numerical terms; examples include profit and market share.

Qualitative measures are those which cannot be expressed in numerical terms, but which may be supported by numerical data. For example quality may be evidenced by the number of complaints.

Monetary and non-monetary measures

Another classification distinguishes between monetary and non-monetary performance measures. Monetary measures are sometimes known as financial performance measures, and include turnover, profit, and return on capital employed.

Non-monetary performance measures include market share; capacity utilisation; labour turnover, etc. Monetary and non-monetary performance measures may be expressed either in absolute terms or relative to other measures. Index numbers may also be used to show trends over a period of time.

The areas of performance criteria, as we have already discussed, will vary. Some of the criteria, and the control and measurement used, are set out in the table below:

Area	Possible criteria
Financial performance	<ul><li>cost</li><li>profitability</li><li>liquidity</li><li>budget variance analysis</li><li>capital structure</li><li>market ratios</li><li>level of bad debts</li><li>return on capital employed</li></ul>
Competitiveness	<ul><li>sales growth by product or service</li><li>measures of customer base</li><li>relative market share and position</li></ul>
Activity	<ul><li>sales units</li><li>labour/machine hours</li><li>number of passengers carried</li><li>number of material requisitions serviced</li><li>number of accounts reconciled</li></ul> Whichever measurement is used it may be compared against a pre-set target.

Productivity	• efficiency measurements of resources planned against those consumed
	• measurements of resources available against those used
	• productivity measurements such as production per person or per hour or per shift
Quality of service	• quality measures in every unit
	• evaluate suppliers on the basis of quality
	• number of customer complaints received
	• number of new accounts lost or gained
	• rejections as a percentage of production or sales
Customer satisfaction	• speed of response to customer needs
	• informal listening by calling a certain number of customers each week
	• number of customer visits to the factory or workplace
	• number of factory and non-factory manager visits to customers
Quality of working life	• days absence
	• labour turnover
	• overtime
	• measures of job satisfaction
Innovation	• proportion of new products and services to old ones
	• new product or service sales levels

3.3 Responsiveness

A reduction in lead time can be achieved by addressing the problems that cause delays.

They include:

- order entry delays and errors
- wrong blueprints or specifications
- long set-up times and large lots
- high defect counts
- machines that break down
- operators who are not well trained
- supervisors who do not co-ordinate schedules
- suppliers that are not dependable
- long waits for inspectors or repair people
- long transport distances
- multiple handling steps
- stock record inaccuracies.

3.4 Quality

Quality is difficult to measure and control. In most companies, poor quality cost includes such items as manufacturing (or any other function's) rework, warranty costs, cost of repair or return of goods from suppliers and inspection costs. In service industries the quality of service is measured by customers' letters of complaint. This is not a very good measurement as it only measures those customers prepared to write and many customers either remain silent or take their custom elsewhere.

Rewards based on quality are a good measurement of success as everyone becomes involved in the measurement and control process. One of IBM's cable suppliers paid a premium for 0.0 to 0.2 percent defects; for a 0.21 to 0.3 percent defect level they knocked $2 off the price of a cable; for 0.31 percent and over, there was a $4 reduction. With the system in place, a defect rate that had averaged 0.11 percent for years rapidly dropped to 0.04 in 60 days – and stayed there.

3.5 Flexibility

Flexibility concerns the organisation's ability to react quickly to changing customer demands and the external environment. Global market segmentation, better-informed consumers, increasingly complex products and the rapid change in tastes and fashions mean that speed and flexibility of response are essential organisational characteristics.

Some ways of measuring and controlling flexibility as a criteria can include measuring:

- product/service introduction flexibility
- product/service mix flexibility
- volume flexibility
- delivery flexibility.

Flexibility in a service industry such as a travel agency could include measures of the average time taken for one assistant to respond to a customer's service request.

3.6 Efficiency and effectiveness

Efficiency is the ratio of output to input.

However, this ratio allows for 100% efficiency to be achieved by high output in relation to high input but the same result can be obtained where both input and output are low.

Effectiveness, according to Reddin, is 'the extent to which a manager achieves the output requirements of his or her position'.

This assumes that the outputs have been identified and made measurable.

Examples of differences between 'effective' managers and 'efficient' managers, are that efficient managers seek to solve problems and reduce costs, whereas effective managers seek to produce creative alternatives and increase profits. On this basis, the management activities of planning, organising, motivating and controlling are more concerned with efficiency rather than effectiveness.

3.7 Financial performance measures

The three main financial performance measures are:

- cost
- profit
- return on capital employed.

These correspond to the use of cost centres, profit centres and investment centres within a responsibility accounting system.

Cost may be measured in total or as a cost per unit of output. The two most commonly-used comparisons are against a pre-set target or as a comparison over time. If trend comparisons are to be made comparing costs over time it is important to recognise the cost behavioural effects of differing activity levels and the use of indices may make the information easier to understand.

Profit is often measured relative to turnover, though for trend comparisons an absolute measurement may be used. It should be remember that profit is a function of activity and is affected by the behavioural aspects of the underlying costs. When making comparisons with pre-set targets the effects of differing activity levels must be recognised.

DEFINITION

Efficiency is the ratio of output to input.

DEFINITION

Effectiveness 'the extent to which a manager achieves the output requirements of his or her position'.

KEY POINT

Main financial performance measures:
- cost
- profit
- return on capital employed.

KEY POINT

Return on capital employed =
$$\frac{\text{Profit}}{\text{Capital employed}} \times 100$$

Return on capital employed is a relative measure usually expressed as a percentage calculated by:

$$\text{Return on capital employed} = \frac{\text{Profit}}{\text{Capital employed}} \times 100$$

KEY POINT

Valuation bases:

- gross book value
- net book value
- replacement cost.

Capital employed is equal to net assets so the question is how should the net assets be valued? It is generally accepted that the value of working capital will be small relative to net assets so the problem is the valuation of fixed assets. Three valuation bases exist:

- gross book value
- net book value
- replacement cost.

Replacement cost is preferred because it represents the opportunity value of the investment. However, if replacement cost is to be used to value the assets, profits should be measured on an inflation-adjusted basis so as to be consistent.

4   Ratio analysis

One important means of assessing performance both of companies by outside observers and of divisions by senior management is by the use of assorted accounting ratios. The reason for this use of several ratios is the difficulty of getting a true picture of performance by using just one figure. The starting point for ratio analysis, the primary performance measure, is the return on capital employed (ROCE) or return on investment (ROI) which can then be split down into 'secondary ratios'. The two secondary ratios are the asset turnover ratio, which then leads to various liquidity ratios, and the net profit percentage, which can be investigated further by calculating additional profitability measures.

The whole process is best shown as a ratio pyramid or ratio tree.

4.1   Ratio pyramid

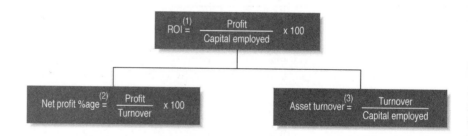

They are linked since $(1) = (2) \times (3)$.

After this there is no clear relationship although:

Net profit percentage can be investigated by finding:

$$\text{Gross profit percentage} = \frac{\text{Gross profit}}{\text{Turnover}} \times 100$$

and

$$\text{Operating ratio} = \frac{\text{Various expenses}}{\text{Turnover}} \times 100$$

Asset turnover can be investigated by finding:

$$\frac{\text{Turnover}}{\text{Fixed assets}} \quad \text{and} \quad \frac{\text{Turnover}}{\text{Net current assets}}$$

The first pair of ratios (or group of ratios) would require careful study if the net profit percentage indicated problems over profitability to determine whether this was due to an unduly low margin or poor control of overheads. The second pair of ratios would indicate whether sufficient sales were being generated and whether working capital was being sufficiently well controlled. If a problem was detected in this last area then various liquidity ratios would be found, such as:

$$\text{Current ratio} = \frac{\text{Current assets}}{\text{Current liabilities}}$$

$$\text{Quick ratio (Acid test ratio)} = \frac{\text{Quick assets (CAs} - \text{Stock)}}{\text{Current liabilities}}$$

$$\text{Debtors period} = \frac{\text{Debtors}}{\text{Daily credit sales}}$$

$$\text{Stock period} = \frac{\text{Stock}}{\text{Daily cost of sales}}$$

$$\text{Creditors period} = \frac{\text{Creditors}}{\text{Daily credit purchases}}$$

These ratios could be found using year-end figures or average figures. In some divisionalised companies some of these liquidity ratios are less important since the assets are managed centrally. Comparison would be made with group standards, other divisions, other periods and other firms in the same business.

5   Productivity measures

5.1   What is a productivity measure?

A **productivity measure** is a measure of the efficiency of an operation.

It relates the goods or services produced to the resources used to produce them. The most productive or efficient operation is one that produces the maximum output for any given set of resource inputs or alternatively uses the minimum inputs for any given quantity or quality of output.

5.2   Production and productivity

It is important to be able to distinguish between production and productivity.

Production is the quantity of goods or services that are produced. **Productivity** is a measure of how efficiently those goods or services have been produced.

Production levels are reasonably straightforward for management to control as they can be increased by working more hours or taking on more employees or decreased by cutting overtime or laying off employees. Production levels can also be increased by increasing productivity and vice versa.

Productivity however is perhaps more difficult for management to control as this can only be increased by producing more goods or services in a set period of time or alternatively reaching set production targets in a shorter period of time.

5.3   Types of productivity measures

Productivity measures are usually given in terms of labour efficiency. However the measures are not restricted to labour and can also be expressed in terms of other resource inputs of the organisation such as the machine hours used for production.

KEY POINT

Labour control ratios:

● production-volume ratio

● capacity ratio

● productivity or efficiency
ratio.

The productivity measures that are to be examined are productivity ratios, production per labour hour, production per employee, production per machine hour and production per machine.

Productivity is often analysed using three labour control ratios:

● production-volume ratio

● capacity ratio

● productivity or efficiency ratio.

Example

Suppose that the budgeted output for a period is 2,000 units and the budgeted time for the production of these units is 200 hours.

The actual output in the period is 2,300 units and the actual time worked by the labour force is 180 hours.

5.4   Production/volume ratio

The production/volume ratio assesses the overall production. Over 100% indicates that overall production is above planned levels and below 100% indicates a shortfall compared to plans.

The production/volume ratio is calculated as:

$$\frac{\text{Actual output measured in standard hours}}{\text{Budgeted production hours}} \times 100$$

$$\text{Standard hour} = \frac{2{,}000 \text{ units}}{200 \text{ hours}} = 10 \text{ units}$$

$$\text{Actual output measured in standard hours} = \frac{2{,}300 \text{ units}}{10 \text{ units}} = 230 \text{ standard hours}$$

$$\text{Production/volume ratio} = \frac{230}{200} = 115\% \ (2{,}300 \div 2{,}000)$$

This shows that production is 15% up on planned production levels.

5.5   Capacity ratio

KEY POINT

The **capacity ratio** provides
indications for worker capacity in
terms of the hours of working time
that have been possible in a
period.

The **capacity ratio** provides indications for worker capacity in terms of the hours of working time that have been possible in a period.

The capacity ratio is calculated as follows:

$$\text{Capacity ratio} = \frac{\text{Actual hours worked}}{\text{Budgeted hours}} \times 100$$

$$\text{Capacity ratio} = \frac{180 \text{ hours}}{200 \text{ hours}} = 90\%$$

Therefore this organisation had only 90% of the production hours anticipated available for production.

5.6   Efficiency ratio

KEY POINT

The **efficiency ratio** is a useful
indicator of productivity, with the
benchmark again being 100%.

The **efficiency ratio** is a useful indicator of productivity, with the benchmark again being 100%.

The efficiency ratio is calculated as follows:

$$\frac{\text{Actual output measured in standard hours}}{\text{Actual production hours}}$$

The efficiency ratio is often referred to as the productivity ratio:

$$\text{Efficiency ratio} = \frac{230}{180} \times 100\% = 127.78\%$$

This can be proved. The workers were expected to produce 10 units per hour, the standard hour. Therefore, in the 180 hours worked it would be expected that 1,800 units would be produced. In fact 2,300 units were produced. This is 27.78% more than anticipated (500/1,800).

5.7   Other productivity measures

In addition to the three measures shown, productivity can be measured by ratios such as:

- production per labour hour
- production per employee
- production per machine hour
- production per machine.

6   Cost per unit

If management is to have control of the operations of an organisation then it must be informed of all the facts that are necessary. One vital piece of information will be the cost of the products that the organisation makes.

This cost per product or cost per unit is necessary in order to make a large number of management decisions, such as determining the selling price of the product, assessing the profitability of the product and comparing the actual cost of the product to the standard or budgeted cost.

Cost per unit is therefore a vital piece of management information and a very important performance indicator.

KEY POINT

Cost per unit is a vital piece of management information and a very important performance indicator.

ACTIVITY 4

Given below are the standard costs and actual cost information for product Y.

Standard costs

10 kg of material G56 @ £4.50 per kg

3 hours of labour @ £5 per hour

Direct expenses of £2.00 per unit

Actual costs

During March 30,000 units of product Y were produced. The costs actually incurred were as follows:

	£'000
Direct materials	1,200
Direct labour	480
Direct expenses	80

Show the standard direct cost per unit and the actual direct cost per unit for March.

Feedback to this activity is at the end of the chapter.

7   The use of ratios

7.1   Advantages of ratios

The main advantage of the use of a ratio, such as return on investment (ROI), also known as return on capital employed (ROCE), is that it allows comparisons to be made with other operations of different sizes.

Generally one will set targets for performance measures, but occasionally all that is required of a segment of a business is that it improves on last year, or it tries to achieve an ROI that puts it in the top 25% of divisions, or its ROI is comparable with the best company in the same industrial sector. Such comparisons are possible despite the different sizes of the operations.

7.2   Disadvantages of ratios

The use of a relative measure, such as ROI, does have particular problems.

A division may be profitable with a high ROI, but if it is only a small part of the business it will have little effect on the overall profitability of the business.

It is possible to manipulate ROI figures in a manner not desirable in the eyes of senior management. What is required is for a business segment to improve ROI (profit ÷ capital employed) by aiming to increase profit with little extra capital employed. Some middle managers will seek to improve ROI by keeping capital employed as low as possible with little effect on profit if possible. The former policy is desirable, the latter not.

8   Performance measures in manufacturing

The performance measures used in manufacturing may be either qualitative or quantitative and will be different for various parts of the business, and for differing manufacturing environments. Some specific measures for these areas are discussed in the following paragraphs.

8.1   Performance measures and sales

Sales may be measured in absolute terms and compared with targets, but other measures may also be used to identify the success of the selling activity. These include:

● profitability by customer

● market share

● customer satisfaction

● orders as a percentage of quotations (i.e. what proportion of jobs tendered for are converted into actual sales orders).

Each of these may be supported by numerical values which can be compared against targets, and trends may be established from one period to another.

8.2   Performance measures and materials

In respect of performance there are three aspects to materials:

● purchase

● storage

● usage.

Each of these aspects must be monitored.

Purchasing performance may be measured using price variances, especially if planning and operating causes are separated.

Storage may be measured by considering:

- average stock levels
- stock losses
- number of stockouts.

Usage of materials may be monitored using:

- usage variances, analysed into planning and operating causes
- wastage rates
- rejection rates.

8.3   Performance measures and labour

KEY POINT

Labour measures:

- variance analysis
- idle time
- absenteeism
- labour turnover.

Traditional variance analysis may be used to identify performance against a target in terms of rate and efficiency variances, especially if planning and operating causes are separated.

In addition idle time and absenteeism should be measured; these may be indicators of employee morale which could also be measured qualitatively by management.

Labour turnover is another performance measure which should be used. Comparisons can be made on a trend basis. Where possible the reasons for leaving should be identified and analysed.

8.4   Performance measures and overhead

Many of the overhead costs incurred are fixed in nature, so the use of variances merely places an accounting value on the underlying cause.

It is important to measure the utilisation of assets, relative to the available capacity and to identify the cause of any differences, e.g. machine breakdown.

8.5   Performance measurement in specific order environments

Specific order environments include job, batch, and contract situations where items are made to specific customer requirements using common skills. However each item or job is different in its finished form because it is customer-specific.

The measures used may vary slightly between job, batch and contract environments but the general principles are the same.

KEY POINT

Specific order measures:

- time taken
- suppliers' performances.

Costs will be compared with estimates and any significant differences investigated to identify their cause. Where common tasks can be identified they may be the subject of standard times and costs which will allow traditional variance analysis to be used.

Time taken may also be compared with estimates and for more complex work (e.g. contracts) the use of network analysis may be appropriate.

Suppliers' performances on delivery, quality of supply and price should also be monitored as failures by suppliers may be a cause of any differences in cost/time performance of the organisation.

8.6   Performance measures in process environments

Process environments are those where homogeneous items are made and later sold from stock to customers who may not be identifiable at the time of production. Typically there are a limited number of items which are made, often from a continuous process.

KEY POINT

Process measures:

- output per input unit
- output per shift
- wastage per good output unit.

It is easy in such environments to set targets against which actual performance can be measured because the output may be clearly defined.

Cost may be controlled against a standard using traditional variance analysis.

Activity and the quality of output may be measured using:

- output per input unit (yield)
- output per shift
- wastage per good output unit.

9   Service industries

Service environments exist to provide a service to a variety of customers. Some of such services (e.g. accountancy/law) are specific to a particular client's needs and are therefore similar to the jobbing environment explained earlier. Other services (e.g. retailing and transport) are not customer-specific.

The four key differences between the products of service industries and those of manufacturing are as follows:

- intangibility – the output being a performance rather than tangible goods
- heterogeneity – the variability in standard of output performance due to the heavy reliance on human input
- simultaneity of production and consumption – precluding advance verification of specification or quality
- perishability – the inability to carry stocks of the product to cover unexpectedly high demand.

These differences pose problems in measuring and controlling performance. A well-defined set of performance measures, both financial and non-financial, is essential.

9.1   Measures of financial performance in service industries

KEY POINT

Typical ratios for a service company:

- turnover per product group
- turnover per 'principal' in say a management consultancy
- % staff costs to turnover
- % space costs to turnover
- % training costs to turnover
- % net profit
- current ratio
- quick asset ratio
- % market share
- % market share increase year by year.

Conventional financial analysis distinguishes four types of ratio: profitability, liquidity, capital structure and market ratios. Analysis of a company's performance using accounting ratios involves comparisons with past trends and/or competitors' ratios. As is well known, such time-series and cross-sectional analyses are problematical. Typical ratios for a service company could include any or all of the following:

- turnover per product group
- turnover per 'principal' in say a management consultancy
- % staff costs to turnover
- % space costs to turnover
- % training costs to turnover
- % net profit
- current ratio
- quick asset ratio
- % market share
- % market share increase year by year.

The 'untraceability' of common costs to product outputs and the high level of stepped fixed costs will also make the use of financial ratios problematical.

We shall now consider performance measurement in three service industries.

9.2   Performance measures in professional services

Accountancy and law are two examples of professional services. Such services tend to be specific to a client's needs, though the service provided is based on common skills and knowledge.

Whilst perishability may not be quite so relevant to professional services (workloads are generally reasonably well in advance and can be scheduled) the other three service characteristics will pose problems. The success of such a business can depend upon the performances of a few key personnel; the ultimate measurement of which will be customer satisfaction, which will directly impact upon financial performance. However, control systems should operate such that poor performance is identified prior to the point of losing important clients!

Performance may be measured in quantitative terms by considering chargeable time as a proportion of time available.

Qualitative measures centre around client satisfaction and the ability to adapt to clients' needs.

9.3   Performance measures in retail services

Retail services sell products to the general public. Their performance should therefore be measured in terms of profitability and customer satisfaction.

It is a business that could perhaps be said to be between manufacturing and pure service. It deals with tangible goods, the quality of which can be checked in advance and which can be stocked; however, the success of a retail business may also depend upon the service provided by the personnel involved (cashiers, shop assistants, store managers, etc.).

The balance of emphasis between goods and service-related performance measures should be dictated by the relative importance placed upon these by the customer. For example, the quality of service provided by individual employees is unlikely to have the same impact on customer spending in large supermarkets as it would in the smaller, more personal shops.

Profitability can be measured in total, per product line, and per square metre of floor space. These may be compared with industry averages and as trends over time.

Customer satisfaction can be measured by monitoring the number of customer complaints and returns. Returns may be caused by poor stock control.

Stock control should be monitored by the rate of stock turnover, and the value and volume of stock losses. These losses should be analysed between perished and obsolete (out-of-date) stocks.

9.4   Performance measures in transport operations

Transport operations provide a service to convey goods or passengers from one place to another.

To some extent, the service output of a transport business is more easily standardised and tangibly measured than other service businesses. The objective is clear – to get the goods or passengers intact from A to B within a given time at minimum cost.

Cost measures will inevitably play a large part in the performance measure system, along with timing targets (particularly for public transport systems – the introduction of 'Passenger Charters' directly penalises operations that don't meet specified timetable criteria).

The service provided by personnel will probably be more important to passenger transport services than those relating to goods, although the customers may, in fact, have less choice between suppliers and thus be less able to reflect their satisfaction or otherwise in financial performance.

Costs may be analysed into standing (fixed) costs and running (variable) costs and those may be compared with pre-set targets. Costs per unit may also be calculated and trends established over time.

Other measures which may be used include the frequency of late arrival and the extent of the lateness involved. These factors will impact on customer satisfaction.

9.5   Internal quality measurement in service industries

Inspection and monitoring of the inputs to the service process is important for all organisations. The quality of the solicitors in a practice or the number and grades of staff available in a consultancy organisation are crucial to the provision of service quality. Multibroadcast measure the number of shop refits per month and BAA monitor the availability and condition of equipment and facilities.

Many service companies use internal mechanisms to measure service quality during the process of service delivery. Multibroadcast use managers to formally inspect the premises, goods and service provided by the staff using detailed checklists covering, for example, the correct pricing of items, correct layout of displays and attitude of staff to the customers. BAA have advanced systems to monitor equipment faults and the terminal managers are expected to report any problems they see.

The quality of the service may be measured after the event, that is, by measuring the results by outputs of the service. For example, Multibroadcast measure the number of service calls they have to make for each of their products, in order to assess product reliability.

9.6   Service quality measures – key points

- Providing a high level of service quality may be a source of competitive advantage.
- Achieving high service quality means ensuring all the factors of the service package meet customer requirements.
- There are twelve factors of service quality: reliability, responsiveness, aesthetics, appearance, cleanliness, tidiness, comfort, friendliness, communication, courtesy, competence, access, availability and security.
- The relative importance of the factors will vary from company to company and between customers.
- Service quality can be measured using external customer satisfaction measures and internal organisational quality systems at different stages of the service process.
- Both internal and external measures of the service quality factors are required to facilitate target setting, the tracking of the costs of changing quality targets and the linking of pay to quality performance.
- Quality control systems vary between professional, service shop and mass service organisations.

10   Performance measures in non-profit making organisations

Non-profit making organisations often have as one of their objectives the concept of value for money. Thus it is important to measure cost and performance against targets to establish whether the objective is being met.

10.1 Performance measures in education

Education is an example of a non-profit-making organisation whose objectives include the provision of a value-for-money service.

The costs of the service must be compared against budgets but other performance indicators may be used in total for the establishment and within each faculty/department. These measures include the following:

Overall

- numbers of students
- amount of research funding received
- proportion of successful students (by grade)
- quality of teaching
- number of publications by staff.

Faculty

- cost per student
- staff : student ratios
- availability of learning resources
- number of courses available.

11 Benchmarking

As mentioned in the particular context of service companies above, comparison of an organisation's performance with that of others will be an important part of the overall performance measurement system. Benchmarking is the increasingly popular practice of identifying an appropriate organisation whose performance may be used as a comparator, or benchmark, for this purpose. An inter-firm comparison helps to put the company's resources and performance into perspective and reflects the fact that it is the relative position of a company which matters in assessing its capabilities. The performance of different organisations, subsidiaries or investment centres can be compared ('benchmarked') by calculating suitable financial ratios for each of them to ascertain which are better or worse than the average.

11.1 Obtaining information for benchmarking

Benchmarking against competitors involves the gathering of a range of information about them. Financial information will generally be reasonably easy to obtain, from published accounts, financial press etc. Some product information may be obtained by acquiring their products and examining them in detail to ascertain the components used and their construction ('reverse engineering'). Literature will also be available in the form of brochures, trade journals, etc.

However, most non-financial information, concerning competitors' processes, customer and supplier relationships, customer satisfaction etc. will not be so readily available.

To overcome this problem, benchmarking exercises are generally carried out with organisations taken from within the same group of companies (intra-group benchmarking) or from similar but non-competing industries (inter-industry benchmarking).

To find out the level of investment in fixed assets of competitors, the business can use physical observation, information from trade press or trade association announcements, supplier press releases as well as their externally published financial statements, to build a clear picture of the relative scale, capacity, age and cost for each competitor. The method of operating these assets, in terms of hours and shift patterns, can be established by observation, discussions with suppliers and customers or by asking existing or ex-employees of the particular competitor. If the method of operating can be ascertained it should enable a combination of internal personnel management and industrial engineering managers to work out the likely relative differences in labour costs. The rates of pay and conditions can generally be found with reference to nationally-negotiated agreements, local and national press advertising for employees, trade and employment associations and recruitment consultants. When this cost is used alongside an intelligent assessment of how many employees would be needed by the competitor in each area, given their equipment etc. a good idea of the labour costs can be obtained.

Another difference which should be noted is the nature of the competitors' costs as well as their relative levels. Where a competitor has a lower level of committed fixed costs, e.g. lower fixed labour costs due to a larger proportion of temporary workers, it may be able to respond more quickly to a downturn in demand by rapidly laying off the temporary staff. Equally, in a tight labour market and with rising sales, it may have to increase its pay levels to attract new workers.

In some industries, one part of the competitor analysis is surprisingly direct. Each new competitive product is purchased on a regular basis and then systematically taken apart, so that each component can be identified as well as the processes used to put the parts together. The respective areas of the business will then assess the costs associated with each element so that a complete product cost can be found for the competitive product.

A comparison of similar value activities, e.g. cost structures, between organisations is useful when the strategic context is taken into consideration. For example, a straight comparison of resource deployment between two competitive organisations may reveal quite different situations in the labour cost as a percentage of the total cost. The conclusions drawn from this, however, depend upon circumstances. If the firms are competing largely on the basis of price, then differentials in these costs could be crucial. In contrast, the additional use of labour by one organisation may be an essential support for the special services provided which differentiate that organisation from its competitors.

One danger of inter-firm analysis is that the company may overlook the fact that the whole industry is performing badly, and is losing out competitively to other countries with better resources or even other industries which can satisfy customers' needs in different ways. Therefore, if an industry comparison is performed it should make some assessment of how the resources utilisation compares with other countries and industries. This can be done by obtaining a measurement of stock turnover or yield from raw materials.

Example of research and development indices

A typical analysis of the research and development expenditure of UK companies could take the following approach. Comparisons could be made with previous years, between industry sectors and also with international competitors. Some examples of the data that might result are as follows:

(a) **Change on previous year**

	% increase in spend
All industry	12
Aerospace	27
Chemicals	7
Food	2
Leisure	46
Service industries	5

(b) **Inter-industry comparisons**

	Research and development per employee (£'000s)	Research and development / sales (%)
Aerospace	2.32	3.33
Chemicals	2.72	3.29
Food	1.01	1.22
Leisure	0.22	0.37
Service industries	2.59	2.65

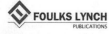

(c)   **International comparisons of research and development per employee (£'000s)**

	UK	USA	Germany
All industry	1.53	3.73	4.32
Aerospace	2.34	2.42	17.48
Chemicals	3.02	4.96	5.57
Leisure	0.21	4.85	n/a
Service industries	5.82	n/a	1.89

(d)   **International comparisons of research and development/sales (%)**

	UK	USA	Germany	Japan
All industry	1.69	3.80	5.09	3.71
Aerospace	3.34	4.20	23.78	n/a
Chemicals	3.56	4.50	5.79	3.88
Leisure	0.36	6.80	n/a	3.62
Service industries	4.51	n/a	2.75	n/a

The evidence seems to be that UK firms are not doing enough to match the efforts of their main competitors in other countries.

11.2 Intra-group benchmarking

Intra-group benchmarking involves the co-operation between companies within a group. Divisions or other operating units within the group companies with similar products and practices pool information about their processes. A centrally-appointed working party will analyse the information and identify the best aspects from each company. These will then be developed into a group policy.

11.3 Inter-industry benchmarking

Inter-industry benchmarking involves co-operation between non-competing businesses with similar processes, supplier and customer bases. For example, a book printer/publisher may liase with an audio product manufacturer/distributor (CDs, tapes, etc). Both will benefit from information obtained from a benchmarking relationship, without the danger of one gaining competitive advantage over the other, as may occur with intra-group benchmarking.

12   Management performance measures

12.1 Methods

A range of methods are available for assessing the performance of managers and the divisions that they run. The most common are listed below:

- return on investment (ROI)
- residual income (RI)
- variance analysis
- ratio analysis
- other management ratios – under this heading would come contribution per key factor and sales per employee or square foot as well as industry-specific ratios such as transport costs per mile, brewing costs per barrel, overheads per chargeable hour, etc.
- other information – such as staff turnover, market share, new customers gained, innovative products or services developed.

Whilst it is common to focus on one key measure of performance, it is important to keep an eye on, and stress the relevance of, a range of measures in order that performance in its widest sense is assessed.

12.2 Points on performance measures

The information system and reports that a company produces on manager and divisional performance should follow three simple principles.

- **Timeliness** – any report should be produced sufficiently quickly after the end of an accounting period (week, month, quarter) to allow corrective action to be taken on any unsatisfactory performance. There is a balance to maintain here between the speed with which information is produced, the accuracy of that information and the cost of producing the figures.

- **Goal congruence** – the performance measures used, the assessment criteria, should not encourage divisional managers to make decisions which shows their divisions performing well against the criteria set, but adopting strategies which are against the well-being of the company as a whole. An example might be a sales department that is judged on total volume of sales made irrespective of the price charged or the credit-worthiness of the customers.

- **Controllability** – the important measure of divisional performance will be linked to profit but care has to be taken in deciding how that profit is calculated. Managers should only be judged on those factors they can control.

12.3 Divisional v managerial performance

The main board of a divisionalised company will wish to assess two aspects of performance.

- the personal performance of the divisional manager
- the economic performance of the manager's divisions.

The type of measures used and the way in which they are evaluated will vary according to who or what is being assessed.

An organisation will compare the performance of divisions and set targets for managers, but this will have to be done with caution. Targets set should take into account:

- the difficulty of the economic environment in which a division is operating
- the motivational value of tough or lenient targets for the divisional manager concerned.

Added to the difficulty or leniency of targets, the question must be asked of profit-based measures, 'which profit to use?' To answer this question the pro-forma below shows a profit and loss account (section of a performance report) for a division.

	£'000	£'000
Outside sales		X
Internal transfers		X
		X
Variable cost of goods sold and transferred	(X)	
Other variable divisional costs	(X)	
		(X)
Contribution		X
Depreciation on controllable fixed assets	(X)	
Other controllable fixed costs	(X)	
		(X)
Controllable operating profit (1)		X
Interest on controllable investment		(X)
Controllable residual income before tax (2)		X
Non controllable divisional fixed costs	(X)	
Apportioned head office costs	(X)	
Interest on non-controllable investment	(X)	
		(X)
Net residual income before tax (3)		X

Notice the following features of this statement:

- Absence of tax charges – it is generally felt that the tax charge of a company cannot be controlled at divisional level and therefore any profit-based measures should use pre-tax profits.

- Inclusion of interest charges – this is a contentious issue and is discussed further when explaining the two main measures ROI and RI.

- Which profit? – A divisional manager's performance should be assessed by reference to figures (1) or (2) whereas the division, which received the benefits from head-office costs and other non-controllable elements even if the manager cannot influence them, should be assessed by reference to figure (3).

12.4 Return on investment (ROI)

Return on investment (ROI), or return on capital employed, is calculated for an investment centre for a particular period as follows:

$$ROI = \frac{\text{Earnings before interest and tax}}{\text{Capital employed}} \times 100$$

If assessing the performance of a manager, the earnings figure should be controllable operating profit and capital employed should be controllable investment. When assessing a division's performance costs and assets that are not controllable at divisional level could be included, although all interest costs are usually excluded. This is very similar to the return on capital employed (ROCE) traditionally used to analyse capital investment projects; the only difference is that here the profits from all projects for a single year are compared to the book value of all investments, whereas in investment appraisal the profits of a single investment project over the several years of that investment's life are compared to the book value of that one single investment.

Advantages of ROI

- As a relative measure it enables comparisons to be made with divisions or companies of different sizes. It could be argued that it is particularly appropriate for profit centres rather than investment centres since the former are not in a position to increase overall profit by undertaking further capital investments.

- It is used externally and is well understood by users of accounts.

- The primary ratio splits down into secondary ratios for more detailed analysis as mentioned above and discussed further later.

- ROI forces managers to make good use of existing capital resources and focuses attention on them, particularly when funds for further investment are limited.

- The nature of the measure is such that it can clearly be improved not just by increasing profit but by reducing capital employed; it therefore encourages reduction in the level of assets such as obsolete equipment and excessive working capital.

Disadvantages of ROI

The disadvantages fall into two categories: those that are problems common to *both* ROI and RI; and those that are specific to ROI.

Specific disadvantages

- Disincentive to invest – a divisional manager will not wish to make an investment which provides an adequate return as far as the overall company is concerned if it reduces the division's current ROI. By the same token existing assets may be sold if, by doing so, ROI is improved even though those assets are generating a reasonable profit.

- ROI improves with age – on the other side of the coin most conventional depreciation methods will result in ROI improving with the age of an asset, being

unsatisfactory initially then improving as the net book value of assets improves. This might encourage divisions hanging on to old assets and again deter them from investing in new ones.

- Corporate objectives of maximising total shareholders' wealth or the total profit of the company are not achieved by making decisions on the basis of ROI. In this way, as a relative measure, it can be compared to the internal rate of return whose use is also dysfunctional.

General problems

Whether it be ROI or RI that are used, there are certain problems common to both measures.

- Calculation of profit – apart from issues such as its controllability mentioned earlier, there is some scope, even within the strictures of a group accounting policy, for some variation in treatment of depreciation. Also the need to increase profit may lead to cutting down on discretionary costs such as training, advertising and maintenance which, whilst improving short-term profit figures, will jeopardise the long-term future of a business. Standards for these should be set and monitored.

- Asset measurement – again group policies should ensure a consistent treatment, but comparison is difficult when some divisions buy and some lease assets. Thought has to be given to the treatment of permanent bank overdrafts; are these current liabilities or a source of finance?

- Conflict with investment decisions – the performance of a division will be influenced by investment decisions that it makes; however those decisions should be made on the basis of NPV calculations, whereas the subsequent performance of the division is assessed by a different criterion. Clearly there is likely to be a problem when a long-term investment decision is accepted, but the short-term effect on profit is detrimental.

ACTIVITY 5

The Arcadia division of Botten Ltd currently has an investment base of £2.4m and annual profits of £0.48m. It is considering the following three investments, funds for which will be supplied by the company.

Project	A	B	C
Initial outlay (£'000)	1,400	600	400
Annual earnings (£'000)	350	200	88

You are required to find the current ROI of the Arcadia division, the ROI of each investment and the ROI of Arcadia with each of the three additional investments added to current earnings in turn.

Feedback to this activity is at the end of the chapter.

ACTIVITY 6

McKinnon Ltd sets up a new division in Blair Atholl investing £800,000 in fixed assets with an anticipated useful life of 10 years and no scrap value. Annual profits before depreciation are expected to be a steady £200,000.

You are required to calculate the division's ROI for its first three years by expressing annual (post-depreciation) profits as a percentage of the book value of assets at the start of each year.

Feedback to this activity is at the end of the chapter.

13   Residual income (RI)

In view of the disadvantages of ROI, particularly its tendency to induce under-investment, most management authors recommend that the performance of investment centres is assessed by calculating an absolute measure of profitability and residual income as follows:

RI = Controllable profit – Imputed interest charge on controllable divisional investment

The two figures shown in the earlier profit and loss account were residual income figures; one (with controllable profit and controllable investment) being used to assess a manager's performance, the other (with all costs included) being used to assess the performance of the division.

13.1   Advantages of RI

Residual income overcomes many of the disadvantages of ROI.

- It reduces the problem of under investing or failing to accept projects with ROIs greater than the group target but less than the division's current ROI.

- As a consequence it is more consistent with the objective of maximising the total profitability of the group.

- It is possible to use different rates of interest for different types of asset.

- The cost of financing a division is brought home to divisional managers.

However, it will suffer from the same problems associated with profit and asset measurement, and potential conflict with NPV investment decisions, as the ROI.

Despite these advantages, and that there are few significant disadvantages that are specific to RI apart from the difficulty of comparison with different sized enterprises, it is not as widely used as ROI.

ACTIVITY 7

Division Z has the following financial performance:

Operating profit	£40,000
Operating assets	£150,000
Cost of borrowing	10%

Would the division wish to accept a new possible investment costing £10,000 which would earn profit of £2,000 pa if the evaluation was on the basis of

(a)   ROI?

(b)   Residual income?

Feedback to this activity is at the end of the chapter.

14   Behavioural implications of performance measures

14.1   Measuring staff performance

The purpose of providing targets and measuring performance is often intended to motivate staff to achieve those targets, but this will only be achieved through involvement and the development of goal congruence. Staff may well see the measurement of performance as a policing device particularly if it is used to assess their personal performance rather than that of the unit they manage.

It must be remembered that managerial performance depends on a number of factors; sometimes good results will occur despite poor management whereas in other areas average results will only occur due to very good management.

14.2 Toughness of targets

A performance measure (monthly profit, weekly output, even something as straight forward as the time taken to reply to a customer or client enquiry) needs to be accepted by the manager or member of staff concerned. If that person feels that the target profit or target output level is too tough then they will be demotivated.

By the same token, if the required standard is too easy they may relax down to the level set as a target. It is suggested by some authors that a target should be set that the manager or member of staff can aspire to, as such it is likely to be slightly tougher than they can actually achieve.

This leaves two problems. How can that optimal standard that achieves maximum performance be identified? What is to be done when, inevitably, the target isn't quite met?

14.3 Budget pressure

Much has been written about the stress put on managers to 'perform'. The existence of, say, a target profit will add to that pressure. This approach to management and performance evaluation has been described as a 'budget constrained' style. One way to reduce the budget pressure is by the use of several performance measures. A manager can then say: 'I haven't hit my target profit, but I have recruited my required number of new customers and have kept staff turnover down to the required level'.

14.4 'Short-termism'

In order to achieve cost savings there are a limited number of things that a manager can do easily. One of these is to cut back on discretionary costs such as entertaining, advertising, training, maintenance. All these cuts will produce a short-term profit improvement; the problem comes with long-term profitability. Cut advertising and future sales may fall, cut training and staff may leave or become less efficient, cut maintenance and plant and machinery will become less productive. Measures are needed to ensure adequate levels of training and maintenance.

14.5 Inter-divisional competitiveness

When performance measures are used there needs to be some incentive to achieve given targets. This may be bonuses, it may be promotion. However, this can have 'dysfunctional' results (sub-optimal results, counter-productive outcomes). Managers may make decisions that make life difficult for other managers. This may simply be a purchasing department buying cheap material making life difficult for a production department. It may involve coercing staff to leave one department and work for another. Managers and staff need to be aware of the overall good of the company.

14.6 Controllability and responsibility

It is clearly desirable that managers' performance should only be assessed by reference to costs or other factors that are under their control. It is worth pointing out two issues here. First, that fewer costs are controllable in the short run than in the longer term. For instance, if an insurance premium is too high, a remedy could be to change insurance companies, but this would involve a penalty if the change took place mid year. The second issue is that of joint responsibility for costs. The classic example being total material cost, responsibility being shared between the purchasing and production managers.

14.7 Goal congruence

Any performance measure should attempt to achieve goal congruence. An example of an inappropriately-thought-out measure would be a sales manager whose performance is assessed purely on the basis of the sales revenue achieved or, worse still, on the number of items sold.

KEY POINT

If the manager feels that the target profit or target output level is too tough then they will be demotivated.

If the required standard is too easy they may relax down to the level set as a target.

KEY POINT

One way to reduce the budget pressure is by the use of several performance measures.

KEY POINT

Measures are needed to ensure adequate levels of training and maintenance.

KEY POINT

When performance measures are used there needs to be some incentive to achieve given targets but managers and staff need to be aware of the overall good of the company.

KEY POINT

Considerations in setting performance measures: toughness of targets, budget pressure, short-termism, inter-divisional competitiveness, controllability and responsibility, and needing to achieve goal congruence.

On the face of it, this would seem an excellent performance measure for a sales manager until it was found that the manager was making sales at drastically reduced prices resulting in items being sold at a loss. There must be 'strings' attached – only sell at standard prices. Even so there are potential problems , for example, if it were then discovered that the customers for the sales refused to pay, being far from credit-worthy organisations. More strings required – no bonus till the cash is received from debtors.

Important considerations in setting performance measures include: toughness of targets, budget pressure, short-termism, inter-divisional competitiveness, controllability and responsibility, and needing to achieve goal congruence.

Conclusion

This chapter has explained the features of responsibility accounting and the factors to be considered when designing a responsibility accounting system.

Performance measures were then considered that may be used in different industries and organisations.

SELF-TEST
QUESTIONS

Responsibility accounting

1   What is responsibility accounting? (1.1)

Designing a responsibility accounting system

2   Why is it important to distinguish controllable costs and uncontrollable costs? (2.1)

Performance criteria

3   Identify seven different areas of performance measures relevant to a business. (3.2)

Productivity measures

4   What is a productivity measure? (5.1)

Performance measures in manufacturing

5   Distinguish between quantitative and qualitative performance measures. (8.1 – 8.6)

Service industries

6   Explain the use of performance measures in service environments. (9.1 – 9.6)

Benchmarking

7   What is meant by benchmarking? (11.1)

Management performance measures

8   Define return on investment (ROI). (12.4)

Residual income

9   Define residual income. (13)

Behavioural implications

10   Explain the behavioural implications of using performance measures. (14.1 – 14.7)

Theta Ltd

The best preparation of examination questions and for application of your knowledge in practice is often to tackle a larger question which looks at several factors surrounding an idea – such an example is the following question. Do attempt this question – it will help consolidate your knowledge in this area – but do remember to give yourself extra time.

Theta Ltd compares the performance of its subsidiaries by return on investment (ROI) using the following formula:

Profit

- Depreciation is calculated on a straight-line basis.
- Losses on sale of assets are charged against profit in the year of the sale.

Capital employed

- Net current assets, at the average value throughout the year.
- Fixed assets, at original cost less accumulated depreciation as at the end of the year.

Theta Ltd, whose cost of capital is 14% per annum, is considering acquiring Alpha Ltd, whose performance has been calculated on a similar basis to that shown above except that fixed assets are valued at original cost.

During the past year, apart from normal trading, Alpha Ltd was involved in the following separate transactions:

(A) It bought equipment on 1 November 20X4 (the start of its financial year) at a cost of £120,000. Resulting savings were £35,000 for the year; these are expected to continue at that level throughout the six years' expected life of the asset after which it will have no scrap value.

(B) On 1 November 20X4 it sold a piece of equipment that had cost £200,000 when bought exactly three years earlier. The expected life was four years, with no scrap value. This equipment had been making a contribution to profit of £30,000 per annum before depreciation and realised £20,000 on sale.

(C) It negotiated a bank overdraft of £20,000 for the year to take advantage of quick payment discounts offered by creditors; this reduced costs by £4,000 per annum.

(D) To improve liquidity, it reduced stocks by an average of £25,000 throughout the year. This resulted in reduced sales with a reduction of £6,000 per annum contribution.

The financial position of Alpha Ltd for the year from 1 November 20X4 to 31 October 20X5, excluding the outcomes of transactions (A) to (D) above, was:

	£'000
Profit for the year	225
Fixed assets	
Original cost	1,000
Accumulated depreciation	475
Net current assets (average for the year)	250

Calculate the ROI of Alpha Ltd using its present basis of calculation:

(i) if none of the transactions (A) to (D) had taken place

(ii) if transaction (A) had taken place but not (B), (C) or (D)

(iii) if transaction (B) had taken place but not (A), (C) or (D)

(iv) if transaction (C) had taken place but not (A), (B) or (D)

(v) if transaction (D) had taken place but not (A), (B) or (C).

Taxation is to be ignored.   **(10 marks)**

For the answer to this question, see the 'Answers' section at the end of the book.

FEEDBACK TO ACTIVITY 1

	(a)	(b)	(c)
Cost units	Room or Meal	Chargeable hour	Widget
Cost centres	Housekeeping	Library	Assembly
	Reception	Word-processing	Machining
	Kitchen	Maintenance	Maintenance
	Administration	Administration	Administration
Revenue centres	Room	Audit	Shops
	Meal	Accountancy	Showrooms
		Taxation	
Investment centres	Hotels	Area offices	Factories
			Shops
			Showrooms

FEEDBACK TO ACTIVITY 2

The dangers of including uncontrollable costs in a performance report are as follows:

(a) Managers might be demotivated if their performance is apparently affected by costs over which they have no influence.

(b) Uncontrollable cost information can divert managers' attention away from what they actually are responsible for.

(c) The manager who is responsible for the costs in question might feel that they are not his or her responsibility as they are reported elsewhere.

FEEDBACK TO ACTIVITY 3

Cost leaders will tend to focus on measuring their resource utilisation and controlling costs along the value chain.

FEEDBACK TO ACTIVITY 4

Standard direct cost per unit

	£
Direct materials 10kg × £4.50	45.00
Direct labour 3 hours × £5	15.00
Direct expenses	2.00
	62.00

Actual direct cost per unit

$$= \frac{\text{Actual total direct costs}}{\text{Number of units produced}}$$

$$= \frac{£1{,}200{,}000 + £480{,}000 + £80{,}000}{30{,}000 \text{ units}} = \frac{£1{,}760{,}000}{30{,}000 \text{ units}} = £58.67$$

The standard direct cost per unit was £62.00 and the actual direct cost per unit for March was £58.67.

FOULKS LYNCH
PUBLICATIONS

Return on investment, $\text{ROI} = \dfrac{\text{Earnings}}{\text{Capital investment}} \times 100$

(a) **Current position**

$\text{ROI} = \dfrac{480}{2,400} \times 100 = 20\%$

(b) **Additional investments**

A: $\text{ROI} = \dfrac{350}{1,400} \times 100 = 25\%$

B: $\text{ROI} = \dfrac{200}{600} \times 100 = 33\tfrac{1}{3}\%$

C: $\text{ROI} = \dfrac{88}{400} \times 100 = 22\%$

(c) **Potential position**

Arcadia + A: $\text{ROI} = \dfrac{830}{3,800} \times 100 = 21.8\%$

Arcadia + B: $\text{ROI} = \dfrac{680}{3,000} \times 100 = 22.7\%$

Arcadia + C: $\text{ROI} = \dfrac{568}{2,800} \times 100 = 20.3\%$

Note that although all three projects have returns that are greater then the current 20%, once project B is accepted the ROI rises to 22.7% making C look less attractive. It would be worth Arcadia's while accepting projects A and B, if this were possible since this would raise its ROI to: $1,030 \div 4,400 = 23.4\%$.

FEEDBACK TO ACTIVITY 6

$$\text{ROI} = \frac{\text{Earnings before interest and tax (but after depreciation)}}{\text{Capital employed (book value at start of year)}} \times 100$$

Year	Opening book value of assets £'000	Annual depreciation £'000	Closing book value of assets £'000	Pre-dep'n profits £'000	Post-dep'n profits £'000	ROI %
1	800	80	720	200	120	$\frac{120}{800} = 15\%$
2	720	80	640	200	120	$\frac{120}{720} = 17\%$
3	640	80	560	200	120	$\frac{120}{640} = 19\%$

Note that ROI increases, despite no increase in annual profits, merely as a result of the book value of assets falling. It would be more appropriate to use the average book value of assets, although the use of opening book values is common.

FEEDBACK TO ACTIVITY 7

(a)   Current ROI = $\frac{£40,000}{£150,000}$ = 26.7%

If the investment is accepted, revised ROI = $\frac{£42,000}{£160,000}$ = 26.3%

i.e. reject the project

(b)   Current RI = £40,000 − (10% × £150,000) = £25,000

Revised RI = £42,000 − (10% × £160,000) = £26,000

i.e. accept the project

Note here is a classic example of ROI giving the wrong conclusion in that a project that was worthwhile as far as the company was concerned is rejected since it reduces the division's current ROI.

FOULKS LYNCH
PUBLICATIONS

Chapter 26

COSTS AND DECISION-MAKING

In the preceding chapters we have looked at the use of costing techniques and standard costs, for product costing, pricing and performance reporting. This chapter looks at the principles to be applied in making decisions regarding production levels, mixes and one-off situations, such as proposals to accept special orders, to shut down parts of the business, etc. Again much of this material should be familiar to you but it has been included because it can be relevant to your understanding of the limiations of costing systems as a source of information for decision-making.

Objectives

By the time you have finished this chapter you should be able to do the following:

- describe and distinguish between relevant and non-relevant costs

- apply and evaluate limiting factor analysis

- evaluate make or buy problems, shutdown decisions, additional shift decisions and overtime, accepting or rejecting special orders, and further processing

- describe and apply cost-volume-profit analysis

- describe and evaluate different product pricing approaches.

1 Information for decision-making

1.1 The decision-making process

There are four basic stages in making a decision.

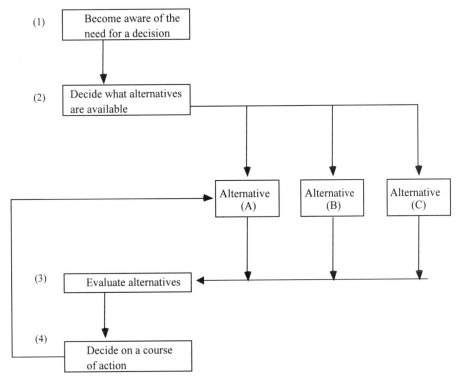

Although the accountant may be involved in all four stages, his main concern is with the evaluation process.

In evaluating the alternatives, the information used will be both **quantitative** (expressed in numerical terms, both financial and non-financial) and **qualitative** (which cannot easily be quantified, e.g. opinions, effects on customer/employee/ supplier relations, environmental considerations, etc).

We are mainly concerned with quantitative information here (usually costs and revenues), but you may also be required to discuss non-financial aspects of a decision in an examination question.

1.2 Marginal costs and revenues

The key concept in virtually all decisions of the nature we are considering here is that of **marginal costs and revenues.**

In its loosest sense, a marginal cost/revenue is an effect on total costs of an action taken, and can take the form of:

- a **relevant** or **opportunity** cost/revenue relating to a particular (often one-off) decision

- a **variable cost/selling price per unit** relating to decisions regarding production levels, mixes etc in applications of **contribution analysis**

- an **avoidable fixed cost** relating to decisions regarding shutdown, curtailment, or further processing decisions.

Although you may think that this chapter is made up of a number of distinct techniques, all the decisions will basically be made by comparing marginal costs with marginal revenues.

2 Use of relevant and opportunity costs

We have looked at this topic in the context of product costing. As it is a fundamental principle in decision-making, we shall briefly review it here.

2.1 Which costs/revenues are relevant to a decision?

The first point to note is that there is only one hard and fast rule about what will be a relevant cost/revenue in a particular decision:

A **change** in **future cash** payments or receipts arising as a result of the action taken.

You must not get into the habit of thinking 'variable costs are always relevant and fixed costs never are', because it is not as simple as that. Consider the following examples:

- If use is being made of materials that are already in stock and will otherwise be scrapped, their cost will be irrelevant to the decision as it will not affect future cashflows.

- If an extra supervisor is needed to take on an extra order their (fixed) salary will be relevant to the decision.

However, the following types of costs can generally be regarded as irrelevant:

(1) **Sunk costs.** Costs which have already been incurred, e.g. costs already incurred in market research. The information gained from the research will be useful in making the decision, but the costs are irrelevant as the decision will not change them.

(2) **Book values and accounting depreciation.** Both of these figures are determined by accounting conventions. For decision-making purposes it is the economic considerations which are important.

(3) **Common costs.** Costs which are common to all alternative courses of action are irrelevant to decision-making.

DEFINITION

Opportunity cost is the value of a
benefit sacrificed in favour of an
alternative course of action.

2.2   The relevant costs of materials

In any decision situation the cost of materials relevant to a particular decision is their
opportunity cost. This can be represented by a decision tree.

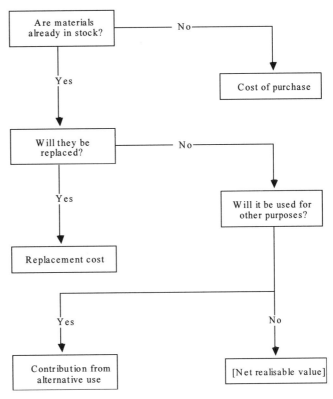

This decision tree can be used to identify the appropriate cost to use for materials.

2.3   The relevant cost of labour

A similar problem exists in determining the relevant costs of labour. In this case the
key question is whether spare capacity exists and on this basis another decision tree can
be produced.

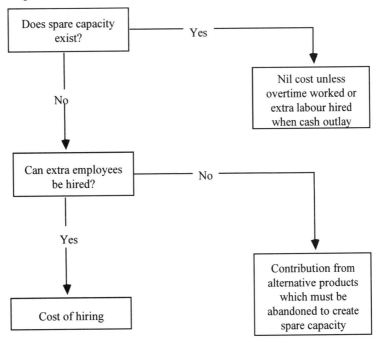

Again this can be used to identify the relevant opportunity cost.

ACTIVITY 1

Z Ltd has 50kg of material P in stock which was bought five years ago for £70. It is no longer used but could be sold for £3/kg.

Z Ltd is currently pricing a job which could use 40kg of material P. What is the relevant cost of P which should be included in the price?

Feedback to this activity is at the end of the chapter.

3 Contribution in decision-making

DEFINITION

Contribution = sales value – variable costs of sale.

It is considered more informative to present product profitability statements on a contribution basis. The term **contribution** describes the amount which a product provides or contributes towards a fund out of which fixed overhead may be paid, the balance being net profit.

3.1 Product comparisons

KEY POINT

Contribution is **directly linked** to the level of activity and is thus more useful for decision making than profit.

Where two or more products are manufactured in a factory and share all production facilities, the fixed overhead can only be apportioned on an arbitrary basis, and should not be allowed to affect the view of their relative worth.

Example

Gadgetry Ltd manufactures a single product which is marketed in three grades of finish – Presentation, De Luxe and Standard. The variable cost of the basic unit is £6 and the cost of finishing and packing is as follows:

Presentation model	£4
De Luxe model	£2
Standard model	£1

The selling prices are as follows.

Presentation model	£15
De Luxe model	£12
Standard model	£10

The marketing manager has estimated demand for next year as follows:

Presentation model	20,000 units
De Luxe model	30,000 units
Standard model	40,000 units

The production manager has estimated the production capacity of the factory at 150,000 pa. Fixed costs have been estimated at £100,000 for the forthcoming year.

An enquiry has been received from a manufacturer who is considering using the basic unit as a sub-assembly in his own product and who, at an acceptable price, would be willing to buy 30,000 units a year.

The company's pre-tax profit objective for the next year is £300,000.

Required:

(a) Calculate the lowest price which could be quoted for the supply of the 30,000 units.

(b) Comment upon any business policy matters that you consider relevant in these circumstances.

Solution

(a) The lowest acceptable price, based on the company's profit objective for next year, is calculated as follows:

	Contribution per unit	Estimated sales units	Contribution £
Presentation model	£5	20,000	100,000
De Luxe model	£4	30,000	120,000
Standard model	£3	40,000	120,000
			340,000
Fixed costs			100,000
Estimated net profit			240,000
Balance required to meet objective			60,000
Profit objective			300,000

To achieve the profit objective, the 30,000 additional units need to obtain a contribution of £60,000, i.e. £2 per unit. Thus, the lowest selling price will be the variable cost of the basic unit, £6 plus £2 contribution = £8 per unit.

(b) Relevant policy matters to be considered by Gadgetry Ltd would include the following:

    (i)   Any price in excess of £6 per unit would increase the net profit of Gadgetry.

    (ii)   The requirement for Gadgetry's basic unit implies that the manufacturer's product may be in competition with Gadgetry's products.

    (iii)   The special order represents an increase of one-third of estimated output. It is likely that such a substantial increase would necessitate a reappraisal of estimated costs.

The special order would raise Gadgetry's production to 80% of capacity – if demand for Gadgetry's products suddenly increased, the company would be unable to take advantage and would lose sales of its more profitable products.

3.2   Other applications of contribution analysis

The contribution principle is used in a variety of decision-making problems. Those considered in the following sections are as follows:

- **Cost volume profit (CVP) analysis** – assessing the effects of differing activity levels on costs and profits, including break-even points.

- **Limiting factor analysis** – to determine optimum production mix.

- **Make or buy decisions** – to decide whether to manufacture in-house or buy in.

4   Cost volume profit (CVP) analysis

CVP analysis is generally applied to the long-term product(s) of a business and uses cost behaviour theory to answer various questions.

- What level of sales is needed to break even?

- What is the margin of safety offered by the expected or budgeted activity level?

- What level of activity is needed to achieve a particular level of profit?

- What will be the effect on profit of changes in costs or selling prices?

It is based on the following assumptions about the long-term costs, revenues and activity levels involved:

- Costs can be classified as either fixed or variable.
- Over the time scale and activity range under review, unit variable costs remain constant and total fixed costs remain constant.
- Unit sales price remains constant.
- The costs and relationships are known.

4.1 Contribution target

Under the assumptions outlined above, unit contribution and total fixed costs can be assumed to be constant at all levels of output in the relevant range. This gives us the basic structure of profit.

	£	£
Selling price per unit	x	
Less: variable costs per unit	(x)	
=		
Contribution per unit	x	
Contribution per unit × volume = **Total contribution**		x
Less: Total fixed costs		(x)
= **Total profit**		x

DEFINITION

Activity to achieve target point =

Target contribution
(target profit + fixed costs)
Unit contribution

Thus if we need to achieve a certain target profit (e.g. a profit of zero if our aim is simply to break even) we can work backwards.

$$\text{Total contribution target} = \text{Target profit} + \text{fixed costs}$$

$$\text{Volume target} = \frac{\text{Total contribution target}}{\text{Unit contribution}}$$

For **break-even**, profit target = 0, and volume target becomes $\dfrac{\text{Fixed costs}}{\text{Unit contribution}}$

Example

Company	:	Widgets Ltd
Product	:	Widgets
Selling price	:	£3 per unit
Variable costs	:	Raw materials, £1 per unit
Fixed costs	:	Factory rent, £500 pa.

(a) How many widgets must be sold per annum to break even?

$$\text{Volume target} = \frac{\text{Contribution target}}{\text{Selling price} - \text{variable costs per unit}}$$

$$= \frac{£500 + £0}{£3 - £1} = 250 \text{ widgets.}$$

At sales volume of 250 units per annum, Widgets Ltd will make nil profit or loss.

		£
Sales	250 × £3	750
Variable costs	250 × £1	250
		500
Fixed costs		500
Profit/(loss)		Nil

(b) If rent goes up by 10% and Widgets Ltd aims to make £200 pa profit, what annual output is needed?

$$\text{Volume target} = \frac{\text{Contribution target}}{\text{Unit contribution}} = \frac{£500 + £50 + £200}{£3 - £1} = 375 \text{ widgets}$$

(c) Assuming the maximum possible output of Widgets Ltd is 250 widgets pa, what selling price would achieve the required profit target of £200 (assuming the increased rent)?

Contribution target = Fixed costs + Profit target

               = £550 + £200 = £750

and

Total contribution = Volume × (Selling price per unit − Variable costs per unit)

∴   750   =   250 × (SP − 1)

       750   =   250 SP − 250

    1,000   =   250 SP

The required selling price (SP) is therefore £4 per unit, giving:

			£
Sales	:	250 widgets × £4	1,000
Variable costs	:	250 × £1	250
Contribution			750
Fixed costs:			550
Profit			200

KEY POINT

- Any change in selling price or variable costs will alter unit contribution.

- Changes in fixed costs or profit required will affect the contribution target.

The simple example above illustrates that, given the cost/selling price structure, a range of alternative predictions can be easily calculated. Any change in selling price or variable costs will alter unit contribution. Changes in fixed costs or profit required will affect the contribution target.

4.2   Contribution to sales ratio

In the above illustration, it was assumed that Widgets Ltd had sold only one product. If it had produced three products, say widgets, gidgets and shmidgets and the unit contribution of each product was different, then it would be uninformative to assess total volume in terms of units.

If, however, the relative proportion of each product sold could be assumed to remain similar or if each product has the same ratio of contribution to sales value, then similar calculations could be made for the business as a whole. Output would be expressed in terms of sales revenue rather than numbers of units, i.e:

$$\text{Contribution to sales ratio (C/S ratio)} = \frac{\text{Contribution in £}}{\text{Sales in £}}$$

Note: you may encounter the term profit to volume (or P/V) ratio, which is synonymous with the contribution to sales ratio. Profit to volume is an inaccurate description, however, and should not be used. The C/S ratio is conveniently written as a percentage.

Example

Widgets Ltd operating statement for year 3 shows.

	Widgets	*Gidgets*	*Schmidgets*	*Total*
Sales units	100	40	60	200
	£	£	£	£
Sales value	400	240	300	940
Variable costs	220	130	170	520
Contribution	180	110	130	420
Fixed costs				350
Profit				70
C/S ratio	45%	46%	43%	44½%

$$\text{Break-even volume in sales value} = \frac{\text{Fixed costs}}{\text{C / S ratio}}$$

$$= \frac{£350}{44\frac{1}{2}\%} = £786.50$$

Thus, the business must sell about £790 of a mixture of widgets, gidgets and shmidgets before it starts to make a profit. The calculation in this instance would be acceptably accurate because the three products have almost identical C/S ratios. If the ratios were significantly different, however, use of the total C/S ratio would imply that the proportions of widgets, gidgets and schmidgets to total sales remained the same over the range of output considered.

4.3 Margin of safety

The difference between budgeted sales volume and break-even sales volume is known as the **margin of safety**. It indicates the vulnerability of a business to a fall in demand. It is often expressed as a percentage of budgeted sales.

Example

The following details relate to a shop which currently sells 25,000 pairs of shoes annually

Selling price per pair of shoes	£40
Purchase cost per pair of shoes	£25

Total annual fixed costs

	£
Salaries	100,000
Advertising	40,000
Other fixed expenses	100,000

Answer each part independently of data contained in other parts of the requirement.

(a) Calculate the break-even point and margin of safety in number of pairs of shoes sold.

(b) Assume that 20,000 pairs of shoes were sold in a year. Calculate the shop's net income (or loss).

(c) If a selling commission of £2 per pair of shoes sold was to be introduced, how many pairs of shoes would need to be sold in a year in order to earn a net income of £10,000?

(d) Assume that for next year an additional advertising campaign costing £20,000 is proposed, whilst at the same time selling prices are to be increased by 12%.

What would be the break-even point in number of pairs of shoes?

Solution

(a) Break-even point $= \dfrac{\text{Total fixed costs}}{\text{Contribution per pair}}$

Contribution per pair $=$ Selling price − Variable cost $= 40 - 25 = 15$

Break-even point $= \dfrac{100,000 + 40,000 + 100,000}{15}$

$= 16,000$ pairs

Margin of safety $=$ Current level of sales − Break-even sales

$= 25,000 - 16,000$

$= 9,000$ pairs

(b) Net income from sale of 20,000 pairs.

	£
Contribution: $20,000 \times 15$	300,000
Less: Fixed costs	240,000
Net profit	60,000

(c) Sales volume for a required profit $= \dfrac{\text{Total fixed cost} + \text{Required profit}}{\text{Contribution per pair}}$

$= \dfrac{240,000 + 10,000}{15 - 2}$

Sales volume for a net income of £10,000 $=$ 19,231 pairs.

Note: because of the need for a whole number answer, actual net income will be:

$(19,231 \times 13) - 240,000$ i.e. £10,003.

(d) Break-even point $= \dfrac{240,000 + 20,000}{\left(15 + \left(40 \times \dfrac{12}{100}\right)\right)}$

Break-even point $= \dfrac{260,000}{19.8} = 13,132$ pairs.

Note: again this whole number answer results in just above break-even point being achieved, i.e:

	£
Contribution: 13,132 × 19.8 =	260,013.60
Less: Fixed costs	260,000.00
Net income	13.60

5 Product mix decisions – limiting factors

All businesses which aim to maximise profit find that the volume of output and sales is **restricted.** For many, **sales demand** is the limiting factor and therefore the business will seek to make the maximum profit by concentrating its selling efforts on those products which yield high contributions.

Other limiting factors may prevent sales growth, e.g. shortage of building space, machine capacity, skilled labour, or the necessary materials. In such cases it is important for the business to obtain maximum profit by concentrating its efforts on those products which yield high contributions relative to the amount of the limiting factor they consume, known as factor analysis.

Example

Two products – Alpha and Gamma – are given a final finish by passing them through a spraying process. There is considerable demand for both products but output is restricted by the capacity of the spraying process. The product details are as follows.

	Alpha £	Gamma £
Selling price	10.00	15.00
Variable cost	6.00	7.50
Contribution	4.00	7.50
Finishing time in spraying process	1 hour	3 hours

Without any restriction in the capacity of the spraying process, Gamma is the more profitable product and should be promoted (assuming that the sales of each product do not affect the other).

KEY POINT

To maximise profits, efforts should be concentrated on the products with the highest contribution per unit of limiting factor (**key factor analysis**).

- However, as the spraying process is the limiting factor, it is important for the business to use the capacity of the process as profitably as possible, i.e. to earn the maximum contribution (and thus profit) for each spraying hour.

- The contributions per spraying hour are £4.00 for Alpha and £2.50 for Gamma and, therefore, it is Alpha which should be promoted.

- This can be proved by assuming a fixed number of spraying hours per week, say 45.

	Alpha	Gamma
Number of units to be sprayed in 45 hours	45	15
Contribution per unit	£4.00	£7.50
Total contribution	£180.00	£112.50

5.1 Other considerations regarding the limiting factor

In the long run management must seek to remove the limiting factor. In the example above, management should be attempting to increase the capacity of the spraying process. Thus, any one limiting factor should only be a short term problem. However, as soon as it is removed, it will be replaced by another limiting factor.

Even in the short run management may be able to find ways round the bottleneck, e.g. overtime working or sub-contracting might be solutions to the situations described.

It may not always be easy to identify the limiting factor. In practice, as already stated, several limiting factors may operate simultaneously. Even in examination questions where there is only one limiting factor, it may be necessary to investigate several possible limiting factors.

Other parameters may set minimum production levels, e.g. there may be a contract to supply Gamma so that certain minimum quantities must be produced.

5.2   Additional resources

Example

X Ltd makes three products – A, B and C – for which unit costs, machine hours and selling prices are as follows:

	Product A	*Product B*	*Product C*
Machine hours	10	12	14
	£	£	£
Direct materials £1 per kg	14 (14 kg)	12 (12 kg)	10 (10 kg)
Variable overhead	18 (12 hours)	12 (8 hours)	6 (4 hours)
Marginal cost	38	30	22
Selling price	50	40	30
Contribution	12	10	8

Sales demand for the period is limited as follows:

A	4,000
B	6,000
C	6,000

However, as a matter of company policy it is decided to produce a minimum of 1,000 units of Product A. The supply of materials in the period is unlimited but machine hours are restricted to 200,000 and labour hours to 50,000.

Indicate the production levels that should be adopted for the three products in order to maximise profitability, and state the maximum contribution.

Solution

First, determine which is the limiting factor at the potential sales level.

	Sales potential (units)	*Total machine hours*	*Total labour hours*
Product A	4,000	40,000	48,000
Product B	6,000	72,000	48,000
Product C	6,000	84,000	24,000
		196,000	120,000

Thus the limiting factor is the labour hours. The next stage is to calculate contribution per labour hour.

Product A $\dfrac{£12}{12} = £1.00$

Product B $\dfrac{£10}{8} = £1.25$

Product C $\dfrac{£8}{4} = £2.00$

 FOULKS LYNCH
PUBLICATIONS

Thus, production should be concentrated on C up to maximum available sales, then B and finally A.

However, a minimum of 1,000 units of A must be produced. Taking these factors into account, the production schedule is as follows:

	Units produced	Labour hours	Cumulative labour hours	Limiting factor
Product A	1,000	12,000	12,000	Policy to produce 1,000 units
Product C	6,000	24,000	36,000	Sales
Product B	1,750	14,000	50,000	Labour hours

5.3   Shadow prices

A **shadow price** is the loss or gain in contribution which would occur if the availability of a scarce resource were to change by one unit of that resource.

Using the example of X Ltd above, the loss or gain of one labour hour would affect the production of product B.

Product B takes 8 hours to produce and yields a contribution of £10 per unit. An alteration in the labour hours available by one would therefore alter production of B by one-eighth of a unit, and change contribution by $\frac{1}{8}$th of £10 or £1.25 (i.e. B's contribution per hour).

The shadow price therefore also represents the maximum amount which should be paid in order to obtain an extra hour or avoid losing an hour. In this example this is £1.25 (or very slightly less) since this is the value in contribution terms of the hour. This is, of course, in addition to the normal cost of one hour because this has already been included in the marginal cost of the product.

6   Make or buy decisions

Occasionally a business may have the opportunity to purchase, from another company, a component part or assembly which it currently produces from its own resources and managers must consider:

- Is the alternative source of supply available only temporarily or for the foreseeable future?

- Is there spare production capacity available now and/or in the future?

6.1   Spare capacity

If the business is operating below maximum capacity, production resources will be idle if the component is purchased from outside. The fixed costs of those resources are irrelevant to the decision in the short term as they will be incurred whether the component is made or purchased. Purchase would be recommended, therefore, only if the buying price were less than the variable costs of internal manufacture.

In the long term, however, the business may dispense with or transfer some of its resources and may purchase from outside if it thereby saves more than the extra cost of purchasing.

Example

A company manufactures an assembly used in the production of one of its product lines. The department in which the assembly is produced incurs fixed costs of £24,000 pa. The variable costs of production are £2.55 per unit. The assembly could be bought outside at a cost of £2.65 per unit.

The current annual requirement is for 80,000 assemblies per year. Should the company continue to manufacture the assembly, or should it be purchased from the outside suppliers?

Solution

A decision to purchase outside would cost the company £(2.65 – 2.55) = 10p per unit, which for 80,000 assemblies would amount to £8,000 pa. Thus, the fixed costs of £24,000 will require analysis to determine if more than £8,000 would actually be saved if production of the assembly were discontinued.

6.2   Other considerations affecting the decision

Management would need to consider other factors before reaching a decision. Some would be quantifiable and some not.

- **Continuity and control of supply.** Can the outside company be relied upon to meet the requirements in terms of quantity, quality, delivery dates and price stability?

- **Alternative use of resources.** Can the resources used to make this article be transferred to another activity which will save costs or increase revenue?

- **Social/legal.** Will the decision affect contractual or ethical obligations to employees or business connections?

6.3   Capacity exhausted

If a business cannot fulfil orders because it has used up all available capacity, it may be forced to purchase from outside in the short term (unless it is cheaper to refuse sales). In the longer term management may look to other alternatives, such as capital expenditure.

It may be, however, that a variety of components is produced from common resources and management would try to arrange manufacture or purchase to use its available capacity most profitably. In such a situation the limiting factor concept makes it easier to formulate the optimum plans. Priority for purchase would be indicated by ranking components in relation to the excess purchasing cost per unit of limiting factor.

Example

Fidgets Ltd manufactures three components used in its finished product. The component workshop is currently unable to meet the demand for components and the possibility of sub-contracting part of the requirement is being investigated on the basis of the following data:

	Component A £	Component B £	Component C £
Variable costs of production	3.00	4.00	7.00
Outside purchase price	2.50	6.00	13.00
Excess cost per unit	(0.50)	2.00	6.00
Machine hours per unit	1	0.5	2
Labour hours per unit	2	2	4

You are required:

(a) to decide which component should be bought out if the company is operating at full capacity.

(b) to decide which component should be bought out if production is limited to 4,000 machine hours per week.

(c) to decide which component should be bought out if production is limited to 4,000 labour hours per week.

Solution

(a) Component A should always be bought out regardless of any limiting factors, as its variable cost of production is higher than the outside purchase price.

(b) If machine hours are limited to 4,000 hours.

	Component B	*Component C*
Excess cost	£2	£6
Machine hours per unit	0.5	2
Excess cost per machine hour	£4	£3

Component C has the lowest excess cost per limiting factor and should, therefore, be bought out.

This can be proved as follows.

	Component B	*Component C*
Units produced in 4,000 hours	8,000	2,000
	£	£
Production costs	32,000	14,000
Purchase costs	48,000	26,000
Excess cost of purchase	16,000	12,000

(c) If labour hours are limited to 4,000 hours.

	Component B	*Component C*
Excess cost	£2	£6
Labour hours	2	4
Excess cost per labour hour	£1	£1.50

Therefore, component B has the lowest excess cost per limiting factor and should be bought out.

This can be proved as follows:

	Component B	*Component C*
Units produced in 4,000 hours	2,000	1,000
	£	£
Production costs	8,000	7,000
Purchase costs	12,000	13,000
Excess cost of purchase	4,000	6,000

7 Evaluating strategic operating proposals

Management will require information to evaluate proposals aimed to increase profit by changing operating strategy. The cost accountant will need to show clearly the effect of the proposals on profit by:

• pin-pointing the changes in costs and revenues

• quantifying the margin of error which will cause the proposal to be unviable.

Examples of strategic operating proposals include:

• Utilisation of space capacity

• Special contract pricing

• Closure of a business segment

• Temporary shutdown

7.1   Example

A company produces and sells one product and its forecast for the next financial year is as follows.

	£'000	£'000
Sales 100,000 units @ £8		800
Variable costs		
Material	300	
Labour	200	
		500
Contribution (£3 per unit)		300
Fixed costs		150
Net profit		150

As an attempt to increase net profit, two proposals have been put forward:

(a) To launch an advertising campaign costing £14,000. This will increase the sales to 150,000 units, although the price will have to be reduced to £7.

(b) To produce some components at present purchased from suppliers. This will reduce material costs by 20% but will increase fixed costs by £72,000.

Solution

Proposal (a) will increase the sales revenue but the increase in costs will be greater.

	£'000
Sales 150,000 × £7	1,050
Variable costs	750
	300
Fixed costs plus advertising	164
Net profit	136

Proposal (a) is therefore of no value and sales must be increased by a further 7,000 units to maintain net profit.

Advertising cost	=	£14,000
Contribution per unit	=	£2
∴ Additional volume required	=	7,000 units

Proposal (b) reduces variable costs by £60,000 but increases fixed costs by £72,000 and is therefore not to be recommended unless the total volume increases as a result of the policy (e.g. if the supply of the components were previously a limiting factor). The increase in sales needed to maintain profit at £150,000 (assuming the price remains at £8) would be:

Reduced profits at 100,000 units	=	£12,000
Revised contribution per unit	=	£3.60
∴ Additional volume required	=	3,333 units

Examples of strategic operating proposals include:

- utilisation of space capacity
- special contract pricing
- closure of a business segment
- temporary shutdown.

7.2 Utilisation of spare capacity

Where production is below capacity, opportunities may arise for sales at a specially reduced price, for example, export orders or manufacturing under another brand name. Such opportunities are worthwhile if the answer to two key questions is 'Yes':

(1) Is spare capacity available?

(2) Does additional revenue (Units × Price) exceed additional costs (Units × Variable cost)?

However, the evaluation should also consider the following questions:

- Is there an alternative more profitable way of utilising spare capacity (e.g. sales promotion, making an alternative product)?
- Will fixed costs be unchanged if the order is accepted?
- Will accepting one order at below normal selling price lead other customers to ask for price cuts?

The longer the time period in question, the more important are these other factors.

Example

At a production level of 8,000 units per month, which is 80% of capacity, the budget of Export Ltd is as follows.

	Per unit £	8,000 units £
Sales	5.00	40,000
Variable costs.		
Direct labour	1.00	8,000
Raw materials	1.50	12,000
Variable overheads	0.50	4,000
	3.00	24,000
Fixed costs	1.50	12,000
Total	4.50	36,000
Budgeted profit	0.50	4,000

An opportunity arises to export 1,000 units per month at a price of £4 per unit.

Should the contract be accepted?

Solution

(a) Is spare capacity available? Yes

		£
(b) Additional revenue	1,000 × £4	4,000
Additional costs	1,000 × £3	3,000
Increased profitability		1,000

FOULKS LYNCH
PUBLICATIONS

Therefore, the contract should be accepted.

(Note that fixed costs are not relevant to the decision and are therefore ignored.)

7.3 Special contract pricing

A business which produces to customer's order may be working to full capacity. Any additional orders must be considered on the basis of the following questions:

(1) What price must be quoted to make the contract profitable?

(2) Can other orders be fulfilled if this contract is accepted?

In such a situation the limiting factor needs to be recognised so that the contract price quoted will at least maintain the existing rate of contribution per unit of limiting factor.

Example

Oddjobs Ltd manufactures special purpose gauges to customers' specifications. The highly skilled labour force is always working to full capacity and the budget for the next year shows the following:

	£	£
Sales		40,000
Direct materials	4,000	
Direct wages 3,200 hours @ £5	16,000	
Fixed overhead	10,000	
		30,000
Profit		10,000

An enquiry is received from XY Ltd for a gauge which would use £60 of direct materials and 40 labour hours.

(a) What is the minimum price to quote to XY Ltd?

(b) Would the minimum price be different if spare capacity were available but materials were subject to a quota of £4,000 per year?

Solution

(a) The limiting factor is 3,200 labour hours and the budgeted contribution per hour is £20,000 ÷ 3,200 hours = £6.25 per hour. Minimum price is therefore:

	£
Materials	60
Wages 40 hours @ £5	200
	260
Add: Contribution 40 hours @ £6.25	250
Contract price	510

At the above price the contract will maintain the budgeted contribution (check by calculating the effect of devoting the whole 3,200 hours to XY Ltd).

Note, however, that the budget probably represents a mixture of orders, some of which earn more than £6.25 per hour and some less. Acceptance of the XY order must displace other contracts, so the contribution rate of contracts displaced should be checked.

(b) If the limiting factor is materials, budgeted contribution per £ of materials is £20,000 ÷ 4,000 = £5 per £1.

Minimum price is therefore:

	£
Materials/wages (as above)	260
Contribution £60 × 5	300
Contract price	560

Because materials are scarce, Oddjobs must aim to earn the maximum profit from its limited supply.

7.4 Closure of a business segment

Part of a business may appear to be unprofitable. The segment may, for example, be a product, a department or a channel of distribution. In evaluating closure the cost accountant should identify:

- loss of contribution from the segment
- savings in specific fixed costs from closure
- penalties, e.g. redundancy, compensation to customers, etc
- alternative use for resources released
- non-quantifiable effects.

Example

Harolds department store comprises three departments – Menswear, Ladies' Wear and Unisex. The store budget is as follows.

	Mens £	Ladies £	Unisex £	Total £
Sales	40,000	60,000	20,000	120,000
Direct cost of sales	20,000	36,000	15,000	71,000
Department costs	5,000	10,000	3,000	18,000
Apportioned store costs	5,000	5,000	5,000	15,000
Profit/(loss)	10,000	9,000	(3,000)	16,000

It is suggested that Unisex be closed to increase the size of Menswear and Ladies' wear

What information is relevant or required?

Solution

Possible answers are as follows:

(a) Unisex earns £2,000 net contribution (store costs will be re-apportioned to Mens/Ladies).

(b) Possible increase in Mens/Ladies sales volume.

(c) Will Unisex staff be dismissed or transferred to Mens/Ladies?

(d) Reorganisation costs, e.g. repartitioning, stock disposal.

(e) Loss of custom because Unisex attracts certain types of customer who will not buy in Mens/Ladies.

FOULKS LYNCH
PUBLICATIONS

7.5 Comparing segment profitability

When presenting information for comparing results or plans for different products, departments etc, it is useful to show gross and net contribution for each segment. The information in the example above would be presented in the following form:

	Menswear £'000	Ladies Wear £'000	Unisex £'000	Total £'000
Sales	40	60	20	120
Direct cost of sales	20	36	15	71
Gross contribution	20	24	5	49
Department costs	5	10	3	18
Net contribution	15	14	2	31

Note that the store costs, if shown, would only appear in the total column. In addition, the statement should include performance indicators relevant to the type of operation. For a department store, such indicators would include:

(a) C/S ratios (based on **gross** contribution)

(b) gross and net contribution per unit of floor space

(c) gross and net contribution per employee.

For a manufacturing company, more relevant indicators would include:

(a) contribution per labour/machine hour

(b) added value/conversion cost per hour

(c) added value/conversion cost per employee.

7.6 Temporary shut-down

When a business has experienced trading difficulties which do not appear likely to improve in the immediate future, consideration may be given to closing down operations temporarily. Factors other than cost will influence the decision.

(1) Suspending production and sales of products will result in their leaving the public eye.

(2) Dismissal of the labour force will entail bad feeling and possible difficulty in recruitment when operations are restarted.

(3) Danger of plant obsolescence.

(4) Difficulty and cost of closing down and restarting operations in certain industries, e.g. a blast furnace.

The temporary closure of a business will result in additional expenditure, e.g. plant will require protective coverings, services will be disconnected. In the same way, additional expenditure will be incurred when the business restarts.

On the other hand, a temporary closure may enable the business to reorganise efficiently to take full advantage of improved trading conditions when they return.

In the short term a business can continue to operate while marginal contribution equals fixed expenses. In periods of trading difficulty, as long as some contribution is made towards fixed expenses, it will generally be worthwhile continuing operations.

KEY POINT

In the short term a business can continue to operate while marginal contribution equals fixed expenses.

Example

A company is operating at 40% capacity and is considering closing down its factory for one year, after which time the demand for its product is expected to increase substantially. The following data applies.

	£
Sales value at 40% capacity	60,000
Marginal costs of sales at 40% capacity	40,000
Fixed costs	50,000

Fixed costs which will remain if the factory is closed amount to £20,000. The cost of closing down operations will amount to £4,000.

Prepare a statement to show the best course of action.

Solution

Statement of profit or loss

Continuing operation	£	Temporary closure	£
Sales	60,000	Fixed expenses	20,000
Marginal cost of sales	40,000	Closing down costs	4,000
Contribution to fixed costs	20,000		
Fixed costs	50,000		
Net loss	(30,000)		(24,000)

Ignoring non-cost considerations, the company will minimise its losses by closing down for one year.

Note that the marginal contribution of £20,000 does not cover the difference between existing fixed costs and those that remain on closure (i.e. £(50,000 – 24,000) = £26,000 compared to £20,000).

Conclusion

We have looked at a lot of different decision-making scenarios in this chapter. We have used various techniques – opportunity costs, contribution analysis, key factor analysis etc – but they are all linked by the basic principle that we are comparing marginal costs with marginal revenues in some form or another.

SELF-TEST QUESTIONS

Use of relevant and opportunity costs

1   Give three types of cost which will generally not be relevant in decision-making. (2.1)

Contribution in decision-making

2   Define and explain contribution. (3)

Cost volume profit (CVP) analysis

3   What are the assumptions of CVP analysis? (4)

4   Explain how to compute a target volume to achieve a target profit. (4.1)

Make or buy decisions

5   When might key factor analysis be used in the context of a make or buy decision? (6.3)

Evaluating strategic operating proposals

6   In a closure decision, list five factors that should be considered. (7.4)

EXAM-TYPE
QUESTION

Hard and soft

A company produces a hard grade and, by additional processing, a soft grade of its product.

A market research study for next year has indicated very good prospects not only for both the hard and soft grades but also for a light grade produced after still further processing.

The raw material is imported and there is a possibility that a quota system will be introduced allowing only a maximum of £300,000 pa of material to be imported.

The company's marketing policy has been to sell 60% of its capacity (or of its allocation of material if the quota is introduced) in the most profitable grade. It has been decided that this policy should continue if it is to produce three grades, but that only 15% of its capacity (or material allocation) should be sold in the least profitable grade.

The budgeted prime costs and selling prices per ton for each grade are as follows:

	Hard	Soft	Light
	£	£	£
Selling price	70	95	150
Direct material cost	15	20	25
Direct wages (@ £2.50 per hour)	15	25	45

For next year the company's annual production capacity is 225,000 direct labour hours and its fixed overhead is £500,000. Variable overhead is 20% of direct wages.

Fixed overhead is at present absorbed by a rate per ton produced.

Required:

(a) State which of the three grades of product will be most profitable and which will be least profitable in the short term assuming that such volume as can be produced can be sold:

    (i)   if the materials quota does not operate

    (ii)   if the materials quota does come into force.   **(10 marks)**

(b) If the materials quota does come into force, calculate the budgeted profit for next year from the company's marketing policy if:

    (i)   only light grade is produced

    (ii)   all three grades are produced in accordance with present policy.

             (10 marks)

             (Total: 20 marks)

For the answer to this question, see the 'Answers' section at the end of the book.

CASE STUDY
TYPE QUESTION

In your exam you will be expected to answer a 50 marks case study question drawing from various areas of the syllabus. To complete our section on management accountancy an example of such a case study is included for you to attempt.

Kwan Tong Umbago Ltd

The budgeted balance sheet data of Kwan Tong Umbago Ltd is as follows:

1 March 20X0

	Cost	Depreciation to date	Net
	£	£	£
Fixed assets			
Land and buildings	500,000	–	500,000
Machinery and equipment	124,000	84,500	39,500
Motor vehicles	42,000	16,400	25,600
	666,000	100,900	565,100

Working capital		
Current assets		
Stock of raw materials (100 units)	4,320	
Stock of finished goods (110 units)*	10,450	
Debtors (January £7,680, February £10,400)	18,080	
Cash and bank	6,790	
	39,640	
Less: Current liabilities		
Creditors (raw materials)	3,900	
		35,740
		600,840
Represented by		
Ordinary share capital (fully paid) £1 shares		500,000
Share premium		60,000
Profit and loss account		40,840
		600,840

* The stock of finished goods was valued at marginal cost.

The estimates for the next four month period are as follows:

	March	April	May	June
Sales (units)	80	84	96	94
Production (units)	70	75	90	90
Purchases of raw materials (units)	80	80	85	85
Wages and variable overheads at £65 per unit	£4,550	£4,875	£5,850	£5,850
Fixed overheads	£1,200	£1,200	£1,200	£1,200

The company intends to sell each unit for £219 and has estimated that it will have to pay £45 per unit for raw materials. One unit of raw material is needed for each unit of finished product.

All sales and purchases of raw materials are on credit. Debtors are allowed two months' credit and suppliers of raw materials are paid after one month's credit. The wages, variable overheads and fixed overheads are paid in the month in which they are incurred.

Cash from a loan secured on the land and buildings of £120,000 at an interest rate of 7.5% is due to be received on 1 May. Machinery costing £112,000 will be received in May and paid for in June.

The loan interest is payable half yearly from September onwards. An interim dividend to 31 March 20X0 of £12,500 will be paid in June.

Depreciation for the four months, including that on the new machinery is:

–   Machinery and equipment £15,733

–   Motor vehicles £3,500

The company uses the FIFO method of stock valuation. Ignore taxation.

Required:

(a)   Calculate and present the raw materials budget and finished goods budget in terms of units, for each month from March to June inclusive.   **(5 marks)**

(b)   Calculate the corresponding sales budgets, the production cost budgets and the budgeted closing debtors, creditors and stocks in terms of value. **(8 marks)**

(c)   Prepare and present a cash budget for each of the four months.   **(10 marks)**

(d)   Prepare a master budget i.e. a budgeted trading and profit and loss account for the four months to 30 June 20X0, and budgeted balance sheet as at 30 June 20X0.   **(15 marks)**

(e)   Advise the company about possible ways in which it can improve its cash management.   **(12 marks)**

(Total: 50 marks)

For the answer to this question, see the 'Answers' section at the end of the book.

**FEEDBACK TO
ACTIVITY 1**

40kg @ £3/kg = £120

Answers to exam-type questions

Private v public sector objectives

Tutorial note: This is a fairly wide ranging question and you need to apply a general knowledge of business operations as well as specific knowledge of financial management. A wide variety of answers would be acceptable; the major points are covered in the following essay plan.

Financial objectives

(i) State owned enterprise

    1   Overall objective is commonly to fulfil a social need.

    2   Because of problems of measuring attainment of social needs the government usually sets specific targets in accounting terms.

    3   Examples include target returns on capital employed, requirement to be self financing, cash or budget limits.

(ii) Private sector

    1   Firm has more freedom to determine its own objectives.

    2   Stock market quotation will mean that return to shareholders becomes an important objective.

    3   Traditionally financial management sees firms as attempting to maximise shareholder wealth. Note that other objectives may exist, e.g. social responsibilities, and the concept of satisficing various parties is important.

Strategic and operational decisions

The major change in emphasis will be that decisions will now have to be made on a largely commercial basis. Profit and share price considerations will become paramount. Examples of where significant changes might occur are:

Financing decision: The firm will have to compete for a wide range of sources of finance. Choices between various types of finance will now have to be made, e.g. debt versus equity.

Dividend decision: The firm will now have to consider its policy on dividend payout to shareholders.

Investment decision: Commercial rather than social considerations will become of major importance. Diversification into other products and markets will now be possible. Expansion by merger and takeover can also be considered.

Threat of takeover: If the government completely relinquishes its ownership it is possible that the firm could be subject to takeover bids.

Other areas: Pricing, marketing, staffing etc, will now be largely free of government constraints.

CHAPTER 4

EXAM-TYPE QUESTION

Stock markets

The Stock Market is a financial intermediary which brings together individuals with different financial requirements. One of its functions is to enable those who need funds to be matched with those who have a surplus of funds. One example of this might be when a private company goes public, the owner realising some of his assets by selling off part or all of his interest in the company. Alternatively, companies needing money to carry out investment projects can raise the funds by issuing securities in the primary market.

The secondary market is the other most important role carried out by a Stock Exchange. This refers to the purchase and sale of secondhand shares and bonds, those which are already held by investors, rather than newly-issued securities.

Long-term capital can be defined in a number of ways, but the usual period over which long-term funds are lent is ten years or more. There are very many types of long-term capital which a company may issue, but essentially it has a choice of three basic categories: ordinary shares, preference shares or loan stock.

Ordinary shares, or equity, are held by the owners of the company. Each share represents a share in the assets of the company and entitles its owner to a dividend paid out of the profits of the company. The dividend is variable both upwards and downwards, although in practice, dividends per share tend to rise slowly over time. In general, ordinary shares also confer the right to vote on their owner.

Preference shares do not represent ownership of the company, nor do they carry votes. They are entitled to a fixed dividend, which must be paid before the ordinary shareholders receive a dividend. If profits are not high enough to pay the dividend it remains unpaid, although if the shares are cumulative, all unpaid dividends must be paid as soon as the company makes sufficient profits. Preference shares are more akin to loan stock than they are to equity.

Loan stock has many different names, the most familiar ones being debentures or bonds. This is debt capital, normally carrying fixed rate interest. The loan is usually made for a specific number of years, after which it is repaid (although a company may issue irredeemable loan stock, which is never repaid). This is different from ordinary and preference shares, which are usually not redeemed by the company; investors wishing to realise their investment sell their shares on to other investors.

The main advantage of raising long-term funds on the Stock Market is the fact that it provides a regulated and ordered way of finding individuals or organisations with money they want to lend. In addition to this function, the secondary market gives assurance to investors that they will be able to realise their investments when they need to. As large volumes of securities are traded on the Stock Market every day, people are relatively safe in tying up their money for apparently long periods of time. Should they need funds, they can liquidate their investments by selling the securities on to somebody else. This means that companies do not have to find investors who are willing to lend money indefinitely or for many years at a time.

Raising equity or debt both have advantages and disadvantages. Equity is useful as the dividends paid depend on profits, so can be reduced or cancelled in times of difficulty. On the other hand, bringing in new shareholders dilutes the control of the company and subjects the original owners to controls and regulations which they may find onerous.

Debt receives a fixed interest payment which is tax deductible, unlike dividends. This makes debt a fairly cheap form of finance, as the payment of interest is offset to a certain extent by the saving of tax. However, debt agreements usually carry with them the right of the debt holders to force the company into liquidation if interest payments are not met.

One of the main criticisms levelled at the Stock Market and those who provide funds through it, is the short-termism. Share ownership, although perhaps wider than it once was, is concentrated in the hands of a few large institutions, such as pension funds, insurance companies and investment and unit trusts. These institutions are often accused of being interested only in short-term gains,

concentrating on dividend payouts and fast capital growth. This means that companies are forced into making short-term decisions to satisfy the institutions, rather than considering the longer term and, for example, carrying out research and development, which may use up cash in the present, but will increase future profits.

Another area of complaint is the lack of funds available for risky or small ventures. Not only are the big institutions reluctant to make such investments, but the cost of raising money on the Stock Exchange makes it prohibitive for all but the largest companies. Other sources of capital, in particular venture capital companies, are needed.

Finally, a company always risks not having its shares fully subscribed by the public, although issues are usually underwritten to ensure that shares can be placed with some investor. The most notorious underwriting problem in the UK was encountered by the British Government, when it sold off shares in British Petroleum around the time of the Stock Market crash in October 1987. The issue was under-subscribed, forcing the Government to turn to the underwriters, who were extremely reluctant to fulfil their role of buying the outstanding shares.

CHAPTER **5**   EXAM-TYPE QUESTION

Ewden plc

(a) Comparison of the two balance sheets reveals that Ewden has suffered a significant fall in liquidity – cash balances have fallen sharply from £1.5m (probably an unnecessarily high level) in 20X2 to just £0.1m in 20X3 while an overdraft of £0.2m has appeared, reflecting a reduction in net cash resources of £1.6m. However, company profitability remains satisfactory, indicating that the run-down in liquidity has been required to finance the acquisition of assets.

Analysis of the financial statements reveals that Ewden has been able to reinvest £3.0m of retained earnings (plus an unspecified amount of depreciation provisions) in order to fund a substantial net increase in fixed assets of £3.0m, presumably to support an output expansion. It is possible that this significant capacity increase might have been obtained via acquisition of another company. Such a large increase implies that during the past recession, Ewden had cut back its capacity in order to reduce costs.

But as well as an increase in fixed assets, Ewden has invested £0.8m in stocks and £1.0m in debtors. This substantial investment in working capital is partially offset by an increase in trade and other creditors of £0.2m making a total increase in working capital of £1.6m.

No additional external long-term finance has been raised, so the increased investment in fixed assets and working capital has had to be financed by a significant reduction in cash balances and the opening-up of a bank overdraft, resulting in a heavy net outflow of liquid resources of £1.6m.

Overtrading is the term applied to a company which rapidly increases its turnover without having sufficient capital backing, hence the alternative term 'under-capitalisation'. Output increases are often obtained by more intensive utilisation of existing fixed assets, and growth tends to be financed by more intensive use of working capital. Overtrading companies are often unable or unwilling to raise long-term capital and thus tend to rely more heavily on short-term sources such as creditors and bank overdrafts. Debtors usually increase sharply as the company follows a more generous trade credit policy in order to win sales, while stocks tend to increase as the company attempts to produce at a faster rate ahead of increases in demand. Overtrading is thus characterised by rising borrowings and a declining liquidity position in terms of the quick ratio, if not always according to the current ratio.

The accounts indicate some of the signs of overtrading, although the case is not proven.

Checking Ewden's ratios against the common symptoms of overtrading we see the following.

(i)   Fall in the liquidity ratios. For Ewden, the current ratio falls from 2.25 to 2.04, which does not seem to indicate a serious decline in liquidity, although the extent of the decline in the quick ratio, (i.e. excluding stocks), from 1.55 to 1.13, might give more cause for concern, especially as the bulk of its quick assets (96%) are in the form of debtors.

(ii)   Rapid increase in turnover – 33% for Ewden.

(iii)   Sharp increase in the sales-to-fixed assets ratio. For Ewden, this has remained steady at 1.33 because the increase in sales has been supported by an increase in fixed assets, suggesting that the output increase was well-planned.

(iv)   Increase in stocks in relation to turnover. For Ewden, the increase is from 11.7% (43 days) to 13.8% (50 days), which is marked but hardly dramatic. Measured against cost of sales, the equivalent figures are 20% (73 days) for 20X2 and 24% (88 days) for 20X3, a more pronounced increase in stockholding.

(v)   Increase in debtors. Ewden's accounts receivable rise as a percentage of sales from 13.3% (49 days) to 16.3% (59 days). This does seem to represent a significant loosening of control over debtors

(vi)   Increase in the trade credit period. The ratio of trade creditors to cost of goods sold rises slightly from 21.4% (78 days) to 21.8% (80 days). The trade credit period is considerably longer (80 days versus 59 days) than the debtor collection period, suggesting that the company is exploiting the generosity of suppliers in order to enhance sales.

(vii)   Increase in short-term borrowing and a decline in cash balances. Clearly, this has happened to Ewden.

(viii) Increase in gearing. Taking the ratio of long and short-term debt-to-equity as the appropriate measure, gearing has actually fallen (from a relatively low level of 21% to 18%) despite the opening of the overdraft, primarily due to the increase in equity via retentions.

(ix)   Fall in the profit margin. In terms of its gross profit margin (operating profit-to-sales), Ewden actually achieves an increase from 42% to 43%, although there is a marginal fall in the ratio of profit after tax-to-sales from 31.7% to 31.3%. This does not suggest that Ewden is using aggressive price discounting in an attempt to increase sales.

It seems that Ewden's liquidity is under pressure but the company displays by no means all the classic signs of overtrading. Ewden might consider issuing further long-term securities if it wishes to support a further sales surge. If sales are expected to stabilise, the recent increase in capacity should be sufficient to produce the desired output, enabling the liquidity position to be repaired via cash flow, which was substantial in 1993, before allowing for the financing of the capital investment.

(b)   **The discount**

At December 20X3, debtors were £2.6m. The debtor collection period was: £2.6m/£16m × 365 = 59 days.

The 2% discount would lower this to 10 days for 50% of customers reducing average debtor days to:

(50% × 59) + (50% × 10) = 34.5 days

The cost of the discount (ignoring any beneficial impact on sales volume) would be:

(2% × 50% × £16m) = £160,000

The revised sales value estimate would be (£16m – £160,000) = £15.84m

Average debtors would become $\dfrac{34.5}{365}$ × £15.84m = £1,497,206

The interest saving would be 18% × (£2.6m – £1.497m) = £198,540

Set against the cost of the discount, the net benefit would be:

(£198,540 – £160,000) = £38,540

Factoring

Reduction in debtor days = (59 – 45)	=	14 days
Reduction in debtors = $\dfrac{14}{365}$ × £16m	=	£613,699
Interest saving = (18% × £613,698)	=	£110,466
Administrative savings	=	£100,000
Service charge = (1.5% × £16m)	=	£240,000
Net cost = (£240,000) + £100,000 + £110,466	=	(£29,534)

The figures imply that the discount policy is preferable but this relies on the appropriate percentage of customers actually taking up the discount and paying on time. Given that debtor days are currently 59, it seems rather optimistic to expect that half of Ewden's customers will be sufficiently impressed by the discount as to advance their settlement by 49 days. Conversely, the assessment of the value of using the factor depends on the factor successfully lowering Ewden's debtor days. Any tendency for the factor to retain these cash flow benefits for himself, rather than passing them on to Ewden, will further increase the net cost of the factoring option. In this respect, the two parties should clearly specify their expectations and requirements from the factoring arrangement.

CHAPTER **6**   EXAM-TYPE QUESTION

Comfylot plc

Key answer tip: This question requires an analysis of three possible strategies to improve cash flow. The first two strategies involve working capital management changes. Calculate the extra costs and the extra benefits of each strategy in turn. Remember that holding debtors has an opportunity cost.

For the third alternative, the company is projecting an increase in sales from extra advertising. Rather than calculate an expected value, the company will find it more useful to know the cost/saving implications of all three possible increases in sales.

FOULKS LYNCH
PUBLICATIONS

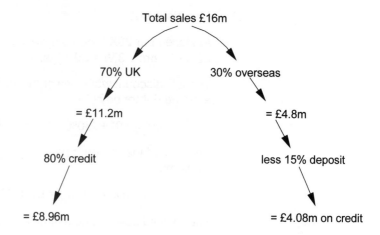

(1)   The costs and savings of domestic factoring can be identified as follows:

Costs of using the factor

	£
Factor charges service fee of 1.5% of all £8.96m credit sales	*134,400*
Redundancy payments	*15,000*

80% of the debts are factored at 15.5% The loans only last whilst the debt is outstanding (average 57 days).

The cost of this is therefore:

	£
80% × £8.96m × 15.5% × 57/365	*173,505*
Investment in the remaining 20% debtors has an opportunity	
cost (15%) = 20% × £8.96m × 15% × 57/365	*41,977*
Total cost	*364,882*

Savings from using the factor

	£
Administration	*85,000*
Bad debts (0.75% × £8.96m) (the factoring is non-recourse)	*67,200*
Current opportunity cost of debtors £8.96m × 57/365 × 15%	*209,885*
	362,085

The net cost of domestic factoring will be £2,797 next year. But redundancy is a non-recurring cost so savings would be expected thereafter.

(2)   The costs and savings associated with the cash discount can be identified as follows:

Costs	£
Administration	*25,000*
Cost of the discount itself (£8.96m × 0.4 × 0.015)	*53,760*
	78,760

Savings

Reduction in bad debts 0.25% × £8.96m   22,400

The discount results in some earlier payment which will reduce the overall level of debtors from the existing (£8.96m × 57/365 =) £1,399,233 to (£8.96m × 40% × 7/365) + (£8.96m × 60% × 57/365) = £908,274.

The opportunity cost of this reduction in the level of debtors of:

                                                                   £

£490,959 is multiplied by 15%   73,644
                                                               _____

                                                                96,044
                                                               _____

The introduction of this cash discount will save a net £17,284.

(3)   The cost/saving implications of all three possible increases in sales will provide the most useful information.
       Existing costs are:

                                                                   £

Export sales = £4.8m less deposit 15% ∴ credit sales = £4.08m

The opportunity cost of debtors = £4.08m × 75/365 × 15% =   125,753

Bad debts = £4.08m × 1.25% =   51,000
                                                               _____

                                                               176,753
                                                               _____

Calculations of the net benefit or loss under each projected possible increase in sales are as follows:

	20%	25%	30%
Sales	£4.896m	£5.1m	£5.304m
	_____	_____	_____
Opportunity cost of debtors(note 1)	160,964	167,671	174,378
Bad debts(note 2)	73,440	76,500	79,560
	_____	_____	_____
	234,404	244,171	253,938
Less: Current cost (see above)	176,753	176,753	176,753
	_____	_____	_____
Net extra costs	57,651	67,418	77,185
Extra administration	30,000	40,000	50,000
Advertising	300,000	300,000	300,000
	_____	_____	_____
Total extra cost	387,651	407,418	427,185
Extra contribution			
£960,000 × 0.35	336,000		
£1.2m ×0.35		420,000	
£1.44m × 0.35			504,000
	_____	_____	_____
Net benefit (loss) (note 3)	(51,651)	12,582	76,815
	_____	_____	_____

Notes:

(1)   Multiply 80/365 × 15% × £4.896m for 20% sales
                                        × £5.100m for 25% sales
                                        × £5.304m for 30% sales

(2)   Multiply the sales figures by 1.5%.

(3)   But the benefits of this year's advertising expenditure may spill over and increase next year's contribution.

CHAPTER 7   EXAM-TYPE QUESTION

Cash management

Tutorial note: part (a) requires a fairly standard discussion of the motives for, and costs of, holding cash. In part (b), speeding up banking will effectively reduce the firm's overdraft requirement. In this question there are no extra costs given for banking daily but they can exist and should be mentioned in your discussion.

(a) The reasons for holding cash are as follows:

(i) The transaction motive

Cash will be required for the day-to-day operations of the business, e.g. to pay creditors, to buy stocks or to make dividend payments.

(ii) The speculative motive

The company will need cash to finance risky business ventures, e.g. the purchase of a machine to carry out a speculative project.

(iii) The precautionary motive

Contingent losses may materialise e.g. legal claims against the company. Cash will need to be held to satisfy such contingencies as they arise.

The company must, therefore, maintain a sufficient level of cash to satisfy the above three requirements. Any cash in excess of this level will result in lower profits. It is true that surplus cash can be invested in the short term to earn interest, and in this respect cash is different from other assets, but such returns will nearly always be less than the return which can be earned on the business's other assets. Thus, in general, cash is really the same as any other working capital asset and should be subject to similar management and control. Surplus cash which can only be invested at low short-term interest rates or, worse still, which is lying idle, is not being properly utilised and will result in decreased profitability.

On the other hand, if the company is holding too little cash it may encounter liquidity problems. Such a shortage of cash could mean that the company is forced to reject certain worthwhile investment opportunities owing to lack of funds, or that its very survival is threatened. Many profitable companies have been forced into liquidation or sale purely as a consequence of cash flow problems.

Proper cash budgeting and planning procedures should ensure that a company does not fall into the trap of holding too little or too much cash.

(b) AB Credit Collection Co

Annual collections $= £5,200,000$

$\therefore$ Weekly collections (average) $= \dfrac{5,200,000}{52} = £100,000$ per week

$\therefore$ Average daily collections $= \dfrac{£100,000}{5} = £20,000$ per day

Annual overdraft rate $= 9\%$

$\therefore$ Daily overdraft rate $= \dfrac{9\%}{365}$

$= 0.0246\%$

Cost of not banking daily = sums not banked × days not banked × daily overdraft rate

		£
Monday	£20,000 × 4 days × 0.0246% =	19.68
Tuesday	£20,000 × 3 days × 0.0246% =	14.76
Wednesday	£20,000 × 2 days × 0.0246% =	9.84
Thursday	£20,000 × 1 day × 0.0246% =	4.92
Friday No change to banking pattern		–
Total weekly cost of not banking daily		49.20

Annual cost $= £49.20 × 52$

$= £2,558.40$

Assumptions

- There are 52 weeks in a year, five days each week, and collections are made on each of these days.
- Takings are evenly spread daily and weekly.
- Bankings are used to reduce the overdraft and thus the overdraft rate is suitable for calculating the annual cost of weekly banking. If the company were able to make use of the funds released in other ways then a different rate may be appropriate. For example, if the company had available investment opportunities, then the cost of capital should be used.

It appears that a daily remitting system would save the company £2,558 pa. However, this must be assessed in the light of the possible effects on agents and costs. At present agents may be earning interest prior to remitting collections to head office and might resent the change in company policy. Also, what effect will the new system have on the number of agent defaults?

CHAPTER **8**　　　　E X A M - T Y P E　 Q U E S T I O N

G plc

(a)

	Price £1.60	Price £1.28
Capital to raise	£768,000	£768,000
Suggest price	£1.60	£1.28
No of shares to issue	480,000	600,000
Current no in issue	1,200,000	1,200,000
Therefore rights issue	4 for 10	1 for 2
	(2 for 5)	

2 for 5

Current value of 5 shares (x 1.80)	9
Value of 2 new shares (x 1.60)	3.2
Theoretical value of 7 shares	12.2
Theoretical ex rights price	12.20/7　= £1.74

The value of each right is £1.74 – £1.60 = £0.14.

1 for 2

Current value of 2 shares (x 1.80)	3.60
Value of 1 new share (x 1.28)	1.28
Theoretical value of 3 shares	4.88
Theoretical ex rights price	4.88/3　= £1.63

The value of each right is £1.63 – £1.28 = £0.35.

(b) The price set for a rights issue is relatively important since the wealth of the shareholders will be unaffected whatever price is determined (since the finance is being raised from the existing body of shareholders and they will automatically participate in any gains).

Therefore the important criterion relates to the success of the issue in terms of its attractiveness to the shareholders. As such it is essential that the issue price.

In addition, it may be noted from the calculation in (i) that the market value of a right is greater the lower the issue price. Although under perfect market conditions this factor is irrelevant, it may nevertheless enhance the attractiveness of the issue in the eyes of the shareholders

Therefore, in practice, the price set for a rights issue tends to be approximately 20% below the prevailing market price of the shares currently in issue. This would give an issue price of around £1.44 (£1.80 × 80%)

(c) The following factors might invalidate the ex – rights price and market values calculated above.

(1) The ex-rights price has been computed on the assumption that the current market price of the company's existing shares will remain at the same effective level until the rights issue takes place and immediately

after. Therefore any factors influencing and changing the share price during that time will render the ex-rights price inaccurate.

(2) The current share price (assuming the semi-strong form of the efficient market hypothesis is true) should reflect the information available concerning the earnings and net present value to be derived from the investment of the new funds. Any further information which becomes available may alter the share price and invalidate the ex-rights price.

(3) The increased number of shares resulting from the rights issue may depress the marketability and therefore the price.

(4) The reaction of shareholders to the issue could influence the share price. For instance, a reluctance to take up the rights could depress the share price.

CHAPTER **9**   EXAM-TYPE QUESTION

Nolipival plc

(a)   **Advantages of convertible loan stock over ordinary shares**

(i)   Convertible loan stock is much cheaper than equity finance. This is due to the security associated with its status as debt, making it very low risk, together with the attractiveness of the option to convert to equity if conditions are favourable.

(ii)   It shares initially all the other advantages of debt finance such as the interest being corporation tax deductible and the issue costs being less than those for an issue of new equity.

(iii)   Until conversion takes place, the existing shareholders' control of the company will be unaffected.

Advantages of convertible loan stock over debenture stock

(i)   Convertibles are cheaper than ordinary debentures since they have all the advantages of debt but in addition have the attraction of conversion to equity. They therefore bear only upside risk until after conversion has taken place.

(ii)   Because its term as debt is likely to be only short-term its conditions of issue will be less restrictive.

(iii)   Provided conditions are favourable and conversion takes place, convertible debt is self-liquidating. In other words redemption effectively takes place with no cash flow implications for the company.

(b)   (i)   Debentures with a floating rate of interest

Such debentures are likely to be advantageous to both borrowers and lenders in circumstances where the market interest rates are volatile. The coupon rate of the debenture may be adjusted to reflect the current market rate of interest. Therefore if interest rates fall the borrower's costs also fall due to a decrease in the coupon rate and the borrower avoids being committed to a high fixed rate of interest. On the other hand, if interest rates rise this will be reflected in an increase in the coupon rate and higher interest payments to lenders.

Due to the matching of the coupon rate to the market rate of interest, the market price of the debentures will be much more stable. This may be attractive to lenders and therefore such debentures will be a means for borrowers of readily obtaining required funds.

(ii) Zero-coupon bonds

As with the floating rate debentures, zero-coupon bonds are attractive in times of volatile interest rates. No interest is payable on the bonds, but the interest is effectively accrued and accounted for in the redemption value of the bond, or reflected in its current market value. Therefore the lender may sell the bond at any time during its life and recover an amount of interest which reflects the current market rates applicable during the period of ownership. The lender has therefore not been locked in to a low fixed rate of interest, but has been able to participate in higher rates, if there has been an interest rate rise since the issue of the bonds. Similarly the cost to the borrower will reflect the interest rates prevailing during the period of issue, as such interest rates will be incorporated in the final redemption value.

The cash flow effect of zero-coupon bonds represents another advantage to the borrower.

Short-term cash flows are preserved since no interest payments are made during the life of the bond.

CHAPTER 10

EXAM-TYPE QUESTION

Ratios – B Ltd

(a) (i) **Ratios of particular significance to shareholders**

	20X1	20X2
Earnings per share	$\dfrac{9{,}520}{39{,}680} \times 100$	$\dfrac{11{,}660}{39{,}680} \times 100$
	= 23.99p	= 29.39p
Dividend cover	$\dfrac{9{,}520}{2{,}240}$	$\dfrac{11{,}660}{2{,}400}$
	= 4.25 times	= 4.86 times

(ii) **Ratios of particular significance for trade creditors**

	20X1	20X2
Current ratio	$\dfrac{92{,}447}{36{,}862}$	$\dfrac{99{,}615}{42{,}475}$
	= 2.51	= 2.34
Quick ratio	$\dfrac{92{,}447 - 40{,}145}{36{,}862}$	$\dfrac{99{,}615 - 50{,}455}{42{,}475}$
	= 1.42	= 1.16

(b) Earnings per share has increased by 22.5% due to improved profits. There has been no change in share capital. The dividend cover (the number of times the ordinary dividend is covered by the available profits) has increased because the percentage of profits paid out as a dividend has decreased. The dividend itself has gone up 7% which is clearly not as much as the earnings improvement. The company is adopting a cautious policy but the dividend looks secure.

The current ratio is decreasing but it is still at an acceptable level. The quick ratio (measure of the company's liquidity) is also decreasing and at a faster rate due to the increasing investment in stock (current ratio is down

approximately 7% and the quick ratio about 18%). The quick ratio is above the generally desired level of 1 but the company should watch this area carefully.

Return on capital employed has remained constant. The ratio of turnover to fixed assets has reduced dramatically due to the high investment in fixed assets. These should help increase turnover and profitability in future years.

CHAPTER 11   EXAM-TYPE QUESTIONS

Question 1: Oracle plc

The Oracle cash flow is as follows:

Year	Cash flow	Discount factor	Present value	Discount factor	Present value
	£	(15%)	£	(10%)	£
0	(15,000)	1.00	(15,000)	1.00	(15,000)
1	1,500	0.870	1,305	0.909	1,364
2	2,750	0.756	2,079	0.826	2,272
3	4,000	0.658	2,632	0.751	3,004
4	5,700	0.572	3,260	0.683	3,893
5	7,500	0.497	3,727	0.621	4,657
			(1,997)		190

(i) Net present value @ 15% = (£1,997)

(ii) Net present value @ 10% = £190

Question 2: Tom

(a) **Future value**

$$= £80 \times \left(\frac{1.005^{24} - 1}{0.005} \right) = £80 \times (1.12716 - 1)/0.005 = £80 \times 25.432 = £2,034.56.$$

Compound forward for 5 years at 8%

$$= £2,034.56 \times (1.08)^5 = £2,034.56 \times 1.46933$$

$$= £2,989.44.$$

(b) APR = 9.38%, then the monthly rate is $1.0938^{\frac{1}{12}} - 1 = 0.0075\%$.

(Note: If you cannot calculate this easily on your calculator, take the APR of 9.38% and divide by 12 to get an approximate monthly rate. 9.38%/12 = 0.7816%. The monthly interest rate is almost certain to be a round number, and it will be a bit less than 0.7817%. So try 0.75%. If the monthly interest rate is 0.75%, what is the APR?
The APR is 1.0075)^{12}-1 = 0.0938 or 9.38%.)

Applying the annuity formula to the present value of an annuity:

$$£4,000 = A/0.0075 \times \left[1 - \left(\frac{1}{1.0075} \right)^{24} \right]$$

$$£4,000 = A/0.0075 \times [1 - (1/1.1964135)]$$

$$£4,000 = A/0.0075 \times [1 - 0.83583]$$

$$0.0075 \, (£4,000) = 0.16417A$$

$$£30 = 0.16417 \, A$$

$$A = £182.74$$

CHAPTER **12**   E X A M - T Y P E   Q U E S T I O N

Basics

Year	Equipment	Working capital	Cash profits	Net cash flow
	£	£	£	£
0	(90,000)	(20,000)		(110,000)
1			37,000	37,000
2			48,000	48,000
3	5,000	20,000	26,000	51,000

Year	Net cash flow	Discount factor at 8%	Present value at 8%	Discount factor at 12%	Present value at 12%
	£		£		£
0	(110,000)	1.000	(110,000)	1.000	(110,000)
1	37,000	0.926	34,262	0.893	33,041
2	48,000	0.857	41,136	0.797	38,256
3	51,000	0.794	40,494	0.712	36,312
			+ 5,892		- 2,391

(a)   The **NPV** at 8% is + £5,892, indicating that the project is financially worthwhile.

(b)   **IRR**

$$\text{IRR} = 8\% + \left[\frac{5,892}{(5,892 + 2,391)} \times (12 - 8)\% \right]$$

= 8% + 2.8%

= 10.8%

CHAPTER **13**   E X A M - T Y P E   Q U E S T I O N

Breckall plc

(a)   *Tutorial notes*

(1)   As different items are inflating at different rates the only realistic approach is to discount money cash flows at the money discount rate. This is particularly true as taxation is involved and the amount of tax payable will be based upon a taxable profit figure which in turn is determined by items subject to various rates of inflation.

(2)   The general procedure will be as follows.

   • determine the corporation tax liability

   • determine other relevant cash flows (in money terms)

   • discount these cash flows to present value at the money discount rate.)

Calculation of corporation tax liability

	1	2	3	4	5	
	£,000	£,000	£,000	£,000	£,000	
Sales (5% rise pa)	3,675	5,402	6,159	6,977	6,790	
Materials (10% rise pa)	588	907	1,198	1,537	1,449	
Labour (10% rise pa)	1,177	1,815	2,396	3,075	2,899	
Overheads (5% rise pa)	52	110	116	122	128	Note 2
Capital allowances	1,125	844	633	475	1,423	Note 1
Taxable profit	733	1,726	1,816	1,768	891	
Tax (35%)	256	604	636	619	312	

Notes

1 **Capital allowances**

	Opening balance £'000	Capital allowance £'000
Year 1	4,500	1,125
Year 2	3,375	844
Year 3	2,531	633
Year 4	1,898	475
Year 5	1,423	1,423 (balancing allowance)

This assumes that the first capital allowance is available in the first year and that the balancing allowance is taken in year 5. Note that capital allowances are based upon original cost of assets.

2 **Depreciation is replaced by the capital allowance**

Interest is not deducted in calculating the tax liability. The tax deductibility of interest will have been allowed for in the calculation of the money discount rate.

Discount relevant cash flows to present value

Cash flow estimates (£'000)

	Year 0	Year 1	Year 2	Year 3	Year 4	Year 5	Year 6
Inflows							
Sales	–	3,675	5,402	6,159	6,977	6,790	–
Outflows							
Materials	–	588	907	1,198	1,537	1,449	–
Labour	–	1,177	1,815	2,396	3,075	2,899	–
Overheads (note 3)	–	52	110	116	122	128	–
Fixed assets	4,500						
Working capital (note 4)	300	120	131	144	156	(851)	–
Taxation (note 5)			256	604	636	619	312
Net cash flows	(4,800)	1,738	2,183	1,701	1,451	2,546	(312)
Discount factors at 15%		0.870	0.756	0.658	0.572	0.497	0.432
Present values	(4,800)	1,512	1,650	1,119	830	1,265	(135)

NPV = £1,441,000 and on this basis the project should be accepted.

3 Once again interest is not included. The cost of interest is taken care of in the discounting process. If we were to charge interest against cash flow and include it in the discounting process we would be double counting. **This is a *very* common examination trap and should be avoided.**

4   We require the *incremental* investment in working capital each year. Adjusting for inflation this is:

Year 0	300		
Year 1	$(400 \times 1.05) - 300$	=	120
Year 2	$(500 \times 1.05^2) - (400 \times 1.05)$	=	131
Year 3	$(600 \times 1.05^3) - (500 \times 1.05^2)$	=	144
Year 4	$(700 \times 1.05^4) - (600 \times 1.05^3)$	=	156
Year 5	$(700 \times 1.05^5) - (700 \times 1.05^4)$	=	42
Year 5	refund of working capital assumed (700×1.05^5)	=	893
Year 5	Net		(851)

5   Tax payment lagged by one year

(b)   ***Tutorial note*** This is a roundabout way of asking what is the IRR of the project.

By normal trial and error procedures the IRR may be determined as follows:

Year	Cash flow	20% discount factor	PV	27% discount factor	PV
0	(4,800)		(4,800)		(4,800)
1	1,738	0.833	1,448	0.787	1,368
2	2,183	0.694	1,515	0.620	1,353
3	1,701	0.579	985	0.488	830
4	1,451	0.482	699	0.384	557
5	2,546	0.402	1,023	0.303	771
6	(312)	0.335	(105)	0.238	(74)
			765		5

The discount rate would have to change from 15% to approximately 27% to produce a net present value of zero. This is a change of approximately 80%.

CHAPTER 14

EXAM-TYPE QUESTION

Mentor Products plc

(a)   The combinations leading to a negative net cash flow are listed in the following table (£'000s):

0	Year 1	2	3	Probability			Net cash flow
(42)	10	10	10	$0.3 \times 0.1 \times 0.3$	=	0.009	(12)
(42)	10	10	20	$0.3 \times 0.1 \times 0.5$	=	0.015	(2)
(42)	10	20	10	$0.3 \times 0.2 \times 0.3$	=	0.018	(2)
(42)	15	10	10	$0.4 \times 0.1 \times 0.3$	=	0.012	(7)
(42)	20	10	10	$0.3 \times 0.1 \times 0.3$	=	0.009	(2)
				Total		0.063	

The total probability of a negative cash flow is 0.063.

Tutorial note: the probabilities are obtained using the multiplication law for mutually exclusive outcomes:

$P(A \text{ and } B \text{ and } C) = P(A) \times P(B) \times P(C)$

(b) Calculation of average (expected) cash flows (£'000s).

| | Year 1 | | | | Year 2 | | | | Year 3 | | |
CF	Prob	CF × Prob		CF	Prob	CF × Prob		CF	Prob	CF × Prob	
10	0.3	3		10	0.1	1		10	0.3	3	
15	0.4	6		20	0.2	4		20	0.5	10	
20	0.3	6		40	0.3	12		30	0.2	6	
				30	0.4	12					
		―				―				―	
Expected cash flows		15				29				19	
		―				―				―	

Discounting the expected CF to obtain present values (£'000s):

Year	Expected cash flow	Discount factor	Present value
0	(42)	1.000	(42.000)
1	15	0.870	13.050
2	29	0.756	21.924
3	19	0.658	12.502
			――――
			5.476
			――――

The expected net present value is £5,476.

(c) Allocate the digits 0 to 9 to the cash flows each year such that the number of digits is proportional to the probability (£'000s).

| | Year 1 | | | Year 2 | | | Year 3 | |
CF	Prob	digits	CF	Prob	digits	CF	Prob	digits
10	0.3	0-2	10	0.1	0	10	0.3	0-2
15	0.4	3-6	20	0.2	1-2	20	0.5	3-7
20	0.3	7-9	30	0.4	3-6	30	0.2	8-9
			40	0.3	7-9			

Select digits from the table of random numbers and record the corresponding cash flows (£'000s).

| Set | Year 0 CF | Year 1 D factor = 0.870 | | | Year 2 D factor = 0.756 | | | Year 3 D factor = 0.658 | | | NPV |
		RN	CF	DCF	RN	CF	DCF	RN	CF	DCF	
1	(42)	4	15	13.05	2	20	15.12	7	20	13.16	(0.67)
2	(42)	7	20	17.40	4	30	22.68	9	30	19.74	17.82
3	(42)	6	15	13.05	8	40	30.24	4	20	13.16	14.45
4	(42)	5	15	13.05	0	10	7.56	0	10	6.58	(14.81)
5	(42)	0	10	8.70	1	20	15.12	3	20	13.16	(5.02)
											―――
											11.77
											―――

The average net present value is 11.77/5 (£'000s) = £2,354.

Three out of five outcomes are negative. The probability of a negative value is therefore 3/5 = 0.6. However, probabilities are based on the relative frequency in a large number of trials. In practice, many hundreds of simulations would need to be carried out.

In comparing this result with part (a), it should also be remembered that the cash flows in part (a) are higher because they have not been discounted, leading to a lower probability of a negative net cash flow.

CHAPTER 15

EXAM-TYPE QUESTION

Question 1: Ceder Ltd

(a)

Calculation of tax liability

	Year 1 £	Year 2 £	Year 3 £	Year 4 £	Year 5 £	Year 6 £
Standard						
Operating cash flows	20,500	22,860	24,210	23,410		
Capital allowance	12,500	9,375	7,031	21,094*		
	8,000	13,485	17,179	2,316		
Taxation (35%)	2,800	4,720	6,013	811		
De-luxe						
Operating cash flows	32,030	26,110	25,380	25,940	38,560	35,100
Capital allowance	22,000	16,500	12,375	9,281	6,961	20,883*
	10,030	9,610	13,005	16,659	31,599	14,217
Taxation (35%)	3,511	3,363	4,552	5,831	11,060	4,976

* Including balancing allowance

Forecast after-tax cash flows

	Year 0 £	Year 1 £	Year 2 £	Year 3 £	Year 4 £	Year 5 £
Standard						
Fixed assets	(50,000)					
Working capital	(10,000)				10,000**	
Operating cash flows		20,500	22,860	24,210	23,410	
Taxation			(2,800)	(4,720)	(6,013)	(811)
	(60,000)	20,500	20,060	19,490	27,397	(811)
Discount factor (12%)		0.893	0.797	0.712	0.636	0.567
Present values	(60,000)	18,307	15,988	13,877	17,424	(460)

Payback period is approximately three years.

Net present value is £5,136.

	Year 0 £	Year 1 £	Year 2 £	Year 3 £	Year 4 £	Year 5 £	Year 6 £	Year £
Standard								
Fixed assets	(88,000)							
Working capital	(10,000)						10,000**	
Operating cash flows		32,030	26,110	25,380	25,940	38,560	35,100	
Taxation			(3,511)	(3,363)	(4,552)	(5,831)	(11,060)	(4,9
	(98,000)	32,030	22,599	22,017	21,388	32,729	34,040	(4,9
Discount factor (14%)	0.877	0.769	0.675	0.592	0.519	0.456	0.400	
Present values	(98,000)	28,090	17,379	14,861	12,662	16,986	15,522	(1,9

Payback period is approximately four years.

Net present value is £5,510.

** Assumes working capital is released immediately. In reality some time-lag will exist.

Normally the project with the highest NPV would be selected. However, as the projects have unequal lives, it can be argued that although the de-luxe has a higher NPV, this is only achieved by operating for two more years. If the machines are to fulfil a continuing production requirement the time factor needs to be considered.

The annual equivalent cost approach is not appropriate as both machines have different level of risk. In this situation the most useful approach is to assume infinite reinvestment in each machine and calculate their NPVs to infinity.

$$NPV\, \infty\ =\ \frac{\begin{array}{c}\text{NPV of the investment} \div \text{Present value of an}\\ \text{annuity of appropriate years and discount rate}\end{array}}{\text{Discount rate}}$$

Standard

$$NPV\, \infty\ =\ \frac{5{,}136 \div 3.037\,*}{0.12}\ =\ £14{,}093$$

De luxe

$$NPV\, \infty\ =\ \frac{5{,}510 \div 3.889\,*}{0.14}\ =\ £10{,}120$$

* The present values of annuities are taken for four and six years as these are the useful lives of the projects.

As the standard machine has the higher NPV ∞, it is recommended that this machine should be purchased.

An alternative approach to the problem of different lives might be to assume a reinvestment rate for the shorter investment and to use this rate to equalise the lives of the investments.

(b) Lease payments are usually made at the start of the year.

			Cash flows			
	Year 0 £	Year 1 £	Year 2 £	Year 3 £	Year 4 £	Year 5 £
Lease						
Cost of machine saved	50,000					
Capital allowance lost			(4,375)	(3,281)	(2,461)	(7,383)
Lease payments	(15,000)	(15,000)	(15,000)	(15,000)		
Tax relief on lease		5,250	5,250	5,250	5,250	
Net cash flow of lease	35,000	(9,750)	(14,125)	(13,031)	2,789	(7,383)
Discount factor (7.15%) A		0.933	0.871	0.813	0.759	0.708
	35,000	(9,097)	(12,303)	(10,594)	2,117	(5,227)

Net present value is (£104).

As the net present value is negative, it appears that the purchase of the machine is the recommended alternative.

The choice of discount rates in lease versus buy analysis is contentious. The approach used here is to regard the lease as an alternative to purchasing the machine using debt finance. The discount rate is, therefore, the amount that the company would have to pay on a secured loan on the machine, the loan being repayable on the terms that are implicit in the lease rental schedule. This discount rate is the after-tax cost of the equivalent loan, 11% (1-0.35) = 7.15%.

This discount rate is only likely to be valid if leases and loans are regarded by investors as being equivalent, and all cash flows are equally risky.

FOULKS LYNCH
PUBLICATIONS

Question 2: Arctica

Key Answer Tip: In part (a) the train of thought required is (i) what effects may the reduction of authorities' capital expenditure have (on government borrowing, business activity, inflation, etc) and (ii) what economic policy/ objective would these effects fit in with? The latter is what the question is essentially asking.

In part (b), first ensure you are happy with what is meant by 'public sector' and 'private sector'. In general, parts of case study question are linked, and in this case the main part of the question concerns a regional authority project, which we are told is to be discounted at a lower rate than a similar project that may be undertaken by a private sector company. This should guide you in both the meaning of the sector terminology, and in the likely direction of the difference between the rates. You now have to think why this may be so.

In part (c) (i) there is a lot of information to assimilate. Try to break it down, extracting the essential data in some brief notes:

- Current vehicle fleet - resale values
- Replacement fleet - capital and overhaul costs; resale values (note: a decision needs to be made as to the final overhaul); number of vehicles required; running costs (need an expected value)
- Summer months, hire contract possibility - income
- Alternative option, contracting out - annual fee
- Discount rate - need to choose which is appropriate

Now identify the cash flows (mainly costs) associated with the two options and compare them in present value terms over the same time period. As the examiner says in his comments, there are a variety of possible approaches here. Don't forget to complete the requirement by explaining your answer - interpret the results of your computations in words, and add any other considerations that you think are relevant.

In part (c) (ii) the maximum sub-contract fee will be that which makes the PV of the costs of this option equal to that of the in-house option. So look back at your computation for the sub-contract option, substitute 'x' for the fee, equate the result to that for the in-house option and solve for x. This is, in fact, finding the equivalent annual cost (EAC) of the in-house option.

Although the terminology used in part (d) is different, you are basically repeating the exercise in (c)(ii), with a different PV of costs of the in-house option to aim at. When removing of the contract hire income from the PV computation, don't start again from scratch - start with the net flows for each year and adjust out the income (you could also do this in PV terms).

Part (e) is *not* a 'write all you know about sources of finance' question. It is very specifically related to the organisation and economic environment in the question. It is simply a waste of time writing about sources that are only open to private sector companies. Note also that 'discuss' requires greater explanation than (say) 'outline'.

(a)   Central governments apply periodic restrictions on public expenditure, both current and capital, as part of their discretionary fiscal policy. Such intervention in the economy seeks to smooth the oscillations of the business cycle by adjusting the balance between public expenditure and revenue from taxes. Specifically, when an economic downturn is expected, the government will plan to operate a budget deficit i.e. spend more than its tax revenue, in order to inject demand into the economy when economic activity is flagging, and conversely, when an economic expansion, with consequent inflationary pressures, is expected.

       This contra-cyclical budgetary policy can dampen fluctuations in the economy, thus increasing business confidence and readiness to invest. However, successful operation of this policy requires considerable skill in forecasting future economic trends, perception in recognising the need to act

and speed in putting appropriate measures into effect so that they have an impact when required.

When a government wishes to restrict its expenditure it is often easier to cut capital expenditure. Although once approved and begun, capital projects acquire a momentum which is difficult to reverse, design specifications can be changed for subsequent phases of a lengthy project, later phases postponed or cancelled, or projects yet to be undertaken can be delayed indefinitely.

(b) Private sector companies are obliged to earn a return at least as great as the opportunity cost incurred by the owners who subscribe capital to them, that is, to at least match the returns offered by comparable investments in which they might otherwise have invested. This reflects the required compensation to reward the individual for waiting for his money, (his rate of 'time preference'), plus some compensation for risk.

In the public sector, many investments such as civil engineering works, have far longer lives than private sector projects, and may also involve costs and benefits which are not priced by the market – so-called externalities such as pollution or congestion costs. For these reasons, it is often argued that a different discount rate should be applied to public sector projects.

One approach is to adopt the social rate of time preference argument. Society has a longer time horizon than private individuals and to reflect this, a lower rate of discount is warranted, so as not to over-discount the distant benefits which would be valued by future generations.

However, this approach may overlook the opportunity cost incurred by society in undertaking the project in question. Since capital can be invested in a number of ways, it is appropriate to examine what projects and hence what returns are foregone by allocating capital to particular uses. Consequently, the correct discount rate would reflect the rate of return on the best alternative use of public funds, including all externalities – the so-called social opportunity cost return.

(In the Arctica example, the government requires a return of 5% in real terms, below the yield on comparable private sector investments. In the UK in recent years, the Treasury has tended to overlook the externalities argument and focus on the post-tax returns which would otherwise have been achieved in the private sector. In this case, it is more likely that the lower percentage reflects the differential advantage enjoyed by the government in raising capital compared to private sector companies.)

(c) (i) Evaluation of alternatives

The optimal course of action from a financial viewpoint is that which minimises the present value of the net costs of meeting the service targets.

The offer

The present value of the annual contract payments sought by Dumpex is found by applying the six-year annuity factor at 5% to the annual payments:

Present value = £1m × PVIFA$_{5,6}$ = £1m × 5.076 = £5.08.

Purchase of new fleet

Expected value of operating costs (£m)

= (0.2 × 1.5) + (0.5 × 0.8) + (0.3 × 0.3) = 0.3 + 0.4 + 0.09 = 0.79

Cash flow profile (£m)

Year

Item	0	1	2	3	4	5	6
Outlay	(0.50)						
Residual values	0.01						0.02
Overhaul*			(0.14)		(0.14)		
Operating costs		(0.79)	(0.79)	(0.79)	(0.79)	(0.79)	(0.79)
Contract income		0.20	0.16	0.12	0.08	0.04	
Net outflows	(0.49)	(0.59)	(0.77)	(0.67)	(0.85)	(0.75)	(0.77)
Discount factor	1.000	0.952	0.907	0.864	0.823	0.784	0.746
Present value	(0.49)	(0.56)	(0.70)	(0.58)	(0.70)	(0.59)	(0.57)

Present value of net outflows = (4.19) (i.e. £4.19m).

Note: the overhaul profile recognises that the expenditure in year 6 of £0.14m required to make the vehicles saleable for £5,000 each is uneconomic. The best alternative is to sell for scrap.

Based upon this information, the in-house option is less costly i.e. the net present value of in-house costs is less than the present value of the contracted-out costs. This may be because Dumpex seeks a higher return for an activity of this degree of risk, and/or it must provide for tax liabilities. However, there remains the uncertainty surrounding the period over which Arctica can expect to receive income from the quarry company. In addition, the operating costs are based on expected values – a run of bad winters could result in costs higher than the contracted-out figure.

(ii) To encourage Arctica to contract out the operation, an annual fee which generates the same or lower present value would have to be offered. The equivalent contract fee is found by dividing the present value of outflows by the appropriate annuity factor i.e:

£4.19m/5.076 = £0.83m

which is considerably below the unofficial offer of £1m.

(d) There is a distinct danger that the in-house cost is understated as the income from the quarry contract is highly unreliable. As a form of sensitivity analysis, the impact of losing all income from that source can be assessed. The break-even value of the contract fee can be found by removing the given contract income figures from the cash flows, finding the present value of the resulting cost stream and converting it into an equivalent annuity i.e. the annual figure which yields the same present value as the series of costs which Arctica expects to incur.

Cash flow profile from part (c) (£m)

Year

	0	1	2	3	4	5	6
Net outflows	(0.49)	(0.59)	(0.77)	(0.67)	(0.85)	(0.75)	(0.77)
Contract income		(0.20)	(0.16)	(0.12)	(0.08)	(0.04)	
Revised net outflows	(0.49)	(0.79)	(0.93)	(0.79)	(0.93)	(0.79)	(0.77)
Discount factor	1.000	0.952	0.907	0.864	0.823	0.784	0.746
Present value	(0.49)	(0.75)	(0.84)	(0.68)	(0.77)	(0.62)	(0.57)

Total present value = (4.72) (i.e. £4.72m).
Hence to break even, the fee for the contract with Dumpex would have to be:

[Present value of costs]/$PVIFA_{5,6}$ = £4.72/5.076 = £0.93m.

This means that to cover the risk attaching to the contract with the quarry company, Arctica would have to pay an annual fee to Dumpex of £0.93m, a little below the unofficial tender of £1m. However, it is likely that the latter figure is above the minimum valuation which Dumpex attaches to the contract, being merely an 'opener' in the negotiation process. There seems to be scope for negotiation.

(e)   Possible alternative sources of finance including the following.

(i)   *Private finance input.* In some countries, (e.g. in the UK under the Private Finance Initiative), efforts are being made to involve the private sector in partially or wholly financing public sector investment. This reflects the government's conviction that some services may be more efficiently provided by the private sector. In the case of Arctica, there may be scope for operating a joint venture, sharing control with a private sector company willing to assume a portion of the financial outlay and associated risk in return for a guaranteed service contract.

(ii)   *Official aid sources.* If the central government is unwilling to fund the project, Arctica may look to external funding agencies such as the range of loan facilities offered by the European Investment Bank, or grants from the European Union Regional Fund which aims to promote economic development in less-developed areas of the EU.

(iii)   *Leasing.* Leasing is a means of transferring expenditure from capital account to revenue account. Instead of incurring a 'lumpy' investment outlay at the outset of the project, the authority may arrange to pay a series of rentals to a leasing company for the use of the asset(s) concerned. With a finance lease, the length of the agreement approximates to the lifetime of the asset(s), and the contract cannot easily be cancelled without prohibitive penalty clauses. Hence, the lessee (user) assumes the risk of equipment obsolescence and idle time. An operating lease is similar to a plant-hire contract whereby the equipment is rented for a limited period corresponding to the requirements of a particular task. Operating leases are usually more expensive than finance leases per period of use, but, as in the case of Arctica, where there are long periods of idle time, they may represent the soundest option.

CHAPTER **16**   EXAM-TYPE QUESTION

RH Ltd

(a)   (i)   Marginal costing statement

	Six months ending 31 March 20X3		Six months ending 30 September 20X3	
	£'000	£'000	£'000	£'000
Sales		980		1,120
Variable cost of sales				
opening stock	-		73.5	
production cost				
8,500 units @ £49		416.5		
7,000 units @ £49			343.0	
	416.5		416.5	
less closing stock				
1,500 units @ £49	73.5			
500 units @ £49			24.5	
		343		392
		637		728

	£'000	£'000
Variable selling costs	196	224
	—	—
Contribution	441	504
Fixed costs		
production (W1)	160.0	160.0
selling etc,	90.0	90.0
	—	—
	250	250
	—	—
Profit	191	254
	—	—

(ii) Absorption costing statement

	Six months ending 31 March 20X3		Six months ending 30 September 20X3	
	£'000	£'000	£'000	£'000
Sales		980		1,120
Cost of sales				
opening stock	-		103.5	
production cost				
8,500 units @ £69	586.5			
7,000 units @ £69			483.0	
	——		——	
	586.5		586.5	
less closing stock				
1,500 units @ £69	103.5			
500 units @ £69			34.5	
	——			
		483		552
		——		——
		497		568
(under)/over-absorption (W2)		10		(20)
		——		——
Gross profit		507		548
Selling etc, costs				
variable	196		224	
fixed	90		90	
	——		——	
		286		314
		——		——
Profit		221		234
		——		——

Workings

(W1) Fixed production overhead is £20 per unit and the normal level of activity is 16,000 units per annum. The budgeted overhead per annum is therefore 16,000 × 20 = £320,000. The budgeted overhead per six-month period is therefore £160,000. The question states that there are no variances apart from a volume variance, therefore, actual overheads are as expected in the budget.

(W2) Under/over-absorption is the difference between overheads incurred and overheads absorbed

1st 6 months

	£'000
Overhead incurred (W1)	160
Overhead absorbed	
8,500 units × £20/unit	170
	——
Over-absorption	10
	——

2nd 6 months

	£'000
Overhead incurred (W1)	160
Overhead absorbed	
7,000 units × £20/unit	140
Under-absorption	20

(b) The difference in profit = fixed production OAR × change in stock

	1st 6 months £'000	2nd 6 months £'000
Marginal costing profit	191	254
Stock difference		
Increase 1,500 units × £20/unit	30	
Decrease 1,000 units × £20/unit		(20)
Absorption costing profit	221	234

(c) Marginal costing is useful in the following business situations:

(1) Shutdown decisions. Using absorption costing it may appear that a product is unprofitable and should be discontinued. The product will have been charged with a share of fixed costs, however, which will usually remain at the same level, regardless of whether the product is continued or not. In the short term at least the focus should be on contribution and if the product has a positive contribution it should be continued.

(2) Limiting factor decisions. When there is a scarce resource, production should be organised so that those products which give the highest contribution per unit of scarce resource are given the highest priority. Fixed costs can and should be ignored as they will be the same irrespective of which products are made.

(3) Make or buy decisions. When a company has the choice of making or buying a component/product it should choose the cheaper option. The focus should be on variable costs alone as again the fixed costs will not change whichever option is chosen.

Question 2: ABC terms

(a) Activity-based costing is a method of costing which is based on the principle that activities cause costs to be incurred, not products. Costs are attributed to activities and the performance of those activities is then linked to products.

A cost driver is the factor that causes costs to be incurred (e.g. placing an order or setting up a machine).

(b) (i) Cost per set-up
$$\frac{£4,355}{1+6+2+8} = \frac{£4,355}{17} = £256$$

Cost per order
$$\frac{£1,920}{1+4+1+4} = \frac{£1,920}{10} = £192$$

Cost per handling of materials
$$\frac{£7,580}{2+10+3+12} = \frac{£7,580}{27} = £281$$

Cost per spare part
$$\frac{£8,600}{2+5+1+4} = \frac{£8,600}{12} = £717$$

Cost per machine hour (No. of m/c hours = 125 + 1,250 + 600 + 10,500)

$$= \frac{£37,424}{12,475} = £3.00/hr$$

 FOULKS LYNCH
PUBLICATIONS

Costs are then attributed to products using the cost driver rates calculated above, for example:

Product A requires one machine set-up, therefore 1 × £256 = £256
Product B requires six machine set-ups, therefore 6 × £256 = £1,536
and so on.

Product	A	B	C	D
	£	£	£	£
Activities:				
Set-ups	256	1,536	512	2,048
Orders	192	768	192	768
Handling	562	2,810	843	3,372
Spare parts	1,434	3,585	717	2,868
Machine time	375	3,750	1,800	31,500
	2,819	12,449	4,064	40,556
No. of units	500	5,000	600	7,000
Cost per unit	£5.64	£2.49	£6.77	£5.79

The costs are then totalled and divided by the number of units to give the cost per unit for each product.

(ii)   The activity-based costing approach attributes more costs to products A, B and C and less to product D than the traditional method of accounting for overhead costs. The activity-based costing method gives a more accurate cost by relating it to the resources used to manufacture each product, consequently these costs are more useful for decision-making than those provided by the traditional method.

CHAPTER 18   EXAM-TYPE QUESTION

Simplo Ltd

(a) Operating statement – Period 6

	£	£
Original budgeted contribution (1,600 units @ £32)	51,200	
Budget revision variances		
Selling price (1,600 units @ £10)	16,000 (F)	
Labour rate (1,600 units × 3 hours × 60p)	2,880 (A)	
		13,120 (F)
Revised budgeted contribution (1,600 @ £40.20)		64,320
Sales volume variance		
Additional capacity (W1)	37,520 (F)	
Productivity reduction (W2)	2,680 (A)	
Idle time (W3)	2,680 (A)	
Stock increase (W4)	16,080 (A)	
		16,080 (F)
Revised standard contribution for actual sales (2,000 @ £40.20)		80,400

Other variances

	F	A
	£	£
Selling price (W5)		8,000
Material usage (W6)		600
Wage rate (W7)	3,040	

		1,320	
Labour efficiency (W8)		1,320	
Labour idle time (W9)		1,320	
	3,040	11,240	8,200 (A)
Actual contribution			72,200

(b) The operating statement shows that the change in selling price and the effect of the wage rate increase combined so that the contribution from the budgeted sales was expected to be £64,320.

The actual sales achieved exceeded those expected because a greater number of units were produced albeit at a lower efficiency than expected and the incidence of lost time due to a machine breakdown and a power failure. Management needs to consider the costs/benefits of implementing planned maintenance to avoid future machine breakdowns and expenditure on a generator to be used in the event of power failure. Consideration should also be given to the policy of manufacturing items for stock. Should production be restricted or demand stimulated?

Management should consider whether the payment of a lower wage rate than anticipated has caused the efficiency variance and the operational problems referred to in connection with the material usage variance.

Workings

(W1) $[(7,600/3) - 1,600] \times £40.20 = 37,520$ F

(W2) $[(7,600 - 200) - (2,400 \times 3)]/3 \times £40.20 = 2,680$ A

(W3) $(200 \text{ hours}/3) \times £40.20 = 2,680$ A

(W4) 400 units @ £40.20 = 16,080 A

(W5) $2,000 \text{ units} \times (£110 - £106) = 8,000$ A

(W6) $[(2,400 \times 5) - 12,060] \times £10 = 600$ A

(W7) $(£6.60 - £6.20) \times 7,600 \text{ hours} = 3,040$ F

(W8) $[(7,600 - 200) - (2,400 \times 3)] \times £6.60 = 1,320$ A

(W9) 200 hours @ £6.60 = 1,320 A

CHAPTER 19   EXAM-TYPE QUESTION

Chemical company

(a) Variance calculations

Standard cost card

Materials	Gallons	£/gallon	£
P	5	0.70	3.50
Q	5	0.92	4.60
Input	10 gallons	(at £0.81)	8.10
Normal loss	1 gallon		-
Output	9 gallons	(at £0.90)	£8.10

FOULKS LYNCH
PUBLICATIONS

Standard cost of actual production = 92,070 × £0.90 = £82,863

	Actual qty in actual mix at actual price →		Actual qty in actual mix at standard price		Actual qty in → std. mix at standard price		→ Std. qty std. mix standard p
	Gallons	£	Gallons	£	Gallons	£	Gallons
	45,000	36,000	45,000	31,500			
	55,000	53,350	55,000	50,600		at 81p	
	100,000	89,350	100,000	82,100	100,000	81,000	ε

Materials cost variances

			£
Mix	£81,000 – £82,100	=	1,100 (A)
Yield	£82,863 – £81,000	=	1,863 (F)
Usage	£82,863 – £82,100	=	763 (F)
Price	£82,100 – £89,350	=	7,250 (A)
Total	£82,863 – £89,350	=	6,487 (A)

(b) **Usefulness of mix variances**

Manufacturing processes often entail the combination of a number of different materials to obtain one unit of finished product. Examples of such processes are chemicals, paints, plastics, fabrics and metal alloys.

The basic ingredients can often be combined in a variety of proportions (or mixes), without perhaps affecting the specified quality characteristics or properties of the finished product.

The sub-analysis of variances into mix and yield components can provide a valuable aid to management decisions as these two variances are often interrelated. The use of a different mixture of raw materials may reduce the co of the mix but could produce an adverse yield effect. However, a yield varianc can arise for reasons other than a change in the mixture of raw materials, for example due to poor management supervision or deliberate wastage of materials by operatives.

A change in the mixture of raw materials may also affect other variances, in particular labour and variable overhead efficiency variances.

A study of mix variances (and of other related variances) may be particularly important when management is experimenting with the introduction of a material substitute.

CHAPTER **20**

EXAM-TYPE QUESTION

Cash budget

	Jul £'000	Aug £'000	Sep £'000	Oct £'000	Nov £'000	Dec £'000	Tota £'000
Receipts							
Sales	210	200	200	200	200	200	1,210
New issue of share capital	-	-	-	30	-	-	30
Payments							
Expenses and purchases	160	150	150	150	150	150	910
Expenses and purchases	24	24	24	24	24	24	144
Plant	12	25	13	-	50	-	100
Stock	-	20	-	-	-	-	20

Tax	-	-	-	-	-	30	30
Dividends	-	24	-	-	-	-	24
	196	243	187	174	224	204	1,228
Surplus/(deficiency)	14	(43)	13	56	(24)	(4)	12
Opening balance	40	54	11	24	80	56	52
Closing balance	54	11	24	80	56	52	64

CHAPTER 21   EXAM-TYPE QUESTION

Budget drawbacks

(a) Many writers on motivational theory have suggested that the leadership style is likely to be reflected in the organisation structure, and hence on the budgetary system developed.

Hopwood pointed out that although the budgeting process appears to be technical and formal (and therefore may appear bureaucratic) it is really an informal bargaining process, whereby managers compete for organisational resources.

If the budgeting system is seen to be bureaucratic, the workforce may perceive it to be a pressure device by management to force employees to achieve higher performance ratings for no extra benefits. This could lead to a 'them' and 'us' solution.

However in the current economic climate, and in a rapidly changing situation, only those firms with efficient managers are likely to be successful. These managers will adopt systems that include both adaptive and dynamic elements that can not be regarded as bureaucratic.

(b) A flexible budget allowance is calculated on the basis of a single output based activity indicator, e.g. budgeted fixed overhead cost + (budgeted variable overhead cost per unit × the actual number of units produced). These variable costs tend to vary with input rather than output. Thus variable absorption rates based on input rather than output and variable overhead absorption rates based on input of machine/direct labour hours are used to estimate the flexible budget allowance.

However, for control purposes the budget is flexed on the basis of an output rather than an input indicator to ensure that input inefficiencies are not covered up. In this manner, the typical flexible budget can be of some value as a control device.

(c) The application of contingency theory to management accounting tells us that there is no universal appropriate accounting system applicable to all organisations in all circumstances. It depends upon the circumstances. Therefore the circumstances will determine to what extent managerial participation in the budgeting process will lead to higher levels of motivation and thus lead to enhanced managerial performance. Certainly there are clear examples where real participation has shown benefits, but it may not be a universal truth.

FOULKS LYNCH PUBLICATIONS

A manufacturing company

(a) Zero base budgeting may be defined as 'a method of budgeting whereby all activities are re-evaluated each time a budget is set'. It basically involves starting budget preparation with a 'clean sheet' and only including items in the budget if they can be justified and represent the most cost effective way of achieving the objective.

Incremental budgeting contrasts with this approach in that it involves using the previous year's budget as the starting point, i.e. last year's budget is implicitly assumed to be reasonable. Incremental adjustments are then made to last year's budget to allow for changes in volume and price level. The disadvantage of this latter approach is that it too easily takes previous budgets as still being valid, even though operating conditions may change, significantly affecting the budget in the next period.

Committed costs are costs which 'arise from having property, plant, equipment and a functioning organisation. Little can be done in the short run to change committed costs' (Horngren). By their nature decisions regarding whether they are incurred are made on a long-term basis, via preparation of the capital budgets. In the assumed context of annual operating budgets these costs would not be affected when zero based budgeting is used.

Engineered costs are 'costs that result from a clear-cut, measured relationship between inputs and outputs' (Horngren). These costs are therefore specific to the activity level achieved. The amount included under zero base budgeting will therefore be changed in line with the projected activity level.

Discretionary costs are costs, the level of which is a matter of policy (e.g. research and development). The amount incurred is therefore not governed by the activity level. Here the manager, under zero base budgeting, must justify, perhaps using cost benefit analysis, the amount of expenditure to include in the budget.

(b)	*Committed*	*Engineered*	*Discretionary*
(i) Safety	Cost of meeting legal requirements, e.g. guards on machines	Protective clothing	Expenditure on literature promoting safety awareness
(ii) Maintenance	Cost of tools, etc needed by maintenance staff	Cost of spare parts. Cost of services needed at specific intervals (e.g. every 10,000 hours)	Cost of having the factory painted
(iii) Accounting	Cost of maintaining statutory books and producing published accounts	Invoicing and postage costs per order. Computer processing time	Staff examination and training costs. Cost of management training.

(c) Ways in which profitability may be improved by the allocation of additional fund to the following areas:

(i) Safety

- Less absenteeism (due to reduction in industrial accidents) and associated production time lost (labour and machine idle time).
- Higher staff morale (feeling of well being due to safety procedures).

- May attract better staff and reduce labour turnover.
- Reduction in insurance premiums if the number of industrial accidents is lower than average.

(ii) Maintenance

- Improved reliability of machinery, i.e. less breakdowns, if there is planned maintenance and it will reduce idle time costs.
- May reduce material wastage.
- Reduced power consumption if production is completed in a shorter time period.
- Life of machines may be extended.
- Shorter production lead times would improve quality of service provided to customers, possibly resulting in increased sales.

(iii) Accounting

- Improved information, e.g. faster and more detailed, if computers are used, resulting in better decisions.
- Computer systems may enable number of staff to be reduced.
- More time available for credit control – reduce payment period taken by debtors.
- More time to improve stock control, e.g. identify slow moving items.

CHAPTER 24	EXAM-TYPE QUESTION

D & E Ltd

(a)   Scatter graph of electricity cost against production

Notes:

(i)   Choose the scales so that the graph fits the paper.

(ii)   Do not attempt to draw a line through the scatter graph unless the question requires it.

(iii) Label the axes and state the units

(b)   The regression line of Y on X is Y = a + bX where

$$b = \frac{n\Sigma XY - \Sigma X\Sigma Y}{n\Sigma X^2 - (\Sigma X)^2} \qquad \text{and } a = \frac{\Sigma Y - b\Sigma X}{n}$$

ΣX = 320

ΣY = 130

n = 10

$$b = \frac{10\times4{,}728 - 320\times130}{10\times12{,}614 - (320)_2} = \frac{5{,}680}{23{,}740}$$

    = 0.239

$$a = \frac{130 - 0.239\times320}{10}$$

    = 5.34

The least squares regression line of electricity costs (Y) on production (X) is therefore

Y   =   5.34 + 0.239X

Where Y is in £'000 and X in '000 units.

Explanation

Assuming there is an approximately linear relationship between production and electricity costs, which is shown to be reasonable by the scatter graph, the electricity costs are made up of two parts, a fixed cost (independent of the volume of production) of £5,340 and a variable cost per unit of production of £239 per 1,000 units (or 23.0p per unit).

(c)   For quarter 11, X = 15, hence

$Y = 5.34 + 0.239$

$= 8.93$

The predicted electricity cost for quarter 11 is therefore £8,930.

For quarter 12, X = 55, hence

$Y = 5.34 + 0.239$

$= 18.5$

The predicted electricity cost for quarter 12 is therefore £18,500

(d)   There are two main sources of error in the forecasts:

(i)   The assumed relationship between Y and X

The scatter graph shows that there can be fairly wide variations in Y for a given X. Also the forecast assumes that the same conditions will prevail over the next two quarters as in the last ten quarters.

(ii)   The predicted production for quarters 11 and 12

No indication is given as to how these planned production values were arrived at, so that it is not possible to assess how reliable they are. If they are based on extrapolation of a time series for production over the past ten quarters, they will be subject to the errors inherent in such extrapolations.

Provided conditions remain similar to the past ten quarters, it can be concluded that the forecasts would be fairly reliable but subject to some variation.

Note: methods for calculation of confidence limits for forecasts are available, but are outside the scope of this syllabus. At this level it is impossible to quantify the reliability, so that comments can only be in general terms, although a correlation coefficient would be worth calculating if time allowed.

(e)   The management accountant can use time series analysis to help make assumptions about the future. It can be particularly helpful during the budget preparation period, e.g. sales forecasting, predicting future product demand. However, the use of time series data rests on the assumption that the historical relationships between past and future sales will continue.

It can enable the management accountant to detect/identify trends, e.g. by using graphical representations and/or moving averages. These can be classified into:

–   seasonal trends, i.e. those fluctuations which change every year, and

–   cyclical trends, i.e. changes which take place every so many years, e.g. every five years

–   abnormal, irregular or erratic fluctuations, i.e. 'one off happenings.'

EXAM-TYPE QUESTION

Constructing an index number

(a) There are four main considerations to be borne in mind when constructing an index number.

 (i) *The purpose of the index number*

 Unless the purpose is defined clearly, the eventual usefulness of the final index will be suspect. In other words it must be designed to show something in particular.

 (ii) *Selection of items for inclusion in an index*

 The main principles to be followed here are that the items selected must be unambiguous, relevant to the purpose, and of ascertainable value.

 Since index numbers are concerned largely with making comparisons over time periods, an item selected one year must be clearly identified (i.e. in terms of size, weight, capacity, quantity, etc,) so that the same items can be selected the following year for comparison.

 (iii) *Selection of appropriate weights*

 Deciding on the level of importance to attach to each change from one year to the next, or the relative importance of each item to the whole list.

 (iv) *Selection of a base year*

 Care must be exercised so that an 'abnormal' year is not chosen in relation to the characteristic being measured. If an abnormally 'high' year is chosen, all subsequent changes will be understated; whereas if an abnormally 'low' year is chosen, all subsequent changes will be overstated in percentage terms.

(b) **Laspeyre Price Index**

$$\frac{\sum p_1 q_0}{\sum p_0 q_0} \times 100$$

	q_0 (20X1 quantities)	$q_0 p_0$ (20X1 total expenditure)	$q_1 p_1$ (20X8 total expenditure)	q_1 (20X8 quantities)	$p_1 = \dfrac{p_1 q_1}{q_1}$	$p_1 q_0$
	lbs	£	£	lbs	£	£
Butter	3,500	280	700	3,500	0.20	700
Potatoes	8,500	85	700	7,000	0.10	850
Apples	2,000	100	250	2,500	0.10	200
Meat	6,000	1,200	3,250	6,500	0.50	3,000
Total	20,000	£1,665	£4,900	19,500		£4,750

$$\frac{\sum p_1 q_0}{\sum p_0 q_0} \times 100 = \frac{£4,750}{£1,665} \times 100$$

$$= 285.3\%$$

Note: In column 6, the 20X8 prices are obtained by dividing the 20X8 total expenditure (column 4) by the 20X8 quantities (column 5).

(c) The major weakness of a Laspeyre Index is that it uses a consumption pattern that may well have changed considerably over the years. Since, when the price of a particular commodity rises considerably, there is usually some slackening in demand (providing it is not totally inelastic), a Laspeyre Index, still using the original quantities as weights, may place too much importance

on this item and therefore will tend to overstate the general level of price increases.

An alternative index to be considered is the Paasche Index, which uses a current pattern of consumption to weight its prices. However, while it overcomes the weakness of a Laspeyre Index it does have its own weaknesses, which should be considered before changing over.

CHAPTER **25**   EXAM-TYPE QUESTION

Theta Ltd

ROI using Alpha's basis

(i)

	£'000
Profit	225
Capital employed:	
Fixed assets (at cost)	1,000
Net current assets	250
	1,250

$$\text{ROI} = \frac{225}{1,250} \times 100 = 18.0\%$$

(ii)

	£'000
Profit	225
Add: Savings less depreciation	
$(35,000 - \frac{120,000}{6})$	15
	240
Capital employed:	
Fixed assets (at cost)	1,000
Add: Purchases (at cost)	120
	1,120
Net current assets	250
	1,370

$$\text{ROI} = \frac{240}{1,370} \times 100 = 17.52\%$$

(iii)

	£'000
Profit as stated	225
Less: Contribution lost	30
	195
Add: Depreciation not charged	20
	215
Capital employed:	
Fixed assets (at cost)	1,000
Less: Disposals (at cost)	200
	800
Net current assets	250
	1,050

$$\text{ROI} = \frac{215}{1,050} \times 100 = 20.48\%$$

Note: As the net current assets are average for the year the inflow of £20,000 realised for sale of asset has not been included. Similarly in (ii) above it is

assumed that the machine was purchased out of additional funds and not from existing cash resources (a common assumption in this style of question).

(iv)

	£'000
Profit	225
Add: Reduction in cost	4
	229
Capital employed:	
Fixed assets (at cost)	1,000
Net current assets	250
	1,250

$$ROI = \frac{229}{1,250} \times 100 = 18.3\%$$

Note: The reduction in creditors is offset by bank overdraft therefore no change in 'net' current assets. Overdraft interest ignored.

(v)

	£'000
Profit	225
Less: Lost contribution	6
	219
Capital employed:	
Fixed assets	1,000
Net current assets (£250,000 – £25,000)	225
	1,225

$$ROI = \frac{219}{1,225} \times 100 = 17.9\%$$

CHAPTER 26

EXAM-TYPE QUESTION

Hard and soft

(a) In the short term, whatever decision the company makes regarding the mix of products to be produced and sold, the fixed overhead can be assumed to remain the same. It is necessary, therefore, to base the decision on the contribution earned by each product.

	Hard		Soft		Light	
	£	£	£	£	£	£
Selling price		70		95		150
Direct material	15		20		25	
Direct wages	15		25		45	
Variable overhead	3		5		9	
		33		50		79
Contribution		37		45		71
Hours per unit		6		10		18
Contribution per hour		£6.167		£4.500		£3.944
Contribution per £1 material		£2.467		£2.25		£2.84

(i) If the materials quota does not operate, the company's production capacity is limited to 225,000 labour hours, in which case it must seek to obtain the greatest contribution for each labour hour. The hard grade gives the greatest contribution per hour and therefore this is the most profitable.

(ii) If the materials quota comes into force, the company must obtain the maximum contribution from each £1 spent on material. The light grade give the greatest contribution per £1 of material and this is therefore the most profitable.

Note: this applies only if the materials quota provides production which is with the production capacity of 900,000 hours. Let's test this.

$$\frac{£300,000}{£25} \times 18 = 216,000 \text{ hours}$$

As this is within the labour constraint, conclusion (ii) is correct.

(b) (i)

	Light
Material	£300,000
Budgeted units	12,000
Contribution per unit	£71
	£
Total contribution	852,000
Fixed overhead	500,000
Budgeted profit for year	352,000

(ii)

	Hard	Soft	Light	Total £
Material allocation	£75,000 (25%)	£45,000 (15%)	£180,000 (60%)	300,00
Budgeted units	5,000	2,250	7,200	
Contribution per unit	£37	£45	£71	
Total contribution	£185,000	£101,250	£511,200	797,45
Fixed overhead				500,00
Budgeted profit for year				297,45

CHAPTER 26

CASE STUDY QUESTIONS

Kwan Tong Umbago Ltd

(a) **Budgets for stocks**

	Units			
	March	*April*	*May*	*June*
Raw materials				
Opening stock	100	110	115	110
Add: Purchases	80	80	85	85
	180	190	200	195
Less: Used in production	70	75	90	90
Closing stock	110	115	110	105
Finished production				
Opening stock	110	100	91	85
Add: Production	70	75	90	90
	180	175	181	175
Less: Sales	80	84	96	94
Closing stock	100	91	85	81

(b) Sales and other budgets

	March	April	May	June	Total
			Units		
Sales (at £219 per unit)	£17,520	£18,396	£21,024	£20,586	£77,526
Production cost					
Raw materials (using FIFO)	3,024*	3,321**	4,050	4,050	14,445
Wages and variable costs	4,550	4,875	5,850	5,850	21,125
	£7,574	£8,196	£9,900	£9,900	£35,570

Debtors
Closing debtors = May + June sales = £41,610

Creditors
June, raw materials = 85 units × £45 = £3,825

$$* \quad \left(£4,320 \times \frac{70}{100}\right) = £3,024$$

$$** \quad \left(£4,320 \times \frac{30}{100}\right) = £1,296 + 45 \text{ units at } £45 = £3,321$$

Closing stocks
Raw materials 105 units × £45 = £4,725
Finished goods 81 units × £110 = £8,910
(Material £45 per unit + Lab & overhead £65 per unit)

(c) Cash budget

	March £	April £	May £	June £
Balance b/f	6,790	4,820	5,545	132,415
Add: Receipts				
Debtors (two months credit)	7,680	10,400	17,520	18,396
Loan	–	–	120,000	–
(A)	14,470	15,220	143,065	150,811
Payments				
Creditors (one month's credit)	3,900	3,600	3,600	3,825
Wages and variable overheads	4,550	4,875	5,850	5,850
Fixed overheads	1,200	1,200	1,200	1,200
Machinery	–	–	–	112,000
Interim dividend	–	–	–	12,500
(B)	9,650	9,675	10,650	135,375
Balance c/f (A) – (B)	4,820	5,545	132,415	£15,436

(d) Master budget

Budgeted trading and profit and loss account for the four months to 30 June 20X0

	£	£
Sales		77,526
Less: Cost of sales		
Opening stock finished goods	10,450	
Add: Production cost	35,570	
	46,020	
Less: Closing stock finished goods	8,910	
		37,110
		40,416

Less:	Expenses	
	Fixed overheads (4 × £1,200)	4,800
Depreciation		
	Machinery and equipment	15,733
	Motor vehicles	3,500
	Loan interest (two months)	1,500
		25,533
		14,883
Less:	Interim dividends	12,500
		2,383
Add:	Profit and loss account balance b/f	40,840
		43,223

Budgeted balance sheet as at 30 June 20X0

Employment of capital	Cost	Depreciation to date	Net
	£	£	£
Fixed assets			
Land and buildings	500,000	–	500,000
Machinery and equipment	236,000	100,233	135,767
Motor vehicles	42,000	19,900	22,100
	778,000	120,133	657,867

Working capital		
Current assets		
Stock of raw materials		4,725
Stock of finished goods		8,910
Debtors		41,610
Cash and bank balances		15,436
		70,681
Less: Current liabilities		
Creditors	3,825	
Loan interest owing	1,500	
		5,325
		65,356
		723,223

Capital employed	£
Ordinary share capital £1 shares (fully paid)	500,000
Share premium	60,000
Profit and loss account	43,223
	603,223
Secured loan (7 ½ %)	120,000
	723,223

(e) Possible ways in which the company can improve its cash management are as follows:

- Employing a *treasury function* to invest surplus cash and thereby improving the productivity of the capital employed. Even a small company such as Kwan Tong Umbago Ltd could switch funds from its bank current account to an account on which it can earn some interest. Many businesses fail to make full use of their cash budget, in that it provides them with an indication of when they will have surplus cash in addition to highlighting when they have a shortage.

- Its cash budget can only be as accurate as the data which it uses to estimate the figures. To arrive at more relevant and realistic estimates it may be possible to use computer packages, e.g. which take account of the numerous variables involved, and statistical techniques such as time series analysis for forecasting sales.

- It may be possible to improve its *credit control*. It currently takes around two months to collect the amounts owing from its debtors whilst paying off its creditors within one month.

  It needs to make an effort to collect what is owing more quickly without offering cash discounts which could prove to be expensive, e.g. by more prompt invoicing and chasing slow payers, etc. It could take a little longer to pay creditors provided that it does not lose cash discounts. A small percentage cash discount does have a high implicit annual interest cost!

- It could generate more cash by identifying and disposing of surplus assets, e.g. unwanted stocks of raw materials and/or finished goods, production and/or office equipment which is no longer required, provided that it can find a buyer. Finding a buyer of the surplus assets may not be easy. Another benefit of disposing of surplus assets which can have a significant impact on cash, is that the disposal may free valuable production, office or storage space. It may also be possible to secure a reduction in insurance premiums at the next renewal date relating to the assets disposed of.

- The company's cash position may also be improved via using more debt financing. The company is low geared and a large proportion of its fixed assets have not already been pledged as security. This should enable it to benefit from low cost financing, e.g. secured loans or debentures, but would expose it to a higher degree of risk caused by the obligation to make regular payments of capital and interest.

- The management could also consider other ways of financing assets, e.g. renting or leasing plant and machinery. This should enable them to generate the payments out of the earnings of the plant and machinery concerned.

- Finally, the company could opt to make greater use of sub-contractors which frees it from having to find additional sums for financing the expansion involved. The sub-contractor would have to finance the purchase of the necessary fixed assets, the remuneration of its labour force and the purchase and holding of stocks of raw materials, work in progress and finished goods. The downside from the company's point of view would be the problem of exercising quality control over the supplier.

Tutorial note: The first two of these suggestions are probably inappropriate for the company whose main problem is low profitability - ROCE = 2% - due to an appalling asset turnover ratio.

Index

FOULKS LYNCH
PUBLICATIONS

TEXTBOOK REVIEW FORM

Thank you for choosing the Official Text for the ACCA professional qualification. As we are constantly striving to improve our products, we would be grateful if you could provide us with feedback about how useful you found this textbook.

Name: ....

Address: ....

....

Email: ....

Why did you decide to purchase this textbook?

Have used them in the past	☐
Recommended by lecturer	☐
Recommended by friend	☐
Saw advertising	☐
Other (please specify)	☐

Which other Foulks Lynch products have you used?

Examination kit	☐
Distance learning	☐
Lynchpins	☐

How do you study?

At a college	☐
On a distance learning course	☐
Home study	☐
Other	☐

Please specify ....

Overall opinion of this textbook

	Excellent	Adequate	Poor
Introductory pages	☐	☐	☐
Syllabus coverage	☐	☐	☐
Clarity of explanations	☐	☐	☐
Clarity of definitions and key points	☐	☐	☐
Diagrams	☐	☐	☐
Practice questions	☐	☐	☐
Self-test questions	☐	☐	☐
Layout	☐	☐	☐
Index	☐	☐	☐

If you have further comments/suggestions or have spotted any errors, please write them on the next page.

Please return this form to: Veronica Wastell, Publisher, Foulks Lynch, FREEPOST 2254, Feltham TW14 0BR

Other comments/suggestions and errors

ACCA Order Form

4 The Griffin Centre, Staines Road, Feltham, Middlesex, TW14 0HS, UK.
Tel: +44 (0) 20 8831 9990 Fax: + 44 (0) 20 8831 9991
Order online: www.foulkslynch.com Email: sales@ewfl-global.com

Examination Date:
Jun 04 ☐ **Dec 04** ☐
(please tick the exam you intend to take)

		Textbooks £20.95	Revision Series £11.95	Lynchpins £6.50	Distance Learning Courses £95.00
Part 1					
1.1	Preparing Financial Statements (UK)	☐	☐	☐	☐
1.1	Preparing Financial Statements (International)	☐	☐	☐	☐
1.2	Financial Information for Management	☐	☐	☐	☐
1.3	Managing People	☐	☐	☐	☐
Part 2					
2.1	Information Systems	☐	☐	☐	☐
2.2	Corporate & Business Law	☐	☐	☐	☐
2.2	Corporate & Business Law (Scottish)	☐			
2.3	Business Taxation – FA 2003	☐	☐	☐	☐
2.3	Business Taxation – FA 2003 (Hong Kong)	☐			
2.4	Financial Management & Control	☐	☐	☐	☐
2.5	Financial Reporting (UK)	☐	☐	☐	☐
2.5	Financial Reporting (International)	☐	☐	☐	☐
2.6	Audit & Internal Review (UK)	☐	☐	☐	☐
2.6	Audit & Internal Review (International)	☐	☐	☐	☐
Part 3					
3.1	Audit & Assurance Services (UK)	☐	☐	☐	☐
3.1	Audit & Assurance Services (International)	☐	☐	☐	☐
3.2	Advanced Taxation – FA 2003	☐	☐	☐	☐
3.2	Advanced Taxation – FA 2003 (Hong Kong)	☐			
3.3	Performance Management	☐	☐	☐	☐
3.4	Business Information Management	☐	☐	☐	☐
3.5	Strategic Business Planning & Development	☐	☐	☐	☐
3.6	Advanced Corporate Reporting (UK)	☐	☐	☐	☐
3.6	Advanced Corporate Reporting (International)	☐	☐	☐	☐
3.7	Strategic Financial Management	☐	☐	☐	☐

Postage, Packing and Delivery:

Textbook & Revision Series	First	Each Extra	Lynchpins	First	Each Extra	Distance Learning (Per subject)	Each
UK	£5.00	£2.00		£2.00	£1.00		£6.00
Europe (incl ROI and CI)	£7.00	£4.00		£3.00	£2.00		£15.00
Rest of World	£22.00	£8.00		£8.00	£5.00		£40.00

Product Sub Total £.............. | Post & Packing £.................... | Order Total £................... | (Payment in UK £ Sterling)

Customer Details
☐ Mr   ☐ Mrs   ☐ Ms   ☐ Miss   Other ....
Initials:................................. Surname: ....
Address: ....
....
....
Postcode: ....
Telephone: ....
Fax: ....
Email address: ....

Delivery Address – if different from above
Address: ....
....
Postcode: ....
Telephone: ....

Payment
1   I enclose Cheque/Postal Order/Bankers Draft for £.....................
    Please make cheques payable to '**Foulks Lynch**'.
2   Charge MasterCard/Visa/Switch card number:

☐☐☐☐ ☐☐☐☐ ☐☐☐☐ ☐☐☐☐

Valid from: ☐☐☐☐   Expiry date: ☐☐☐☐

Issue no: (Switch only) ☐☐

Signature: .... Date: ....

Declaration
I agree to pay as indicated on this form and understand that
Foulks Lynch Terms and Conditions apply (available on request).
Signature: .... Date: ....

Notes: Prices are correct at time of going to print but are subject to change

For delivery – | United Kingdom | – 5 working days
please | Eire & EU Countries | – 10 working days
allow: | Rest of World | – 10 working days

Notes: All orders over 1kg will be fully tracked & insured.
Signature required on receipt of order. Delivery times
subject to stock availability. A telephone number or email address is required
for orders that are to be delivered to a PO Box number.